Other Titles in McGraw-Hill's Data Warehousing and Data Management Series

Data Warehousing, Data Mining, and OLAP

Alex Berson

Stephen J. Smith

McGraw-Hill

New York   San Francisco   Washington, D.C.   Auckland   Bogotá
Caracas   Lisbon   London   Madrid   Mexico City   Milan
Montreal   New Delhi   San Juan   Singapore
Sydney   Tokyo   Toronto

Library of Congress Cataloging-in-Publication Data

Berson, Alex.
 Data warehousing, data mining, and OLAP / Alex Berson, Stephen J. Smith.
  p.   cm.
 Includes bibliographical references and index.
 ISBN 0-07-006272-2
 1. Data warehousing. 2. Data mining. 3. Online data processing.
 I. Smith, Stephen J. II. Title.
 QA76.9.D37B47   1997
 005.74—dc21   97-27472
                                                   CIP

McGraw-Hill

*A Division of The **McGraw·Hill** Companies*

1 2 3 4 5 6 7 8 9 0 DOC/DOC 9 0 2 1 0 9 8 7

ISBN 0-07-006272-2

The sponsoring editor for this book was John Wyzalek, the editing supervisor was Bernard Onken, and the production supervisor was Pamela A. Pelton. It was set in Century Schoolbook by North Market Street Graphics.

Printed and bound by R. R. Donnelley & Sons Company.

 This book is printed on recycled, acid-free paper containing a minimum of 50% recycled de-inked fiber.

To Irina, Vlad, and Michelle
Alex Berson

To Samuel, who needs a chance
Steve Smith

Contents

Part 3.   Business Analysis   221

Foreword

Ever since the dawn of business data processing, managers have been seeking ways to increase the utility of their information systems. In the past, much of the emphasis has been on automating the transactions that move an organization through the interlocking cycles of sales, production, and administration. Whether accepting an order, purchasing raw materials, or paying employees, most organizations process an enormous number of transactions and in so doing gather an even larger amount of data about their business.

Despite all the data they have accumulated, what users really want is information. What can they learn from the data about how to satisfy their best customers, how to allocate their resources most efficiently, and how to minimize losses? When there are millions of trees, how can one draw meaningful conclusions about the forest? In conjunction with the increased amount of data, there has been a shift in the primary users of computers, from a limited group of information systems professionals to a much larger group of knowledge workers with expertise in particular business domains, such as finance, marketing, or manufacturing. Data warehousing is a collection of technologies designed to convert heaps of data to usable information. It does this by consolidating data from diverse transactional systems into a coherent collection of consistent, quality-checked databases used only for informational purposes. Not only are data warehouses among the largest databases (frequently more than a terabyte), but they often have large numbers of users with diverse requirements. Consequently, they need carefully thought out architectures that take advantage of the most advanced multitier client/server computing tools.

Data warehouses are used in three primary ways. First, they enhance the traditional information presentation technologies (reports and graphs) by bringing the data necessary for their creation into a single source. This consolidation eliminates one of the biggest sources of error and delay: the fragmentation of data in diverse transaction databases. Second, data warehouses are used to support online analytical processing (OLAP). Whereas traditional query and report tools describe what is in a database, OLAP goes further in helping the user answer why certain things are true. The user forms a hypothesis about a relationship and verifies it with a series of queries against the data. For example, an analyst might hypothesize that people with low incomes and high debt are bad credit risks, and analyze the database with OLAP to verify (or disprove) this assumption.

However, the very size and complexity of data warehouses make it difficult for any user, no matter how knowledgeable in the application of data, to formulate all possible hypotheses that might explain something such as the behavior of a group of customers. How can anyone successfully explore databases containing 100 million rows of data, each with thousands of attributes?

The newest, hottest technology to address these concerns is data mining. Data mining (the third major application of data warehouses) uses sophisticated statistical analysis and modeling techniques to uncover patterns and relationships hidden in organizational databases—patterns that ordinary methods might miss.

Data mining is different from OLAP because, rather than verifying a hypothesis, it is used to generate a hypothesis. Say, for example, an analyst wants to identify the risk factors for granting credit. The data mining tool might discover that people with high debt and low incomes are bad credit risks (as before), but it might also discover a pattern that the analyst did not think to try, such as the fact that debt-to-income ratio and age are determinants of risk. Here is where data mining and OLAP complement each other. Before acting on the pattern, the analyst needs to know the financial implication of using the discovered pattern to govern who gets credit. The OLAP tool can allow the analyst to answer those kinds of questions. Together, data warehouses, OLAP, and data mining are transforming the way businesses use data. The resulting insights are producing dramatic returns on investment. A survey that Two Crows Corporation recently conducted provided strong evidence of corporate satisfaction. Of those organizations far enough along to have formed an opinion, all of them plan to continue to expand their present use of data mining.

In this book, Alex Berson and Steve Smith have brought together these different pieces of client/server computing, data warehousing, OLAP, and data mining and have provided an understandable and coherent explanation of how data mining works and how it can be used from the business perspective. I believe that this synergy among data warehouses, OLAP, and data mining will produce a new and significantly improved way of doing business across the enterprise that provides a real competitive advantage to those who make the most effective use of these technologies. This book will be a useful guide.

Herb Edelstein
President, Two Crows Corporation

Preface

The last few years have seen a growing recognition of information as a key business tool. Those who successfully gather, analyze, understand, and act upon information are among the winners in this new information age. Therefore, it is only reasonable to expect the rate of producing and consuming information to grow. We can define *information* as that which resolves uncertainty. We can further say that *decisionmaking* is the progressive resolution of uncertainty and is a key to a purposeful behavior by any mechanism (or organism). In general, the current business market dynamics make it abundantly clear that, for any company, information is the very key to survival.

If we look at the evolution of the information processing technologies, we can see that while the first generation of client/server systems brought data to the desktop, not all of this data was easy to understand, unfortunately, and as such, it was not very useful to end users. As a result, a number of new technologies have emerged that are focused on improving the information content of the data to empower the knowledge workers of today and tomorrow. Among these technologies are data warehousing, metadata repositories, online analytical processing (OLAP), and data mining. In some ways, these technologies are the manifestation of the maturity of the client/server computing model and its applicability to a wide variety of business problems.

Therefore, this book is about the need, the value, and the technological means of acquiring and using information in the information age.

From that perspective, this book is intended to become the handbook and the guide for anybody who's interested in, planning, or working on data warehousing and related issues. This audience is quite large, and includes both technology and business people. Among them are information technology managers, business analysts, marketing managers, product planners, client/server application developers, systems and database administrators, information security officers, data center operations staff, and data networking specialists. Data warehousing and its advantages, features, and usage are discussed against the background of the evolution of the computing models, hardware and software innovations for parallel processing, client/server architecture and implementations, and database management systems. Using these topics as a foundation, the book proceeds to analyze the components of a data warehouse, including data sourcing and transformation tools, parallel database technology, metadata management, query, reporting, OLAP, data mining tools, and information delivery over the Web. Armed with the knowledge of data warehousing technology, the reader continues into a discussion on the principles of business analysis, models and patterns, and an in-depth analysis of data mining. The book ends with a brief look into the future potential of these technologies.

Why This Book Is Needed

The amount of information related to the subject of data warehousing is tremendous. Moreover, as technologies continue to mature, areas like OLAP, data mining, the World Wide Web, and parallel database technologies continue to attract the attention of developers, strategists, and users alike. At the same time, the amount of information about some of these technologies is still limited, while the hype surrounding other technologies (e.g., data mining) continues to further complicate the choices. To sort through all the available information, to separate hype from reality, and to find a cohesive and complete description of data warehousing and its effect on business is extremely difficult.

The main premise of this book is that, to date, several technologies have matured independently of one another, and no one as yet has thought a great deal about how to put the pieces together. These technologies include the following:

- Data warehouse–enabled relational database systems that are designed to support very large databases (VLDB) at significantly higher levels of performance and manageability.

- Data sourcing and transformation tools that can help acquire, understand, and clean up data stored in legacy and traditional online transaction processing (OLTP) systems before it gets loaded into a data warehouse.

- OLAP that is driven by the business need for an information view that can be rapidly assimilated and manipulated by business users and by the technology need to adapt standards-based solutions (e.g., relational database technology) and to leverage the opportunities available through the Web.

- Data mining that is enabled by new algorithms that provide easy-to-use and understandable techniques and that is driven by the business need to automatically solve well-defined business problems.

Never before has there been an opportunity to combine these technologies into one integrated system. To date, there are a number of very good books on various aspects of data warehousing. Unfortunately, most of the books published to date focus on a specific topic and a specific technology, without recognizing that the technologies have vastly greater value together—each improves the utility of the other like interlocking puzzle pieces. This book reveals how the technologies and architectures work together and what value they provide to the end user. This book presents the big picture by showing the businessperson how a data warehouse can be made useful to him or her.

Another unique aspect of this book is that it contains a lot of material, some of which can be found in various vendor publications and in specialized research and trade literature. That is especially important because a significant portion of the available information is being changed on a regular basis. Various emerging standards and continuous product updates are examples of the dynamic nature of this material. The technologies and tools described in this book require a detailed knowledge of different hardware and software platforms. Specifically, the hardware platforms described in this book include midrange systems, parallel processors, workstations, and servers. Operating systems include UNIX, Windows/NT, NetWare, and OS/2. Database management systems discussions are focused on key features of SYBASE, ORACLE, INFORMIX, MS SQL Server, DB2, and Red Brick. The book discusses object-relational database technology of universal servers, a star schema design, and the effect of the Web on all components of data warehousing. Readers are also introduced to technologies and products from Arbor Software, Cognos, Constellar, Evolutionary Technologies, Informatica, Information Builders, LogicWorks, MicroStrategies, Prism Solution, and Vality, among many others.

Unfortunately, even if one decides to read all the available literature, it would be very difficult to obtain a clear picture of how all these technologies and products fit together to deliver value to a business enterprise. That is why the authors' personal experiences in developing large-scale data warehousing projects and extended involvement with commercial parallel computing, OLAP, machine learning, artificial intelligence, and the Internet proved to be invaluable in writing this book.

Who This Book Is For

This book has been written as a result of the authors' experiences in participating in several large-scale data warehousing projects and in developing OLAP and data mining solutions for various industry segments.

For the discussion of the architecture, advantages, and benefits of data warehousing, the authors met with many business and IT managers, systems integrators, system administrators, database and data communications specialists, and system programmers, all of whom may be potential readers of this book.

This book can be used as a guide for system integrators, designers of data warehouse and data mart systems, data and database administrators considering the issues of parallel relational database systems, OLAP designers, and those who are planning to implement and support data mining. Webmasters, network specialists, and information security officers will find this book useful for implementing a distributed data warehouse or for deploying Web-enabled analysis tools throughout an enterprise.

Some specific data warehouse components described in the book can help IT managers, system administrators, DBAs, network and communications specialists, and application developers to make informed decisions when selecting platforms and products to implement a data warehouse or a data mart. The maturity of various OLAP and data mining technologies has enabled the authors to discuss design, implementation, and operational issues at such a level of detail that the book should be an invaluable tool for any professional in solving a whole spectrum of issues and concerns related to data warehousing.

Finally, those readers who are looking into such advanced topics as object-relational database systems, high-performance commercial computing, OLAP, and data mining will find this book extremely useful.

Prerequisite

The authors assume readers have little or no previous knowledge about data warehousing. This book is targeted at two classes of readership: business professionals—including sales and marketing managers, product planners, and financial experts—and technology professionals. Both groups of readers can understand this book—no previous data warehousing experience is necessary. Readers with any degree of knowledge of information technology can benefit from this book. Those who deal with only COBOL batch programs will find this book useful. Those with CICS, SQL, DB2 or any other database expertise, including DBA experience, will benefit. UNIX, Windows and Windows/NT, OS/2, and NetWare application developers, systems and network administrators, and LAN specialists should not have any problems reading this book.

Style Used

The book has been structured as a self-teaching guide. The introduction to data warehousing, its relationship to the client/server architecture, and an overview of data warehousing technology components and their roles is placed in the first part. The rest of the book is dedicated to specific technologies and methodologies designed to implement a data warehouse, with an in-depth discussion of business analysis, OLAP, data mining, and data visualization. The book concludes with a brief look at prevailing trends and directions in the data warehouse market.

The book includes a fair amount of diagrams, figures, examples, and illustrations in an attempt to present a lot of rather complicated material in as simple a form as possible. Data warehousing is a complex, involved, and often-misunderstood subject; so, whenever possible, theoretical issues are explained with practical examples. Therefore, the authors have made a serious effort to explain complex issues of parallel relational database systems, OLAP, and data mining, using both simple examples and theoretical discussions. For those readers interested in theory, the book provides sufficient theoretical overview of star schema design, parallel systems, artificial intelligence, and predictive modeling.

This book is about a very dynamic subject. All material included in the book is current at the time of writing. The authors realize that as data warehousing continues to evolve, and as vendors continue to improve and expand on their product quality and functionality, changes will be necessary. The authors intend to revise the book if a significant development in the data warehousing arena makes it necessary to add, delete, or change parts of the text.

What Is Included

Part I begins with an introduction to the business imperative and the technology roadmap of data warehousing. This part discusses the relationship between a data warehouse and client/server architecture and provides an overview of parallel system architectures and the corresponding developments in the area of database systems.

Part II starts with an in-depth analysis of data warehouse architecture and components, and discusses the design, technical, and implementation considerations of building a data warehouse. This part describes how a relational database technology can be leveraged for the high scalability and very large database support required by a data warehouse. Star schema design, bitmap indexes, and other innovative techniques are also discussed in this part. Finally, this part provides an overview of data extraction, transformation, and cleanup tools, as well as a discussion on the importance of metadata and the issues surrounding its management.

Part III begins to introduce the reader to the technical considerations related to business analysis. Query and reporting tools, OLAP, and the ideas behind models, patterns, statistics, and artificial intelligence are discussed in this part.

Part IV focuses on data mining. Decision trees, neural networks, clustering, nearest neighbor, fuzzy logic, genetic algorithms, and rule induction are among the techniques discussed in this part. In addition, a discussion on how to select the right technique is presented.

Part V concludes with a discussion on data visualization and an in-depth look at the current trends and future directions in the data warehouse arena.

The *appendixes* include an article on the value of data mining, OLAP guidelines, an analysis of common mistakes made when building a data warehouse, and an extensive bibliography.

Acknowledgments

First, I am grateful to Steve Smith for his knowledge, persistence, attention to details, and dedication, without which this book would not have happened. Very special thanks to my many friends and colleagues at Merrill Lynch for providing a creative and challenging atmosphere. Working with people like George Lieberman, Joe Hollander, Scott Ryles, John Ginelli, Tom Musmanno, Steve Wolfe, Guy Pujol, Joe Frediani, and many others gave me an opportunity to learn and work in a very stimulating and challenging environment on the leading edge of computer technology.

I also have to thank my numerous friends at ADT, Cognizant, Informix, IBM, Pilot Software, and ICS, specifically Peter Meekin, Eric Kim, Larry Johnson, and John Pezzullo.

I am very grateful to Dr. Ramon Barquin for his invaluable help and kindness by allowing me to include his insightful "10 Mistakes . . ." in this book.

I would like to thank all those who have helped me with clarifications, criticism, and valuable information during the writing of this book, including Herb Edelstein, who not only provided many thoughtful insights, but was patient enough to read the entire manuscript and make may useful suggestions. And, of course, this book would never have been finished without the invaluable assistance and thoroughness of McGraw-Hill editors and M.R. Carey of North Market Street Graphics.

Finally, the key reason for this book's existence is my family. My very special thanks to Irina, Vlad, Michelle, and the rest of my family for giving me time to complete the book, for understanding its importance, and for never-ending optimism, support, and love. I am especially grateful to my son Vlad for his help in designing the illustration material (and my personal home page on the Web).

Alex Berson

Since this is my first book I'd like to give credit where credit is due—to my high school teachers, who taught me how to write and started me out in science. I might have figured it out on my own later, but perhaps not. For me, there is no doubt that my ability to write at all rests with the patient encouragement of my teachers Ms. Durish, Mrs. Meys, and Mr. Palmer—and the less than patient but humorous encouragement of Mr. Rullo (though this is probably not exactly what they were expecting when they were making me read Dickens, Sartre, and Hardy).

Alex—thanks for your optimism and good sense to "just keep writing"—this book could, of course, not have happened without you.

Thanks to my parents for making me take piano lessons—which made me want to study instead. Thanks to Noel for giving me the time (sorry I ran a little bit late). Thanks to Debbie, for always checking to see if I was done yet. And special thanks to Samantha, Nathaniel, Emily, Sheri, and Irene.

And, finally, my sincerest appreciation to my colleagues and teachers who have taught me a great deal about what I have written here today: Mario Bourgoin, Joe Yarmus, Kurt Thearling, Emily Stone, Gary Drescher, Brij Masand, Jim Hutchinson, Xiru Zhang, Kris Carlson, Dave Waltz, Danny Hillis, Craig Stanfill, Craig Shaefer, Stewart Wilson, Tommy Poggio, Charles Leiserson, Ron Rivest, Alan Zaslavsky, Jim Clark, Eric Kim, Herb Edelstein and Peter Meekin.

Steve Smith

Foundation

Information (and energy) are at the core of everything around us. Our entire existence is a process of gathering, analyzing, understanding, and acting on the information. There is no reason to expect an end to what we call an information age. On the contrary, it is only reasonable to expect the rate of producing and consuming the information to grow. Indeed, information can be defined as "that which resolves uncertainty" and the decision making, as the progressive resolution of uncertainty. Since purposeful behavior by any mechanism (or organism) depends on sequential decision making, it is clear that information is required not just to exist, but to survive. Therefore, this book is about the need, the value, and the means of acquiring and using the information in the information age.

The first generation of client/server systems has brought data to the desktop, often as an implementation of decision support systems (DSSs) and executive information systems (EISs). Unfortunately, not all of this data was easy to understand and, as such, was not very useful to end users. In addition, these applications were focused on presenting data to high-level executives.

To improve the information content of the data and to empower knowledge workers of today and tomorrow, the latest "hot" technologies that have emerged on the client/server arena are focused on filtering unnecessary data and presenting the valuable information in a user-friendly, intuitive, and easy to understand way. Among these technologies are data warehousing, metadata repositories, on-line analytical processing (OLAP), and data mining. These technologies are a manifestation of the maturity of the client/server computing model and its applicability to a wide variety of business problems. Discussion of these technologies and their business implications is the main focus of this book.

1

Introduction to Data Warehousing

The 1990s may be remembered as the decade during which organizations began to recognize the strategic use of data as a discipline entirely different from operational use. Operational database systems have been traditionally designed to meet mission-critical requirements for on-line transaction processing and batch processing. In contrast, strategic data usage is characterized by online ad hoc query processing or batch intelligence-gathering functions for decision support.

Businesses are desperate for systems which deliver competitive advantage. Efficiency is no longer the key to business success; flexibility and responsiveness have taken its place. When we add to this the emergence of a worldwide communications infrastructure, then the situation starts to look quite interesting. Within a few years we will see many business transactions conducted through this infrastructure, with the potential for a real-time mode of business operation. Those organizations that have harnessed the power of information will have a massive competitive advantage over their rivals, and key to this will be an effective data warehousing strategy.

A data warehouse has emerged as a recognition of the value and role of information. It is the means for this strategic data usage. A data warehouse is not the same as a DSS. Rather, a data warehouse is a platform with integrated data of improved quality to support many DSS and EIS applications and processes within an enterprise. Data warehousing improves the productivity of corporate decision makers through consolidation, conversion, transformation, and integration of operational data, and provides a consistent view of an enterprise.

As a clarification point, DSS and EIS systems are very similar in that they present information for decision making; however, EIS applications typically allow greater flexibility in "slicing and dicing" data in a style most acceptable to senior decision makers. EIS can also be characterized by canned reports supporting unpredictable drill-down functionality, high performance, and high usability targeted toward managers rather than analysts.

In short, data warehousing is a blend of technologies aimed at effective integration of operational databases into an environment that enables strategic use of data. These technologies include relational and multidimensional database management systems, client/server architecture, metadata modeling and repositories, graphical user interfaces, and much more.

1.1   Why All the Excitement?

The 1996 study by the International Data Corporation (IDC) on the financial impact of data warehousing focused on what the economists label the *productivity paradox*. This refers to the fact that until the early 1990s, the benefits of technology were running well behind the pace of investment. The IDC report states that information technology (IT) investments have not delivered the expected benefits. Indeed, with the IT investment portfolio measured at about $464 billion (U.S.) spent on technology around the world in 1994 alone, senior managers are justifiably asking for more evidence of net benefits than ever before.

One of the reasons for this poor return on investment (ROI) is that traditionally computing technology was focused on automating routine clerical tasks, improving efficiency of existing processes, and collecting data. Unfortunately, even though large amounts of data have been collected, until recently, the value of this data was difficult to understand and use.

With the advent of data warehousing, companies can use information already collected as raw data to get large ROI, to obtain and sustain a significant competitive advantage. According to IDC, some of the reasons for seeing large financial returns in data warehousing implementations are

- The ability to focus on business processes and perform a complete financial analysis of these processes, thus enabling organizations to make decisions based on an understanding of the entire system rather than using rough estimates based on incomplete data.

- The ability to rationalize and automate the process of building an integrated enterprisewide information store rather than developing many individual DSSs and the corresponding infrastructure.

- The hardware, software, and storage costs related to the development, deployment, and maintenance of large informational data stores continue to decline.

- The benefits of data warehousing can be easily extended to strategic decision making, which can yield very large and tangible benefits.

- The ability to simultaneously understand and manage both the macro and micro perspectives of the organization can save organizations countless hours of manual work and can help avoid making costly mistakes that can be a result of assumptions made on incomplete or incorrect data.

The IDC study concluded that an average 3-year ROI in data warehousing reached 401 percent, with over 90 percent of the surveyed companies reporting a 40+ percent ROI, half of the companies reporting over 160 percent ROI, and a quarter showing returns greater than 600 percent! Although the detailed analysis of the IDC report is beyond the scope of this book, we will use its findings to demonstrate how data warehousing and related technology can and should be used to achieve these enviable results.

1.2 The Need for Data Warehousing

The data warehouse is an environment, not a product. It is an architectural construct of information systems that provides users with current and historical decision support information that is hard to access or present in traditional operational data stores. In fact, the data warehouse is a cornerstone of the organization's ability to do effective information processing, which, among other things, can enable and *share* the discovery and exploration of important business trends and dependencies that otherwise would have gone unnoticed.

In principle, the data warehouse can meet informational needs of knowledge workers and can provide strategic business opportunities by allowing customers and vendors access to corporate data while maintaining necessary security measures. There are several reasons why organizations consider data warehousing a critical need. These drivers for data warehousing can be found in the business climate of a global marketplace, in the changing organizational structures of successful corporations, and in the technology.

From a *business perspective,* in order to survive and succeed in today's highly competitive global environment, business users demand business answers mainly because

- Decisions need to be made quickly and correctly, using all available data.
- Users are business domain experts, not computer professionals.
- The amount of data doubles every 18 months, which affects response time and the sheer ability to comprehend its content.
- Competition is heating up in the areas of business intelligence and added information value.

In addition, the necessity for data warehouses has increased as organizations distribute control away from the middle-management layer that has traditionally provided and screened business information. As users depend more on information obtained from information technology systems—from critical-success measures to vital business-event-related information—the need to provide an information warehouse for the remaining staff to use becomes more critical.

There are several *technology reasons* for the existence of data warehousing. First, the data warehouse is designed to address the incompatibility of informational and operational transactional systems. These two classes of information systems are designed to satisfy different, often incompatible, requirements. At the same time, the IT infrastructure is changing rapidly, and its capabilities are increasing, as evidenced by the following:

- The price of computer processing speed in MIPS (million instructions per second) continues to decline, while the power of microprocessors doubles every 2 years.
- The price of digital storage is rapidly dropping.
- Network bandwidth is increasing, while the price of high bandwidth is decreasing.
- The workplace is increasingly heterogeneous in terms of hardware and software.
- Legacy systems need to, and can, be integrated with new applications.

1.3   Paradigm Shift

The emergence and wide acceptance of data warehousing can be closely linked to another significant phenomenon: client/server architecture. Both can be linked to several fundamental changes in today's computing.

1.3.1   Computing paradigm

The first change can be characterized as a shift in a computing paradigm. A traditional view of computing can be that of a computer user that accesses a powerful tool—the computer—via a communication network. The emphasis here was on a need to access a known computer program that resided on a known, possibly remote, system, as was the case in host-based and master-slave computing.

A new way of computing is emerging now. Users use computers to solve problems and to request services. There is an implied understanding that the services the users require may not be found in a single system, but rather are distributed across a network. Users use their individual computers as entry points to get access to this distributed computing power. The global nature of today's business, the proliferation of workgroup computing and LAN/WAN environments, the strong focus on shared and reusable resources, the attention given to the promise of the Information Superhighway, and the wide use of global networking services such as the Internet and the World Wide Web (WWW) are the evidence of this shift in computing paradigm (see Fig. 1.1).

This shift can be also observed in the way distributed client/server computing is being positioned in the enterprise. As more and more mission critical applications are being placed (ported to or developed for) on this new environment, the early client/server solutions proved to be inadequate to solve today's business problems. This inadequacy affects both the run time and the development aspects of the client/server computing. The major changes affecting the way

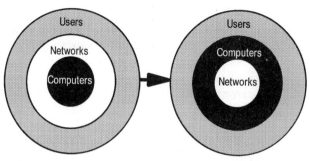

Figure 1.1   Computing paradigm shift.

client/server computing is implemented do not invalidate the client/server architecture, but rather introduce a set of additional, more demanding requirements on the environment. Among these trends, the following appear most prevalent:

- *Object orientation.*   The promise of development productivity of the object-oriented analysis, design, and programming cannot be ignored any longer. The implicit or explicit acceptance of object orientation by information technology practitioners, coupled with the emergence of object-oriented standards and the availability of related development and run-time tools, results in the need to adopt the client/server model to handle objects, mostly in the form of object request brokers.

- *Middleware.*   The layer in the client/server architecture that transforms a simple two-tier client/server computing model into a more complex client-middleware-server model.

- *Storage and handling of complex data.*   The ability to store and manipulate complex types of data (possibly defined by users) such as video, images, text, and spatial and time series data in new object-relational database systems as if they were traditional data types.

- *High-performance commercial parallel computing and very large database (VLDB) processing.*   Traditional servers are often incapable of handling large volumes of data, a large number of users, and high demands on performance and throughput required of the new breed of applications (data mining, multimedia, speech and character recognition, visualizations, etc.). Computer engineers and scientists turn their attention to different computer architectures and new ways of database processing to satisfy these demands. Massively parallel processors and parallel databases are examples of these efforts.

1.3.2   Business paradigm

An impartial observer may notice that the advancements in computing technology manifests itself in the change in the way we do business. Indeed, proprietary systems and mainframe-based computing of the 1960s and 1970s moved a traditional business enterprise from the manual back and front office to an automated back office and the proliferation of on-line transaction processing (OLTP). Essentially, though, these automated systems were designed to duplicate traditional manual operations, and while these innovations improved the processing speed and throughput, they did not change the way the businesses worked.

However, the rapidly changing market dynamics, competitive pressures, globalization of the commercial markets, reduced profit margins, and other similar factors forced business to review their structures, approaches, and strategies. Users are demanding more value for the money, and are well aware of the competitive offerings. The world map is changing as previously closed markets become available, and the speed of market penetration as well as the flexibility and adaptability of the products and services differentiate successful enterprises from previously inconceivable business failures.

The role of information technology.   Let's look at the business paradigm shift (see Fig. 1.2) from the IT perspective. In most organizations, information technology has become synonymous with automation. The past 30 years have seen IT projects aimed at the automation of business processes. The financial justification for these projects has been quite simple; we spend X and save Y, where Y is hopefully greater than X. However, in today's global and highly competitive business environment the information technology has another, potentially much more important, role to play outside of business automation, and that is as a *provider of information.*

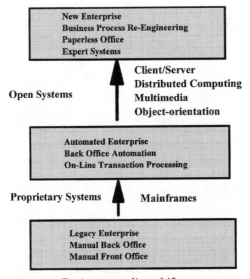

Figure 1.2   Business paradigm shift.

A common and natural misconception among many IT users is that we are already using information systems. Indeed, the proliferation of desktop technologies now enables almost any business manager to manipulate quite large amounts of data and perform quite complex calculations. Much of this, however, is ineffective and the current infatuation with the technologies hides the fact that we seldom know which questions to ask, or which questions can be asked.

Indeed, we can informally define automation as a set of processes that are concerned with the efficiency of predictable, repetitive tasks; automation cannot say anything about whether such a process is desirable in the first place and how it might evolve. Information, on the other hand, is a level above automation and is fundamentally derived from an act of comparison. Generating a monthly sales report is an act of automation unless some comparative process is added (e.g., actual versus forecast). Most businesses have already realized the majority of benefits that might be derived from automation, and attention is turning to other ways in which competitive advantage might be leveraged. Many businesses are starting to realize that information might be the ultimate weapon to achieve a sustainable competitive advantage.

Information always prompts action, and understanding its value transforms a computer from a giant calculator to a giant logical machine that is used in the realm of business information. In fact, data warehousing, with its associated technologies, is a clear manifestation of this fundamental shift. Following this shift, we can reasonably assume that data warehousing represents a first tentative step in a movement that will eventually make the current commercial use of information technologies look quite modest.

Aggressive rightsizing, business process reengineering, changes resulting from the introduction of workgroup computing to the way the front office works, a prominent role given to decision support systems and their users— executives and information workers, paperless office, just-in-time delivery of products, and services that exceed customer expectations are just a few examples of what a new business enterprise may need to use to stay competitive. And technologies such as client/server computing, distributed computing, object orientation, multimedia, extensive use of artificial intelligence and expert systems for data visualization and data mining, voice and image recognition, personal communication systems, and handheld computers may help businesses to achieve these goals.

1.4 Business Problem Definition

The business problems solved by data warehousing and complementary technologies all have one common trend—they provide the organizations with a sustainable competitive advantage. For example, consider the business application domains of decision support. It is a general category of applications that enables organizations to make informed and rational decisions about all aspects of their business, including, but not limited to:

- *Customer retention.*   Sophisticated customer retention programs begin with modeling those customers who have defected to identify patterns that led to their defection. These models are then applied to the current customers to identify likely defectors so that preventive actions can be initiated.

- *Sales and customer service.*   In today's highly competitive environment, superior customer service creates the sales leaders. When information is properly aggregated and delivered to front-line sales and service professionals, customer service is greatly enhanced. If customer information is available, rule-based software can be employed to automatically recommend products. These programs have already shown phenomenal gains in cross-selling ratios.

- *Marketing.*   Marketing depends heavily on accurate information to execute retention campaigns, lifetime value analysis, trending, targeted promotions, etc. Indeed, only by having a complete customer profile can promotions be targeted, and targeting dramatically increases response rates and thus decreases campaign costs. Direct mail costs are directly proportional to the completeness and accuracy of customer data.

- *Risk assessment and fraud detection.*   An accessible customer base significantly reduces the risk of entering into undo risk. For example, a mail order retailer can identify payment patterns from different customers at the same address, identifying potentially fraudulent practices by an individual using different names. An insurance company can identify its complete relationship with a client who may have different kinds of policies totaling more than an acceptable level of exposure. A bank can identify fiscally related companies that may be in financial jeopardy before extending a loan.

If we decide to categorize the business problems best addressed by data warehousing, we may first classify them into

- *Retrospective analysis,* which focuses on the issues of past and present events. For example, an organization may have to decide that it requires an in-depth analysis of the performance of the sales organization for the last 2 years across different geographic regions, demographics, and types of products.

- *Predictive analysis,* which focuses on predicting certain events or behavior based on historical information. For example, an organization may want to build a predictive model which describes the attrition rates of their customers to the competition and also defines steps that would reduce the attrition with a certain degree of confidence.

These two classes of business problems can be further classified by considering the following application types and techniques:

- *Classification.*   This technique is used to classify database records into a number of predefined classes based on certain criteria. For example, a credit card company may classify customer records as good, medium, or poor risk. A classification system may then generate a rule stating that "A customer who earns more than $40,000, is between 45 and 55 years of age, and lives within a particular zip code is a good credit risk."

- *Clustering and segmentation.* This technique is used to segment a database into subsets, or clusters, based on a set of attributes. For example, in the process of understanding its customer base, an organization may attempt to segment the known population and thus discover clusters of potential customers on the basis of attributes never used before for this kind of analysis (e.g., type of school they attended, number of vacations per year). Clusters can be created either statistically or by using artificial-intelligence (AI) methods. Clusters can be analyzed automatically by a program, or by using visualization techniques.

- *Associations.* These techniques identify affinities among the collection as reflected in the examined records. These affinities are often expressed as rules, for example, "Sixty percent of all the records that contain items A and B also contain C and D." The percentage of occurrences (in this case 60) is the confidence factor of the association. Association technique is often applied to market basket analysis, where it uses point-of-sales transaction data to identify product affinities.

- *Sequencing.* This technique helps identify patterns over time, thus allowing, for example, an analysis of customers' purchases during separate visits. It could be found, for instance, that a customer who buys engine oil and filter during one visit will buy gasoline additive the next time. This type of analysis is particularly important for catalog companies. It's also applicable in financial applications to analyze sequences of events that affect the prices of financial instruments.

To put it another way, many organizations are faced with a wealth of data that is maintained, and stored, but the inability to discover valuable, often previously unknown, information hidden in the data prevents these organizations from transforming this data into knowledge and wisdom. The business desire is, therefore, to extract valid, previously unknown, and comprehensible information from large databases and use it for profit.

To fulfill these goals, organizations need to follow these steps:

- Capture and integrate both the internal and external (e.g., purchased) data into a comprehensive view that encompasses the whole organization.

- "Mine" the integrated data for information.

- Organize and present the information and knowledge in ways that expedite complex decision making.

To do all these things, organizations need to integrate various components of a decision support application into a data warehouse that organizes data in ways that facilitate analysis. Throughout the book, we'll show how the business problems defined above can be addressed by properly implementing and using a data warehouse and companion technologies such as on-line analytical processing (OLAP) and data mining.

1.5   Operational and Informational Data Stores

Corporations have a variety of on-line transaction processing systems (e.g., financial, order entry, work scheduling, and point-of-sale systems) which create operational data. Operational data focuses on transactional functions such as bank card withdrawals and deposits. This data is part of the corporate infrastructure; it is detailed, nonredundant, and updateable; and it reflects current values. It answers such questions as "How many gadgets were sold to a customer number 123876 on September 19?"

Informational data, on the other hand, is organized around subjects such as customer, vendor, and product. It focuses on providing answers to problems posed by decision makers, such as "What three products resulted in the most frequent calls to the hotline over the past quarter?" Informational data is often summarized, is redundant to support varying data views, and is nonupdateable. In an operational system, a single data record can change constantly, while decision support requires that the record be stored as a series of snapshots of instances of that record over time.

Informational data is obtained from operational data sources (including any or all applications, databases, and computer systems within the enterprise). Since operational data is fragmented and inconsistent (for example, names and addresses for customers might be handled differently on each system), it must be "cleaned up" to conform to consistent formats, naming conventions, and access methods in order for it to be useful in decision support.

Data warehousing is designed to provide an architecture that will make corporate data readily accessible and usable to knowledge workers and decision makers. This differs from the operational systems which

- Are organized by application
- Support daily business processing on a detailed transactional level
- Are update-intensive
- Use current data
- Are optimized for high performance
- Access few records per transaction, often direct access by primary key
- Support a large number of relatively short transactions
- Support a large number of concurrent users

While the majority of informational and operational databases use the same underlying relational database management system (DBMS) technology, the following characteristics of informational data illustrate its difference from operational data:

- *Data access.*   This tends to be ad hoc, rather than predefined, structured access.
- *Data model (schema).*   This reflects end-user analysis needs, while an operational data model is normalized to support automicity, consistency, isolation, and durability (ACID) properties.
- *Time base.*   Recent, aggregated, derived, and historical data, while operational data tends to be current data or a snapshot of recent data.
- *Data changes.*   Informational data changes are mostly periodic, scheduled batch updates, while operational data is subject to continuous high-frequency changes.
- *Unit of work.*   Informational data is queried, while operational data is subject to concurrent update, insert, and delete.
- *Records range accessed per transaction.*   Millions for informational data versus tens for operational.
- *Number of concurrent users.*   Typically, hundreds for informational versus thousands for operational.
- *Transaction volume.*   Relatively low for informational data but high for operational data.
- *Types of users.*   Analytical, managerial vs. clerical, operational users; frequently, a user of the operational data is another system.
- *Number of indexes.*   Often many complex, compound versus few, simple.

These differences between the informational and operational databases are summarized in the following table.

	Operational data	Informational data
Data content	Current values	Summarized, archived, derived
Data organization	By application	By subject
Data stability	Dynamic	Static until refreshed
Data structure	Optimized for transactions	Optimized for complex queries
Access frequency	High	Medium to low
Access type	Read/update/delete Field-by-field	Read/aggregate Added to
Usage	Predictable Repetitive	Ad hoc, unstructured Heuristic
Response time	Subsecond (<1 s) to 2–3 s	Several seconds to minutes

Operational data store.   An interesting variation on the theme is an idea of rationalizing and integrating operational systems for the purpose of performing the decision support and analysis on the operational, transactional data. In other words, an operational data store (ODS) is an architectural concept to support day-to-day operational decision support and contains current value data propagated from operational applications. This causes the data maintained in the ODS to be subjected to frequent changes as the corresponding data in the operational system changes. ODS provides an alternative to operational DSS applications accessing data directly from the OLTP systems, thus eliminating the performance impact that such DSS activities can have on the OLTP systems.

We can use the frequency of update—real time or near real time, periodic, or overnight—to categorize ODS systems. Although ODS architecture is quite different from that of a data warehouse, ironically, the last two categories make the ODS quite similar to a data warehouse. That's why many of the application requirements of the ODS can be accomplished through well-defined access directly to the operational data or by enhancing the extraction process used to populate the data warehouse. However, some significant challenges of the ODS still remain. Among them are

- Location of the appropriate sources of data
- Transformation of the source data to satisfy the ODS data model requirements
- Complexity of near-real-time propagation of changes from the operational systems to the ODS (including tasks to recognize, obtain, synchronize, and move changes from a multitude of disparate systems)
- A DBMS that combines effective query processing with transactional processing capabilities that ensure the ACID transaction properties
- A database design that is optimized to support the most critical DSS activities and at the same time reduce the number of indexes to minimize the impact on update performance

Functionally, operational data stores provide a centralized view of near-real-time data from operational systems. Although most data warehouses are refreshed daily (the warehouse data is of daily periodicity), in certain situations (e.g., inventory movement, freight balancing) a rapid analysis is required to manage the business, and, if the data exists in separate files, a central ODS may facilitate this analysis. In addition, the ODS can also serve as a replacement for change logs used to refresh other DSS files in the enterprise.

1.6   Data Warehouse Definition and Characteristics

A data warehouse can be viewed as an information system with the following attributes:

- It is a database designed for analytical tasks, using data from multiple applications.

- It supports a relatively small number of users with relatively long interactions.

- Its usage is read-intensive.

- Its content is periodically updated (mostly additions).

- It contains current and historical data to provide a historical perspective of information.

- It contains a few large tables.

- Each query frequently results in a large result set and involves frequent full table scan and multitable joins.

A formal definition of the data warehouse is offered by W. H. Inmon: "A data warehouse is a subject-oriented, integrated, time-variant, nonvolatile collection of data in support of management decisions." In other words, a data warehouse combines:

- One or more tools to extract fields from any kind of data structure (flat, hierarchical, relational, or object; open or proprietary), including external data

- The synthesis of the data into a nonvolatile, integrated, subject-oriented database with a metadata "catalog"

There are a number of other terms related to the data warehouse. Following are some informal definitions of these terms:

- *Current detail data.* Data that is acquired directly from the operational databases, and often represents an entire enterprise. The current detail data is organized along subject lines (customer profile data, customer activity data, demographic data, sales data, etc.).

- *Old detail data.* This represents aged current detail data, or the history of the subject areas; this data is what makes trend analysis possible.

- *Data mart.* An implementation of the data warehouse in which the data scope is somewhat limited compared to the enterprisewide data warehouse. A data mart may contain lightly summarized departmental data and is customized to suit the needs of a particular department that owns the data; in a large enterprise, data marts tend to be a way to build a data warehouse in a sequential, phased approach; a collection of data marts composes an enterprise-wide data warehouse; conversely, a data warehouse may be construed as a collection of subset data marts. More on data marts can be found in Part 2 of this book.

- *Summarized data.* Data that is aggregated along the lines required for executive-level reporting, trend analysis, and enterprisewide decision making; summarized data volumes are much smaller than current and old detail data.

- *Drill-down.*   An ability of a knowledge worker to perform business analysis in a top–down fashion, traversing the summarization levels from highly summarized data to the underlying current or old detail; for example, if highly summarized geographic sales data indicates a reduction in sales volumes in North America, an analyst can drill down into the state, county, city, and even the address of the sales offices with the worst sales records.

- *Metadata.*   One of the most important aspects of data warehousing; it is data about data, and contains the location and description of warehouse system components; names, definition, structure, and content of the data warehouse and end-user views; identification of authoritative data sources (systems of record); integration and transformation rules used to populate the data warehouse; a history of warehouse updates and refreshments; metrics used to analyze warehouse performance vis-à-vis end-user usage patterns; security authorizations; and so on.

While users' needs from a data warehouse will differ from company to company, similarities will exist. The following classification defines and describes some data warehouse attributes:

- A data warehouse provides a mechanism for separating operational and informational processing, with information being the domain of the warehouse. Since the warehouse is populated by data created by the operational environment, the flow of information is usually one-way, from the operation data stores to the data warehouse.

- A holistic perspective that eliminates the vertical, line-of-business orientation of the operational data and provides an integrated perspective across the enterprise. The data warehouse is designed to help resolve inconsistencies in data formats, semantics, and usage across multiple operational systems.

- Part of a warehouse's function will include processing the data from its raw form in the operational databases. Data warehouse procedures include aggregating, reconciling, and summarizing data to make it more relevant and useful for users.

- The data content of the warehouse is a subset of all data in an organization. Even though the warehouse contains data originating from the operational environment, the contents of the warehouse are unique. Within the informational landscape, however, the warehouse should be considered as a universal set of all data emanating from inside and outside the company.

- Collecting data throughout the enterprise can result in an overwhelming amount of information. An effective means to navigate through the data maze can make a big difference as to whether the warehouse is used.

- Frequently, data from outside the company contributes to the decision-making process. Incorporating external data and mapping it to the appropriate applications are important data warehouse functions and should be transparent to the user.

- Automating the data extraction and the required frequency of updates needs to be the warehouse's responsibility. Often, subsets of informational data need to be replicated for remote sites. Since data consolidation needs to precede replication, the warehouse becomes a logical place for the consolidation to occur. Monitoring the data replication process to ensure that remote sites are synchronized with events at the central site also falls under the purview of the warehouse solution.

Although these attributes are normally associated with a data warehouse, they may not be immediately required by an organization's data warehouse implementation. But planning ahead for future needs will result in a data warehouse solution that is flexible.

1.7 Data Warehouse Architecture

Data warehouse architecture is based on a relational database management system server that functions as the central repository for informational data. In the data warehouse architecture, operational data and processing is completely separate from data warehouse processing (see Fig. 1.3).

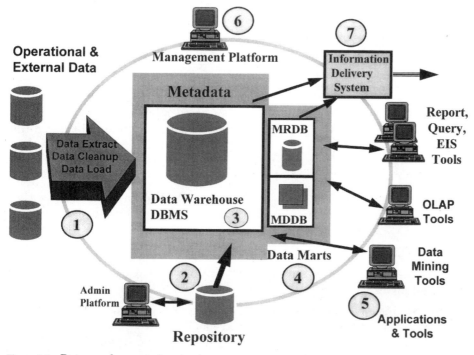

Figure 1.3 Data warehouse environment.

The source data for the warehouse is the operational applications. As the data enters the data warehouse, it is transformed into an integrated structure and format. The transformation process may involve conversion, summarization, filtering, and condensation of data. Because data within the data warehouse contains a large historical component (sometimes covering 5 to 10 years), the data warehouse must be capable of holding and managing large volumes of data as well as different data structures for the same database over time.

The data warehousing architecture shown on Fig. 1.3 clearly identifies seven data warehouse components:

- Data sourcing, cleanup, transformation, and migration tools
- Metadata repository
- Warehouse database technology
- Data marts
- Data query, reporting, analysis, and mining tools
- Data warehouse administration and management
- Information delivery system

A detailed discussion on these components starts in Chap. 6 and continues throughout the book.

A note on operational data stores. The data warehouse architecture shown in Fig. 1.3 can be extended to include operational data stores (ODSs) discussed in Sec. 1.5. An ODS can be used for decision support activities against the operational data as well as a staging area for the data acquisition into the data warehouse (see Fig. 1.4, item 7). The operational data store can sustain the same frequency of updates as the underlying operational (legacy) data, thus providing a consistent view of operational data for decision support and analysis.

In fact, if we consider that ODS is the result of a business need for operational data integration, then we can contrast it with a data warehouse in the following way:

- ODS is subject-oriented, similar to a classic definition of a data warehouse
- ODS is integrated, in the same sense as a data warehouse

However

- ODS is volatile, while a data warehouse is nonvolatile.
- ODS contains very current data, while a data warehouse contains both current and historical data.
- ODS contains detailed data only, and not precalculated summaries and aggregates, as is typical for a data warehouse. Indeed, having aggregates and summaries stored in the ODS practically defeats the main reason for its

existence, since ODS can be update-intensive and near-real-time accurate. If summaries are stored in the ODS, then every update will force an automatic change to these summaries, which is often a resource-intensive and time-consuming operation.

In relationship to a data warehouse, ODS may be used as a data staging area for data warehouse data sourcing. Conversely, the ODS does not have to act as the data staging area for the warehouse, especially if the data warehouse needs to acquire data from external sources that may not be found in the ODS. In this case, the data warehouse can be sourced separately from the ODS, or an additional data source can be included in the data warehouse data extraction component (Fig. 1.4, item 1).

Specifically, the two-tiered data warehouse is a "fat" client model, in which client system functions include user interface, query specification, data analysis, report formatting, aggregation, and data access. The data warehouse server performs data logic, data services, file services, and maintains metadata (see Fig. 1.5).

The two-tiered architecture lacks the scalability and flexibility of the multi-tiered model. Multitiered data warehouse architecture reflects the multitiered client/server model (see Fig. 1.6).

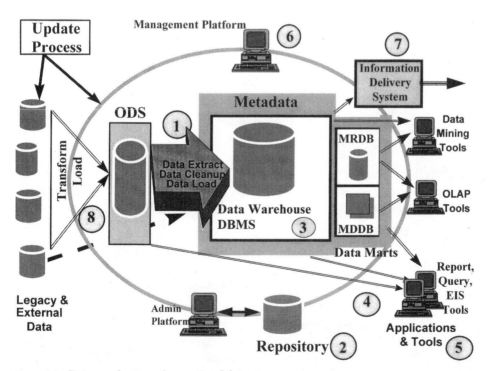

Figure 1.4 Data warehouse and operational data stores.

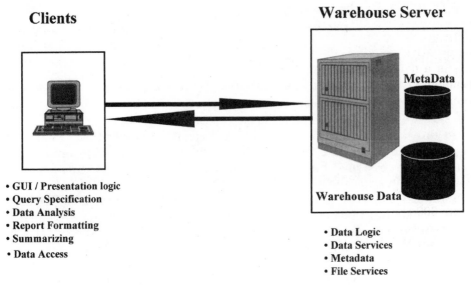

Figure 1.5   Two-tier data warehouse architecture.

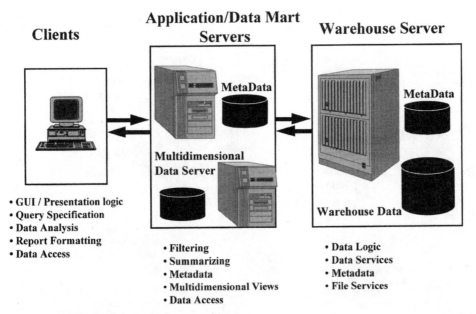

Figure 1.6   Multitiered data warehouse architecture.

This architecture solves the scalability and flexibility issues of the two-tiered data warehouse. Application servers perform data filtering, aggregation, and data access; support metadata; and provide multidimensional views. [*Note:* Alternatively, application servers can be data mart servers, with all the benefits of a dependent data mart environment already integrated into a single scalable architecture (this topic is discussed further in Chap. 6). A client system is left with graphical user interface (GUI), query specification, data analysis, report formatting, and data access.]

1.8 Chapter Summary

The beginning of this chapter briefly reviewed the IDC study on the financial impact of data warehousing. We firmly believe that a technology that can generate 600+ percent return on investment with an average payback of 2.3 years deserves very serious discussion. This discussion is done throughout the book, and it progresses from the introduction of data warehousing to its relationship to client/server architecture, to the analysis of the various warehousing components, to mapping of the technology, and finally to the set of business problems that data warehousing is designed to address.

2

Client/Server Computing Model and Data Warehousing

The previous chapter introduced the concepts of data warehousing, briefly named its components, and indicated one of the architectural foundations of data warehousing: the client/server computing model. This chapter takes a closer look at client/server architecture and one of its most important implications on data warehousing: the notion of specialization of clients and servers.

2.1 Overview of Client/Server Architecture

The term *client/server* originally applied to a software architecture that described processing between two programs: an application and a supporting service. At that time, the client program and the server program did not have to be physically separated; they could be a calling program and a called program running simultaneously on the same machine. Thus, client/server discussions were originally limited to interactions between one client and one server. As computer science and the theory of programming evolved, however, the concepts of some programs capable of providing services or managing resources on behalf of a number of other programs became widely accepted. In fact, the client/server computing model represents a specific instance of distributed cooperative processing, where the relationship between clients and servers is the relationship between hardware and software components.

The client/server computing model covers a wide range of functions, services, and other aspects of the distributed environment. Our discussion of the client/server architecture begins with a look at the evolution of distributed application environments and an introduction to open systems and standards.

2.1.1 Host-based processing

The client/server computing model implies a cooperative processing of requests submitted by a client, or requester, to the server which processes the requests and returns the results to the client.

Client/server cooperative processing is really a special form of distributed processing, in which resources (and tasks affecting the resources) are spread across two or more discrete computing systems. While distributed systems are a relatively new phenomenon, operating-system-level distribution is well known and widely used. One example may be the distribution of arithmetical and input/output (I/O) functions between a central processing unit (CPU) and an I/O channel controller. Other examples include the distribution of network control functions among an IBM host running the Virtual Telecommunications Access Method (VTAM) and a communication controller running the Network Control Program (NCP), or a distribution of operating system functions among multiple CPUs in a multiprocessor such as the IBM 3090/600 (six processors). However, for the purpose of this book, let's consider processing environments as they are viewed by a particular application.

Distributed systems evolved from the most primitive environment to support application processing. It is the host-based processing environment (Fig. 2.1) that does not have any distributed application processing capabilities. Host-based application processing is performed on one computer system with attached unintelligent, "dumb," terminals. A single stand-alone PC or an IBM mainframe with attached character-based display terminals are examples of the host-based processing environment. From an application processing point of view, host-based processing is totally nondistributed.

2.1.2 Master-slave processing

The next-higher level of distributed application processing is master-slave processing (Fig. 2.2). As the name implies, in a master-slave system, slave computers

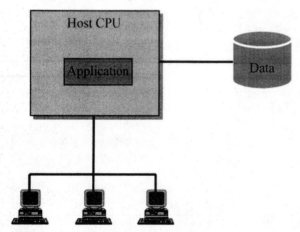

Figure 2.1   Host-based processing environment.

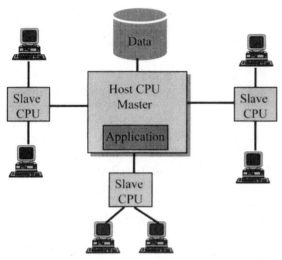

Figure 2.2   Master-slave processing environment.

are attached to the master computer and perform application-processing-related functions only as directed by their master.

Application processing in a master-slave environment is somewhat distributed, even though the distribution of the processing tends to be unidirectional—from the master computer to its slaves. Typically, slave computers are capable of some limited local application processing, such as on-screen field validation, editing, or function key processing. An example of a master-slave processing environment is a mainframe (host) computer, such as IBM 3090, used with cluster controllers and intelligent terminals.

2.1.3 First-generation client/server processing

The client/server processing model has emerged as a higher level of shared-device processing typically found in local area networks (LANs).

In a shared-device LAN processing environment (see Fig. 2.3), personal computers (PCs) are attached to a system device that allows these PCs to share a common resource—a file on a hard disk and a printer are typical examples. In LAN terminology, such shared devices are called *servers* (a file server and a printer server in our example). The name "server" is appropriate, since these shared devices are used to receive requests for service from the PCs for generic, low-level functions. In a typical LAN-based shared-device processing environment, these PC requests are usually limited to services related to shared file or print processing (a common file can be read by several PCs, and some report pages can be sent by multiple PCs to the same printer). The obvious drawback of such an approach is that all application processing is performed on individ-

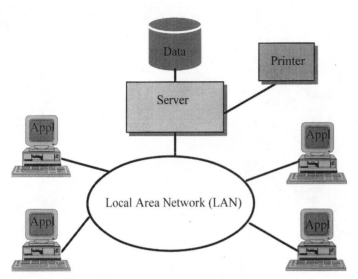

Figure 2.3   Shared-device processing environment.

ual PCs, and only certain functions (print, file I/O) are distributed. Therefore, an entire file has to be sent to a PC that issued a READ request against this file. If a file has to be updated, the entire file is locked by the PC that issued the update request. An example of shared-device processing can be Novell's Net-Ware or Microsoft's LAN Manager, which allows a local area network to have a system dedicated exclusively to the file and/or print services.

The client/server processing model (Fig. 2.4) is a natural extension of shared-device processing. Evolutionary, as local area networks grew in size and number of supported workstations, the shared-device system, both file servers and print servers, also grew in capacity and power. Gradually, these servers became capable of serving a large number of workstations. At the same time, the role of the workstations was also changing—the workstations were becoming "clients" of the servers. The main reason for the change was that in a large LAN environment sharing of file and print services among the workstations in a LAN group was representing only a fraction of a typical application. The significant part of the application functionality was also a good candidate for sharing among LAN users. Therefore, some of the application processing was distributed to a new server: the server that receives requests from applications running on workstations (clients) and processes them for each of its clients. In this model, application processing is divided (not necessarily evenly) between the client and the server. The processing is actually initiated and partially controlled by the service requester—the client, but not in a master-slave fashion. Instead, both the client and the server cooperate to successfully execute an application. A database server such as the SYBASE SQL Server is an example of the client/server processing environment.

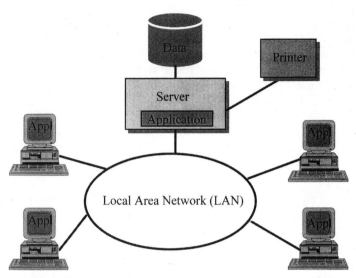

Figure 2.4   Client/server processing environment.

An advantage of the client/server approach can be illustrated by comparison between a file server and a database server. For example, if a PC application needs particular records from a shared file, it sends a request to read the entire file to a file server, which makes this entire file available to the PC. The application running on this PC has to search the file to select requested records. The computing resources of the file server are used to process the entire file, while PC resources are used to run an application that reads every record of the file. If every file record is sent to the PC for processing, a significant portion of the available resources is used inefficiently, and communication lines are overburdened.

In the case of a database server, an application running on a PC sends a record READ request to its database server. The database server processes the database file locally, and sends only the requested records to the PC application. Both the client and the server computing resources cooperate to perform the requested query. To summarize, architecturally, client/server processing requires

- Reliable, robust communications between clients and servers
- Client/server cooperative interactions that are initiated by a client
- Application processing distribution between a client and its server
- Server-enforced control over what services or data clients can request
- Server-based arbitration of conflicting client requests

2.1.4   Second-generation client/server

The client/server computing model has undergone rapid evolution from a "simple" two-tiered client/database-server model to a multitiered, widely distributed, data-rich cooperative distributed environment. The client requests are no longer limited to "just" relational data. The second generation of client/server computing deals with servers dedicated to applications, data, transaction management, systems management, and the like. Data structures supported by this enhanced computing model range from relational to multidimensional to unstructured to multimedia. Clients are now mobile, and the remote access is universally accepted and planned for.

Indeed, the second generation of client/server computing is characterized by a multitiered architecture which promotes migration of the application logic from the client to the application server in a three-tiered environment (see Fig. 2.5).

At the same time, server-based application logic becomes less monolithic, and the advancements in the middleware and application development techniques allow for construction of applications from smaller reusable components. The increasing scalability requirements for data size and performance, advancements in the middleware, and distributed systems enable application logic to be distributed across multiple servers. And finally, an integration of distributed architectures with the object models leads to evolution of procedural client/server systems to a distributed object computing model.

The actual development of a distributed cooperative client/server environment is not a trivial task. To fulfill the requirements of cooperative processing between a client and a server, several questions have to be answered. Among these questions are

- How do the clients and servers find each other across the network?

- Since clients and servers often reside on separate systems (in separate address spaces), how do they (clients and servers) share information?

- How can clients and servers that run on many heterogeneous platforms under many operating systems synchronize their processing across many network protocols?

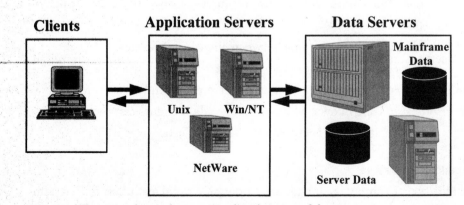

Figure 2.5 Three-tiered second-generation client/server model.

These and other questions are addressed by the client/server architecture in general and the suite of emerging distributed computing standards in particular.

2.2 Server Specialization in Client/Server Computing Environments

The client/server computing paradigm is becoming the dominant force influencing computing in the 1990s. The demands for new systems capabilities follow and are often ahead of the advances in computing technology. At the same time, computing environments are undergoing an evolution from general-purpose centralized systems toward architectures characterized by the collective power of many specialized systems interconnected via advanced networks. Indeed, even nature has successfully demonstrated similar trends. Consider single-cell organisms that evolved into more complex specialized multicellular creatures because more complex systems offer greater capabilities. Cells became specialized because relatively small specialized parts can evolve to achieve the desired functionality more successfully than large general-purpose parts. In a computing environment, cells are individual systems. Combining the specialized systems into a collective computing entity can be accomplished by making all system nodes interconnected in a network and allowing the nodes to enter into desired internode relationships.

In the client/server paradigm, the application components (presentation logic, business logic, database logic, DBMS) and data are distributed across the network. Network nodes can be classified as clients (those who request services) and servers (those who perform requested services). Clients and servers cooperate through a two-party relationship established for each client/server pair, even though there can be a many-to-one relationship between a collection of clients and their server.

Cooperative client/server processing does not entail interactions between equals. For example, it is a client who initiates the application, and as a result, an interaction with its server. It is also true that client systems, not servers, interface directly with end users. Generally speaking, there are certain functions that clients perform best in a client/server environment. Similarly, there are other functions best performed by servers. For instance, DBMSs usually run on servers, not on clients. In the data warehousing environment in particular, the optimum design should call for the server specialization aimed at achieving the highest possible scalability, performance, and throughput when supporting diverse and sophisticated user community performing complex analysis on very large databases.

Server specialization is best reflected in the functionality and design of database servers. Basically, database servers should be able to provide large amounts of a fast-disk storage, significant processing power, and the ability to run many applications (clients) simultaneously. However, as technology continues to evolve, specialization is extending to such functions as communications, terminal emulation, fax (facsimile transmission), library management, and electronic mail (e-mail). The focus of this chapter is the functional and architectural specialization of servers. This specialization is illustrated through examples of the server's hardware architecture and operating system implementations.

2.3 Server Functions

Architecturally, a server is a logical process that provides services to requesting processes. In client/server computing, a client initiates the client/server interaction by sending a request to its server. The functions that a server should perform are determined, in large part, by the types of requests that clients can send to the servers. Conversely, a server that is unable to perform a function requested by a client cannot participate in a cooperative client/server interaction. Ideally, a client should not be sending an unsupported request to such a server. In general, however, once clients and servers are interconnected in a network, the following functions may be required of servers by users:

- *File sharing.* In a workgroup environment, clients may have a need to share the same data file (for example, an insurance rates file in an insurance office). The rates file is placed in a shared-file processor—*file server*—and clients send their file I/O requests to the file server. Usually, a file server provides a client with the access to the entire file, so that when one client updates a shared file, all other clients are unable to access this file. Another typical use of file servers is a file transfer between clients.

- *Printer sharing.* In a workgroup environment, one high-capacity printer may replace all individual client printers. Then all clients may send file print requests to a *print server*. A print server maintains a queue of all files to be printed, sending each print file, in turn, to a shared printer (usually a high-output high-quality printer). Typically, all individual print files are printed with a special separator page that indicates the client name and file name.

- *Database access.* In a client/server environment, application processing is divided between client and server systems. Servers may execute some portion of the business logic and database logic. Similar to file servers, *database servers* provide clients with access to data that resides on a server. However, DBMSs are more sophisticated than basic file I/O access methods. DBMSs provide concurrent data access with various levels of locking granularity and data integrity. DBMSs eliminate data redundancy, allow for user-transparent data distribution, and even allow parts of application-specific data access logic to be incorporated into the DBMS itself. Clients request access to desired data (contrary to a file server's access to the entire file), and all necessary manipulation on the required data is performed at the database server. Thus, multiple clients can access a database concurrently.

- *Communication services.*   In a workgroup environment that is connected to a remote host processor, all communications software and hardware can be concentrated on a special *communication server,* to which clients may forward their communication requests for processing.
- *Fax.*   Facsimile services, that usually require special equipment and software, are now more frequently trusted to dedicated *fax servers.* Clients send and receive fax documents by requesting appropriate services from a fax server.

Other client-requested functions (see, e.g., Fig. 2.6), such as electronic mail and library, network, resource, and configuration management, are being handled in today's client/server environment by appropriate servers.

A server node in a client/server model can be specialized to perform its particular function in the most efficient way. However, besides individual, function-specific specialization, servers as a class of systems can be specialized to satisfy the following general-purpose requirements:

- *Multiuser support.*   Even in a small workgroup environment, a server should be able to service multiple concurrent clients. Clients running different tasks would expect a server to support multitask processing. Note that

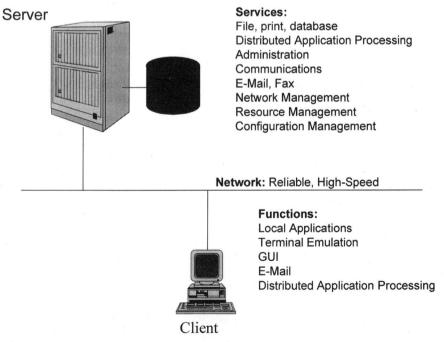

Server

Services:
File, print, database
Distributed Application Processing
Administration
Communications
E-Mail, Fax
Network Management
Resource Management
Configuration Management

Network: Reliable, High-Speed

Functions:
Local Applications
Terminal Emulation
GUI
E-Mail
Distributed Application Processing

Client

Figure 2.6   Client/server functions.

multitasking can be implemented in a single-user system (like OS/2), and is a necessary but not sufficient requirement for multiuser support (multitasking system is not equivalent to a multiuser system).

- *Scalability.*   Scalability is the property of a system which permits an incremental increase in capacity, performance, throughput, the number of supported users, etc., by adding required computing resources as needed and without changing the applications. As the number of applications and their resource requirements and the number of users grow, a server should be able to satisfy these increasing demands on its resources, i.e., should provide scalable performance. Scalability does not mean that users should buy an overcapacity server system at an extra cost. On the contrary, the system should satisfy current requirements and, at the same, time should be easy to expand. This expansion can be achieved by a *vertical* scaling of a server (perhaps by adding or upgrading a CPU or a hard-disk unit), or by a *horizontal* scaling, in which multiple servers cooperate transparently to share the workload. Since vertical scalability does not require additional administrative support as a system scales up, it is often the preferred method of developing scalable systems. Horizontal scalability can be implemented in loosely coupled systems and distributed environments (e.g., databases and applications) as these are becoming more mature and provide better support. One drawback of horizontal scalability in loosely coupled systems is the requirement for additional system administration support, which can affect the degree of scalability an organization can afford. A less attractive and more expensive alternative to scalability would be to replace the system every time it reaches the limits of its capacity, especially given the rapid change of today's business requirements.

- *Performance and throughput.*   A server system should provide performance and throughput levels satisfactory to the business needs and user requirements in a multiuser client/server environment. For example, even if business requirements do not call for subsecond response time for every business transaction, users would hardly appreciate a system that takes more than a few seconds to respond to every user action. Similarly, if a workload on a server increases with the addition of new users, neither the performance nor the throughput should suffer. Since, like any other business requirements, application and user demands on a server can grow quite rapidly, a server system should be able to provide scalable and easily tunable performance and throughput.

- *Storage capacity.*   As the number of users and applications running on a server increases, and as advances in storage technology drive the costs of physical storage down, the demand for extra storage and faster access times becomes one of the critical requirements for a server system. The storage demands come from operating systems that need additional storage to implement new advanced features, from users that desire to store various data files on a server, and from applications such as DBMS and computer-aided software engineering (CASE) tools that are some of the major storage consumers. For example, if a workstation that is running a CASE tool requires at least 32 Mbytes of RAM (random-access memory) and 300 Mbytes of hard-disk space, a server may need 128 to 512 Mbytes of RAM and 2 to 5 Gbytes of disk space to support several of these workstations.

■ *Availability.*   As more and more mission-critical applications are migrated or deployed into a client/server environment, the availability of the server system becomes an essential business requirement. Similar to the mainframe data center environment, today's servers are expected to be up and running most of the time, and the 24 × 7 (24 h, 7 days a week) uptime for a server is not at all unusual. The key factors affecting availability are the server robustness and on-line administration. *Robustness* implies that the server system reduces the importance of any particular failure and recovers from it transparently and automatically. Hardware and software fault tolerance, including features like hot and warm standby servers, disk duplexing and mirroring, and the use of RAID (redundant array of inexpensive disks) disk subsystems, are all designed to improve server robustness. *On-line administration* is aimed to provide continuous operations, where both planned and unplanned outages are reduced or even eliminated. Operations such as database reorganization, backup and recovery, starting and stopping of server processes, system monitoring and configuration, user administration, and application and system upgrades should ideally be performed on line, without taking the server down.

■ *Multimedia.*   As new applications and technologies become available, the demand for multimedia storage support is increasing. Image, video, and sound applications are becoming more and more popular. So, the requirements for a server system may include the ability to store not only digitized images on disk but also hypertext on an optical storage device [WORM (write once–read many), CD-R (CD-recordable), and DVD (diversified video disk)] and video and sound data on videocassettes, compact disks, and video disks.

■ *Networking and communications.*   Client/server communications happen over a communication network. Both client and server systems should have built-in networking capabilities. Without networking there is no client/server interaction and, therefore, no clients and servers. If a system is designed with the networking requirements in mind, the system hardware and software architectures can be optimally integrated with the networking interfaces and protocols.

It will become clear in subsequent discussion that these server requirements are essential to data warehousing implementations.

2.4   Server Hardware Architecture

Discussion of the high-performance aspects of server platform specialization will be concentrated on specialization and advances in the server hardware architecture. This analysis of the server hardware architecture trends is intended to clarify often misused and misunderstood technological jargon used by some hardware vendors, at the same time giving readers a reference point that can be used when a server purchasing decision is to be made. The discussion will focus on three popular server architecture features: *reduced instruction set computer* (RISC), *symmetric multiprocessing* (SMP), and *massively parallel processor* (MPP) architectures.

2.5 System Considerations

The basic principles of computer design describe, among other things, the factors that affect computer performance. In general, these factors include CPU architecture, the size and implementation methods of the instruction set, the ability of compilers to optimize for performance, computer chip technology, and the operating system. In terms of the application, CPU architecture, technology, and instruction set are the resources that the compilers and operating systems should be capable of exploiting to achieve the highest possible performance. Ideally, system's hardware architecture, operating systems, and enabling software (i.e., compilers) are all balanced and tuned according to the nature of the application in order to achieve the highest possible performance and throughput. For example, applications that tend to be easily vectorized can benefit from running on a computer equipped with a vector facility (e.g., a supercomputer like the Cray Y-MP). Many applications, on the other hand, are not vectorizable, and can best operate on systems with scalar performance. These applications may take advantage of a superscalar CPU design (i.e., the IBM POWER, PowerPC, and Digital ALPHA). Other architectures include distributed memory, massively parallel systems, and clustered systems. In either case, in order to fully utilize often expensive hardware solutions, operating systems should be aware of the hardware configurations, and the compilers should be able to produce machine code optimized for these platforms.

Thus, the underlying instruction set becomes one of the critical performance factors. Indeed, computer performance can be described by the following symbolic formula:

$$\text{Performance} = \frac{1}{(\text{cycle time}) \times (\text{path length}) \times (\text{cycles/instruction})}$$

The *cycle time* is the opposite of the system clock rate, and is limited mostly by the underlying chip technology. Most of today's personal computers and workstations can operate at speeds ranging from 75 to 200 MHz, although some high-end workstations offer commercial CPUs with higher speed. In general, faster clock speed may require new, higher-density chip technologies. The shorter the cycle time, the higher the performance.

Path length describes the number of machine instructions necessary to execute one command. The shorter the path length, the higher the resulting performance. CPU architecture, the underlying instruction set, and optimizing compilers are the factors that can reduce the path length.

The *cycles-per-instruction* factor describes how many computer cycles are necessary to execute one instruction. This number can vary from less than 1 (in RISC architectures) to greater than 1 in traditional CISC architectures. If the number is less than 1, then more than one instruction can be executed in one CPU cycle. Thus, performance is better. Computer designers continuously introduce innovative solutions to improve the cycles-per-instruction ratio. Superscalar and superpipelining are the two best known approaches to this problem. Other factors affecting computer performance include memory access times, external storage characteristics, and I/O data transfer rates; and in a networking environment, communications and networks.

Some systems can be optimized best for commercial environments, which are generally characterized by integer processing, transaction processing, file and disk subsystems manipulation, and a significant number of attached low- to medium-function terminals and workstations. Other systems may be best suited to scientific environments, which are generally characterized by very high-floating-point performance requirements, and few high-function graphical workstations attached to the central server via very high-speed interconnections. Still other systems may be designed to achieve a careful balance between integer and floating-point performance, thus extending the system's applicability to both commercial and scientific worlds. In any event, when system designers wish to address the performance issue, they may concentrate their efforts on one of the following:

- Shortening the instruction path length
- Improving the cycles-per-instructions ratio
- Speeding up the system clock

The designers may attempt to achieve the desired performance for the mix of integer and floating-point instructions, thus creating a universal high-performance architecture.

2.6   RISC versus CISC

In the early 1980s some system designers argued that the then-current chip architectures could yield higher performance if new architectures would adopt the same principles as some of the best optimizing compilers; that is, optimizing compilers could produce almost as good code as the best programmers could write in Assembler language. Analyzing the compiled code, David Patterson of the University of California at Berkeley found that compilers used the simplest instructions of an available instruction set. These simple instructions could be used more efficiently than the complex instructions when the system hardware was optimized for this task. Unfortunately, the opposite was true. Traditional computer architectures were optimized for more complex instructions. The instructions in these architectures were decoded by the microcode that was placed in the microprocessor hardware. Patterson proposed the *reduced instruction set computer* (RISC), as opposed to the traditional *complex instruction set computer* (CISC). In RISC architectures instructions are decoded directly by the hardware, thus increasing the speed of the processing.

Originally, a RISC processor contained only the simplest instructions extracted from a CISC architecture, and the hardware was optimized for these instructions. Not only did the RISC design contain the simplest instructions, but the number of available instructions was significantly lower than with a comparable CISC design. Beginning in 1980, Patterson's group undertook the task of implementing RISC prototype processors, called RISC I and RISC II. RISC I contained 44,000 transistors, was completed in 19 months, and outperformed a Digital VAX 11/780 by a ratio of 2 to 1. An interesting historical fact is that the first RISC machine (although not identified by that name) was the IBM 801 System—a result of a research project conducted by IBM from 1975 to 1979.

Note that, besides the performance, the apparent simplicity of RISC architecture provides another advantage—a designer can realize the RISC design in silicon chips faster. Therefore, time to market can be reduced and the latest in technology can be used in a current design more quickly than comparable CISC design.

The simplicity of RISC architecture is relative. Second-generation RISC designs introduced more complex instruction sets and increased the number of instructions (sometimes comparable to CISC design). In recent years, designers began exploring a richly diverse set of RISC architectures and implementations. This diversity is most apparent in the recent RISC implementations from Digital: the ALPHA chip and the IBM/Motorola/Apple PowerPC chip. Even though both are superscalar implementations, these two implementations represent very different philosophies for achieving high-performance: complexity versus simplicity. The PowerPC architecture defines powerful instructions, such as *floating-point multiply/add* and *update load/store,* that get more work done with fewer instructions. The ALPHA architecture simplicity, on the other hand, lends itself to very high-clock-rate implementations. Therefore, the real performance leverage in the second-generation RISC design is achieved by a carefully balanced tradeoff between an optimized definition of the instruction set, machine organization, and processor logic design.

An important RISC feature is that each instruction is simple enough to be executed in one CPU cycle. In a "simple" RISC architecture, this may be true for a simple integer addition, but a floating-point addition may be simulated by several single-cycle instruction. To alleviate this and other similar problems, second-generation RISC architecture may be improved by a *superscalar* implementation (IBM's RS/6000 and PowerPC and Digital's ALPHA are examples of the superscalar RISC implementation). Superscalar design splits the processor into separate units so that the processor can sustain execution of two or more instructions per clock cycle. For example, the branch processor decodes instructions and assigns them to the other two units: integer processor and floating-

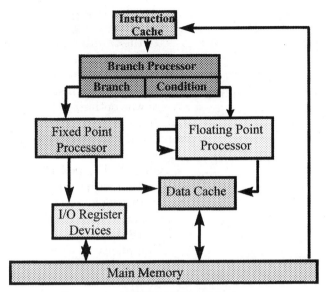

Figure 2.7   Superscalar RS/6000 RISC architecture.

point processor. Figure 2.7 illustrates the logical view of IBM RS/6000 super-scalar POWER RISC implementation.

Each of the three processors can perform several instructions simultaneously. Integer and floating-point units contain multiple buffers to handle new operations before old ones are completed, and the branch can initiate multiple instructions. The resulting instruction "pipeline" in effect breaks instruction processing into a series of stages connected like stations in an assembly line. In the RS/6000 example, the five-stage pipelining and superscalar design allows up to four instructions (one fixed point, one floating-point, one branch, and one condition) or five simultaneous operations per cycle (three integer operations—fixed-point, branch, and condition; and two floating-point operations that constitute one floating-point instruction—multiply and add). That's why a superscalar RISC machine performs well in commercial, high-performance integer processing environments and in scientific, floating-point-intensive applications. Multiple vendors continuously work on the innovations in superscalar design, which result in frequent leapfrogging in performance among the vendors. For example, the next generation of the POWER architecture (POWER2) practically doubles the number of simultaneous instruction by integrating additional integer and floating-point units into the design. And the PowerPC chips (a result of a joint IBM/Motorola/Apple venture) offer even higher levels of price performance with a relatively low cost and power consumption.

A fundamental implementation technique used in RISC architectures is *pipelining,* a technique that allows more than one instruction to be processed at the same time. A typical pipelined CPU uses several execution steps, or

stages, to execute one cycle-long instruction. The first-generation RISC implementations developed in the 1980s tended to look alike, with simple five-stage
instruction pipelines (see Fig. 2.8).

Pipelining achieves high performance through the parallelism of processing
several instructions at once, each in a different pipeline stage. To optimize the
performance and increase the throughput of the pipeline, designers increase
clock rates and introduce higher granularity of stages, known as *superpipelining*. For example, MIPS R4000 uses eight-stage pipelining, and Digital's
ALPHA uses parallel pipelines with different numbers of stages: 10 for floating
point and 7 for integer and load and store instructions.

In a well-designed pipeline, all stages contain logic with approximately the
same execution times. A careful balance between the number of instructions,
clock speed, and the number of pipeline stages in superscalar RISC implementations will result in even higher performance levels of microcomputers, and
workstations capable of hundreds of SPECint92 and SPECfp92 [Standard Performance Evaluation Corp. (SPEC) benchmarks for the integer and floating-
point performance] will be available in the near future at the cost of a regular
PC. In recent years, designers began exploring a richly diverse set of architectures and implementations. This diversity is most apparent in the recent RISC
implementations from Digital—the ALPHA chip and the PowerPC chip from
IBM/Motorola/Apple. Both are superscalar implementations; that is, they can
sustain execution of two or more instructions per clock cycle. Otherwise, these
two implementations represent very different philosophies for achieving high
performance.

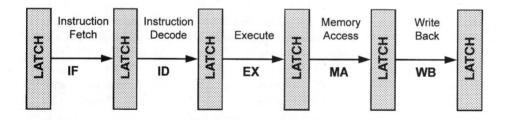

Clock Cycle:	0	1	2	3	4	5	6	7
Instruction 1	IF	ID	EX	ME	WB			
Instruction 2		IF	ID	EX	ME	WB		
Instruction 3			IF	ID	EX	ME	WB	
Instruction 4				IF	ID	EX	ME	WB

An instruction sequence flowing down the pipeline

Figure 2.8   "Classic" five-stage pipeline.

The PowerPC architecture defines powerful instructions, such as *floating-point multiply/add* and *update load/store,* which get more work done with fewer instructions. The ALPHA architecture simplicity, on the other hand, lends itself to very high-clock-rate implementations (see Table 2.1).

The ALPHA processor can afford to execute more instructions if it can issue them faster. The typical example is *load and store* instructions that transfer only 32-bit or 64-bit quantities. As a result, ALPHA implementations have a shorter cache load path, and the cache can be accessed with a faster clock.

The PowerPC uses independent pipelines, buffering, and out-of-order dispatching, and it does a lot of computation in each pipe stage. Advanced branch handling and out-of-order dispatch lead to more efficient use of pipes and more overlap among loop iterations. The ALPHA has tightly coupled pipelines, little buffering, and in-order issuing, and it does relatively less work in each pipe stage.

The PowerPC gains performance by design cleverness; the ALPHA gains performance by design simplicity. This tradeoff is a classic one, and the fact that both philosophies lead to viable processors is probably an indication that either choice is satisfactory as long as the implementation is done well.

The performance advantage of the RISC architecture has to be leveraged by optimizing compilers and operating systems. To date, many UNIX-based operating systems and Microsoft's Windows/NT are capable of supporting RISC architecture.

2.7   Multiprocessor Systems

Multiprocessing is becoming an indispensable tool for improving the performance of computer systems struggling to support ever more complex and demanding applications. In fact, multiprocessing systems and parallel database

TABLE 2.1   Summary of RISC Architectural Characteristics

Feature	PowerPC 601	ALPHA 21064
Basic architecture	Load/store	Load/store
Instruction length	32 bits	32 bits
Byte/halfword load and store	Yes	No
Condition codes	Yes	No
Conditional moves	No	Yes
Integer registers	32	32
Integer register size	32/64 bits	64 bits
Floating-point registers	32	32
Floating-point register size	64 bits	64 bits
Floating-point format	IEEE 32-bit, 64-bit quantities	IEEE, VAX 32-bit, 64-bit quantities
Virtual address	52–80 bits	43–64 bits
32/64 mode bit	Yes	No
Segmentation	Yes	No
Page size	4 kbytes	Implementation-specific
Clock frequency, MHz	66–100 (PowerPC 604)	166–275 (ALPHA 21064A)
SPECint92	63–160 (PowerPC 604)	70–170 (ALPHA 21064A)
SPECfp92	72–165 (PowerPC 604)	105–290 (ALPHA 21064A)

technology promise to elevate client/server computing to new levels in performance, throughput, scalability, and availability. Generally, adding processors creates the possibility of performing several computing tasks in parallel, thus speeding up the overall execution of the program. As CPU costs decrease, users find that adding processors to their existing multiprocessor hardware is significantly more economical than either adding computer systems or replacing existing systems with more powerful uniprocessor systems. Conversely, adding entire computers to increase throughput has its drawbacks:

- Adding processors usually results in addition of expensive peripheral devices.

- Stand-alone uniprocessors cannot share memory unless they are networked at an additional expense. To speed up applications, an operating environment including appropriate load balancing software must be in place to distribute and synchronize applications, usually at additional cost and complexity.

- Adding faster uniprocessors is more expensive than obtaining the same performance by increasing the number of processors.

Therefore, designers are focusing on computing architectures where the processing units are physically close and are often integrated by a single operating system. In such a system, the processing units (PUs) speed up a single computational task by executing it jointly (in parallel). These *parallel* systems have high-performance computing as their objective, but also add such objectives as synchronicity, reliability, resource sharing, and extensibility. An additional and important goal is to achieve *linear* speed-up and scale-up; for example, doubling the number of processors cuts the response time in half (linear speed-up) or provides the same performance on twice as much data (linear scale-up). In addition to these general objectives, multiprocessing systems and specialized parallel database management systems address a number of key business requirements:

- The need for fast response time on complex queries—a requirement for decision support systems (DSSs) and data warehousing.

- The need to support large (and growing) data sets. This is especially true for very large database (VLDB) support, that goes beyond parallel query execution—parallel execution of database utilities that load, back up, and create an index is the only way to effectively manage large databases that exceed hundreds of gigabytes (Gbytes) and even terabytes (Tbytes).

- The need to support a large number of concurrent users.

- The need for increasingly high transaction rates for on-line transaction processing (OLTP) applications.

- The need to effectively support new large-size data types like multimedia, image, text, voice, full-motion video, and new application classes such as data warehouse, multimedia Internet access, home shopping, and video-on-demand.

As client/server computing matures into its second generation, multiprocessor systems become the mainstream computing platform for high-end servers, and demonstrate the clear need and advantages of server specialization. This chapter takes a closer look at the hardware configurations of multiprocessing systems. Multiprocessor systems can be classified by the following:

- Degree of coupling that measures how strongly the PUs are connected by evaluating the ratio of the amount of data exchanged among PUs to the amount of local processing performed by PUs in executing a task

- Interconnection structure that determines the network topology—bus, star, ring, tree, etc.

- Component interdependence that determines the level of dependence between PUs

The principal distinction between different classes of multiprocessor systems is the degree of coupling between the processors and the memory. Specifically, multiple-processor parallel systems have either *shared* or *distributed memory*. Additionally, these systems can be implemented with an either *shared-* or *distributed-disk* subsystem, although the impact of shared versus distributed memory is much more severe from the general architecture and programming model viewpoints. In fact, a shared-memory system is typically the one with a shared-disk design, while the distributed-memory systems may have either shared or distributed disk implementations.

While in general the topology of a distributed system can change because of communication link failure, interprocess communications in distributed-memory parallel systems, for instance, are more reliable and predictable.

2.7.1   SMP design

A *shared-memory* multiprocessor [typically, a symmetric multiprocessor (SMP)] incorporates a number of processors, called *processing units* (PUs), that share a common memory, common I/O and various other common system resources. In other words, this is a *tightly coupled* design, in which an SMP machine coordinates interprocess communications (IPCs) through a global memory that all PUs share. A typical shared memory multiprocessor consists of a relatively small number (4 to 30 on average) of processors. Processors select tasks to be executed from a common task pool, and are interconnected via a high-speed common system bus, thereby providing extremely efficient interprocessor communications.

Shared-memory multiprocessing ensures that any processor completing one task is immediately put to work on another, next available task. All PUs share a single copy of an operating system, and each PU executes a task selected from a common task pool. (*Note:* Not every operating system can support SMP. An SMP system requires an operating system that can take advantage of the shared-memory multiple-processor configuration. The operating system requirements for the SMP are discussed later in this chapter.)

Typically, in order to reduce the volume of shared memory traffic, each PU has one or more memory caches. One or more memory controllers may be included in this architecture to support the high-memory-access requirements of multiple PUs.

A system in which all PUs in a shared-memory multiprocessor have equal capabilities and can perform the same functions is called a *symmetric multiprocessor* (SMP) (Fig. 2.9). Each PU in an SMP system can run user applications as well as any portion of the operating system, including such operations as I/O interrupt, operating system kernel functions, and I/O drivers. In addition, any task can be executed on any PU and can migrate from PU to PU as system load characteristics change.

The SMP implementation has a significant positive effect on scalability. Indeed, if a system designates one PU to perform a particular task (e.g., service I/O interrupts), this PU will become overloaded as the number of I/O requests increases, and overall system performance will degrade.

SMP architecture provides two high-level features:

■ *Seamless execution.* This is the ability of an SMP system to seamlessly, transparently to the user, support existing applications. In truly seamless

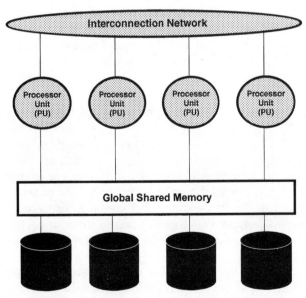

Figure 2.9 Symmetric shared-memory multiprocessor.

implementations, all applications originally written for a uniprocessor will be able to run on an SMP system unmodified. By taking full advantage of multiprocessing, applications can achieve significant performance gains. This is especially important for servers running DBMSs and supporting transaction processing.

- *Limited scalable performance.*   This encompasses two components: computational growth and I/O growth. Computational growth can be achieved by adding processing elements, while I/O growth can be a result of adding peripherals and/or I/O buses. It is important to note that the addition of a PU increases the overall system performance up to a limit. The per PU increase is not equal to the performance of the individual PU, but rather corresponds to a fraction of this PU performance. As the number of PUs grows, various factors such as system bus and memory subsystem design, cache sizes, and the need to keep certain memory regions protected as they keep data specific to a given PU, all affect the resultant performance. Another obstacle to the SMP scalability is a feature called *cache coherency*—a frequency at which a cache has to be repeatedly emptied and filled as tasks continue to get scheduled and preempted (interrupted) for the execution on a given PU.

2.7.2   SMP features

If asked to name only the two most important SMP characteristics, it could be the following:

- The most significant benefit would be the use of a familiar traditional programming paradigm. Since the memory is shared, every program assumes that all memory is available for storage and retrieval. It is, in fact, the responsibility of the operating system (sometimes assisted by the hardware microcode) to ensure that multiple programs or threads of execution do not "step on" each other and corrupt each other's memory content. Today's SMP machines support standards-based operating systems and application enablers (compilers, tools, database management systems, etc.).

- The most significant drawback is related to the limited scalability—the throughput of an SMP system does not demonstrate a linear growth in the direct proportion to the number of PUs. Depending on the PU and system bus speed, the SMP throughput does not increase (and can even decrease, due to the local cache coherency problem) when the number of PUs exceed some (machine-specific) number, typically less than 30.

Nevertheless, within its scalability limitations, SMP-based systems provide the ability to increase performance incrementally. Therefore, SMP systems has become a mainstream of today's server platform. They allow for future upgradability, and represent a cost-effective solution for such applications as DBMS, gateways, and transaction processing. Typically, these applications are composed of smaller, relatively independent tasks that can be assigned to numerous processors. Applications such as these are ideally suited to run on servers in a client/server environment.

Providing symmetry in shared-memory systems has an impact on both hardware and software architectures. Specifically, an operating system design becomes more complex on an SMP system. In fact, without an SMP-capable operating system it is very difficult to realize the potential scalability benefits of a symmetric multiprocessor. Software features supporting scalable SMP performance include capabilities to execute the operating system kernel, I/O interrupts, and I/O drivers on all PUs.

2.7.3   SMP operating systems

Let's take a closer look at an SMP-capable operating system. Such an operating system is designed to assign work to available PUs based on a particular load-balancing algorithm. This work is represented by processes and lighter, finer-granularity threads. A *thread,* which is defined by POSIX as a single sequential flow of control within a process, allows developers to write cooperative routines, all sharing access to the same data in memory. Therefore, an operating system that does not support threads can take advantage of the SMP hardware only on the large-grain process level, while a threads-capable operating system can be much more efficient when running multiple applications as well as single multithreaded applications.

Shared-memory protection.   The SMP operating system complexity is related to the locking strategy that is designed to prevent simultaneous updates to data structures and codes in SMP common shared memory. The locking strategy is designed to address the shared-memory nature of SMP systems, where an SMP-aware operating system has to be able to prevent processes from modifying each other's memory and system resources. In other words, the SMP OS must make sure that processor 1 does not let process A modify memory that process B, running on processor 2, is using. Since typically there is no master PU in an SMP, the processors must let each other know about the processes they run and the memory area they use.

Dynamic load balancing.   This feature is another critical requirement of an SMP software architecture. Indeed, if a PU has been added to an SMP system, the operating system and application software should be able to take advantage of the additional PU by dynamically redistributing the load among all available PUs.

Various SMP operating systems handle memory protection, multithreading support, and load balancing differently, with various effects on scalability and performance. For example, Windows/NT is multithreaded and SMP-capable, with the multithreaded NT kernel managing resource allocation by acting as a nonpreemptable master scheduler of processes and threads. Windows/NT memory protection is based on its nonpreemptable microkernel architecture and protected subsystems, which copy data structures for a thread to a different memory area when this thread is passed to a new subsystem. While this approach limits the possibility for a conflict, copying data structures is time-consuming.

UNIX operating systems vary in the way they support multithreading and SMP. Open Software Foundation's OSF/1 operating system supports SMP by defining an IEEE POSIX 1003.4 *P-Threads* standard-compliant threads. HP-UX and Sun Solaris are both multithreaded and SMP-capable, while UNIX System V Release 4 (SVR4) is not multithreaded but supports SMP by using child processes that the operating system spawns on different PUs. Solaris is using a complex system of reader and writer locks to ensure memory protection.

Scalable software architectures are designed not only to take advantage of the SMP hardware architecture transparently and seamlessly but also to provide for an easy entry into parallel computing, where multiple applications can run simultaneously. There are several techniques for developing parallel applications capable of achieving maximum performance in a multiprocessing system, including problem partitioning (dividing a problem into several smaller independent parts) and data decomposition for load balancing.

2.8   SMP Implementations

High-performance SMP systems offer comparable or higher performance than do traditional uniprocessors, while promising an impressive incremental performance scalability within the design limits. Properly designed SMP systems allow for seamless execution and the ability of existing applications to execute transparently without modifications. That is why several SMP systems available today are used as DBMS servers, communication gateways, and transaction processing platforms.

Some popular shared-memory systems include products like Pyramid Technology's high-end machines, which combine SMP implementation with RISC technology, Sequent Computers Symmetry series, Sun Ultra series (3000, 4000, and 6000), and HP's Enterprise Server (both T and K series). Even such a well-known supercomputer maker as Cray Research is serious about SMP architecture, as demonstrated by its CRAY SUPERSERVER 6400 (Sun Super-SPARC-based, 4- to 64-PU SMP system running Solaris 2).

Today's SMP servers are quite powerful, and often exceed performance ratings traditionally attributed to high-end mainframes and supercomputers. Consider the SMP offering from a well-known and reliable UNIX server vendor—the T-500. The system combines HP's advanced PA-RISC processor architecture with symmetric multiprocessing software and a balanced high-end memory and I/O bus. HP Corporate Business Server T-500 uses up to 12 state-of-the-art RISC-based processors, each equipped with a large, high-speed cache memory (1 Mbyte per CPU for instructions and data each). This system is designed to be independent of the semiconductor and implementation technologies. Therefore, the T-500 can take advantage of leading-edge technologies as they develop. For example, the use of CMOS VLSI technology enables the entire CPU to be integrated into a single-circuit-board module. The resulting reduction in complexity reduces system cost while increasing performance and reliability.

A system like T-500 is designed for growth by incorporating a 64-bit virtual address capability with the total addressing range of 256 terabytes (Tbytes). It offers a high-speed processor memory bus capable of accessing main memory at the bandwidth of 1 gigabyte per second (Gbyte/s). This bus is designed to minimize bus contention. Special hardware features ensure processor cache coherency—a well-known problem in SMP designs. Not only such a system is designed for high-performance computing. To satisfy commercial customers running large databases, the T-500 supports eight I/O channels with an aggregate I/O throughput of 256 Mbytes/s. Its HP-UX operating system support is standards-based and is compliant with POSIX 1003.1 and 1003.2, FIPS 151-1, and X/Open Portability Guide Issue 4 (XPG4).

3

Parallel Processors and Cluster Systems

The previous chapter discussed the specialization of clients and servers in a distributed client/server environment, focusing on server specialization for higher scalability, performance, throughput, ability to handle very large databases, and other important functionality. This specialization was analyzed in the examples of the microprocessors architectures such as CISC and RISC, and shared-memory architectures such as symmetric multiprocessors like SMP. This chapter continues this discussion by taking a closer look at distributed-memory architectures that are finding its way into successful implementations of very large data warehouses.

3.1 Distributed-Memory Architecture

As was described above, SMP machines have an inherent architectural limitation on scalability. One solution that avoids this limitation is a nontrivial approach employed by distributed memory massively parallel processors (MPPs) and clusters of uniprocessors and SMP systems. These systems are often called *shared-nothing* systems, since neither the PUs nor the local memory are shared, thus eliminating the main reason for the limited scalability of the SMP.

A common attribute of a *distributed-memory* machine, whether an MPP or a cluster, is a high-performance interconnection network that interconnects PUs and their local memory units. An interconnection network can be a high-speed "external" LAN (for typical SMP clusters), high-speed "internal" switch, a connection tree, a hypercube, a star, a mesh, etc. Many of these solutions are proprietary innovative designs, but the standardization efforts move into this area as well; for example, there is a new interconnection system called the Scalable Coherent Interconnect (SCI), which is an IEEE standard.

3.1.1 Shared-nothing architectures

In a distributed-memory machine, all PUs are connected to each other via an intercommunication mechanism and communicate by passing messages (see Fig. 3.1). In other words, distributed-memory systems are considered *loosely coupled* multiprocessor systems. Although both MPP and cluster systems adhere to the same distributed-memory computing model, they can be differentiated from one another by a number of attributes. For example, in the MPP design, a *proprietary* interconnect provides very high-bandwidth and low-latency communication between nodes. An MPP operating system that is designed to take advantage of this proprietary scalable interconnection network is responsible for the inter-PU communications. These systems were originally designed to solve numeric-intensive processor-bound Grand Challenge problems, and were once limited to specialized communities focused around a handful of centralized and extremely expensive computing facilities. MPP operating systems are optimized for the programs that are often easily partitionable for the parallel execution. As the number of PUs increases, these systems demonstrate excellent scalability due to the nature of the applications they are designed to handle. Often, such an MPP system can contain and effectively use hundreds and even thousands of PUs.

One obvious drawback of the distributed memory architecture is it's requirement for a "new" distributed programming paradigm. Indeed, a traditional programming paradigm assumes that all memory is available to the CPU for storing and retrieving the data. In a distributed-memory system, a program the executes an instruction such as a = a + 1 has to first locate the variable a in its local or remote memory (in the latter case, the processor needs to issue special instructions to retrieve the value of a from the remote location and to send it to this processor's memory). The result is a need for a *new operating system* design, *new compilers, new* programming *languages,* etc.

Distributed-memory systems can be classified by their interconnect architectures, or by the way the messages are passed and synchronized. Parallel architectures can be divided into contemporary *multiple-instruction multiple-data* (MIMD) and older *single-instruction multiple-data* (SIMD) machines. In *MIMD* systems (such as Intel Paragon's XP/S and IBM's SP) multiple processors can simultaneously execute different instructions on different data. Therefore, MIMD systems are inherently asynchronous computers that can synchronize processes by either accessing control data (semaphores, switches, etc.) in shared memory, or by passing synchronization messages in distributed-memory systems. MIMD systems are best suited to *large-grain* parallelism (on a subroutine and task level). An extension of MIMD is the *multiple-program multiple-data* (MPMD) model, in which multiple processors concurrently execute multiple programs accessing different data. The MPMD model supports parallel database processing for the commercial applications of the MPP technology as well as clusters of uniprocessors and SMPs.

SIMD machines (such as the Thinking Machine Corporation's CM-2, MasPar's MP-1 and MP-2) are by design synchronous parallel computers in which

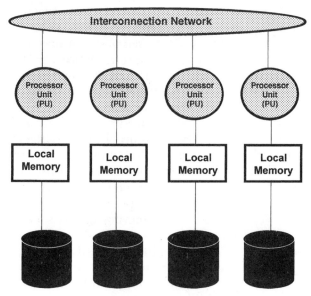

Figure 3.1   Distributed memory architecture.

all PUs execute the same instruction at the same time (or remain idle). SIMD machines are typically controlled by a central control unit that broadcasts a single instruction to all PUs, at which time PUs execute that instruction in synchronous fashion on their local data. *Fine-grained* (instruction-level) parallelism is best suited for SIMD machines.

In general, distributed-memory MPP and cluster systems promise a tremendous increase in scalable performance and throughput. Arguably, distributed-memory systems are the result of the shift in the computing paradigm, discussed in Chap. 1, and could become a dominant enterprise server architecture for mission-critical applications of today and tomorrow.

3.1.2   Shared-disk systems

A shared-nothing distributed-memory system can be very effective for those problems that lend themselves to be easily partitioned. Sometimes called "embarrassingly parallel," these problems can be solved by concurrently executing the same instruction against different data records read from individual disks. For example, consider a counting problem—count all records in the file that contain amounts greater than $100 in a MONEY field. Assuming a uniform distribution of the MONEY values throughout the file, to solve this problem on a shared-nothing machine could be as simple as

- Partitioning the file into equal parts
- Running a program like IF MONEY > $100 ADD 1 TO COUNT on all processors
- Adding all COUNT values to get the final answer

If the file contains 1,000,000 records, partitioning it in 1000 parts can theoretically speed up the performance of the query by 1000 times relative to a sequential (nonparallel) execution. However, if the problem becomes more complex (i.e., multilevel selection criteria), or if the data is not uniformly distributed, the problem cannot be solved as effectively by blind partitioning; the elapsed time of the overall operation will be skewed toward the partitioned that has the most occurrences of the MONEY field that satisfy the selection criteria.

One way to reduce this data skew is a variation of distributed-memory shared-nothing architecture in which the memory is distributed but the disk storage is shared (see Fig. 3.2). Such a system has many scalability characteristics of the distributed-memory MPP system, but also provides a single image of the disk subsystem that can be easily managed by a database management system.

In fact, this architecture assumes that all processors have direct access to all disks. To make this design effective for parallel database access, an extra software layer called a *distributed cache manager* is required to globally manage cache concurrency among processors. While the shared-disk design helps reduce DBMS dependency on data partitioning, it also introduces a potential limitation on the overall system scalability for distributed-memory systems.

3.2   Research Issues

Amdahl law.   Although hardware parallelism is clearly a desired and beneficial approach to achieve scalability, it does have some practical limitations that do not depend on the particular approach (SMP, MPP, etc.) discussed above. Consider Amdahl's law of scalability, which states that every process in the uni-

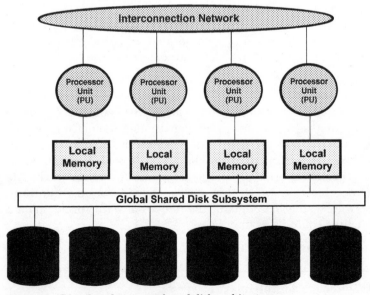

Figure 3.2   Distributed memory shared-disk architecture.

verse has a component that is inherently sequential (e.g., a process of dividing a single query into subqueries and distributing these subqueries to individual processor to be processed in parallel). Specifically,

$$T_N = \frac{T_1(p)}{N} + T_1(1-p),$$

where T_N is computing time using N processors, T_1 is computing time using 1 processor, and p is the percent that can be parallelized. Thus, the speed limit as N approaches infinity is $1/(1-p)$.

As long as p stays below 100%, you will always be limited by this inherently nonscalable component, and thus cannot get a perfect scalability. Therefore, a significant challenge facing computer designers is to make that nonscalable component as small as possible.

The theoretical approach to increase the p is to leverage capabilities of distributed-memory architectures in shared-nothing environments or applying similar principles to shared-resource environments [e.g., using nonuniform memory access (NUMA) or cache-only memory access (COMA) architectures, discussed in Sec. 3.4]. Since distributed-memory architecture uses a different computing and programming paradigm, its emergence in the commercial marketplace is surrounded by a number of active theoretical and practical issues. The bulk of the issues is related to what is known as the *paradigm integration* caused by the advent of high-power MPP machines and low-latency high-bandwidth intercommunication networks. Paradigm integration means that a new MPP-compliant program should combine both task and data parallelism with a single application. The need for the paradigm integration is driven by the code reuse requirement in a parallel architecture, heterogeneous models that combine multidisciplines of the numeric-intensive tasks, data visualization, and commercial computing. The latter deserves a special interest because of its often contradictory on-line transaction processing (OLTP) and decision support system (DSS) requirements. Another important feature of commercial high-performance computing is the requirements and design complexity of parallel database management systems capable of very complex query and very large database processing. The discussion on parallel database management system can be found in Chap. 4.

Some of the current MPP research issues are listed below.

- *Traditional performance measurements.* These measurements [million instructions per second, million floating-point operations per second (MIPS, MFLOPS)] have to be redefined for MPP/SMP systems, since they do not reflect real performance characteristics.

- *Scalability.* How MPP system performance is affected by the problem size, or by the number of PUs.

- *Operating systems.* Operating systems designed for distributed and parallel processing are in their infancy; operating system design and construction is an open problem, especially given the state of accepted standards in the area of microkernels, interprocess communications, object-oriented operating systems, load balancing, etc.

- *Task scheduling.* This is a rather complex issue that has lead so far to a number of heuristic solutions, each of which may or may not work under different circumstances.

- *Innovative programming methods.* Traditional sequential shared-memory programming methods may not work or may not be able to take advantage of the distributed-memory architecture; issues like MIMD-based programming, data-parallel programming, functional programming, and tuple-space programming are just a few research items researchers are working on.

- *Compilers and optimization work.* This focuses mostly on two directions. The *implicit* approach modifies existing languages or introduces new ones that help conceal the underlying system from the programmer (the preferred way for commercial computing). Obviously, this approach shifts a burden of parallel complexity to the compiler developer; currently, there is a shortage of good parallel compilers. The *explicit* approach extends existing languages, or introduces new languages to express parallelism directly. This approach has a serious impact on existing programmer's skill set.

- *Database systems.* Many vendors and researchers in a scientific community are working diligently to develop truly parallel database management systems. Oracle, IBM, Informix, and Sybase already have versions of their products targeted for *specific* MPP environments (i.e., there is a production version of Oracle 7 for several MPP systems). Full-function Parallel DBMS (PDBMS) development is facing the same issues of reliability, scalability, performance, etc. that the rest of the MPP community is forced to deal with.

- *Heterogeneous processing, reliability, and code portability.* These are "traditional" distributed-system issues that are becoming even more pressing with the advent of MPP and clusters, especially in the commercial arena.

The advent of the revolutionary distributed-memory architectures is a clear indication of the necessity and benefits of the server specialization. Indeed, the specialization would not go that far if the set of business problems facing the server did not require extraordinary measures.

3.3 Cluster Systems

As was mentioned above, the distributed-memory MIMD/MPMD architecture maps well onto a collection of loosely coupled uniprocessors or SMPs connected by local area networks.

In a cluster environment, each PU executes a copy of a *standard* operating system, and the inter-PU communications are performed over an open-systems-based interconnect (e.g., Ethernet, TCP/IP) by either special operating systems extensions or by an add-on software components.

The relatively low bandwidth and high latency of the interconnection network limit the cluster's ability to efficiently communicate data between nodes. In fact, many clustered systems are more sensitive to communications, data sharing, and synchronization requirements than are MPP systems, since the communication in clusters is frequently over a standard communication network, and typically is based on standard communications protocols [e.g., Transmission Control Protocol/Internet Protocol (TCP/IP)], although systems using Fiber Distributed Data Interface (FDDI), Asynchronous Transfer Mode (ATM), High Performance Parallel Interface (HiPPI), and Fiber Channel Standard (FCS) are capable of supporting an extremely high bandwidth (e.g., up to a 800-mbit/s link speed for HiPPI, 1065 Mbits/s for FCS). While the major cost element of the MPP system is the high-speed internal interconnection network, clusters of uniprocessors and SMPs shift the cost to the large number of software licenses that result from the need to install operating system software on each node in the cluster. On the positive side, cluster systems are often designed for high availability by providing shared access to disks and better balancing between processor-bound and I/O-bound tasks. As such, cluster systems can be successfully deployed for both the scientific and commercial applications. The promise of unlimited scalability; the availability and price performance of the SMP systems; the continuous growth in server performance and throughput requirements; the emergence of new application classes; the need to support new data types, large amounts of data, and large user communities; and the improvements in parallel database management system software all lead major server vendors to start the race to develop commercial distributed memory SMP clusters.

The latest developments in machine hardware architectures result in significant improvements in all three approaches. SMP systems continue to improve the performance of the interconnect (system bus) and the operating system, thus increasing SMP scalability beyond today's levels. Modern cluster systems demonstrate many characteristics of the MPP system, including a very high-speed scalable interconnection mechanism, a compact "cluster in the box" packaging, and support for hundreds of PUs. In turn, MPP systems are evolving to utilize SMP nodes, thus increasing per-PU power and taking advantage in intranode shared memory architecture (see Fig. 3.3). The net result of these developments is that the distinction between MPP and clusters will become blurred as architectures continue to converge.

An example of these developments in MPP in cluster systems can be found in existing and emerging products. Although IBM has a clear lead with its SP and follow-on systems, many established vendors, including Hewlett-Packard, Sun, and Sequent, have plans to deliver competitive offerings within the next 2–3 years. These vendors plan to leverage their expertise in operating systems and SMP implementation by developing innovative interconnect technologies and using standards-based very high-speed communications protocols.

Probably one of the best justifications for the server specialization is the price/performance characteristics of the latest in server designs. Traditionally, system performance is measured in MIPS, SPECmarks, or a somewhat more meaningful transactions per second (TPS). The cost of each TPS rating is quite

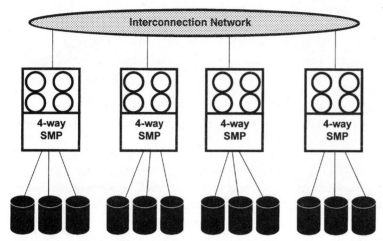

Figure 3.3 Distributed memory cluster of four-way SMP nodes.

high for a high-end mainframe. The price/performance characteristics of specialized server systems compare very favorably with those of a mainframe-class machine. In fact, it is not unusual to achieve an order-of-magnitude improvement in price/performance when using a specialized high-end server. And as technology continues to advance, the price/performance of specialized servers is getting even better, thus justifying architectural specialization for a server platform.

3.4 Advances in Multiprocessing Architectures

As was described in this and previous chapters, the scalability of a classic shared-memory architecture has an inherent limitation—because of the need to keep cache lines coherent, the scalability of a shared-memory system is reduced as the number of processing nodes increases. To overcome this inherent limitation but still maintain a familiar programming model, the designers have developed two innovative architectures:

- *Cache-coherent nonuniform memory access* (CC-NUMA), embraced by such vendors as Data General, Sequent, and Silicon Graphics

- *Cache-only memory architecture* (COMA), exemplified by SICS Data Diffusion Machine and Kendal Square Research's KSR-1

In a NUMA-style system, the (physical) address on a memory bus of a processing node is used to determine the home-node memory location of a particular data element. The cache hierarchy on each processing node is constructed to replicate and hold copies of data from not only the local memory but also the memory of remote nodes. A hardware coherence and directory mechanism serves to keep these cached copies consistent. While the caching helps reduce the access latency to otherwise remote memory, the total available memory is restricted to the size of the cache on each node.

A typical new-generation CC-NUMA system consists of multiple four-processor standard high-volume (SHV) motherboards. These are joined by a standards-based interconnect technology that implements CC-NUMA across the entire system. In a Data General implementation, each SHV motherboard contains four Intel Pentium Pro processors, with as much as 512 kbytes of cache per processor, and dual I/O channels (see Fig. 3.4). In this architecture, the cache memory (called level 2, or L2) runs at processor speed and is accessible with each processor cycle. Requested data not found in cache is read from main memory and copied into L2 cache. Data not found in a main memory of the requesting motherboard must be retrieved from a "far" memory of another SHV motherboard via a fast interconnect, that is based on ANSI-standard Scalable Coherent Interface (SCI) technology, that can move data at a speed of 1 Gbyte/s. The interconnect maintains a level 3 (L3) cache to store data requested from "far" memory locations. The multiple cache hierarchy (L2 and L3) help reduce the penalty for accessing data from adjacent nodes.

In a COMA machine, additional hardware, including tag and state memory, is added to the dynamic random-access memory (DRAM) of each node to convert it into a kind of cache called "attraction memory." This additional hardware enables disassociation of the actual data location in the machine from the physical addresses produced by the processors. Doing so enables data to be replicated and migrated automatically on demand around the machine, creating a flexible platform for applications.

In short, a COMA machine provides a very flexible and scalable platform for a wide variety of applications, but at the expense of additional memory system overhead and even more importantly, a complex attraction-memory coherence controller implementation. Thus, a NUMA machine, although enforcing tighter constraints in terms of the degree of data replication and migration an appli-

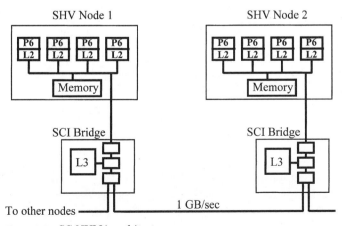

Figure 3.4   CC-NUMA architecture.

cation may use, and incurring a slightly higher cost of incorrect data place-ment, is easier to implement and is, therefore, a more popular approach.

3.5 Optimal Hardware Architecture for Query Scalability

To summarize, let's review the optimal hardware architecture for query scala-bility. Parallel query database algorithms (discussed in detail in Chap. 4) are used heavily as the technical foundation for the creation, maintenance, and analysis of very large data warehouses. These parallel database implementa-tions include parallel table scans, joins, sorts, merges, parallel index creation, parallel database load, backup and recovery, and other database operations. The parallel database architectures take advantage of the parallel hardware architectures of the underlying system in order to increase scalability.

3.5.1 Uniformity of data access times

In terms of hardware architecture, parallel query algorithms operate on data that resides in one of four possible containers: local memory, local disk, remote memory, and remote disk. As long as data resides on local memory or a disk, data access times are uniform and, in general, parallel algorithms scale quite well. But if the data resides on a remote memory or a remote disk, the system architecture can grossly influence data access times, causing system-architecture-induced data skew. This data skew can have a signifi-cantly negative impact on parallel query performance. In fact, if data access times are not uniform because of the way parallel system nodes are con-nected, system-architecture-induced data skew can become so severe that the effect of parallelism is lost, effectively serializing the execution of an appar-ently parallel algorithm.

Data skew is often thought to be a database-software- or data-layout-dependent problem. Although this can certainly be true, system-architecture-induced parallelism can cause data skew that no software or a clever database administration technique can resolve. Indeed, if an algorithm assumes even data distribution across all processors, then having nonbalanced data distrib-ution can cause one processor to process more data than the other processors have to do, thus causing everybody to wait for this processor to finish. So, the apparent solution is to redistribute the data evenly across all nodes of a mul-tiprocessing system. However, that's where system hardware architecture tax-onomy becomes a factor.

3.5.2 System architecture taxonomy and query execution

The system architecture taxonomy magnifies the effects of nonuniform data distribution by orders of magnitude. First, let's look at data access times from different computer components, as shown in the following table:

Container type	Access time
Local memory	A few microseconds
Remote memory	Hundreds of microseconds to a few milliseconds
Local disk	Tens of milliseconds
Remote disk	10–30 ms

As you can see, the difference in access time between different containers is in the orders of magnitude, which means that having data in local memory and on a remote disk, for example, will cause a data skew of 10,000 times! That's why shared-memory symmetric multiprocessors (SMPs) with their inherently uniform access times can demonstrate good scalability in low-node configurations. As was shown in the previous sections, SMPs are limited in scalability as a result of cache coherency and the scalability limits of the system bus, which is the main shared resource. Designers continue to lower the latency and increase the bus bandwidth (by making the bus shorter, increasing the clock speed, and widening the unit of data transfer over the bus), but these efforts are beginning to slow down by reaching the limits of physical laws of the universe (e.g., speed of light).

The short system bus scalability problem is eliminated in shared-nothing architectures. However, the way loosely coupled shared-nothing architecture nodes are connected together can greatly influence the amount of data skew, thus determining how well a given shared-nothing architecture can scale. In other words, the architecture of the system interconnect is critical in determining the latency incurred when a given node has to access data from a remote node.

Indeed, in a four-node MPP system, each node can be connected to either two (in a daisy-chained topology; Fig. 3.5) or three other nodes, and a remote node access in a fully connected mesh results in a maximum of one hop (see Fig. 3.6). As the number of nodes increases, this type of interconnection becomes more expensive and difficult to implement (e.g., in an eight-node configuration, each node will have to have seven connections for a one-hop connectivity). Therefore, designers have developed various interconnection topologies that maintain a small number of per-node connection but at the same time manage to reach remote nodes in a small number of hops. In general, the maximum number of nodes a given node can be connected to is called *connection density*.

There are many other interconnect topologies, including toroidal 2-D mesh, 3-D mesh (see Fig. 3.7), toroidal 3-D mesh, tree, hypercube, and cross-bar switch (see Fig. 3.8), all with different connection densities. All these interconnection architectures, with the exception of the cross-bar switch, are asymmetric models, meaning that some nodes are closer than others to a specific node. Therefore, these topologies require different number of hops when accessing data from the neighboring node or a remote node, thus producing system-architecture-induced data skew by design, regardless of how evenly the data is distributed across nodes. In fact, the less dense the connection model, the more asymmetric it becomes.

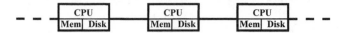

Daisy-chained network

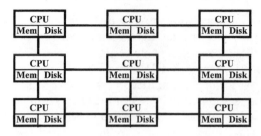

2-D mesh

Figure 3.5 Daisy-chained and 2-D mesh topologies.

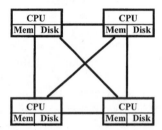

Figure 3.6 Fully connected four-node mesh.

The cross-bar switch, on the other hand, is a symmetric model. Borrowed from telephone switching designs, this technology creates a direct, point-to-point connection between every node.

Let's review the architectural taxonomy of the interconnect.

Topology	Connection density	Example
Flat, daisy-chained network	2	Many
2-D mesh	4	Pyramid R1000 Unisys OPUS
3-D mesh	6	Tandem
Tree	3	Teradata
Hypercube	N, where 2^N is the number of nodes	nCube
Cross-bar switch	N/A	IBM SP, NCR WorldMark 5100

In conclusion, hardware architectures can have a serious impact on system scalability. All asymmetric interconnection models can produce system-architecture-induced data skew. The symmetric cross-bar interconnection model is the architecture of choice for loosely coupled shared-nothing system as well as for new system designs, including NUMA.

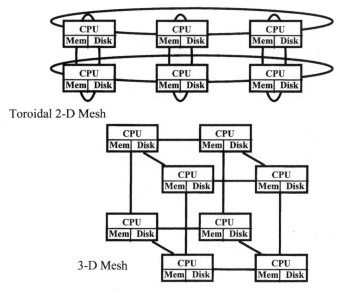

Toroidal 2-D Mesh

3-D Mesh

Figure 3.7   Toroidal 2-D mesh and 3-D mesh.

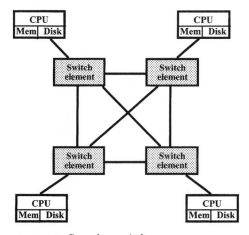

Figure 3.8   Cross-bar switch.

3.6   Server Operating Systems

Naturally, server specialization is not limited to its hardware architecture. The server *operating system* determines how quickly the server can fulfill client requests, how many clients it can support concurrently and reliably, and how efficiently the system resources such as memory, disk I/O, and communications components are utilized.

3.6.1 Operating system requirements

In order to analyze available server operating systems, first let's consider some general requirements attributed to a server operating system in a client/server environment. By design, a server operating system has to support multiple users performing multiple, often conflicting, tasks concurrently. Therefore, a reasonable server operating system has to demonstrate at least the following:

- *Multiuser support.*
- *Preemptive multitasking.* This feature allows a server to allocate time and resources among multiple tasks evenly or on the basis of priorities; in preemptive multitasking one (possibly a higher-priority) task can interrupt another task when necessary; preemptive multitasking contrasts with a cooperative multitasking (e.g., implemented by Microsoft Windows), in which one application has to be coded to give up control to another application.
- *Multithreaded design.* This allows a server operating system to employ lightweight processes to serve multiple requests, and to distribute threads to multiple CPUs in a multiple-CPU server; like multitasking within a single task, multiple threads can execute concurrently within a single process, thus reducing resource requirements and improving concurrency.
- *Memory protection.* This is a necessary feature designed to prevent multiple concurrent tasks from violating each other's memories.
- *Scalability.* The server operating system should be able to scale up as the number of users and applications increases.
- *Security.* A server operating system has to provide its clients with a secure environment that protects each client and the corresponding resources.
- *Reliability and availability.* Clearly, a server that serves tens and even hundreds of users should not go down at will, especially if it runs mission-critical applications; a server operating system should protect the system from the ill effects of an abnormally terminating application (crash protection).

In addition to these requirements, servers (and clients) should be evaluated according to the operating system architecture, which is an important but often ignored characteristic of an operating system.

3.6.2 Microkernel technology

In the traditional operating system, operating system services such as process management, virtual memory management, network management, file system services, and device management are all built into the kernel. The result is a large, complex, and often inflexible kernel that is difficult to enhance or port to different hardware platforms. These system kernels traditionally support uniprocessors and are inherently less secure. The new operating system architecture is based on the *microkernel* technology, originally developed by Carnegie Mellon University. By design, the microkernel is relatively small and highly secure. It provides only the basic system services, such as task and thread management, interprocess communications, virtual memory services, input/output services, and interrupt services. These services are made available to the user-level tasks through a set of microkernel interface functions.

Unlike the traditional kernel-based operating system approach, services such as file system, network services, and device drivers operate outside the microkernel as user-level servers, thus reducing complexity, increasing portability, and requiring fewer interactions between user tasks and the microkernel to perform operating system services. What is more, this architecture results in a highly modular operating system that can support multiple operating system "personalities" by configuring the outside services as needed. For example, the microkernel technology which is based on Carnegie Mellon's Mach 3.0 microkernel is used by IBM to allow DOS, OS/2, and AIX operating system "personalities" to coexist on a single machine.

In general, the benefits of the microkernel-based operating system can be summarized as follows:

- Simplified architecture
- Extensibility
- Portability
- Enhanced real-time support
- Multiprocessor support
- Robust system security

All of these benefits make a microkernel-based operating system a good candidate for the ideal server operating system.

3.7 Operating System Implementations

The next few sections will look at several of the most popular server operating systems, and will try to emphasize their strengths, weaknesses, and market potential.

3.7.1 UNIX

UNIX is a mature and established operating system. Developed in the late 1960s, UNIX acquired a significant customer base and demonstrated its many strong features on real-life applications. Today, UNIX continues to increase its market share on an annual basis.

There are numerous UNIX versions developed by multiple vendors to run on practically any platform imaginable. Similarly, there are thousands of applications available to run on UNIX platforms. Overall, UNIX is a true multiuser, multithreaded, fully preemptive multitasking operating system. It is portable to the majority of hardware platforms available today, including CISC (e.g., Intel) and RISC (e.g., RS/6000, PowerPC, Motorola, SPARC, MIPS). It is a scalable operating system, designed to run on SMP and even MPP machines. UNIX advanced features include built-in networking, numerous operating system utilities, crash protection, administration, and diagnostics. UNIX is a secure system. It is C1- and C2-secure, and is certifiable for B1 and B2 levels of security for distributed systems.

Applications developed for UNIX running on a particular platform are (generally speaking) source-code-compatible with other hardware platforms that support UNIX, which enhances applications portability, especially for such applications as DBMS, Network File System, and Source Code Library. The portability and scalability make UNIX an attractive server operating system.

The picture is a little different on the client system side. Multiple available UNIX versions cause confusion among independent software vendors (ISVs) and users alike. The lack of common UNIX kernel code and a common windowing application programming interface (API) set continues to cause some hesitation on the user's part to adopt UNIX as the operating system of choice throughout the corporation. This lack of unity discourages some ISVs from developing shrink-wrapped software for UNIX, which may seriously affect vendors' efforts to position UNIX as a client operating system, but it probably has a little, if any, effect on the adoption and growth of UNIX as a server operating system.

UNIX operating system, tools, and applications have influenced the specification of many standards and, in fact, stimulated the emergence of open systems. The adherence to such standards as FIPS (Federal Information Processing Standard), SVID (System V Interface Definitions), XPG4 (X/Open Portability Guide), and POSIX common operating system services, shell, tools, and real-time extensions further enhances portability. UNIX alliance vendors are working on bringing together various UNIX version. The Common Open Software Environment (COSE) is a standard being developed by most major UNIX OS vendors, including Hewlett-Packard, IBM, Novell, SunSoft, and the Santa Cruz Operation. COSE specifies how each UNIX version should look, feel, and act.

3.7.2 Windows/NT

Microsoft's Windows/NT (New Technology) is an advanced operating system for Intel and RISC processors. By design, Windows/NT offers the best features of OS/2 and UNIX operating system.

Windows/NT supports 16-bit DOS and Windows applications, OS/2 character-based applications, 32-bit native applications, preemptive multitasking, multithreading, and crash protection. Windows/NT provides advanced LAN and multiuser capabilities required by a server OS.

Although not yet ported to as many hardware platforms as UNIX, Windows/ NT is architected to be hardware-independent. It supports several RISC processors (e.g., MIPS and Digital ALPHA) and C1- and C2-level security certification, and is POSIX-compliant (POSIX 1003.1—Base Functions); all these features are missing from OS/2. Windows/NT offers software fault tolerance through a transaction-oriented recoverable file system (NTFS), disk mirroring, and memory-mapped files that simplify virtual memory operations.

In addition, Windows/NT offers Windows-like user interface, which makes it very easy to use by most current Windows and DOS users, of which there are millions. The scope and promised functionality of NT has markedly affected the direction of the UNIX community during the past 2 years, causing UNIX vendors to seriously consider bringing different versions of UNIX together by developing standards for a common kernel, common APIs, and common look and feel.

The current version of Windows/NT (version 4) has an advanced user interface similar to that of Windows 95, and supports such important features like Plug-and-Play. Many industry experts believe that NT will slow the progress of UNIX and erect impassable barriers on the advancement of nonportable operating systems. At the same time, an analysis of market trends leads to the conclusion that Windows/NT will not destroy UNIX's momentum.

3.7.3 OS/2

OS/2 was the first operating system specifically designed to provide the preemptive multitasking for the Intel processor. Early versions of OS/2 (versions 1.x) were plagued with many problems and therefore were not adopted by the majority of the organizations as the operating system of choice. The shortcomings of OS/2 version 1 included heavy hardware requirements, poor performance, single-processor support, and the lack of applications and ISV support.

With the release of OS/2 version 2, this operating system became a stable platform that can provide advanced operating system features for workstations and servers alike. OS/2 version 2 can run 16-bit DOS and Windows applications as well as 32-bit applications specifically designed to take advantage of the 32-bit addressing and processing power of the operating system. OS/2 is a multitasking and multithreaded operating system, and currently supports a total of 4096 threads and processes, with 64,000 semaphores per process. OS/2 uses Named Pipes as the preferred interprocess communication (IPC) mechanism, and can use most popular network protocols to connect local and remote processes into a client/server system. OS/2 uses an add-on product—LAN Server—to provide LAN and multiuser capabilities required by a server OS.

OS/2 can address up to 512 Mbytes of virtual memory, with automatic paging to and from disk. One of the OS/2 strengths is its stability and "crashproof" memory protection. If a DOS, Windows, or native OS/2 application develops a serious problem, only this application can terminate; the rest of the system remains active, and applications such as a DBMS can continue to serve its clients.

OS/2 supports the High-Performance File System (HPFS), which is faster than DOS File Allocation Table (FAT) file system. HPFS uses an intelligent cache system and lays out files to minimize disk fragmentation. OS/2 can be tuned to optimize the use of I/O devices such as SCSI and SCSI-2 high-performance adapters.

A number of significant improvements have been implemented in the current version of OS/2—OS/2 Warp Version 3. OS/2 Warp, Version 3 is optimized to provide high performance in low-memory environments, with a host of new features that make it even easier to use. It's enriched with a suite of full-function applications, plus built-in access to the information highway (BonusPak for OS/2 Warp). The enhanced Workplace Shell can be customized to place favorite functions in the LaunchPad. OS/2 Warp provides for a quick and simple installation. For a notebook user, the Plug and Play feature allows the system to automatically identify the PCMCIA(TM) cards installed in the computer. BonusPak for OS/2 Warp provides access to IBM's Internet Connection Service. Using the IBM WebExplorer and Gopher features allows users to find and retrieve data from thousands of databases worldwide. FTP or Gopher allows users to download software, news, weather maps, images, and more. WebExplorer includes built-in e-mail support and World Wide Web access.

The features available in OS/2 Warp include

- Addressability: 32-bit
- Preemptive multitasking:
  - ⇨ Concurrent processing of multiple DOS, Windows, and OS/2 applications
  - ⇨ Fast and easy movement among applications
  - ⇨ Protection between applications
- Ease-of-use facilities:
  - ⇨ Workplace Shell object-based user interface
  - ⇨ On-line tutorial
  - ⇨ Contextual Help
  - ⇨ Fast, graphical installation
- System requirements:
  - ⇨ i386™ SX microprocessor (or compatible) or higher
  - ⇨ VGA (Video Graphics Array) display (minimum)
  - ⇨ Fax/modem (9600 baud or higher for on-line access to the Information Superhighway)
- Memory requirements:
  - ⇨ 4 Mbytes minimum

- Disk-space requirements:
  - ⇨ 35 to 50 Mbytes of free hard-disk space, depending on the installation options selected
  - ⇨ Up to 30 Mbytes of additional free space (user-selectable) (required by BonusPak for OS/2 Warp)

One of the limiting factors in OS/2 acceptance is its inability to run on non-Intel processors. This diminishes OS/2 portability and scalability as a server operating system.

3.7.4 NetWare

Novell's NetWare is another popular server operating system, especially for file and print services, although it is used today as a database server OS as well. NetWare offers many of the same facilities found in advanced operating systems such as OS/2, Windows/NT, and UNIX, but not without some severe limitations.

NetWare (version 3.11 and above) is a true 32-bit operating system with a heavy emphasis on networking. In fact, it would be more accurate to call NetWare a *network operating system* (NOS). Its advanced file server features make NetWare one of the best in the networking world.

NetWare runs on Intel platforms only, which is a definite limitation. To achieve greatest performance, NetWare allows application developers to extend the system services associated with the file server by using NetWare Loadable Modules (NLMs). NLMs become a part of the NetWare kernel and run alongside the services already included in the NOS. Therefore, NLMs can demonstrate very strong performance, but not without the price. NLMs are not memory-protected—Intel 386 and higher processors provide four levels of protection known as rings; ring 0 has the highest number of privileges and is usually reserved for the operating system itself, while ring 3 has the lowest number of privileges. NLMs run at ring 0 and are able to get at and corrupt memory areas reserved for operating system processes and I/O device drivers, thus bringing an entire system down.

Unlike traditional virtual memory operations, NetWare does not page-code to and from memory, which prevents additional NLMs to be loaded once the memory limitation has been reached—a severe impact on scalability. NetWare does not support preemptive multitasking, which means that NetWare cannot stop a running application to allow another application to continue execution. In addition, NetWare does not support threads, which limits server ability to support such services as remote procedure calls (RPCs).

3.7.5 OS summary

In the absence of other major portable operating systems, UNIX and Windows/NT should dominate the market for the server operating system, especially for new applications. The industry will probably choose between UNIX and Windows/NT mostly on vendor and marketing issues rather than on technical issues. Indeed, these two operating systems are quite similar in their technical capabilities, and one will be able to do almost anything that another can.

UNIX is capable of handling most types of workloads today. Windows/NT is still relatively new, but could be ready to compete for most types of workloads in the near future. Application portability provided by these two environments and the freedom of choice of hardware platform available for these operating systems are the drivers that will foster their continued growth.

Today's trends in computing architecture emphasize the value of openness, portability, and interoperability. Therefore, the possibility of survival of nonportable operating systems is rather small, even though several established operating systems are technically superior to UNIX and Windows/NT today in many ways. An example of such a nonportable operating system is IBM's MVS.

4

Distributed DBMS Implementations

Database management systems are the information backbone of today's organizations. Current technology and business requirements make it increasingly clear that distributed systems will play a major role in the advanced computing environments of today and of the future. Client/server computing, network computing, and peer-to-peer computing are just several examples of such environments. As these environments assume mission-critical roles in the enterprise, several trends affecting the DBMS technology are becoming evident. One of these trends forces the DBMS technology to enable the development and support of distributed environments, while another trend is driving the complexity and the sheer volume of the data toward the next generation of DSS and OLTP applications: data warehousing and on-line complex processing, or OLCP. A clear indication of this trend can be found in the advancements in the area of commercial high-performance computing, in the amount of data that organizations are trying to process on the emerging client/server platforms, and in the general high level of expectations developers and users alike place on the client/server distributed DBMS. These new OLCP-capable database management systems can provide businesses with a quantum leap in the ability to *understand,* not just process, huge amounts of data. This understanding will allow organizations to obtain strategic competitive advantage by managing the business more efficiently, recognizing and adapting to trends, avoiding mistakes and bad business decisions, and providing customers with answers and value-added information directly, in a common, integrated platform.

Today, evaluating and choosing a database management system is steadily becoming one of the first system decisions management information system (MIS) managers must make. And, with the data warehousing requirements steadily pushing the limits of the traditional RDBMS technology, the task of selecting an appropriate DBMS becomes even more critical. Therefore, this chapter is intended to discuss some practical, technical RDBMS implementation trends and features that client/server RDBMS designers and users alike should be aware of.

4.1   Implementation Trends and Features of Distributed Client/Server DBMS

The volume of information flowing through enterprises has grown tremendously over the last several years. Until recently, enterprise databases could store only characters, numbers, and dates in a well-structured DBMS. Today, technology enables businesses to store large amounts of information, especially unstructured information. New infrastructures are being developed to allow virtually any authorized user to access this information (i.e., the World Wide Web).

The database world is changing considerably:

- New DBMS technologies are replacing accepted architectures—for example, data replication instead of two-phase commit. Replication is easier to understand and far easier to implement than two-phase commit protocols. Replication can be used for various applications, including
    - ⇨ Populating data warehouses
    - ⇨ Remote backup and fault tolerance
    - ⇨ Mobile computing and support of disconnected clients
    - ⇨ Local access of information
- Not only do new data types—image, voice, animation, multimedia, full-motion video—need to be stored and retrieved, but new applications such as video-on-demand impose new demands on DBMS technologies.
- Databases grow steadily in size, and the support for very large databases (VLDBs) presents new technical challenges.
- The need for load balancing between systems requires new capabilities from distributed DBMSs.
- Several key technologies are maturing and will be used extensively during the coming years, such as parallel DBMS functions.
- The relational DBMS is being extended to coexist with other models, such as object databases.

Distributed relational database systems make special demands on the database logical and physical design, and on the database management system architecture and functionality as well. At the very least, a distributed RDBMS must

- Maintain data integrity by providing local and global locking mechanisms, and by supporting database commit and rollback transaction integrity
- Automatically detect deadlocks and perform transaction and database recovery

- Be intelligent enough to optimize data access for a wide variety of application requests

- Have an architecture that is capable of taking advantage of the high-powered platforms it runs on

- Overcome the traditional DBMS bottleneck—input/output (I/O)—by tuning the DBMS engine and I/O subsystem to achieve high data throughput and high I/O rates

- Provide support for optimum space management, which is especially important if the underlying platform is a resource-constrained microcomputer

- Support database security and administration facilities for distributed data and applications locations, preferably from a single, centralized location

And all this must be done by a distributed RDBMS reliably and within acceptable performance and throughput parameters, especially in multiuser distributed on-line transaction processing and complex data warehousing environments.

Therefore, the users must take a close look at the actual technology of a given product. It is important to see how each particular product is implemented regardless of the hardware platform. At the same time, it is as important to understand how a DBMS can take advantage of a particular hardware or software platform, and what advanced features (if any) a given DBMS product offers to satisfy and possibly exceed customer expectations. In this respect, it is important to understand how a selected RDBMS is engineered for one or more of the increasingly popular hardware architectures:

- Shared-memory symmetric multiprocessors (SMPs)

- "Shared-nothing" distributed-memory massively parallel processors (MPPs) and loosely coupled *clusters*

This is not an insignificant consideration. Granted, these emerging high-performance computing solutions appear more expensive than traditional uniprocessors. But in return, they promise an unprecedented scalability for higher performance and throughput. And that scalability is extremely important today, when client/server applications are pushing the capacity and performance of network servers to their engineered limits. In fact, these new DBMS technologies pursue two goals: speed-up (an ability to execute the same request on the same amount of data in less time) and scale-up (an ability to obtain the same performance on the same request as the database size increases). Moreover, the key here is to achieve *linear* speed-up and scale-up—doubling the number of processors cuts the response time in half (linear speed-up) or provides the same performance on twice as much data (linear scale-up).

So, let's examine some key requirements for a database server architecture that have to be considered for the implementation of complex mission-critical distributed systems.

4.1.1   RDBMS architecture for scalability

In a distributed multiuser client/server environment, a database management system resides at the database server and should be architected as a server component of the client/server computing model. As such, the DBMS server should be designed to receive and process a variable number of concurrent database requests from multiple remote users.

Scalability.   The server RDBMS should process client requests efficiently, and the performance and throughput characteristics of the RDBMS should not change as the number of concurrent users, database size, etc., grows. To maintain these characteristics, additional computing resources (e.g., CPU, memory, disks) may have to be added to the system at a relatively small incremental cost, with a *predictable* effect on the system, and *without changing the application or administrative practices*. This property of the system is often referred to as system *scalability*.

There are two approaches to achieve scalability:

1. The *external* approach, which increases the number of servers in the environment and lets multiple server systems run concurrently to share the workload. Loosely coupled systems running distributed databases support external scalability. More often than not, this approach requires additional administrative support.

2. *Internal* (in-system) scalability implies a single system that can be scaled up by adding a computing resource such as faster CPU, or more CPUs, or more memory, etc., to the existing server platform. This approach should not require additional software components as scale goes up, and, therefore, should not require a change in administrative practices.

Both types of scalability dictate that an RDBMS should be able to effectively use all available computing resources, thus supporting an incremental approach to capacity planning. In effect, from a capacity planning perspective, a truly scalable RDBMS is equivalent to a *free hardware upgrade*.

Internal scalability is the focus of this discussion, since today it is achievable on multiprocessor machines: SMPs, MPPs, and clusters. These multiprocessor platforms allow the addition of processors without changing either the applications or the administrative process.

To provide scalability, a server RDBMS architecture should support

- *Extensibility.*   The DBMS should not be specialized for a particular system configuration (e.g., a certain number of processors), and should automatically take advantage of the new configuration, without the need for reinstallation; this can be achieved by a sophisticated task scheduling algorithm that can assign new tasks to additional resources in a load-balanced, predictable fashion, and by dividing large tasks (e.g., complex database queries) into a set of small subtasks that can be performed in *parallel*. By definition, a *parallel scalable* RDBMS provides predictable extensibility. The principles of a parallel scalable DBMS are discussed later in this chapter.

- *Limitation-free architecture.*   If a DBMS has built-in architectural limitations (limits on the number and size of supported tables, number of concurrent connections, etc.), it will not scale, regardless of how well it can parallelize tasks and operations.

- *Application transparency.*   An application should not be aware of the platform architecture, configuration, and the changes to the platform implemented to achieve the next level of performance and throughput; ideally, migrating from one platform to another (e.g., from an SMP to an MPP) should not require application changes, even though the DBMS itself may have to adapt to a new processing model (in this case, from a shared-memory model to a distributed-memory model).

Multithreading.   Operating in a limited resource environment (server system) under the control of an operating system, the DBMS designers can follow different strategies to achieve server efficiency.

One strategy is to create an operating system server process (task) for every DBMS client, which typically results in, among other things, additional operating system overhead (e.g., context switching), and additional CPU and memory requirements (see Fig. 4.1). A unit of context management under the control of a single process is called a *thread.* A thread can be either implemented within the server process, or via operating system services. The latter

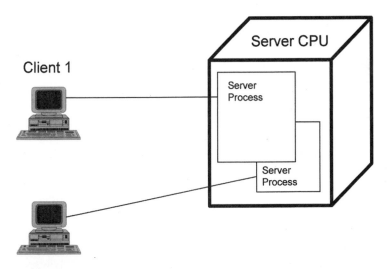

Figure 4.1   Single-threaded architecture.

is considerably more expensive for process creation, destruction, and context switching. We will call this a *single-threaded* architecture.

A considerably more efficient approach is to launch a separate thread for each separate task (like a client connection supported by a server). Such a "lightweight" task can be controlled by the DBMS server rather than the operating system (see Fig. 4.2). In principle, threads can clone themselves and thus perform concurrent tasks.

Threads do not incur operating system overhead after being launched. A true multithreaded architecture provides a high degree of resource sharing (e.g., threads can share memory space with other threads) and tends to make system performance more stable with respect to the number of users and additional server functionality. In general, a multithreaded DBMS server architecture is preferable to a single-threaded one. A multithreaded database server can manage all the resources needed by the RDBMS itself (including buffers, disk I/O, locking, and logging), which essentially makes it a special-purpose operating system dedicated to the DBMS operations by scheduling threads execution.

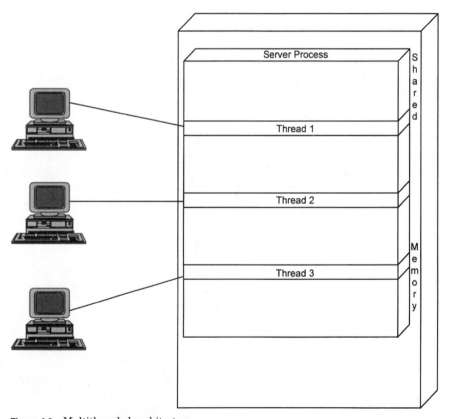

Figure 4.2 Multithreaded architecture.

The multithreaded scheduler can be either preemptive or nonpreemptive. *Nonpreemptive* threads execute until they give up control of the CPU or until a specified time interval (time slice) has expired, and therefore an "unfriendly" thread can block every other one from running. This approach imposes some requirements on the operating system and DBMS design, as well as some limitations on the system scalability. *Preemptive* threads can be interrupted by a scheduler when another thread requires the processor and satisfies some requirements (e.g., new thread's priority, thread class, the state of the current thread) imposed by the scheduler to initiate the switchover. Preemptive thread scheduling is effective for database servers that must share resources between DBMS and non-DBMS applications.

Among UNIX-based RDBMS server implementations, the SYBASE SQL Server is one example of the multithreaded server architecture. The latest release of the SYBASE SQL Server extends the concept of the multithreaded architecture to symmetric multiprocessing hardware platforms.

4.1.2 RDBMS performance and efficiency features

Relational DBMS server performance is usually measured by using standard benchmarks as well as some proprietary application transaction mix. Because many external factors affect RDBMS performance (operating system environment, hardware platform, etc.), benchmarks usually demonstrate some particular small aspect of the performance picture as a whole and can be unreliable as a predictor for any specific environment or configuration.

Clearly, a well-designed database server should be able to manage appropriate resources transparently from the application, and use these resources efficiently. For example, the way the database server allocates and manages the system and shared memory, and the locking strategy in effect, all determine some overall performance characteristics of the RDBMS. However, there are certain relational DBMS design features that quite definitely affect its performance. Some of these features are applicable to the performance of the individual database engines, while others—such as global optimization—affect the performance of the entire distributed database system.

Server-enforced integrity and security. Data integrity and security are critical requirements for database management systems. *Integrity features,* such as referential and domain integrity, assure the accuracy and consistency of data, while *database security* refers to authorization and control of data access. Integrity and security can be implemented in several different ways. For example, integrity constraints and security procedures can be included in every application. In the client/server computing model, it may mean duplication of the relevant code on every client running these applications. However, the more efficient approach would call for the implementation of the integrity and security features centrally, directly at the DBMS server level. Such DBMS server architecture will provide for higher application reliability, reduced development and maintenance costs, and increased database security.

Global optimization.   As was discussed in the previous chapters, the performance of a relational DBMS is determined largely by the capabilities of the query optimizer. One of the rules of distributed database specifies that in a truly distributed database system, the optimization must take into account not only local but also global factors, including distributed nodes and network characteristics.

Typical cost-based optimization selects the access path for a given query on the basis of the estimated cost of the query processing. Usually, the optimizer calculates the cost in such units as the number of I/O operations and/or CPU cycles, and takes into account the number of records needed to satisfy the query, availability of indexes, and various statistical information about data organization. These statistics are accumulated and maintained by the RDBMS in its internal system catalog. Optimization becomes even more critical in distributed query processing. Indeed, consider an application that attempts to join two database tables that are distributed to two different locations.

The size of each node's databases and relevant tables, the network speed, and the processing and I/O power of each node are among the major factors that affect the performance of a distributed query. The distributed (global) query optimization requires access to a global database directory or catalog in order to obtain necessary node characteristics and statistical information about the remote databases.

Without global query optimization, a distributed relational DBMS may perform extremely inefficiently. Such a system may send all the records of the bigger table to another, remote, location, for selection and join, and then send the results back. As the complexity of the queries exceeds the two table join requirements, each additional table and/or database increases the number of choices for and the complexity of the optimizer.

Therefore, an efficient implementation of global query optimization is a rather difficult task that only a handful of RDBMS vendors attempt to undertake. Products like Informix support global optimization with certain limitations, and even then the quality of optimization decreases with the complexity of the query.

Parallel relational DBMS processing.   A special case of global query optimization is the query optimization in distributed-memory parallel systems (clusters and MPPs). Often, this is referred to as *parallel query processing*. Generally speaking, parallel RDBMS processing offers the solution to the traditional problem of poor RDBMS performance for complex queries and very large databases. Intuitively, it is quite clear that accessing and processing portions of the database by individual threads in parallel (instead of monolithic, sequential access of the entire large database) can greatly improve the performance of the query. This is especially important for data warehousing supporting complex decision support systems (DSSs) and batch processing.

4.1.3 Types of parallelism

Database vendors started to take advantage of parallel hardware architectures by implementing multiserver and multithreaded systems designed to handle a large number of client requests efficiently. This approach naturally resulted in the *interquery parallelism,* in which different server threads (or processes) handle multiple requests at the same time. Interquery parallelism has been successfully implemented on SMP systems, where it increased the throughput and allowed support of more concurrent users. However, without changing the way the DBMS processed queries, interquery parallelism was limited—even though multiple queries were processed concurrently, each query was still processed serially, by a single process or thread. In other words, if a query consists of a table scan, and join and sort operations, then this would be the order in which these operations execute, and each operation would have to finish before the next one could began.

To improve the situation, many DBMS vendors developed versions of their products that utilized *intraquery parallelism.* This form of parallelism decomposes the serial SQL query into lower-level operations such as scan, join, sort, and aggregation (see Fig. 4.3, case 1). These lower-level operations then are executed concurrently, in parallel. By dedicating multiple resources to processing a single request can be processed faster. Operations other than queries—INSERTs, DELETEs, UPDATEs, index creation, database load, backup, and recovery—can also be parallelized and thus speeded up.

Parallel execution of the tasks within SQL statements (intraquery parallelism) can be done in a number of ways:

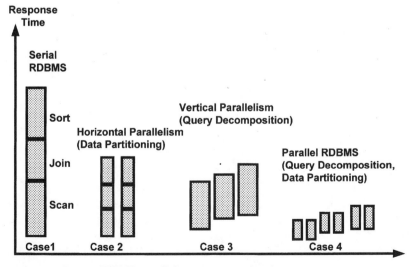

Figure 4.3 Types of DBMS parallelism.

- *Horizontal parallelism.* This means that the database is partitioned across multiple disks, and parallel processing occurs within a specific task (i.e., table scan) that is performed concurrently on different processors against different sets of data. Indeed, if the entire database is partitioned into a number of smaller segments, each located on its own (logical) device, then the total query can be decomposed into an equal number of subqueries, all running in parallel against a corresponding partition of the database. The resulting execution time is significantly reduced in comparison with a sequential query (Fig. 4.3, case 2). Obviously, this approach requires a multiprocessor server. However, as illustrated in Fig. 4.4, processor-based parallelism does not reduce a traditional DBMS bottleneck: I/O. It is only logical, then, that the multiprocessor server and a parallel RDBMS should benefit from the server architecture that supports parallel I/O. As illustrated in Fig. 4.5, additional performance improvements can be achieved by placing data partitions on separate physical devices (preferably connected via separate I/O buses). The optimizer can partition the query on the basis of the data partitioning rules (e.g., key ranges, hash algorithms).

- *Vertical parallelism.* This occurs among different tasks; all component query operations (i.e., scan, join, sort) are executed in parallel in a pipelined fashion. This approach requires a much higher level of sophistication from the DBMS engine. It assumes that the RDBMS engine can decompose the query on the basis of its functional components (in our example, scan, join, and sort). Once decomposed, the query components can start executing in parallel, with a minimum delay between the execution steps (vertical parallelism). Ideally, as database records are processed by one step (e.g., scan), they are *immediately* given to the next step (e.g., join), thus eliminating the wait time inherited in sequential query processing. In this case (Fig. 4.3, case 3), the query decomposer and the optimizer can allocate different query components to available processors from the processor pool.

- *Hybrid approach.* Finally, parallel scaleable RDBMS can employ a combination approach, in which the query decomposer and the optimizer can partition the query both horizontally (based on the data partitioning algo-

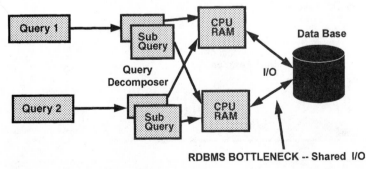

Figure 4.4 Shared-I/O bottleneck.

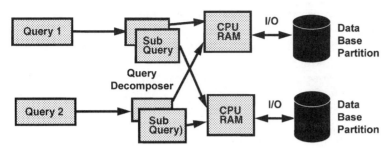

Figure 4.5 Parallel scalable RDBMS, MPP, and parallel I/O.

rithm) and vertically (based on the functional composition of the query). The hybrid approach can result in the highest utilization of computing resources available in an MPP database server, and will provide for the best scalability, performance, and throughput of the DBMS (see Fig. 4.3, case 4).

The ability to decompose and process large queries in parallel is applicable to on-line transaction processing as well. In OLTP and especially OLCP environments, parallel query processing can supplement an overall multithreaded approach in which individual threads can be executed on separate processors. In other words, to take full advantage of the parallel hardware architectures and to achieve high performance of complex queries in a very large database (VLDB) environment, a relational RDBMS should be able to balance the workload of individual threads across multiple processors and decompose a complex query into multiple subqueries that can be executed in parallel.

Several major DBMS vendors offer various degrees of availability of parallel query processing, frequently coupled with a particular platform on which the query decomposer was developed. Most prominent among them are Oracle with the Parallel Query and Parallel Server Options (version 7 and above), Informix OnLine Dynamic Scalable Architecture (version 7 and above), and SYBASE MPP (formerly, Navigation Server).

Locking granularity. Locking preserves data integrity by preventing multiple updates to the same records simultaneously. Some servers permit manual locking, but, in reality, automatic locking in a database management system is imperative. The importance of locking becomes especially clear in a parallel RDBMS environment, in which multiple users execute various steps of complex queries across multiple data partitions.

Users or processes that are locked out from access must wait until the required data is freed (locks are released). When this happens, the user's response time, and thus a perception of DBMS performance, suffers. For instance, table-level update locks, as a rule, result in poor performance. While locking, in itself, preserves data from corruption, it could limit the number of users simultaneously accessing the RDBMS.

If a DBMS locks an entire database for each user, then the DBMS becomes, in effect, a single-user DBMS. Therefore, the size of locks the RDBMS can impose on a database (locking granularity) becomes very important.

Ideally, the RDBMS should lock only those records that are being updated. The smallest level of granularity in commercial databases is the row level. *Row*-level locking implies that the database can use a lock granularity of a single row. This means that multiple users can simultaneously update different rows on the same page. Each user locks only the row on which the operation is performed, and does not interfere with other users in the same page. Row-level locking permits the highest degree of concurrency by allowing users not to lock each other out. For example, Oracle and Informix RDBMSs support row-level locking. The disadvantage of row-level locking is its significant overhead. Also, since each lock requires a certain amount of memory and/or disk space, the number of locks imposed on a database (and therefore, the number of users) may be limited by the amount of available space. Some RDBMS servers can *escalate* locks from one level (e.g., row) to a higher level (e.g., data page or a table), and release lower-level locks when their number exceeds the user-defined limit. For example, IBM's DB2 supports lock escalation.

The next level of locking granularity is the *page* level. Thus, when one user updates a row, the entire page is locked and other users are blocked from updating, and sometimes even reading, rows in that page. Page-level locking introduces moderate overhead at the cost of reduced concurrency.

Table-level locking means that the database can lock an entire table at a time. This level is useful for locking a table for batch updates, locking out users for maintenance or reporting, etc.

Finally, *database*-level locking means that the entire database can be locked with a single command. Obviously, this level of locking practically eliminates concurrency.

Deadlock detection. Locking is associated with another performance problem: deadlocks. A *deadlock* occurs when program A locks a record that program B needs, and program B locks the record that program A needs. Each program must wait until the other completes, which is impossible. Thus, a deadlock (sometimes known as a "deadly embrace"), has occurred. The DBMS server should automatically detect deadlocks and use appropriate algorithms to resolve them. As with global optimization, deadlock detection becomes much more complicated in a distributed environment. The time criterion might not be sufficient, since network delays and slow response time may be confused with a lock at a remote site. A truly distributed RDBMS server should be capable of resolving "distributed" deadlocks, even though the majority of the available DBMS implementations use some simple, time-out-based rules to resolve deadlocks.

Clustered indexes. Indexes usually represent separate data structures (e.g., various B-tree structures) that contain record keys and pointers to the corresponding records. Indexes can be used to access records directly by the key values, and can also guarantee uniqueness of the keys (if the keys are defined as unique). Indexes should be constantly maintained—kept in sync with the key values of the records when the data is updated, added, or deleted. Even though index maintenance can negatively affect RDBMS performance, lack of indexes could result in serious performance degradation in direct (by full or partial key) data access. In this respect, clustered indexes are most important. Clustered indexes are usually built on a primary (as opposed to foreign) key, require the data to be sorted in ascending or descending key order, and are also sorted in the same order as the data (see Fig. 4.6). Thus, clustered indexes can significantly improve record search and sequential retrieval in key order by reducing the required number of input/output operations. [*Note:* Some RDBMS products (e.g., Ingres, Centura) reduce or completely eliminate index I/O by supporting *hash indexes,* where records can be found by a key stored at locations calculated by a special algorithm. Hash indexes facilitate direct access and can coexist with indexes in the same RDBMS.]

In addition to clustered indexes, some RDBMS products support *clustered tables.* Tables are said to be clustered when they are stored close to each other on a disk based on a commonly used join key. Clustered tables help speed up the data access if two tables are always accessed by the same join key.

An RDBMS optimizer can improve the access path by automatically determining whether an index should be used for a given query. That is because index I/Os also consume resources and affect performance. Advanced optimizers, such as the one found in DB2, maintain index statistics and can actually determine whether a clustered index is still clustered after heavy insert/delete

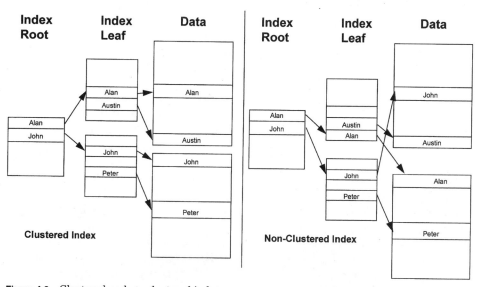

Figure 4.6   Clustered and nonclustered indexes.

activity, before the decision is made to use the index. Despite the importance of clustered indexes, to date only few products support them (e.g., Sybase, Oracle, and IBM's DB2).

Dirty reads.   Some RDBMS products support a fast-read mode without data integrity where the database system can scan the data as it currently exists on disk or in memory, regardless of whether the data has been committed. Even though dirty reads offer measurable performance advantages, their use has to be balanced against the potential exposure to inaccurate data.

Asynchronous I/O.   RDBMS input/output is potentially a source of performance bottleneck. Properly designed database management systems should minimize the number of actual physical disk I/O and spread the cost of I/O operations across many users. One technique that facilitates reduction in the number of disk accesses is asynchronous I/O. This technique involves overlapping I/O operations with other work that the RDBMS server has to perform. In this case, the server does not wait for the completion of the I/O. Such an overlapping can be improved even further when the data is updated in shared buffers and the data writes are forced to disk only when the data buffers are full. The consistency of data in this case is guaranteed by write-ahead logging to a shared transaction log. In IBM system environments, asynchronous I/O is frequently implemented on an operating system level, as well as by a DBMS itself (e.g., DB2). UNIX-based databases, however, must be designed to implement asynchronous I/O. Oracle, Sybase, and Informix all offer asynchronous I/O capabilities in UNIX environments.

In addition to asynchronous I/O, the I/O performance of the UNIX file systems can be improved by using "raw I/O." RDBMS products such as SYBASE SQL Server use raw devices to bypass UNIX file system buffering schema and often offer much higher performance than that of the UNIX file systems and buffer managers.

Stored procedures.   Stored procedures are collections of SQL statements and flow-control directives (e.g., IF, THEN, ELSE) that are parsed, verified, compiled, bound, and stored at the DBMS server. Stored procedures allow for the input and output parameters, user-declared variables, and conditional execution typical of any programming language. Stored procedures can call other procedures and can be executed on remote relational DBMS servers. Stored procedures not only enhance the efficiency and flexibility of SQL but also dramatically improve RDBMS performance. Indeed, because of the nonnavigational nature of SQL, the access path selection is performed by the relational DBMS optimizer when an SQL statement is bound (parsed, verified, etc.). This process is resource-intensive—the corresponding instruction path length may be measured in several thousands of machine instructions. If it has to be performed every time a SQL statement is executed, the resulting performance will be greatly decreased (this type of SQL access is called *dynamic* SQL).

The SQL statements are *static* when they are parsed, verified, compiled, bound, and stored in the RDBMS server before they are executed, or the first time they are executed. If SQL statements are static, the consecutive executions will be done at a much smaller expense and, therefore, more rapidly. Some RDBMS systems (e.g., DB2) implement static SQL in such a way that the SQL statements are parsed and compiled before execution during the program preparation process. The resulting objects are stored in appropriate RDBMS libraries (i.e., Database Request Modules and DB2 Plans), from which they can be recalled. Other products (e.g., SYBASE SQL Server) parse and compile SQL statements the first time they are executed, and may store the results in memory (usually in a shared-procedure cache). Of course, even though there is no need to recall procedures from the libraries, one drawback of the latter technique is the possibility of the compiled stored procedure being paged out in a very active environment.

Regardless of the implementation technique, stored procedures improve the performance of SQL statements by eliminating costly preprocessing overhead. They also reduce network traffic by eliminating the need to send lengthy SQL statements from applications to RDBMS servers. In a typical UNIX-based client/server environment, for example, a stored procedure can be processed in one-fifth the time it takes to process a single embedded SQL command.

Cursor support. *Cursors* are programming constructs that allow applications to process the returned result set one record at a time. The result set can be derived from executing a single or multiple SQL queries in a single database connection. The record-at-a-time processing is typical of and required by OLTP systems. All RDBMS cursor implementations permit at least a unidirectional (forward) access of the result set. Some RDBMS products also allow backward scrolling, which is useful for many retrieval applications.

4.2   DBMS Connectivity

Heterogeneous data access. An advanced RDBMS implementation should be able to support the distribution of applications and data over networks and, as such, should be able to interconnect with like (homogeneous) and unlike (heterogeneous) systems and databases. Homogeneous connectivity is often built into the relational database system itself. Some distributed RDBMS products even offer distributed data consistency by supporting two-phase commit protocols.

Heterogeneous databases are much more difficult to interconnect; data structure, access, language can all be different, dissimilar. A traditional approach to heterogeneous DBMS connectivity is to build gateways that allow foreign database management systems to look like the native DBMS from an application's perspective. Sometimes, gateways allow third-party software vendors' programming tools and foreign databases to access data in the selected DBMS. However, because of the difference in heterogeneous DBMS architectures and supporting environments (e.g., SYBASE SQL Server on a UNIX server and DB2 on IBM MVS mainframes), gateways do not provide for seamless data access. Gateways may involve connection between different networks [e.g., Ethernet and System Network Architecture (SNA)], different communication protocols [e.g., TCP/IP and Advanced Program-to-Program Communications (APPC)], different data representation [e.g., American Standard Code for Information Interchange (ASCII) and Extended Binary-Coded Decimal Interchange Code (EBCDIC)], etc. Therefore, gateways are rarely used to support database transactions that span multiple heterogeneous environments, where all data consistency is guaranteed by a distributed heterogeneous two-phase commit protocol. Such implementations will require a cross-platform transaction manager that can interface with all participating heterogeneous databases. Such TP managers are being designed within the guidelines of the open systems. For example, X/Open has proposed XA (eXtended Architecture) interfaces for open systems TP managers, and the OSF Distributed Computing Environment, among other products, has selected these interfaces for its TP manager.

Nevertheless, today gateways solve a critical need to interconnect new and existing RDBMSs. Gateways play an important role by providing access to heterogeneous systems, especially when critical business data and legacy applications all reside on an organization's mainframes. Almost all gateways available today offer access to IBM's DB2. Better gateway implementations use Advanced Program-to-Program Communications (APPC/LU6.2) to provide real-time read-write access to mainframe data. Some gateways, such as MDI Database Gateway, OmniSQL Gateway, and Net/Gateway from Sybase, are DBMS-extensible, and allow UNIX-based RDBMS to interactively access *any* mainframe data available via CICS/MVS (IBM's transaction monitor for IBM mainframes).

Middleware. A generalized access to heterogeneous databases is probably a function of the middleware layer of the advanced client/server architecture. Some middleware solutions include ODBC from Microsoft and DRDA from IBM. A detailed discussion of the middleware is outside the scope of this book.

Remote procedure calls. If gateways represent one of the most popular way to access heterogeneous data from one hardware or software platform to another, server-to-server and client-to-server RDBMS connectivity is best supported via the mechanism of remote procedure calls (RPCs). Remote procedure calls represent a connectionless mechanism by which one process can execute another process residing on a different, usually remote, system, possibly running a different operating system. Any parameters needed by a subroutine are passed between the calling and called processes. A database RPC is a clearly defined request for a service or data issued over a network to an RDBMS server by a client or another server. Unlike traditional remote procedure calls, database RPCs (e.g., SYBASE RPC) can call stored procedures and allow the DBMS server to return multiple records (rows) in response to a single request. Since database RPCs eliminate the need for a client to send lengthy SQL statements and to receive individual records separately, they greatly reduce network traffic. In addition, RPCs can help implement heterogeneous DBMS connectivity by solving the language incompatibility problems. One system can call a remote procedure on another system without concern to the remote system's language syntax.

4.3   Advanced RDBMS Features

Database triggers and rules. Advanced relational DBMS implementations should provide users with the ability to initiate (trigger) certain user-defined actions based on a particular data-related event. *Triggers,* which can be viewed as a special type of stored procedure, are often used to implement referential integrity constraints. For example, a user may attempt to insert data into or update a table field which represents a foreign key (see discussion on referential integrity in previous chapters). The appropriate trigger can be designed to check the new field value against the values of the primary key. Similarly, delete actions can be controlled (e.g., prevented or cascaded) using user-developed delete triggers. In general, triggers can call other triggers or stored procedures, and are powerful tools for application development. Centrally located on the server (in SYBASE SQL Server, for example), triggers can improve RDBMS performance, although they require programming efforts, especially when implementing referential integrity.

Therefore, dictionary-based declarative referential integrity implementations are preferable to those using triggers. Declarative referential integrity provides better documentation and clarity by using standard nonprocedural SQL statements to define referential integrity constraints. DB2 and DB2/2 both support declarative referential integrity.

If triggers are often used to support referential integrity, RDBMS rules are used to implement user-defined domain constraints. For example, a database rule may say that the state code must be one of the approved two-character codes: NY, NJ, or CA.

Products that support database-resident rules facilitate the development of applications by implementing many business rules centrally as RDBMS rules. CA/Ingres and SYBASE SQL Server are just two examples that implement RDBMS-resident rules.

Image support. Today, business requirements often include the need to support multimedia, in particular, image applications. Ideally, a RDBMS selected for a client/server, distributed environment, should also support special IMAGE data types, known as *binary large objects* (BLOBs). These represent very large (up to several gigabytes) fields that are used to store images, graphics, long text documents, and even voice recordings. Ideally, the RDBMS should be capable of not only storing and retrieving BLOBs but also making BLOB fields available through the use of standard SQL like any other data element. Several RDBMSs available today (e.g., Oracle and Sybase) provide BLOB support. In addition, some RDBMS vendors and standards groups, such as SQL Access Group, are working on SQL extensions that would allow BLOB manipulations from SQL statements. Conversely, object-oriented DBMS (OODBMSs) are probably even better suited to handle this problem.

Graphical front-end development tools. Users of distributed RDBMSs all demand an advanced graphical suite of application development tools. Today, users can see two trends in the front-end tools for DBMS application development. Some RDBMS products (like Ingres, Informix, and Oracle, to name just a few) integrate graphical application development tools as an integrated solution. Oracle even offers computer-aided software engineering (CASE) tools to facilitate application development. Other RDBMS vendors rely on third-party front-end tool vendors to supply application development tools that can construct applications efficiently for a given RDBMS. Examples of such tools are JAYCC, Uniface, and Neuron Data. Intimate knowledge of the underlying database system often results in better application performance when integrated front-end–DBMS solutions are used. On the other hand, independent front-end tool vendors often offer better and more open graphical user interfaces (GUIs), and allow users to be more flexible about choosing the best database management system. Whatever the case, front-end tools must be considered when selecting a RDBMS.

On-line analytical processing (OLAP) and multidimensional databases (MDDBs). Often, system designers and users like to differentiate operational databases, designed for OLTP applications, from data warehouse databases designed to support decision support systems (DSSs). Aside from purely operational consideration (availability, multiuser support, etc.), databases designed for DSS should easily lend themselves to support ad hoc analytical queries. Sometimes, the analytical needs appears to exceed the two dimensions (rows and columns) of the classic relational data model. This multidimensional on-line analytical processing may employ multidimensional DBMS to allow users to

- View data from many different viewpoints
- Easily switch from one viewpoint to another
- Drill down into the data with a parent-child relationship between the data points

A detailed discussion of OLAP tools and multidimensional databases can be found in Chap. 13.

Object-oriented DBMS. The object-oriented approach continues to grow in acceptance. Object-oriented analysis and design and object-oriented programming are becoming a desired and preferred way of developing applications rapidly and efficiently because of the ability to reuse application code and entire business objects. The need for and the benefits of OODBMS are the driving forces that result in developing new database system models: OODBMS and object-relational DBMS (ORDBMS). Therefore, while OODBMS discussions are beyond the scope of this book, a few comments should be made for the purpose of completeness. The development of the new OODBMS follows two major approaches: (1) extending the relational model to accommodate object concepts and (2) building radically different, nonrelational database systems. Approach 1 leads to development of ORDBMS. It is pursued by many vendors (including traditional RDBMS vendors) and is facilitated by the ANSI SQL committee and SQL Access Group (SAG) working toward the object-oriented extensions to SQL (SQL3). Approach 2 is promoted by OODBMS vendors and Object Database Management Group, or ODMG (a subset of the OMG) that believe that the relational data model is not suited for the object-oriented approach. Their efforts are focused on developing a common set of standards for OODBMS, a set that is probably quite different from the one being developed by the ANSI.

It is a fair assumption that both approaches will eventually result in an object DBMS model that will incorporate the best features of both worlds. Some OODBMS products on the market today, such as GemStone from Servio Corporation and ObjectStore (Object Design Inc.), are examples of the new generation of object-oriented database management systems that provide access to objects through the applications written in C, C++, and SmallTalk. Others, such as Matisse (ADB Inc.), Objectivity/DB (Objectivity), and UniSQL (UniSQL Inc.), support object databases through the standard SQL interfaces, including ODBC. Significant developments in this area are reflected in products like Informix Universal Server, Oracle 8, and DB2 Universal Database (see Chap. 5 for more details).

4.4   RDBMS Reliability and Availability

The key factors affecting DBMS availability are *robustness*—the ability to reduce the affects of any particular failure, coupled with the ability to recover from failures automatically; and *manageability*—the ability to administer a DBMS on line, often from a remote site. Although availability is critical to any DBMS model (relational, nonrelational, object), the following discussion focuses on how these factors affect the design of relational database system.

4.4.1   Robustness, transactions recovery, and consistency

A database transaction treats one or more SQL statements as a single *unit of work,* which is the atomic unit of database recovery and consistency. Consistency in RDBMS prevents simultaneous queries and data modification requests from interfering with each other and prevents access to partially changed and not yet committed data.

A RDBMS should provide for automatic database consistency by implementing the proper levels of locking, validating logical and physical database consistency, and supporting two-phase commit protocols.

Consistency checking should be performed automatically during transaction and database recovery. There are two major types of recovery: transaction recovery from a system or application failure and system recovery from media failure. *Transaction recovery* means that, in case of system or application failure, all committed changes must be made permanent—committed data must be written to a database device (disk). At the same time, all data affected by this transaction but not yet committed is recovered (rolled back) to the pretransaction state completely and automatically. The direction of the recovery process is backward—from the point of failure to the last point of consistency. In the case of media failure (i.e., disk crash), an RDBMS must be designed to perform point-in-time recovery, which includes restoration of the lost data using the most current backup, and forward recovery of data from the point of the latest backup to the point immediately before the media failure. Transaction logs are usually used to store changes to the database and perform recovery procedures: before-change image (for backward recovery) and after-change image (for forward recovery). Often, a RDBMS uses an automatic checkpoint mechanism to maintain the currency of the transaction log. The majority of the database products available today support various degrees of database consistency and recovery.

Shared log files. Technically speaking, the mechanism a DBMS employs to ensure the integrity of database transactions is database *logging*. DBMS logging requires that every change to the database be automatically written to the database log file. These change records can be used by the DBMS to recover from an in-flight transaction failure (ROLLBACK) and for the point-in-time forward recovery. Advanced RDBMS implementations allow one physical write to the log file to contain the COMMIT/ROLLBACK information for several transactions. The resulting reduction in log I/O improves RDBMS update performance, allows for the efficient use of resources, and facilitates multiuser support.

On-line backup and recovery. The database backup and recovery mechanisms should be able to operate dynamically, on line, while the RDBMS server continues to operate. Indeed, in a multiuser, multidatabase environment, a backup of one database should not prevent users from accessing other databases, even on the same physical system. This is especially true when many organizations authorize database owners to be responsible for backing up their databases and corresponding transaction logs. On-line recovery should allow a database to recover automatically from an application or transaction failure (i.e., perform automatic rollback), and support a forward recovery procedure. On-line backup and recovery should be a mandatory feature for RDBMS products selected for real-time, OLTP environments (e.g., banking, brokerage, ticket reservation, air traffic control).

4.4.2   Fault tolerance

While backup and recovery are important availability features, a database management system concerned with their robustness must also employ hardware and software measures typically found in fault-tolerant systems. Hardware fault tolerance requires a physical system implementation in which all (or the majority of) the components are duplicated, so that when one component fails, the "hot" standby takes over immediately. Among the fault-tolerant measures found in DBMSs are the ability to work with RAID (redundant array of inexpensive disks) devices, disk mirroring, and duplexing. In addition to protecting from disk failures, these measures often help optimize I/O performance.

Disk mirroring.   Several vendors supply hardware fault-tolerant solutions (e.g., Tandem and Stratus computers). Unfortunately, these solutions are rather expensive and lock RDBMS developers and users into a particular vendor or product. Several RDBMS vendors offer software-based fault tolerance by providing disk mirroring for transaction logs and/or databases. For example, SYBASE SQL Server supports disk mirroring for either the transaction log or the database itself.

Mirroring a transaction log protects against the loss of any committed transaction (see Fig. 4.7), while mirroring a database guarantees continuous operation in the event of media failure. Indeed, mirroring a database means nonstop recovery (see Fig. 4.8).

Disk mirroring requires the availability of a separate physical disk drive device on a RDBMS server, and actually duplicates all writes to the primary device on the mirror. Disk mirroring has an added advantage in that both disks—the primary and the mirror—are available for read operations. Some RDBMS products take advantage of this fact by routing read requests to the disk drive that provides better response time.

4.5 RDBMS Administration

Relational DBMS administration for high availability has two aspects: remote administration and on-line administration.

Remote administration.   Users looking for a distributed RDBMS solution should select RDBMS to support database administration (DBA) functions from any

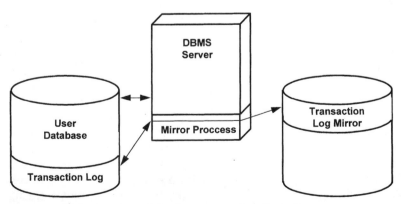

Figure 4.7   Disk mirroring: minimum guaranteed configuration.

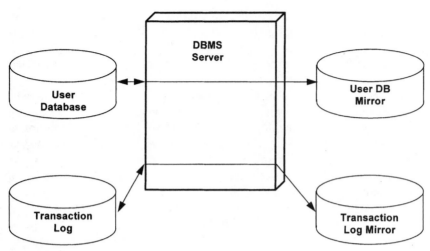

Figure 4.8 Disk mirroring on multiple disks.

site. Database administration includes installing the database system software, managing disk storage, creating and managing database objects, performing backup and recovery, providing database security, managing database users and their permissions and privileges, controlling database and table access, monitoring and tuning system performance, and determining and solving system problems. In a distributed environment, these tasks may have to be done at each database location. Thus, users should require that RDBMS vendors provide database administration facilities that allow limited DBA staff to perform the necessary administration functions rapidly, conveniently, and from any (preferably centralized) location. Indeed, if remote database administration is not available, an organization has to face two unattractive choices: send DBAs to the database location as the need arises or maintain qualified DBA personnel at each location. If a network contains hundreds or even thousands of nodes, either choice becomes economically unfeasible.

Most RDBMS products available to date, especially products that operate in UNIX-based environments, provide at least some degree of remote database administration. Noticeable among them are solutions that are based on the Tivoli Management Environment (TME) framework. Examples can be found in such database implementations as Oracle, Sybase, and Informix.

On-line administration. Administrative tasks such as performance tuning, resource management, database recovery, and archiving often interfere with the RDBMS availability requirements. On-line administration implies continuous operation of the DBMS irrespective of the administrative actions taken against it. For example, traditional RDBMS administration tasks such as initiating a backup, adding a new user, modifying a user profile, and creating database objects, should be performed on line, without stopping the database system and interrupting ongoing activities.

Client/Server RDBMS Solutions

There are several DBMS products designed to work in client/server environments based on various hardware and operating system platforms. To demonstrate how the architectural and design features previously discussed apply to the major RDBMS products, the following discussion focuses on some of these products: Sybase, Oracle, Informix, DB2/6000, and Microsoft SQL Server.

5.1 State-of-the-Market Overview

When one decides to analyze the database management market, several trends become clear:

- The relational DBMS (RDBMS) market continues to mature; and that maturity extends to traditional capabilities of RDBMS servers, thus pushing specialized technologies into small niches.

- The Internet phenomena coupled with mobile computing begin to move the focus from a traditional client/server database transactions to a long "over-the net" transaction model; the entire transaction becomes network-resident.

- Data warehousing continues to push the scalability and query performance limits of a traditional RDBMS technology.

- Support for complex data types encapsulated as spatial, textual, time series, image, video, and sound objects becomes a real business need.

- The need for data interoperability is more frequently addressed by function sharing than by data sharing.

- Data replication becomes a widely acceptable form of data distribution, and RDBMS solutions will continue the integration with the most robust messaging and queuing products.

Given these trends, the major RDBMS vendors—Oracle, Sybase, Informix, IBM, and Microsoft—continue to leapfrog each other in several areas of database technology, with major efforts directed toward the Internet transactions; improved scalability to support very large databases and advanced processing techniques such as OLAP; sophisticated data replication aimed at mobile users like salesforce automation; and the ability to handle (not just access but perform data manipulation operations) on complex data types. The latter is serving as a battleground among relational DBMS vendors, object database vendors (e.g., Versant, ObjectStore, Objectivity, Matisse), object-relational DBMS vendors (e.g., Illustra/Informix, Omniscience, UniSQL), and a small group of highly specialized vendors (e.g., MapInfo, MediaDB, Arcinfo). Clearly, a complete analysis of all these players is well beyond the scope of this book. Therefore, the following sections look at the products from the current RDBMS market leaders as a good indication of where the technology is moving. This chapter discusses the products from these vendors in a very general way. For example, a discussion on Oracle's Universal Server and Informix's joint development with Illustra are mentioned very briefly.

Scalability features of these products are closely tied to the data warehousing ambitions of these key vendors, and are discussed in much more detail in Chaps. 8 and 9.

5.2   Oracle

Oracle is one of the largest RDBMS vendors. The Oracle RDBMS is available on practically every hardware platform and every operating system. Currently in version 8, Oracle provides parallel query processing capabilities, and as such, is the first commercial RDBMS that is available on several SMP and MPP platforms. Oracle offers not just a relational database management system, but the entire suite of integrated software tools, including an Integrated Computer Aided Software Engineering (I-CASE) toolset. Some of the strongest features of Oracle RDBMS are

- Hardware and system software portability
- Wide communication protocol support
- Distributed processing capabilities
- Parallel query processing
- Active data dictionary
- SQL support:
  - ⇨ Procedural (PL/SQL)
  - ⇨ SQL precompiler support
  - ⇨ ANSI SQL support
  - ⇨ Extended SQL support (SQL*Plus)

Oracle front-end tools include SQL*FORMS graphical tools for application development, SQL*ReportWriter, and SQL*Menu products.

The Oracle RDBMS offers standard SQL implementation with several useful extensions and two programming interfaces: low-level Oracle Call Interface and embedded SQL with SQL precompilers. The Oracle RDBMS offers sophisticated concurrency control, row-level locking, contention-free queries, event-related triggers, and asynchronous I/O. In addition, Oracle supports shared databases via its Oracle Parallel Server option with the Global Cache system, in which multiple Oracle instances residing on multiple systems can share the same database located on a shared disk.

Beginning with version 7, the Oracle RDBMS supports cost-based optimization, clustered indexes, stored procedures, database triggers, disk mirroring, server-enforced integrity constraints, BLOB data types, on-line backup/recovery, and on-line, remote database administration.

The Oracle distributed RDBMS implementation is facilitated by the SQL*Net and SQL*Connect products. These components allow Oracle to support distributed queries and updates, data location transparency, site autonomy, heterogeneous DBMS access, and network independence. Oracle's SQL*Net is a heterogeneous network interface and supports DECnet, TCP/IP, SNA LU0, LU2 and APPC/LU6.2, Novell's IPX/SPX, Named Pipes, NetBIOS, X.25, OSI, Async, and Banyan Vines, to name just a few. The Oracle SQL*Connect heterogeneous DBMS connectivity facility supports access to DB2, SQL/DS, and VAX RMS. One of the most important components of the Oracle RDBMS is its active data dictionary, which is a set of read-only tables containing information about the database and database objects (tables, views, indexes, synonyms, sequences, and clusters). The data dictionary provides information about user names, user privileges, table constraints, column default values, primary and foreign keys, object space allocation, and audit data, and is, in fact, a database reference guide for all database users.

As mentioned before, Oracle was the first commercial RDBMS that successfully ventured into the high-performance scalable commercial computing arena with the support of very large databases. To that end, Oracle's architecture uses simulated multithreading, with one server process used for each concurrently executing user request, but allowing users to share a set of processes. Incoming processes are dispatched to a server process assigned from the process pool, with the number of both servers and dispatchers tunable by the system administrator. One drawback of this approach is that the entire process (and not a lightweight thread) can be blocked while waiting for the I/O, memory, or other system resources. Despite these drawbacks, Oracle uses process switching to facilitate its port to an SMP or MPP architecture. An add-on Oracle Parallel Server (OPS) option for loosely coupled clusters and MPP, together with the Parallel Query Option (PQO) are designed to take advantage of SMP and MPP architectures by allowing separate instances of Oracle to run on individual processors, while sharing access to database files. Oracle solves the critical issue of memory and cache management in multiprocessor environments by implementing a global lock manager and the GigaCache system, which provide for cache coherency and in-cache data integrity. Oracle 8, released in July 1997, offers significant improvements in very large database support, including increased scalability, robust data partitioning, and enhanced availability.

5.2.1 System management

Oracle Enterprise Manager (OEM), released in 1996, consists of a systems management framework and applications for managing the Oracle database (v.7.3 and higher) and database extensions. The framework consists of a management server/console and intelligent agents that ship with every Oracle v.7.3 database. The framework provides a graphical console, and basic event and job scheduling subsystems (utilized by the management applications). Standard and extended applications enable a graphical drag-and-drop interface to perform database administration tasks (in addition to the command-line and script-based interfaces). Additional capabilities are included in the Performance Pack applications, which enable performance monitoring, tuning, diagnostics, and resource analysis. The provides a consistent centralized Oracle RDBMS management across the wide variety of platforms that Oracle supports, many of which are not addressed by the database-tool-independent software vendors. The management server/console is available on Windows NT or 95, with a Java-enabled Web interface.

While OEM is aimed at Oracle-only installations, Oracle also has a solution for heterogeneous database environments. This solution is based on the Tivoli TME framework for systems management, and is called the *Enterprise Server Manager* (ESM) (developed by a U.K. DBMX Ltd.). ESM provides Oracle-only schemas and user management capabilities along with event and performance management layered on top of the Tivoli framework, and is accessible through the Tivoli/Enterprise Console (T/EC). DBMX is also working to integrate ESM functionality into OEM to enable the OEM-intelligent agents to communicate management events to the T/EC.

5.2.2 Oracle Universal Server

Beginning with its version 7.3, Oracle has announced the availability of its Universal Server (see Fig. 5.1). Oracle Universal Server leverages its relational database server to create a new generation of powerful information management systems. Oracle Universal Server allows users to store, manipulate, retrieve, and share many data types, including business records, documents, messages, images, audio, and video, in transaction processing applications and data warehouses.

Oracle Universal Server allows users to securely and reliably deliver these powerful applications to a large number of users over any type of network, and

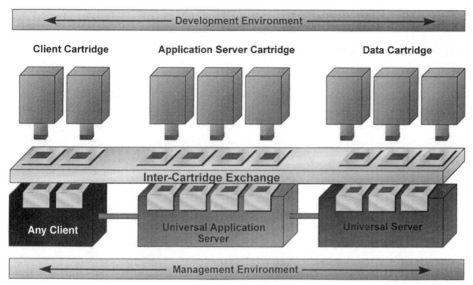

Figure 5.1 Oracle Universal Server and Network Computing Architecture.

regardless of the hardware and software platforms. Universal Server integrates several add-on facilities, including ConText Option, Messaging Option, OLAP Option, and Spatial Data Option. Two of these facilities are described below.

5.2.3 Oracle ConText Option

Business information is more than just structured data stored in databases. In fact, about 85 percent of all corporate data is text, buried in manuals, reports, e-mail, and Web pages. Text in all its forms represents a vast and valuable information resource. However, tapping that resource and incorporating it with structured information has largely been an unrealized goal. While robust, SQL-based relational databases were used for structured data, proprietary and hard-to-scale retrieval engines were used for text.

The Oracle ConText Option is the text management solution tightly integrated with its database. It enables organizations to leverage text information sources as quickly and easily as structured data. It combines the scalability of the Oracle Server and its SQL-based tools with advanced text-retrieval technology to help users extract the information needed. Together, these technologies allow enterprises to integrate large-scale document databases with mission-critical applications and provide users with fast, efficient access to text-based information. The ConText Option is designed for managing and accessing any information source, from historical news archives to cutting-edge Web content.

The ConText Option provides four key advantages:

- **Database-quality architecture.** Users can manage text with the scalability, security, integrity, fault tolerance, and administrative ease of a relational database. Unlike specialized text-retrieval applications, the ConText Option incorporates text at the data repository level. This way, new and existing Oracle applications can take advantage of text assets via robust, parallel, multiprocessor architectures. These systems can support many noncurrent users and millions of documents in multigigabyte to terabyte databases—a scalable solution for data warehousing, electronic commerce, OLTP, and distributed environments.

- **Standards-based development environment.** While stand-alone text-retrieval products often require separate development environments, the ConText Option supports retrieval via standard SQL, treating text data as a peer to relational data. A variety of standard tools, ranging from Forms interfaces to sophisticated Web environments, can combine structured data searches with intelligent text searches and text reductions in a single query. The result is a unified environment for rapidly developing new text-enabled applications, or for easily performing "hot upgrades" to text capabilities of existing systems.

- **Advanced text-retrieval technology.** Using the ConText Option's advanced text-retrieval, text-reduction, and classification features, users can pinpoint required information quickly within very large databases. These advanced features for text retrieval, reduction, and classification include
  - ⇨ Automatic text reduction
  - ⇨ Automatic classification
  - ⇨ Soundex fuzzy matches
  - ⇨ Proximity searches
  - ⇨ Boolean logic
  - ⇨ Multilingual stemming
  - ⇨ Relevance ranking
  - ⇨ Term weighting
  - ⇨ Thesaurus support
  - ⇨ Stop lists

- **Extensible framework.** The ConText Option's extensible framework integrates new languages, formats, specialized search engines, and services within the same unified database. This preserves the enterprise's investment in storage and retrieval applications. For example, the ConText Option currently supports several major European languages, Japanese, and most popular formats, including HTML (HyperText Markup Language) and PDF

(Portable Document Format). Chinese and Korean will be available in upcoming releases.

5.2.4   Oracle Spatial Data Option

The Oracle Spatial Data Option available beginning with release 7.3 is an extension to the Oracle7 Server for the management of spatial information. It enables spatial data to be efficiently stored, accessed, and manipulated in the database in the same manner as structured data. A database that has been spatially enabled offers a distinct advantage because it includes a critical, but often neglected, element of the decision-making process: location.

With the Oracle Spatial Data Option, users can take advantage of the spatial data. For example, an insurance company may want to predict its financial exposure during a catastrophe such as a flood. Using Oracle Spatial Data Option, the company can efficiently query the database to quickly find policyholders whose location is within the actual or predicted flood zones. Since all the types of data are within one enterprisewide database, the company can combine this location information with other business data such as value of policies, names of policyholders, and telephone numbers. Thus, the company can quickly deploy the right resources to assist their policyholders and limit the company's financial exposure.

Spatial data management is a horizontal technology with broad application in many market segments. Spatial information technology is pivotal to the retail market, real estate, banking, insurance, and horizontal business applications, including data warehousing and mission-critical systems. The Oracle Spatial Data Option is a key component of any information system in which location is an important part of the decision-making process.

5.3   Informix

The Informix OnLine Dynamic Server (available starting with release 6) is a completely reengineered RDBMS product based on the Informix Dynamic Scalable Architecture (DSA). The Informix OnLine Dynamic Server offers a number of fully integrated advanced features at no extra cost, including

- True multithreaded architecture
- Distributed DBMS capabilities
- Symmetric multiprocessing (SMP)
- Parallel disk I/O and utilities
- Hot standby support
- Multiprotocol network support
- Parallel query processing
- Table partitioning

- Partition-level backup and restore

- Support for large databases

Informix Dynamic Scalable Architecture supports multiple concurrent threads, which are scheduled according to resource availability independently of the mechanism used by the platform's operating system. The scheduler itself is nonpreemptive, and assigns tasks from the multiple, different priority *ready queues* on a FIFO (first-in first-out) basis. The architecture supports two additional queue types: the *wait* queue (where threads waiting for and event such as resource availability are placed) and the *sleep* (inactive threads) queue.

Informix OnLine Dynamic Server SMP support is provided via the true multi-threading feature of the DSA. In essence, although it looks like a single server to the user, the DSA schedules multiple virtual processors, each of which runs multiple threads by context switching. A virtual processor is assigned to a particular CPU and belongs to one of the processor classes. The number of virtual processors can be altered dynamically by users for some classes and automatically by the system for other classes.

Parallel disk I/O, parallel utilities, and parallel query processing features are integrated into the DSA, which divides each atomic database operation into multiple concurrent threads. In addition, each database operation is data-flow-driven, and begins its processing as soon as input data is available. In turn, the output of each database operation is fed to the next operation for processing. This approach allows concurrent threads to be assigned in parallel to sort, merge, scan, join, selection, and projection operations (see case 3 in Fig. 4.3): *vertical parallelism*. Similarly, this architecture allows different tasks to run in parallel: *horizontal parallelism* (as in case 4, Fig. 12.3). The latter can benefit from data partitioning supported by the DSA in three modes: index key partitioning, hash partitioning, and expression partitioning (partitions are established based on a SQL expression).

To achieve the highest levels of scalability and performance, Informix announced its support for loosely coupled clusters and MPP systems in the Release 8 eXtended Parallel Server (XPS). Other Informix OnLine features include software disk mirroring, on-line backup and recovery, asynchronous parallel I/O, flexible monitoring facilities for the configuration information and DBMS activity, and cost-based optimization. Informix OnLine supports BLOBs for image, graphics, voice, and large text objects. In fact, Informix is so efficient in multimedia applications that it is often chosen as the underlying DBMS for commercial image systems. Informix distributed database support is provided by Informix Star (ISTAR), and includes distributed cost-based optimization, data location transparency, and distributed queries. For heterogeneous DBMS connectivity, Informix uses third-party software vendors to implement its mainframe gateway strategy.

Overall, Informix OnLine offers an innovative server architecture, relatively few hardware and software requirements, an impressive software development tools (Informix/4GL and NewEra), and excellent performance.

5.3.1 Features

To enable customers with the ability to move and manage information among regional offices and data centers, data marts and data warehouses, and relational databases and mainframes, Informix is enhancing its Informix-OnLine database servers—all of which are based on Informix's Dynamic Scalable Architecture (DSA)—with comprehensive replication and advanced systems management products. Furthermore, Informix has Web-enabled its OnLine database family with the Internet technology from Netscape.

Another important set of features available from Informix is the Distributed Enterprise Solution. This complete set of desktop-to-data center functionality represents the Informix distributed enterprise solution, which can be further enhanced with the best-of-breed technology from Informix partners. This solution applies to all industries using distributed OLTP and decision support applications. In particular, companies within financial services, manufacturing, retail, and telecommunications can use Informix's distributed enterprise solution for branch office automation to improve customer service, marketing, and sales efforts.

Informix's data replication feature is designed to support both Informix and heterogeneous database environments, providing customers with the flexibility to disseminate and consolidate information across geographically dispersed database servers according to their replication needs and database software investments. Informix's replication solution is scalable, and is integrated within a single database server.

Informix's comprehensive replication support consists of three products that work together within the enterprise: Informix-Workgroup Replication, Informix-Enterprise Replication, and Praxis International Inc.'s OmniReplicator for heterogeneous replication. To manage both Informix and heterogeneous replication support, Informix provides Replication Manager, with easy-to-use wizards, built into its OnLine family of database servers. Replication Manager is accessed using Informix's suite of systems management tools.

Systems management. Informix's advanced management solution consists of Informix's own automated, scalable systems management tool and integrated support for third-party systems management tools and SNMP (Simple Network Management Protocol)-based enterprise management frameworks.

The Informix-Enterprise Command Center (IECC) is a scalable, automated systems management tool that allows customers to manage one to thousands of database servers easily from a central console. Because of its object-oriented, CORBA/IIOP-based architecture, IECC is Java-enabled, allowing users to create "lights out" systems management automation and to customize application management objects. IECC also offers users the flexibility to manage distributed databases from a Web browser or Microsoft Windows PCs, providing universal systems management from any desktop regardless of platform or location.

IECC is a completely open platform designed to allow third-party systems management applications and network management tools to easily interoperate, providing complete systems management in heterogeneous environments. Informix partners with the leading systems management tool vendors, including BMC Software, Inc., Compuware Corp., Hewlett-Packard Co., Platinum Technology, Inc. and Tivoli Systems, Inc. IECC, with SNMP support, enables users to plug in network management tools, such as CA-Unicenter, HP Open View, IBM Net View, and Sun Solstice, into Informix's central-console systems management solution.

Web-enabled environment.   Informix has expanded its Web-enabled database solution to the entire family of OnLine database products using Netscape Communications Corp.'s Internet software. The integration of Informix's OnLine databases with Netscape's Internet software offers customers a high-performance, scalable database solution that connects distributed enterprises via the Web for either Internet or intranet applications. Using this solution, companies can cost-effectively deploy information stored in Informix OnLine databases to and from data centers and remote sources using an easy-to-use browser interface, as well as traditional client/server applications.

Informix also offers Answers OnLine, a built-in, knowledge-based inference engine with several critical assistance features that are installed with Informix's OnLine databases and is easily accessed via the Web. Using Answers OnLine, customers have access to a product documentation library, answers to commonly asked questions, development and integration guides, and training videos and materials. Answers OnLine is also customizable to enable customers to add and distribute any information required in the enterprise.

Answers OnLine is installed and linked automatically to Informix's OnLine databases using the Web browser and server. This enables all database users within the distributed enterprise to receive simultaneous Answers OnLine updates via a direct link to Informix's corporate Web site.

5.3.2 Informix Universal Server

With the acquisition of Illustra Information Technologies in 1996, Informix found itself in a position to rapidly develop what it calls a Universal Server (see Fig. 5.2).

Universal Server, announced in December 1996, is designed to intelligently manage complex data, not as BLOBs, but natively as objects. This means very high-performance query and transaction access to rich, complex data—exactly the requirements emerging from the new classes of applications. Universal Server provides an SQL interface for rapid application development and maintenance, as well as continuing to deliver the scalability and manageability of the Informix Dynamic Scalable Architecture (DSA) product line. Using Universal Server, users have freedom to define both the structure and behavior of data needed to define their particular applications. The server can make intelligent choices to optimize access to the complex data, and users can define

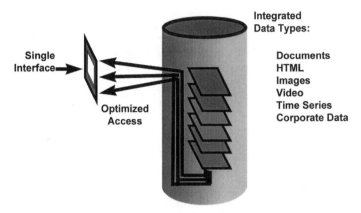

Figure 5.2   Informix Universal Server.

functions that manipulate the data right in the server itself, or take advantage of datatype and function extensions written by others.

User-defined data types.   The new abstract data types (ADTs) can be user-defined and created from scratch or by *inheriting* structure from another type. Structure, rules (triggers), operators, functions, and aggregates can all be inherited. Informix Universal Server is a strongly typed system, meaning that unlike data types cannot be directly compared, but must instead be cast into a comparable form. The Universal Server supports the definition of casting functions to do just that.

User-defined functions.   Informix Universal server extends the concept of stored procedures by allowing functions written in a high-level language to occupy the same position in the Object-Relational RDBMS (ORDBMS) as stored procedures do in an RDBMS. These user-defined functions (UDFs) allow developers to encapsulate both the data and the behavior in a single known object. The Universal Server enables developers to define any arbitrary complex function to execute in either the server or the client. The functions can be written in C, C++, Java, and Informix's Stored Procedure Language (SPL). A part of the function definition includes instructing the system about the I/O and CPU costs of the function, so that the optimizer can make intelligent choices about how to optimize the query in which the function is embedded.

Functions can be overloaded, meaning that there can be several functions with the same name but different parameter list (the sequence of parameters and their types form the function's *signature*). The Universal Server invokes the right function by examining its signature.

A special case of user-defined functions is *user-defined aggregates*, which are aimed at multidimensional analysis. Since functions and aggregates inherit

Informix's Dynamic Scalable Architecture parallel features, user-defined aggregates are easily parallelizable.

Informix Universal Server supports *triggers* on SELECT statement, enabling the DBMS to take actions when it detects a user reading particular data from the database. This ability to record usage patterns is especially valuable when using the Universal Server to provide HTML pages for the World Wide Web access.

Informix Universal Server can be extended to manage new kinds of data by means of *DataBlade* modules, which define new data structures, new functions that manipulate them, and optionally, new access methods to provide fast access to the data. Informix provides a software development kit to create DataBlade modules from existing C or C++ class definitions and C subroutines. A single Universal Server can be loaded with many DataBlade modules simultaneously, and customers can extend and even replace the functionality of these modules. A DataBlade module is very different from the object wrapper technique used by some RDBMS vendors. Object wrappers attempt to provide object capabilities by layering an object simulator on top of a regular relational DBMS. The problem with an object wrapper is that the optimizer and access methods do not understand the object concepts. There is no way to provide high-performance, content-based queries against complex data. In addition, the simulator layer has to create the objects at run time, using only classic RDBMS technology, which is an expensive and slow operation. Often, this will force an object wrapper to perform multiple slow table scans because it is unable to express the query efficiently to the underlying RDBMS, whereas an ORDBMS can perform a fast index lookup.

In an ORDBMS, by contrast, data is stored as structures, and the internal details are accessible to functions running in the server. ORDBMS function definitions include instructions to the optimizer about the I/O and CPU cost of the function so that the optimizer can choose an intelligent query plan.

Access methods. Some new data types are not well served by the B-trees, hashing, and bitmap indexes the available from traditional RDBMS vendors. Examples of data poorly served by such indexes include images and 2-D and 3-D geographic data for which the standard access methods are ineffective. Without an appropriate access method, data manipulation is prohibitively slow, even on very fast computers. It also slows linearly (or worse) as the data size increases. Adding a new access method to a typical RDBMS is a very complex task that can be performed only by senior vendor engineering staff, while an ORDBMS is designed for pluggable access methods. While adding a new access method (or index type) is not a typical development activity, it is an important part of ORDBMS extensibility because it is required for high-performance access to many nontraditional data types. Informix Universal Server supports efficient access methods, including R-tree and Rlink-tree for multidimensional data, and Doc-tree for text retrieval blades.

5.4   Sybase

5.4.1   SYBASE SQL Server

Sybase Client/Server architecture is a proven solution for integrating heterogeneous data and applications.

Some particular strengths of SYBASE SQL Server are

- 32-bit multithreaded architecture—SYBASE implements multithreading in the engine, and does not use operating system threads.

- Dynamic (on-line) backup for continuous operations—Sybase published the benchmark results rating the Sybase Backup Server at 45 Gbytes/h.

- Database triggers and stored procedures, with trigger self-recursion.

- Server-enforced business rules and referential integrity.

- Support for user-defined data types.

- Cost-based optimization.

- ANSI standard SQL support.

- Clustered indexes.

- Cursor support.

- Asynchronous I/O.

- Multilevel locking.

- Operating system support—UNIX, Windows NT, OS/2, VMS.

- Access control, security, and remote database administration—SYBASE supports *role-based* security and database auditing by roles; stored procedure executions can be limited by roles.

SYBASE supports software disk mirroring and provides integrated graphical application development environment—the *PowerBuilder*.

Distributed databases are supported by remote procedure calls (RPCs) and remote stored procedures, gateways, and open client–server interfaces that are based on the ISO Remote Database Access (RDA) protocol. Data location transparency and programmable two-phase commit for multisite updates are enhanced via the use of RPCs.

The Open Client is a programmable interface which manages all communications between clients and the SQL Server. SYBASE Open Server provides a consistent method of receiving SQL requests or RPC from SYBASE applications and passing them to a non-SYBASE application.

For heterogeneous (relational, nonrelational databases, and files) data access, SYBASE provides the Open Connectivity solutions which include MDI Gateway and OmniSQL Gateway that allow a SYBASE application to access non-SQL Server data, including legacy (mainframe) data available through the Customer Information Control System (CICS).

The follow-on to SYBASE SQL Server 4.x was a major product release called *SYBASE System 10.* System 10 does not refer to just the SQL Server but to an entire family of products. For example, OmniSQL Gateway, Replication Server, and Navigation Server are components of the System 10 release. Other examples include systems management tools to manage local and distributed client/server environments. Among these tools are

- *Enterprise SQL Server Manager* (ESSM)—a graphical systems management tool for distributed DBMS that is based on the Tivoli Management Environment (TME) framework.
- *SQL Server Monitor*—a graphical tool used to monitor SQL Server performance. Up to 300 parameters can be monitored concurrently.
- *SQL Debug*—a source level debugger for Transact-SQL code.

Other systems management features include support for the system's estimation of storage space allocation, reports on the status of integrity constraints, and threshold violation by database segment. The system can determine when to rebuild the index following the sort order change. SYBASE also supports chargeback statistics per user on the basis of CPU and I/O usage.

Virtual Server Architecture.   SYBASE SQL Server design is based on Sybase's Virtual Server Architecture (VSA), which allows it to utilize coarse-grain parallel processing features on symmetric multiprocessing (SMP) systems. SQL Server can be run as a single process (does not utilize SMP) or as multiple cooperating processes.

Asynchronous I/O.   The SQL Server engine uses an asynchronous device I/O on platforms that support it. SQL Server allows the user to partition a physical device into several logical devices. Each logical database device uses a separate thread, providing asynchronous I/O capability even within one physical device.

Because a separate thread is used for each logical device, the SQL Server can write concurrently to different database devices. The asynchronous I/O capability also allows for nonserial writes within mirrored devices. This means that the system can queue up writes immediately to both sides of mirrored devices. Without asynchronous I/O, the system would have to wait for each write to finish before starting another.

Client-Side asynchronous I/O.   Client applications can benefit greatly from the use of asynchronous programming capabilities. Asynchronous applications are designed to make efficient use of time by performing other work while waiting for server operations to complete. The new Open Client Client-Library (CT-Library) provides programmers with a set of routines for asynchronous programming. These asynchronous I/O capabilities allow client applications to use one connection for multiple actions.

Replication. Sybase has implemented data replication services as a variant of the publisher/subscriber model. The replication processing and control logic are built into a separate product called Replication Server. Replication Server keeps copies of data up-to-date at multiple sites providing client applications with access to local data instead of remote, centralized databases. The Replication Server provides reliable data and transaction delivery despite network failures and automatically synchronizes data after failure. Replication Server has an open architecture allowing organizations to build a replicated data system from existing systems and applications. Systems can be expanded incrementally as the organization grows and business requirements change.

Parallel query processing. Sybase has implemented parallel query processing as a separate product called *SYBASE MPP* (previously known as the *Navigation Server*). SYBASE MPP provides high-speed access to large volumes of data by partitioning the data across multiple SYBASE SQL Servers and by using parallel concurrent access to multiple processors.

SYBASE MPP product is designed to provide support for very large database (VLDB) environments that are typical for data warehousing. SYBASE MPP is designed to handle thousands of users, very high transaction rates, and complex decision support applications.

The query optimizer. SYBASE SQL Server supports both syntax-based and cost-based optimization. Syntax-based optimization is based on the form of the SQL expression. The advantage of syntax-based optimization is low overhead on the server. With cost-based optimization, statistics are kept on the database tables. The optimizer makes use of the statistical data to determine the best plan for the execution of a particular query.

5.4.2 Performance improvements in SYBASE System 11

SYBASE System 11—the long-awaited follow-on to SYBASE System 10—addresses many of the performance and scalability issues of System 10. Some of the System 11 improvements include

- Multiple-buffer choices—named *variable-size buffer caches* for improved I/O performance
- Increased data I/O size (blocks up to 16 kbytes)
- Parallel log writes
- Improved "cache hit ratio" for enhanced SMP performance
- Parallel data partitioning (data can be added to several partitions concurrently)
- Parallel lock manager (concurrent control to several types of transaction locks)

- Multiple network engines, which eliminate the System 10 single-network engine (Engine 0) limitation
- Update-in-place (System 10 performs updates as a combination of delete and insert operations)
- Nonblocking ("dirty") reads
- Optimizer enhancements for subquery processing (typical in decision support applications)

5.5   IBM

5.5.1   Background

Advances in client/server architecture and distributed computing, the emergence of open-system standards and wide acceptance by users of open-system goals, continue to change the computing environment, as well as information systems market directions and trends. One of the most noticeable changes in the computer industry today is that the market for traditional mainframe and even minicomputers is shrinking, while the market for microprocessor-based solutions and local area networking is expanding. These market changes and customer demands for the availability of distributed, open, client/server products have led IBM to accept and embrace the client/server computing architecture and ideas of interoperability and support for open systems. As a result, IBM extended the range of available services by providing connectivity, network management, distributed database, shared files, presentation services, mail exchange, and common languages not only among its operating environments—MVS (Multiple Virtual Storage), OS/2, and AIX (Advanced Interactive eXecutive)—but also interoperability among multiuser, multivendor systems. In the context of distributed data management, however, this chapter briefly discusses a relatively new addition to the DB2 family: DB2 Universal Database.

5.5.2   DB2 Universal Database

This product, designed to compete directly with Informix Universal Server and Oracle Universal Server, combines DB2 Common Server 2.1 and DB2 Parallel Edition 1.2 into a single product. As such, in addition to traditional alphanumeric data, DB2 Universal Database can also manage audio, image, text, and video data types. As in the case of Informix, in the DB2 implementation the term "universal" refers to the ability of the DBMS to support a wider set of data types and a higher degree of extensibility of functions than other relational DBMSs. In fact, as you can see from the list of features above, DB2 Common Server had the functionality to support audio, image, text, and video before both of its competitors.

The code base for this version is a consolidation of the code of DB2 Common Server v.2.1 and DB2 Parallel Edition v.1.2, and is used for DB2 implementations under AIX, Windows NT, HP-UX, Sun Solaris, Siemens-Nixdorf's Sinix, and OS/2.

Features. DB2 Universal Database inherits the best of its parents: DB2 Common Server and DB2 Parallel Edition. The product supports nested triggers and stored procedures, referential and domain integrity, user-defined data types, and user-defined functions (UDFs).

The user-defined data types and user-defined functions are very similar to those of Informix, and demonstrate the same object properties of encapsulation, inheritance, and overloading. IBM's unique Query-by-Image-Content (QBIC) technology provides a strong foundation for developing UDFs, which can execute in the database engine address space as well as in a separate address space for added protection. IBM Universal Database allows users to embed UDFs directly into the SQL statements in accordance with the SQL3 standard.

UDFs allow developers to define any function that is invoked from a standard SQL statement similar to built-in scalar and aggregate functions. For example, a user may define a function called *DISTANCE* that calculates a distance from the destination based on current coordinates. Such a function may be invoked as part of a standard SELECT statement.

Similar to DataBlade in functionality, DB2 provides *relational extenders,* which are function libraries that can be added to the database to extend its object orientation. IBM provides relational extenders to handle text, image, video, audio, and fingerprint data. Specifically, DB2 Universal Database supports:

- Nested triggers and stored procedures that can operate on a row or a statement level

- Check constraints, used to embed business rules into the database and enforce domain integrity

- User-defined data types

- User-defined functions (UDFs)

- Relational extenders: function libraries that can be added to the database to extend its object orientation

- Visual development language

- Support for database partitions

- Support for raw devices on all UNIX versions

- Support for object-oriented programming and VisualAge (a variant of SmallTalk) programming language

- Support for multimedia applications by providing features that facilitate image storage and manipulation

- Enhancements in query optimization, performance, and scalability

- A suite of data warehousing and connectivity products that includes
  - ⇨ DataGuide—an information catalog (metadata) facility
  - ⇨ DataJoiner—a tool that allows a single query to access heterogeneous data sources (including DB2, Sybase, Oracle, IMS, and VSAM)

⇨ DataPropagator—a data replication system that supports relational and nonrelational (e.g., IMS) systems

⇨ Visualizer—an end-user data access tool with graphical query and charting capabilities

Access to host data.   One of the clear advantages of DB2 is its transparent access to distributed corporate data. This connectivity is based on IBM's Distributed Relational Database Architecture (DRDA). DB2 Universal Database, as its predecessor DB2 Common Server, uses Distributed Database Connection Services/6000 (DDCS/6000)—an implementation of the DRDA Application Requester (AR) for the AIX platform. Using DDCS, DB2 can directly participate in the distributed unit of work with any DRDA-compliant RDBMS, including DB2/MVS, SQL/DS (VM and VSE), and Database Manager for OS/400.

In addition to providing direct connection to these RDBMSs, DDCS can act as a gateway for remote database clients, including DOS, MS Windows, AIX, and OS/2 clients using TCP/IP and SNA APPC/LU6.2 protocols.

Transaction management.   DB2 provides full transactional support in compliance with X/Open's XA transactional interfaces. As XA-compliant resource manager, DB2 can participate in the CICS-controlled two-phase commit. In addition, since CICS/MVS APIs are supported by CICS/6000, a mainframe COBOL/CICS/DB2 application can be easily ported to an AIX platform running CICS/6000 and DB2. DB2 can support other XA-compliant transaction managers, including Transarc's Encina.

Administration.   DB2 administration and management is facilitated by the Database System Monitor, which allows the gathering of real-time statistical information for the entire DBMS, individual databases, tables, and applications. DataHub is an IBM database administration tool that provides remote administration of heterogeneous database management systems and unattended database operations. Visual Explain is an easy-to-use tool for analyzing and tuning SQL statements. Database Director is a bundled client-side software that aids in database administration. It allows a DBA to define databases and specify their locations. Once the location directory is complete, access to the database is transparent to users and applications, regardless of the database location.

DB2 Backup and Recovery is an integrated facility that supports on-line backup operations. Parallel backup of table spaces is supported starting with Common Server version 2. Database restore and forward recovery procedures are also supported. Remote backup to MVS and VM systems is supported via Adstar Distributed Storage Manager (ADSM). Other administration tools provide graphical support for database configuration, directory management, recovery, and user and user group security.

Application development. The development environment includes a visual development language that is similar to Visual Basic with extensions that support used-defined functions and stored procedures. Object-oriented VisualAge and graphical VisualGen (a GUI builder) are components of the DB2 application development environment. Multimedia application support includes tools such as Ultimedia Manager and Ultimedia Query that facilitate image storage and manipulation. DB2 Universal Database BLOBs can be up to 2 Gbytes in size, and several BLOB columns can be defined in a single table. DB2 provides functions that support searching BLOBs for text or images, and concatenation to other text BLOBs. In addition, users can define their own functions (UDFs) to perform various operations on multimedia data.

Additional application development support includes a rich set of APIs and software developer's toolkits that provide static and dynamic SQL, declarative referential integrity, ODBC, call-level interface (CLI), SQL precompiler, and embedded SQL from C, C++, FORTRAN, COBOL, and REXX programs. The ANSI-standard SQL support is extended to include a subset of the ISO/ANSI SQL3 standard: compound SQL statements and the VALUE scalar function. The compound SQL allows application developers to group several SQL statements into a single executable block. The VALUE function returns the first nonnull result from a series of expressions.

An application development tool—DB2 Stored Procedure Builder—is used to develop client-side GUI applications, server-based stored procedures, and user-defined functions.

Performance and scalability. Many RDBMS performance-enhancement features are incorporated into the DB2 Universal Database design. Among them are row-level locking, highly advanced cost-based query optimizer, buffer manager, stored procedures, and triggers. DB2 Universal Database supports database partitions via table spaces that segregate storage for data, indexes, and binary large objects (BLOBs). Table spaces may span devices; they can be extended and backed up without stopping the database. All UNIX versions of the product support raw devices for improved I/O performance.

DB2 Universal Database advanced optimization techniques include support for recurring SQL (useful for optimization and routing problems such as finding the best route for delivery trucks or airplanes), and the ability to rewrite complex queries as a series of simpler ones—a very valuable feature for ad hoc client/server applications. Query speed-up technologies include big block reads (ability to read several disk pages in a single I/O operation), and read-ahead feature, in which data pages are read in anticipation of their use.

DB2 Universal Database is designed for scalability by supporting symmetric multiprocessing and distributed-memory systems (MPP). By incorporating parallel query processing into DB2 Universal Database, it can achieve significant performance levels running on the SMP systems from IBM, HP, and Sun, as well as on shared-nothing systems like IBM SP.

5.6   Microsoft

5.6.1   Background

Before the breakup with Sybase in 1994, Microsoft offered its version of SQL Server, which was based on SYBASE SQL Server version 4.2. That version of the product has successfully penetrated the market for small database servers. Its integration with Windows NT and GUI-oriented administration tools reduced the learning time and offered good price performance, low ownership costs, and an easy migration path to the UNIX-based SYBASE SQL Server product.

5.6.2   MS SQL Server

However, now the two companies—Sybase and Microsoft—follow different development paths, and their products, although still named *SQL Server,* are diverging in features, interfaces, and architecture. The following section briefly discusses Microsoft's SQL Server.

The first release of SQL Server 6 has confirmed Microsoft's intention to replace the Sybase process and memory management architecture in favor of an approach optimized for Windows NT. Although this approach limits SQL Server 6 to a single operating system (Windows NT), it makes a lot of sense from Microsoft's point of view to leverage robust and scalable Windows NT services rather than include them in the database engine. For example, SQL Server 6 uses Windows NT threads. The threads are scheduled by the Windows NT scheduler, and can share the same address space, all without incurring the overhead associated with thread creation and dispatching. The number of threads is configurable using a single system parameter. In addition to the internal architecture of the engine, SQL Server 6 offers many new and improved features. Several features of MS SQL Server 6 are covered as follows.

Architecture.   SQL Server architecture is a parallel symmetric server architecture with automatic workload balancing across multiple processors. It includes true multithreaded kernel for improved transaction performance and scalability, full on-line transaction processing with automatic rollback and rollforward recovery, a cost-based query optimizer with statistics-based query cost analysis for improved response, asynchronous I/O that supports parallel access to multiple disk devices for greater throughput, and a high-speed page locking with configurable lock escalation—automatic deadlock detection and resolution.

Scalability and parallelism.   One of the more interesting features of SQL Server 6 is Parallel Data Scan. With Parallel Data Scan, SQL Server 6 launches multiple NT threads for reading data from disk to memory in parallel. The DBMS performance is improved significantly since Parallel Data Scan increases the probability that required data pages are already in memory (clearly, this feature can especially benefit SMP systems with a large memory and good disk striping capability). However, the retrieved rows of data are still processed sequentially, via a single thread, which significantly reduces the potential benefit of the Parallel Data Scan. In fact, the SQL Server 6 parallelism is limited, and it does not apply to operations such as sorting, filtering, and SQL statement parsing. SQL Server 6 determines when to perform Parallel Data Scan on the basis of disk access pattern, and not on the decision by the optimizer.

Built-in replication.   SQL Server 6 has built-in replication capabilities that are not an add-on product but are part of the core engine. Replication to ODBC subscribers, including IBM DB2, Oracle, SYBASE, and Microsoft Access, allows SQL Server data to be distributed to non-SQL Server systems. Configuring and managing data replication is simple using the SQL Enterprise Manager.

Similar to SYBASE, SQL Server 6 replication is based on the primary-site strategy. All data at replicated targets is read-only, and is subscribed to; SQL Server 6 follows the publisher/subscriber model. SQL Server 6 replication reads data changes from the log—there is a log reader task that runs continuously and captures log changes while they are still in memory. This design clearly minimizes negative impact on transaction performance and throughput.

SQL Server 6 replication is integrated with the SQL Server performance monitor to display important replication-related statistics graphically.

SQL Scheduler.   This is a scheduling and execution facility that runs a distributed task for each distributed subscriber database. The SQL Scheduler can run continuously to minimize the latency, or in a timed batch mode, which improves replication for large databases and narrow network bandwidth.

Distributed management.   SQL Server 6 offers a graphical capability to manage multiple SQL Servers from a single management workstation. This capability is built on 32-bit OLE (Object Linking and Embedding) objects called *distributed-management objects* (DMO). DMOs encapsulate all SQL Server management functions such as starting and stopping the server, accessing system catalog and stored procedures, managing devices and databases, managing publications and subscriptions for the replication services, handling alerts, and running Transact-SQL commands (SQL Server programming language). Microsoft supplies a management application—SQL Enterprise Manager—that uses DMOs to provide a graphical easy-to-use management environment.

Administration.   In the area of database administration, SQL Server 6 improves both performance and productivity. Specifically, SQL Server 6 offers improved versions of such utilities and commands as backup and recovery, indexing, database consistency checking, and even updating optimizer statistics. Backup and recovery can be performed in parallel, by striping the backup across multiple devices, and by loading the database from multiple devices. Also, SQL Server 6 supports backup over Named Pipes, which enables backups on remote systems, or via a third-party backup product. Another attractive feature is the ability to preview information in the dump file prior to loading it into a database. Both backup and restore (DUMP and LOAD commands) are automatically logged in the Windows NT event log.

Availability, reliability, and fault tolerance.   SQL Server supports mirrored database devices with automatic failover on device failure for fault tolerance; RAID 5 disk striping with parity for improved performance, reliability, and fault tolerance; unattended on-line backup with guaranteed data consistency for high availability; protected user contexts, which can isolate faults to a single user thread; point-in-time recovery to restore database or transaction logs to a specific time; and server fault tolerance, allowing automatic failover to a backup or standby server.

Distributed transactions.   The Distributed Transaction Coordinator is new in SQL Server 6.5. It makes distributed applications easier to create by automating the management of transactions across multiple servers, saving valuable time previously spent individually coding client applications. Distributed Transaction Coordinator (DTC) manages transactions that span two or more SQL Server systems, guaranteeing transaction integrity and recoverability. Its transparent two-phase commit supports server-to-server procedures and simplifies application development.

Security.   SQL Server provides single-log-in ID for network and database, enhanced security and reduced administrative complexity, password and network data steam encryption for improved internetwork data security, and stored procedure encryption to preserve integrity and security of server-based procedural application code.

Rich development environment.   Developing the right client/server database applications is crucial. SQL Server helps users develop richer applications efficiently and easily, for benefits in cost savings and a true competitive advantage. For instance

- Desktop integration and support for industry standards make it easy to develop and deploy feature-rich database applications.
- A wide range of development tools for customization over multiple interfaces, such as Microsoft Access, Visual FoxPro, Visual Basic, Visual C++, PowerBuilder, SQL Windows, are available.
- Seamless management of transactions across multiple servers. Distributed Transaction Coordinator (DTC) enables implementation of a transparent two-phase commit without writing code.
- Numerous off-the-shelf solutions offer a broad choice of third-party solutions.

Cursors.   SQL Server 6 provides very attractive and frequently requested server-side cursors, which can improve network performance by allowing data manipulation without returning rows to the client system. And what's more, these cursors support forward and backward (bidirectional) scrolling. The cursors can be engaged via API calls to the DB-Library for C and the ODBC SQL Server driver.

Other features include

- Integrated Visual Basic for Application (VBA) macro language for automated operations.

- Event notification.

- Mail and messaging integration; SQL Mail enhancements make it possible to send and receive electronic mail with Microsoft Exchange or populate Exchange public folders with data from SQL Server.

- High-performance access to information on the Web via new Web Assistant that enables users to populate the Web server with SQL data through a variety of methods.

- Robust host connectivity via TransAccess products that support bidirectional distributed processing and data sharing between the mainframe and the network, allow mainframe transaction programs to act as server for Windows NT-based applications, or, alternatively, as enterprise clients that initiate and interact with SQL Server.

- Enhancements to data warehousing include new OLAP query extensions, CUBE, and ROLLUP.

- A *data pipe* capability, using EXEC and INTO, allows SQL Server to programmatically retrieve information from multiple sources and populate SQL Server tables with the results.

The list of features is much longer than this section of the book indicates. Suffice it to say that Microsoft's SQL Server is an advanced relational database management system that is closely integrated with Windows NT and capable of providing cost-effective and functionally rich solutions.

5.6.3   Data warehousing market positioning

Microsoft is clearly taking a number of steps designed to help it become a serious player in the data warehousing market. Its recently announced comprehensive strategy aimed at simplifying the implementation of data warehousing solutions using Microsoft SQL Server is proof of this trend. The strategy includes the Active Data Warehousing Framework, an extensible set of Component Object Model (COM) based interfaces; the Microsoft Alliance for Data Warehousing, a coalition of industry partners; significant product enhancements; and consulting services.

The Active Data Warehousing Framework includes a metadata model, data acquisition and transformation services, data distribution and replication, and administration, making it easier for third-party vendors to integrate their products with Microsoft SQL Server in a complete data warehousing solution. Alliance members include Business Objects, Execusoft, Informatica, NCR, Pilot Software, Platinum Technologies, Praxis International, and SAP AG.

Data Warehousing

As was stated in Chap. 1, the data warehouse is the means for strategic data usage. It is not the same as a decision support system. Rather, a data warehouse is a platform with integrated data of improved quality to support many decision support and analytical applications and processes within an enterprise. If implemented and used properly, the data warehouse can be a cornerstone of the organization's ability to do effective information processing, which, among other things, can enable and share the discovery and exploration of important business trends and dependencies that otherwise would have gone unnoticed. The goal of data warehousing is to improve the productivity of corporate decision makers through consolidation, conversion, transformation, and integration of operational data, and to provide a consistent view of an enterprise. This part of the book deals with a number of data warehousing-specific issues, including

- *Data warehousing components (Chap. 6)*
- *The process of building a data warehouse (Chap. 7)*
- *Analysis of multiprocessor architectures as they relate to data warehousing (Chap. 8)*
- *Database technologies used in data warehousing (Chap. 9)*
- *Data cleanup, transformation, and replication tools (Chap. 10)*
- *Metadata (Chap. 11)*

6

Data Warehousing Components

The data warehouse is an environment, not a product. It is an architectural construct of an information system that provides users with current and historical decision support information that is hard to access or present in traditional operational data stores. Data warehousing is a blend of technologies and components aimed at effective integration of operational databases into an environment that enables strategic use of data. These technologies include relational and multidimensional database management systems, client/server architecture, metadata modeling and repositories, graphical user interfaces, and much more.

6.1 Overall Architecture

The data warehouse architecture is based on a relational database management system server that functions as the central repository for informational data. In the data warehouse architecture, operational data and processing is completely separate from data warehouse processing. This central information repository is surrounded by a number of key components designed to make the entire environment functional, manageable, and accessible by both the operational systems that source data into the warehouse and by end-user query and analysis tools (see Fig. 6.1).

Typically, the source data for the warehouse is coming from the operational applications [an exception might be an operational data store (ODS), discussed briefly in Chap. 1]. As the data enters the data warehouse, it is transformed into an integrated structure and format. The transformation process may involve conversion, summarization, filtering, and condensation of data. Because data within the data warehouse contains a large historical component (sometimes covering 5 to 10 years), the data warehouse must be capable of holding and managing large volumes of data as well as different data structures for the same database over time.

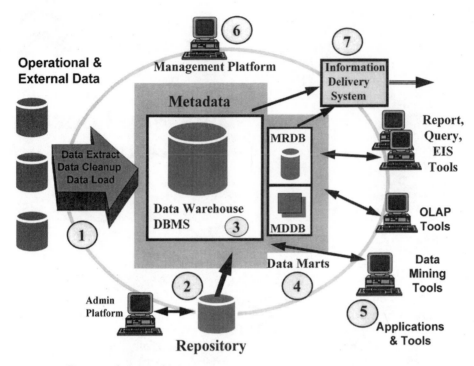

Figure 6.1 Data warehouse architecture.

The following section takes a close look at the seven major data warehousing components identified in Fig. 6.1.

6.2 Data Warehouse Database

The central data warehouse database is a cornerstone of the data warehousing environment. Marked as item 2 on the architecture diagram (in Fig. 6.1), this database is almost always implemented on the relational database management system (RDBMS) technology. However, a warehouse implementation based on traditional RDBMS technology is often constrained by the fact that traditional RDBMS implementations are optimized for transactional database processing. Certain data warehouse attributes such as very large database size, ad hoc query processing, and the need for flexible user view creation including aggregates, multitable joins, and drill-downs, have become drivers for different technological approaches to the data warehouse database. These approaches include

■ Parallel relational database designs that require a parallel computing platform, such as symmetric multiprocessors (SMPs), massively parallel processors (MPPs), and/or clusters of uni- or multiprocessors (this technology was discussed in Chaps. 2 and 3 and is discussed further in Chaps. 7 to 9).

■ An innovative approach to speed up a traditional RDBMS by using new index structures to bypass relational table scans. This is discussed in more detail in Chap. 9.

■ Multidimensional databases (MDDBs) that are based on proprietary database technology or implemented using already familiar RDBMS. Multidimensional databases are designed to overcome any limitations placed on the warehouse by the nature of the relational data model. This approach is tightly coupled with the on-line analytical processing (OLAP) tools that act as clients to the multidimensional data stores. These tools architecturally belong to a group of data warehousing components jointly categorized as the data query, reporting, analysis, and mining tools (Fig. 6.1, item 4).

6.3 Sourcing, Acquisition, Cleanup, and Transformation Tools

A significant portion of the data warehouse implementation effort is spent extracting data from operational systems and putting it in a format suitable for informational applications that will run off the data warehouse.

The data sourcing, cleanup, transformation, and migration tools (identified as item 1 on the architecture diagram) perform all of the conversions, summarizations, key changes, structural changes, and condensations needed to transform disparate data into information that can be used by the decision support tool. It produces the programs and control statements, including the COBOL programs, MVS job-control language (JCL), UNIX scripts, and SQL data definition language (DDL) needed to move data into the data warehouse from multiple operational systems. It also maintains the metadata. The functionality includes

■ Removing unwanted data from operational databases

■ Converting to common data names and definitions

■ Calculating summaries and derived data

■ Establishing defaults for missing data

■ Accommodating source data definition changes

The data sourcing, cleanup, extract, transformation, and migration tools have to deal with some significant issues as follows:

■ *Database heterogeneity.* DBMSs are very different in data models, data access language, data navigation, operations, concurrency, integrity, recovery, etc.

■ *Data heterogeneity.* This is the difference in the way data is defined and used in different models—homonyms, synonyms, unit incompatibility (U.S. vs. metric), different attributes for the same entity, and different ways of modeling the same fact.

These tools can save a considerable amount of time and effort. However, significant shortcomings do exist. For example, many available tools are generally useful for simpler data extracts. Frequently, customized extract routines need to be developed for the more complicated data extraction procedures. The vendors prominent in this arena include Prism Solutions, Evolutionary Technologies Inc. (ETI), Vality, Praxis, and Carleton.

6.4 Metadata

Metadata is data about data that describes the data warehouse. It is used for building, maintaining, managing, and using the data warehouse. Metadata can be classified into

- Technical metadata, which contains information about warehouse data for use by warehouse designers and administrators when carrying out warehouse development and management tasks. Technical metadata documents include
  - ➪ Information about data sources
  - ➪ Transformation descriptions, i.e., the mapping method from operational databases into the warehouse, and algorithms used to convert, enhance, or transform data
  - ➪ Warehouse object and data structure definitions for data targets
  - ➪ The rules used to perform data cleanup and data enhancement
  - ➪ Data mapping operations when capturing data from source systems and applying it to the target warehouse database
  - ➪ Access authorization, backup history, archive history, information delivery history, data acquisition history, data access, etc.
- Business metadata contains information that gives users an easy-to-understand perspective of the information stored in the data warehouse. Business metadata documents information about
  - ➪ Subject areas and information object type, including queries, reports, images, video, and/or audio clips
  - ➪ Internet home pages
  - ➪ Other information to support all data warehousing components. For example, the information related to the information delivery system (see Sec. 6.8) should include subscription information, scheduling information, details of delivery destinations, and the business query objects such as predefined queries, reports, and analyses.
  - ➪ Data warehouse operational information, e.g., data history (snapshots, versions), ownership, extract audit trail, usage data

Equally important, metadata provides interactive access to users to help understand content, find data. One of the issues dealing with metadata relates to the fact that many data extraction tool capabilities to gather metadata remain fairly immature. Therefore, often there is a need to create a metadata interface for users, which may involve some duplication of effort.

Metadata management is provided via a metadata repository and accompanying software. Metadata repository management software can be used to map the source data to the target database, generate code for data transformations, integrate and transform the data, and control moving data to the warehouse. This software, which typically runs on a workstation, enables users to specify how the data should be transformed, such as data mapping, conversion, and summarization.

As users' interactions with the data warehouse increase, their approaches to reviewing the results of their requests for information can be expected to evolve from relatively manual analysis for trends and exceptions to agent-driven initiation of the analysis based on user-defined thresholds. The definition of these thresholds, configuration parameters for the software agents using them, and the information directory indicating where the appropriate sources for the required information can be found are all stored in the metadata repository as well.

One of the important functional components of the metadata repository is the information directory. The content of the information directory is the metadata that helps technical and business users exploit the power of data warehousing. This directory helps integrate, maintain, and view the contents of the data warehousing system.

From a technical requirements point of view, the information directory and the entire metadata repository

- Should be a gateway to the data warehouse environment, and thus should be accessible from any platform via transparent and seamless connections

- Should support an easy distribution and replication of its content for high performance and availability

- Should be searchable by business-oriented key words

- Should act as a launch platform for end-user data access and analysis tools

- Should support the sharing of information objects such as queries, reports, data collections, and subscriptions between users

- Should support a variety of scheduling options for requests against the data warehouse, including on-demand, one-time, repetitive, event-driven, and conditional delivery (in conjunction with the information delivery system)

- Should support the distribution of the query results to one or more destinations in any of the user-specified formats (in conjunction with the information delivery system)

- Should support and provide interfaces to other applications such as e-mail, spreadsheet, and schedulers

- Should support end-user monitoring of the status of the data warehouse environment (in conjunction with the administration and management components, discussed in Sec. 6.7).

At a minimum, the information directory components should be accessible by any Web browser, and should run on all major platforms, including MS Windows, Windows NT, and UNIX. Also, the data structures of the metadata repository should be supported on all major relational database platforms.

These requirements define a very sophisticated repository of metadata information. In reality, however, existing products often come up short when implementing all these requirements. Additionally, most of the other data warehousing components employ their own set of metadata definitions, often with a narrow scope defined specifically to enable this particular component. Therefore, a critical requirement for a robust full-featured metadata repository is the ability to integrate various metadata stores provided by multiple data warehouse tools and components.

Since the ability to do the extracts periodically and to refresh and update the synthesized data via copy management tools is very important for the well-being of a data warehouse, the maintenance of the information directory becomes one of the key critical issues in data warehousing.

The relative immaturity of metadata repositories is also reflected in the state of terminology. For example, some data warehousing vendors name the metadata repository as a dictionary or encyclopedia. And very few of the current metadata repository architectures clearly identify its internal components such as information directory (discussed above).

Examples of metadata repositories include R&O's Rochade, Prism Solution's Directory Manager, and Platinum Technologies' Information Repository.

6.5   Access Tools

The principal purpose of data warehousing is to provide information to business users for strategic decision making. These users interact with the data warehouse using front-end tools. Many of these tools require an information specialist, although many end users develop expertise in the tools. Both dynamic and preplanned analyses are enabled in a high-performance environment because joins, summations, and periodic reports are preplanned and results are usually moved to servers as close to end users as possible for immediate access.

Although ad hoc requests, regular reports, and custom applications are the primary delivery vehicles for the analysis done in most data warehouses, many development efforts in the data warehousing arena are focusing on exceptional reporting also known as *alerts,* which let a user know when a certain event has occurred. For example, if the data warehouse is designed to assess the risk of currency trading, an alert can be activated when a certain currency rate drops below a predefined threshold. When an alert is well synchronized with the key objectives of the business, it can provide warehouse users with a tremendous advantage.

The end-user tools area spans a number of components. For example, all end-user tools use metadata definitions to obtain access to data stored in the warehouse, and some of these tools (e.g., OLAP tools) may employ additional and/or intermediary data stores (i.e., multidimensional database). These additional data stores play a dual role—they may act as specialized data stores for a given end-user tool, or just be a subset of the data warehouse covering a specific subject area, such as a data mart.

For the purpose of this discussion let's divide these tools into five main groups:

- Data query and reporting tools
- Application development tools
- Executive information system (EIS) tools
- On-line analytical processing tools
- Data mining tools

These topics are discussed in the following sections.

6.5.1 Query and reporting tools

This category can be further divided into two groups: *reporting* tools and *managed query* tools.

Reporting tools can be divided into production reporting tools and desktop report writers.

- Production reporting tools will let companies generate regular operational reports or support high-volume batch jobs, such as calculating and printing paychecks.
- Report writers, on the other hand, are inexpensive desktop tools designed for end users.

Managed query tools shield end users from the complexities of SQL and database structures by inserting a metalayer between users and the database. The *metalayer* is the software that provides subject-oriented views of a database and supports point-and-click creation of SQL. These tools are designed for easy-to-use, point-and-click, and visual navigation operations that either accept SQL or generate SQL statements to query relational data stored in the warehouse. Some of these tools proceed to format the retrieved data into easy-to-read reports, while others concentrate on the on-screen presentation. These tools are the preferred choice of the users of business applications such as segment identification, demographic analysis, territory management, and customer mailing lists. As the complexity of the questions grows, these tools may rapidly become inefficient. The reporting and query tools are discussed further in Chap. 12.

6.5.2 Applications

Often, the analytical needs of the data warehouse user community exceed the built-in capabilities of query and reporting tools. Or, the tools will require such a complex set of queries and sophisticated data models that the business users may find themselves overwhelmed by the need to become SQL and/or data modeling experts. This situation will almost certainly defeat the ease-of-use attraction of the query and reporting tools. In this case, organizations will often rely on a true and proven approach of in-house application development using graphical data access environments designed primarily for client/server environments. Some of these application development platforms integrate well with popular OLAP tools, and can access all major database systems, including Oracle, Sybase, and Informix. Examples of these application development environments include PowerBuilder from PowerSoft, Visual Basic from Microsoft, Forté from Forté Software, and Business Objects from Business Objects. Application development tools are discussed further in Chap. 12.

6.5.3 OLAP

On-line analytical processing (OLAP) tools. These tools are based on the concepts of multidimensional databases and allow a sophisticated user to analyze the data using elaborate, multidimensional, complex views. Typical business applications for these tools include product performance and profitability, effectiveness of a sales program or a marketing campaign, sales forecasting, and capacity planning. These tools assume that the data is organized in a multidimensional model which is supported by a special multidimensional database (MDDB) or by a relational database designed to enable multidimensional properties [multirelational database (MRDB)]. A detailed discussion on OLAP and multidimensional databases is presented in Chap. 13.

6.5.4 Data mining

A critical success factor for any business today is its ability to use information effectively. This strategic use of data can result from opportunities presented by discovering hidden, previously undetected, and frequently extremely valuable facts about consumers, retailers and suppliers, business trends, and direction and significant factors. Knowing this information, an organization can formulate effective business, marketing, and sales strategies; precisely target promotional activity; discover and penetrate new markets; and successfully compete in the marketplace from a position of informed strength. A relatively new and promising technology aimed at achieving this strategic advantage is known as *data mining*.

Let's define data mining as the process of discovering meaningful new correlations, patterns, and trends by digging into (mining) large amounts of data stored in warehouses, using artificial-intelligence (AI) and statistical and mathematical techniques. In these areas, data mining can reach beyond the capabilities of the OLAP, especially since the major attraction of data mining is its ability to build *predictive* rather than *retrospective* models.

Data mining is not specific to any industry—it requires intelligent technologies and the willingness to explore the possibility of hidden knowledge that resides in the data. Industries that are already taking advantage of data mining include retail, financial, medical, manufacturing, environmental, utilities, security, transportation, chemical, insurance, and aerospace industries, with the early success stories coming primarily from the retail, financial, and medical sectors. The organizations using data mining techniques report gaining insights into their respective businesses by revealing implicit relationships, patterns, surprisingly significant facts, trends, exceptions, and anomalies previously unavailable through the human analysts. These experiences show that, although data mining is still an emerging discipline, it has a huge potential to gain significant benefits in the marketplace. Most organizations engage in data mining to

- *Discover knowledge.* The goal of knowledge discovery is to determine explicit hidden relationships, patterns, or correlations from data stored in an enterprise's database. Specifically, data mining can be used to perform:
  - ⇨ Segmentation (e.g., group customer records for custom-tailored marketing)
  - ⇨ Classification (assignment of input data to a predefined class, discovery and understanding of trends, text document classification)
  - ⇨ Association (discovery of cross-sales opportunities)
  - ⇨ Preferencing (determining preference of customer's majority)

- *Visualize data.* Analysts must make sense out of a huge amount of information stored in corporate databases. Prior to any analysis, the goal is to "humanize" the mass of data they must deal with and find a clever way to display the data.

- *Correct data.* While consolidating massive databases, many enterprises find that the data is not complete and invariably contains erroneous and contradictory information. Data mining techniques can help identify and correct problems in the most consistent way possible. The number of applications within this category is somewhat limited because of the difficult nature of the correction process. Replacing missing values or correcting what can be perceived as "wild" values requires judgment calls that are difficult to provide automatically.

The strategic value of data mining is time-sensitive, especially in the retail-marketing and finance sectors of the industry. Indeed, organizations that exploit the data first will gain a strategic advantage in serving and attracting customers. Consequently, the benefits derived from the data mining process provide early adopters of the technology with a timely competitive advantage.

Using data mining to build predictive models in decision making has several benefits. A model should explain why a particular decision was made. Adjusting a model on the basis of feedback from future decisions will lead to experience accumulation and true organizational learning. Finally, a predictive model can be used to automate a decision step in a larger process. For example, using a model to instantly predict whether a consumer will default on credit card payments will allow automatic adjustment of credit limits rather than depending on expensive staff making inconsistent decisions.

A detailed discussion on data mining is presented in Part 4 of this book.

6.5.5   Data visualization

Data warehouses are causing a surge in popularity of data visualization techniques for looking at data. Data visualization is not a separate class of tools; rather, it is a method of presenting the output of all the previously mentioned tools in such a way that the entire problem and/or the solution (e.g., a result of a relational or multidimensional query, or the result of data mining discovery) is clearly visible to domain experts and even casual observers.

Data visualization goes far beyond simple bar and pie charts. It is a collection of complex techniques that currently represent an area of intense research and development focusing on determining how to best display complex relationships and patterns on a two-dimensional (flat) computer monitor. Similar to medical imaging research, current data visualization techniques experiment with various colors, shapes, 3-D imaging, sound, and virtual reality to help users to really see and feel the problem and its solutions.

6.6   Data Marts

The concept of the data mart is causing a lot of excitement and attracts much attention in the data warehouse industry. Mostly, data marts are presented as an inexpensive alternative to a data warehouse that takes significantly less time and money to build. However, the term *data mart* means different things to different people. A rigorous definition of this term is a data store that is subsidiary to a data warehouse of integrated data. The data mart is directed at a partition of data (often called a *subject area*) that is created for the use of a dedicated group of users. A data mart might, in fact, be a set of denormalized, summarized, or aggregated data. Sometimes, such a set could be placed on the data warehouse database rather than a physically separate store of data. In most instances, however, the data mart is a physically separate store of data and is normally resident on a separate database server, often on the local area network serving a dedicated user group. Sometimes the data mart simply comprises relational OLAP technology which creates highly denormalized star schema relational designs or hypercubes of data for analysis by groups of users with a common interest in a limited portion of the database. In other cases, the data warehouse architecture may incorporate data mining tools that extract sets of data for a particular type of analysis. All these types of data marts, called *dependent data marts* because their data content is sourced from the data warehouse, have a high value because no matter how many are deployed and no matter now many different enabling technologies are used, the different users are all accessing the information views derived from the same single integrated version of the data.

Unfortunately, the misleading statements about the simplicity and low cost of data marts sometimes result in organizations or vendors incorrectly positioning them as an alternative to the data warehouse. This viewpoint defines *independent data marts* that in fact represent fragmented point solutions to a range of business problems in the enterprise. This type of implementation should rarely be deployed in the context of an overall technology or applications architecture. Indeed, it is missing the ingredient that is at the heart of the data warehousing concept: data integration. Each independent data mart makes its own assumptions about how to consolidate the data, and the data across several data marts may not be consistent.

Moreover, the concept of an independent data mart is dangerous—as soon as the first data mart is created, other organizations, groups, and subject areas within the enterprise embark on the task of building their own data marts. As a result, you create an environment in which multiple operational systems feed multiple nonintegrated data marts that are often overlapping in data content, job scheduling, connectivity, and management. In other words, you have transformed a complex *many-to-one* problem of building a data warehouse from operational and external data sources to a *many-to-many* sourcing and management nightmare.

Another consideration against independent data marts is related to the potential scalability problem: the first simple and inexpensive data mart was most probably designed without any serious consideration about the scalability (for example, you wouldn't consider an expensive parallel computing platform for an "inexpensive" and "small" data mart). But, as usage begets usage, the initial small data mart needs to grow (i.e., in data sizes and the number of concurrent users), without any ability to do so in a scalable fashion.

We would like to make it clear that the point-solution-independent data mart is not necessarily a bad thing, and it is often a necessary and valid solution to a pressing business problem, thus achieving the goal of rapid delivery of enhanced decision support functionality to end users. The business drivers underlying such developments include

- Extremely urgent user requirements
- The absence of a budget for a full data warehouse strategy
- The absence of a sponsor for an enterprisewide decision support strategy
- The decentralization of business units
- The attraction of easy-to-use tools and a mind-sized project

To address data integration issues associated with data marts, the recommended approach proposed by Ralph Kimball is as follows. For any two data marts in an enterprise, the common dimensions must conform to the *equality and roll-up rule,* which states that these dimensions are either the same or that one is a strict roll-up of another.

Thus, in a retail store chain, if the purchase orders database is one data mart and the sales database is another data mart, the two data marts will form a coherent part of an overall enterprise data warehouse if their common dimensions (e.g., time and product) conform. The time dimensions from both data marts might be at the individual day level, or, conversely, one time dimension is at the day level but the other is at the week level. Because days roll up to weeks, the two time dimensions are conformed. The time dimensions would not be conformed if one time dimension were weeks and the other time dimension, a fiscal quarter. The resulting data marts could not usefully coexist in the same application.

In summary, data marts present two problems: (1) scalability in situations where an initial small data mart grows quickly in multiple dimensions and (2) data integration. Therefore, when designing data marts, the organizations should pay close attention to system scalability, data consistency, and manageability issues. The key to a successful data mart strategy is the development of an overall scalable data warehouse architecture; and the key step in that architecture is identifying and implementing the common dimensions.

6.7   Data Warehouse Administration and Management

Data warehouses tend to be as much as 4 times as large as related operational databases, reaching terabytes in size depending on how much history needs to be saved. They are not synchronized in real time to the associated operational data but are updated as often as once a day if the application requires it.

In addition to the main architectural components already described, almost all data warehouse products include gateways to transparently access multiple enterprise data sources without having to rewrite applications to interpret and utilize the data. Furthermore, in a heterogeneous data warehouse environment the various databases reside on disparate systems, thus requiring internetworking tools. Although there are no special data warehousing internetworking technologies, and a typical data warehouse implementation relies on the same communications software as messaging and transaction processing systems (e.g., NetWare, TCP/IP protocols, products that use DCE technology), the need to manage this infrastructure component is obvious.

To summarize, managing data warehouse includes

- Security and priority management
- Monitoring updates from multiple sources
- Data quality checks

- Managing and updating metadata
- Auditing and reporting data warehouse usage and status (for managing the response time and resource utilization, and providing chargeback information)
- Purging data
- Replicating, subsetting, and distributing data
- Backup and recovery
- Data warehouse storage management [e.g., capacity planning, hierarchical storage management (HSM), purging of aged data]

6.8   Information Delivery System

The information delivery component is used to enable the process of subscribing for data warehouse information and having it delivered to one or more destinations of choice according to some user-specified scheduling algorithm. In other words, the information delivery system distributes warehouse-stored data and other information objects to other data warehouses and end-user products such as spreadsheets and local databases. Delivery of information may be based on time of day, or on a completion of an external event. The rationale for the delivery system component is based on the fact that once the data warehouse is installed and operational, its users don't have to be aware of its location and maintenance. All they may need is the report or an analytical view of data, at a certain time of the day, or based on a particular, relevant event. And of course, with the proliferation of the Internet/Intranet (INET) and the World Wide Web (WWW or the Web), such a delivery system may leverage the INET and convenience of browsers by delivering warehouse-enabled information to thousands of end users via the ubiquitous worldwide network.

In fact, the World Wide Web is changing the data warehousing landscape since at the very high level the goals of both the Web and data warehousing are the same: easy access to information. The value of data warehousing is maximized when the right information gets into the hands of those individuals who need it, where they need it, and when they need it the most. However, many corporations have struggled with complex client/server systems to give end users the access they need. The issues become even more difficult to resolve when the users are physically remote from the data warehouse location. The Web removes a lot of these issues by giving users an universal and relatively inexpensive access to data. Couple this access with the ability to deliver the required information on demand, or according to a schedule, or based on a predefined set of events, and the result is a Web-enabled information delivery system that allows users dispersed across continents to perform a sophisticated business-critical analysis, and to engage in collective decision making that is based on timely and valid information.

Chapter

7

Building a Data
Warehouse

There are several reasons why organizations consider data warehousing a critical need. These drivers for data warehousing can be found in the business climate of a global marketplace, in the changing organizational structures of successful corporations, and in the technology.

From a *business perspective,* to survive and succeed in today's highly competitive global environment, business users demand business answers mainly because

- Decisions need to be made quickly and correctly, using all available data.
- Users are business domain experts, not computer professionals.
- The amount of data is doubling every 18 months, which affects response time and the sheer ability to comprehend its content.
- Competition is heating up in the areas of business intelligence and added information value.

In addition, the necessity for data warehouses has increased as organizations distribute control away from the middle-management layer, which has traditionally provided and screened business information. As users depend more on information obtained from information technology (IT) systems—from critical-success measures to vital business-event-related information—the need to provide an information warehouse for the remaining staff to use becomes more critical.

There are several *technology reasons* for the existence of data warehousing. First, the data warehouse is designed to address the incompatibility of informational and operational transactional systems. These two classes of information systems are designed to satisfy different, often incompatible, requirements. At the same time, the IT infrastructure is changing rapidly, and its capabilities are increasing, as evidenced by the following:

- The price of MIPS (computer processing speed) continues to decline, while the power of microprocessors doubles every 2 years.
- The price of digital storage is rapidly dropping.
- Network bandwidth is increasing, while the price of high bandwidth is decreasing.
- The workplace is increasingly heterogeneous with respect to both the hardware and software.
- Legacy systems need to, and can, be integrated with new applications.

These business and technology drivers often make building a data warehouse a strategic imperative. This chapter takes a close look at what it takes to build a successful data warehouse.

7.1   Business Considerations: Return on Investment

7.1.1   Approach

The information scope of the data warehouse varies with the business requirements, business priorities, and even magnitude of the problem. The subject-oriented nature of the data warehouse means that the nature of the subject determines the scope (or the coverage) of the warehoused information. Specifically, if the data warehouse is implemented to satisfy a specific subject area (e.g., human resources), such a warehouse is expressly designed to solve business problems related to personnel. An organization may choose to build another warehouse for its marketing department. These two warehouses could be implemented independently and be completely stand-alone applications, or they could be viewed as components of the enterprise, interacting with each other, and using a common enterprise data model. As defined earlier, the individual warehouses are known as *data marts*. Organizations embarking on data warehousing development can chose one of the two approaches:

- The *top–down approach,* meaning that an organization has developed an enterprise data model, collected enterprisewide business requirements, and decided to build an enterprise data warehouse with subset data marts
- The *bottom–up approach,* implying that the business priorities resulted in developing individual data marts, which are then integrated into the enterprise data warehouse

The bottom–up approach is probably more realistic, but the complexity of the integration may become a serious obstacle, and the warehouse designers should carefully analyze each data mart for integration affinity.

7.1.2 Organizational issues

Most IS organizations have considerable expertise in developing operational systems. However, the requirements and environments associated with the informational applications of a data warehouse are different. Therefore, an organization will need to employ different development practices than the ones it uses for operational applications.

The IS department will need to bring together data that cuts across a company's operational systems as well as data from outside the company. But users will also need to be involved with a data warehouse implementation since they are closest to the data. In many ways, a data warehouse implementation is not truly a technological issue; rather, it should be more concerned with identifying and establishing information requirements, the data sources to fulfill these requirements, and timeliness.

7.2 Design Considerations

To be successful, a data warehouse designer must adopt a *holistic* approach—consider *all* data warehouse components as parts of a single complex system and take into the account *all* possible data sources and *all* known usage requirements. Failing to do so may easily result in a data warehouse design that is skewed toward a particular business requirement, a particular data source, or a selected access tool.

In general, a data warehouse's design point is to consolidate data from multiple, often heterogeneous, sources into a query database. This is also one of the reasons why a data warehouse is rather difficult to build. The main factors include

- Heterogeneity of data sources, which affects data conversion, quality, timeliness

- Use of historical data, which implies that data may be "old"

- Tendency of databases to grow very large

Another important point concerns the experience and accepted practices. Basically, the reality is that the data warehouse design is different from traditional OLTP. Indeed, the data warehouse is *business*-driven (not IS-driven, as in OLTP), requires *continuous* interactions with end users, and is *never finished,* since both requirements and data sources change. Understanding these points allows developers to avoid a number of pitfalls relevant to data warehouse development, and justifies a new approach to data warehouse design: a business-driven, continuous, iterative warehouse engineering approach. In addition to these general considerations, there are several specific points relevant to the data warehouse design.

7.2.1 Data content

One common misconception about data warehouses is that they should not contain as much detail-level data as operational systems used to source this data in. In reality, however, while the data in the warehouse is formatted differently from the operational data, it may be just as detailed. Typically, a data warehouse may contain detailed data, but the data is cleaned up and transformed to fit the warehouse model, and certain transactional attributes of the data are filtered out. These attributes are mostly the ones used for the internal transaction system logic, and they are not meaningful in the context of analysis and decision making.

The content and structure of the data warehouse are reflected in its *data model*. The data model is the template that describes how information will be organized within the integrated warehouse framework. It identifies major subjects and relationships of the model, including keys, attributes, and attribute groupings. In addition, a designer should always remember that decision support queries, because of their broad scope and analytical intensity, require data models to be optimized to improve query performance. In addition to its effect on query performance, the data model affects data storage requirements and data loading performance.

Additionally, the data model for the data warehouse may be (and quite often is) different from the data models for data marts. The data marts, discussed in the previous chapter, are sourced from the data warehouse, and may contain highly aggregated and summarized data in the form of a specialized denormalized relational schema (star schema) or as a multidimensional datacube. The key point is, however, that in a dependent data mart environment, the data mart data is cleaned up, is transformed, and is consistent with the data warehouse and other data marts sourced from the same warehouse.

7.2.2 Metadata

As already discussed, metadata defines the contents and location of data (data model) in the warehouse, relationships between the operational databases and the data warehouse, and the business views of the warehouse data that are accessible by end-user tools. Metadata is searched by users to find data definitions or subject areas. In other words, metadata provides decision-support-oriented pointers to warehouse data, and thus provides a logical link between warehouse data and the decision support application. A data warehouse design should ensure that there is a mechanism that populates and maintains the metadata repository, and that *all* access paths to the data warehouse have metadata as an entry point. To put it another way, the warehouse design should prevent any direct access to the warehouse data (especially updates) if it does not use metadata definitions to gain the access.

7.2.3 Data distribution

One of the biggest challenges when designing a data warehouse is the data placement and distribution strategy. This follows from the fact that as the data volumes continue to grow, the database size may rapidly outgrow a single server. Therefore, it becomes necessary to know how the data should be divided across multiple servers, and which users should get access to which types of data. The data placement and distribution design should consider several options, including data distribution by subject area (e.g., human resources, marketing), location (e.g., geographic regions), or time (e.g., current, monthly, quarterly). The designers should be aware that, while the distribution solves a number of problems, it may also create a few of its own; for example, if the warehouse servers are distributed across multiple locations, a query that spans several servers across the LAN or WAN may flood the network with a large amount of data. Therefore, any distribution strategy should take into account all possible access needs for the warehouse data.

7.2.4   Tools

A number of tools available today are specifically designed to help in the implementation of a data warehouse. These tools provide facilities for defining the transformation and cleanup rules, data movement (from operational sources into the warehouse), end-user query, reporting, and data analysis. Each tool takes a slightly different approach to data warehousing and often maintains its own version of the metadata which is placed in a tool-specific, proprietary metadata repository. Data warehouse designers have to be careful not to sacrifice the overall design to fit a specific tool. At the same time, the designers have to make sure that all selected tools are compatible with the given data warehouse environment and with each other. That means that all selected tools can use a common metadata repository. Alternatively, the tools should be able to source the metadata from the warehouse data dictionary (if it exists) or from a CASE tool used to design the warehouse database. Another option is to use metadata gateways that translate one tool's metadata into another tool's format. If these requirements are not satisfied, the resulting warehouse environment may rapidly become unmanageable, since every modification to the warehouse data model may involve some significant and labor-intensive changes to the metadata definitions for every tool in the environment. And then, these changes would have to be verified for consistency and integrity.

7.2.5   Performance considerations

Although the data warehouse design point does not include subsecond response times typical of OLTP systems, it is nevertheless a clear business requirement that an ideal data warehouse environment should support interactive query processing. In fact, the majority of end-user tools are designed as interactive applications. Therefore, "rapid" query processing is a highly desired feature that should be designed into the data warehouse. Of course, the actual performance levels are business-dependent and vary widely from one environment to another. Unfortunately, it is relatively difficult to predict the performance of a typical data warehouse. One of the reasons for this is the unpredictable usage patterns against the data. Thus, traditional database design and tuning techniques don't always work in the data warehouse arena. When designing a data warehouse, therefore, the need to clearly understand users informational requirements becomes mandatory. Specifically, knowing how end users need to access various data can help design warehouse databases to avoid the majority of the most expensive operations such as multitable scans and joins. For example, one design technique is to populate the warehouse with a number of denormalized views containing summarized, derived, and aggregated data. If done correctly, many end-user queries may execute directly against these views, thus maintaining appropriate overall performance levels.

7.2.6   Nine decisions in the design of a data warehouse

The job of a data warehouse designer is a daunting one. Often the newly appointed data warehouse designer is drawn to the job because of the high visibility and importance of the data warehouse function. In effect, management says to the designer: "Take all the enterprise data and make it available to management so that they can answer all their questions and sleep at night. And please do it very quickly, and we're sorry, but we can't add any more staff until the proof of concept is successful."

This responsibility is exciting and very visible, but most designers feel overwhelmed by the sheer enormity of the task. Something real needs to be accomplished, and fast. Where do you start? Which data should be brought up first? Which management needs are most important? Does the design depend on the details of the most recent interview, or are there some underlying and more constant design guidelines that you can depend on? How do you scope the project down to something manageable, yet at the same time build an extensible architecture that will gradually let you build a comprehensive data warehouse environment?

These questions are close to causing a crisis in the data warehouse industry. Much of the recent surge in the industry toward "data marts" is a reaction to these very issues. Designers want to do something simple and achievable. No one is willing to sign up for a galactic design that must somehow get everything right on the first try. Everyone hopes that in the rush to simplification, the long-term coherence and extendibility of the design will not be compromised. Fortunately, a pathway through this design challenge achieves an implementable immediate result, and at the same time it continuously augments the design so that eventually a true enterprise-scale data warehouse is built. The secret is to keep in mind a design methodology, which Ralph Kimball calls the "nine-step method" (see Table 7.1).

As a result of interviewing marketing users, finance users, salesforce users, operational users, first- and second-level management, and senior management, a picture emerges of what is keeping these people awake at night. You

TABLE 7.1   Nine-Step Method in the Design of a Data Warehouse

1. Choosing the subject matter
2. Deciding what a fact table represents
3. Identifying and conforming the dimensions
4. Choosing the facts
5. Storing precalculations in the fact table
6. Rounding out the dimension tables
7. Choosing the duration of the database
8. The need to track slowly changing dimensions
9. Deciding the query priorities and the query modes

can list and prioritize the primary business issues facing the enterprise. At the same time, you should conduct a set of interviews with the legacy systems' DBAs, who will reveal which data sources are clean, which contain valid and consistent data, and which will remain supported over the next few years.

Preparing for the design with a proper set of interviews is crucial. Interviewing is also one of the hardest things to teach people. I find it helpful to reduce the interviewing process to a tactic and an objective. Crudely put, the tactic is to make the end users talk about what they do, and the objective is to gain insights that feed the nine design decisions. The tricky part is that the interviewer can't pose the design questions directly to the end users. End users don't have opinions about data warehouse system design issues; they have opinions about what is important in their business lives. End users are intimidated by system design questions, and they are quite right when they insist that system design is IT responsibility, not theirs. Thus, the challenge of the data mart designer is to meet the users far more than half way.

In any event, armed with both the top–down view (what keeps management awake) and the bottom–up view (which data sources are available), the data warehouse designer may follow these steps:

Step 1: choosing the subject matter of a particular data mart.   The first data mart you build should be the one with the most bang for the buck. It should simultaneously answer the most important business questions and be the most accessible in terms of data extraction. According to Kimball, a great place to start in most enterprises is to build a data mart that consists of customer invoices or monthly statements. This data source is probably fairly accessible and of fairly high quality. One of Kimball's laws is that the best data source in any enterprise is the record of "how much money they owe us." Unless costs and profitability are easily available before the data mart is even designed, it's best to avoid adding these items to this first data mart. Nothing drags down a data mart implementation faster than a heroic or impossible mission to provide activity-based costing as part of the first deliverable.

Step 2: deciding exactly what a fact table record represents.   This step, according to R. Kimball, seems like a technical detail at this early point, but it is actually the secret to making progress on the design. As explained in Chap. 9, the fact table is the large central table in the dimensional design that has a multipart key. Each component of the multipart key is a foreign key to an individual dimension table. In the example of customer invoices, the "grain" of the fact table is the individual line item on the customer invoice. In other words, a line item on an invoice is a single fact table record, and vice versa. Once the fact table representation is decided, a coherent discussion of what the dimensions of the data mart's fact table are can take place.

Step 3: identifying and conforming the dimensions. The dimensions are the drivers of the data mart. The dimensions are the platforms for browsing the allowable constraint values and launching these constraints. The dimensions are the source of row headers in the user's final reports; they carry the enterprise's vocabulary to the users. A well-architected set of dimensions makes the data mart understandable and easy to use. A poorly presented or incomplete set of dimensions robs the data mart of its usefulness. Dimensions should be chosen with the long-range data warehouse in mind. This choice presents the primary moment at which the data mart architect must disregard the data mart details and consider the longer-range plans. If any dimension occurs in two data marts, they must be exactly the same dimension, or one must be a mathematical subset of the other. Only in this way can two data marts share one or more dimensions in the same application. When a dimension is used in two data marts, this dimension is said to be *conformed*. Good examples of dimensions that absolutely must be conformed between data marts are the customer and product dimensions in an enterprise. If these dimensions are allowed to drift out of synchronization between data marts, the overall data warehouse will fail, because the two data marts will not be able to be used together. The requirement to conform dimensions across data marts is very strong. Careful thought must be given to this requirement before the first data mart is implemented. The data mart team must figure out what an enterprise customer ID is and what an enterprise product ID is. If this task is done correctly, successive data marts can be built at different times, on different machines, and by different development teams, and these data marts will merge coherently into an overall data warehouse. In particular, if the dimensions of two data marts are conformed, it is easy to implement drill across by sending separate queries to the two data marts, and then sort-merging the two answer sets on a set of common row headers. The row headers can be made to be common only if they are drawn from a conformed dimension common to the two data marts.

With these first three steps correctly implemented, designers can attack the last six steps (see Table 7.1). Each step gets easier if the preceding steps have been performed correctly.

7.3 Technical Considerations

A number of technical issues are to be considered when designing and implementing a data warehouse environment. These issues include

- The hardware platform that would house the data warehouse
- The database management system that supports the warehouse database
- The communications infrastructure that connects the warehouse, data marts, operational systems, and end users
- The hardware platform and software to support the metadata repository
- The systems management framework that enables centralized management and administration of the entire environment.

Let's look at some of these issues in more detail.

7.3.1 Hardware platforms

Since many data warehouse implementations are developed into already existing environments, many organizations tend to leverage the existing platforms and skill base to build a data warehouse. This section looks at the hardware platform selection from an architectural viewpoint: what platform is best to build a successful data warehouse from the ground up.

An important consideration when choosing a data warehouse server is its capacity for handling the volumes of data required by decision support applications, some of which may require a significant amount of historical (e.g., up to 10 years) data. This capacity requirement can be quite large. For example, in general, disk storage allocated for the warehouse should be 2 to 3 times the size of the data component of the warehouse to accommodate DSS processing, such as sorting, storing of intermediate results, summarization, join, and formatting. Often, the platform choice is the choice between a mainframe and non-MVS (UNIX or Windows NT) server.

Of course, a number of arguments can be made for and against each of these choices. For example, a mainframe is based on a proven technology; has large data and throughput capacity; is reliable, available, and serviceable; and may support the legacy databases that are used as sources for the data warehouse. The data warehouse residing on the mainframe is best suited for situations in which large amounts of legacy data need to be stored in the data warehouse. A mainframe system, however, is not as open and flexible as a contemporary client/server system, and is not optimized for ad hoc query processing. A modern server (nonmainframe) can also support large data volumes and a large number of flexible GUI-based end-user tools, and can relieve the mainframe from ad hoc query processing. However, in general, non-MVS servers are not as reliable as mainframes, are more difficult to manage and integrate into the existing environment, and may require new skills and even new organizational structures.

From the architectural viewpoint, however, the data warehouse server has to be specialized for the tasks associated with the data warehouse, and a mainframe can be well suited to be a data warehouse server. Let's look at the hardware features that make a server—whether it is mainframe-, UNIX-, or NT-based—an appropriate technical solution for the data warehouse.

To begin with, the data warehouse server has to be able to support large data volumes and complex query processing. In addition, it has to be *scalable,* since the data warehouse is never finished, as new user requirements, new data sources, and more historical data are continuously incorporated into the warehouse, and as the user population of the data warehouse continues to grow. Therefore, a clear requirement for the data warehouse server is the scalable high performance for data loading and ad hoc query processing as well as the ability to support large databases in a reliable, efficient fashion. Chapter 4 briefly touched on various design points to enable server specialization for scalability in performance, throughput, user support, and very large database (VLDB) processing.

Balanced approach.   An important design point when selecting a scalable computing platform is the right balance between all computing components, for example, between the number of processors in a multiprocessor system and the I/O bandwidth. Remember that the lack of balance in a system inevitably results in a bottleneck!

Typically, when a hardware platform is sized to accommodate the data warehouse, this sizing is frequently focused on the number and size of disks. A typical disk configuration includes 2.5 to 3 times the amount of raw data. An important consideration—disk throughput comes from the actual number of disks, and not the total disk space. Thus, the number of disks has direct impact on data parallelism. To balance the system, it is very important to allocate a correct number of processors to efficiently handle all disk I/O operations. If this allocation is not balanced, an expensive data warehouse platform can rapidly become CPU-bound. Indeed, since various processors have widely different performance ratings and thus can support a different number of disks per CPU, data warehouse designers should carefully analyze the disk I/O rates and processor capabilities to derive an efficient system configuration. For example, if it takes a CPU rated at 10 SPECint to efficiently handle one 3-Gbyte disk drive, then a single 30 SPECint processor in a multiprocessor system can handle three disk drives. Knowing how much data needs to be processed should give you an idea of how big the multiprocessor system should be. Another consideration is related to disk controllers. A disk controller can support a certain amount of data throughput (e.g., 20 Mbytes/s). Knowing the per-disk throughput ratio and the total number of disks can tell you how many controllers of a given type should be configured in the system.

The idea of a balanced approach can (and should) be carefully extended to all system components. The resulting system configuration will easily handle known workloads and provide a balanced and scalable computing platform for future growth.

Optimal hardware architecture for parallel query scalability.   An important consideration when selecting a hardware platform for a data warehouse is that of scalability. Therefore, a frequent approach to system selection is to take advantage of hardware parallelism that comes in the form of shared-memory symmetric multiprocessors (SMPs), clusters, and shared-nothing distributed-memory systems (MPPs). As was shown in Chap. 3, the scalability of these systems can be seriously affected by the system-architecture-induced data skew. This architecture-induced data skew is more severe in the low-density asymmetric connection architectures (e.g., daisy-chained, 2-D and 3-D mesh), and is virtually nonexistent in symmetric connection architectures (e.g., cross-bar switch). Thus, when selecting a hardware platform for a data warehouse, take into account the fact that the system-architecture-induced data skew can overpower even the best data layout for parallel query execution, and can force an expensive parallel computing system to process queries serially.

7.3.2 Data warehouse and DBMS specialization

To reiterate, the two important challenges facing the developers of data warehouses are the very large size of the databases and the need to process complex ad hoc queries in a relatively short time. Therefore, among the most important requirements for the data warehouse DBMS are performance, throughput, and scalability.

The majority of established RDBMS vendors has implemented various degrees of parallelism in their respective products. Although any relational database management system—such as DB2, Oracle, Informix, or Sybase—supports parallel database processing, some of these products have been architected to better suit the specialized requirements of the data warehouse.

In addition to the "traditional" relational DBMSs, there are databases that have been optimized specifically for data warehousing, such as Red Brick Warehouse from Red Brick Systems. The DBMS features designed to satisfy the high performance and scalability requirements of a data warehouse are briefly discussed in Chap. 12. The next chapter looks into the DBMS characteristics for performance and scalability from the data warehouse viewpoint.

7.3.3 Communications infrastructure

When planning for a data warehouse, one often neglected aspect of the architecture is the cost and efforts associated with bringing access to corporate data directly to the desktop. These costs and efforts could be significant, since many large organizations do not have a large user population with direct electronic access to information, and since a typical data warehouse user requires a relatively large bandwidth to interact with the data warehouse and retrieve a significant amount of data for the analysis. This may mean that communications networks have to be expanded, and new hardware and software may have to be purchased.

7.4 Implementation Considerations

A data warehouse cannot be simply bought and installed—its implementation requires the integration of many products within a data warehouse. The caveat here is that the necessary customization drives up the cost of implementing a data warehouse. To illustrate the complexity of the data warehouse implementation, let's discuss the logical steps needed to build a data warehouse:

- Collect and analyze business requirements.
- Create a data model and a physical design for the data warehouse.
- Define data sources.
- Choose the database technology and platform for the warehouse.
- Extract the data from the operational databases, transform it, clean it up, and load it into the database.
- Choose database access and reporting tools.
- Choose database connectivity software.
- Choose data analysis and presentation software.
- Update the data warehouse.

When building the warehouse, these steps must be performed within the constraints of the current state of data warehouse technologies.

7.4.1   Access tools

Currently, no single tool on the market can handle all possible data warehouse access needs. Therefore, most implementations rely on a suite of tools. The best way to choose this suite includes the definition of different types of access to the data and selecting the best tool for that kind of access. Examples of access types include

- Simple tabular form reporting
- Ranking
- Multivariable analysis
- Time series analysis
- Data visualization, graphing, charting, and pivoting
- Complex textual search
- Statistical analysis
- Artificial intelligence techniques for testing of hypothesis, trends discovery, definition, and validation of data clusters and segments
- Information mapping (i.e., mapping of spatial data in geographic information systems)
- Ad hoc user-specified queries
- Predefined repeatable queries
- Interactive drill-down reporting and analysis

- Complex queries with multitable joins, multilevel subqueries, and sophisticated search criteria

In addition, certain business requirements often exceed existing tool capabilities and may require building sophisticated applications to retrieve and analyze warehouse data. These applications often take the form of custom-developed screens and reports that retrieve frequently used data and format it in a predefined standardized way. This approach may be very useful for those data warehouse users who are not yet comfortable with ad hoc queries.

There are a number of query tools on the market today. Many of these tools are designed to easily compose and execute ad hoc queries and build customized reports with little knowledge of the underlying database technology, SQL, or even the data model (i.e., Impromptu from Cognos, Business Objects, etc.), while others (e.g., Andyne's GQL) provide relatively low-level capabilities for an expert user to develop complex ad hoc queries in a fashion similar to developing SQL queries for relational databases. Business requirements that exceed the capabilities of ad hoc query and reporting tools are fulfilled by different classes of tools: OLAP and data mining tools. The technology behind these tools is discussed later in the book.

7.4.2   Data extraction, cleanup, transformation, and migration

As a component of the data warehouse architecture, proper attention must be given to *data extraction,* which represents a critical success factor for a data warehouse architecture. Specifically, when implementing data warehouse, several selection criteria that affect the ability to transform, consolidate, integrate, and repair the data should be considered:

- The ability to identify data in the data source environments that can be read by the conversion tool is important. This additional step may affect the timeliness of data delivery to the warehouse.

- Support for flat files, indexed files [e.g., Virtual Storage Access Method (VSAM)] and legacy DBMSs [e.g., Information Management System (IMS) and Computer Associates' CA-IDMS] is critical, since the bulk of corporate data is still maintained in data stores of this type.

- The capability to merge data from multiple data stores is required in many installations. Using data replication technologies (see Chap. 11) helps—a data-change capture facility provides the functionality of reading log data to obtain only the changed data to be transferred. This reduces the amount of data that must be loaded into the data warehouse for periodic updating of the data warehouse.

- The specification interface to indicate the data to be extracted and the conversion criteria is important.

- The ability to read information from data dictionaries or import information from repository products is desired. This can reduce the amount of specification effort required.

- The code generated by the tool should be completely maintainable from within the development environment.

- Selective data extraction of both data elements and records enables users to extract only the required data.

- A field-level data examination for the transformation of data into information is needed. For example, a user-exit feature is important for users who may need to perform more sophisticated operations on the data than can be achieved using the facilities provided with the tool.

- The ability to perform data-type and character-set translation is a requirement when moving data between incompatible systems.

- The capability to create summarization, aggregation, and derivation records and fields is very important.

- The data warehouse database management system should be able to perform the load directly from the tool, using the native API available with the RDBMS; alternatively, the system should support the capability to create a flat file and then use the load utility provided by the RDBMS.

- Vendor stability and support for the product are items that must be carefully evaluated.

Vendor solutions.   Some vendors have emerged that are more focused on fulfilling requirements pertaining to data warehouse implementations as opposed to simply moving data between hardware platforms.

The extraction tools briefly described in the following paragraphs illustrate three separate approaches to the warehousing extraction function. Prism markets a primarily model-based approach, while Information Builders markets a gateway approach. SAS products could handle all the warehouse functions, including extraction. Several extraction tools are discussed in more detail in Chap. 11.

Prism solutions.   Prism Warehouse Manager maps source data to a target database management system to be used as a warehouse. Warehouse Manager generates code to extract and integrate data, create and manage metadata, and build a subject-oriented, historical base. The standard conversions, key changes, structural changes, and condensations needed to transform operational data into data warehouse information are automatically created. Prism Warehouse Manager can extract data from multiple source environments, including DB2, IDMS, IMS, VSAM, RMS, and sequential files under UNIX or MVS. Target databases include Oracle, Sybase, and Informix. Prism Solutions has strategic relationships with Pyramid and Informix.

Carleton's PASSPORT. PASSPORT is positioned in the data extract and transformation niche of data warehousing. The product currently consists of two components. The first, which is mainframe-based, collects the file-record-table layouts for the required inputs and outputs and converts them to the Passport Data Language (PDL). The second component is workstation-based and is used to create the metadata directory from which it builds the COBOL programs to actually create the extracts. The user must transfer the PDL file from the mainframe to a location accessible by PASSPORT. The metadata directory is stored in a relational database (e.g., DB2 Common Server). The product itself runs on Windows and OS/2. The Windows version shows a graphical representation of the workflow that operates using the standard expand, collapse, drill-down, etc., metaphor. Carleton's PASSPORT can produce multiple output files from a single execution of an extract program. Carleton is partnering with Sybase on the integration of PASSPORT with SYBASE Open Client and Open Server.

Information Builders Inc. The EDA/SQL family of products provides SQL access to and a uniform relational view of relational and nonrelational data residing in over 60 different databases on 35 different platforms. EDA/SQL implements a client/server model that is optimized for higher performance. EDA/SQL supports copy management, data quality management, data replication capabilities, and standards support for both ODBC and the X/Open CLI. IBI's product is the component of almost every systems supplier's legacy data access strategy, including Amdahl, IBM, Digital Equipment, HP, and Bull as well as many database and tool vendors.

SAS Institute Inc. SAS begins with the premise that most mission-critical data still resides in the data center and offers its traditional SAS System tools as a means to serve all data warehousing functions. Its data repository function can act to build the informational database. SAS Data Access Engines serve as extraction tools to combine common variables, transform data representation forms for consistency, consolidate redundant data, and use business rules to produce computed values in the warehouse. SAS views serve the internetworking and refresh roles, and SAS' reporting, graphing, and decision support products act as the front end. In addition to interacting with SAS System databases, SAS engines can work with hierarchical and relational databases and sequential files.

7.4.3 Data placement strategies

As a data warehouse grows, there are at least two options for data placement. One is to put some of the data in the data warehouse into another storage media; e.g., WORM, RAID, or photo-optical technology. The data selected for transport to the alternate storage media is detailed and older and there is less demand for it. The bulk storage can be handled either by the data warehouse server or another server used exclusively for handling the bulk storage media.

The second option is to distribute the data in the data warehouse across multiple servers. Some criteria must be established for dividing it over the servers—by geography, organization unit, time, function, etc. Another factor in determining how data should be divided among multiple data warehouse servers is the pattern of usage, such as what data is accessed and how much data is accessed, and any joins, sorts, or other processing that occurs after the data is accessed. However the data is divided, a single source of metadata across the entire organization is required. Hence, this configuration requires both corporationwide metadata and the metadata managed for any given server.

Data replication.   Where most users require only a small subset of the corporate data, using data replication or data movers to place only the data that is relevant to a particular workgroup in a localized database can be a more affordable solution than data warehousing. In many cases, often only a small portion of the data a company collects will be relevant. Many companies use data replication servers to copy their most needed data to a separate database where decision support applications can access it. Replication technology creates copies of databases on a periodic basis, so that data entry and data analysis can be performed separately. Thus, end users' ad hoc queries and analytical processing are prevented from competing with operational applications for server resources.

Similar process can be used to move data into distributed data marts. This situation can arise in organizations where the data is stored centrally in a corporate data warehouse, and then needs to be delivered for the analysis to remote users at widely distributed locations. For example, the New York corporate headquarters of an international corporation collect critical data on various financial transactions into the enterprisewide data warehouse. The corporation has developed a robust multidimensional model to perform complex multivariant analysis using an OLAP tool. The financial analysts who benefit from this data reside in New York and in regional locations (London, Tokyo, Frankfurt). As soon as data becomes available to produce the required multidimensional database, this data is then securely replicated to all locations, loaded into local copies of the multidimensional data mart, and analyzed locally using the OLAP tool.

Database gateways.   Aside from the high cost of development, many data warehouse solutions require the use of a database gateway. While traditional gateway technology provides LAN users with the ability to easily access small amounts of mainframe data, it is not optimized for moving large files. Networks can be slowed by multiple concurrent user requests for similar data through a gateway. Because gateway queries are not predictable, the DBMS cannot be tuned for gateway access. Gateway access for decision support will often compete with production applications for resources.

7.4.4 Metadata

A frequently occurring problem in data warehousing is the problem of communicating to the end user what information resides in the data warehouse and how it can be accessed. The key to providing users and applications with a roadmap to the information stored in the warehouse is the metadata. It can define all data elements and their attributes, data sources and timing, and the rules that govern data use and data transformations. Metadata needs to be collected as the warehouse is designed and built. Since metadata describes the information in the warehouse from multiple viewpoints (input, sources, transformation, access, etc.), it is imperative that the same metadata or its *consistent* replicas be available to all tools selected for the warehouse implementation, thus enforcing the integrity and accuracy of the warehouse information. The metadata also has to be available to all warehouse users in order to guide them as they use the warehouse. Even though there are a number of tools available to help users understand and use the warehouse, these tools need to be carefully evaluated before any purchasing decision is made. In other words, a well-thought-through strategy for collecting, maintaining, and distributing metadata is needed for a successful data warehouse implementation. An interesting approach to metadata repository management is offered by Prism's Directory Manager. This product is designed to integrate and manage all metadata definitions throughout the warehouse environment. The Directory Manager can:

- Import business models from CASE tools (Bachman, ADW, IEF, and any other CDIF-compliant CASE tools).

- Import metadata definitions from the Prism Warehouse Manager (the transformation and extraction component of the Prism product suite).

- Export metadata into catalogs, dictionaries, or directories of many DSS access tools.

- Create flexible customized views based on end-user requirements using graphical front-end application.

In other words, Prism Directory Manager may be the right tool to solve the problem of creating and managing a unified metadata repository to support the entire data warehousing environment. A more detailed discussion on metadata management tools is offered in Chap. 10.

7.4.5 User sophistication levels

Data warehousing is a relatively new phenomenon, and a certain degree of sophistication is required on the end user's part to effectively use the warehouse. A typical organization maintains different levels of computer literacy and sophistication within the user community. The users can be classified on the basis of their skill level in accessing the warehouse. For example, let's define three classes of users:

- *Casual users.* These users are most comfortable retrieving information from the warehouse in predefined formats, and running preexisting queries and reports. These users do not need tools that allow for sophisticated ad hoc query building and execution.

- *Power users.* In their daily activities, these users typically combine predefined queries with some relatively simple ad hoc queries that they create themselves. These users can also engage in drill-down queries to further analyze the results of simple queries and reports. These users need access tools that combine the simplicity of predefined queries and reports with a certain degree of flexibility.

- *Experts.* These users tend to create their own complex queries and perform a sophisticated analysis on the information they retrieve from the warehouse. These users know the data, tools, and database well enough to demand tools that allow for maximum flexibility and adaptability.

Therefore, when implementing the warehouse, an analysis of the end-user requirements has to be coupled with an evaluation of the user sophistication levels, and the selected end-user tools have to satisfy both the business needs and the capabilities and preferences of the end users.

7.5 Integrated Solutions

Most data warehouse vendor solutions consist of a relational database used for the data warehouse, data warehouse management software, and data access and reporting tools, along with the necessary database connectivity software. What follows is a brief look at some of the solutions available on the market today.

A number of vendors participate in data warehousing by providing a suite of services and products that go beyond one particular component of the data warehouse. These vendors tend to establish internal centers of data warehousing expertise and often engage in partnership relationships with specialized independent software vendors for the products and expertise.

Digital Equipment Corp.   Digital has combined the data modeling, extraction, and cleansing capabilities of Prism Warehouse Manager with the copy management and data replication capabilities of Digital's ACCESSWORKS family of database access servers in providing users with the ability to build and use information warehouses. ACCESSWORKS runs on the Digital Open VMS platform and provides the necessary data access back-end gateways and front-end connections.

Hewlett-Packard.   Hewlett-Packard's client/server-based HP Open Warehouse comprises multiple components, including a data management architecture, the HP-UX operating system, HP 9000 computers, warehouse management tools, an Allbase/SQL relational database, and the HP Information Access query tool. HP offers single-source support for the full HP Open Warehouse solution. This allows customers to choose components that best suit their needs, without having to work with multiple vendors for support. HP also provides a suite of consulting services for designing and implementing a data warehouse. HP Open Warehouse integrates a number of third-party products, including Red Brick Warehouse from Red Brick Systems, Prism Warehouse Manager from Prism Solutions, EXTRACT from Evolutionary Technologies, Enterprise Data Access/SQL from IBI, and Open Development Environment from Open Environment Corp.

IBM. The IBM Information Warehouse framework consists of an architecture; data management tools; OS/2, AIX, and MVS operating systems; hardware platforms, including mainframes and servers; and a relational DBMS (DB2). Other components of the IBM Information Warehouse family include:

- *DataGuide/2*—provides a catalog of shared data and information objects which can be listed and described in everyday business terms, and searched with key words. Once the information is identified, DataGuide/2 can start applications to retrieve and process it.

- *DataPropagator*—automates data replication across an enterprise, using a graphical user interface (see discussion on DataPropagator in Chap. 11).

- *DataRefresher*—provides copy management capability for moving large amounts of data from a broad range of data sources.

- *DataHub*—manages complex client/server relational database environments and provides the base for IBM's family of copy management and replication tools.

- *Application System* (AS)—provides a set of general data access, query, reporting, and charting facilities and specialized tools for planning or modeling, project management, linear programming, document processing, and application development.

- *Personal Application System/2* (PAS/2)—decision support software designed for Windows and OS/2 PCs. The user can select from a list of decision support objects that can manage and analyze data, produce reports and charts of the data, and create procedures to automate regular work. Optionally includes business planning, project management, statistical analysis, and application development.

- *Query Management Facility* (QMF)—a host-based facility that provides query, reporting, and graphics functions from menu options.

- *IBM FlowMark*—workflow management product designed to help database administrators document their system management tasks and automatically execute these tasks.

Sequent. Sequent Computer Systems Inc.'s DecisionPoint Program is a decision support program for the delivery of data warehouses dedicated to on-line complex query processing (OLCP). The program combines Sequent symmetric multiprocessing (SMP) architecture with a variety of client/server products and services, including UNIX-based Sequent Symmetry 2000 Series, Red Brick Warehouse for Red Brick Systems, and ClearAccess Query Tool from Clear-Access Corp. DecisionPoint is targeted at information service organizations seeking to meet the data access demands of knowledge workers and executives. ClearAccess Query Tool provides DecisionPoint users with a transparent window into the Red Brick Warehouse. Using a graphical interface, users query the data warehouse by pointing and clicking on the warehouse data items they want to analyze. Query results are placed on the program's clipboard for pasting onto a variety of desktop applications, or they can be saved to a disk.

Conclusion.   Clearly, this is not a complete list. Database vendors are all positioning themselves as providers of integrated data warehouse services and products. Oracle, Sybase, and Informix all offer integrated data warehouse solutions that are based on recent acquisitions, development of in-house consulting expertise, and strategic partner alliances.

7.6   Benefits of Data Warehousing

Data warehouse usage includes

- Locating the right information
- Presentation of information (reports, graphs)
- Testing of hypothesis
- Discovery of information
- Sharing the analysis

Using better tools to access data can reduce outdated, historical data. Likewise, users can obtain the data when they need it most, often during business-decision processes, not on a schedule predetermined months earlier by the IS department and computer operations staff.

Data warehouse architecture can enhance overall availability of business intelligence data, as well as increase the effectiveness and timeliness of business decisions.

7.6.1   Tangible benefits

Successfully implemented data warehousing can realize some significant tangible benefits. For example, conservatively assuming an improvement in out-of-stock conditions in the retailing business that leads to a 1 percent increase in sales can mean a sizable cost benefit (e.g., even for a small retail business with $200 million in annual sales, a conservative 1 percent improvement in sales can yield additional annual revenue of $2 million or more). In fact, several retail enterprises claim that data warehouse implementations have improved out-of-stock conditions to the extent that sales increases range from 5 to 20 percent. This benefit is in addition to retaining customers who might not have returned if, because of out-of-stock problems, they had to do business with other retailers.

Other examples of tangible benefits of a data warehouse initiative include the following:

- Product inventory turnover is improved.

- Costs of product introduction are decreased with improved selection of target markets.

- More cost-effective decision making is enabled by separating (ad hoc) query processing from running against operational databases.

- Better business intelligence is enabled by increased quality and flexibility of market analysis available through multilevel data structures, which may range from detailed to highly summarized. For example, determining the effectiveness of marketing programs allows the elimination of weaker programs and enhancement of stronger ones.

- Enhanced asset and liability management means that a data warehouse can provide a "big" picture of enterprisewide purchasing and inventory patterns, and can indicate otherwise unseen credit exposure and opportunities for cost savings.

7.6.2   Intangible benefits

In addition to the tangible benefits outlined above, a data warehouse provides a number of intangible benefits. Although they are more difficult to quantify, intangible benefits should also be considered when planning for the data warehouse. Examples of intangible benefits are:

- Improved productivity, by keeping all required data in a single location and eliminating the rekeying of data

- Reduced redundant processing, support, and software to support overlapping decision support applications

- Enhanced customer relations through improved knowledge of individual requirements and trends, through customization, improved communications, and tailored product offerings

- Enabling business process reengineering—data warehousing can provide useful insights into the work processes themselves, resulting in developing breakthrough ideas for the reengineering of those processes

8

Mapping the
Data Warehouse to a
Multiprocessor Architecture

A number of key technology aspects of data are extremely important to understanding and successfully implementing a data warehouse. One of the key technologies is the database management systems used in data warehousing. Therefore, this chapter attempts to provide a closer look at the relational and specialized database technology for data warehousing and maps these technologies to the multiprocessing hardware architectures discussed in the previous chapters.

8.1 Relational Database Technology for Data Warehouse

Although the basics of parallel database technology were already discussed in Chap. 4, this section attempts to avoid repetition of that discussion and provide a data warehouse-centric viewpoint on the technology and its implications.

The organizations that embarked on data warehousing development deal with ever-increasing amounts of data. Generally speaking, the size of a data warehouse rapidly approaches the point where the search for better performance and scalability becomes a real necessity. This search is pursuing two goals:

- *Speed-up*—the ability to execute the same request on the same amount of data in less time

- *Scale-up*—the ability to obtain the same performance on the same request as the database size increases

An additional and important goal is to achieve *linear* speed-up and scale-up; doubling the number of processors cuts the response time in half (linear speed-up) or provides the same performance on twice as much data (linear scale-up).

These goals of linear performance and scalability can be satisfied by parallel hardware architectures, parallel operating systems, and parallel database management systems. Parallel hardware architectures are based on multiprocessor systems designed as a shared-memory model [symmetric multiprocessors (SMPs)], shared-disk model, or distributed-memory model [massively parallel processors (MPPs), and *clusters* of uniprocessors and/or SMPs].

8.1.1 Types of parallelism

Database vendors started to take advantage of parallel hardware architectures by implementing multiserver and multithreaded systems designed to handle a large number of client requests efficiently. This approach naturally resulted in *interquery parallelism,* in which different server threads (or processes) handle multiple requests at the same time. Interquery parallelism has been successfully implemented on SMP systems, where it increased the throughput and allowed the support of more concurrent users. However, without changing the way the DBMS processed queries, interquery parallelism was limited; even though multiple queries were processed concurrently, each query was still processed serially by a single process or a thread. In other words, if a query consists of a table scan, or join and sort operations, then this would be the order in which these operations execute, and each operation would have to finish before the next one could begin.

To improve the situation, many DBMS vendors developed versions of their products that utilized *intraquery parallelism.* This form of parallelism decomposes the serial SQL query into lower-level operations such as scan, join, sort, and aggregation (see Fig. 8.1, case 1). These lower-level operations then are executed concurrently, in parallel. By dedication of multiple resources to the processing, a single request can therefore be processed faster. Operations other than queries—INSERTs, DELETEs, UPDATEs, index creation, database load, backup, and recovery—can also be parallelized and thus speeded up.

Parallel execution of the tasks within SQL statements (intraquery parallelism) can be done in either of two ways:

- *Horizontal parallelism,* which means that the database is partitioned across multiple disks, and parallel processing occurs within a specific task (i.e., table scan) that is performed concurrently on different processors against different sets of data (Fig. 8.1, case 2)

- *Vertical parallelism,* which occurs among different tasks—all component query operations (i.e., scan, join, sort) are executed in parallel in a pipelined fashion. In other words, an output from one task (e.g., scan) becomes an input into another task (e.g., join) as soon as records become available (see Fig. 8.1, case 3)

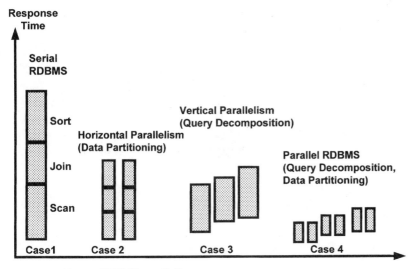

Figure 8.1   Types of DBMS parallelism.

A truly parallel DBMS should support both horizontal and vertical types of parallelism concurrently (see Fig. 8.1, case 4).

8.1.2   Data partitioning

Data partitioning is a key requirement for effective parallel execution of database operations. It spreads data from database tables across multiple disks so that I/O operations such as read and write can be performed in parallel. Partitioning can be done randomly or intelligently.

Random partitioning includes random data striping across multiple disks on a single server. Another option for random partitioning is *round-robin partitioning,* in which each new record is placed on the next disk assigned to the database. Although random partitioning can be effective in reducing I/O contention for multiple concurrent requests against the same table, its effectiveness can be significantly reduced depending on data distribution and query selectivity; since DBMS does not know where each record (row) resides, it is possible that all partitions may have to be fully scanned in order to satisfy a query.

Intelligent partitioning assumes that DBMS knows where a specific record is located and does not waste time searching for it across all disks. Intelligent partitioning allows a DBMS to fully exploit parallel architectures and also enables higher availability. For example, not only can the DBMS avoid reading certain disk segments where the selection criteria is not met, intelligent partitioning also allows query processing even if a disk partition is unavailable, as long as the DBMS determined that the partition data is not required to satisfy the query. Intelligent partitioning techniques include:

- *Hash partitioning.* A hash algorithm is used to calculate the partition number (hash value) based on the value of the partitioning key for each row.

- *Key range partitioning.* Rows are placed and located in the partitions according to the value of the partitioning key (all rows with the key value from A to K are in partition 1, L to T are in partition 2, etc.).

- *Schema partitioning.* This is an option not to partition a table across disks; instead, an entire table is placed on one disk, another table is placed on a different disk, etc. This is useful for small reference tables that are more effectively used when replicated in each partition rather than spread across partitions.

- *User-defined partitioning.* This is a partitioning method that allows a table to be partitioned on the basis of a user-defined expression (e.g., use state codes to place rows in one of 50 partitions).

Since a table can be partitioned in only one way at a time, the partitioning choice has to satisfy database access requirements; a wrong partitioning method can create "hot spots" which defeat the advantages of parallel hardware and software. For example, if a table is partitioned by key ranges and accessed by a non-partitioned key, the processing may be totally ineffective, and may result in performance characteristics that are worse than that of a serial database.

8.2 Database Architectures for Parallel Processing

Software parallelism is a natural follow-on to hardware parallel architectures. In addition to the parallel operating system, an adaptable parallel database software architecture is required to take advantage of parallelism in shared-memory and distributed-memory environments. In fact, the parallel database architecture is what determines the ultimate scalability of the solution. There are three main DBMS software architecture styles: shared-everything architecture, shared-disk architecture, and shared-nothing architecture.

8.2.1 Shared-memory architecture

Shared-memory or *shared-everything* style is the traditional approach to implementing an RDBMS on SMP hardware. It is relatively simple to implement, and has been very successful up to the point where it runs into the scalability limitations of the shared-everything architecture. The key point of this approach is that a single RDBMS server can potentially utilize all processors, access all memory, and access the entire database, thus providing the user with a consistent single system image (see Fig. 8.2).

In shared-memory SMP systems, the DBMS assumes that the multiple database components executing SQL statements communicate with each other by exchanging messages and data via the shared memory. All processors have access to all data, which is partitioned across local disks (see Fig. 8.2).

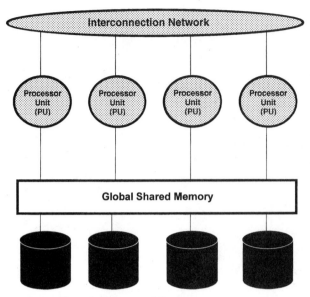

Figure 8.2 Shared-memory architecture.

Several design points can significantly affect the scalability of this architecture. Among them is a key design approach of *process-based* implementation (e.g., Oracle 7.x running on UNIX platforms) or *threads-based* implementation. The latter approach has variations of an RDBMS implementing its own threads (e.g., SYBASE SQL Server, Informix OnLine), or using the operating system threads (e.g., Microsoft SQL Server running on NT). In general, threads provide better resource utilization and faster context switching, thus providing for better scalability. At the same time, threads that are too tightly coupled with the operating system may limit RDBMS portability. Overall, the scalability of shared-memory architectures is limited. SMP systems do not demonstrate a linear growth in direct proportion to the number of processors. Depending on the processor and system bus speed, the SMP throughput does not increase (and can even decrease, due to a local cache coherency problem) when the number of processors exceeds some (machine-specific) number.

8.2.2 Shared-disk architecture

Shared-disk architecture implements a concept of shared ownership of the entire database between RDBMS servers, each of which is running on a node of a distributed memory system (see Chaps. 3 and 4 for more details). Each RDBMS server can read, write, update, and delete records from the same shared database, which would require the system to implement a form of a distributed lock manager (DLM) (see Fig. 8.3). DLM components can be found in hardware, the operating system, and/or a separate software layer, all depend-

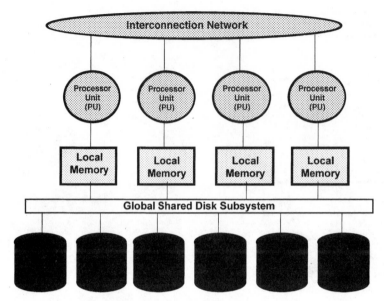

Figure 8.3   Distributed-memory shared-disk architecture.

ing on the system vendor. The complexity of the necessary coordination performed by the DLM is hidden from users and application developers, thus providing for a single system image. As with every shared-something approach, this architecture imposes some constraints to the scalability. For example, in the worst-case scenario, if all nodes are reading and updating the same data, the RDBMS and its DLM will have to spend a lot of resources synchronizing multiple buffer pools (similar to a cache coherency problem in SMP systems). This problem, sometimes called "pinging," can have a significantly negative effect on scalability. Another potential bottleneck is the DLM itself, since it may have to handle significant message traffic in a highly utilized RDBMS environment. RDBMS designers and administrators are constantly working on improving the overall performance of the system.

On the positive side, shared-disk architectures can reduce performance bottlenecks resulting from *data skew* (an uneven distribution of data), and can significantly increase system availability. The shared-disk distributed-memory design eliminates the memory access bottleneck typical of large SMP systems, and helps reduce DBMS dependency on data partitioning.

Latest releases of Oracle Parallel Server and DB2/MVS running in the IBM's Parallel Sysplex and utilizing its coupling facility are examples of maturity and robustness of this architecture.

8.2.3   Shared-nothing architecture

In a shared-nothing distributed-memory environment (Fig. 8.4), the data is partitioned across all disks, and the DBMS is "partitioned" across multiple

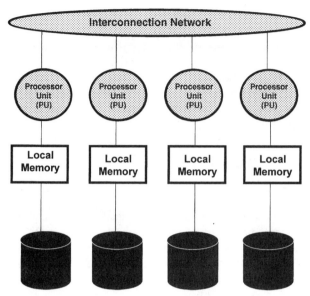

Figure 8.4 Distributed-memory architecture.

coservers, each of which resides on individual nodes of the parallel system and has an ownership of its own disk and, thus, its own database partition. A shared-nothing RDBMS parallelizes the execution of a SQL query across multiple processing nodes. Each processor has its own memory and disk, and communicates with other processors by exchanging messages and data over the interconnection network. This architecture is optimized specifically for the MPP and cluster systems.

The shared-nothing architectures offer near-linear scalability. Theoretically, the number of processor nodes is limited only by the hardware platform limitations (and budgetary constraints), and each node itself can be a powerful SMP system. However, the shared-nothing distributed-memory architecture is the most difficult to implement. There are a number of reasons for that difficulty—it requires a new programming paradigm, new operating system or parallel extensions to an existing one, new compilers, new or enhanced programming languages, etc. (See Chap. 3 for more details.) From a parallel DBMS viewpoint, however, a number of issues and requirements are unique to the shared-nothing architecture. These requirements include:

- *Support for function shipping.* Decomposed SQL statements have to be routed to and executed on the processor that has the needed data in order to drastically reduce the interprocessor communications.

- *Parallel join strategies.* A join between two tables is called a *colocated* join when the rows to be joined reside on the same partition. However, if the rows of the two tables reside on different partitions (e.g., are controlled by different processors), a parallel DBMS has to be able to select an effective strategy to perform the join with minimum interprocessor communication traffic. Choices include *redirected* joins, in which the rows of one table are sent to the node where the corresponding rows of another table reside or the matching rows of both tables are sent to a third node to be joined; *repartitioned* joins, where the rows of both tables are repartitioned on the join column and then redirected to enable colocated joins; and *broadcast* joins, where the entire table is sent to all nodes. The data shipment from one processor node to another is an implied requirement for these strategies.

- *Support for data repartitioning.*   When one of the processors or a local disk fails, the DBMS must be able to repartition the database across remaining processor nodes automatically.

- *Query compilation.*   This is the process of selecting an access path throughout the database. The shorter the path, the quicker is the query. The DBMS optimizer uses statistical information about data partitioning, data values, cardinality, indexes, etc. stored in the database catalog to make optimal choices. In a distributed-memory environment, each processor node contains its own database partition and, thus, may have its own database catalog. The DBMS should be able to compile the query on any processor node using both the local and the global catalog.

- *Support for database transactions.*   Since a parallel distributed memory DBMS is in fact a distributed DBMS, it should comply with many of the rules for a distributed DBMS. For example, a global lock manager and global deadlock detection mechanism are required to support database transactions in a distributed-memory system.

- *Support for the single system image of the database environment.*   A parallel DBMS has to be managed as a single logical entity, and must present a consistent view to database administrators and developers regardless of how many processor nodes it is supporting.

8.2.4   Combined architecture

Interserver parallelism of distributed-memory architecture means that each query is parallelized across multiple servers (e.g., processor nodes of the MPP or clusters), while *intraserver parallelism* of the shared-memory architecture means that a query is parallelized within the server (i.e., across multiple processors of an SMP). Clearly, each approach has its own advantages and disadvantages.

A true, flexible, constraint-free architecture should take full advantage of its operating environment and, at the same time, reduce the disadvantages associated with a particular approach. In other words, a combined hardware architecture could be a cluster of SMP nodes (see Chap. 3 for details). Then, a combined parallel DBMS architecture should support interserver parallelism of distributed-memory MPPs and clusters and intraserver parallelism of SMP nodes.

8.3   Parallel RDBMS Features

Data warehouse development requires a good understanding of all architectural components, including the data warehouse DBMS platform. Understanding the basic architecture of warehouse DBMS is the first step in evaluating and selecting a product. Understanding the specific features of the product and how these features are implemented helps users make an intelligent decision when choosing a particular DBMS. First, let's look at what state-of-the-art parallel features the developers and users of the warehouse should demand from the DBMS vendors:

- *Scope and techniques of parallel DBMS operations.*   This includes queries (SQL statements based on the SELECT verb), and other Data Manipulation Language (DML) operations such as INSERT, DELETE, and UPDATE, and DBMS utilities. In queries, many atomic operations (i.e., scan, sort, join) can all be parallelized both horizontally and vertically. Existing DBMS products perform these parallel operations differently—some can parallelize a table scan, but not an index scan; some support vertical parallelism but limit the pipeline to a small number of concurrent tasks. Clearly, the fewer the limitations on parallelism, the better the product can leverage the parallel hardware platform. Similarly, parallel execution of INSERT, DELETE, and UPDATE operations is extremely valuable not only for OLTP but also for query processing; indeed, when a DBMS creates a temporary table to sort or join large tables, an INSERT operation is involved to populate the table. These operations require locking strategies that are optimized for parallel execution. There, a DBMS that uses multiple log files, for example, is better positioned to reduce an update bottleneck. Finally, a DBMS that supports parallel database load, backup, reorganization, and recovery is much better positioned to handle very large databases (VLDBs).

- *Optimizer implementation.*   A cost-based optimizer that is cognizant of the parallel environment and data partitioning will produce an execution plan that is the most efficient and results in the shortest execution path. The optimizer has to be able to recognize the parallel environment it operates in, and automatically invoke strategies best suited for a given situation. For example, different approaches should be taken when a query is executed in a shared-nothing environment, where the main goal is to minimize interprocessor communications, compared with a shared-memory SMP system, in which the interprocessor communications are done via a shared memory and are not nearly as expensive.

- *Application transparency.*   Basically, an application developer should not be aware that the database application is designed for a parallel DBMS environment. At a minimum, a parallel DBMS should not force a developer to modify an existing application to take advantage of the parallel system. That should be true not only for queries but also for DBMS server features such as stored procedures, triggers, and rules.

- *The parallel environment.* This is a complementary requirement to the application transparency. DBMS needs to be aware of the parallel environment. Such an awareness allows the DBMS server to take full advantage of the existing facilities on a very low level.

- *DBMS management tools.* These tools should help configure, tune, administer, and monitor a parallel DBMS as effectively as if it were a serial DBMS. Because a given data-partitioning schema frequently results in unbalanced hot-spot data partitioning, a tool that allows a DBA to repartition the database dynamically could prove invaluable.

- *Price/performance.* In terms of performance and scalability, a parallel DBMS should demonstrate near-linear speed-up and scale-up. The key, however, is to obtain these characteristics at reasonable costs. Industry-standard benchmarks can be used to measure price and performance of a parallel DBMS. Transaction Processing Council's TPC-C measures price and performance of complex transactions, while TPC-D is designed to measure price and performance of decision support queries.

8.4   Alternative Technologies

In addition to parallel database technology, a number of vendors are working on other solutions improving performance in data warehousing environments. These include

- Advanced database indexing products
- Specialized RDBMSs designed specifically for data warehousing
- Multidimensional databases

The multidimensional databases and specialized relational databases are covered in the next chapters that discuss on-line analytical processing (OLAP). This section describes new programming techniques used to speed up relational queries.

Advanced indexing techniques.   A new approach to increasing performance of a relational DBMS is to use innovative indexing techniques to provide rapid direct access to data. SYBASE IQ is an example of a product that uses a bitmapped index structure of the data stored in the SYBASE DBMS. In fact, SYBASE IQ is a database product that accepts queries and attempts to resolve them through its proprietary bitmapped index structures. More information on SYBASE IQ can be found in the next chapter.

Products like this promise increased performance without deploying expensive parallel hardware systems. However, the close relationship between the database data and its index structure may be an obstacle to OLTP processing (indexes need to be rebuilt when the underlying data is changed). This non-updatable nature of the index has a negative effect on scalability.

While the bitmapped indexes significantly accelerate data access, they are best suited for low-cardinality data, and tend to lose their effectiveness for high-cardinality data. It is also unclear how such a technique can handle new data types such as image, voice, and multimedia.

8.5 Parallel DBMS Vendors

This section provides an overview of several vendor's strategies and products for parallel database processing.

8.5.1 Oracle

Oracle supports parallel database processing with its add-on Oracle Parallel Server option (OPS) and Parallel Query Option (PQO). The OPS was originally designed for loosely coupled clusters of shared-disk systems (e.g., VAX-clusters), and it enables multiple instances of Oracle running on multiple computers to share the same data using a distributed cache manager. The PQO is optimized to run on SMPs or in conjunction with the OPS, and is supported on all Oracle platforms except NetWare and OS/2—all these are targeted for the future.

With the acquisition of IRI Software, Oracle now is positioned to offer a comprehensive data warehousing solution that complements its parallel DBMS offering.

Architecture. The fundamental component of Oracle's design is the notion of the virtual shared-disk capability. Oracle considers this point a key that makes almost every hardware platform commercially viable. The Oracle Parallel Server option is required on any distributed-memory platform (MPP or clusters), where the shared-disk software is provided by the operating system vendor. Oracle uses the process-based approach, and has a lot of experience with interquery parallelism. For intraquery parallelism, Oracle offers the extracost PQO. PQO uses a shared-disk architecture which assumes that each processor node has access to all disks. PQO supports parallel execution of queries that include at least one full table scan, user-defined functions, and subselects statements. PQO supports parallel operations such as index build, database load, backup, and recovery. The users have full access to all database functionality in parallel environments.

Data partitioning. Oracle has chosen the approach that allows its customers to move into a parallel environment without having to deal with the administrative overhead of partitioning data. Oracle 7 supports random striping of data across multiple disks. Because of their random nature, partitions cannot be backed up and recovered at the partition level, and Oracle 7 cannot skip partitions that don't contain relevant data. (Data partitioning is significantly improved in Oracle 8.) Oracle supports dynamic data repartitioning, which is done in memory using key range, hash, or round-robin methods to facilitate joins where data spans nodes. Starting with version 7.3, Oracle supports processor affinity, which helps increase locality of reference and thus eliminates a shared-disk overhead in certain workloads.

Parallel operations. Oracle has rectified a number of deficiencies found in releases prior to 7.3. For example, it supports hash joins. Its optimizer is now parallel-aware, and generates a parallel plan instead of a serial plan, which had to be parallelized, although Oracle may execute all queries serially unless two conditions are met: (1) the optimizer must encounter at least one full table scan and (2), the DBMS must be instructed to parallelize operations. The instructions can be specified as a start-up parameter for the Oracle instance, as a parallelization factor assigned by a DBA at a table level, or as optimizer hints that are submitted with each individual query.

The Oracle PQO query coordinator breaks the query into subqueries, and passes these to the corresponding pool server processes. The server processes work in parallel, and return their results to the coordinator for any post-processing. The Oracle PQO can parallelize most SQL operations, including joins, scans, sorts, aggregates, and groupings. In addition, Oracle can parallelize the creation of indexes, database load, backup, and recovery. When executing in parallel, PQO supports both horizontal and vertical parallelism. Vertical parallelism is currently limited to two levels—in a query that contains scan, join, and sort, only two operations can be pipelined.

8.5.2 Informix

Informix Software has partnered with Sequent Computers in reengineering its DBMS engine to build in full parallelism from the ground up (Sequent had an exclusive 6-month window before the product was ported to other platforms). Informix runs on a variety of UNIX platforms, and its release 7 of the product is available on Windows NT. Informix OnLine release 8, also known as *XPS* (eXtended Parallel Server), supports MPP hardware platforms that include IBM SP, AT&T 3600, Sun, HP, and ICL Goldrush, with Sequent, Siemens/Pyramid, and others to follow.

Architecture. Informix developed its Dynamic Scalable Architecture (DSA) to support shared-memory, shared-disk, and shared-nothing models. It is threads-based architecture. Parallel query processing implementation was first available for the shared-memory SMP systems, with other parallel architecture support built into subsequent releases. Informix OnLine release 7 is a shared-memory implementation that supports parallel query processing and intelligent data partitioning. The next release of the product (Informix 8) allows a partitioned table to be distributed across nodes on the network, and is designed to support MPP and clusters. The XPS version of Informix supports distributed-memory architectures and can support shared-disk environments to handle node failures.

Data partitioning.   Informix OnLine 7 supports round-robin, schema, hash, key range, and user-defined partitioning methods. Both data and indexes can be partitioned. The number of partitions is user-defined. Repartition is done dynamically, on line, and in parallel.

Parallel operations.   All database functionality is preserved in parallel versions of the product. Informix OnLine 7 executes queries, INSERTs, and many utilities in parallel. Release 8 adds parallel UPDATEs and DELETEs. Informix supports multiple physical logs on each processing node. Full parallel point-in-time recovery is available. The cost-based optimizer is fully aware of the parallel environments and generates parallel query execution plans.

Partnerships.   Informix has established several strategic relationships that provide added functionality to its product line:

- Data modeling, through its relationship with Prism Solutions.
- Management tools for data extract, transformation, and maintenance, through Prism and Carleton Corp.
- Open systems, through relationships with all the hardware vendors that offer scalable, high-end, open systems hardware solutions.
- Front-end and gateway access—like Oracle and Sybase, Informix has relationships with several vendors, including Business Objects, Inc.; Clear Access/ Fairfield Software; Gupta Technologies; Information Advantage, Inc.; IBI; PowerSoft Corp.; Trinzic Corp.; and Uniface Corp.

8.5.3   IBM

IBM's parallel client/server database product—DB2 Parallel Edition (DB2 PE)—is a database that is based on DB2/6000 server architecture. Originally, DB2 PE was targeted mostly for IBM SP and clusters of RS/6000, all running AIX, although the company may decide to port the product to other platforms in the future. The first release of the product was not optimized to support SMP systems, triggers, and BLOBs. The current version—DB2 Universal Database—aims to close the gap between DB2 PE and functionality-rich DB2/6000 version 2 (see Chap. 4 for more details).

Architecture.   DB2 PE is a shared-nothing architecture in which all data is partitioned across processor nodes. Its version 1.x was process-based as opposed to threads-based. The system comprises a number of coordinator processes and agent processes, each running on different nodes and owning a partition of a database. This approach matches very well with a distributed-memory MPP architecture of single processor IBM SP. It is yet unclear how well it will perform on a system with SMP nodes.

   All database operations and utilities are fully parallelized where possible. IBM internal and some customer benchmarks show that the product demonstrates excellent scalability. Although DB2 PE can run on a LAN-based cluster of RS/6000, its design is optimized for high-performance SP with its very high-speed internal interconnect. True to the shared-nothing architectural model, DB2 PE does not implement a virtual shared disk or a distributed lock manager, although the product can take advantage of shared memory when communicating across virtual nodes on SMP systems. Each DB2 PE instance has its own log, its own memory, and its own storage devices. This allows for easy customization—nodes can be added and deleted relatively quickly. Each node is aware of other nodes and how the data is partitioned.

Data partitioning. DB2 PE supports hash partitioning and *node groups* that allow a table to span multiple nodes. The DBA can choose to partition a table on a table-by-table basis, depending on the application workload. The DBA can rebalance (repartition) data across nodes when nodes are added or deleted, or to improve application access to the database. Rebalancing is done on line. The master system catalog for each database is stored on one node and cached on every other node. Data definition statements are automatically routed to the master catalog node, and changes are cascaded to other nodes.

Parallel operations.   Parallelism is built into the basic architecture. All database operations (query processing, INSERTs, DELETEs, UPDATEs, load, backup, recovery, index creation, table reorganization, etc.) are fully parallelized. Many database utility operations (e.g., load, backup, restore) are done at the partition level. DB2 PE breaks SQL statements into fragments for each node, executing the same low-level processing in a parallel environment that is possible on a single node. DB2 PE's cost-based optimizer is aware of the parallel environment, data partitioning, and the cost of internodal messaging. DB2 PE supports function shipping (preferred) and a variety of join strategies, including colocated, redirected, broadcast, and repartitioned joins.

8.5.4   Sybase

Sybase has implemented its parallel DBMS functionality in a product called *SYBASE MPP* (formerly *Navigation Server*). It was jointly developed by Sybase and NCR (formerly AT&T GIS), and its first release was targeted for the AT&T 3400, 3500 (both SMP), and 3600 (MPP) platforms. AT&T had an exclusive 6-month window before the product was ported to other platforms that include IBM SP, Sun, and HP. Sybase has developed another product aimed at improving DBMS performance—SYBASE IQ (see a brief discussion on advanced indexing technologies in Sec. 8.4)—and now faces the challenge of rationalizing positions of both the SYBASE MPP and SYBASE IQ for data warehousing and VLDB processing.

Architecture.   SYBASE MPP is designed to make multiple distributed SQL Servers look like a single server to the user. It is a shared-nothing system that partitions data across multiple SQL Servers and supports both function shipping and data repartitioning. SYBASE MPP is an Open Server application that operates on top of existing SQL Servers. In other words, the database engine itself (SQL Server) is not aware of the parallel environment; all the knowledge about the environment, data partitions, and parallel query execution is maintained by SYBASE MPP software. Therefore, some server-based features, such as triggers or any cross-server integrity constraints, are difficult to use in this release of the product. This architecture also means that SQL Servers have to send data to a coordinator for the query if, for example, a SQL statement includes a join involving data that is not local to a given SQL Server. Moreover, the query is not decomposed for the parallel environment—the entire SQL statement has to be sent to the SQL Server.

SYBASE MPP performs a unique two-level optimization—SQL statements are always optimized on a global level by SYBASE MPP, and ad hoc queries are also optimized by the individual SQL Servers, which allows SQL Servers to effectively use local indexes. Internal benchmarks and early customer experiences show that SYBASE MPP demonstrates near-linear scalability on shared-nothing AT&T 3600.

SYBASE MPP consists of specialized servers:

- *Data Server*—the smallest executable unit of parallelism that consists of SQL Server, Split Server (performs joins across nodes), and Control Server (coordination of execution and communications). Precompiled parallel plans are translated into appropriate SQL statements in the form of stored procedures for each Data Server.

- *DBA Server*—handles optimization, DDL statements, security, and global system catalog.

- *Administrative Server*—a graphical user interface for managing SYBASE MPP.

In addition to these servers, SYBASE MPP is supplied with the Configurator—a tool for the initial planning and ongoing management of SYBASE MPP configuration and data partitioning based on database design, planned transactions, and performance and capacity requirements. To date, Sybase is the only vendor that offers automated user assistance in designing parallel databases.

Data partitioning. SYBASE MPP supports hash, key range, and schema partitioning. Indexes are partitioned to match their table partitioning. Each SQL Server maintains its own local indexes and statistics.

Parallel operations. All SQL statements and utilities are executed in parallel across SQL Servers, but in the first release of the product, all processing at the SQL Server level remains serial. Therefore, SYBASE MPP supports horizontal parallelism, but the vertical parallelism support is limited to the capabilities of the SQL Server engine (a more robust vertical parallelism becomes available with SYBASE System 11 internal parallel capabilities).

8.5.5 Microsoft

SQL Server (version 6.5 is the current version at the time of this writing) has the least parallel functionality of the big 5 RDBMS vendors, and, because it is based only on Windows NT, it is totally dependent on NT development organizations within Microsoft to bring the NT's parallel capabilities to match the best UNIX operating systems. Beginning with Windows NT 3.5.1, SQL Server 6 was able to provide interquery parallelism and scalability for up to four processors on an SMP hardware.

SQL Server architecture is shared-everything design optimized for SMP systems. SQL Server is tightly integrated with the NT operating system threads, and thus its scalability is highly dependent on NT scalability beyond four processors. Windows NT version 4 is designed to provide scalability for up to eight processors. Scalability beyond the eight processors is being addressed via Microsoft's cluster strategy, which proposes to link groups of four-processor SMP systems (such as Intel's Pentium Pro motherboard) together in NT clusters. The first stage of the cluster development is being done by Microsoft with its hardware partners such as Compaq, Digital, HP, NCR, and Tandem (known as the *Wolfpack group*), and its first implementation on Compaq and Digital running SQL Server 6.5 became available in 1996. This is a two-node, shared-disk hardware model, but since SQL Server does not support shared-disk software models, it cannot provide concurrent database access from the two nodes. Instead, it provides a good failover capability between servers and nodes.

The next stage of NT cluster development relies on shared-nothing NT cluster hardware and the NT environment. Microsoft has licensed many of Tandem's patents for shared-nothing software, and will develop a shared-nothing version of SQL Server.

8.5.6 Other RDBMS products

The vendor products discussed here represent a significant part of the parallel DBMS market. However, this market is not limited to these products. In fact, several established vendors and products have been developing parallel database solutions for a number of years. Let's look at two vendors: Teradata and Tandem.

NCR Teradata. Teradata, introduced in 1983, initially ran only on specialized platforms, although NCR has recently moved it to UNIX, and the current version runs on NCR 4500 and 5100S (SMP machines). Teradata employs hardware components as part of its architecture, and has been traditionally seen as a proprietary architecture, although it demonstrates very good scalability. Its architecture is a mature, fully parallel shared-nothing architecture that resembles SYBASE Navigation Server, but is enhanced by leveraging hardware design. Its main drawback is its high cost and lack of DBMS functionality useful in OLTP environments. The Teradata RDBMS version 2 no longer relies on proprietary hardware, but is still limited to Intel processors and UNIX SVR4 (System V release 4). Although still shared-nothing in design, Teradata can now operate on shared-memory systems (NCR 4500 and 5100S), shared-disk clusters (NCR 5100C), and shared-nothing systems (NCR 5100M). Teradata has been successfully used for very large decision support systems. For example, Teradata supports Wal-Mart's multiterabyte data warehouse for optimizing inventory.

Tandem NonStop SQL/MP. This is the latest version of Tandem's NonStop SQL RDBMS. Introduced in 1987, NonStop SQL was optimized for high-performance OLTP applications and high availability—fault tolerance was always Tandem's trademark. This focus on high availability led to development parallel database utilities that were fast and dynamic; the database remains available at all times. NonStop SQL/MP is closely tied to and runs on Tandem's proprietary NonStop operating kernel and Himalaya distributed-memory servers. Similar to Teradata, despite its proprietary nature, NonStop SQL/MP is a mature parallel DBMS product. It uses a shared-nothing architecture, supports key range partitioning on the primary key, and parallelizes queries, other DML functions, and utilities. Log files are also partitioned, so that the concurrency is high and the recovery is fully parallel. The optimizer is aware of the environment and can generate both serial and parallel plans—it is designed to choose the lowest-cost option. Data can be repartitioned dynamically in memory to optimize join or to parallelize a previously nonpartitioned table. NonStop SQL/MP is a highly scalable parallel RDBMS that is well suited both for decision support processing against large databases and high-throughput OLTP. In fact, Tandem has published audited TPC-C benchmark results that demonstrated almost 100 percent linear scalability in supporting a large number of concurrent users on the database size reaching 1.3 Tbytes. The major weaknesses of NonStop SQL/MP include its lack of standards compliance (at the time of this writing, NonStop SQL conformed to SQL89, not SQL92) and the fact that it currently runs only on Tandem's proprietary Himalaya platforms.

8.5.7 Specialized database products

The two products described as follows represent software (Red Brick) and hardware (White Cross) approaches to specialized data warehouses.

Red Brick Systems. Red Brick Warehouse is an example of a specialized multirelational approach to multidimensional requirements of modern data warehousing. Red Brick offers a relational data warehouse product specialized for decision support. The product is designed for query-intensive environments. Red Brick Warehouse consists of three components:

- *Table Management Utility,* a high-performance load subsystem that loads and indexes operational data
- Database Server, which stores and manages the warehoused information

- *RISQL Entry Tool,* an interactive query tool that provides decision support extensions and direct user access to the Red Brick Warehouse database

Red Brick Warehouse is architected to work with very large databases (500+ Gbytes), and can load and index data at up to 1 Gbyte/h. Incremental load capabilities update the Red Brick Warehouse with only the most current data.

Red Brick supports specialized indexes that include traditional B-Tree, STAR, and PATTERN index structures. STAR indexes are built automatically when tables are created, and maintain relationships between primary and foreign keys using a STAR schema approach (see Chap. 9). PATTERN indexes are fully inverted text indexes that greatly reduce search time for partial character string matching. RISQL provides access to data stored in the Red Brick Warehouse and offers SQL extensions via functions such as rankings, running averages, and cumulative totals, which are necessary for data analysis and decision support. RISQL Reporter is a report generator that provides enhanced report formatting, columnar formatting, and batch reporting capabilities.

Red Brick follows the ISO SQL 92 standard and has strategic relationships with Sequent, IBM, Sun, Sybase, and HP as well as many of the tool suppliers through a variety of relationship programs (Prism Solutions, Brio Technology, Trinzic, Microsoft, Clear Access, HP, Pilot Software, etc.).

White Cross Systems Inc.   White Cross Systems, a U.K.-based firm, offers a massively parallel processing (MPP) data server as a specialized means of handling a data warehouse. Its WX 9020 system features over 300 processors, 6 Gbytes of memory, 120 Gbytes of mass storage, and the capability to add additional WX 9020 systems to scale up to meet performance or I/O constraints. The mass storage uses RAID technology. A separate communications processor lets the WX 9020 run as a separate server, interacting with user applications using standard SQL.

DBMS Schemas for Decision Support

As a natural outgrowth of tremendous progress in the automation of operational systems, businesses in almost every industry have begun to implement data warehouses. Having found that they possess a wealth of untapped data, these businesses are using data warehouses to unlock these treasure chests of information.

However, some of the methods and tools that served so well to create operational systems are not nearly as well suited to the different demands of the data warehouse. This is particularly true in the field of relational database management systems (RDBMSs). Traditional on-line transaction processing (OLTP) database systems were simply not designed to suit data warehousing requirements (this was briefly discussed in Chaps. 6 to 8). Data warehousing projects were forced to choose between a data model and a corresponding database schema that is intuitive for analysis but performs poorly and a model-schema that performs better but is not well suited for analysis. As data warehousing continued to mature, new approaches to schema design resulted in schemas better suited to the business analysis that is so crucial to successful data warehousing. The schema methodology that is gaining widespread acceptance for data warehousing is the *star* schema. This chapter provides a brief overview of this methodology and its benefits and describes the performance problems that result when traditional OLTP RDBMSs are used to process queries involving star schemas. In addition, this chapter also describes other innovative approaches to implementing data warehouse databases, including bitmapped indexing and columnwise storage techniques. All these technologies are illustrated in the examples of various vendor implementations, including Red Brick Systems, Oracle, and Sybase.

9.1   Data Layout for Best Access

Businesses across all industries have developed considerable expertise in implementing efficient operational systems such as payroll, inventory tracking, and purchasing. Indeed, the original objectives in developing an abstract model known as the *relational model* were to address a number of shortcomings of nonrelational database management and application development. For example, the early database systems were complex to develop and difficult to understand, install, maintain, and use. The required skill set was expensive, difficult to attain, and in short supply.

Since the relational model is based on mathematical principles and predicate logic, existing relational database management systems (RDBMSs) offer powerful solutions for a wide variety of commercial and scientific applications. From the IT viewpoint, a key element of the database design expertise is focused on developing data modeling and relational database schema so that the corresponding RDBMS can achieve maximum operational efficiency.

The typical requirements for the RDBMS supporting operational systems are based on the need to effectively support a large number of small but simultaneous read and write requests. Database schema definition often focuses on maximizing concurrency and optimizing insert, update, and delete performance by defining relational tables that map very efficiently to operational requests while minimizing contention for access to individual records.

The demands placed on the RDBMS by a data warehouse are very different. A data warehouse RDBMS typically needs to process queries that are large, complex, ad hoc, and data-intensive. Not only are there significant technological differences in how these systems consume computing resources, but the nature of what is being done requires a fundamentally different approach to defining the database schema.

Indeed, solving modern business problems such as market analysis and financial forecasting requires query-centric database schemas that are array-oriented and *multidimensional* in nature. These business problems are characterized by the need to retrieve large numbers of records from very large data sets (hundreds of gigabytes and even terabytes) and summarize them on the fly.

9.2   Multidimensional Data Model

The multidimensional nature of business questions is reflected in the fact that, for example, marketing managers are no longer satisfied by asking simple one-dimensional questions such as "How much revenue did the new product generate?" Instead, they ask questions such as "How much revenue did the new product generate by month, in the northeastern division, broken down by user demographic, by sales office, relative to the previous version of the product, compared with the plan?"—a six-dimensional question. One way to look at the multidimensional data model is to view it as a cube (see Chap. 13 for more details). The multidimensional cube is the foundation of the multidimensional database technology that is not relational by nature. This technology is discussed in more detail in Chap. 13. Since we have stated that the major database technology for data warehousing is the relational database (RDBMS), this chapter will look at the database schema design as it pertains to relational database technology.

9.3   Star Schema

The multidimensional view of data that is expressed using relational database semantics is provided by the database schema design called *star schema*. The basic premise of star schemas is that information can be classified into two groups: facts and dimensions. *Facts* are the core data element being analyzed. For example, *units* of individual items sold are facts, while dimensions are attributes about the facts. For example, *dimensions* are the product types purchased and the date of purchase (see Fig. 9.1).

Asking the business question against this schema is much more straightforward because we are looking up specific facts (UNITS) through a set of dimensions (MARKETS, PRODUCTS, PERIOD). It's important to notice that, in the typical star schema, the fact table is much larger than any of its dimension tables. This point becomes an important consideration of the performance issues associated with star schemas.

Consider a typical business analysis problem: Find the share of total sales represented by each product in different markets, categories, and periods, compared with the same period a year ago. To do so, you would calculate the percentage each number is of the total of its column, a simple and common

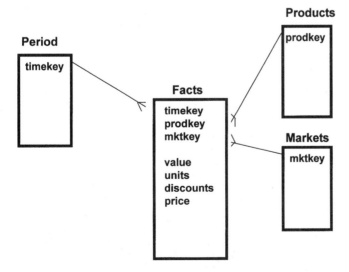

Facts Table primary key = {timekey:prodkey:mktkey}

Figure 9.1   Star schema.

concept. However, in a classic relational database these calculations and display would require definition of a separate view, requiring over 20 SQL commands. The star schema is designed to overcome this limitation of the two-dimensional relational model.

9.3.1   DBA viewpoint

A star schema is a relational schema organized around a central table (fact table) joined to a few smaller tables (dimensional tables) using foreign key references. The *fact table* contains raw numeric items that represent relevant business facts (price, discount values, number of units sold, dollar value, etc.). The facts are typically additive and are accessed via dimensions. Since the fact tables are presummarized and aggregated along business dimensions, these tables tend to be very large.

Smaller tables are the *dimensional tables,* which define business dimension in terms already familiar to the users. These dimensional tables contain a non-compound primary key (mktkey, timekey, etc.) and are heavily indexed. Dimensional tables typically represent the majority of the data elements. These tables appear in constraints and GROUP BY clauses, and are joined to the fact table using foreign key references. Typical dimensions are time periods, geographic and demographic regions, products, promotions and discounts, sales representatives, office numbers, account numbers, vendors, distributors, etc.

Once the star schema database is defined and loaded, the queries that answer questions similar to the one described here are relatively simple, and, what's more, the actual database work to arrive at the answer is minimal compared to a standard relational model.

A star schema can be created for every industry—consumer packaged goods, retail, telecommunications, transportation, insurance, health care, manufacturing, banking, etc.

9.3.2   Potential performance problems with star schemas

Although most experts agree that star schemas are the preferred modeling method for data warehousing, there are a number of RDBMS issues associated with star schema implementation. In general, if a query-centric star schema is hosted on a traditional RDBMS optimized for OLTP processing, the result may be poor performance.

Indexing.   As every DBA knows, using indexes can enforce the uniqueness of the keys, and can also improve read performance. Since the tables in the star schema design typically contain the entire hierarchy of attributes (e.g., in a PERIOD dimension, this hierarchy could be *day* → *week* → *month* → *quarter* → *year*), one approach is to create a multipart key of day, week, month, quarter, year. While this approach is acceptable in normalized designs, it presents some problems in the star schema model:

- It requires multiple metadata definitions (one for each key component) to define a single relationship (table); this adds to the design complexity, and sluggishness in performance.

- Since the fact table must carry all key components as part of its primary key, addition or deletion of levels in the hierarchy will require physical modification of the affected table, which is a time-consuming process that limits flexibility.

- Carrying all the segments of the compound dimensional key in the fact table increases the size of the index, thus impacting both performance and scalability.

One alternative to the compound key is to concatenate the keys into a single key (e.g., the key contains all the attributes—day, week, month, quarter, year). This approach solves the first two problems, but the size of the index still remains a problem. The best approach is to drop the use of "meaningful" keys in favor of using an artificial, *generated* key, which is the smallest possible key that will ensure the uniqueness of each record. Note that the meaningful keys (day, week, etc.) do not need to disappear; they can simply be moved to nonkey attributes. The resulting star schema design consists of a single fact table, with a primary key that has only one key column per dimension, where each key is a generated key. The generated key approach allows for the highest levels of flexibility, low maintenance, and highest possible performance.

Level indicator.   Another potential problem with the star schema design is that in order to navigate the dimensions successfully, the dimensional table design often includes a level of hierarchy indicator for every record. Every query that is retrieving detail records from a table that stores details and aggregates must use this indicator as an additional constraint to obtain a correct result. The level is a useful tool for the environments that are tightly controlled by the DBA and DA staff, and very few ad hoc queries are allowed. If the user is not aware of the level indicator, or its values are incorrect, the otherwise valid query may result in a totally invalid answer.

The best alternative to using the level indicator is the *snowflake* schema. In this schema, aggregate fact tables are created separately from detail tables. In addition to the main fact tables the snowflake schema contains separate fact tables for each level of aggregation, thus making it impossible to make a mistake of selecting PRODUCT detail record when querying PRODUCT-SUMMARY table. Of course, the snowflake schema is even more complicated than a star schema, and often requires multiple SQL statements to get an answer.

Other problems with the star schema design.   While the potential problems described above are by and large the schema design problems, and can be addressed by the DBA and DA staff, the next set of problems are related to the relational DBMS engine and optimization technology.

Pairwise join problem. As was stated previously, traditional OLTP RDBMS engines are not designed for the rich set of complex queries that can be issued against a star schema. In particular, the need to retrieve related information from several tables in a single query—"join processing"—is severely limited. Many OLTP RDBMSs can join only two tables at a time. If a complex join involves more than two tables, the RDBMS needs to break the query into a series of pairwise joins. Pairwise joining was not a severe limitation for the simple requests that dominated OLTP databases; however, such join techniques cannot perform adequately in a data warehouse environment. The limitation of the pairwise join is best illustrated in an example. Using our example star schema (Fig. 9.1), if you wanted to list the share of total sales represented by each product in different markets, categories, and periods, you would need to join data from four tables: FACTS, PERIODS, MARKETS, and PRODUCTS. A traditional OLTP RDBMS would have to select two tables to join initially, say, PRODUCTS and FACTS. These two tables would be joined, and an intermediate result consisting of PRODUCTS joined to FACTS would be generated. This intermediate join result would be joined with another table, perhaps MARKETS, to produce another intermediate join result. This process would continue, generating a number of intermediate results in order to generate the full result. These intermediate results can be large and very costly to create. When it comes to dealing with complex queries, traditional OLTP RDBMSs face even worse problems because the order in which the joins are done dramatically affects query performance. As an extreme example, if the join of MARKETS to FACTS results in the selection of only a single record, subsequent joins would be joining only this one record. However, if FACTS is joined to PRODUCTS first, an intermediate result might be generated that contains every single row in FACTS. Because selecting the order of the pairwise joins can have such a dramatic performance impact, traditional OLTP RDBMS optimizers spend a lot of CPU cycles in the effort to find the best order in which to execute those joins.

Unfortunately, because the number of combinations to be evaluated grows exponentially with the number of tables being joined, the problem of selecting the best order of pairwise joins rarely can be solved in a reasonable amount of time. As was shown by Kiyoshi Ono and Guy M. Lohman in their publication "Measuring the Complexity of Join Enumeration in Query Optimization" (*Proceedings of the 16th VLDB Conference,* Brisbane, Australia; Aug. 13–16, 1990), the number of ways to pairwise join a set of N tables is $N!$ (N factorial). For example, a five-table query has $5! = (6 \times 5 \times 4 \times 3 \times 2 \times 1) = 120$ combinations. For a 7-table query, there would be $(7 \times 6 \times 5 \times 4 \times 3 \times 2 \times 1) = 5040$ combinations; for a 10-table query, there would be 3,628,800 combinations; and so on. Clearly the number of combinations that the RDBMS optimizer needs to evaluate can grow very quickly.

Even these numbers are misleading because when evaluating a join between two tables, the RDBMS optimizer may have many different join algorithms with which the tables could be joined. Each of these algorithms may need to be evaluated for every combination. For example, if there are five possible join algorithms, the RDBMS may need to evaluate $10! \times 5 = \sim 18$ million combinations for a 10-table query. This problem is so serious that some databases will not run a query that tries to join too many tables. Also, a typical RDBMS will decide the order in which to do the pairwise joins (i.e., will select a query plan) before the query begins to execute, thus delaying the execution of a query even further.

Star schema join problem.   Because the number of pairwise join combinations is often too large to fully evaluate, many RDBMS optimizers limit the selection on the basis of a particular criterion, often by picking combinations of tables that are directly related. Using our example star schema, this criterion would say that joining FACTS and PRODUCTS tables would be preferable to joining PRODUCTS and MARKETS. This strategy works reasonably well with traditional OLTP schemas that contain a rich network of interrelated tables, but unfortunately, in a data warehousing environment this strategy is very inefficient for star schemas. Indeed, in a typical star schema, the only table directly related to most other tables is the fact table. This means that the fact table is a natural candidate for the first pairwise join.

Unfortunately, the fact table is typically the very largest table in the query, so this strategy invariably leads to selecting a pairwise join order that generates a very large intermediate result set. Generating large intermediate result sets severely affects query performance.

Underlying these performance issues is the assumption that the RDBMS can accurately select the best of two pairwise join orderings for the limited set of orderings to be evaluated. Unfortunately, in a typical RDBMS optimized for OLTP, the query is analyzed and the plan is selected on the basis of estimates of how large the intermediate results will be. These estimates are derived from statistics gathered from the data itself, and are often imprecise. As in any computational environment, the propagation of errors only makes matters worse; an error in the first estimate is magnified with each new estimate, so even the smallest errors become tremendously magnified. The net effect is that, more often than not, the traditional RDBMS may dismiss the optimal ordering as being too costly because of errors in the cost estimation process.

9.3.3   Solutions to performance problems

The performance problems associated with the way relational DBMS technology is implemented, have been addressed by the RDBMS vendors with various degrees of success, although some of these solutions are constrained by the very infrastructures that have made these RDBMSs so successful in OLTP applications.

A common optimization that provides some relief for the star schema join problem is to look at more combinations of pairwise join orderings. All major RDBMS vendors, including Sybase, Informix, CA Ingres, Oracle, and Teradata, implement this minimal enhancement. The basic idea of this optimization is to get around the pairwise join strategy of selecting only related tables. In other words, the optimization strategy allows these products to join unrelated tables.

When two tables are joined and no columns "link" the tables, every combination of the two tables' rows are produced. In terms of relational algebra, this is called a *cartesian product*. For example, if the PRODUCTS table had two rows ("bolts," "nut") and the MARKETS table had three rows ("East," "West," "Central"), the cartesian product would contain six rows: "bolt"/"East," "bolt"/"West," "bolt"/"Central," "nut"/"East," "nut"/"West," and "nut"/"Central."

Normally, the RDBMS optimizer logic would never consider cartesian products as reasonable pairwise join candidates, but for star schemas, considering these cartesian products sometimes improves query performance. Generating cartesian products can sometimes improve query performance because the fact table in a star schema is typically much larger than its dimension tables. Remember that one of the problems with selecting related tables to join is that the fact table is chosen very early on for a pairwise join. This can be a very bad choice because a very large intermediate result may be generated because of the sheer size of the fact table. Alternatively, if a cartesian product of all dimension tables is first generated (by successive pairwise joins), the join to the fact table can be deferred until the very end. The key benefit is that the large fact table does not find its way into any of the intermediate join results. The key cost is the need to generate the cartesian product of the dimension tables. As long as the cost of generating the cartesian product is less than the cost of generating intermediate results with the fact table, this optimization has some benefit.

Unfortunately, this simple optimization does not solve all performance problems. This strategy is viable only if the cartesian product of dimension rows selected is much smaller than the number of rows in the fact table. For example, if there were 20,000 PRODUCTS rows, 300 MARKETS rows, and 3,000 DATE rows, the final intermediate result size could be $20,000 \times 300 \times 3,000 = {\sim}18,000,000,000$ rows! Using this strategy, the query processing would probably take a very long time to complete, and the RDBMS would be better off by using the more traditional pairwise join ordering. In other words, the multiplicative nature of the cartesian join makes the optimization helpful only for relatively small problems. Unfortunately, a typical data warehouse is not small. Therefore, it is only natural that a growing number of RDBMS vendors use hardware and software parallelism as the answer to these problems (parallel RDBMS technologies are discussed in Chap. 8). Parallelism appears particularly attractive in light of the maturity and availability of high-performance parallel systems, including symmetric multiprocessing (SMP) and massively parallel processing (MPP) systems. As was discussed in Chap. 8, parallelism can help reduce the execution time of a single query (speed-up) or handle additional work without degrading execution time (scale-up). Unfortunately, parallelism can only reduce—not eliminate—the performance degradation issues related to star schemas. When applied to traditional brute-force pairwise join strategies, parallel RDBMS tries to solve the performance problem by throwing enough computing resources at the problem to make execution time bearable. This brute-force approach has its limitations. For example, assume that the best pairwise algorithm processes a certain multitable query in 500 s. Assuming that this algorithm is perfectly parallelizable, on a 10-

CPU multiprocessor system it would process the query in 50 s. If, on the other hand, the original serial query processing takes 50,000 s, its parallelization would yield the execution time of 5000 (almost 2 h). Therefore, parallelism alone may not be sufficient to optimize star schema processing. The next section looks at some schema innovations that help alleviate the performance problems discussed above. We will discuss these innovations on the example of the technologies pioneered by one of the data warehousing vendors: Red Brick.

9.4 STARjoin and STARindex

Despite the seriousness of the performance problems inherited in a traditional star schema processing, the relational model is nevertheless well suited to data warehousing. That fact is reinforced by the realities of SQL standardization, the wealth of RDBMS-related tools, and available expertise. In short, a RDBMS is the natural choice for the data repository of the data warehouse.

The question is how to come up with a new way to efficiently process complex queries against data warehouse databases without suffering from the performance and optimization problems discussed in the previous section. The answer may be an RDBMS design that implements parallelizable multitable joins in a single pass. One RDBMS that has implemented such a solution is Red Brick's RDBMS. Red Brick calls this technique the STARjoin (trademark).

A *STARjoin* is a high-speed, single-pass, parallelizable multitable join. Red Brick's RDBMS can join more than two tables in a single operation. Moreover, even when joining only two tables, STARjoin outperforms many join methods implemented by traditional OLTP RDBMSs.

The core technology in STARjoin is an innovative approach to indexing. The use of indexes to accelerate query processing has long been a standard capability incorporated into all RDBMS products. When indexes are defined on selected columns of a table and the query selectivity is limited to those columns, the RDBMS can use the index to very quickly identify the rows of interest.

Red Brick's RDBMS supports the creation of specialized indexes, called *STARindexes,* to dramatically accelerate join performance. The STARindexes are different from traditional index structures like B-tree or bitmap indexes. STARindexes are created on one or more foreign key columns of a fact table. Unlike traditional indexes that contain information to translate a column value to a list of rows with that value, a STARindex contains highly compressed information that relates the dimensions of a fact table to the rows that contain those dimensions. STARindexes are very space-efficient; therefore, they can be built and maintained very rapidly.

The presence of a STARindex allows Red Brick's RDBMS to rapidly identify which target rows of the fact table are of interest for a particular set of dimensions. Also, because STARindexes are created over foreign keys, no assumptions are made about the type of queries which can use the STARindex. In other words, STARindexes do not constrain the kind of queries or types of joins that can be done, but accelerate queries that join related tables.

There are few similarities and some significant differences between STARindexes and traditional multicolumn indexes. One difference is that a typical multicolumn index references a single table whereas the STARindex can reference multiple tables. Another key difference is that, with multicolumn indexes, if a query's WHERE clause does not constrain on all the columns in the composite index, the index cannot be fully used unless the specified columns are a leading subset.

For example, a composite index on columns A, B, and C can be used if the query constrains are contiguous from left to right. In other words, the index will be used if the query constrains include columns A, B, and C; if columns A and B are constrained; or if just A is constrained; but not if columns A and C are constrained. Unlike multicolumn indexes, the STARindex can be fully utilized regardless of patterns of constraint processing. Additionally, to overcome some inherent issues of key ordering, Red Brick supports the creation and maintenance of any number of STARindexes on a table to ensure that an optimal index is always available.

Given the power and flexibility of STARindexes, the STARjoin algorithm can make use of their existence to efficiently identify all the rows required for a particular join. For example, instead of generating a full cartesian product of dimension tables, which then can be joined to the fact table, the STARjoin using STARindex could efficiently join the dimension tables to the fact table without the penalty of generating the full cartesian product. This is because the STARindex allows the STARjoin to quickly identify which regions of the cartesian product space contain rows of interest (in much the same way that a B-tree index can quickly identify which rows contain column values of interest). The STARjoin algorithm thus is able to generate a cartesian product in regions where there are rows of interest and bypass generating cartesian products over regions where there are no rows.

To better understand the significant performance benefit of STARjoins, consider this example. Assume that there are 500 possible PRODUCTS, 200 MARKETS, 300 PERIODS, and one million FACTS in the data warehouse database. Further assume that a particular query selects 50 PRODUCTS, 20 MARKETS, and 30 PERIODS that ultimately will select 1000 of the FACTS.

A traditional pairwise join strategy would generate 111,000 rows. A cartesian product would perform better in generating $50 \times 20 \times 30 = 30,000$ intermediate rows plus 1000 FACTS rows—31,000 rows.

A well-constrained STARjoin would actually generate only slightly more combinations than exist in the selected rows of the FACTS table—on average about 10 percent more for a total cost of $1000 + (1000 \times 10 \text{ percent}) = 1100$ rows. Even though a row count represents a very imprecise method of determining the cost of a query, it provides a good way to compare the costs of the approaches.

Red Brick claims that its RDBMS, using proprietary STARjoin technology, can perform the multitable joins typical of data warehouse applications 10 to

20 times faster than traditional pairwise join techniques. And for very large data warehouses, where even these levels of performance are insufficient, Red Brick supports a fully parallel STARjoin.

The ability of STARjoin to join multiple tables in a single pass simplifies the selection of an execution plan. However, the possible presence of multistar indexes complicates the solution of selecting the best index to accelerate a given query. The Red Brick RDBMS solves this problem by supporting an incremental optimization model. The basic idea is to determine which sections of the query can be reasonably estimated and then run them. The actual (not estimated) results of this step are used to estimate the next step, eliminating the problem of propagating estimation errors. The query plan can even change in midquery if the actual data is radically different from statistics used to compose the original estimate. Red Brick's RDBMS uses this technique to select the appropriate STARindex only after it has become clear how many rows there are in the dimension tables to be joined. The resulting index selection is far better than could be achieved with an estimation approach to optimization.

Moreover, this technique controls the degree of parallelism by allowing the RDBMS to assign parallel processing only to the large queries and let the small queries run without parallelism; this approach makes the most efficient use of system resources.

9.5 Bitmapped Indexing

A new approach to increasing performance of a relational DBMS is to use innovative indexing techniques to provide rapid direct access to data. SYBASE IQ is an example of a product that uses a bitmapped index structure of the data stored in the SYBASE DBMS.

9.5.1 SYBASE IQ

SYBASE IQ is based on the indexing technology developed by Expressway Technologies, which Sybase acquired in 1994. After devoting almost 2 years to improvements in performance and tight integration with SQL Server technology and interfaces, Sybase has released SYBASE IQ as a stand-alone database that is targeted as an "ideal" data mart solution that is optimized to handle multiuser ad hoc queries.

Overview. SYBASE IQ is not just a bitmap index running in a relational database; it is a separate SQL database. Data is loaded into SYBASE IQ very much as into any relational DBMS. Once loaded, SYBASE IQ converts all data into a series of bitmaps, which are then highly compressed and stored on disk. SYBASE IQ can satisfy all SQL queries within its own engine. Unlike other bitmap index implementations, SYBASE IQ indexes do not point to data stored elsewhere—all data is contained in the index structure.

Sybase positions SYBASE IQ as a read-only database for data marts, with a practical size limitation currently placed at 100 Gbytes (note that there is no theoretical limit to the database size that SYBASE IQ can support).

Sybase engineers claim that SYBASE IQ does not require special schemas to operate efficiently in decision support environments. However, it was the experience of many SYBASE IQ early users that the product is more effective on denormalized tables that at the extreme resemble star schema designs.

Data cardinality. In general, bitmap indexes are used to optimized queries against low-cardinality data—that is, data in which the total number of potential values is relatively low. For example, state code data cardinality is 50 (50 potential values), and gender cardinality is only 2 (male and female). For low-cardinality data, each distinct value has its own bitmap index consisting of a bit for every row in the table. If the bit for a given index is "on," the value exists in the record (see Fig. 9.2). Here, a 10,000-row employee table that contains the "gender" column is bitmap-indexed for this value. The bitmap index representation is a 10000-bit-long vector, which has its bits turned on (value of 1) for every record that satisfies "gender" = "M" condition.

Bitmap indexes can become cumbersome and even unsuitable for high-cardinality data where the range of potential values is high. For example, values like "income" or "revenue" may have an almost infinite number of values. One obvious solution is to express these types of data in ranges of values, such as $10 to $50 and $51 to $100. Unfortunately, this approach limits the capabilities of bitmap indexes, and often is not effective or meaningful to solve particular business problems. Another solution is to use traditional B-tree index

Empl-Id	Gender	Last name	First Name	Address
1001234	M	Smith	John	10 Main Street
1001235	F	Johnson	Mary	20 Broadway
1001237	F	Anders	Cathy	7 Broad Street
1002456	M	Peter	Steve	44 Tall Blvd.

1 0 0 1 1 1 0 0 0 1 0 1 0 1 1 0 0 0 1 1 1 1 0 0 1 0 0 1 0 1 0 0 0 1

Record 1
Record 2

Record N

Figure 9.2 Bitmap index.

structures. However, the B-tree indexes can often grow to large sizes because as the data volumes and the number of indexes grow, they require frequent maintenance as data is added to, updated, or deleted from the database. Finally, B-tree indexes can significantly improve the query performance if the query type is known in advance, and the index is built to reflect the known access path. The B-tree index could be quite ineffective for ad hoc queries typical of data warehousing applications.

SYBASE IQ uses a patented technique called Bit-Wise (Sybase trademark) technology to build bitmap indexes for high-cardinality data. The technique is so advanced that where most traditional bitmap index techniques are limited to about 250 distinct values for high-cardinality data, the SYBASE IQ high-cardinality index starts at 1000 distinct values!

Index types.   The first release of SYBASE IQ provides five index techniques (subsequent releases may discontinue one of the indexes). Selecting the right index depends on the cardinality of the data and how the data is accessed. Most users apply two indexes to every column. One is a default index called the *Fast Projection index,* and the other is either a low- or high-cardinality index.

For low-cardinality data SYBASE IQ provides.

- *Low Fast index,* which is optimized for queries involving scalar functions like SUM, AVERAGE, and COUNTS

- *Low Disk index,* which is optimized for disk space utilization at the cost of being more CPU-intensive

Similarly, for high-cardinality data, SYBASE IQ supports High Group and High Non-Group indexes. Both support aggregates and range retrieval queries, but the High Group index is additionally optimized to support GROUP BY queries.

Performance.   SYBASE IQ technology achieves very good performance on ad hoc queries for several reasons:

- *Bitwise technology.*   This allows rapid response to queries containing various data types, supports fast data aggregation and grouping, often resolves queries without performing table scans, and can even eliminate ongoing DBA tuning activity due to the inherent high performance.

- *Compression.*   SYBASE IQ uses sophisticated algorithms to compress data into bitmaps. Early users of SYBASE IQ report that data stored in SYBASE IQ occupies about one-fourth the amount of disk storage typically allocated for a traditional RDBMS. Therefore, queries can run faster because SYBASE IQ can hold more data in memory, minimizing expensive I/O operations (note that using 64-bit architectures like Digital's ALPHA 8400 will provide even higher performance to SYBASE IQ).

- *Optimized memory-based processing.*   SYBASE IQ caches data columns in memory according to the nature of user's queries. As an example, for multi-dimensional ad hoc queries SYBASE IQ stored columns that comprise query dimensions in memory, which significantly speeds up the processing.

- *Columnwise processing.*   Unlike many relational database systems on the market (including SYBASE SQL Server), SYBASE IQ scans columns, not rows (see Fig. 9.3). For the low-selectivity queries (those that select only a few attributes from a multiattribute row) the technique of scanning by columns drastically reduces the amount of data the engine has to search.

- *Low overhead.*   As an engine optimized for decision support, SYBASE IQ does not carry an overhead associated with traditional OLTP-designed RDBMS performance. For example, SYBASE IQ does not support two-phase commit and therefore does not incur the additional processing overhead.

- *Large block I/O.*   Block size within SYBASE IQ (prior to compression) can be tuned from 512 bytes to 64 kbytes, so that the system can read as much information as necessary in a single I/O.

- *Operating-system-level parallelism.*   SYBASE IQ breaks low-level operations like sorts, bitmap manipulation, load, and I/O, into nonblocking operations that the operating systems can schedule independently and in parallel. This can leverage multiprocessing capabilities of SMP systems with little performance degradation.

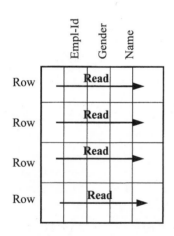

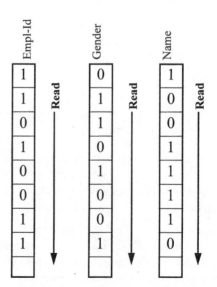

Traditional Row-based processing   **SYBASE IQ Column-wise processing**

Figure 9.3   SYBASE IQ columnwise processing.

- *Prejoin and ad hoc join capabilities.* SYBASE IQ allows users to take advantage of known join relationships between tables by defining them in advance and building indexes between tables. Join indexes are supplemented by a variety of join algorithms, including sort-merge, nested loop, and others.

Also, the DSS Query Processor acts as the intelligent query optimizer that chooses the best available access methods and algorithms for executing each individual query.

Shortcomings of indexing. Although SYBASE IQ provides many advanced unique and truly beneficial features, the product is not perfect. Some of the tradeoffs that users should be aware of when choosing to use SYBASE IQ include

- *No updates.* SYBASE IQ does not support updates, and therefore is unsuitable for applications that require even a small number of updates. Users would have to update the source databases, and then load the updated data into SYBASE IQ on a periodic basis.

- *Lack of core RDBMS features.* Even though it is positioned as a stand-alone database, SYBASE IQ does not support all the robust features of SYBASE SQL Server, such as backup and recovery. Currently, it does not support stored procedures, a fast data-integrity checker, certain types of parallelism, data replication, complex data types, Transact-SQL extensions such as support for positive and negative numbers and many simple calculations, and SQL extensions for user-defined functions like ranking.

- *Less advantageous for planned queries.* SYBASE IQ advantages are most obvious when running ad hoc queries. Even though SYBASE IQ can run exceedingly well on preplanned queries, its advantages here are not as compelling. In a typical preplanned query environment, DBAs optimize the database design to achieve a high level of performance by applying appropriate indexes and denormalizing the database schema.

- *High memory usage.* SYBASE IQ takes advantage of available system memory. Although this is a design point for SYBASE IQ, and its designers consciously traded memory access for the expensive I/O operation, for budgetary and system configuration considerations, this may appear as a constraint.

9.5.2   Conclusion

Products such as SYBASE IQ promise increased performance without deploying expensive parallel hardware systems. However, the close relationship between the database data and its index structure may be an obstacle to OLTP processing (indexes need to be rebuilt when the underlying data is changed). This nonupdatable nature of the index has a negative effect on scalability. As was already stated, while the bitmapped indexes significantly accelerate data access, it is unclear how such a technique can handle new data types such as image, voice, and multimedia.

9.6 Column Local Storage

Another approach to improve query performance in the data warehousing environment has been pioneered by the vendors of parallel systems. For example, Thinking Machines Corporation has developed an innovative data layout solution that improves RDBMS query performance many times. Implemented in its CM-SQL RDBMS product, this approach is based on storing data columnwise, as opposed to traditional rowwise storage.

Indeed, a traditional RDBMS approach to storing data in memory and on the disk is to store it one row at a time, and each row can be viewed and accessed as a single record (see Fig. 9.4). This approach works well for OLTP environments in which a typical transaction accesses a record at a time. However, for a set processing typical of the ad hoc query environment in data warehousing, the goal is to retrieve multiple values of several columns. For example, if a problem is to calculate average, maximum, and minimum salary, the columnwise storage of the salary field requires a DBMS to read only one record (see Fig. 9.4).

Thus, if the database supports columnwise storage, then the desired column value from many rows can be stored as a single physical record in memory and on the hard drive. The benefits are obvious—a single I/O can retrieve a long record containing a subset of the column's domain. Couple this approach with a parallel RDBMS and hardware architecture, and the resulting performance

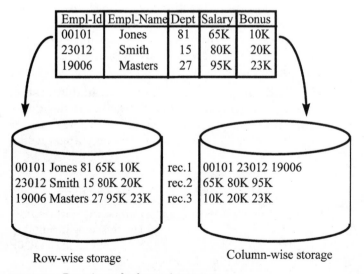

Figure 9.4   Rowwise and columnwise storage.

improvements can be quite drastic. Of course, this approach requires a radical change in the way RDBMS handles physical-to-logical I/O mapping, and works best with low-selectivity queries (a query which contains only a few column names in its SELECT clause). The effectiveness of columnwise storage is reduced where the selectivity approaches 30 percent.

9.7   Complex Data Types

So far, discussion of the best DBMS architecture for data warehousing has been limited to traditional alphanumeric data types. One clearly pronounced trend in data management is the need to support complex data types. These data types include text, image, full-motion video, and sound. The support required is beyond storing these usually large data objects [often called binary large objects (BLOBs)]. What's required by business is much more than just storage; the ability to retrieve the complex data type like an image by its content, the ability to compare the content of one image to another in order to make rapid business decisions, and the ability to express all of this in a single SQL statement are among the emerging requirements for the data warehousing DBMS. In other words, the complex data types that represent complex real-life objects have to be handled like objects, with their behavior encapsulated inside the object or inherited from other objects.

An example of the advantages of handling complex data types is an insurance company that wants to predict its financial exposure during a catastrophe such as a flood. Using a database that can support complex (spatial) data, the company can efficiently query the database to quickly find policyholders whose locations are within the actual or predicted flood zones. And, since all the types of data are within one enterprisewide database, the company can combine this location information with other business data such as value of policies, names of policyholders, and telephone numbers. Thus, the company can quickly deploy the right resources to assist their policyholders and limit the company's financial exposure.

Some new data types are not well served by the B-trees, hashing, and bitmap indexes available from traditional RDBMS vendors. Examples of data poorly served by such indexes include images and 2-D and 3-D geographic (spatial) data for which the standard access methods are ineffective.

The modern data warehouse DBMS has to be able to efficiently store, access, and manipulate complex data types in the database in the same manner as structured data. This is not a trivial undertaking—the DBMS has to be able to define not only new data structures, but also new *functions* that manipulate them, and often, new *access methods* to provide fast access to the data. Without an appropriate access method, manipulating the data is prohibitively slow, even on very fast computers. It also slows linearly (or worse) as the data size increases. Also, adding a new access method to a typical RDBMS is a very complex task that can be performed only by vendor engineering.

The solution is a database system in which new data structures, functions, and access methods can be easily implemented as part of the core DBMS functionality. Such a DBMS is known as *object-relational DBMS* (ORDBMS). In an ORDBMS, data is stored as structures, and the internal details are accessible to functions running in the server. ORDBMS function definitions include instructions to the optimizer about the I/O and CPU cost of the function so that the optimizer can choose an intelligent query plan. Functions execute on the server—close to the data—bringing higher levels of efficiency, because data does not have to be moved out of the server to be manipulated.

An alternative approach is to use the object wrapper technique. Object wrappers attempt to provide object capabilities by layering an object simulator on top of a regular relational DBMS. The problem with an object wrapper is that the optimizer and access methods do not understand the object concepts. There is no way to provide high-performance, content-based queries against complex data. In addition, the simulator layer has to create the objects at run time, using only classic RDBMS technology, which is an expensive and slow operation. Often, this will force an object wrapper to perform multiple slow table scans because it is unable to express the query efficiently to the underlying RDBMS.

Support for complex data types is a horizontal technology with broad applications in many vertical market segments. For example, spatial information technology is pivotal to the retail market, real estate, banking, insurance, and horizontal business applications, including data warehousing and mission-critical systems. To put it briefly, the support for spatial data is a key requirement of any information system in which location is an important part of the decision-making process. Vendors who are capable of supporting these kinds of requirements include Oracle, with its Spatial Data Option and ConText Option; Informix, with the Informix Universal Server with DataBlades; and IBM, with Universal Database and its SQL extenders (see Chap. 5 for more details on these products).

10

Data Extraction, Cleanup, and Transformation Tools

As a key component of the data warehouse architecture, the set of tools that support data sourcing, extraction, cleanup, and transformation represents a critical success factor for any data warehouse project. This chapter looks at the requirements for these kinds of tools, and analyzes a number of vendor solutions available in the market.

10.1 Tool Requirements

The tools that enable sourcing of the proper data contents and formats from operational and external data stores into the data warehouse have to perform a number of important tasks that include

- Data transformation from one format to another on the basis of possible differences between the source and the target platforms.

- Data transformation and calculation based on the application of the business rules that force certain transformations. Examples are calculating age from the date of birth, or replacing a possible numeric gender code with a more meaningful "male" and "female" and data cleanup, repair, and enrichment, which may include corrections to the address field based on the value of the postal zip code.

- Data consolidation and integration, which may include combining several source records into a single record to be loaded into the warehouse.

- Metadata synchronization and management, which includes storing and/or updating metadata definitions about source data files, transformation actions, loading formats, and events, etc.; thus, the entire data sourcing process is controlled by and documented in the metadata repository.

When implementing a data warehouse, several selection criteria that affect the tool's ability to transform, consolidate, integrate, and repair the data should be considered:

- The ability to identify data in the data source environments that can be read by the conversion tool is important. This additional step may affect the timeliness of data delivery to the warehouse.

- Support for flat files, indexed files (e.g., VSAM) and legacy DBMSs (e.g., IMS and CA-IDMS) is critical, since the bulk of corporate data is still maintained in data stores of this type.

- The capability to merge data from multiple data stores is required in many installations. Using data replication technologies helps—a data-change capture facility provides the functionality of reading log data to obtain only the changed data to be transferred. This reduces the amount of data that must be loaded into the data warehouse for periodic updating of the data warehouse.

- The specification interface to indicate the data to be extracted and the conversion criteria is important.

- The ability to read information from data dictionaries or import information from repository products is desired. This can reduce the amount of specification effort required.

- The code generated by the tool should be completely maintainable from within the development environment.

- Selective data extraction of both data elements and records enables users to extract only the required data.

- A field-level data examination for the transformation of data into information is needed. For example, a user-exit feature is important for users who may need to perform more sophisticated operations on the data than can be achieved using the facilities provided with the tool.

- The ability to perform data-type and character-set translation is a requirement when moving data between incompatible systems.

- The capability to create summarization, aggregation, and derivation records and fields is very important.

- The data warehouse database management system should be able to perform the load directly from the tool, using the native API available with the RDBMS; alternatively, the system should support the capability to create a flat file and then use the load utility provided by the RDBMS.

- Vendor stability and support for the product are items that must be carefully evaluated.

10.2   Vendor Approaches

The rapid growth of data warehousing has given birth to vendors that are more focused on fulfilling requirements pertaining to data warehouse implementations as opposed to simply moving data between hardware platforms.

The tasks of capturing data from a source data system, cleaning and transforming it, and then loading the results into a target data system can be carried out either by separate products, or by a single integrated solution. More contemporary integrated solutions can fall into one of the categories described below.

- *Code generators* create tailored 3GL/4GL transformation programs based on source and target data definitions, and data transformation and enhancement rules defined by the developer. This approach reduces the need for an organization to write its own data capture, transformation, and load programs. Code generation products employ data manipulation language statements to capture a subset of the data from the source system. Some also support the capture of changes to source data by processing the recovery log files of the source system. With most products, user-written programs or exits can be called for performing additional data transformation and enhancement. Code generation products are used for data conversion projects, and for building an enterprisewide data warehouse, when there is a significant amount of data transformation to be done involving a variety of different flat file, nonrelational, and relational data sources. The main issue with this approach is the management of the large number of programs required to support a complex corporate information system. Each group of related data sources will result in a generated program that copies data from the source system to a target system. Often many of these point-to-point programs may be required to support the needs of an installation. Managing and coordinating such an environment is difficult and error-prone. Vendors recognize this issue, and some are developing management components employing techniques such as workflow methods and automated scheduling systems.

- Database *data replication* tools employ database triggers or a recovery log to capture changes to a single data source on one system and apply the changes to a copy of the source data located on a different system. Most replication products do not support the capture of changes to nonrelational files and databases, and often do not provide facilities for significant data transformation and enhancement. These point-to-point tools are used for disaster recovery and to build an operational data store, a data warehouse, or data mart when the number of data sources involved is small, and a limited amount of data transformation and enhancement is required.

- Rule-driven *dynamic transformation engines* (also known as *data mart builders*) capture data from a source system at user-defined intervals, transform the data, and then send and load the results into a target environment, typically a data mart. To date most products have supported only relational data sources, but products are now emerging that handle nonrelational source files and databases. Data to be captured form the source system is usually defined using query language statements, and data transformation and enhancement is done based on a script or function logic defined to the tool. Some products also allow user-written code to be called for doing additional data transformation and enhancement. With most tools in this category, data flows from source systems to target systems through one or more servers, which perform the data transformation and enhancement. These transformation servers can usually be controlled from a single location, making the job of managing such an environment much easier.

The data extraction, transformation, and clean tools described in Secs. 10.4 and 10.5 illustrate these different approaches to the warehousing extraction function. From a data warehouse architecture point of view, we'll concentrate on tools that implement two of the approaches—code generators and dynamic transformation engines.

10.3 Access to Legacy Data

Today, many businesses are adopting client/server technologies and data warehousing to meet customer demand for new products and services, and to obtain a competitive advantage. For better or for worse, the majority of information required to support business applications and analytical power of data warehousing is locked behind mainframe-based legacy systems.

Thus, the need to achieve seamless integration of heterogeneous environments and to provide an enterprisewide access to legacy system becomes paramount for any organization that wants to meet the objectives of both user community and IT organization while protecting their heavy financial investment in hardware and software and utilizing an important strategic resource. To meet this goal, many organizations turn to middleware solutions that can manage the interaction between the new applications and growing data warehouses on one hand and the back-end legacy systems on the other hand.

The middleware strategy is the foundation for tools such as Enterprise/Access from Apertus Corporation, which is discussed in this section. Enterprise/Access is designed for scalability and manageability in a data warehousing computing environment. It is a development tool that enables the rapid development of transparent, production-quality client/server interfaces to legacy applications and databases. With Enterprise/Access, legacy systems on virtually any platform can be connected to a new data warehouse via client/server interfaces without the significant time, cost, or risk involved in reengineering application code. Enterprise/Access provides a three-tiered architecture that defines how applications are partitioned to meet both near-term integration and long-term migration objectives:

- The data layer provides data access and transaction services for management of corporate data assets. This layer is independent of any current business process or user interface application. It manages the data and enforces the business rules for data integrity.

- The process layer provides services to manage automation and support for current business processes. It allows modification of the supporting application logic independent of the underlying data or user interface.

- The user layer manages user interaction with process and/or data layer services. It allows the user interface to change independently of the underlying business processes.

With Enterprise/Access, a data warehouse data store can be developed as a virtual shared corporate database that can access legacy systems. Two virtual database models for Enterprise/Access can be applicable to the development of data warehouses:

- In the first model, Enterprise/Access acts as the virtual database. The host interfaces and the business transactions are defined entirely in Enterprise/Access. This model is used when building a generalized architecture and modernizing applications. Migration is not an issue at this point.
- In the second model, Enterprise/Access and Open Gateway use a SQL Server as a virtual database. Host interfaces are located in Enterprise/Access while business logic is implemented via stored procedures. This model is used when migrating legacy system functionality to a relational database, such as SYBASE.

Enterprise/Access developers build services that communicate with legacy applications and map application-specific messages, such as terminal screens or reports, into the client/server interface. These services are stored in a central repository so that they can be simultaneously shared by multiple client applications and easily reused or enhanced. Enterprise/Access provides a consistent API that allows developers to access relational databases, such as SYBASE, ORACLE, and INFORMIX, from within their services. This interface is designed to allow the rapid integration of new database systems as required as well as the interchange of database systems without changes to service code.

Enterprise/Access provides broad communications support, enabling access to virtually any legacy application or database. Communications methods include terminal emulation, peer-to-peer communication, and RDBMS. Enterprise/Access provides protocol independence that supports multiple standard protocols, including 3270/SNA, 3270/BSC, Telnet 3270, Telnet VT100/VT220, Async Device VT100/VT220, SNA, and APPC/LU6.2. Enterprise/Access uses Protocol Agents that insulate developers from communications details and allow new protocols to be easily added to the system. These Protocol Agents support specific protocol implementations and are dynamically loaded in accordance with the communications requirements of a given service.

The Enterprise/Access toolkit is an open-systems environment that supports industry-standard interfaces and facilitates tool independence. Enterprise/Access services can be accessed via any tool supporting the Sybase SQL Server API and Microsoft Open Database Connectivity (ODBC), such as PowerSoft PowerBuilder, Microsoft Access and Visual Basic, Microsoft Visual C++, and Blythe Omnis 7.

10.4   Vendor Solutions

The following subsections discuss tools from Prism Solutions, SAS Institute, Carleton Corporation, Vality Corporation, Evolutionary Technologies, and Information Builders.

10.4.1   Prism Solutions

While Enterprise/Access focuses on providing access to legacy data, Prism Warehouse Manager provides a comprehensive solution for data warehousing by mapping source data to a target database management system to be used as a warehouse. Warehouse Manager generates code to extract and integrate data, create and manage metadata, and build a subject-oriented, historical base. The standard conversions, key changes, structural changes, and condensations needed to transform operational data into data warehouse information are automatically created. Prism Warehouse Manager can extract data from multiple source environments, including DB2, IDMS, IMS, VSAM, RMS, and sequential files under UNIX or MVS. Target databases include ORACLE, SYBASE, and INFORMIX. Prism Solutions has strategic relationships with Pyramid and Informix. Prism Solution is discussed in more detail in the next chapter, which focuses on metadata.

10.4.2   SAS Institute

SAS starts with the premise that most mission-critical data still resides in the data center and offers its traditional SAS System tools as a means to serve all data warehousing functions. Its data repository function can act to build the informational database. SAS Data Access Engines serve as extraction tools to combine common variables, transform data representation forms for consistency, consolidate redundant data, and use business rules to produce computed values in the warehouse. SAS views serve the internetworking and refresh roles, and SAS reporting, graphing, and decision support products act as the front end. In addition to interacting with SAS System databases, SAS engines can work with hierarchical and relational databases and sequential files.

10.4.3   Carleton Corporation's PASSPORT and MetaCenter

As was already mentioned, the process of migrating and moving legacy data to a new data warehouse environment can be costly and time-consuming. And once it is built, managing the warehouse, from scheduling updates through metadata browsing, can be rather difficult and time consuming. Carleton's PASSPORT and the MetaCenter products are positioned to fulfill these data extraction and transformation needs of data warehousing.

PASSPORT. PASSPORT is a sophisticated metadata-driven, data-mapping, and data-migration facility. PASSPORT Workbench runs as a client on various

PC platforms in the three-tiered environment, including OS/2 and Windows, and is used to develop PASSPORT applications to meet data warehousing and data migration needs.

The product currently consists of two components. The first, which is mainframe-based, collects the file, record, or table layouts for the required inputs and outputs and converts them to the Passport Data Language (PDL). The second component is workstation-based and is used to create the meta-data directory from which it builds the COBOL programs to actually create the extracts. The user must transfer the PDL file from the mainframe to a location accessible by PASSPORT. The metadata directory is stored in a relational database (such as DB2/2). Carleton's PASSPORT can produce multiple output files from a single execution of an extract program.

Overall, PASSPORT offers

- A metadata dictionary at the core of the process

- Robust data conversion, migration, analysis, and auditing facilities

- The PASSPORT Workbench, a graphical user interface (GUI) workbench that enables project development on a workstation, with uploading of the generated application to the source data platform

- Native interfaces to existing data files and RDBMS, helping users to leverage existing legacy applications and data

- A comprehensive fourth-generation specification language and the full power of COBOL

PASSPORT can assist the various personnel who design, implement, maintain, or use data warehouses, including business systems analysts and those involved in joint application design (JAD) sessions, data warehouse designers and implementors, data warehouse administrators, and end users.

PASSPORT highlights. Carleton PASSPORT includes a number of facilities and features which are briefly discussed below.

- *Data Access.* This facility is data-dictionary-driven, and provides input data selection, automatic file and data matching, selective random access, automatic handling of multiple record types, intelligent joins, data sampling, and single or multiple record access.

- *Data Analysis and Auditing.* This facility provides
  - ⇨ Audit reports, including Duplicates report, Sequence Checking report, Cross Tabulation report, File Footing report, Stratification report, and Statistical Summary report
  - ⇨ Audit Facilities, including SAMPLE Command, AGE Function, DATE Keyword, and ENCRYPT Option

- *Language and Design.* This facility supports predefined calculations, arithmetic operations, relational and boolean operations, range operations, arrays, input data sorts, work fields and system fields, conditional processing, internal and external subroutines, and loop processing.

- *Passport Data Language* (PDL). This has a free-form command structure, with English-like command syntax.

- *Run-time environment.* This supports dynamic work fields and error-limit control.

- *Report Writing.* This facility supports an unlimited number of line formats, unrestricted output line contents, variable page size, controlled horizontal and vertical spacing, and dynamic printing.

Additionally, PASSPORT provides the *System Activity Report,* which includes syntax checking, error trapping, run-time messages, file activity summary, report activity summary, and path analysis.

Other features of Carleton PASSPORT include

- *Centralized metadata repository.* This is an enterprise-level, common, single-master metadata repository that provides global access, provides central information change management and control, and enables metadata accuracy and integrity.

- *Business metadata.* Carleton's PASSPORT provides for metadata in business English—in addition to a technical description—for end users to access. This business metadata is stored in a relational format that is accessible by any SQL-based query tool.

- *Load image formats for target DBMS.* PASSPORT formats data for loading into any target RDBMS, including DB2, Informix, Oracle, Sybase, and Red Brick. For example, PASSPORT's DB2 internal load file format provides for very efficient loading into DB2, several times faster than the DB2 external load format.

- *Optional user exits.* PASSPORT provides support for user exits, where users can optionally invoke previously written routines.

- *Browsing capabilities.* PASSPORT provides metadata in a relational format that is easily accessible by any end-user query tool. Metadata is collected and stored in a format that is optimized to support a wide range of browsing and querying requirements.

The MetaCenter. The *MetaCenter,* developed by Carleton Corporation in partnership with Intellidex Systems, Inc., is an integrated tool suite that is designed to put users in control of the data warehouse. The MetaCenter features a seamless development and management system for a multitiered data warehouse environment that manages

- Data extraction
- Data transformation
- Metadata capture
- Metadata browsing
- Data mart subscription
- Warehouse control center functionality
- Event control and notification

At the heart of the MetaCenter solution is the *Metadata Dictionary,* which contains both business and technical rules used in the extract process to populate the data warehouse. The metadata may be linked to tool-specific dictionaries, data repositories, and logical design tools, as well as extract program definitions. The Intellidex feature of the MetaCenter provides tools to synchronize physical and logical layers, providing a "control center" for the data warehouse.

The MetaCenter, in conjunction with PASSPORT, provides a number of sophisticated capabilities:

- *Data extraction and transformation.* The PASSPORT Workbench provides data transformation capabilities to support the complex data migration requirements often associated with populating a data warehouse. Developers can automatically generate COBOL extract programs from the metadata that describes where the data is, what it looks like, and how it should be processed. Extract programs pull data from legacy systems, then manipulate, scrub, and transform the data for use in the data warehouse.

- *Event management and notification.* The Intellidex Scheduler serves as the warehouse "traffic cop." Data movement and subscription events are executed and monitored by the Scheduler via its event monitors. The Scheduler sends notification to the various responsible administrators via e-mail.

- *Data mart subscription.* Data warehouse users can subscribe to the data they need using business terminology, without having to understand the complexities of database nomenclature. Subscriptions, or specific requests for data, are authorized by the warehouse administrator, who acts as the "gatekeeper" to the enterprisewide data warehouse. Users are then notified via e-mail (the Intellidex Control Center includes MAPI support) that their data request has been completed and the results are waiting to be viewed.

- *Control Center Mover.* This unit works with the Scheduler to automatically move each data request. The Mover provides seamless connectivity and data pumping between the data warehouse and the data marts. The Administrator Module manages user profiles that allow specific functions such as requesting, browsing, searching, and reporting.

Overall, Carleton's PASSPORT and the MetaCenter products provide a wide range of sophisticated capabilities that include data extraction, transformation, scrubbing, and metadata management.

10.4.4   Vality Corporation

Vality Corporation's *Integrity* data reengineering tool is used to investigate, standardize, transform, and integrate data from multiple operational systems and external sources. Its main focus is on data quality. Indeed, focusing on avoiding the "GIGO" (garbage in, garbage out) principle, Integrity feeds high-quality information to critical information systems by reengineering data prior to migration into the target system. Integrity is a specialized, multipurpose data tool that organizations apply on projects such as

- Data audits
- Data warehouse and decision support systems
- Customer information files and householding applications
- Client/server business applications such as SAP R/3, Oracle, and Hogan
- System consolidations
- Rewrites of existing operational systems
- Year 2000 projects (by finding every instance of dates within code)

Benefits of the Integrity tool.   The Integrity tool

- Attains and maintains the highest quality data—needed to minimize bad decisions caused by erroneous and missing information.
- Builds accurate, consolidated views of customers, suppliers, products, and other corporate entities, thus enhancing decision support, enabling cross-product marketing, supporting business reengineering and workflow initiatives, and improving customer service and customer retention through enhanced knowledge of the business process.
- Surfaces essential business information, buried in legacy data, which is needed to build and validate the data model and ensure that it accurately reflects how you do business.
- Simplifies, expedites, and lowers the cost of data migration. The tool consumes few programming resources and can help reduce the clerical staff needed to handle exception reports.

Integrity does not compete with data extraction tools. Rather, Integrity complements extraction products by feeding them clean, consolidated, accurate information.

Integrity attains high levels of data accuracy and quality by being able to "understand" and handle the value in each field of each record occurrence. Working at the record-occurrence level, Integrity detects, classifies, and specifies data from any source for proper mapping to any target. That is in contrast with metadata-based propagation tools that cannot ensure data quality because they map at the metalevel, not the lower record-occurrence level.

As a value-added service, Vality provides IT organizations with a data reengineering survey to identify specific data problems in their projects and prescribe the data tasks needed to fix them. Survey results enable users to

- Assess the risks of exposing a new information system to existing data

- Gauge whether Integrity would warrant the organization's investment

Overall, Integrity is a comprehensive and mature tool that provides organizations with a critical ability to assess and improve the quality of data put into the data warehouse.

10.4.5 Evolutionary Technologies

Another example of the data extraction and transformation tools is the ETI-EXTRACT Tool Suite from the Evolutionary Technologies, Inc. This product automates and expedites the migration of data between dissimilar storage environments, potentially allowing organizations to save up to 95 percent of the time and cost of manual data conversion. The product's data manipulation capabilities, combined with code-generation technology and a customized implementation methodology, enables users to

- Populate and maintain data warehouses

- Move to new architectures, such as distributed client/server, while preserving their investment in legacy systems

- Integrate disparate systems

- Migrate data to new databases, platforms, and applications

The ETI-EXTRACT Tool Suite is a flexible solution that

- Supports data collection, conversion, and migration from a variety of platforms, operating systems, and database management systems to any other environment—including proprietary systems.

- Automatically generates and executes programs in the appropriate languages for source and target platforms and produces any necessary JCL and scripts to move the data and execute conversion programs.

- Provides a powerful metadata facility that allows users to track information about stored data. This facility provides the ability to access, export, and merge metadata, including critical information such as schema definitions, source-to-target mapping, business rules and/or data transformation logic, and interdatabase relationships.

■ Provides a sophisticated graphical interface that allows users to indicate how to move data, through simple point-and-click interaction.

Product overview. The ETI-EXTRACT Tool Suite (in its third release at the time of this writing) automates the migration of data between different storage systems. It produces all the necessary programs to retrieve, transform, and move data from any data access system to any other, regardless of hardware or software platform, in any programming language. The ETI-EXTRACT Tool Suite is used for generating programs required to populate and refresh data warehouses; to test, transform, and migrate large production databases; to create the data bridge programs required to reengineer applications or implement new applications; and to support migrations to architectures such as client/server.

ETI-EXTRACT combines program generation functionality with extensible data selection and transformation facilities able to handle complex conditional data manipulations. In addition, it offers administration capabilities that expand users' control over heterogeneous environments, as well as an intuitive graphical user interface that makes easy the process of specifying data collection and transformation instructions and generating all the necessary programs. All ETI-EXTRACT functions are accessed through the industry-standard Motif/Windows-style point-and-click interface that makes it simple to learn and easy to use. The interface features intuitive icons that identify objects and provide visual cues and important information. Multifunction consolidated windows in a spreadsheet-style format are dynamically user-configurable for increased productivity and specially designed to use a minimum of pop-up windows for clean, uncomplicated screen layouts. An object-action paradigm further simplifies and minimizes user interaction.

ETI-EXTRACT generates programs in the appropriate language for the source and target systems. This extensible tool can produce programs in many programming languages, such as C, COBOL, RPG, and even proprietary languages such as SAP's ABAP/4 language. The generated programs are transferred and executed directly on the source and target for maximum processing efficiency.

A key feature is ETI-EXTRACT's ability to support conditional data selection and transformation that can be done programmatically. Selection and transformation criteria and rules are specified via a point-and-click menu-driven process that displays only those processing options and instructions valid in the current context, so that the generated code will be correct and efficient by construction. As the selection and transformation logic is being specified, a corresponding string of text is automatically created as well that describes in clear and simple language (i.e., English) exactly what will be done to the data affected. This descriptive string is included in the conversion metadata. The ETI-EXTRACT Tool Suite also provides a broad range of metadata management options. It automatically captures all the relevant metadata, including the information about the source and target systems and any business rules and conditional selection and transformation logic applied to any data values. And through its Metadata Facility, described later, the ETI-EXTRACT enables users to interactively view metadata, produce impact analysis reports to facilitate maintenance as changes occur in operational systems, and even merge metadata from multiple different sources and export metadata as needed to any other repository or storage facility.

The ETI-EXTRACT Tool Suite consists of two sets of productivity tools—the Master Toolset and the Data Conversion Toolset—which include the Conversion Editor, the Executive, the Workset Browser, and the Metadata Facility.

The Master Toolset. The Master Toolset is a set of interactive editors that allows a systems programmer, known as a *Master User,* to define to the MetaStore database everything required to be able to read and write to any database management system or file system in the enterprise environment. This information for a specific data access system is called an ETI-EXTRACT *Data System Library* (DSL). Once this initial setup work is done, the DBMS or file system can serve as a source or target for data migration between data stored in that environment and data stored in any other DBMS or file system defined to the MetaStore database. Specifically

- The *Environment Editor* allows the specification of each different platform and system operating environment to be accessed.

- The *Schema Editor* provides easy access for browsing or updating schema information.

- The *Grammar Editor* offers a simplified means for defining customized conditional retrieval, transformation, and populate logic to meet environment-specific needs.

- The *Template Editor* enables rapid specification of programming rules to shape the way data retrieval, conversion, and populate programs are generated, including conformance to rules for corporate coding standards.

The Conversion Editor. This is an interactive set of tools that provides a graphical point-and-click interface for defining the mapping of data between the various source data systems and target data systems. The Conversion Editor enables a Conversion Specialist user who is knowledgeable about the data involved but who may not be a programmer to specify all the instructions for selectively collecting, transforming, and physically moving the data. The Conversion Editor features a user-configurable screen that visually links sources and targets in an easy-to-read spreadsheet-style layout. The Conversion Editor allows users to

- Selectively retrieve data from one or more database management systems or file formats
- Create programs that test and transform data as required
- Merge data from multiple systems to create a new database
- Populate any number of database management systems or file formats

Once the Conversion Specialist has specified the desired conversion parameters, the Conversion Editor uses this information to generate all the programs required to complete the entire conversion, as well as a script that allows the execution of the generated programs to be controlled from the ETI-EXTRACT host. Because all the data retrieval and manipulation instructions, including all business rules and transformations, are specified within the Conversion Editor, all this important information is automatically captured and stored as metadata in the ETI-EXTRACT MetaStore database.

Other components of the ETI-EXTRACT Tool Suite.   These include

- The *ETI-EXTRACT Executive,* which provides process control and automatic job execution capability. Once a set of source code programs has been generated, the Executive uses the generated execution script along with the network and file transfer protocols already in place in the environment to physically transfer the generated programs to the appropriate source and target computer systems. The Executive automatically launches the compilation of individual programs, controls the execution of the compiled programs, and monitors the entire process of retrieving, transforming, and moving the data between systems.

- The *ETI-EXTRACT Workset Browser,* which provides a user-customizable desktop metaphor with intuitive graphical icons that represent the processes and objects that can be selected and manipulated. Worksets allow one database to be accessed by many users and others to be accessed by only one. The Workset Browser provides a check-in/check-out mechanism that enables multiple concurrent users to work with the same databases or files without risking the integrity of the data.

- The *ETI-EXTRACT Metadata Facility,* which features the MetaStore database, the Metadata Exchange Library (MDX), an interactive metadata browsing mechanism, and a report-generation capability. These components combine to provide metadata capture, access, reporting, and integration.

- The *MetaStore Database,* which is an object-oriented database that provides many capabilities, including concurrent multiuser support, impact analysis reporting, and versioning capabilities. It provides a centralized place to capture and store all the metadata used by the Conversion Editor as well as metadata from other sources. The MetaStore database's versioning feature allows users to establish a comprehensive and detailed audit trail and simplify point-in-time access to historical data. The interactive browsing facility provides a means of viewing the metadata stored in the MetaStore database as needed. The report-generation capability enables the same types of information to be printed out for review.

- The *Metadata Exchange Library* (MDX), which allows metadata to be managed just like any other type of enterprise data. With MDX, a user simply employs the Conversion Editor to indicate graphically how to export metadata from the MetaStore database to any other enterprise repository or catalogue, import metadata from other sources into the MetaStore database, and even merge metadata from multiple sources. The Conversion Editor then generates the programs required to export, merge, and import the requested metadata.

Overall, the ETI-EXTRACT Tool Suite is a comprehensive and mature data extraction and transformation tool.

10.4.6 Information Builders

The final example of a product that can be used as a component for data extraction, transformation, and legacy access tool suite for building data warehouses is EDA/SQL from Information Builders. The EDA/SQL family of products provides SQL access to and a uniform relational view of relational and non-relational data residing in over 60 different databases on 35 different platforms. EDA/SQL implements a client/server model that is optimized for higher performance. EDA/SQL supports copy management, data quality management, data replication capabilities, and standards support for both ODBC and the X/Open CLI. IBI's product is the component of almost every systems supplier's legacy data access strategy, including Amdahl, IBM, Digital Equipment, HP, and Bull as well as many database and tool vendors.

10.5 Transformation Engines

The following subsections discuss two of the currently available dynamic transformation engine tools—Informatica's Powermart Suite and Constellar Hub.

10.5.1 Informatica

Informatica's product, PowerMart Suite, has to be discussed in conjunction with the Metadata Exchange Architecture (MX) initiative. This is a multicompany metadata integration initiative. Informatica joined forces with Andyne, Brio, Business Objects, Cognos, Information Advantage, Infospace, IQ Software, and MicroStrategy to deliver a "back-end" architecture and publish API specifications supporting its technical and business metadata. Informatica's product, the PowerMart suite, captures technical and business metadata on the back-end that can be integrated with the metadata in front-end partners' products, presenting a unified view of metadata across the enterprise.

MX provides a set of application program interfaces (APIs) that OLAP, query, and access tool vendors can use to integrate their products with Informatica's open metadata repository. The Informatica Repository is the foundation of the PowerMart suite in which business and technical metadata is stored—for example, subject areas, table names and formats, data elements, and detailed data mappings and data transformations. PowerMart creates and maintains the metadata repository automatically as the various PowerMart tools are applied to the tasks of schema design and source data extraction and transformation.

PowerMart.   Informatica's flagship product—PowerMart Suite—consists of the following components:

- *PowerMart Designer* is made up of three integrated modules—Source Analyzer, Warehouse Designer, and Transformation Designer. The Source Analyzer reads schema information from the operational systems in order to determine the formats and structure of the operational database. It analyzes RDBMS catalogs, as well as COBOL source code and database definition scripts (e.g., IMS DBDGENs), to extract data structure information. Warehouse Designer is used to design the data mart model. A major feature of the Warehouse Designer is the Star Schema Design Wizard, which allows designs to be made by leveraging the operational schema design and stepping the user through the creation of the warehouse design. Transformation Designer visually displays the operational database-to-data mart mapping that is automatically created by PowerMart. The mapping can be modified or deleted using drag-and-drop techniques.

- *PowerMart Server* runs on a UNIX or Windows NT platform. It consists of an Extractor, Transformation Engine, and Loader. Each of these three processes operates independently and takes full advantage of hardware server parallelism for high data throughput and scalability.

- The *Informatica Server Manager* is responsible for configuring, scheduling, and monitoring the Informatica Server. It operates in one of three modes: session configuration, session monitoring, and PowerCapture configuration.

- The *Informatica Repository* is the metadata integration hub of the Informatica PowerMart Suite. The metadata information stored in the Informatica Repository is utilized and viewed by the Repository Manager and the Metadata Browser. The Repository Manager is used to create and maintain the Informatica Repository and the metadata that is contained within it. The Metadata Browser is used to browse and view the metadata in the Repository. Analysis of the data mart database field dependencies as well as operational database field dependencies, can also be viewed.

- *Informatica PowerCapture* allows a data mart to be incrementally refreshed with changes occurring in the operational system, either as they occur (for critical real-time warehousing) or on a scheduled basis. This is accomplished by using the log mechanisms in the operational database to extract the information. This ensures that the online performance of the operational systems is not adversely affected.

10.5.2   Constellar

The Constellar Hub consists of a set of components supporting the distributed transformation management capabilities. The product is designed to handle the movement and transformation of data for both data migration and data distribution in an operational system, and for capturing operational data for loading into a data warehouse.

Constellar employs a hub and spoke architecture to manage the flow of data between source and target systems. At the core of this environment are one or more multithreaded transformation hubs that perform data transformation based on rules defined and developed using the Migration Manager. Transformation hubs run as servers on either UNIX or Windows NT, and make extensive use of Oracle tools, databases, and recovery features for handling and maintaining both data and metadata.

Each of the spokes represents a data path between a transformation hub and a data source or target. A hub and its associated sources and targets can be installed on the same machine, or may run on separate networked computers. Product pricing is based on the number of hubs and spokes in the configuration. Constellar supports data sources and targets for flat files, ORACLE databases, and databases and files supported by Oracle's database gateway products.

The Constellar data capture component selects records from local or remote databases using SQL data manipulation statements and loads the records into internal staging tables for processing by the transformation hub. Records can also be extracted from local and remote files. The extract component can handle files containing repeating groups, fixed and variable length records, and multiple record types. Only the records and fields required for transformation are loaded into the staging area. Depending on performance requirements, the developer can choose to use the Oracle load utility or SQL to populate the staging tables. For simple file-to-file transformations, the staging area can be bypassed entirely, and selected records passed straight to the transformation hub. Multiple extract processes can be run on the same machine with the transformation hub. The use of staging tables adds overhead to the transformation process, but has the advantage that when data needs to be acquired and integrated from many different source systems, and possibly at different times of the day, it can first be accumulated into the staging area and then transformed when all the required data has been assembled. This makes it easier to manage a large transformation project.

The transformation hub performs the tasks of data cleanup and transformation. The hub supports

- Record reformatting and restructuring.
- Field level data transformation, validation, and table lookup.
- File and multifile set-level data transformation and validation.
- The creation of intermediate results for further downstream transformation by the hub.

Data is transformed in a two-step process. The *collate* step filters and joins source records, which are then passed to the *transform* step, where field-level transformation rules are applied. Output records from these two steps are inserted into the staging area. For simple file-to-file transformations, the staging area can be bypassed, and records inserted straight into the target database.

The Constellar load component consists of *Export* and *Send*. Export writes transformed records from the staging tables to target databases and files, while Send transfers result files to remote machines. Multiple export processes can be run on the same machine as the transformation hub, or on a remote one.

Constellar development environment.   The rules and procedures that control how data is extracted, transformed, and exported are defined using the Migration Manager. This tool supplies the developer with a Windows-based point-and-click interface for defining sources, targets, and transformations. These definitions are stored in a set of relational tables known as the *metadata dictionary*. This dictionary can be shared by one or more transformation hubs, and can be replicated for recovery purposes using either Oracle symmetric replication or Constellar Hub transformation services.

Metadata

Metadata, or the information about the enterprise data, is emerging as a critical element in effective data management, especially in the data warehousing arena. Vendors as well as users have began to appreciate the value of metadata. At the same time, the rapid proliferation of data manipulation and management tools has resulted in almost as many different "flavors" and treatments of metadata as there are tools.

Thus, this chapter discusses metadata as one of the most important components of a data warehouse, as well as the infrastructure that enables its storage, management, and integration with other components of a data warehouse. This infrastructure is known as *metadata repository,* and it is discussed in the examples of several repository implementations, including the repository products from Platinum Technologies, Prism Solution, and R&O.

11.1 Metadata Defined

Metadata is one of the most important aspects of data warehousing. It is data about data stored in the warehouse and its users. At a minimum, metadata contains

- The location and description of warehouse system and data components (warehouse objects).

- Names, definition, structure, and content of the data warehouse and end-user views.

- Identification of authoritative data sources (systems of record).

- Integration and transformation rules used to populate the data warehouse; these include the mapping method from operational databases into the warehouse, and algorithms used to convert, enhance, or transform data.

- Integration and transformation rules used to deliver data to end-user analytical tools.

- Subscription information for the information delivery to the analysis subscribers (see Chap. 1 for a description of information delivery system).

- Data warehouse operational information, which includes a history of warehouse updates, refreshments, snapshots, versions, ownership authorizations, and extract audit trail.

- Metrics used to analyze warehouse usage and performance vis-à-vis end-user usage patterns.

- Security authorizations, access control lists, etc.

As data that describes the data warehouse, metadata is used for building, maintaining, managing, and using the data warehouse. Equally as important, metadata provides interactive access to users to help understand content, find data.

In a complex and multicomponent environment such as a data warehouse, different tools must be able to freely and easily access, and in some cases manipulate and update, the metadata created by other tools and stored in a variety of different storage facilities. One approach to achieve this goal is to establish at least a minimum common denominator of interchange standards and guidelines to which the different vendors' tools can comply. This approach has been offered by the leading data warehousing vendors, and is known as the *Metadata Interchange Initiative.*

11.2   Metadata Interchange Initiative

The Metadata Interchange Initiative was launched by the founding members (Arbor Software, Business Objects, Cognos, ETI, Platinum Technology, and Texas Instruments) to bring industry vendors and users together to address a variety of difficult problems and issues with regard to exchanging, sharing, and managing metadata. This is intended as a coalition of interested parties with a common focus and shared goals, not a traditional standards body or regulatory group in any way.

The group's charter is *to develop the standard specifications for metadata interchange format and its support mechanism (Metadata Interchange/Standard).* The most important goal of the metadata interchange standard is to define an extensible mechanism that will allow vendors to exchange common metadata as well as carry along "proprietary" metadata.

The founding members agreed on the initial goals, including

- Creating a vendor-independent, industry-defined and -maintained standard access mechanism and standard application programming interface (API) for metadata

- Enabling users to control and manage the access and manipulation of metadata in their unique environments through the use of interchange-standards-compliant tools

- Allowing users to build tool configurations that meet their needs and to incrementally adjust those configurations as necessary to add or subtract tools without impact on the interchange standards environment

- Enabling individual tools to satisfy their specific metadata access requirements freely and easily within the context of an interchange model

- Defining a clean, simple interchange implementation infrastructure that will facilitate compliance and speed up adoption by minimizing the amount of modification required to existing tools to achieve and maintain interchange standards compliance

- Creating a process and procedures not only for establishing and maintaining the interchange standards specification but also for extending and updating it over time as required by evolving industry and user needs

The heart of the interchange standard specification is the *core-set components,* which represent the minimum common denominator of metadata elements and the minimum points of integration that must be incorporated into tools products for compliance. Compliance with the interchange standard requires support for all relevant core set components and integration points in accordance with the approved specifications. The interchange standard also provides for an approved set of optional and extension components that are relevant only to a particular type or class of tool or a specific application or architecture. Because these are used by more than one tool or application, they can and should conform to the standard definition and set of access parameters, but because they are not generic across all tools, architectures, or applications, they would not be eligible for the core set, nor required for compliance.

The Metadata Interchange Standard defines two distinct metamodels:

- The *application metamodel*—the tables, etc., used to "hold" the metadata for a particular application

- The *metadata metamodel*—the set of objects that the metadata interchange standard can be used to describe

These represent the information that is common to (i.e., represented by) one or more classes of tools, such as data extraction tools, replication tools, user query tools, and database servers.

Metadata Interchange Standard framework.   Implementation of the interchange standard metadata model must assume that the metadata itself may be stored in any type of storage facility or format: relational tables, ASCII files, fixed-format or customized-format repositories, and so on. Therefore, the interchange standard metadata access methodology must be based on a framework that will translate an access request into the interchange standard syntax and format for the metamodel of choice.

The Metadata Interchange Coalition defines several approaches to consider in accomplishing this:

- *Procedural approach.*   This is predicated on each individual tool's interaction with the defined API. In this approach, the intelligence to communicate with the API is built into the tool wherever the tool may need to create, update, access, or otherwise interact with the metadata. This approach enables the highest degree of flexibility in terms of evolving the standard metadata implementation, but at the same time, it requires a great deal of up-front effort on the part of the tool vendors to retrofit this logic into the tools to achieve compliance.

■ *ASCII batch approach.*   This approach relies instead on the ASCII file format that contains the description of the common metadata components and standardized access requirements that make up the interchange standard metadata model. In this approach, the entire ASCII file containing the metadata interchange standard schema and access parameters is reloaded whenever a tool accesses the metadata through the standard API. This approach requires only the addition of a simple import/export function to the tools. However, this approach is resource- and processing-intensive and would likely be prohibitively inefficient.

■ *Hybrid approach.*   This is an approach that would follow a data-driven model. By implementing a table-driven API that would support only fully qualified references for each metadata element, a tool could interact with the API through the standard access framework and directly access just the specific metadata object needed.

Figure 11.1 graphically illustrates the proposed layers for the proposed metadata interchange standard.

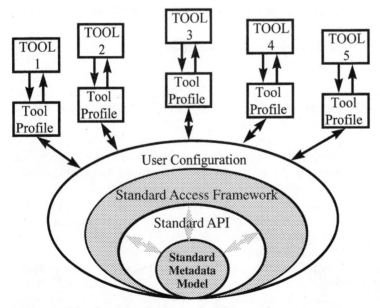

Figure 11.1   Metadata interchange standard framework.

The components of the Metadata Interchange Standard Framework are

- The *Standard Metadata Model,* which refers to the ASCII file format used to represent the metadata that is being exchanged.

- The *Standard Access Framework,* which describes the minimum number of API functions a vendor must support.

- *Tool Profile,* which is provided by each tool vendor. The Tool Profile is a file that describes what aspects of the interchange standard metamodel a particular tool supports.

- The *User Configuration,* which is a file describing the legal interchange paths for metadata in the user's environment. This file allows customers to constrain the flow of metadata from tool to tool in their specific environments. This file is used by the functions in the Interchange Standard Access Framework to determine if the metadata model file should be imported by any particular tool.

This framework defines the means by which various tool vendors will enable metadata interchange. The Metadata Interchange Standard is a promising step toward defining a common and effective way to enable cross-platform and cross-tool management of metadata. This or similar standards may also be used to define the structure and APIs for a focal point of metadata management: the metadata repository.

11.3   Metadata Repository

The data warehouse architecture framework, defined in Chap. 1, represents a higher level of abstraction than the Metadata Interchange Standard Framework, and by design, includes the metadata interchange framework as one of its components. Specifically, the data warehouse architecture (see Fig. 11.2) defines a number of components, all of which interact with each other via the architecturally defined layer of metadata. The metadata itself is housed in and managed by the metadata repository (Fig. 11.2, component 2). Metadata repository management software can be used to map the source data to the target database, generate code for data transformations, integrate and transform the data, and control moving data to the warehouse. This software, which typically runs on a workstation, enables users to specify how the data should be transformed, such as data mapping, conversion, and summarization.

To reiterate, metadata defines the contents and location of data (data model) in the warehouse, relationships between the operational databases and the data warehouse, and the business views of the warehouse data that are accessible by end-user tools. Metadata is searched by users to find data definitions or subject areas. In other words, metadata provides decision-support-oriented pointers to warehouse data, and thus provides a logical link between warehouse data and the decision support application. A data warehouse design

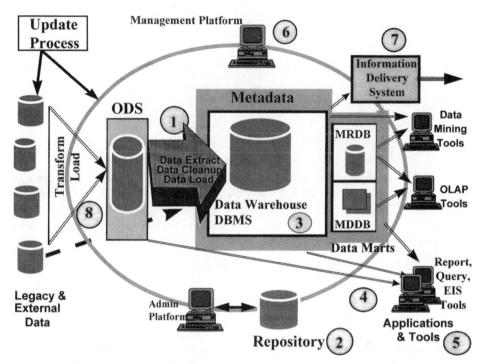

Figure 11.2 Data warehouse architecture.

should ensure that there is a mechanism that populates and maintains the metadata repository, and that *all* access paths to the data warehouse have metadata as an entry point. To illustrate the variety of access paths available into the data warehouse, and at the same time to show how many tool classes can be involved in the process, consider the diagram shown in Fig. 11.3, where the metadata access and collection is indicated by double lines.

To put it another way, the warehouse design should prevent any direct access to the warehouse data (especially updates) if it does not use metadata definitions to gain the access.

Having such metadata repository implemented as a part of the data warehouse framework provides the following benefits:

- It provides a comprehensive suite of tools for enterprisewide metadata management.

- It reduces and eliminates information redundancy, inconsistency, and under-utilization.

- It simplifies management and improves organization, control, and accounting of information assets.

- It increases identification, understanding, coordination, and utilization of enterprisewide information assets.

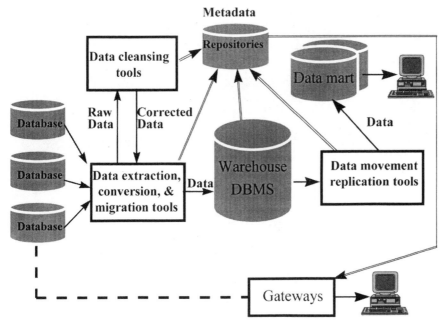

Figure 11.3   Tool landscape and metadata integration points.

- It provides effective data administration tools to better manage corporate information assets with full-function data dictionary.
- It increases flexibility, control, and reliability of the application development process and accelerates internal application development.
- It leverages investment in legacy systems with the ability to inventory and utilize existing applications.
- It provides a universal relational model for heterogeneous RDBMSs to interact and share information.
- It enforces CASE development standards and eliminates redundancy with the ability to share and reuse metadata.

11.4   Metadata Management

A frequently occurring problem in data warehousing is the inability to communicate to the end user what information resides in the data warehouse and how it can be accessed. The key to providing users and applications with a roadmap to the information stored in the warehouse is the metadata. It can define all data elements and their attributes, data sources and timing, and the rules that govern data use and data transformations. Metadata needs to be collected as the warehouse is designed and built. Since metadata describes the information in the warehouse from multiple viewpoints (input, sources, transformation, access, etc.), it is imperative that the same metadata or its *consistent* replicas be available to all tools selected for the warehouse implementation, thus enforcing the integrity and accuracy of the warehouse information. The metadata also has to be available to all warehouse users in order to guide them as they use the warehouse. Even though there are a number of tools available to help users understand and use the warehouse, these tools need to be carefully evaluated before any purchasing decision is made. In other words, a well-thought-through strategy for collecting, maintaining, and distributing metadata is needed for a successful data warehouse implementation.

11.5   Implementation Examples

The following sections briefly describe the metadata repository implementation approaches adopted by Platinum Technologies, R&O, Prism Solutions, and LogicWorks.

11.5.1   PLATINUM Repository

PLATINUM Repository is a client/server repository toolset for managing enterprisewide metadata. The PLATINUM Repository is built as an open-systems solution for organizations implementing enterprisewide systems management strategies.

The PLATINUM Repository toolset allows companies to manage, maintain, and access corporate data, applications, and systems in a complex, heterogeneous client/server environment. The users and warehouse administrators can effectively reconcile and manage a wealth of dispersed corporate data by integrating business information and providing easy access to ever-increasing amounts of corporate knowledge. PLATINUM's *Global Data Dictionary repository* provides a "data junction" functionality for all corporate information and a metadata model to achieve a consistent view of corporate information.

PLATINUM Repository is designed for use in situations when a company needs reliable, systemwide solutions for managing the metadata, or when a company needs a tool to document warehouse sources, targets, and translation rules, and requires an interface with popular warehouse-building and analysis tools. Another example of a potential use of PLATINUM Repository is when a corporation is looking to rationalize data under management, develop and enforce naming standards, implement CASE model management, perform legacy system and data structure impact analysis, and to do all of it over a variety of platforms.

PLATINUM also provides a companion product—PLATINUM Data Shopper, which is a GUI tool for accessing repository metadata and data warehouse contents.

Technical features.   Repository clients support OS/2, Windows 95, Windows NT, and ISPF interface. The repository engine supports OS/2 and Windows NT. The engine scales to HP-UX, AIX, Sun Solaris, and other UNIX platforms. The repository database may reside on DB2/MVS or any platform running ORA-CLE or SYBASE SQL Server.

11.5.2   R&O: The ROCHADE Repository

The ROCHADE Repository is a client/server-based application that has its roots in document management in the early 1980s. Over the last 10 years it has been ported to many platforms and been reimplemented as a client/server application utilizing TCP/IP, APPC, and NetBIOS.

ROCHADE was specifically written as an extensible and scalable metadata storage and manipulation application to achieve three major competitive advantages:

- *Performance*—subsecond response time over WAN environments.

- *Scalability*—ROCHADE can be run anywhere from a laptop to a mainframe.

- *Capacity*—R&O maintains that its product supports very large repository implementations. For example, one customer installation is built on ROCHADE manipulating close to 7 Gbytes of metadata.

One drawback of ROCHADE was its proprietary database implementation for the metadata storage. R&O is moving toward an implementation based on a standard RDBMS.

11.5.3   Prism solutions

An interesting approach to metadata repository management is offered by Prism's *Directory Manager*. This product is designed to integrate and manage all metadata definitions throughout the warehouse environment. The Directory Manager can

- Import business models from CASE tools (Bachman, ADW, IEF, and any other CDIF-compliant CASE tools)

- Import metadata definitions from the Prism Warehouse Manager (the transformation and extraction component of the Prism product suite described in Chap. 10)

- Export metadata into catalogs, dictionaries, and directories of many DSS access tools

- Create flexible customized views based on end-user requirements using graphical front-end application

In other words, Prism Directory Manager is positioned as the tool aimed at solving the problem of creating and managing a unified metadata repository to support the entire data warehousing environment.

Prism Directory Manager allows users to build, store, and navigate an integrated Information Directory of the metadata in a data warehouse. Similar to the card catalog at a library, Prism Directory Manager assists users in finding relevant information for analysis by providing integrated views of business and technical data in the warehouse. It shows where it came from, how it was transformed, and how it has changed over time. Users can create their own customized views of the metadata to fit their business requirements. Prism Directory Manager consists of three components:

- *Information Directory*—the actual directory containing appropriate entries
- *Directory Builder*—customizes views, imports and exports metadata, and sets up relationships
- *Directory Navigator*—navigates the metadata and launches queries into the warehouse

Prism Directory Manager provides a single integration point for managing informational metadata in a data warehouse environment. It builds an extensive view of warehouse information expressed in both business and technical terms. This integrated view allows users to better understand the business information available in the warehouse in context with its physical implementation. By defining the contents of a data warehouse and the structure of the data over a broad spectrum of time, Prism Directory Manager answers users' questions about

- What data exists in the data warehouse
- Where to find the data
- What the original sources of the data are
- How summarizations were created
- What transformations were used
- Who is responsible for correcting errors
- What queries can be used to access the data
- How business definitions have changed over time
- What underlying business assumptions have been made

To build the Information Directory, Prism Directory Manager imports metadata from several sources, including the technical metadata collected by Prism Warehouse Manager during data warehouse development, as well as business metadata from CASE tools and flat files. Prism Directory Manager offers a choice of server databases for the Information Directory, including DB2, ORACLE, SYBASE, INFORMIX, and Watcom.

The Directory Manager includes the ability to share new types of metadata, via a metadata exchange capability called a *MetaLink*. The MetaLink establishes a common layer of metadata between Prism Directory Manager and data warehouse access and analysis tools. Starting with release 2.5, Prism Directory Manager also supports Teradata as a server database on UNIX platforms, and a Windows 95 client for both Directory Builder and Directory Navigator that connect users to the Information Directory.

Prism Directory Manager enhances data warehouse use in several ways:

- Users can identify and retrieve relevant information for analysis with easy, point-and-click navigation of the metadata and one-step launch of query tools.
- Customized navigational paths can be built for different groups of users, enabling more independent querying and filtering of metadata information.
- Business analysts can navigate a data warehouse independently, reducing the need for IS support and increasing the quality of business decisions.

Prism's metadata enhances the accuracy, timeliness, and integrity of data stored in the warehouse, resulting in more confident analysis and decision making.

By providing a single integration point for managing data warehouse metadata, Prism Directory Manager simplifies the population of metadata and makes the metadata more consistent and accurate throughout the warehouse environment.

The ability to exchange metadata among the various data warehouse components greatly reduces the amount of data entry and manual administration needed for managing data warehouse metadata.

Prism Directory Manager serves as the foundation for the storage and management of metadata for all of Prism's data mart, enterprise, and data warehousing solutions. This metadata acts as the centralized card catalog which documents where information is stored and how the data is changed throughout the data warehousing process. By linking its metadata with the industry's leading warehousing tools and repositories, Prism provides a single source of consistent and accurate metadata across the corporate enterprise. This greatly eases the ability to manage, navigate, and access business information intelligently, while protecting a company's initial investment in information systems.

Interoperability with metadata repositories. In order to meet the pressing customer and vendor requirement for a unified, standard interface to manage and share all business and technical information throughout the enterprise, Prism Solutions, Inc. has opened its metadata directory to exchange data with repositories from PLATINUM Technology, R&O (both discussed in the previous sections), and with HP Intelligent Warehouse. HP Intelligent Warehouse is integrated with the Prism Directory Manager through Prism's MetaLinks. This enables HP's Intelligent Warehouse and DataMart Manager users who manage heterogeneous access environments to have full access to the metadata stored in the Prism Information Directory. By providing a common interface to Prism Information Directory's metadata, users can leverage their investment in data access and reporting tools, such as Cognos' Impromptu, Business Objects' BusinessObjects, and Brio Technology's BrioQuery to conduct business analysis across heterogeneous network systems.

Prism Information Directory's information model supports full warehouse metadata exchange with PLATINUM's Repository (PR/MVS release 3.4 and later) and R&O's ROCHADE (version 5.0 and later) repositories through the CDIF standard.

Prism supports ODBC and SQL for open access of metadata from analysis and query environments, as well as Internet standards such as Java and HTML for access to warehouse metadata from industry-standard web browsers, such as Netscape Navigator and Microsoft Internet Explorer. In addition, Prism plans to support OMG's CORBA and Microsoft's DCOM for distribution and synchronization of metadata.

Prism is also committed to supporting emerging specifications for metadata exchange, such as the Metadata Coalition's Metadata Interchange Specification version 1.0, described in Sec. 11.2.

The discussion on Prism Directory Manager would be incomplete without mentioning two companion products: Prism Warehouse Manager and Prism Change Manager. *Prism Warehouse Manager* (briefly discussed in Chap. 10) is the software that transforms operational data into usable business information. It generates programs to extract operational data and external data from source databases, integrates the data from the various sources, and then transforms and loads the integrated data to a choice of target databases on mainframe and client/server platforms. An extensive selection of built-in transformations allows users to perform the data conversions, summarizations, key changes, structural changes, and condensations needed to create an historical perspective of information.

To automate metadata acquisition and to ensure consistent data content in the Directory Manager, Prism Solutions offers another product—*Prism Change Manager,* which automates data warehouse maintenance by capturing, transforming, and applying changed data to the data warehouse. Using log tapes as a source, Prism Change Manager captures only relevant changed records via off-line and unattended execution, saving production time and money as well as protecting the performance of operational systems. Current or near-current changed data is captured from fields that were used as source files for the data warehouse, including DB2, Enscribe, IMS, NonStop/SQL, and ORACLE.

As data warehouses grow and mature, tools like Prism Directory Manager, R&O ROCHADE, and PLATINUM Repository become increasingly valuable. Indeed, user requirements change as the business environments change and new markets and products are being constantly introduced. As with any large system, the warehouse performance needs to be constantly tuned. And information content of the warehouse is constantly being updated. All these factors position metadata repository management products as a focal point of warehouse control and management.

11.5.4 LogicWorks Universal Directory

A recent addition to the group of metadata repository tools is Universal Directory™ from LogicWorks. Universal Directory acts as the hub of all data warehousing activity. By centralizing metadata, it improves the way users manage the entire data warehousing development life cycle.

LogicWorks Universal Directory is an information directory that lets users inventory, publish, and search the metadata about their data warehouse. It is designed to ease the burden of developing and maintaining an effective data warehouse.

Information Directory is designed from the ground up to handle the following activities:

- *Inventorying source data.* Metadata provides information about the name, description, characteristics, and the physical location of the source data being inventoried.

- *Designing the data warehouse.* Metadata is used to define the desired information and to identify what, if any, of that information is currently available in the source data.

- *Mapping source to target data.* Metadata identifies the source and target and defines how the source will be transformed to the target.

- *Populating the data warehouse.* Metadata is used to identify the most appropriate source data to use when populating the warehouse.

- *Analyzing data in the data warehouse.* Metadata imparts knowledge about the information being analyzed and defines the resulting asset.

- *Evolving the data warehouse content.* Metadata provides insight into what additional data would be a natural extension to the data already populating the data warehouse.

Universal Directory consists of two major components: the *Universal Explorer* and the *Directory Administrator.* The Universal Explorer provides business users with a set of tools that facilitate the browsing of informational assets contained within the data warehouse or data mart. The Directory Administrator (for data warehousing managers) facilitates the acquisition, maintenance, extensibility, usage, publishing, analysis and security of data warehouse metadata. Both the Directory Administrator and the Universal Explorer use a search engine that allows users to intuitively navigate vast amounts of information, thus increasing the accuracy of searches. It also lets users customize searches to meet specific data warehousing needs and automate the personalization and delivery of metadata.

Universal Explorer. Universal Explorer is a Yahoolike search engine that provides easy access to the information assets that are stored in Universal Directory. It helps users understand the contents of the data warehouse by providing a clear picture of associated metadata objects such as attributes, external documents, and packages. It can also be used to communicate the value, contents, and activities associated with metadata objects so that users can fully understand their context and their importance to the organization.

Universal Explorer's Weblike search engine lets users explore all of the contents of Universal Directory. The search can be narrowed by object type and/or classification, in addition to using simple boolean expressions such as AND, OR, and NOT. A visual analysis tool enables the discovery of related Universal Directory instances by traversing instances of relationships to other object types. The user interface toolbars and navigation can be customized.

Moreover, Universal Explorer allows users to visualize the data warehousing using a star schema diagram. Choosing metadata from a star schema diagram, users can directly query the data warehouse with Sterling Software's CLEAR: Access reporting tool (included with Universal Directory.)

Universal Explorer allows users to organize metadata with user-defined "packages" for easy references. By allowing users to define groups of otherwise unrelated metadata instances as packages and personal folders, Universal Explorer can ease user access and navigation to application-specific data. For example, a word processing document of population specifications can be packaged with a star schema diagram and a source COBOL program to give users an understanding of a particular data warehousing project initiative.

Another useful feature of Universal Explorer is the "What's New" facility that lets users know what's new in the warehouse. Universal Directory lets users monitor the status of the data warehousing environment, or any other Universal Directory news, via a What's New area on the Universal Explorer screen. For example, the What's New box might describe the latest subject areas to be populated into the data warehouse, the most recent source feed, or the refresh schedule for particular tables.

Directory Administrator.   Directory Administrator helps the data warehouse development team inventory, maintain, index, and publish metadata applicable to the data warehouse and other information assets. Metadata can be extended to reflect organization-specific objects, properties, and relationships. This makes the data warehouse easier to build and maintain over time.

Directory Administrator's document import tool automates the process of importing nontraditional metadata such as word processing documents and spreadsheets. The file import facility automates the process of storing and user-defined metadata that can be arranged into comma-separated value (.csv) format, such as web page listings. Directory Administrator's indexing tool supports the establishment of search indices at the time of initial metadata population, or selectively at a later time. Both the documents' metadata and content within the documents can be indexed. Directory Administrator helps categorize the imported information by assigning a classification to each object.

Universal Directory provides users with an extensible metamodel. Although the product is shipped with a default metamodel, by using Directory Administrator's point-and-click metamodel management tools, users can add new properties to an existing object type, add an entirely new object type, and create new associations between object types.

Universal Directory supports capture of metadata from a variety of legacy data sources. The legacy source systems include valuable metadata that needs to be imported into Universal Directory. To assist in this activity, Universal Directory is integrated with Micro Focus Revolve, a legacy system scanner that parses metadata for the Universal Directory from JCL jobs, program code, and copybooks. The analytical and graphical capabilities of Revolve assist in the selection of the right metadata to include in Universal Directory implementation.

From the manageability point of view, metadata instances in Universal Directory can be manually maintained—instances may be added, edited, or deleted as necessary. Users can secure access to the Universal Directory contents by user and by group restrictions by metadata classification. Large groups of metadata instances can be removed as they become unused of outdated.

Finally, Universal Directory can interoperate with other LogicWorks information management tools, most notably ERwin (a database design tool) and ModelMart (a model management tool), both of which are shipped with Universal Directory.

11.6   Metadata Trends

One of the clearly observable trends in the data warehouse arena is the increase in requirements to incorporate external data within the data warehouse. This is necessary in order to reduce costs and to increase competitiveness and business agility. However, the process of integrating external and internal data into the warehouse faces a number of challenges:

- Inconsistent data formats
- Missing or invalid data
- Different levels of aggregation
- Semantic inconsistency (e.g., different codes may mean different things from different suppliers of data)
- Unknown or questionable data quality and timeliness

All these issues put an additional burden on the collection and management of the common metadata definitions. Some of this burden is being addressed by standards initiatives like Metadata Coalition's Metadata Interchange Specification, described in Sec. 11.2. But even with the standards in place, the metadata repository implementations will have to be sufficiently robust and flexible to rapidly adopt to handling a new data source, to be able to overcome the semantic differences as well as potential differences in low-level data formats, media types, and communication protocols, to name just a few.

Moreover, as data warehouses are beginning to integrate various data types in addition to traditional alphanumeric data types, the metadata and its repository should be able to handle the new enriched data content as easily as the simple data types before. For example, including text, voice, image, full-motion video, and even Web pages in HTML format into the data warehouse may require a new way of presenting and managing the information about these new data types. But the rich data types mentioned above are not limited to just these new media types. Many organizations are beginning to seriously consider storing, navigating, and otherwise managing data describing the organizational structures. This is especially true when we look at data warehouses dealing with human resources on a large scale (e.g., the entire organization, or an entity like a state, or a whole country). And of course, we can always further complicate the issue by adding time and space dimensions to the data warehouse. Storing and managing temporal and spatial data and data about it is a new challenge for metadata tool vendors and standard bodies alike.

3

Business Analysis

This part of the book deals with the overview of business analysis as it applies to data warehousing. Indeed, as was stated in Chap. 1, the principal purpose of data warehousing is to provide information to business users for strategic decision making. This decision-making process is the business analysis of the information stored in a data warehouse, and it is enabled by a number of applications, tools, and techniques that can provide various business-focused views to business domain experts.

The next chapter discusses a broad category of query and reporting tools and applications that are designed to perform somewhat traditional reporting functions about the business.

Chapter 13 takes a close look at on-line analytical processing (OLAP), including its roots, purpose, techniques, and available solutions. Chapters 14 to 16 define some theoretical background in the area of business analysis. Specifically, Chap. 14 deals with models and patterns; Chap. 15, with statistics; and Chap. 16, with the disciplines of artificial intelligence.

12

Reporting and Query
Tools and Applications

The principal purpose of data warehousing is to provide information to business users for strategic decision making. These users interact with the data warehouse using front-end tools, or by getting the required information through the information delivery system, as illustrated in Fig. 12.1. Different types of users engage in different types of decision support activities, and therefore require different types of tools (see Table 12.1).

12.1 Tool Categories

There are five categories of decision support tools, although the lines that separate them are quickly blurring:

- Reporting
- Managed query
- Executive information systems
- On-line analytical processing (see Chap. 13 for more details)
- Data mining (see Part 4 for more details)

12.1.1 Reporting tools

Reporting tools can be divided into production reporting tools and desktop report writers. *Production reporting tools* will let companies generate regular operational reports or support high-volume batch jobs, such as calculating and printing paychecks. Production reporting tools include third-generation languages such as COBOL; specialized fourth-generation languages, such as Information Builders, Inc.'s Focus; and high-end client/server tools, such as MITI's SQR.

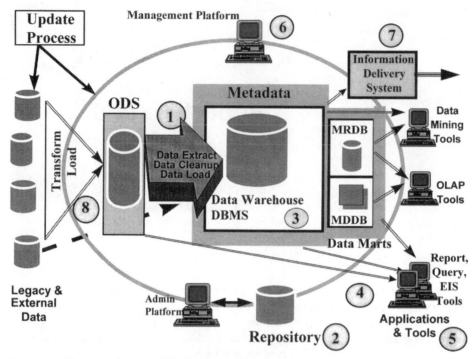

Figure 12.1   Data warehouse architecture.

Report writers, on the other hand, are inexpensive desktop tools designed for end users. Products such as Seagate Software's Crystal Reports let users design and run reports without having to rely on the IS department. In general, report writers have graphical interfaces and built-in charting functions. They can pull groups of data from a variety of data sources and integrate them in a single report. Leading report writers include Crystal Reports, Actuate Software Corp.'s Actuate Reporting System, IQ Software Corp.'s IQ Objects, and Platinum Technology, Inc.'s InfoReports. Vendors are trying to increase the scalability of report writers by supporting three-tiered architectures in which report processing is done on a Windows NT or UNIX server. Report writers also are beginning to offer object-oriented interfaces for designing and manipulating reports and modules for performing ad hoc queries and OLAP analysis.

TABLE 12.1   Users and Related Activities

User	Activity	Tools
Clerk	Simple retrieval	4GL*
Executive	Exception reports	EIS
Manager	Simple retrieval	4GL
Business analysts	Complex analysis	Spreadsheets; OLAP, data mining

* Fourth-generation language.

12.1.2 Managed query tools

Managed query tools shield end users from the complexities of SQL and database structures by inserting a metalayer between users and the database. *Metalayer* is the software that provides subject-oriented views of a database and supports point-and-click creation of SQL. Some vendors, such as Business Objects, Inc., call this layer a "universe." Other vendors, such as Cognos Corp., call it a "catalog." Managed query tools have been extremely popular because they make it possible for knowledge workers to access corporate data without IS intervention.

Most managed query tools have embraced three-tiered architectures to improve scalability. They support asynchronous query execution and integrate with Web servers. Managed query tools vendors are racing to embed support for OLAP and data mining features. Some tool makers, such as Business Objects, take an all-in-one approach. It embeds OLAP functionality in its core 4.0 product. Other vendors, such as Cognos, Platinum Technologies, and Information Builders, take a best-of-breed approach, offering Microsoft Corp. Office-like suites composed of managed query, OLAP, and data mining tools. Other leading managed query tools are IQ Software's IQ Objects, Andyne Computing Ltd.'s GQL, IBM's Decision Server, Speedware Corp.'s Esperant (formerly sold by Software AG), and Oracle Corp.'s Discoverer/2000.

12.1.3 Executive information system tools

Executive information system (EIS) tools predate report writers and managed query tools; they were first deployed on mainframes. EIS tools allow developers to build customized, graphical decision support applications or "briefing books" that give managers and executives a high-level view of the business and access to external sources, such as custom, on-line news feeds. EIS applications highlight exceptions to normal business activity or rules by using color-coded graphics.

Popular EIS tools include Pilot Software, Inc.'s Lightship, Platinum Technology's Forest and Trees, Comshare, Inc.'s Commander Decision, Oracle's Express Analyzer, and SAS Institute, Inc.'s SAS/EIS. EIS vendors are moving in two directions. Many are adding managed query functions to compete head-on with other decision support tools. Others are building packaged applications that address horizontal functions, such as sales, budgeting, and marketing; or vertical industries, such as financial services. For example, Platinum Technologies offers RiskAdvisor, a decision support application for the insurance industry that was built with Forest and Trees. Comshare provides the Arthur family of supply-chain applications for the retail industry.

12.1.4 OLAP tools

OLAP tools provide an intuitive way to view corporate data. These tools aggregate data along common business subjects or dimensions and then let users navigate through the hierarchies and dimensions with the click of a mouse button. Users can drill down, across, or up levels in each dimension or pivot and swap out dimensions to change their view of the data.

Some tools, such as Arbor Software Corp.'s Essbase and Oracle's Express, preaggregate data in special multidimensional databases. Other tools work directly against relational data and aggregate data on the fly, such as MicroStrategy, Inc.'s DSS Agent or Information Advantage, Inc.'s DecisionSuite. Some tools process OLAP data on the desktop instead of a server. Desktop OLAP tools include Cognos' PowerPlay, Brio Technology, Inc.'s BrioQuery, Planning Sciences, Inc.'s Gentium, and Andyne's Pablo. Many of the differences between OLAP tools are fading. Vendors are rearchitecting their products to give users greater control over the tradeoff between flexibility and performance that is inherent in OLAP tools. Many vendors are rewriting pieces of their products in Java. (See a detailed discussion on OLAP in Chap. 13.)

12.1.5   Data mining tools

Data mining tools are becoming hot commodities because they provide insights into corporate data that aren't easily discerned with managed query or OLAP tools. Data mining tools use a variety of statistical and artificial-intelligence (AI) algorithms to analyze the correlation of variables in the data and ferret out interesting patterns and relationships to investigate.

Some data mining tools, such as IBM's Intelligent Miner, are expensive and require statisticians to implement and manage. But there is a new breed of tools emerging that promises to take the mystery out of data mining. These tools include DataMind Corp.'s DataMind, Pilot's Discovery Server, and tools from Business Objects and SAS Institute. These tools offer simple user interfaces that plug in directly to existing OLAP tools or databases and can be run directly against data warehouses.

The end-user tools area spans a number of data warehouse components (see Fig. 12.1). For example, all end-user tools use metadata definitions to obtain access to data stored in the warehouse, and some of these tools (e.g., OLAP tools) may employ additional or intermediary data stores (e.g., data marts, multidimensional databases).

12.2   The Need for Applications

The discussion in this chapter focuses on the tools and applications that fit into the managed query and EIS categories. As was mentioned above, these are easy-to-use, point-and-click tools that either accept SQL or generate SQL statements to query relational data stored in the warehouse. Some of these tools and applications can format the retrieved data into easy-to-read reports, while others concentrate on the on-screen presentation. These tools are the preferred choice of the users of business applications such as segment identification, demographic analysis, territory management, and customer mailing lists. As the complexity of the questions grows, these tools may rapidly become inefficient. Indeed, consider various access types to the data stored in a data warehouse:

- Simple tabular form reporting
- Ad hoc user-specified queries
- Predefined repeatable queries
- Complex queries with multitable joins, multilevel subqueries, and sophisticated search criteria
- Ranking
- Multivariable analysis
- Time series analysis
- Data visualization, graphing, charting, and pivoting
- Complex textual search
- Statistical analysis
- AI techniques for testing of hypothesis, trends discovery, definition, and validation of data clusters and segments
- Information mapping (i.e., mapping of spatial data in geographic information systems)
- Interactive drill-down reporting and analysis

The first four types of access are covered by the combined category of tools we'll call *query and reporting* tools. We can identify three distinct types of reporting:

1. *Creation and viewing of standard reports.* This is today's main reporting activity: the routine delivery of reports based on predetermined measures.

2. *Definition and creation of ad hoc reports.* These can be quite complex, and the trend is to off-load this time-consuming activity to the users. As a result, reporting tools that allow managers and business users to quickly create their own reports and get quick answers to business questions are becoming increasingly popular.

3. *Data exploration.* With the newest wave of business intelligence tools, users can easily "surf" through data without a preset path to quickly uncover business trends or problems. This is the domain of OLAP tools, discussed in the next chapter.

While reporting type 1 may appear relatively simple, types 2 and 3, combined with certain business requirements, often exceed existing tool's capabilities and may require building sophisticated applications to retrieve and analyze warehouse data. These applications often take the form of custom-developed screens and reports that retrieve frequently used data and format it in a pre-defined standardized way. This approach may be very useful for those data warehouse users who are not yet comfortable with ad hoc queries. Therefore, this chapter will also look at some application development environments that may be used to build custom applications for data warehousing.

12.3   Cognos Impromptu

Overview.   Impromptu from Cognos Corporation is positioned as an enterprise solution for interactive database reporting that delivers 1- to 1000+-seat scalability. Impromptu's object-oriented architecture ensures control and administrative consistency across all users and reports. Users access Impromptu through its easy-to-use graphical user interface. Impromptu has been well received by users because querying and reporting are unified in one interface, and the users can get meaningful views of corporate data quickly and easily.

Impromptu offers a fast and robust implementation at the enterprise level, and features full administrative control, ease of deployment, and low cost of ownership. Impromptu is the database reporting tool that exploits the power of the database, while offering complete control over all reporting within the enterprise. In terms of scalability, Impromptu can support a single user reporting on personal data, or thousands of users reporting on data from large data warehouses.

User acceptance of Impromptu is very high because its user interface looks and feels just like the Windows products these users already use. With Impromptu, users can leverage the skills they've acquired from using today's popular spreadsheets and word processors. In addition, Impromptu insulates users from the underlying database technology, which also reduces the time necessary to learn the tool.

The Impromptu Information Catalog.   Impromptu reporting begins with the *Information Catalog,* a LAN-based repository of business knowledge and data-access rules. The Catalog insulates users from such technical aspects of the database as SQL syntax, table joins, and cryptic table and field names. The Catalog also protects the database from repeated queries and unnecessary processing.

Creating a catalog is a relatively simple task, so that an Impromptu administrator can be anyone who's familiar with basic database query functions.

The Catalog presents the database in a way that reflects how the business is organized, and uses the terminology of the business. Impromptu administrators are free to organize database items such as tables and fields into Impromptu's subject-oriented folders, subfolders, and columns. Structuring the data in this way makes it easy for users to navigate within a database and assemble reports. In addition, users are not restricted to fixed combinations or predetermined selections; they can select on the finest detail within a database.

Impromptu enables business-relevant reporting through business rules, which can consist of shared calculations, filters, and ranges for critical success factors. For example, users can create a report that includes only high-margin sales from the last fiscal year for the eastern region, instead of having to use complex filter statements.

Object-oriented architecture. Impromptu's object-oriented architecture drives inheritance-based administration and distributed catalogs. This means that changes to business rules, permission sets, and query activities cascade automatically throughout the enterprise. Such top-to-bottom administration ensures that changes are global and control is precise.

Impromptu implements management functionality through the use of governors. The governors allow administrators to control the enterprise's reporting environment. Some of the activities and processes that governors can control are

- Query activity
- Processing location
- Database connections
- Reporting permissions
- User profiles
- Client/server balancing
- Database transactions
- Security by value
- Field and table security

Organizations can automate Impromptu and its interaction with other OLE-aware desktop applications using standard OLE Automation calls. With this capability, users can automate simple, repetitive tasks or create powerful applications outside Impromptu. In addition, Impromptu offers its own visual automation facility, CognosScript, an environment for building user-defined macros. Users can create custom applications that incorporate Impromptu functionality using either CognosScript or any environment that supports OLE Automation (e.g., Microsoft's Visual Basic or PowerSoft's PowerBuilder).

Reporting. Impromptu is designed to make it easy for users to build and run their own reports. With ReportWise templates and HeadStarts, users simply apply data to Impromptu to produce reports rapidly.

Impromptu's predefined ReportWise templates include templates for mailing labels, invoices, sales reports, and directories. These templates are complete with formatting, logic, calculations, and custom automation. Organizations can create templates for standard company reports, and then deploy them to every user who needs them. The templates are database-independent; therefore, users simply map their data onto the existing placeholders to quickly create sophisticated reports. Additionally, Impromptu provides users with a variety of page and screen formats, known as *HeadStarts*, to create new reports that are visually appealing.

Impromptu offers special reporting options that increase the value of distributed standard reports:

- *Picklists and prompts.* Organizations can create standard Impromptu reports for which users can select from lists of values called *picklists*. For example, a user can select a picklist of all sales representatives with a single click of the mouse. For reports containing too many values for a single variable, Impromptu offers prompts. For example, a prompt asks the user at run time to supply a value or range for the report data. Picklists and prompts make a single report flexible enough to serve many users.

- *Custom templates.* Standard report templates with global calculations and business rules can be created once and then distributed to users of different databases. Users then can apply their data to the placeholders contained in the template. A template's standard logic, calculations, and layout complete the report automatically in the user's choice of format.

- *Exception reporting.* Exception reporting is the ability to have reports highlight values that lie outside accepted ranges. Impromptu offers three types of exception reporting that help managers and business users immediately grasp the status of their business:
    - ⇨ *Conditional filters.* Retrieve only those values that are outside defined thresholds, or define ranges to organize data for quick evaluation. For example, a user can set a condition to show only those sales under $10,000.
    - ⇨ *Conditional highlighting.* Create rules for formatting data on the basis of data values. For example, a user can set a condition that all sales over $10,000 always appear in blue.
    - ⇨ *Conditional display.* Display report objects under certain conditions. For example, a report will display a regional sales history graph only if the sales are below a predefined value.

- *Interactive reporting.* Impromptu unifies querying and reporting in a single interface. Users can perform both these tasks by interacting with live data in one integrated module.

- *Frames.* Impromptu offers an interesting frame-based reporting style. Frames are building blocks that may be used to produce reports that are formatted with fonts, borders, colors, shading, etc. Frames know about their contents and how to display them. Frames, or combinations of frames, simplify building even complex reports. Once a multiframe report is designed, it can be saved as a template and rerun at any time with other data. The data formats itself according to the type of frame selected by the user:

⇨ List frames are used to display detailed information. List frames can contain calculated columns, data filters, headers and footers, etc.

⇨ Form frames offer layout and design flexibility. Form reports can contain multiple or repeating forms such as mailing labels.

⇨ Cross-tab frames are used to show the totals of summarized data at selected intersections, for example, sales of product by outlet.

⇨ Chart frames make it easy for users to see their business data in 2-D and 3-D displays using line, bar, ribbon, area, and pie charts. Charts can be stand-alone or attached to other frames in the same report.

⇨ Text frames allow users to add descriptive text to reports and display binary large objects (BLOBs) such as product descriptions or contracts.

⇨ Picture frames incorporate bitmaps to reports or specific records, perfect for visually enhancing reports.

⇨ OLE frames make it possible for users to insert any OLE object into a report.

■ Impromptu's design is tightly integrated with the Microsoft Windows environment and standards, including OLE 2 support. Users can quickly learn Impromptu using Microsoft Office–compatible user interface that is complete with tabbed dialog boxes, bubble Help, and customizable toolbars. Together with OLE support, users can produce enhanced reports by simply placing data or objects in a document, regardless of the application in which it resides. For example, Impromptu reports can be embedded in spreadsheet files, or placed in a Word document.

Impromptu Request Server.   Starting with version 3.5, Impromptu introduced the new Request Server, which allows clients to off-load the query process to the server. A PC user can now schedule a request to run on the server, and an Impromptu Request Server will execute the request, generating the result on the server. When done, the scheduler notifies the user, who can then access, view, or print at will from the PC. This offers many benefits; for example, users can do their processing when and where they want, either immediately on their PCs or on the server. This frees up the PC to do other things, possibly to run another reporting session. A user can even run the report at night with the PC turned off. Administrators can use this off-peak processing concept to schedule regular and recurring standard reports, which they distribute as part of normal business operations. Administrators can also use server processing to reduce network traffic, to get more effective use out of computing resources and to sequence operations in their centralized environment. The Impromptu Request Server runs on HP/UX 9.X, IBM AIX 4.X, and Sun Solaris 2.4. It supports data maintained in ORACLE 7.x and SYBASE System 10/11.

Supported databases.   Impromptu provides a native database support for ORACLE, Microsoft SQL Server, SYBASE SQL Server, OmniSQL Gateway,

SYBASE NetGateway, MDI DB2 Gateway, Informix, CA-Ingres, Gupta SQL-Base, Borland InterBase, Btrieve, dBASE, Paradox, and ODBC accessing any database with an ODBC driver.

Conclusion.   In summary, Impromptu features include

- *Unified query and reporting interface.*   Impromptu unifies both query and reporting in a single user interface. This allows users to query the database and create standard and sophisticated ad hoc reports—all in the same module.

- *Object-oriented architecture.*   Object-oriented architecture enables inheritance-based administration, so that the requirements of more than 1000 users can be accommodated as easily as a single user. This ensures control and administrative consistency across all users and reports from a central point of control.

- *Complete integration with PowerPlay.*   Cognos business intelligence products provide an integrated solution for users who need to explore trends and patterns and view the underlying details at the same time.

- *Scalability.*   Impromptu's scalability ranges from a single user reporting on personal data to thousands of users reporting on data from large data warehouses. Impromptu's Request Server gives users direct access to the data warehouse and choice of processing location for maximum flexibility.

- *Security and control.*   Security, based on user profiles and classes, determines how the database is accessed, who can access it, and what the user is permitted to see. Impromptu's security features ensure that users have access only to the information they require.

- *Data presented in a business context.*   Impromptu presents information using the terminology of the business. Impromptu can deliver data under headings such as fiscal periods, sales regions, and product groups—whatever makes the most sense in any given business context. This makes report building easier to learn and increases user acceptance.

- *Over 70 predefined report templates.*   Impromptu's predefined, database-independent templates allow users to simply apply data to make reports instantly come alive. Users can quickly and easily create such popular reports as mailing labels, invoices, and sales reports.

- *Frame-based reporting.*   Impromptu provides list, form, cross-tab, chart, text, image, and OLE frames to build reports. Simple and complex reports can be built relatively easily using frames or combinations of frames.

- *Business-relevant reporting.*   Impromptu enables business-relevant reporting through business rules such as shared calculations, filters, and value ranges. This saves time during report creation and maintains consistency of report information across the enterprise.

- *Database-independent catalogs.*   The heart of Impromptu is its information catalog, a LAN-based repository of business knowledge and data-access rules. Since catalogs are independent of the database, they require only minimal maintenance.

12.4   Applications

Often, organizations use a familiar application development approach to build a query and reporting environment for the data warehouse. There are several reasons for doing this:

- A legacy DSS or EIS system is still being used, and the reporting facilities appear adequate.

- An organization has made a large investment in a particular application development environment (e.g., Visual C++, PowerBuilder), and has a sufficient number of well-trained developers to provide required query and reporting solutions.

- A new tool may require an additional investment in developers skill set, software, and the infrastructure, all or part of which was not budgeted for in the planning stages of the project.

- The business users do not want to get involved in this phase of the project, and will continue to rely on the IT organization to deliver periodic reports in a familiar format.

- A particular reporting requirement may be too complicated for an available reporting tool to handle.

All these reasons are perfectly valid and, in fact, in many cases result in a timely and cost-effective delivery of a reporting system for a data warehouse.

Overall, the entire development paradigm is shifting from procedural to object-based. A universal acceptance of languages such as C++ and the proliferation and maturity of Microsoft's Object Linking and Embedding (OLE) are evidence of the growing popularity of object-oriented analysis, design, and programming. Further evidence can be found in the new way of building applications from reusable components—the gains in productivity and software quality can be quite dramatic.

As a result, the market for effective, portable, easy-to-learn, full-featured graphical development tools is very competitive. This market is not static. It continues to grow more competitive as Windows development and operating environments continue to mature, and as de facto industry standards such as OLE, ODBC, MAPI, and HTML continue to proliferate. The universal acceptance of the World Wide Web has added more fuel to the market dynamics. In fact, regardless of whether we are talking about a third-generation language (3GL) such as C++ or a tool like PowerBuilder, the ability to access information via the Web is considered to be a mandatory requirement for any system built today. To discuss new application development methodologies and every popular tool is certainly beyond the scope of this book. Thus, although application development includes 3GL languages such as C and C++, this section discusses the two popular 4GL tools that are often used to develop generic client/server applications. While these tools are not specific data warehousing tools, they are quite applicable to building query and reporting systems for data warehousing. The tools discussed below are PowerBuilder from the PowerSoft division of Sybase, and Forté, from Forté Software.

12.4.1 PowerBuilder

PowerBuilder delivers some of the key attractions of object-oriented application development, including encapsulation of application objects, polymorphism, the ability to inherit forms and GUI objects, and the premise that, once an object has been created and tested, it can then be reused by other applications.

The strength of PowerBuilder isn't just its object orientation, its ability to develop Windows applications, or its affinity toward client/server architecture. One of the greatest benefits attributed to PowerBuilder is its ability to dramatically increase the developer's productivity and shorten the development cycle when creating graphical client/server applications.

PowerBuilder offers a powerful fourth-generation language (4GL), object-oriented graphical development environment, and the ability to interface with a wide variety of database management systems. It can interface with such popular database engines as SYBASE SQL Server, IBM's DB2, Centura's SQLBase, ORACLE Server, Informix OnLine, XDB Server from XDB, and All-base/SQL from Hewlett-Packard.

Object orientation. PowerBuilder supports many object-oriented features. Among them is *inheritance,* which allows developers to change attributes of child classes by modifying these attributes in the parent class of objects. *Data abstraction*—the encapsulation of properties and behavior within the object— is enabled through three classes of objects: window classes, menu classes, and user-defined classes. These classes contain objects that are defined and built by developers looking for enhanced reusability. Indeed, the encapsulation of the code and attributes generalizes the functionality of the objects. Hence, if reusability is desired, objects should be created with clearly defined interfaces and encapsulated data and behavior. *Polymorphism,* another object term, allows one message to invoke an appropriate but different behavior when sent to different object types. Polymorphism support in PowerBuilder means that the same message can be sent to the object and its parent, and both would behave appropriately. A trivial example would be a message to add a title to a document. In the general case, the document class has subclasses of letters, resumes, and status reports, all of which inherit document properties. The message in question can add an appropriate title to each subclass document according to the internal format that was encapsulated into this document.

To add to the list of object-oriented features of PowerBuilder, consider the SQL object that allows programmers to modify the application's data windows at run time. In addition, PowerBuilder supports execution of SQL commands at run time.

Windows facilities. A powerful Windows-based environment, PowerBuilder supports key Windows facilities. These include dynamic data exchange (DDE), dynamic link libraries (DLLs), object linking and embedding (OLE), multiple-document interface (MDI), and a familiar drag and drop metaphor.

PowerSoft also included collaborative workgroup enabling facilities such as the code management feature in its flagship product. PowerBuilder code management supports the ability to check objects in and out of libraries, which facilitates joint workgroup development projects.

Features. PowerBuilder is known for its intuitive user interface, graphical development environment, and ease of use. With PowerBuilder, a developer can define the bulk of an application by creating windows and controls with various painter utilities. This work is done on a client platform running Microsoft Windows, and the entire development environment is designed to take advantage of the available Windows facilities. The PowerBuilder windows and controls can contain program scripts that execute in response to different events that can be detected by PowerBuilder. The scripting language—PowerScript—is a high-level, object-oriented, event-driven programming language similar to Visual Basic.

PowerBuilder controls include standard Windows objects such as radio buttons, push buttons, list boxes, check boxes, combo boxes, text fields, menus, edit fields, and pictures.

Among the events are standard Windows events such as *clicked* and *double-clicked,* which represent pointing-device (i.e., a mouse) handling. PowerBuilder allows developers to define application-specific events and create application messages that are used for communication between application objects.

Creation of a new window is a starting point for a new application. Ideally, this new window closely corresponds with a high-level user's view of the application, which clearly enhances the quality of the application (at least in the user's eyes). Let's examine how a client/server application can be constructed using PowerBuilder painters.

- *Application Painter.* This utility is used first to identify basic details and components of a new or existing application. Existing application maintenance is quite simple—double clicking on the application icon displays a hierarchical view of the application structure. All levels can be expanded or contracted with a click of the right mouse button. Similarly easily, the Application Painter allows creation and naming of a new application, selection of an application icon, setting of the library search path, and defining of default text characteristics. As an event-driven system, the Application Painter has access to application-level events. Among them are Open (triggered when an application starts), Close (triggered when an application is terminated), Idle (triggered when an application remains inactive after a specified period of time), and a number of error events. These events control the main flow of the application. For example, an Open event, when triggered, executes the Open script for the application, which may direct control to initialization statements and open applications windows defined with the Window Painter. The Application Painter can be also used to run or debug the application.

- *Window Painter.* The Window Painter is used to create and maintain the majority of PowerBuilder window objects (with the exception of user-defined objects). Several types of windows are supported by the Window Painter: main, parent, child, pop-up, dialog, and MDI. For a new application, the process usually starts with the creation of a main application window (the one typically displayed first when the application starts). This window, like all others, has several attributes such as title, position, size, color, and font. These attributes, as well as objects within the window (various buttons, boxes, menus, etc.), are defined using the Window Painter. It is important to note that all Window Painter operations are performed in an intuitive graphical fashion, by dragging and dropping and clicking mouse buttons. After the window and controls are created, the developers can select the Script Option to open the *Power-Script Painter,* which allows developers to select from a list of events and global and local variables, all of which can be pasted into the body of the code. From the PowerScript Painter the developer can invoke the Object Browser, which displays attributes of any object, data type, and structure. The selected attributes also can be pasted into the code. Another useful action supported within the Window Painter is the Paste SQL window, which allows a developer to graphically select and paste SQL statements. Windows created with the Window Painter possess such object properties as inheritance, where windows and controls can inherit properties from other windows.

- *DataWindows Painter.* DataWindows are at the heart of many Power-Builder applications. These are powerful dynamic objects that provide access to databases and other data sources such as ASCII files. PowerBuilder applications use DataWindows to connect to multiple databases and files, as well as import and export data in a variety of formats such as dBase, Excel, Lotus, and tab-delimited text. Acting as primary data containers, DataWindows are used for such database operations as ad hoc queries, browsing and editing of tables, report writing, and data exchange with other applications. All basic DataWindows operations are supported transparently, without the need to code in SQL. Using DataWindows Painter, a developer can select a data source using DataWindow options such as Quick Select, SQL Select (DataWindows issues SQL Select statements), Query (a SQL statement created in another object), and External (data retrieval using PowerScript statements). In addition, DataWindows supports execution of stored procedures for those database engines that support this feature. That is one of the reasons why PowerBuilder is so popular with SYBASE developers. Data-Windows allows developers to select a number of presentation styles from the list of tabular, grid, label, and free form. An option in DataWindows allows a user-specified number of rows to be displayed in a display line. Associated with DataWindows Painter is the *Query Painter,* which allows the generation of SQL statements that can be stored in PowerBuilder libraries. These stored SQL statements can be used elsewhere in the current application as well as in other applications.

Thus, using basic Application Painter, Window Painter, and DataWindows Painter facilities, a simple client/server application can be constructed literally in minutes. When more complex applications are to be created, developers can code SQL statements into the scripts associated with other PowerBuilder objects. A rich set of SQL functions is supported, including CONNECT/DIS-CONNECT, DECLARE, OPEN and CLOSE cursor, FETCH, and COMMIT/ROLLBACK. Stored procedures are supported via DECLARE, EXECUTE, UPDATE, and CLOSE procedure statements. PowerBuilder supports such SQL extensions as FETCH PRIOR and SELECT FOR UPDATE, if the DBMS supports these. Dynamic preparation and execution of SQL statements is also supported.

SQL scripts communicate with database engines via a special transaction object (SQLCA is the default), which manages communication parameters, identifies the target database, and monitors the status of database operations. This transaction object is created automatically by PowerBuilder when the application starts up. For database connectivity, PowerBuilder supports ODBC and DRDA. ODBC support comes with an ODBC administration utility, which allows the user to add new data sources; add, modify, and delete users; and install and (re)configure ODBC drivers. In addition, the Administration utility works with database views and stored procedures.

PowerBuilder supplies several other painters. Among them are

- *Database Painter.* This painter allows developers to pick tables from the list box and examine and edit join conditions and predicates, key fields, extended attributes, display formats, and other database attributes.

- *Structure Painter.* This painter allows the creation and modification of data structures and groups of related data elements.

- *Preference Painter.* This is a configuration tool that is used to examine and modify configuration parameters for the PowerBuilder development environment.

- *Menu Painter.* This painter creates menus for the individual windows and the entire application.

- *Function Painter.* This is a development tool that assists developers in creating function calls and parameters using combo boxes. In addition to facilitating the creation of new functions, Function Painter simplifies access to the function arguments and global variables of over 500 functions provided by PowerBuilder.

- *Library Painter.*   This painter manages the library in which the application components reside. It also supports check-in and check-out of library objects for developers.

- *User Object Painter.*   This painter allows developers to create custom controls. Often, these custom controls are graphical objects that modify or combine existing objects. Once created, these custom controls can be treated just like standard PowerBuilder controls.

- *Help Painter.*   This is a built-in help system, similar to the MS Windows Help facility.

Distributed PowerBuilder.   Starting with version 5, the PowerBuilder offers a distributed computing development environment, in which developers can create objects that contain business rules and distribute them onto one or more application servers. This multitiered environment allows for an unlimited number of application servers. Distributed PowerBuilder offers a fast way to develop sophisticated distributed applications. It unites rapid application development and multitiered computing to provide "practical application partitioning." Developers can create distributed applications using PowerBuilder nonvisual objects to define business processing logic. Developers can distribute PowerBuilder objects across the network for increased scalability and centralized management. These distributed objects can also be compiled for optimum performance. Nonvisual user objects can be saved with proxy objects or aliases which store all the information needed to distribute the application onto a remote server. A new transport object is created on the server platform, where it listens for client connection requests. A new client-based connection object requests connection to a remote object. A connection is then created in its own thread for maximum performance. Distributed PowerBuilder supports a distributed computing model in a LAN environment as well as the World Wide Web (either the Internet or an intranet). To this end, PowerBuilder objects provide a high-level interface to distributed services, thus freeing developers from the need to understand the complexities of the underlying communications drivers.

Features.   Distributed PowerBuilder features a broad range of new features that enable the deployment of fast applications anywhere:

- *Fast Compiled Code*—native code generation built on advanced Watcom compiler technology. This significant enhancement improves application performance in a number of key areas, including script execution, mathematical expressions, integer and floating-point arithmetic, function calls, and array processing.

- *Practical application partitioning*—the ability to partition PowerBuilder objects across the network for improved application performance and management.

- *Extended OLE 2 support*—OLE 2 automation is provided for developing, deploying, and accessing OLE 2 automation servers. Any OCX object can "plug and play" directly into PowerBuilder applications, resulting in productive component-based development. Any OCX object can be encapsulated as a PowerBuilder object for inheritance and reuse.

- *Windows 95 Logo compliance*—distributed PowerBuilder supports all the richness of the Windows 95 user interface, including list view and tree view controls, extended controls for Tab, Rich Text Format, long file names, registry, property sheets, and drop-down picture list box.

- *Scalable Team Development—ObjectCycle*—a server-based object management facility that provides versioning, labeling, and reporting functions to assist development teams in doing rapid application development in a workgroup setting.

- *New DataWindows*—Distributed PowerBuilder adds two DataWindow presentation styles: OLE 2 and Rich Text Edit (RTE). OLE-style DataWindows provide a SQL interface to OLE automation servers, making it possible to embed OLE server objects such as Microsoft Word, Microsoft Graph, and Microsoft Excel into the PowerBuilder DataWindow. Rich Text DataWindows offer developers and end users word-processing capabilities within the context of the DataWindow.

- *Advanced Object Browser*—an object browser that is accessible directly from any PowerBuilder painter. This fully integrated browser displays a tabbed interface and allows developers to inspect any object type, including System objects, Enumerated data types, OLE objects, Proxy objects, Structures, Data types, Application, DataWindow, Window, Menu, User objects, and Functions.

- *PowerBuilder Foundation Class Library*—an innovative architecture that offers developers a powerful set of reusable, prebuilt objects and services to accelerate the development of full-featured object-oriented Distributed PowerBuilder applications. Developers can easily customize and extend all PFC classes.

- *PowerScript Editor*—a fully customizable Script Editor that allows developers to easily change font, size, style, color, tab size, and more to match their own programming style. Support for syntax highlighting and automatic indenting reduces typing errors and makes code easier to read. Additional features include drag and drop support for blocks of code, and support for an unlimited number of undo operations.

- *Art, Component, and Sample Productivity Galleries*—three easily accessible productivity galleries. The Art Gallery's assortment of icons and bitmaps adds flair to an application's menus, toolbars, and buttons. The Sample Gallery quickly demonstrates how to build a wide range of applications with features including DataWindows, Pipeline, Inheritance, Mail, MDI, Menu Techniques, and OLE. The Component Gallery provides a collection of prebuilt OCX controls for enhancing and expanding Power-Builder applications.

12.4.2 Forté

In a three-tiered client/server computing architecture, an application's functionality is partitioned into three distinct pieces: presentation logic with its graphical user interface, application business logic, and data access functionality. Typically, in such a partitioned application, the presentation logic is placed on a client, while the application logic resides on an application server, and the data access logic and the database reside on a database or a data warehouse server (see Fig. 12.2).

Forté (from Forté Software, Inc.) is designed to provide application developers with facilities to develop and partition applications to be efficiently placed on the proper platforms of the three-tiered architecture. Forté provides an environment that encourages rapid development, testing, and deployment of distributed client/server applications across any enterprise. Forté's strength is in its ability to implement open, scalable applications that are independent of database management systems, windows managers, communications software, and operating systems.

Application partitioning. Forté allows developers to build a logical application that is independent of the underlying physical environment. Developers build an application as if it were to run entirely on a single machine. Then, Forté automatically splits apart (partitions) the application to run across the clients and servers that constitute the deployment environment. Forté also enables developers to easily modify the partitioning scheme. By supporting tunable application partitioning, Forté increases developer productivity, applications flexibility, performance, and control.

Shared-application services. With Forté, developers build a high-end application as a collection of application components. These components can include

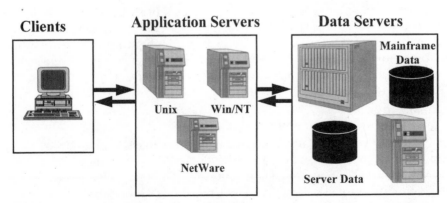

Figure 12.2 Three-tiered client/server architecture.

client functionality such as data presentation and other desktop processing. They can also include shared-application services which provide high-level business functions such as a billing service, a repair scheduling service, or an inventory service. Shared services are built along with desktop functionality using the same set of tools in a unified development environment. When the application is partitioned, Forté installs each shared service on a multiuser computer, where it is accessed simultaneously by many users. There is no need for each user to have his own copy of the service.

Shared-application services form the basis for a three-tiered application architecture in which clients request actions from application services that, in turn, access one or more of the underlying data sources. Each tier (clients, application services, data sources) can be developed and maintained independent of each other.

Business events. Business events automate the notification of significant business occurrences so that appropriate actions can be taken immediately by users and/or application services. For example, in a customer support application, service reps can be notified of critical calls, even if they are busy at the time. In financial services, a trader can be notified when the price of a bond hits a new high. In manufacturing, if a machine fails, shipping schedules can be automatically adjusted and repair technicians can be immediately redeployed.

Forté supports business events with several key technologies. Forté detects events, whether they originate on a user's desktop or in an application service. Forté then sends notification to all the application components that have expressed interest in that event. Each Forté application component can process the arrival of an event, even if it is working on another application task at the time. These capabilities apply to events that flow from clients to servers, from servers to servers, and from servers back to clients.

Forté offers comprehensive life-cycle support through three functional components:

- *Application Development Facility* (ADF). This is based on the distributed object computing framework and is used to define user interfaces and application logic; it includes a GUI designer for building user screens, a proprietary 4GL called *Transactional Object-Oriented Language* (TOOL), a set of standard class libraries, an interactive debugger, and a development repository. Developers construct applications using *workshops* (a set of tools similar to PowerBuilder's painters). A GUI is not a necessary component—Forté supports building distributed client/server applications that do not have a user interface (e.g., a telephone switch support system). Screens and 4GL routines are stored and managed in a repository as objects to permit a modular approach and facilitate reuse.

- *System Generation Facility* (SGF). This assists developers in partitioning the application, generating executables for distribution. Forté's most powerful feature is its ability to automate partitioning of the application into client and server components. SGF automatically puts processes on the appropriate device on the basis of the application's logic and platform inventory—a developer supplies the information about eligible platforms. Forté maps this proposed architecture to the target environment and sets up necessary communications. SGF generates C++ source code for compilation into native executable code on target platforms. To enhance flexibility, Forté allows developers to override the proposed partitioning with a graphical partitioning tool. In addition, application partitions can be replicated for scaleability, load balancing, and fault resilience.

- *Distributed Execution Facility* (DEF). This provides tools for managing applications at run time, including system administration support, a distributed object manager to handle communications between application partitions, and a performance monitor. DEF provides a unified collection of run-time services and control structures to deploy partitions, administer applications, distribute objects, perform load balancing, provide for failover scenarios, and dynamically tune performance. The Forté run-time system supports the partitioned application. It manages the communications among application partitions for high performance. It implements the reliability strategies of partition failover, transactions, and version checking. It provides integration with OLE, DCE, object brokers, RPCs, TP monitors, and wrapped external services. It also includes the Forté performance monitor and application management interface.

Forté generates portable code across all supported platforms that include VMS, HP-UX, Dynix (Sequent), AIX, SunOS, Solaris, and DG-UX. Client support includes MS Windows, Apple Macintosh, and Motif.

Forté provides general-purpose object wrappers to interface with legacy applications. Legacy support is provided via RPCs (Netwise) and gateways (SYBASE/MDI and ORACLE), with integration via DDE and object request broker (Digital's Object Broker). Forté facilitates synchronization of processes by supporting transactions across heterogeneous platforms.

Application development is simplified since developers do not have to know the networking protocol, how the application is partitioned, and on which platforms each partition would run. Forté enables multitasking within applications by providing simple commands to invoke asynchronous communications.

Web and Java integration.   In November 1996, Forté announced release 3.0, a major enhancement of the Forté suite of products for developing, deploying, and managing high-end distributed applications. Release 3.0 provides integration with Java, desktop, and mainframe platforms, and offers new features to improve the management and performance of distributed applications.

Release 3.0 features for extended support of desktop standards, performance, and enhanced legacy integration include the following:

- ActiveX and ActiveX server support: ActiveX objects can be embedded within Forté applications for ease of access to ActiveX component libraries.

- Forté servers can be called from OLE, complementing the previous release feature that allowed Forté to call OLE objects. This makes it easier for other applications to access Forté servers.

- To enhance legacy integration, Forté Software entered into a joint development and marketing agreement with Conextions, Inc., North Andover, Mass. Conextions' Enterprise Access Series provides access to a variety of legacy systems, including IBM mainframes, AS/400, UNIX, VAX VMS, Tandem, and others. Conextions has developed a Forté Developer's Toolkit for Enterprise Access Server, which allows developers to access legacy data and resources as native Forté objects without writing any host-specific code.

- Support for the ability to call Forté Application Servers from C++ modules, complementing a release 2.0 capability for Forté Servers to call C++ modules. This means that investments organizations make in creating Forté Servers can be leveraged by C++ programs.

- Nomadic Services Support for mobile computing. This enables remote users to run an application stand-alone and to then connect to corporate servers at a later time to complete a task.

- An option to generate and compile C++ code for client modules in order to speed up the execution on desktop machines. This complements Forté's ability to generate compiled as well as interpreted servers.

- 4GL Profiler, which provides detailed data on an application's performance, simplifying tuning. Because of increased use of native C++ compiler optimizers, Forté users can anticipate a reduction in memory usage up to 40 percent, depending on the platform employed.

Portability and supported platforms. Forté provides transparent portability across the most common client/server platforms for both development and deployment. Each developer can choose from among Windows, Macintosh, and Motif desktops. Forté masks the differences while preserving the native look and feel of each environment.

Any set of supported platforms can be used for deployment. For example, applications developed with Sybase on UNIX can be deployed with ORACLE on VMS. Organizations have the freedom to alter their technical infrastructure while preserving their investments in developed applications. Server/Hosts platforms include Data General AViiON, Digital Alpha, Open VMS, UNIX, VAX/Open VMS, HP 9000, IBM RS/6000, Sequent Symmetry, Sun SPARC, and Windows NT. Desktop GUI support includes Macintosh, Motif, and Windows. Supported RDBMSs include DB2/6000, INFORMIX, MS SQL Server, ORACLE, Rdb, SYBASE, and any ODBC-compliant database.

12.4.3   Information builders

We will discuss two products from Information Builders: Cactus and FOCUS Fusion.

Cactus.   As a response to products like Forté, Information Builders, Inc. has developed *Cactus,* a new second-generation, enterprise-class, client/server development environment. Designed for today's rapidly expanding, multiplatform topologies, Cactus lets developers create, test, and deploy business applications spanning the Internet, IBM mainframes, midrange servers, LANs, and workstations.

As a three-tiered development environment, Cactus enables creation of applications of any size and scope. The applications are typically a combination of transaction processing, decision support, and batch processing.

Cactus builds highly reusable components for distributed enterprise-class applications through a visual object-based development environment. Typical business applications consist of three primary components: the presentation layer, business logic, and data access. Enterprise-class client/server systems require that these components be built to run where and when required. Using Cactus, an application can be built and packaged for two-tiered, three-tiered, or Web topologies. A drag-and-drop partitioning editor permits developers to move locally developed application components to servers anywhere in an enterprise.

Cactus is easy to learn and use. Developers don't have to go outside the toolbox to create complex applications. Cactus offers an object-based visual programming environment that utilizes the industry's most powerful multiplatform language. Using Cactus, the application developer learns one language on the desktop that can then be partitioned across 35 different operating systems and servers. Cactus provides access to a wealth of VBX, OLE, and ActiveX controls. Developers can integrate these controls into their applications and package them with their finished products. Cactus OCX (OLE custom control) enables products such as Visual Basic, or any other application with OCX support, to include Cactus processing, thereby extending three-tiered capabilities to otherwise two-tiered products.

Web-enabled access.   Cactus offers full application development for the Web with no prior knowledge of HTML, Java, or complex 3GLs. Developers can build traditional PC-based front ends or web applications for industry-standard Net browsers, all from one toolbox.

In addition, developers are insulated from the details of operating systems, networks, and DBMSs on UNIX, NT, MVS, VM/CMS, and CICS. Business functionality is defined at the highest level as if it were running on a single computer. The result is that the developer can focus on the business problem rather than the underlying technology.

Components and features

- *Cactus Workbench*—the front-end interface that provides access to the tool suite via iconic toolbars, push buttons, and menus. The tool components are functionally categorized into database access, business logic, and presentation to enable three-tiered development and deployment. Another IBI product, EDA/Client, is a required component of the Cactus Workbench.

- *Application Manager*—an integrated application repository that manages the data access, business logic, and presentation components created during development and managed during the maintenance phase of a system.

- *Partitioning Manager*—a component that allows developers to drag locally developed procedures and drop them on different Cactus servers anywhere in an enterprise.

- *Object Browser*—offers developers direct access to any portion of a multi-tiered application: database access, business logic, and presentation. The browser enables easy navigation and pinpoint access to all application components.

- *Maintain*—the proprietary language of Cactus. While incorporating a high level of abstraction for productivity, it provides the syntax necessary to perform sophisticated computations.

- *File Painter*—used to build the database access objects. The Object Browser also allows developers to formulate business logic, and the Form Painter enables the creation of presentation components.

- *Application Packager*—used at deployment. It creates an executable program for start-up and installation diskettes for an application. The packaged application can then be run on a Windows machine that has the Cactus Run-time Libraries installed.

- *EDA/Client*—the required "messaging layer" for tier-to-tier communications.

- *Cactus Servers*—the targets of the partitioned applications.

- *Cactus OCX*—an OLE Custom Control that allows any Cactus procedure to be called by a third-party application.

- *Cactus Server Gateway*—the transport layer for Web page delivery to a Web server from Cactus.

FOCUS Fusion.   *FOCUS Fusion,* another tool from Information Builder, is the new multidimensional database technology for OLAP and data warehousing. It is a multidimensional OLAP tool designed to address business applications that require multidimensional analysis of detail product data. As an OLAP tool, FOCUS Fusion is discussed in more detail in the next chapter. It is mentioned here because, in addition to typical OLAP features, FOCUS Fusion provides

- *Fast query and reporting*—Fusion's advanced indexing, parallel query, and rollup facilities provide blistering performance for reports, queries, and analyses—with the scalability users' need to go beyond OLAP to complete data warehouse solutions.

- *Comprehensive, graphics-based administration facilities,* which make Fusion database applications easy to build and quick to deploy.

- *Integrated copy management facilities,* which schedule automatic data refresh from any source into Fusion.
- *A complete portfolio of tightly integrated business intelligence applications* that span reporting, query, decision support, and EIS needs.
- *Open access via industry-standard protocols* such as ANSI SQL, ODBC, and HTTP via EDA/SQL, so that Fusion works with hundreds of desktop tools, including World Wide Web browsers.

In fact, FOCUS Fusion is a comprehensive data warehousing solution that provides functionality used across several data warehousing components, including

- Data extraction, cleansing, and loading for fast deployment
- Three-tiered reporting architecture for high performance, flexibility, and scalability
- OLAP access to precalculated summaries (rollup) with dynamic detail data manipulation capabilities
- Warehouse expansion with smart partitioning without disrupting users
- Simplified metadata change management for simple, quick warehouse expansion

Fusion works with the leading EIS, DSS, and OLAP tools; supports parallel computing environments; and seamlessly integrates with more than 60 different databases on more than 35 platforms, including ORACLE, SYBASE, SAP, Hogan, Microsoft SQL Server, DB2, IMS, VSAM, and many more.

In addition to Fusion and Cactus, Information Builders also develops management-layer tools which monitor and control access to production databases, enabling the warehouse manager to selectively augment the warehouse over time to "tune" it in accordance with users' actual access patterns.

Chapter

13

On-Line Analytical Processing (OLAP)

This chapter continues to build on the foundation laid out in Chap. 9, which discussed the RDBMS architectures and database schema designs best suited for data warehousing. OLAP is an application architecture, not intrinsically a data warehouse or a database management system (DBMS). Whether it utilizes a data warehouse or not, OLAP is becoming an architecture that an increasing number of enterprises are implementing to support analytical applications. The majority of OLAP applications are deployed in a "stovepipe" fashion, using specialized MDDBMS technology, a narrow set of data, and, often, a prefabricated application-user interface. As we look at OLAP trends, we can see that the architectures have clearly defined layers and that a delineation exists between the application and the DBMS. This delineation has given rise to the next generation of OLAP tools, which provide capabilities that utilize RDBMS technology heretofore found only with specialized MDDBMS technology.

The need for the architectural styles, trends, and major players of OLAP are discussed in this chapter.

13.1 Need for OLAP

Solving modern business problems such as market analysis and financial forecasting requires query-centric database schemas that are array-oriented and *multidimensional* in nature. These business problems are characterized by the need to retrieve large numbers of records from very large data sets (hundreds of gigabytes and even terabytes) and summarize them on the fly. The multidimensional nature of the problems it is designed to address is the key driver for OLAP.

The result set may look like a multidimensional spreadsheet (hence the term *multidimensional*). Although all the necessary data can be represented in a relational database and accessed via SQL, the two-dimensional relational model of data and the Structured Query Language (SQL) have some serious limitations for such complex real-world problems. For example, a query may translate into a number of complex SQL statements, each of which may involve full table scan, multiple joins, aggregations and sorting, and large temporary tables for storing intermediate results. The resulting query may require significant computing resources that may not be available at all times and even then may take a long time to complete. Another drawback of SQL is its weakness in handling time series data and complex mathematical functions. Time series calculations such as a 3-month moving average or net present value calculations typically require extensions to ANSI SQL rarely found in commercial products.

Response time and SQL functionality are not the only problems. OLAP is a continuous, iterative, and preferably interactive process. An analyst may drill down into the data to see, for example, how an individual salesperson's performance affects monthly revenue numbers. At the same time, the drill-down procedure may help the analyst discover certain patterns in sales of given products. This discovery can force another set of questions of similar or greater complexity. Technically, all these analytical questions can be answered by a large number of rather complex queries against a set of detailed and presummarized data views. In reality, however, even if the analyst could quickly and accurately formulate SQL statements of this complexity, the response time and resource consumption problems would still persist, and the analyst's productivity would be seriously impacted.

13.2   Multidimensional Data Model

The multidimensional nature of business questions is reflected in the fact that, for example, marketing managers are no longer satisfied by asking simple one-dimensional questions such as "How much revenue did the new product generate?" Instead, they ask questions such as "How much revenue did the new product generate by month, in the northeastern division, broken down by user demographic, by sales office, relative to the previous version of the product, compared the with plan?"—a six-dimensional question. One way to look at the multidimensional data model is to view it as a cube (see Fig. 13.1). The table on the left contains detailed sales data by product, market, and time. The cube on the right associates sales numbers (units sold) with dimensions—product type, market, and time—with the UNIT variables organized as *cells* in an *array*. This cube can be expanded to include another array—price—which can be associated with all or only some dimensions (for example, the unit price of a product may or may not change with time, or from city to city). The cube supports matrix arithmetic that allows the cube to present the dollar sales array simply by performing a *single* matrix operation on all cells of the array {dollar sales = units * price}.

The response time of the multidimensional query still depends on how many cells have to be added on the fly. The caveat here is that, as the number of dimensions increases, the number of the cube's cells increases exponentially. On the other hand, the majority of multidimensional queries deal with summarized, high-level data. Therefore, the solution to building an efficient multidimensional database is to preaggregate (consolidate) all logical subtotals and totals along all dimensions. This preaggregation is especially valuable since typical dimensions are *hierarchical* in nature. For example, the TIME dimension may contain hierarchies for years, quarters, months, weeks, and days; GEOGRAPHY may contain country, state, city, etc. Having the predefined hierarchy within dimensions allows for logical preaggregation and, conversely, allows for a logical drill-down—from the product group to individual products, from annual sales to weekly sales, and so on.

Another way to reduce the size of the cube is to properly handle *sparse* data. Often, not every cell has a meaning across all dimensions (many marketing databases may have more than 95 percent of all cells empty or containing 0). Another kind of sparse data is created when many cells contain duplicate data (i.e., if the cube contains a PRICE dimension, the same price may apply to all markets and all quarters for the year). The ability of a multidimensional database to skip empty or repetitive cells can greatly reduce the size of the cube and the amount of processing.

Dimensional hierarchy, sparse data management, and preaggregation are the keys, since they can significantly reduce the size of the database and the need to calculate values. Such a design obviates the need for multitable joins and provides quick and direct access to the arrays of answers, thus significantly speeding up execution of the multidimensional queries.

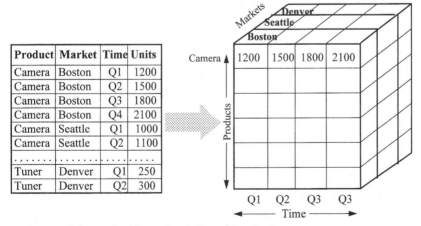

Figure 13.1   Relational tables and multidimensional cubes.

13.3   OLAP Guidelines

Multidimensionality is at the core of a number of OLAP systems (databases and front-end tools) available today. However, the availability of these systems does not eliminate the need to define a methodology of how to select and use the products. Dr. E. F. Codd, the "father" of the relational model, has formulated a list of 12 guidelines and requirements as the basis for selecting OLAP systems. Users should prioritize this suggested list to reflect their business requirements and consider products that best match those needs:

1. *Multidimensional conceptual view.*   A tool should provide users with a multidimensional model that corresponds to the business problems and is intuitively analytical and easy to use.

2. *Transparency.*   The OLAP system's technology, the underlying database and computing architecture (client/server, mainframe gateways, etc.), and the heterogeneity of input data sources should be transparent to users to preserve their productivity and proficiency with familiar front-end environments and tools (e.g., MS Windows, MS Excel).

3. *Accessibility.*   The OLAP system should access only the data actually required to perform the analysis. Additionally, the system should be able to access data from all heterogeneous enterprise data sources required for the analysis.

4. *Consistent reporting performance.*   As the number of dimensions and the size of the database increase, users should not perceive any significant degradation in performance.

5. *Client/server architecture.*   The OLAP system has to conform to client/server architectural principles for maximum price and performance, flexibility, adaptivity, and interoperability.

6. *Generic dimensionality.*   Every data dimension must be equivalent in both structure and operational capabilities.

7. *Dynamic sparse matrix handling.*   As previously mentioned, the OLAP system has to be able to adapt its physical schema to the specific analytical model that optimizes sparse matrix handling to achieve and maintain the required level of performance.

8. *Multiuser support.*   The OLAP system must be able to support a workgroup of users working concurrently on a specific model.

9. *Unrestricted cross-dimensional operations.*   The OLAP system must be able to recognize dimensional hierarchies and automatically perform associated roll-up calculations within and across dimensions.

10. *Intuitive data manipulation.*   Consolidation path reorientation (pivoting), drill-down and roll-up, and other manipulations should be accomplished via direct point-and-click, drag-and-drop actions on the cells of the cube.

11. *Flexible reporting.* The ability to arrange rows, columns, and cells in a fashion that facilitates analysis by intuitive visual presentation of analytical reports must exist.

12. *Unlimited dimensions and aggregation levels.* Depending on business requirements, an analytical model may have a dozen or more dimensions, each having multiple hierarchies. The OLAP system should not impose any artificial restrictions on the number of dimensions or aggregation levels.

In addition to these 12 guidelines, a robust production-quality OLAP system should also support

■ *Comprehensive database management tools.* These tools should function as an integrated centralized tool and allow for database management for the distributed enterprise.

■ *The ability to drill down to detail (source record) level.* This means that the tool should allow for a smooth transition from the multidimensional (preaggregated) database to the detail record level of the source relational databases.

■ *Incremental database refresh.* Many OLAP databases support only full refresh, and this presents an operations and usability problem as the size of the database increases.

■ *Structured Query Language (SQL) interface.* An important requirement for the OLAP system to be seamlessly integrated into the existing enterprise environment.

13.4   Multidimensional versus Multirelational OLAP

These relational implementations of multidimensional database systems are sometimes referred to as *multirelational* database systems. To achieve the required speed, these products use the star or snowflake schemas—specially optimized and denormalized data models that involve data restructuring and aggregation. (The snowflake schema is an extension of the star schema that supports multiple fact tables and joins between them.)

One benefit of the star schema approach (discussed in Chap. 9) is reduced complexity in the data model, which increases data "legibility," making it easier for users to pose business questions of OLAP nature. Data warehouse queries can be answered up to 10 times faster because of improved navigations.

13.5   Categorization of OLAP Tools

On-line analytical processing (OLAP) tools are based on the concepts of multidimensional databases and allow a sophisticated user to analyze the data using elaborate, multidimensional, complex views. Typical business applications for these tools include product performance and profitability, effectiveness of a sales program or a marketing campaign, sales forecasting, and capacity planning. These tools assume that the data is organized in a multidimensional model which is supported by a special multidimensional database (MDDB) or by a relational database designed to enable multidimensional properties (e.g., star schema, discussed in Chap. 9). A chart comparing capabilities of these two classes of OLAP tools is shown in Fig. 13.2.

13.5.1 MOLAP

Traditionally, these products utilized specialized data structures [i.e., multi-dimensional database management systems (MDDBMSs)] to organize, navigate, and analyze data, typically in an aggregated form, and traditionally required a tight coupling with the application layer and presentation layer. There recently has been a quick movement by MOLAP vendors to segregate the OLAP through the use of published application programming interfaces (APIs). Still, there remains the need to store the data in a way similar to the way in which it will be utilized, to enhance the performance and provide a degree of predictability for complex analysis queries. Data structures use array technology and, in most cases, provide improved storage techniques to minimize the disk space requirements through sparse data management. This architecture enables excellent performance when the data is utilized as designed, and predictable application response times for applications addressing a narrow breadth of data for a specific DSS requirement. In addition, some products treat time as a special dimension (e.g., Pilot Software's Analysis Server), enhancing their ability to perform time series analysis. Other prod-

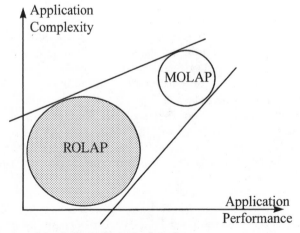

The area of the circles indicate the data size

Figure 13.2   OLAP style comparison.

ucts provide strong analytical capabilities (e.g., Oracle's Express Server) built into the database.

Applications requiring iterative and comprehensive time series analysis of trends are well suited for MOLAP technology (e.g., financial analysis and budgeting). Examples include Arbor Software's Essbase, Oracle's Express Server, Pilot Software's Lightship Server, Sinper's TM/1, Planning Sciences' Gentium, and Kenan Technology's Multiway.

Several challenges face users considering the implementation of applications with MOLAP products. First, there are limitations in the ability of data structures to support multiple subject areas of data (a common trait of many strategic DSS applications) and the detail data required by many analysis applications. This has begun to be addressed in some products, utilizing rudimentary "reach through" mechanisms that enable the MOLAP tools to access detail data maintained in an RDBMS (as shown in Fig. 13.3). There are also limitations in the way data can be navigated and analyzed, because the data is structured around the navigation and analysis requirements known at the time the data structures are built. When the navigation or dimension requirements change, the data structures may need to be physically reorganized to optimally support the new requirements. This problem is similar in nature to the older hierarchical and network DBMSs (e.g., IMS, IDMS), where different sets of data had to be created for each application that used the data in a manner different from the way the data was originally maintained. Finally, MOLAP products require a different set of skills and tools for the database administrator to build and maintain the database, thus increasing the cost and complexity of support.

To address this particular issue, some vendors significantly enhanced their reach-through capabilities. These hybrid solutions have as their primary characteristic the integration of specialized multidimensional data storage with RDBMS technology, providing users with a facility that tightly "couples" the multidimensional data structures (MDDSs) with data maintained in an RDBMS (see Fig. 13.3, left). This allows the MDDSs to dynamically obtain detail data maintained in an RDBMS, when the application reaches the bottom

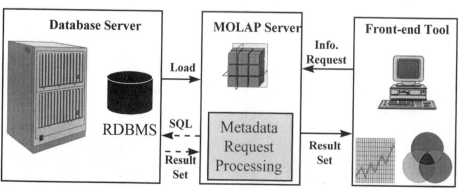

Figure 13.3   MOLAP architecture.

of the multidimensional cells during drill-down analysis. This may deliver the best of both worlds, MOLAP and ROLAP. This approach can be very useful for organizations with performance-sensitive multidimensional analysis requirements and that have built, or are in the process of building, a data warehouse architecture that contains multiple subject areas. An example would be the creation of sales data measured by several dimensions (e.g., product and sales region) to be stored and maintained in a persistent structure. This structure would be provided to reduce the application overhead of performing calculations and building aggregations during application initialization. These structures can be automatically refreshed at predetermined intervals established by an administrator.

13.5.2   ROLAP

This segment constitutes the fastest-growing style of OLAP technology, with new vendors (e.g., Sagent Technology) entering the market at an accelerating pace. Products in this group have been engineered from the beginning to support RDBMS products directly through a dictionary layer of metadata, bypassing any requirement for creating a static multidimensional data structure (see Fig. 13.4). This enables multiple multidimensional views of the two-dimensional relational tables to be created without the need to structure the data around the desired view. Finally, some of the products in this segment have developed strong SQL-generation engines to support the complexity of multidimensional analysis. This includes the creation of multiple SQL statements to handle user requests, being "RDBMS-aware," and providing the capability to generate the SQL based on the optimizer of the DBMS engine. While flexibility is an attractive feature of ROLAP products, there are products in this segment that recommend, or require, the use of highly denormalized database designs (e.g., star schema). The design and performance issues associated with the star schema have been discussed in Chap. 9.

The ROLAP tools are undergoing some technology realignment. This shift in technology emphasis is coming in two forms. First is the movement toward

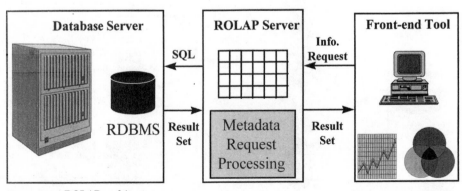

Figure 13.4   ROLAP architecture.

pure middleware technology that provides facilities to simplify development of multidimensional applications. Second, there continues further blurring of the lines that delineate ROLAP and hybrid-OLAP products. Vendors of ROLAP tools and RDBMS products look to provide an option to create multidimensional, persistent structures, with facilities to assist in the administration of these structures. Examples include Information Advantage (Axsys), MicroStrategy (DSS Agent/DSS Server), Platinum/Prodea Software (Beacon), Informix/Stanford Technology Group (Metacube), and Sybase (HighGate Project).

13.5.3   Managed query environment (MQE)

This style of OLAP, which is beginning to see increased activity, provides users with the ability to perform limited analysis capability, either directly against RDBMS products, or by leveraging an intermediate MOLAP server (see Fig. 13.5). Some products (e.g., Andyne's Pablo) that have a heritage in ad hoc query have developed features to provide "datacube" and "slice and dice" analysis capabilities. This is achieved by first developing a query to select data from the DBMS, which then delivers the requested data to the desktop, where it is placed into a datacube. This datacube can be stored and maintained locally, to reduce the overhead required to create the structure each time the query is executed. Once the data is in the datacube, users can perform multidimensional analysis (i.e., slice, dice, and pivot operations) against it. Alternatively, these tools can work with MOLAP servers, and the data from the relational DBMS can be delivered to the MOLAP server, and from there to the desktop.

The simplicity of the installation and administration of such products makes them particularly attractive to organizations looking to provide seasoned users with more sophisticated analysis capabilities, without the significant cost and maintenance of more complex products. With all the ease of installation and administration that accompanies the desktop OLAP products, most of these

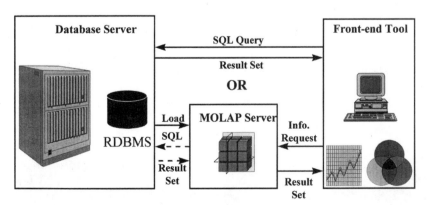

Figure 13.5   Hybrid/MQE architecture.

tools require the datacube to be built and maintained on the desktop or a separate server. With metadata definitions that assist users in retrieving the correct set of data that makes up the datacube, this method causes a plethora of data redundancy and strain to most network infrastructures that support many users. Although this mechanism allows for the flexibility of each user to build a custom datacube, the lack of data consistency among users, and the relatively small amount of data that can be efficiently maintained are significant challenges facing tool administrators.

Examples include Cognos Software's PowerPlay, Andyne Software's Pablo, Business Objects' Mercury Project, Dimensional Insight's CrossTarget, and Speedware's Media.

13.6   State of the Market

OLAP tools provide an intuitive way to view corporate data. These tools aggregate data along common business subjects or dimensions and then let users navigate through the hierarchies and dimensions with the click of a mouse button. Users can drill down, across, or up levels in each dimension or pivot and swap out dimensions to change their view of the data.

Some tools, such as Arbor Software Corp.'s Essbase and Oracle's Express, preaggregate data in special multidimensional databases. Other tools work directly against relational data and aggregate data on the fly, such as MicroStrategy, Inc.'s DSS Agent or Information Advantage, Inc.'s DecisionSuite. Some tools process OLAP data on the desktop instead of a server. Desktop OLAP tools include Cognos' PowerPlay, Brio Technology, Inc.'s BrioQuery, Planning Sciences, Inc.'s Gentium, and Andyne's Pablo. Many of the differences between OLAP tools are fading. Vendors are rearchitecting their products to give users greater control over the tradeoff between flexibility and performance that is inherent in OLAP tools. Many vendors are rewriting pieces of their products in Java.

Database vendors eventually might be the largest OLAP providers. The leading database vendors plan to incorporate OLAP functionality in their database kernels. Oracle, Informix Software, Inc., and—most recently—Microsoft have taken the first step toward this end by acquiring OLAP vendors (IRI Software, Stanford Technology Group, and Panorama, respectively.)

Red Brick Systems' Red Brick Warehouse has always supported SQL extensions that perform simple OLAP functions, such as rank, sorts, and moving averages. Red Brick Warehouse 5.0 also supports data mining algorithms.

13.6.1   Cognos PowerPlay

PowerPlay from Cognos is a mature and popular software tool for multidimensional analysis of corporate data. PowerPlay can be characterized as an MQE tool (see Sec. 13.5.3) that can leverage corporate investment in the relational database technology to provide multidimensional access to enterprise data, at the same time proving robustness, scalability, and administrative control.

Cognos PowerPlay is an open OLAP solution that can interoperate with a wide variety of third-party software tools, databases, and applications. The analytical data used by PowerPlay is stored in multidimensional data sets called *PowerCubes*. Cognos' client/server architecture allows for the Power-Cubes to be stored on the Cognos universal client or on a server. PowerPlay offers a single universal client for OLAP servers that supports PowerCubes located locally, on the LAN, or (optionally) inside popular relational databases. In addition to the fast installation and deployment capabilities, PowerPlay provides a high level of usability with a familiar Windows interface, high performance, scalability, and relatively low cost of ownership.

Specifically, starting with version 5, Cognos PowerPlay client offers

- Support for enterprise-size data sets (PowerCubes) of 20+ million records, 100,000 categories, and 100 measures

- A drill-through capability for queries from Cognos Impromptu (discussed in Chap. 12)

- Powerful 3-D charting capabilities with background and rotation control for advanced users

- Scatter charts that let users show data across two measures, allowing easy comparison of budget to actual values

- Linked displays that give users multiple views of the same data in a report

- Full support for OLE2 Automation, as both a client and a server

- Formatting features for financial reports: brackets for negative numbers, single and double underlining, and reverse sign for expenses

- Faster and easier ranking of data

- A "home" button that automatically resets the dimension line to the top level

- Unlimited undo levels and customizable toolbars

- An enhanced PowerPlay Portfolio that lets users build graphical, interactive, EIS-type briefing books from PowerPlay reports; Impromptu reports; word processing, spreadsheet, or presentation documents; or any other documents or reports

- A 32-bit architecture for Windows NT, Windows 95, and Windows 3.1

- Access to third-party OLAP tools including direct native access to Arbor's Essbase and Oracle's Express multidimensional databases

- PowerCube creation and access within in existing relational databases such as ORACLE, SYBASE, or Microsoft SQL Server right inside the data warehouse.

- PowerCube creation scheduled for off-peak processing, or sequential to other processes

- Advanced security control by dimension, category, and measure—on the client, the server, or both

- Remote analysis where users pull subsets of information from the server down to the client

- Complete integration with relational database security and data management features

- An open API through OLE Automation, allowing both server- and client-based PowerCubes to be accessed by Visual Basic applications, spreadsheets, and other third-party tools and applications

PowerPlay Administrator. As was mentioned above, PowerPlay's capabilities include drill-to-detail using Impromptu. Also, cubes can be built using data from multiple data sources. For the administrators who are responsible for creating multidimensional cubes, new capabilities allow them to populate these PowerCubes inside popular relational databases, and to do the processing off the desktop and on UNIX servers. To provide a robust administration capabilities, Cognos offers a companion tool—PowerPlay Administrator, which is available in Database and Server editions.

In PowerPlay Administrator Database edition, the administrator would continue to model the cube and run the population of the cube process (called *Transform*) on the client platform. The advantage is that data from multiple sources can now be used to generate a PointerCube for the client, and the actual PowerCube can be inside a relational database. This means that existing database management tools and the database administrator can be used to manage the business data, and a single delivery mechanism can be employed for both application and OLAP processing. A sophisticated security model is provided which in effect creates a "master" cube to service a variety of users. This is defined and controlled through the Authenticator, also included with PowerPlay.

The Administrator Server edition of PowerPlay lets users process the population of the cube on a UNIX platform. An administrator uses client Transformer to create a model, and moves it to the UNIX server using the supplied software component called *PowerGrid*. The server Transformer, once triggered, will create the PowerCube, and the only prerequisite is that all data sources be accessible. Once completed, the resulting PowerCube (or PointerCube if the multidimensional database is placed inside an RDBMS) is copied or transferred to the client platform for subsequent PowerPlay analysis by the user. The Authenticator can be used to establish user classes and access security, and can also be used to redirect cube access since all database passwords and locations can be known to the Authenticator.

PowerPlay supports clients on Windows 3.1, Windows 95, and Windows NT. Administrator Database and Server editions execute on HP/UX, IBM AIX, and Sun Solaris, and support PowerCubes in ORACLE 7, SYBASE SQL Server, and Microsoft SQL Server.

13.6.2   IBI FOCUS Fusion

FOCUS *Fusion* from Information Builders, Inc. (IBI) is a multidimensional database technology for OLAP and data warehousing. It is designed to address business applications that require multidimensional analysis of detail product data. FOCUS Fusion complements Cactus (discussed in Chap. 12) and EDA/SQL middleware software to provide a multifaceted data warehouse solution.

FOCUS Fusion combines a parallel-enabled, high-performance, multidimensional database engine with the administrative, copy management, and access tools necessary for a data warehouse solution. Designed specifically for deployment of business intelligence applications in data warehouse environments, Fusion provides

- Fast query and reporting—Fusion's advanced indexing, parallel query, and roll-up facilities provide high performance for reports, queries, and analyses, with the scalability users need to complete data warehouse solutions.

- Comprehensive, graphics-based administration facilities that make Fusion database applications easy to build and deploy.

- Integrated copy management facilities, which schedule automatic data refresh from any source into Fusion.

- A complete portfolio of tightly integrated business intelligence applications that span reporting, query, decision support, and EIS needs.

- Open access via industry-standard protocols like ANSI SQL, ODBC, and HTTP via EDA/SQL, so that Fusion works with a wide variety of desktop tools, including World Wide Web browsers.

- Three-tiered reporting architecture for high performance

- Scalability of OLAP applications from the department to the enterprise

- Access to precalculated summaries (roll-up) combined with dynamic detail data manipulation capabilities

- Capability to perform intelligent application partitioning without disrupting users

- Interoperability with the leading EIS, DSS, and OLAP tools

- Support for parallel computing environments
- Seamless integration with more than 60 different databases on more than 35 platforms, including ORACLE, SYBASE, SAP, Hogan, Microsoft SQL Server, DB2, IMS, and VSAM

FOCUS Fusion's proprietary OverLAP technology allows Fusion to serve as an OLAP front end or shared cache for relational and legacy databases, effectively providing a virtual warehousing environment for the analysis of corporate data. This can simplify warehouse management and lower overall costs by potentially reducing the need to copy infrequently accessed detail data to the warehouse for a possible drill-down.

Fusion components. FOCUS Fusion is a modular tool that supports flexible configurations for diverse needs, and includes the following components:

- *Fusion / Dbserver.* High-performance, client/server, parallel-enabled, scalable multidimensional DBMS. Fusion/DBserver runs on both UNIX and NT and connects transparently to all enterprise data that EDA/SQL can access (more than 60 different databases on over 35 platforms). Fusion/ Dbserver also provides stored procedure and RPC (remote procedure call) facilities.
- *Fusion / Administrator.* Comprehensive GUI-based (Windows) administration utility that provides visual schema definition and bulk load of Fusion databases, multidimensional index definition and build, and roll-up definition and creation. Additionally, Fusion/Administrator automates migration of FOCUS databases to Fusion.
- *Fusion / PDQ.* Parallel data query for Fusion/Dbserver exploits symmetric multiprocessor (SMP) hardware for fast query execution and parallel loads.
- *EDA / Link.* Fusion's client component supports standard APIs, including ODBC and ANSI SQL. EDA/Link provides access to Fusion from any desktop (Windows/95/NT, UNIX, Macintosh, OS/2) or host system (UNIX, MVS, AS/400, VMS, etc.) over TCP/IP and many other network topologies (via EDA Hub Servers) to integrate Fusion into enterprise processes.
- *EDA / WebLink.* Fusion's open browser client that supports Netscape, Mosaic, Internet Explorer, and all other standard HTML browsers. It works with Information Builders' HTML generator to facilitate Web-based warehouse publishing applications.
- *Enterprise Copy Manager for Fusion.* Fully automated assembly, transformation, summarization, and load of enterprise data from any source(s) into Fusion on scheduled basis. It consists of Enterprise Copy Server, Enterprise Copy Client (the graphical Windows-based interface), and Enterprise Source Server (the remote gateway access to source data).
- *EDA Gateways.* Remote data access gateways that provide transparent, live drill through capabilities from Fusion/Dbserver to production databases.

13.6.3 Pilot Software

Pilot Software offers the Pilot Decision Support Suite of tools from a high-speed multidimensional database (MOLAP), Data Warehouse integration (ROLAP), data mining, and a diverse set of customizable business applications targeted after sales and marketing professionals. The following products are at the core of Pilot Software's offering:

- *Pilot Analysis Server.* A full-function multidimensional database with high-speed consolidation, graphical user interface (Pilot Model Builder), and expert-level interface. The latest version includes relational integration of the multidimensional model with relational data stores, thus allowing the user the choice between high-speed access of a multidimensional database or on-the-fly (ROLAP) access of detail data stored directly in the data warehouse or data mart.

- *Pilot Link.* A database connectivity tool that includes ODBC connectivity and high-speed connectivity via specialized drivers to the most popular relational database platforms. A graphical user interface allows the user seamless and easy access to a wide variety of distributed databases.

- *Pilot Designer.* An application design environment specifically created to enable rapid development of OLAP applications.

- *Pilot Desktop.* A collection of applications that allow the end user easy navigation and visualization of the multidimensional database.

- *Pilot Sales and Marketing Analysis Library.* A collection of sophisticated applications designed for the Sales and Marketing business end user (including 80/20 Pareto analysis, time-based ranking, BCG quadrant analysis, trendline, and statistical forecasting). The applications can be modified and tailored to meet individual needs for particular customers.

- *Pilot Discovery Server.* A predictive data mining tool that embeds directly into the relational database and does not require the user to copy or transform the data. The data mining results are stored with metadata into the data warehouse as a predictive segmentation and are embedded into the multidimensional model as a dimension. The discovery server contains a graphical user interface called *Pilot Discovery Server Launch,* which eases building data mining models.

- *Pilot Marketing Intelligence Library.* Currently there are two applications for exposing the value of the data mining results. One allows the user to graphically view the predictive segmentation and rules that describe the prediction; the other allows for profit/loss and return on investment analysis for the data mining results.

- *Pilot Internet Publisher.* A tool that easily allows users to access their Pilot multidimensional database via browsers on the Internet or intranets.

Some of the distinguishing features of Pilot's product offering include the overall complete solution from powerful OLAP engine and data mining engine to their customizable business applications. Within their OLAP offering, these are some of the key features:

- *Time intelligence.* The Pilot Analysis Server has a number of features to support time as a special dimension. Among these are the ability to process data on the fly to convert from the native periodicity (e.g., the data was collected weekly) to the periodicity preferred by the customer viewing the data (e.g., view the data monthly). This feature is accomplished via special optimized structures within the multidimensional database.

- *Embedded data mining.* The Pilot Analysis Server is the first product to integrate predictive data mining (as it is described in this book) with the multidimensional database model. This allows the user to benefit from not only the predictive power of data mining but also the descriptive and analytical power of multidimensional navigation.

- *Multidimensional database compression.* In addition to the compression of sparsity (the removal of cells in the multidimensional database which have no value), Pilot Analysis Server also has special code for compressing data values over time. A new feature called a "dynamic dimension" allows some dimensions to be calculated on the fly when they are attributes of an existing dimension. This allows the database to be much smaller and still provide fast access. Dynamic variables which are also calculated on the fly are also available to further decrease the total size of the database and thus also decrease the time for consolidation of the database.

- *Relational Integration.* Pilot allows for a seamless integration of both MOLAP and ROLAP to provide the user with either the speed of MOLAP or the more space-efficient ROLAP. The users interface with the system by defining the multidimensional model or view that they prefer, and the system self-optimizes the queries into precalculated MOLAP storage or directly in the relation data store depending on the usage pattern and the time/space tradeoff preferences of the end user.

13.7   OLAP Tools and the Internet

The two most pervasive themes in computing have been the Internet/WWW and data warehousing. From a marketing perspective, a marriage of these two giant technologies is a natural and unavoidable event. The reason for this trend is simple; the compelling advantages in using the Web for access are magnified even further in a data warehouse. Indeed:

- The Internet is a virtually free resource which provides a universal connectivity within and between companies.

- The Web eases complex administrative tasks of managing distributed environments.

- The Web allows companies to store and manage both data and applications on servers that can be centrally managed, maintained, and updated, thus eliminating problems with software and data currency.

For these and other reasons (see Chap. 25), the Web is a perfect medium for decision support. Let's look at the general features of the Web-enabled data access.

- The *first-generation Web sites* used a static distribution model, in which clients access static HTML pages via Web browsers. In this model, the decision support reports were stored as HTML documents and delivered to users on request. Clearly, this model has some serious deficiencies, including inability to provide Web clients with interactive analytical capabilities such as drill-down.

- The *second-generation Web sites* support interactive database queries by utilizing a multitiered architecture in which a Web client submits a query in the form of HTML-encoded request to a Web server, which in turn transforms the request for structured data into a CGI (Common Gateway Interface) script, or a script written to a proprietary Web-server API (i.e., Netscape Server API, or NSAPI). The gateway submits SQL queries to the database, receives the results, translates them into HTML, and sends the pages to the requester (see Fig. 13.6). Requests for the unstructured data (e.g., images, other HTML documents, etc.) can be sent directly to the unstructured data store.

- The emerging *third-generation Web sites* replace HTML gateways with Web-based application servers. These servers can download Java applets or

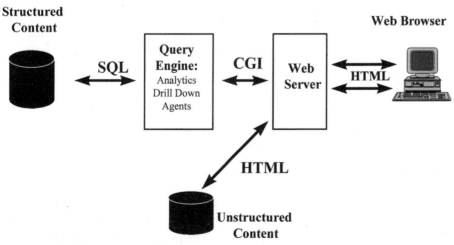

Figure 13.6 Web processing model.

ActiveX applications that execute on clients, or interact with corresponding applets running on servers—servlets. The third-generation Web servers provide users with all the capabilities of existing decision-support applications without requiring them to load any client software except a Web browser.

Not surprisingly, vendors of decision support applications, especially query, reporting, and OLAP tools, are rapidly converting their tools to work on the Web. Vendor approaches for deploying tools on the Web include

- *HTML publishing.* This approach involves transforming an output of a query into the HTML page that can be downloaded into a browser. This approach does not support interactive access to data or reports.

- *Helper applications.* In this approach, a tool is configured as a helper application that resides within a browser. This is the case of a "fat" client, in which, once the data is downloaded, users can take advantage of all capabilities of the tool to analyze data. However, maintaining these helper applications becomes another task for system administrators.

- *Plug-ins.* A variation on the previous approach, plug-ins are helper applications that are downloaded from the Web server prior to their initial use. Since the plug-ins are downloaded from the server, their normal administration and installation tasks are significantly reduced. However, typically plug-ins are browser-specific, and may not run on all platforms or with all browsers. Also, as browsers get updated, these plug-ins may have to be upgraded as well, creating additional administration workload.

- *Server-centric components.* In this approach the vendor rebuilds a desktop tool as a server component, or creates a new server component that can be integrated with the Web via a Web gateway (e.g., CGI or NSAPI scripts).

- *Java and ActiveX applications.* This approach is for a vendor to redevelop all or portions of its tool in Java or ActiveX. The result is a true "thin" client model. There are advantages and disadvantages to both, but this approach appears to be one of the most promising and flexible.

The remainder of this section looks at several OLAP tools from a perspective of Internet/Web implementations.

Arbor Essbase Web. Essbase is one of the most ambitious of the early Web products. It includes not only OLAP manipulations, such as drill up, down, and across; pivot; slice and dice; and fixed and dynamic reporting but also data entry, including full multiuser concurrent write capabilities—a feature that differentiates it from the others.

Since Arbor sells Essbase only as a server, it does not have a client package that might suffer from sales of its Web gateway product. Thus, Essbase Web makes sense from a business perspective. The Web product does not replace administrative and development modules, only user access for query and update.

Information Advantage WebOLAP.   Information Advantage uses a server-centric messaging architecture, which is composed of a powerful analytical engine that generates SQL to pull data from relational databases, manipulates the results, and transfers the results to a client.

Since all the intelligence of the product is in the server, implementing Web OLAP to provide a Web-based client is straightforward. The architecture of Information Advantage's Web product is similar to Essbase's, with a Web gateway between the Web server and the analytical engine—although in this case, the data store and the analytical engine are separate, where Essbase is both a data store and an analytical engine.

MicroStrategy DSS Web.   MicroStrategy's flagship product, DSS Agent, was originally a Windows-only tool, but MicroStrategy has smoothly made the transition, first with an NT-based server product, and now as one of the first OLAP tools to have a Web-access product. DSS Agent, in concert with the complement of MicroStrategy's product suite—DSS Server relational OLAP server, DSS Architect data modeling tool, and DSS Executive design tool for building executive information systems—generates SQL dynamically and relies on the relational database server to perform complex analysis, rather than creating a "cube" like most of the other tools. By inserting a Web gateway between the Web server and the DSS Server engine, MicroStrategy was able to replace the interactive DSS Agent front-end with a Web browser, which passes requests to the DSS Server's API.

Brio technology.   In November 1996, Brio shipped a suite of new products called *brio.web.warehouse.* This suite implements several of the approaches listed above for deploying decision support OLAP applications on the Web. The key to Brio's strategy is a new server component called *brio.query.server.* The server works in conjunction with BrioEnterprise and Brio's Web clients—*brio.quickview* and *brio.insight*—and can off-load processing from the clients and thus enables users to access Brio reports via Web browsers. On the client side, Brio uses plug-ins to give users viewing and report manipulation capabilities.

13.8   Conclusion

It seems clear that all OLAP vendors will position their products to be fully Web-compliant. The scope of functionality and a particular style of implementation will become a market differentiator for these tools.

Server-centric tools, such as Information Advantage and Prodea Beacon from Platinum Technology, and the multidimensional OLAP tools—Arbor's Essbase, Oracle Express, Planning Sciences' Gentia, Kenan Technologies' Acumate ES, Holistic Systems' Holos, and Pilot Software's Pilot Server—appear to be in an excellent position to take advantage of their architectures to provide easy access from a Web browser. Similarly, client-centric tools, such as Business

Objects, Software AG's Esperant, Cognos' PowerPlay, or Brio Technologies' Brio suite of products, are developing and making available robust and full-featured Web-enabled versions of their products (see discussion of Brio Technology above). Their task becomes easier as both Java and ActiveX become more mature and readily available for the Web deployment.

In conclusion, we would like to remind you that the technologies supporting the Internet and the Web continue to advance very rapidly. Therefore, when you evaluate an OLAP product for the Web access, keep in mind that the features you see in the current release should not be the deciding factor—in order to stay competitive, the vendors will continue to improve their products' Web capabilities significantly, sometimes even radically. It is clear that the Web is here to stay and can play a valuable role in data warehousing, even in the short term.

14

Patterns and Models

In the following chapters topics ranging from artificial intelligence to data mining and statistics will be discussed. Although each topic involves a very different scientific discipline and the technologies can differ greatly, they all have two things in common—they all build models and they all extract patterns.

This should not be surprising since, in the end, all these methods are processing data in order to take some efficient and applicable action. In the business domain this might include using a model of consumer bankruptcy in order to decide whether to issue a home mortgage. In the scientific domain it might mean the use of a model that maps the tennis balls scattered on a tennis court by a small mobile robot that automatically removes the balls. Whatever the application, there is always the requirement of the model to assess the current situation and then take action. Those systems that use models to help guide that decision-making process will consequently make better decisions than will those that just take random actions.

This section seeks to define what models and patterns really are and to show some of the commonalties among the techniques that will be described in the following chapters.

14.1 Definitions

14.1.1 What is a pattern? What is a model?

To get a basic insight into what patterns and models are, consider the simple problem of trying to determine the next number in the following sequence: 1212121 . . . ?. If you had to make a guess, you'd probably guess the number 2 since many patterns of a 1 followed by a 2 have occurred in the data. The pattern "12" is found often enough that you have some confidence that there is a predictive model that says "If 1, then 2 will follow."

This is an example of a pattern, a model, and some training examples. In this case detecting the pattern is relatively simple. In other cases, however, detecting the pattern could be much more difficult. Assume, for instance, that you had fewer examples: 121 . . . ? or that the sequence were much longer: 1212123121212 . . . ?. In this case there certainly appears to be a pattern of 121212 => 3, but there is only a single example of it to support the hypothesis.

Both of these examples show how models can be created by detecting the patterns in some historical data and then making calculated guesses about how likely those patterns are to be repeated. A predictive model then has something in common with the small plastic airplane models you may have glued together as a child. In each case we've built a model that is quite a bit smaller than the real thing (either the real airplane or the entire database) but represents some important characteristic of the larger thing that is being modeled. In the case of the model airplane, it is unable to fly, but it nonetheless captures the shape and look of the real thing. In the case of the database model, it captures a pattern in the database that describes an important aspect of the database but certainly does not describe the entire database (for instance, the database may be hundreds of gigabytes in size but the model may only be a few kilobytes in size).

For real-world business applications a model can be anything from a mathematical equation, to a set of rules that describe customer segments, to the computer representation of a complex neural network architecture which translates to several sets of mathematical equations. Some of these more complex models are effectively computer programs that take in data about the current situation and output other data that is used as a prediction for some unknown. The user can then take action on that predicted information. This process can be viewed at a very high level as a black box or an oracle that produces answers to relevant questions as is shown in Fig. 14.1. Here a model is used to make a prediction about a record that represents some new state of the world. The model is a limited reflection of the entire historical database from which it was built.

Although there are many ways to define patterns and models, here is what they mean in the context of data warehousing and data mining.

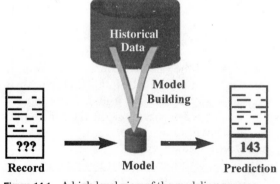

Figure 14.1   A high-level view of the modeling process.

- *Model.*   A description of the original historical database from which it was built that can be successfully applied to new data in order to make predictions about missing values or to make statements about expected values.

- *Pattern.*   An event or combination of events in a database that occurs more often than expected. Typically this means that its actual occurrence is significantly different from what would be expected by random chance.

This definition of a model is fairly general-purpose but is also centered on databases and data warehousing. It is not to say that a plastic replica of an airplane is not also a perfectly good model. Our definition is just more tuned into the type of model that we will be talking about in this book. It might also seem that the definition of a pattern given above is fairly weak, but it does a good job of sifting through the essentials of a pattern. For instance, it is not enough for a pattern simply to repeat; the number of repetitions must be significant. And, in general, no pattern is of any interest if it cannot be successfully applied in new situations.

One final question, then, might be: What is the difference between a pattern and a model? There may not be a crisp dividing line between the two (as, for example, in the number sequence example where the pattern "123" was also the model), but patterns are usually driven from the data and generally reflect the data itself, whereas a model generally reflects a purpose and may not be driven from the data necessarily. For instance, one can build a model of the physical world using the equations of newtonian physics that do a great job of explaining the data of the world (e.g., how fast something falls or how far it flies), but the equations are not really patterns in any sense. On the other hand, most of the models discussed in this book will in fact be driven by data. In this case the biggest distinction between a model and a pattern, besides the fact that models are created for some purpose, is that patterns are usually less complex and there are usually many of them. For example, a model of customer behavior may be very complex and contain hundreds of patterns that have been gleaned from the database.

14.1.2   Visualizing a pattern

The example that has been used so far of finding the patterns in a sequence of numbers could be visualized on a graph. Since human beings are pretty good at picking out visual patterns, they will often try to map their data to a graph in order to "see" it. Sometimes they are able to visually perceive patterns that might not otherwise have been noticed. For instance, the simple example of numbers (121212312121 . . .) that we have been using so far could be mapped to a graph as in Fig. 14.2.

If there are more complicated patterns to be detected like the sequence of numbers shown in Table 14.1, it could be much more difficult to detect any patterns. However, when the data is graphed, even with 10 times as many data

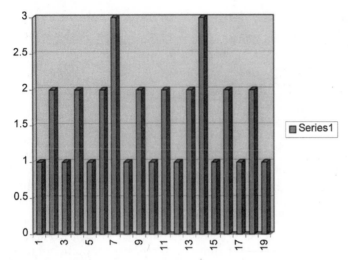

Figure 14.2   A graphical representation of a number sequence.

points, it seems to form a pretty simple and understandable pattern, as is shown in Fig. 14.3.

Even though the data is complicated, these patterns are easy to detect visually because the value to be predicted next varies smoothly with the position on the x axis. A much more complicated situation would arise on a graph where the next value was dependent on the position not only along the x axis but also along some other axis that wasn't being graphed. In most real-world prediction problems the value to be predicted is dependent on many more factors than just one. As we'll see in later chapters, there are very powerful techniques for building these complex models and some new visualization techniques that make it possible to see higher-dimensional data.

14.2   A Note on Terminology

So far we have talked quite a bit about data in terms of the data warehouse—which, more often than not, means talking about the data in terms of how it is

TABLE 14.1   A More Complex Pattern of Numbers

0.0998334166468282E-02	0.198669330795061
0.198669330795061	0.389418342308651
0.29552020666134	0.564642473395035
0.389418342308651	0.717356090899523
0.479425538604203	0.841470984807897
0.564642473395035	0.932039085967226
0.644217687237691	0.98544972998846
0.717356090899523	0.999573603041505
0.783326909627483	0.973847630878195
0.841470984807897	0.909297426825682

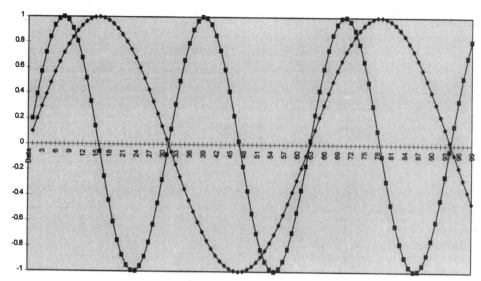

Figure 14.3   A graphical representation of a complex number sequence appears much more understandable.

stored: rows, columns, tables, relations, keys, etc. When we talk about predictive modeling, however, the main consideration is what data is being predicted, what data is to be used to make those predictions, and how much data with historical examples you will need to build your model. Consequently, the focus and terminology for predictive modeling is on the data structures that relate to this important modeling information. Although the physical storage of this data is important for the RDBMS for performance and data management reasons, the number one concern for modeling systems is predictive accuracy. The terminology that reflects this difference is thus slightly different:

- *Database.*   The collection of data that has been collected, on which data analysis will be performed and from which predictive models and exploratory models will be created. This is often called the *historical database* to refer to data that has been collected over time. In machine learning and data mining, there is often differentiation between the training database and the test database. Both of these databases are constructed from the historical database and constitute nonoverlapping subsets of the historical database. As their names imply, one is used for training (building the model), and the other is used for testing the model.

- *Record.*   The atom-level data structure that holds the data pertinent to individuals in the database. A record corresponds to a row of a table in a denormalized database. Each record is made up of values for each field that it contains, including the predictor fields and the prediction field. Many databases have a record for each customer or account. In general, a record represents some state of the world about which a prediction could be made.

- *Field.* The data structure that represents an attribute of a record. Fields correspond to columns in a relational database and to dimensions and measures in a multidimensional database. Fields are also called *attributes, features, variables,* and *dimensions.*

- *Predictor.* A field that could be used to build a predictive model. Some function of the predictor values of a record produces the prediction value for that record. In general, predictors are what fields are called when they are being used for prediction or data exploration.

- *Prediction.* The field that will have a value created for it by the predictive model. It is also the field that is passed to the data mining technique for the model to be built. In general, the prediction field is similar to any other field except in the way it is handled by the predictive model building process.

- *Value.* Each field has a value (e.g., the field *age* for the record representing a customer has the value 34).

In different fields of research each of these concepts gets a slightly different name. Although there are sometimes subtle differences in meaning, these names are often used interchangeably depending on whom you are talking to. Table 14.2 shows how these concepts can be translated between different disciplines. While data mining has not settled on a particularly well defined naming convention, the naming that is used in this book is displayed in that column.

A note on knowledge and wisdom. Along with the concepts of prediction and the automated building of models goes the idea that perhaps some of these systems are doing more than just data processing or computation. Some people believe and will tell you that data mining and particularly artificial intelligence have moved into the realms of intelligence and knowledge creation. For instance, another name used interchangeably for data mining is *knowledge discovery.* Some have even gone so far as to create elaborate hierarchies of intelligence to

TABLE 14.2 Translation of Several Predictive Modeling Concepts

Data mining	Relational databases	OLAP	Statistics	Artificial intelligence
Data set	Table, database	Multidimensional database, cube	Data set, sample	Data set, training set
Record	Row	NA	Record, datum	Example, record
Field	Column	Variable, dimension, measure	Variable	Field, feature, dimension
Predictor	Column	Variable, dimension, measure	Independent variable	Field, feature, dimension
Prediction	Column	Variable, dimension, measure	Dependent variable	Classification target

show how these new technologies can transform data into information, information into knowledge, and knowledge into wisdom. Such claims are interesting to think about, but they belong more in the realm of a philosophical discussion rather than in the practicalities of building and mining a data warehouse.

Data is a fairly well defined concept, and *information*—although many people don't use the term in its strict technical sense—also has a very precise definition. *Knowledge, intelligence,* and *wisdom* are much more difficult to define, and very difficult to recognize even if they do exist. For this reason we will stick to these very well defined, albeit less glamorous, descriptions of what these systems are capable of. In general, you should be wary of vendors or scientists selling these types of modeling systems as more than what they are. They are very powerful in their own right without needing to create humanlike qualities about them.

14.3   Where Are Models Used?

Let's now look at some business problems and see how they would benefit from modeling. The four business problems that we will be working with will be centered around the customer—and, in particular, the customer life-cycle. Any business that stays in business for long has customers, so this should be a reasonable place to start.

14.3.1   Problem 1: selection

In selection, the business is trying to select new prospective customers. The organization may have a long list of possible candidates for customers but may be unsure which prospects are actually desirable. Avoiding customers who are unprofitable or only marginally profitable is a big part of the selection process. If this were high school and the senior prom were coming up soon, selection would be the process where you narrowed down the list of all people you knew to just those whom you wanted to go to the prom with.

In business, this initial list may have been acquired as a list of prospects from a variety of sources, maybe from a magazine's mailing list, a direct coupon mailing, from the government census database, or maybe at random from the phone book. In any case the company would like to be able to concentrate on only those prospects who are going to be good customers. Those who will actually buy the product, pay their bills on time, and can be leveraged into perhaps purchasing other products. This can be a particularly challenging predictive modeling problem because there is often limited information about these prospects in comparison to the information available about long-term customers. Ideally the business would like to build a model based on data available about these prospects that can adequately predict the behavior of potential customers. To do this they would use their large historical database about existing customers to create and test the model before they unleashed it on the real prospect list.

A good example of models that need to be built for selection comes from the telecommunications industry, where long-distance carriers know quite a bit about the long-distance calling habits of their current customers but usually have only limited information on prospects (e.g., age, income, credit history). The model they would like to build would be one that takes this generally available information and can predict what their long-distance telephone usage would be. To do this they use their own historical database that does contain long distance telephone usage to determine which generally available information (predictor fields) can be used to predict long-distance revenue. Having a model of per-customer profitability and revenue allows long-distance providers to more carefully tailor their programs to expend more resources on high-value customers.

14.3.2   Problem 2: acquisition

The second phase in the customer life cycle is that of customer acquisition. If selection is analogous to determining whom you would like to invite to the senior prom, then acquisition is analogous to the process of getting them to agree to go with you. In business terms it means acquiring a customer via some offer or product that is of interest to them. For instance, some of the different plans that are put together by the long-distance phone companies (free minutes, rebates, or simplified pricing) are all acquisition strategies that are carefully crafted and targeted at those prospects who have made the cut in the selection phase. Keep in mind that not all the prospects in the selection phase are created equal. Some prospects may be high-profit and will warrant expensive acquisition strategies. Some prospects will be low-profit customers and warrant very inexpensive strategies.

The challenge to building a model for acquisition comes from modeling which tactic will result in the minimum effort (and expense) but still result in the prospect saying "yes." For example, a selection model can be used as the basis for a prediction about a future customer's value. From this, an acquisition strategy can be formed with the acquisition model in order to acquire the customer at as low a cost as possible. The model would take the known attributes of a given prospect and produce a probability of acquisition for each available tactic. For example, the customer might be 90 percent likely to be acquired if a $100 offer were made, 60 percent likely to be acquired if a 10 percent discount were offered, and 1 percent likely to be acquired through a simple mailed invitation. These models can be based on the past experience of making these offers to other prospects and seeing which ones actually were acquired. Once the models are built and the prospects are modeled, a business decision can be made to optimize overall return on investment.

14.3.3   Problem 3: retention

The next phase of the customer life cycle is retaining customers once they have been acquired. In the prom analogy, retention might correspond to keeping your date throughout the prom without having that person dance with someone else. Unlike your date at the senior prom, customer loyalty is not what it used to be. Given the highly competitive markets of today and the ease with which a competitor can contact and entice away your customers, loyalty is something that must be actively encouraged and monitored.

In the cellular phone and the banking industries, nearly one in every three customers is lost to the competition every year. The bad news is that in these industries, acquiring a new customer costs roughly $300. The really bad news is that the customers who are attriting are often the most profitable ones. Having a model of which customers are at risk of leaving can be invaluable since correcting customer dissatisfaction or countering a competitor's offer before the competitor can contact your customer is far more effective at retaining the customer than even extremely expensive reactive measures taken after the customer has already decided to jump ship to the competition.

Like models for selection and acquisition, a good model for retention has two parts. First, a model is necessary to predict who is at risk and to what degree; second, a model is needed to determine which retention strategy would be most effective (e.g., waiving the membership fee for a credit card, or a lower interest rate or discount restaurant coupons). Again these models can be based on the historical data that has been collected in the past on which customers have attrited and what strategies were successful in preventing their attrition or in winning them back. Especially for attrition, the models need to be constantly updated since what worked last year may no longer work because of changes in the marketplace being carried out by the competition.

14.3.4 Problem 4: extension

Finally after you've landed customers, and managed to retain good customers, you may want to extend the services or products that you sell to them beyond what they initially purchased when they were acquired. In our senior prom analogy, extension would correspond to making sure you got another date after the prom was over. For business this usually means selling another related product to the customer. The good news about extension (and this is true for retention as well) is that you own a significant amount of proprietary data about your customer—information that was not available to you when you were building the models for selection and acquisition, where all you knew about a given customer was what was publicly available. With this additional information (which your competition is not privy to), you have a decided advantage at selling another product.

Extension is also called *cross-selling,* and it can be as simple as a bank trying to sell life insurance to a customer who recently took out a home mortgage, or it could include more complex products such as the balance transfer offer which credit card issuers make to their existing customers, asking these customers to transfer their debt from competing creditors to their card. Modeling which customers will actually be interested in another one of your products is important since the customer can easily be overloaded with solicitations for products in which they are not interested and then not respond to solicitations that they actually might want to purchase. Likewise, if your customers are not solicited for something that they need and you offer but are unaware of it, they will then be susceptible to a solicitation from your competition.

14.4   What Is the "Right" Model?

For any of these pattern detection and predictive systems, there is the hope that the "correct" or "right" model exists. Specifically, this is the underlying model that would completely and perfectly predict what is going on—it is the holy grail to either find this underlying space or come as close as you can to it. One problem is that you have to account for some real-world events such as random noise, data errors, imprecise measures, and missing measures. Now that we have an understanding of what a model is and what it can be used for, we are faced with a few important questions:

- Is there such a thing as a "perfect" model?
- Can one model be better than another?
- How do you judge which model is better?

To answer these questions, let's go all the way back to the early 1800s, when the mathematician Pierre Simon Laplace asserted that if it were possible to know precisely the current state of everything in the universe at a given time, it would then be possible to build a model to perfectly predict all future events from that point forward. Laplace's view has since been tempered by the uncertainties of quantum physics and the Heisenberg uncertainty principle as well as the more recent developments in the field of chaotic systems. Despite this evidence to the contrary, many people still feel that underlying the complex and often seemingly meaningless events that take place. There may be some well-defined model that, if it could be uncovered, would explain and predict much of what is observed.

We will not attempt to here philosophize on whether such a model really is possible for the entire universe, but we can say something fairly practical about what a model is in the domain of the average database and business problem to be solved using predictive modeling.

14.4.1   The perfect model

The perfect model—if such a thing existed—would have several important characteristics:

- It could always be used to make the correct prediction.
- It would not degrade over time.
- It could be used with the data at hand and not require any extraordinary data collection.
- It would be simpler and smaller than the data it was used to model.

For any real-world problem there is no such perfect model. There is always relevant data that can't be collected, or the data that is collected contains errors or has missing values; and almost always the models that are built today are susceptible to change over time. Given these realities, it is still useful to think about what a perfect model might look like and then to see how errors are introduced into the model by the shortcomings of the real world.

To some degree this idea of the correct or perfect model is held by statisticians. In statistics it is believed that for any given predictor there is a "true" distribution of the values of the data that underlies whatever the actual collected data looks like. If the collected data differs from this ideal distribution, it is because of random fluctuations in the finite size of the sample or in simple errors that come with the imperfect collection of data in the real world.

This idea is best explained by example. In Fig. 14.4 a fair six-sided die is tossed repeatedly and the number of times each side comes up is recorded. Because the die is fair, the "true" distribution should look flat—each side should come up the same number of times. But the real world sneaks in, and several troublesome things happen. People recording the data often make mistakes and write down the wrong number. In this hypothetical example the lucky number of the person recording the data is 5, and the person tends to write down that number rather than the actual value. Also the die is thrown only 18 times, so even though the die is fair, just by dumb luck the number 6 comes up many more times than the expected number of 3. So when all is said and done, the values of the die that were expected (in a perfect world) would have been 3 times for each of the six sides. Instead, this underlying distribution is modified by several external effects such as poor and biased data collection and bad luck. So even though there is a true model for the behavior of the die, the data does not necessarily reflect it. In more complex models the same caveats apply. Even if there is a true perfect model underlying the data, real-world effects can cloud its existence so that the data may look quite different. In Laplace's world it could be argued that even the erroneous data collection

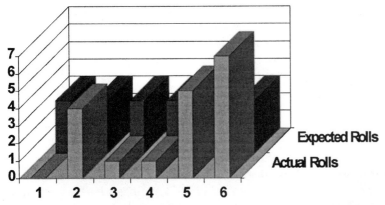

Figure 14.4 The actual and expected number of times each side of a fair die should be rolled.

could have been modeled by modeling the behavior of the person collecting the data. In reality this would be a very hard thing to do.

14.4.2 Missing data

One of the biggest problems in collecting real-world data from which to build predictive models is not having enough of the right data. Consider, for instance, the case in the medical domain where there is some evidence linking very low heart attack rates to people who have had extremely restricted fat-free diets from birth. There is some evidence to support this model, based on the diets of people from around the world, but for the country that is of most interest to the study—the United States—there simply is no record of anyone who has maintained such a restricted diet. Thus there is little to no data that can be used to even begin to extract a pattern, let alone build a comprehensive model. Often the lack of data can be remedied in the business world by proactively collecting it. Specifically the data that is not currently available could be solicited by test marketing campaigns.

In other cases the amount of information collected may be insufficient for construction of a good model (remember that even in Laplace's conjecture he assumed that he could have access to the knowledge about everything in the world at a given time in order to build a good model). For instance, what if you had to predict someone's name, given only their phone number? In general, there is no connection between someone's name and their phone number—or if there is, it will be slight (for instance, in the United States, recent immigrants may live in the same general geographic area, creating a higher concentration of people with the same last name within the same telephone exchange). But even in those cases where there is some connection between name and phone number, it is likely to be slight and highly variable—probably not something you'd want to launch your marketing program against. Much more information than just a person's name would be required in order to build a good model to predict telephone numbers. Unfortunately much of this information is not readily available.

The thing to remember about missing data is that, no matter how hard you try or how large your database is, you will always be missing something that could improve the performance of the model that you are building. Sometimes it will be missing predictors, and sometimes it will be a lack of records. The key is to recognize that in the real world the model you will be making will always be based on missing data and to make allowances for it.

14.5 Sampling

One of the things that we notice about patterns and models is that a model is, by definition, only a small part of the greater space in which something is going on. For instance, the patterns in the data that we have been looking at could probably be recognized without having to see every single example for every possible combination of predictors.

14.5.1   The necessity of sampling

Let's go back to our original case, in which we are trying to predict the next number in the sequence "1212123121212 . . . ," or a more interesting real-world case where we may only have a few examples of fraud in our database of customers. In both examples what is presented to us, and from which we are supposed to build a model, is only a small fraction of the total space of examples which we could be looking at. We do not have in our database, no matter how large it is, an example of every possible customer and all the predictors that describe that person. In fact, even if we have 100 million customer records in our database, this will only be a fraction of the U.S. population—and an even smaller fraction of the total world population. Given that we don't have every example in our database, can we still build a reliable model? The answer is yes. The model will never be as good as it would have been if you had all the possible examples, but it will be a lot better than having no model at all.

There are, of course, other times when you don't have all the possible data points that you might want. Sometimes you just don't have enough data, but other times you may not want to use all the data that you have because it may be difficult to process or store all of it as you are looking for patterns in trying to build a model. In this case you can perform sampling.

Sometimes people will denigrate sampling techniques because they believe that they won't get the right answer from the "right" model unless they use "all" of the data. The problem is that they rarely, if ever, have the opportunity to use all the data. For instance, if you were classifying fraud cases, you might have some information about some people such as their incomes and their credit limits. In general, you know that people who have low incomes and high credit limits are more likely to commit fraud and those who have high incomes but low credit limits are as well. You know that in your credit card company there are credit limits ranging from $100 to $10,000, in $100 increments—which translates to 100 different possible credit limits that people could have. For the customers' income, you could likewise come up with 100 different values from no salary to professional athletes and CEOs making up to $10 million each year. You've picked 100 different salaries and 100 different credit limits—which translates to 10,000 different types of customers based on just income and credit limit. Even in a database of over 1 million customers (a reasonable-sized credit card company), you would be unlikely to find every possible combination of income and credit limit represented by at least one database record. Or consider the case where you represent personal income in $1 increments—now there are $10,000,000 \times 100$ or 1 billion possible types of customers in your database that might or might not be representative of fraud. If you consider that this is just the number of examples that you have with two predictors and how much larger the "space" of examples could be if you added more and more predictors, this would likely mean that your space would be so large that you would never be able to fill in all the empty slots with viable examples of customers. And, of course, this is exactly the problem that you run into in real-world situations. Thus sampling is something that we are doing all of the time whether we'd like to do it or not. The issue then is: If sampling is unavoidable in all but the most pristine academic settings, then maybe we should instead embrace it and make use of it.

14.5.2   Random sampling

One way to make use of sampling is to use it to effectively limit the size of your database in which to find the predictive patterns. For instance, if you had a database of 1 billion examples of people who had committed credit card fraud, you would be hard-pressed to wade through all that data—either by hand or even with a computer in any reasonable amount of time. But if, on the other hand, you were given 10 randomly chosen examples from this huge database that looked like the data in Table 14.3, you might quickly begin to see a pattern: namely, that people aged 42 seem to have a very high likelihood for committing fraud.

By randomly sampling the database, we can see that an impossible problem became feasible and a possible model was offered up almost immediately. Such a model could then be refined and confirmed by further sampling the data with larger numbers of samples. As will be shown in the following section, it can be critical that this sampling be done by some random process in order to avoid any possible bias that would create a less-than-optimal model.

14.6   Experimental Design

A well-thought-out and well-executed experimental design is critical for the eventual success of statistical analysis or for data mining. *Experimental design* refers to the way that the data that is used for analysis is collected and transformed. Sometimes the analyst has very little control over how the data was created or how it was gathered, but sometimes it is possible to control how the data is collected so that it is possible to build a better predictive model. For instance, it is much easier to build a good predictive model if there is a good

TABLE 14.3   Random Sample from Database*

Age	Fraud
42	Yes
13	No
42	Yes
42	Yes
67	No
45	Yes
37	No
41	No
42	Yes

* A small random sample from a much larger database still can show an important predictive pattern.

random sample rather than some sample that is limited in some way and does not represent the population that will eventually be modeled.

The initial inclination may be to avoid sampling completely and instead look at all the possible data or all possible combinations of predictor values. The problem with this approach is that it is almost always unattainable because the number of records could not be acquired, stored, or processed. Almost all modeling has to do with sampling. If you were able to collect all possible data in your database for every possible situation, then it would not be necessary to build a predictive model; it would suffice to simply look up in the database the particular situation now in question and find the answer. In experimental design, determining how to sample, or overcoming poor sampling strategy that can't be controlled, is extremely important.

14.6.1 Avoiding bias

When performing sampling it is important to recognize certain differences in the way that a sample could be collected and to be very aware of any way that the sample was collected without a truly randomized process. Sometimes bias is present in the manner in which the sample was collected. For instance, if you were looking to introduce a new orange-flavored soda to your existing soda line and you wanted to know whether it would sell, you might find it most convenient to conduct taste tests in the town where the soda company's corporate headquarters resides. Gathering data in this way would be easy to do (just walk outside the front door and ask), but it might well result in bias in the test that would throw off the results. For instance, the town population outside the corporate headquarters includes a significant number of soda company employees and their families, neighbors, and friends—all of whom would likely be already familiar with the soda brand and perhaps more favorably predisposed to buying the new soda.

Surprisingly, biased samples such as this are used all the time, with the result that the predictive model behaves differently when used on new data (in this case on different towns across America) than it did when the model was constructed and run on the data in the data warehouse. The best possible way to avoid this kind of bias is to perform a completely random sample. In this case, if you are planning on selling your new soda product across America, the best way to base your taste tests would be to randomly visit some small percentage of all the people across the country. Clearly, this is much more expensive than just asking the people in town. It should also, however, give a much better predictive model about who would eventually purchase the soda.

14.6.2 More on sampling

Even after you have collected your data from a well-thought-out experimental design, you may still want to sample the data when you build your model because of the amount of time that it can take to build a model on a large database. For instance, consider a credit card company with 15 million customer records stored in the data warehouse. The best possible statistical model that could be produced would use all the records, but this might take a very long time. Sampling provides a way to get a very good answer that is often within a very small fraction of the optimal answer with many fewer records. The basic idea is captured in the law of diminishing returns, where, for example, 10,000 records might provide a model that was within 90 percent in accuracy of a model that was built on 10 million customer records. Running on millions of records is preferred for a better prediction, but there is often a cost involved.

Round robin.   One easy way to sample a database is merely to take every nth record in the database. For instance, if you wanted a 1 percent sample of a database of 100 million records you could devise a scheme that took every 100th record in the database (resulting in 1 million records in your sample). This scheme is relatively easy to implement, but it can cause some problems. Since it is not completely random but instead the selection of the sample depends on how the data is laid out in the database, the sample could be biased in some way if there is any pattern at all in the way that the data is stored consecutively in the database.

For instance, consider that perhaps the best way, from the IT perspective, to store customer records is to have one customer record from one state followed by a customer record from the next state so that the first 50 records would be from 50 different states, and then the next 50 records would likewise contain one customer record from every state. Maybe IT did this to balance the query load against a parallel disk system (IT always has its reasons), but the bottom line is that if you used this round-robin approach to sampling and you chose every 50th record, your sample would contain records from only one particular state. The resulting model then would likely be heavily biased by the sample and not be applicable across the entire country. Note that it wouldn't be just every 50th but also any multiple of 50 (100, 150, 200, etc.). Because the way the data may have been laid out may have some pattern or order to it, it could be dangerous to use this particular sampling technique.

Stratified sampling.   Another form of sampling is *stratified sampling*. The idea here is that you may have in your database a value for the prediction column in that database that is particularly important to what you are modeling but occurs in very low concentrations. For instance, it is not uncommon to have a response rate of much less than 1 percent for a targeted mailing. Thus, in 100,000 customer records who received the mailing, only 1000 responded. If, in order to build the model, a 1 percent sample is used, there will be 1000 records but only 10 records that give information about those customers that responded. In such a case it is often better to take a higher proportion of the records which were positive responses in order to build a better model. In this case it might be valuable to take 500 response records and 500 nonresponse records to build the model. Once the model is built, there is one remaining important step that corrects the model back to the original concentrations of response and nonresponse records.

Cluster sampling. One other form of stratified sampling is *cluster sampling,* in which the original database is clustered and then equivalent numbers of records are taken from each cluster to ensure that all important subgroups within the database are represented. For instance, with customer records, the records could be clustered into groups where the customers had similar socio-economic qualities (e.g., old and wealthy, liberal with middle income, blue collar). The sampling procedure would then be to select some samples from each of the clusters to make sure that all major groups were well represented in the model. Normally, if the samples and the database were large enough, random sampling would be adequate to make sure that each group was represented. If, however, there were many of these important subgroups, and some of them contained only a few records, it would be necessary to use this approach to make sure that there was adequate coverage of the groups in the sample.

14.7 Computer-Intensive Statistics

At its most basic level, statistics really is just a matter of counting things, and counting things in context. However, when the numbers become too large or too computationally expensive, other methods are used, such as the formula used to describe a given distribution of data. Using such a formula makes it easy to calculate the mean and variance and other statistics once something is known about the original distribution. Despite the complexities of the math involved, statistics in the real world is always performed on finite numbers of records with finite numbers of different values for predictors. Thus it is always possible to count and experiment to understand how data is behaving in addition to modeling the behavior with a mathematical model.

The difference between these two techniques is roughly captured by statisticians in the terms *parametric techniques* and *nonparametric techniques.* The parametric techniques generally use parameters in a model that closely matches the observed data, and the required estimations of error and variance are calculated from an equation with these parameters in it. Nonparametric techniques, on the other hand, compute the possible answers through experimentation and different types of sampling and resampling of the data.

To understand the difference between parametric and nonparametric techniques, consider an example in which a predictive customer segment has been created from a predictive model that indicates that customers are equally likely to respond as not respond to a marketing offer. Thus the predicted response rate for the segment will be 50 percent. Before you launch a marketing campaign against this segment, however, you—as a skilled marketing person—would also like to know what the error bar is around this prediction. For instance, you know that if the response rate is 40 percent or lower, you will lose money on the campaign. Obviously, then, you'd like to know what the chances are of this happening. If you actually knew what the underlying distribution was for response in that customer segment, you would be able to answer that question.

For instance, you might find that only 10 percent of the time that you launched a campaign against this segment the response would be equal to or less than 40 percent, which might be an acceptable level of risk for you. The question, then, is how you would calculate this downside number. One way that you could do it would be to model the distribution by some other well-known distribution. In this case you might again model this response model in a similar way to flipping a coin. Even if you flip a fair coin 100 times, it is unlikely that it will come up heads 50 times and tails 50 times (although this is the most probable scenario). There is, of course, a very real chance that even with a perfectly fair coin, if you flipped it 100 times, it would come up heads 40 times and tails 60 times. The chance of this happening can be modeled by a binomial random variable, and the chances of this scenario taking place can be calculated. In using this calculation, however, we've made some important assumptions; the main one is that the average response rate of many such campaigns really will be 50 percent if enough campaigns are launched. This is not a strictly valid assumption for a number of reasons:

- The predictive model was built on a sample of the data, and thus the 50 percent response rate predicted is really just an estimate of the actual response rate of the true distribution.

- In real marketing situations the world is constantly changing. What may have been a good model yesterday may not be a good model today. This estimate of the response rate of 50 percent is based on the assumptions that things are not necessarily changing.

For these reasons the assumptions that are made in parametric statistics can sometimes give misleading results. There is another way, however. The other way to calculate the statistics is to perform experiments. If you want to know what the variation in your predictive model will be, you could vary the sampling procedure, take another sample from the database, and see what rate is predicted from that sample. Consider the experiments shown in Table 14.4. Here two different marketing managers in two different companies build predictive models from 1000 customer records by sampling 500 of them. In each case the first model that they build shows a 50 percent response rate. To see how this response rate is affected by the sample of the data, both marketing managers randomly resample the database 10 different times. After this is done, one marketing manager feels comfortable in her estimates of response rate, while the other feels much less confident of his own estimates. And in fact since the first manager has created her own distribution, she can actually cal-

TABLE 14.4   Random Sample Showing Predicted Response of Targeted Customer Segment*

Company	1	2	3	4	5	6	7	8	9	10	Avg.
A	50%	49%	48%	51%	51%	47%	50%	52%	49%	53%	50%
B	50%	57%	33%	55%	64%	50%	43%	67%	36%	45%	50%

* Different models can be either stable or highly variable over different random samples.

culate the chance that 40 percent response might occur simply as a result of random variation. Table 14.4 shows the predicted response from a targeted customer segment over 10 different random samples of 500 records from a 1000 record database. Company A finds that their model is relatively stable and consistent independent of the sample. Company B finds that their predictive model is highly volatile depending on the sample.

14.7.1 Cross-validation

The example above shows how databases can be used to compute the error and variance on some statistics. This can be done for statistics such as the mean, for which there are easy-to-determine formulas for calculating the variance and the error. The nice thing about these nonparametric techniques is that they can also be used to calculate other statistics for which it is nearly impossible to calculate the variance. For instance, there are easy-to-compute formulas to calculate the variance for the sample mean, but there is no easy way to similarly calculate the variance for the sample median. The nice thing about working directly with the data, however, is that it can provide not only an estimate for the particular statistical measure but also the variance or error that goes along with it.

For prediction, there is a similar nonparametric technique called *cross-validation*, in which when the predictive model is built, the prediction is made on one part of the database, and the model is then applied to the other part of the database. Typically these are called the *training database* and the *test database*, respectively. If these two databases are kept completely separate from each other (i.e., no record is contained in both of them), then the performance of the predictive model on the test set will give some measure of the amount of variance in the accuracy that one might expect to see for different databases.

An extension of the cross-validation method is to not just break the database into two pieces once but to randomly repeat this break several times and record the accuracy of the predictive model over each breakup. Each time the database would be randomly broken up into two pieces, the predictive model built on one piece, and the accuracy tested on the other piece. In the limit the database could be broken up into a training set that contained all the records in the database except one, and the one that it didn't contain would be the test database. If the data is broken up in this way, as many training and test sets could be created as there are data points.

In Tables 14.5 and 14.6 cross-validation is used to split the original database into two pieces. One piece is used to build the predictive model, and the other

TABLE 14.5   Training Set Used for Test Set or Cross-Validation

			Training database				
6	Carl	No	27	$5400	High	Brown	M
2	Al	No	53	$1800	Medium	Green	M
7	Donna	Yes	50	$ 165	Low	Blue	F
8	Don	Yes	46	$ 0	High	Blue	M
10	Ed	No	68	$1200	Low	Blue	M

TABLE 14.6   **Test Set Used for Test Set or Cross-Validation**

				Test database			
3	Betty	No	47	$16,543	High	Brown	F
1	Amy	No	62	$ 0	Medium	Brown	F
4	Bob	Yes	32	$ 45	Medium	Green	M
5	Carla	Yes	21	$ 2300	High	Blue	F
9	Edna	Yes	27	$ 500	Low	Blue	F

is used to test it. In this case the split is 50/50; in practice the test database is often smaller than the training database.

14.7.2   Jackknife and bootstrap resampling

In addition to the cross-validation approach to estimating the accuracy of a predictive model, it may also be useful to see how particular statistical measures vary with chance fluctuations in sampling. For instance, if you were given a database with the ages of 100 people in it randomly selected from the general U.S. population, you might wonder what the average age was and how much variability you might see in it simply because only a small sample of people actually made it into the database. Effectively, you'd like to see how sensitive your calculation of the average age is to simple fluctuations in the way that the sample was collected. There are perhaps three ways that you might go about trying to figure this out using nonparametric techniques:

1. Go out and collect another sample of 100 ages from the general population and see how the average age of that sample compares to the first one.

2. Randomly pull one record out of the database and recompute the average age and see how much its value is influenced by just one data point.

3. Create a new database of 100 values from the original database of 100 via random sampling. See how much the average age differs in this new database.

Technique 1 is the most logical: "If you want to see what the variance is on the average age of a 100-value sample, just try it a few times and see how much it varies." Or maybe just calculate the average age across the U.S. population and see how much it differs from the sample calculation. This is, in fact, exactly what you are trying to figure out in the most straightforward way possible. The problem with the technique is, however, that you don't always have the luxury of being able to create multiple sample databases and compare them, or to calculate the value of interest across the entire population.

Consider, for instance, what might happen if you were trying to calculate the average revenue from a cellular phone customer who had been enticed into membership by the offer of a free phone. In this case it is very expensive to create the sample (since you have to give a free phone to each participant). In these cases, which are almost always found in the business world, gathering more data is expensive, so you need to do the best that you can with the sample you've got. This leaves the last two methods as practical ways of estimating how far off from the truth you could be in your estimates by using a sample. The first method, in which a single record is removed is called the "jackknife" technique. The second method, in which a new resampled database is created from the original sampled database, is called the "bootstrap" technique.

The jackknife method was so named by John Tukey with the implication that it was an all-purpose statistical tool. Indeed, the method is very general and can be used in a wide variety of situations. It is also not terribly expensive to compute. In our example of estimating the average age, you might at first think that the average age would not change very much by removing just one data point from the original sample. In general, it would not, but in a data set of 99 children and one octogenarian, pulling that one record of the 80-year-old would have a considerable effect on the average age. If, however, the data set were made up uniformly of teenagers, the average age would not appear to be so greatly affected by the loss of just one data point. The intent of the jackknife method is to provide some sense of how the particular statistic that is being calculated changes with random fluctuations in the sample. To get an even better measure of this fluctuation, the jackknife method creates many of these new databases that are missing one value (in fact, as many of these databases can be created as there are data values or records). The average ages over all these databases are then collected, and the degree to which they vary indicates the sensitivity of the initial result to the limits of the sample.

In the second technique of resampling the original database, the bootstrap method (the name implying that if it were possible to pick oneself up by the bootstraps, a database could be reused and resampled to give even more information), the intent is the same as for the jackknife: create a new database from the original and see how much the average age changes. The bootstrap sample is created via a technique called *random sampling with replacement*. The idea here is that records are sampled from the original database just as if you were pulling winning lottery numbers from a glass jar. Because there is replacement, however, a winning number, once drawn, is placed back into the original glass jar and could be picked again (presumably the lucky winner would be paid out as many times as the number was drawn). With replacement some lottery numbers will yield multiple winners and some numbers will not be drawn at all. For the bootstrap, this corresponds to our example of a database with 100 ages in it from which a bootstrap database of 100 values will be created. Since the initial database had just 100 records and the new sampled database has 100, some of the records from the original database may appear multiple times in the bootstrap database and some will not appear at all. This is similar to the way the original sample of 100 was drawn from the much larger database of the U.S. population. Some of the random fluctuations seen in the sampling from the country down to 100 will be reflected in the bootstrap database created from the 100-value sample.

The jackknife, bootstrap, and cross-validation techniques are all computationally expensive ways to determine how the limited view of the world that is afforded by your sample reflects reality. However, they can provide insight into the extent to which these estimates might vary to enable the business user to estimate risk and make decisions wisely. They do not necessarily replace the calculated analytical results of variance, but they can be used in a much larger number of situations than is possible with other methods, or if these other methods are applied, they may make such simplifying assumptions as to make the results difficult to understand. Certainly one of the great advantages of these techniques is that they make good intuitive sense. To summarize the differences between these methods, consider the example in Table 14.7. Here our original database of 10 people is broken up into two separate databases via the three techniques. Typically multiple such resampled databases would be created for the technique. Each of the three techniques used to estimate variability in the sample database does so by comparing the value obtained in one sample to another. The three techniques are contrasted here, showing which records would be removed (strike-through), retained, or duplicated (underlined) in two resampled databases typical for one iteration of the technique.

14.8   Picking the Best Model

One of the most important things that you need to do when building a predictive model is to make sure that you have picked up the essential patterns in the data that will hold true the next time you apply your model. For instance, when you use cross-validation as previously described, you may well want to test with data from last month and train on data from 2 months ago. Then the model that you built would be tried out on new data "from the future." The performance of this data should provide a great deal of confidence that your model will work next month as well.

Have you ever taken a test in college, say, in physics, where you memorized a couple of specific examples of how to work out problems—the same ones that the professor wrote out on the board during class? Then during the test the professor gave slightly different problems that were just different enough that you were unable to solve them? This is known as "cookbook physics," in which you

TABLE 14.7   Comparison of How Different Resampling Techniques Might Be Used to Create Two New Databases from the Original

Technique	Database 1	Database 2
Jackknife	Al, Amy, Bob, Betty, ~~Carl~~, Carla, Don, Donna, Edna, Ed	Al, Amy, Bob, Betty, Carl, Carla, Don ~~Donna~~, Edna, Ed
Bootstrap	Al, ~~Amy, Bob~~, Betty, Carl, Carla, Don, Donna, _Donna_, Edna, Ed, _Ed_	Al, ~~Amy~~, Bob, _Bob, Bob_, Betty, ~~Carl~~, Carla, _Carla_, Don, ~~Donna~~, Edna, Ed
Cross-validation	Al, Amy, ~~Bob~~, Betty, ~~Carl~~, Carla, Don, ~~Donna, Edna~~, Ed	~~Al, Amy~~, Bob, ~~Betty~~, Carl, ~~Carla~~, ~~Don~~, Donna, Edna, ~~Ed~~

just memorize the equations and a few particular applications but never really understand the whole problem or how the pieces fit together. You knew how to solve the problem in a particular area but were unable to extract the general information or knowledge about the problem itself and how it should be solved if the situation changed slightly. The same thing can happen to predictive models. Consider a predictive model built with an artificial neural network.

A neural network "learns" by being repeatedly presented with examples of the predictors and the prediction (or in statistical parlance, the independent and dependent variables). As the network is presented with more and more examples, it subtly modifies the connection strengths between the different pieces of data coming in and the required answer coming out. By doing this, the network begins to make fewer and fewer mistakes. In some cases the network will result in no mistakes made for the particular prediction after the training data has been run by it enough times. Interestingly, though, the performance of the validation data shows a different behavior. The error rate of the validation data reaches a minimum at one point of learning and then begins to increase after that—even while the error rate of the training data continues to decrease.

This effect is called "overfitting" and corresponds to the above-mentioned physics student who tries to memorize exactly the right thing to do on a handful of physics problems, rather than trying to understand the general rules for predicting physical systems. The neural network at first is extracting general rules for prediction but over time, as the same examples are repeatedly presented to it, the network effectively begins to memorize the answers to the particular examples that it has in the training set. This works well for decreasing the error rate on the training set as the network comes closer and closer to fully memorizing the data. It also means that the network has begun to extract patterns that are not predictive of the problem being solved but are predictive only given some of the idiosyncrasies of the particular database. For instance, you could find the analogous rule that all people named Jonathan David Smith are poor credit risks embedded in the neural network. It may be the case that both the people named Jonathan David Smith in the training database were bad credit risks, but it is unlikely that someone's full name is predictive of credit worthiness. More general predictive models are more likely to hold up under cross-validation and provide good results under a wide variety of conditions. In the next chapters we will see how many different techniques deal with the problem of overfitting.

15

Statistics

Statistics is a branch of mathematics concerning the collection and the description of data. Usually statistics is considered to be one of those scary topics in college along with chemistry and physics. However, statistics is really a much friendlier branch of mathematics because it can be used every day. Statistics was, in fact, born from very humble beginnings to solve real-world problems in business, biology, and gambling! Knowing statistics will help average businesspeople make better decisions by allowing them to figure out risk and uncertainty when all the facts either aren't known or can't be collected. Even with all the data stored in the largest of data warehouses, business decisions still just become more informed guesses. The more and better the data and the better the understanding of statistics, the better the decision that can be made.

Statistics has been around for a long time—easily a century, and arguably many centuries from when the concept of probability first began to gel. It could even be argued that the data collected by the ancient Egyptians, Babylonians, and Greeks were all statistics long before the field was officially recognized. Today data mining has been defined independently of statistics, although "mining data" for patterns and predictions is really what statistics is all about. Some of the techniques that are classified under data mining such as CHAID (chi square automatic interaction detector) and CART (classification and regression trees) really grew out of the statistical profession more than anywhere else, and the basic ideas of probability, independence, and causality and overfitting are the foundation on which both data mining and statistics are built.

15.1 Data, Counting, and Probability

One thing that is always true about statistics is that there is always data involved, and usually enough data so that the average person cannot keep track of all the data in their heads. This is certainly more true today than it was when the modern ideas of probability and statistics were being formulated and refined early in the twentieth century. Today people have to deal with data ranging up into the order of terabytes and have to make sense of it and glean the important patterns from it. Statistics can help greatly in this process by helping you answer several important questions about your data:

- What patterns are there in my database?
- What is the chance that an event will occur?
- Which patterns are significant?
- What is a high-level summary of the data that gives me some idea of what is contained in my database?

Certainly statistics can do more than answer these questions, but for most people today these are the questions that statistics is used to answer. Consider, for example, that a large part of statistics is concerned with summarizing data, and, more often than not, this summarization has to do with counting. One of the great values of statistics is in presenting a high level view of the database that provides some useful information without requiring every record to be understood in detail. This aspect of statistics is the part that people run into every day when they read the daily newspaper and see, for example, a pie chart reporting the number of U.S. citizens of different eye colors, or the average number of annual physician visits for people of different ages. Statistics at this level is used to report important information which may help people make useful decisions. There are many different parts of statistics, but the idea of collecting data and counting it is often at the base of even these more sophisticated techniques. The first step in understanding statistics, then, is to understand how the data is collected into a higher-level form—and one of the most notable ways of doing this is with the histogram.

15.1.1   Histograms

One of the best ways to summarize data is to provide a histogram of the data. In the simple example database shown in Table 15.1, we can create a histogram of eye color by counting the number of occurrences of different eye col-

TABLE 15.1   **An Example Database of Customers with Different Predictor Types**

ID	Name	Prediction	Age	Balance ($)	Income	Eyes	Gender
1	Amy	No	62	0	Medium	Brown	F
2	Al	No	53	1800	Medium	Green	M
3	Betty	No	47	16,543	High	Brown	F
4	Bob	Yes	32	45	Medium	Green	M
5	Carla	Yes	21	2300	High	Blue	F
6	Carl	No	27	5400	High	Brown	M
7	Donna	Yes	50	165	Low	Blue	F
8	Don	Yes	46	0	High	Blue	M
9	Edna	Yes	27	500	Low	Blue	F
10	Ed	No	68	1200	Low	Blue	M

ors in our database. For this example database of 10 records, this is fairly easy to do and the results are only slightly more interesting than the database itself. However, for a database of many more records, this is a very useful way of getting a high-level understanding of the database.

The histogram shown in Fig. 15.1 depicts a simple predictor (eye color) which will have only a few different values regardless of whether there are 100 customer records or 100 million in the database. There are, however, other predictors that have many more distinct values and can create a much more complex histogram. Consider, for instance, the histogram of ages of the customers in the population. In this case the histogram can be more complex but can also be enlightening. Assume that you found that the histogram of your customer data looked as it does in Fig. 15.2.

By looking at this second histogram, the viewer is in many ways looking at all the data in the database for a particular predictor or data column. By looking at this histogram it is also possible to build an intuition about other important factors, such as the average age of the population and the maximum and minimum ages, all of which are important. These values are called *summary statistics*. Some of the most frequently used summary statistics include

- *Max*—the maximum value for a given predictor

- *Min*—the minimum value for a given predictor

- *Mean*—the average value for a given predictor

- *Median*—the value for a given predictor that divides the database as nearly as possible into two databases of equal numbers of records

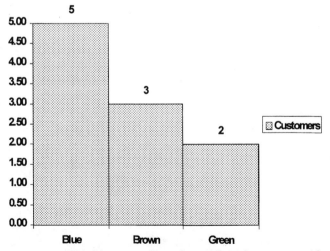

Figure 15.1   This histogram shows the number of customers with various eye colors. This summary can quickly show important information about the database such as that blue eyes are the most frequent.

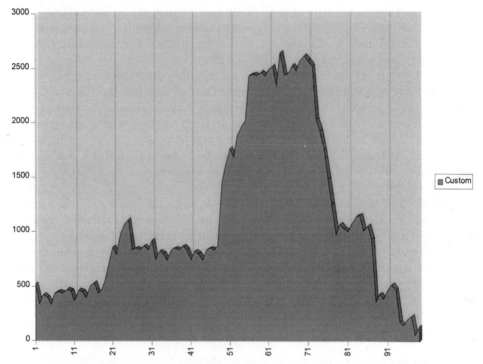

Figure 15.2   This histogram shows the number of customers of different ages and quickly tells the viewer that the majority of customers are over the age of 50.

- *Mode*—the most common value for the predictor

- *Variance*—the measure of how spread out the values are from the average value

When there are many values for a given predictor, the histogram begins to look smoother and smoother (note the difference between the two histograms in Figs. 15.1 and 15.2). Sometimes the shape of the distribution of data can be calculated by an equation rather than just represented by the histogram. This is what is called a *data distribution*. Like a histogram, a data distribution can be described by a variety of statistics. In classic statistics the belief is that there is some "true" underlying shape to the data distribution that would be formed if all possible data were collected. The shape of the data distribution can be calculated for some simple examples. The statistician's job then is to take the limited data that may have been collected and from that make a best guess at what the "true" or at least most likely underlying data distribution might be.

Many data distributions are well described by just two numbers, the mean and the variance. The mean is something most people are familiar with; the variance, however, can be problematic. The easiest way to think about it is that it measures the average distance of each predictor value from the mean value over all the records in the database. If the variance is high, the values are all over the place and very different. If the variance is low, most of the data values are fairly close to the mean. To be precise, the actual definition of the variance uses the square of the distance rather than the actual distance from the mean, and the average is taken by dividing the squared sum by one less than the total number of records. In terms of prediction, a user could make some guess at the value of a predictor without knowing anything else other than the mean and also gain some basic sense of how variable the guess might be on the basis of the variance.

15.1.2 Types of categorical predictors

In looking at the 10-record example database in this book, we see that different columns of data (what we call *predictors* for prediction problems) cannot all be treated in the same way. What, for instance, is the mean of eye color? Or what is the max or min eye color? In this case eye color is a type of predictor called a *nominal* or *unordered categorical,* which is one of three major types of predictors that are used in analysis with not only statistical tools but also all types of data mining and other predictive modeling tools. To understand the distinction between these types of predictors, consider three different ways people might classify shoes:

- *Classify by shoe color*—where there are, say, five possible shoe colors: red, green, blue, black, and white

- *Classify by consumer age group*—where the categorical values are infant, child, teen, and adult

- *Classify by size of foot*—where the actual shoe size corresponds to the length of someone's foot in whole inches, with 10 different values of 4, 5, 6, 7, 8, 9, 10, 11, 12, and 13 in

Each of these predictors is a categorical predictor in the sense that there is a finite number of categories or values that each of these predictors can have (i.e., five possible colors, four age groups, and 10 sizes in inches). A categorical predictor is distinguished from a continuous predictor such as a person's precise age by the finite number of values a categorical can take on, while a continuous predictor could hypothetically take on an infinite number of values (e.g., you could more and more precisely measure someone's age from years to days to microseconds and effectively have an infinite number of possible values). The most important distinction for most algorithms, though, has less to do with the number of possible values (finite = categorical, infinite = continuous) than whether there is any ordering of the values possible. The three main types of ordering categorical predictors are the following:

- *Nominal categorical predictors,* such as shoe color in the example above, have no particular relationship to each other. One cannot, for instance, say that "red" was greater or less than "blue," nor could one say that "white" was between "red" and "green." *Nominal* here derives from *name,* where there is a distinct name for each value but just like a person's name, the name gives no ordering information.

- *Ordinal categorical predictors,* like consumer age group, convey a little bit more information than do nominal predictors. As their name implies, ordinal predictors can be ordered. In the example above, it is possible to say that infant shoes are less than children's shoes and that teen shoes are between children's sizes and adult sizes. Ordinal predictors cannot, however, convey any sense of how much bigger or smaller the relative ordering is. Although it is possible to say that infant is less (younger) than a teenager, it is not possible to say that they are 3 times less or any specific amount less.

- *Interval categorical predictors,* on the other hand, do convey a sense of numeric distance between values. It is possible to say that size 10-in shoes are 2 in away from size 12-in shoes.

These distinctions can be important in determining not only which statistical technique can be used with the particular data but also what kind of other data mining technique could be used. The type of predictor can also have an important impact on how the data needs to be preprocessed. For instance, the extra information about distance contained in the interval categorical can provide better predictive models than just an ordinal or nominal categorical could. In this way a hierarchy is sometimes placed on the type of data going from nominal predictors at the bottom of the hierarchy to interval and continuous predictors at the top of the hierarchy. In general, any statistical method that can accommodate a predictor at one level of the hierarchy can accommodate predictors at higher levels. For instance, if a statistical (or data mining) method can accommodate a nominal predictor, then it could just as easily use an interval predictor by ignoring the extra information about order and distances between the values. Often much effort is exerted in preprocessing data for both statistics and data mining in order to convert predictor types.

15.1.3 Probability

The notion of probability is a critical concept for statistics and for all data mining techniques. Just because probability is familiar to most of us, it should not be deprecated as a very useful and basic device with which to perform predictions and detect patterns. For instance, if you were offered a deal whereby you would be given a million dollars if you could correctly predict the color of an Irish person's tie on St. Patrick's Day, you would likely have little difficulty in predicting green, even if you knew nothing about the individual—whether that person was old or young or even liked the color green. You would pick green (and feel fairly confident in your choice) just because you knew that overall, the probability of that person wearing green would be pretty good. It wouldn't be guaranteed to make you a millionaire, but it would be by far the best chance you'd have.

In the real world, for instance, the benchmark model for predicting tomorrow's stock market price is simply to pick the most probable value—which is yesterday's closing price. This is a surprisingly simple model which has been known to beat out several far more complicated models, and it is based solely on predicting the most likely event with no further information. Even if there were more information, there might be no better predictive model than to look at all the possible outcomes and predict the most likely one. This is called the *a priori probability* because it is the one that exists before any more information is known.

When more information is known, conditions can be placed on the event which will change the probability of it occurring. For instance, there will be some a priori rate of fraud that takes place in the credit card industry (suppose it is one fraudulent transaction out of every million). If, however, we place the condition that we look only at transactions of electronics equipment (which is of high value and easy to quickly resell), we may find that the rate of fraudulent transactions is 10 times higher or one out of every 100,000 transactions. This second kind of probability is called the *conditional probability*. It is used widely in data mining techniques such as decision trees and rule induction, where the rule or description of the segment represents the conditions under which the probability is found to be true.

15.1.4 Bayes' theorem

Sometimes it is not possible to precisely calculate the conditional probability that is most useful but other probabilities related to the predictors in question are available. In some of these cases Bayes' theorem can be used to calculate the correct conditional probability when it otherwise would not have been possible to calculate it. Bayes' theorem states that if you want to know the probability of event A conditional on event B occurring, it can be calculated as the probability of both events A and B occurring divided by the probability of event B. For instance, if you'd like to know what the probability is of a customer responding to your cross-selling marketing offer contingent (conditional) on their receiving a mailing, you could calculate it if you knew the percentage of customers who received the mailing and responded (probability of events A and B occurring) and the percentage of customers who received the mailing (probability of event B occurring). This equation is actually a direct consequence of an even more basic concept in statistics: the idea of independence of events.

15.1.5 Independence

In statistics two events are considered to be independent of each other if the probability of both of them occurring together is equal to the probability of one event multiplied by the probability of the other event. This simple concept can be very powerful because it states that if the two events are not equal, then one event probably influences the other. Thus the degree to which two events are not independent is often used to flag what is and what is not interesting (e.g., interesting rules in rule induction systems or exceptional values in multidimensional databases).

As an example of how events are and are not independent, consider a simple example about a person named Joe. Joe is a fairly fashion-conscious individual but is a little bit peculiar in that he only owns clothes that are either green or red. In fact, exactly half of his shirts are green, and half are red. The same is true of his ties. Joe randomly picks out a shirt each day from his closet. Since this is a random event and half the shirts in his closet are red, then there is a 50 percent chance (or 0.5 probability) that Joe will be wearing a green shirt on any given day (and likewise a 50 percent chance of wearing a red shirt). If Joe were red-green colorblind, then we'd expect that the tie that he picked out would also have a 50 percent chance of being red or 50 percent chance of being green. Because Joe can't tell the difference in color, the two events are independent (the event of Joe picking a shirt can't have an effect on the color of the tie since he can't tell the difference). To see how this independence of events is manifest in the data, consider Table 15.2, where Joe's attire is shown over 12 days' time. From the table we can see that half the time he wore a green shirt and half the time a red shirt (6 out of 12 days = ½). We know that the events are independent of each other because of Joe's colorblindness; what we would expect to see from the data, then, is that the probability of each pair of events (red tie/green shirt, red tie/red shirt, etc.) is equal to the product of the probabilities of each event occurring independently.

This table (Table 15.2) of data may appear to have little relevance to your business problems (unless maybe if you are in the fashion industry), but the types of data it contains and the types of patterns that are being detected are ubiquitous across industry. This table would, for instance, not look a great deal different if it contained transaction records from a convenience store. The data would be captured in a star schema in your data warehouse and could be used to determine the dependence of one purchase event on another (say, between buying ketchup and hamburger buns, or baby diapers and beer). Determining if there is a pattern in the database and some dependence between Joe's choice of shirt and choice of tie requires some counting to be done. This counting is shown in Table 15.3. This table lists information on how many days each pos-

TABLE 15.2   What Joe Wore to Work on 12 Consecutive Days

Day	Shirt color	Tie color
1	Green	Red
2	Red	Red
3	Red	Red
4	Green	Green
5	Red	Green
6	Green	Green
7	Red	Red
8	Green	Green
9	Green	Red
10	Red	Green
11	Green	Red
12	Red	Green

**TABLE 15.3   Count of Various Tie and Shirt
Color Combinations**

Shirt	Tie	Days worn
Green	Green	3
Green	Red	3
Red	Green	3
Red	Red	3

sible combination of red and green shirts and ties could be worn. Each of the four combinations occurs 3 out of 12 days or $\frac{3}{12} = \frac{1}{4}$ of the time.

The chance of Joe wearing a red tie is 50 percent, and the chance that Joe wears a red shirt is 50 percent, and since the two events are independent of each other (since Joe is colorblind he couldn't possibly coordinate the choice of colors), the chance of Joe wearing any one of the four combinations of red and green shirts and ties is equal and $\frac{1}{4}$ each. Interestingly, because these predictors are independent statistical theory states, the chance of any of these four combinations occurring is just the chance of the one predictor having a certain value and then the chance that the other predictor has a certain value. In the case of green shirt and red tie, this is $\frac{1}{2} * \frac{1}{2} = \frac{1}{4}$. So this calculated probability matches the actual data.

Now consider what it might be like if Joe were not colorblind and still had some sense of fashion. In this case you might find that he wears ties and shirts that match most of the time when going to work. The table in the database might then resemble Table 15.4, where the choice of shirt color has a dramatic impact on the choice of tie color. Notice that half the time he wore a green shirt but that he was more likely to wear a green tie with that green shirt. These events are no longer independent.

When Table 15.5 is created, it shows the combinations of all shirt colors and tie combinations and that all the possibilities are no longer equally likely as we previously saw when the shirt color and tie color predictors were independent. It now appears that there is some relationship or correlation between these

**TABLE 15.4   What Joe Would Wear to Work
If He Weren't Colorblind**

Day	Shirt color	Tie color
1	Green	Green
2	Red	Green
3	Red	Red
4	Green	Green
5	Red	Red
6	Green	Green
7	Red	Red
8	Green	Green
9	Green	Green
10	Red	Red
11	Green	Red
12	Red	Red

TABLE 15.5   Count of Various Tie and Shirt Color Combinations*

Shirt	Tie	Days worn
Green	Green	5
Green	Red	1
Red	Green	1
Red	Red	5

* Color-combination counts now indicate that the predictors are not independent.

predictors; in fact, since we know how the data is collected, we could even say that the choice of shirt color causes the choice of tie color. This type of relationship between predictors is aptly called *causal*. We now see that rather than occurring ¼ of the time the color coordinated attire occurs ⅚ of the time—a significant departure from the independence criterion.

This has been a particularly simple example of what independence between predictors is and how it works. It has also displayed the idea of causality. As we'll see in a later section, you truly need to be very careful about assuming that just because two predictors are not independent of each other that one causes the other. In the next section we'll see how independence relates to true causality and how it can be used to make predictions. As a preview to its use for prediction, consider that by looking at how Joe made his selections of clothes each day and putting that data into a table we could get a very good idea of whether Joe's choices of colors were independent. Then, on the basis of that finding, we could make some qualified prediction about whether Joe was colorblind or just "fashion-impaired" (although, of course, there could be other explanations for Joe's inability to dress himself in matching colors). If Joe were our customer, a guess at his color preferences could help us better predict what targeted mailing to send him next.

15.1.6   Causality and collinearity

In the previous section we saw how independence between events can be defined statistically and how the deviation from independence can be a powerful indicator of interesting patterns and predictive information. Independence is so important because the lack thereof implies that one event affects or even causes another event. Causal relationships between predictors is important because these are the relationships that are the most predictable over time, in different places and under a variety of different conditions. Causal relationships are the best at creating repeatable stable predictions that return the most value.

The question then is "What is causal?" As previously mentioned, lack of independence implies causality but doesn't guarantee it. Consider, for instance, that in North America the advent of cold weather does not appear to be independent of massively increased sales in department stores. In fact, as the temperature first starts to decrease to within 10 percent of its annual nadir year after year, sales significantly increase—especially in toy stores. Given this strong lack of independence of the two events, can we then say that a drop in temperature is causing increased department store sales? Probably not, since it is not the temperature but the Christmas season that is driving the department store sales. Christmas is the true causal event for the increased store sales, but cold weather also seems to be a good predictor.

This effect in which one predictor seems to go hand in hand with another but really is not causal is known as *collinearity*. The question then is "If I built a predictive model that was unaware of the concept of Christmas, wouldn't using temperature work nearly as well?" The answer is: If temperature is the only predictor in the database, then probably the best that can be done is to use it. Most of the time it will produce a good model. On the other hand, because it is not truly a causal predictor, things could go wrong. For instance, if the predictive model were applied in the Southern Hemisphere, or on some year when the weather was particularly balmy through December, the prediction could be very far off. On the other hand, even knowing that the event of December 25th was driving the increased purchasing would not be a sufficiently causal model when applied to countries that are not predominantly Christian.

The true meaning of causality then appears to be somewhat difficult to pin down. Clearly it is the holy grail of predictions if it can be achieved. To date it has been easier to describe its behavior than to describe it directly. In general, causal predictors display the following features:

- Predictive models built from the relationship do have some business or scientific value.

- The relationship seems to apply under a wide variety of situations without having to modify the predictive model.

- The relationship between the hypothesized causal event and the outcome is very strong and very far from independence.

15.1.7 Simplifying the predictors

One of the most important tasks that a statistician faces is determining what columns of data (predictors) to use and which to ignore. Sometimes this is done before predictive modeling is ever started in order to provide legally valid models (such as when ethnic background is eliminated as a possible predictor for a home mortgage loan approval). Sometimes predictors are eliminated because they contain future information that would contaminate the predictive model being built. More often than not, though, predictors are eliminated in order to simplify the understanding of the data and to improve the speed at which the models can be built. There are several ways that predictors are determined to be relevant or not relevant to a particular model and also some techniques that create new predictors through mathematical combinations of existing predictors. CART (classification and regression trees) and CHAID (chi square automatic interaction detector) were originally developed not for prediction but as automated ways of adding selected predictors to standard statistical models. They are both relatively efficient at determining relevant predictors. Other techniques that are used to determine the value of predictors include

- *Sensitivity analysis*—which seeks to determine how sensitive and predictive a model is to small fluctuations in the value of a predictor

- *Principal-components analysis*—which seeks to weight the importance of a variety of predictors so that they optimally discriminate between various possible predicted outcomes

- *Factor analysis*—which seeks to reduce the number of total predictors from a large number down to only a few predictors or "factors" that largely affect the predicted outcome.

15.2 Hypothesis Testing

15.2.1 Hypothesis testing on a real-world problem

In statistics there is a technique called *hypothesis testing,* which is used throughout the field. The idea of hypothesis testing is to construct a hypothesis about how the data was created that explains the values in the data and to then test to see how likely it is to be an acceptable explanation. This is in contrast to some of the data mining approaches, which simply seek to create the best predictive model relative to those that could possibly be constructed. For data mining there is, in general, less of a sense of guessing the right model and then seeing if the data fits and more of a sense of building the model from the data.

Hypothesis testing is a three-step process that can be repeated many times until a suitable hypothesis is found:

- The data is observed and an understanding is formed about how the data was collected and created.

- A guess about what process created the data is made (that hopefully explains the data). This is the hypothesis.

- The hypothesis is tested against the actual data by assuming that it is correct and then determining how likely it would be to observe this particular set of data.

This idea of making a guess first and then seeing if it is true should be an intuitively appealing way to convince yourself and others that your prediction is the correct one. For example, one of the most compelling reasons for Einstein's peers to accept his radical theories about light and gravity was that if his theory was correct, it would have meant that light would actually be bent around the sun. This would mean that stars that were behind the sun and normally obscured from view could be seen as if they were in front of the sun.

This was a radical hypothesis but one that Einstein could prove mathematically and with thought experiments, but it was hard to confirm or deny until relevant data could be collected. The data that would confirm his theory was difficult to come by, however, since the sun was so bright that it overwhelmed any starlight. The correct data could, however, be obtained during a solar eclipse because it would block the overpowering light from the sun and the much fainter starlight could be seen. When the next eclipse occurred, Einstein's prediction was matched exactly by the data and his overall theory was much more readily accepted. Up to the point of the solar eclipse, Einstein had good theoretical proof of these theories and his theories could retrospectively explain many phenomena that were at that time not well explained. However, it was his prediction of light bending and its confirmation that truly swayed his audience.

In hypothesis testing it is important not only to make the hypothesis that is or isn't confirmed by the data but also to determine how likely the hypothesis is to explain the data (i.e., is it a perfect match to the data or just a close match?). One way to measure how close a match it is to the hypothesis is to compare the data to the most basic hypothesis, namely, that the data was created merely by chance. For instance, consider if you were a marketer of a soda product and you had two possible brands of cola that you wanted to introduce to the market—a sugarcane-sweetened drink called Cane Cola and a corn-syrup-sweetened drink called Corn Cola.

The two soda brands were identical in marketing, advertising, distribution, and name (arguably equally bad names), and they were also identical in all ingredients except for the way they were sweetened. The product marketing manager's hypothesis is that it doesn't matter which way the drink is sweetened since he believes that the taste is fairly comparable and has already ramped up production on Corn Cola since it is easier to produce. The CEO, however, requires that the marketing manager's hypothesis be validated, and she calls for a taste test. The results of the taste test are captured in Table 15.6. They show that one product is chosen 20 times more often than the other in taste tests. The product manager (who's already invested in Corn Cola) argues that this is just a random perturbation that occurred by chance. Hypothesis testing can be used to see how likely it is that the marketing manager is right.

Now that data has been collected, hypothesis testing can be used. The hypothesis is that this difference in sales of soda occurred purely by chance (as put forward by the product manager hoping to preserve his employment). If this were really true, one would reason that the division of purchases between Cane Cola and Corn Cola would be more evenly divided. Ideally, the split would be 50/50: 24 purchases would be Cane Cola and 24 purchases would be Corn Cola. But a 23/25 split or even a 20/28 split might seem within the realm of possibility. The 4/80 split that was actually observed seems very unlikely.

TABLE 15.6   Marketing Data from Taste Tests of Two Cola Products

	Corn cola (corn syrup sweetened)	Cane cola (sugarcane sweetened)
Taste test selections	4	80

However, you can never directly prove that even this unlikely 4/80 split didn't happen by chance. There is always some possibility that this did happen by chance, just as there is always the chance that other improbable events could occur (such as sinking all the balls on the break in a game of pool or tossing a fair coin 100 times and all of them coming up heads). The question then is not to disprove the hypothesis, since that really can't be done, but rather to see how unlikely an event this taste testing data represents if, in fact, the hypothesis is true. One way to calculate this probability is to convert the current business problem into a simpler problem that is more familiar. In this case this marketing problem can be converted fairly easily into the analogous problem of calculating the chance that a coin can come up heads 4 out of 84 times and still be a fair coin. Since the chance of getting heads on a coin flip is 50 percent and since our working hypothesis is that the choice between sodas is equivalent (since marketing, advertising, packaging, etc. are identical), we can consider the event of choosing one soda over another soda to be similar to the chance of getting heads rather than tails on a coin flip. We know intuitively that if we were betting with someone on coin flips and they owned the coin, we would be very suspicious of the coin if it came up heads only 4 times out of 84. But even in a perfectly random coin toss, this could happen. The question is how often it could happen. One way to answer this question and help confirm or deny the product manager's hypothesis would be to count the total number of different scenarios of taste tests if the choice between the two sodas were equivalent and then see in how many scenarios Corn Cola was preferred 4 or fewer times.

To get started on this more complicated problem, let's first consider a simpler example in which there are just three purchases, one of which is Corn Cola. The hypothesis in this simpler case is still the same: There is no preferred difference in the colas, and the one-out-of-three choice was just a random fluctuation. In this simple case, however, it is very easy to check and see just how often you might see one or fewer Corn Cola sales out of three total sales. If the sodas can be chosen equivalently by three different consumers, then there are only eight possible scenarios. These are displayed in Table 15.7.

TABLE 15.7   Marketing Data from Taste Tests of Sugarcane and Corn Syrup Colas*

Scenario	Consumer Jack	Consumer Jill	Consumer Bob
1	Cane	Cane	Cane
2	Cane	Cane	Corn
3	Cane	Corn	Cane
4	Cane	Corn	Corn
5	Corn	Cane	Cane
6	Corn	Cane	Corn
7	Corn	Corn	Cane
8	Corn	Corn	Corn

* With just three taste test participants, eight different scenarios would be possible if the consumers really had no preference.

In the simpler example shown in Table 15.6, we see that of the eight possible ways that the sodas could have been chosen by the three consumers, corn soda was chosen only once or not at all in scenarios 1, 2, 3, and 5, which is 4 out of 8 times, or half the time. So the actual scenario that was recorded from the preference tests was as likely to happen as to not happen if there was no consumer preference. This is not much of an indictment against the position of the hypothesis of the product manager.

Intuitively, this probably makes sense. If one out of three people buy the given soda, you aren't so suspicious that there might be any difference (just as if a coin came up heads only once in three tries). However, the real problem here probably intuitively feels quite different. Observing only 4 Corn Cola sales out of 84 seems much less likely than 1 out of 3. Luckily, we can see just how unlikely this sequence of events would be by performing exactly the same calculation as before except this time on a larger scale.

To calculate how unlikely the occurrence of 4 out of 84 sales would be, we would need to construct a table similar to Table 15.7. In this case, though, it would have 84 columns (one for each of the consumers) but 2^{84} rows (84 twos multiplied together) or around 20,000,000,000,000,000,000,000,000 rows (for this reason we're not putting this table in the book). The good news is that we don't need to create every possible scenario even on a computer. Instead we can perform a calculation whereby the chances of this 4-out-of-84 event occurring can be calculated. In this case this type of coin flipping problem can be modeled with something known in statistics as a *binomial random variable*. Figuring out the chance of such a scenario occurring then just requires plugging three numbers into a formula:

1. First, you need to plug in the probability of the event that you are testing for (viz., 0.5 since your hypothesis is that either choice of soda is equivalently likely to happen).

2. Second, you need to know the number of trials (or in this case the number of consumer testers = 84).

3. The third thing you need to know is the number of positive events that occurred (in this case 4 purchases of corn syrup cola).

When these equations are used, it is possible to calculate the chance that, if the sodas were considered equivalent by the consumer (our hypothesis), only 4 purchases out of 84 would have occurred by chance. This calculation says that the chance of this happening (and our product manager's hypothesis being valid) is about one out of a billion, billion scenarios. In other words, if every man, woman, and child on earth conducted a taste test every day for their entire life, everyone would have to live to the age of nearly 3 million years before even one such scenario would occur. With some confidence, the CEO can now respond to the product manager that the chance that consumers can't tell the difference between Corn Cola and Cane Cola is very, very unlikely.

15.2.2   Hypothesis testing, *P* values, and alpha

In the cola example a sequence of events was described that helped to decide an important marketing question, and to provide a well-defined measure of how likely an event was to occur. Having this measure is important because it now allows businesspeople to objectively compare a variety of possibilities as opposed to just using their intuition. Let's recap the sequence of events and translate what happened into the language of statisticians. The process that the cola marketing manager went through had several major steps:

1. Collect the data.
2. Make a hypothesis.
3. Convert the problem into a simpler one that was familiar.
4. Calculate how often the observed data would occur if this hypothesis were true.
5. Compare this likelihood of the data occurring to some probability that is familiar and can give a relative sense of likelihood.

The first step was to collect the data. In this case 84 people made a choice between the two colas and their preferences were recorded. It is also important to note that general data about the experiment was collected such as the fact that the advertising and marketing campaigns, packaging, and other relevant attributes of the experiment were kept relatively equivalent. This data was the starting point for the disagreement between the product manager and the CEO.

In the second step the CEO and the product manager both made hypotheses. The CEO's hypothesis was "Something is wrong. Since only 4 out of 84 consumers chose Corn Cola, consumers must significantly prefer Cane Cola." The product manager for the new cola also made a hypothesis: "Nothing is wrong. Consumers like both sodas equally well, but 4 out of 84 just happened by chance and was well within expectations and consistent with his hypothesis."

In statistics the hypothesis of the product manager is called the *null hypothesis,* and it is typically stated that the observed data happened strictly by chance and that there is independence between predictors and often that the events are equally likely to happen. In hypothesis testing it is necessary to show that the null hypothesis is likely to be wrong and thus that the effect being observed is far enough away from what would be expected by random chance that it should be considered to be true.

A way to think about the null hypothesis is by drawing an analogy from the legal profession. The null hypothesis is like the assumption of innocence in a criminal case in a court of law. Disproving the null hypothesis is similar to the requirement to presume innocence until proven guilty beyond a reasonable doubt. The similar phrase for statisticians would read "Presume the null hypothesis unless there is overwhelming evidence that it is not true." The null hypothesis is the status quo hypothesis in that it assumes the simplest explanation for things, and it must be shown that this explanation is dramatically inconsistent with the observed data before another hypothesis is considered.

In the third step of the cola example, the problem of understanding cola preferences was converted into an equivalent, more familiar, problem of coin flipping. By doing this, the statistician is able to calculate how likely the given event was without actually creating a very large table and counting the possibilities. Most often the problem can be converted into some better understood and simpler problem either directly or with a few simplifying assumptions.

The fourth step is to calculate how often the data would have been observed if the null hypothesis were true. In this case the number of times that 4 out of 84 consumers would have chosen corn-sweetened cola but actually had no preference would have been minuscule. In this case the chance of this happening was one out of a billion billion, or a probability of 0.0000000000000000014. In hypothesis testing this probability of the null hypothesis being true is called the P value. If the P value is high, then the null hypothesis is likely to be true. If it is small, as it is in this case, then the null hypothesis is unlikely and should be abandoned for a better hypothesis.

To see how P values can change with different experimental results, consider the case where there are only 18 consumers, 12 of whom chose the sugarcane-flavored cola. Again in this case the CEO may argue that something is wrong with the new product line and the product manager may argue that for only 18 consumer trials, 12 is not that out of the ordinary (of course 9 or 50% would be expected if there were no preference and no random fluctuations in the data). In this case the probability of 12 or more consumers choosing one cola over another was 24 percent—a P value of 0.24. Or nearly one quarter of the time you could see this type of variation even if the consumers had no preference. With a P value of 0.24 it is unlikely that one would reject the null hypothesis, just as in a legal setting it is unlikely that a defendant would be found guilty by a jury if there were a 24 percent chance that that person were innocent. In this case the product manager for the cola would prevail.

The fifth step listed above involves comparison of the P value to something familiar in order to get a relative feel for the likelihood of the null hypothesis. In the first case of 4 out of 84 corn syrup cola selections, the comparison was made against the fact that even all the people on the earth living millions of years could not reproduce this event if it really did just happen by chance. Typically this comparison is chosen as a number which represents the level of significance or how cautious one is being in rejecting or accepting the null hypothesis. The P value is compared to this level of significance, and the null hypothesis is rejected or accepted according to whether the P value is smaller or larger than it. Typically this value is set at 0.05—or, in other words, if this collection of data could occur by chance only 5 percent of the time or less, then it is unlikely that it did just occur by chance and the null hypothesis should be rejected. This value is called *alpha*. The smaller the alpha value, the less chance you take of incorrectly rejecting the null hypothesis.

15.2.3 Making mistakes in rejecting the null hypothesis

Alpha is also often set at 0.01 rather than 0.05 for an even more conservative view in rejecting the null hypothesis. There is no right choice in choosing alpha. It depends on the situation. The difference between the choice of values for alpha often lies in the cost incurred if a mistake is made and the null hypothesis is incorrectly rejected. In the legal analogy these differences in alpha might correspond to the extra caution a jury might take in finding a defendant guilty in a criminal trial for murder (where an incorrect verdict could mean life in prison for an innocent person), as opposed to a civil trial (where the cost of a mistake is purely monetary). In the first case the jury would want to be sure of the person's guilt beyond all reasonable doubt (a small alpha—P value = 0.01 or smaller). In the second case at the civil trial a preponderance of evidence is sufficient (analogous to a larger alpha—maybe a P value of 0.05). Table 15.8 summarizes the results with the two cola examples. In the two examples of consumer choice between colas the null hypothesis is that consumers have no preference. If this is the case, the P value gives the chance of this event occurring. For the first scenario, it is very unlikely that this data was collected by chance; for the second, it could happen nearly 25 percent of the time. Even the second scenario can be used to reject the null hypothesis if alpha is large enough, although typically alpha is 0.01 or 0.05.

There is also the chance that the null hypothesis is incorrectly accepted. In this case if the null hypothesis is incorrectly accepted, the product manager and the CEO will mistakenly believe that consumers have no preference for the colas and will begin production on both. Because there really is a consumer preference, advertising and production dollars will be wasted. If, on the other hand, the consumers really have no preference but the null hypothesis is rejected, the product manager and CEO might incorrectly discontinue the new cola product line and miss out on a new market opportunity.

Statisticians call these two types of error types I and II. They are summarized in Table 15.9 and as follows:

■ *Type I.* The null hypothesis is true (e.g., consumers have no cola preference), but the hypothesis is rejected.

TABLE 15.8 Testing the Null Hypothesis for Different Alpha Values

Cola scenario	P value (probability that this happened by chance if there were no preference)	Reject null hypothesis alpha = 0.01	Reject null hypothesis alpha = 0.25
80 of 84 choose cane cola	0.0000000000000000014	Yes—consumers do have a preference	Yes—consumers do have a preference
12 of 18 choose cane cola	0.24	No—we have not proved that consumers have a preference	Yes—consumers do have a preference

TABLE 15.9 Two Types of Errors that Can Be Made When Either Accepting or Rejecting the Null Hypothesis Incorrectly

	Consumers really don't have a preference	Consumers really prefer Cane Cola
Accept null hypothesis (decide that there is *no* consumer preference)	Correct decision	Type II error (cost = wasted production dollars)
Reject null hypothesis (decide that there is consumer preference)	Type I error (cost = missed market opportunity)	Correct decision

> ■ *Type II.*   The null hypothesis is not true (e.g., consumers do have a cola preference), but the hypothesis is not rejected.

15.2.4 Degrees of freedom

Throughout the sections of this book that deal with modeling, one of the most important ideas introduced is that of *overfitting.* Overfitting is what happens when a predictive model is built on historical data (whether via statistical techniques or data mining), and the model is so complex that it, too, closely models the historical data and the idiosyncrasies in it but does not extract useful general information that can be applied to other databases. To combat this effect, statistics introduces the idea of confidence in the model via hypothesis testing, but it also introduces the idea of *degrees of freedom.*

Generally the degrees of freedom of a particular modeling problem are equivalent to the number of records that are available in the historical database. As a predictive model is created that gets more and more complex (i.e., utilizing more and more predictors or combinations of predictors), the degrees of freedom are used up. As the degrees of freedom are used up, the criterion for the model to be considered valid becomes more and more restrictive. This means that very complex models may predict the historical data quite well and yet still be considered unlikely to be valid, and simpler models (less accurate on the historical data) are preferred. In plain English, this translates to something similar to Occam's razor, which has been used as a guiding principle in physics for many years: "Given a choice of different models that explain the data equally well, always choose the simplest one."

15.3   Contingency Tables, the Chi Square Test, and Noncausal Relationships

15.3.1   Contingency tables

Contingency tables are tables that are used to show the relationship between two categorical predictors or between a predictor and a prediction. For instance, Tables 15.10 and 15.11 are contingency tables that relate two predictors in a database. In Table 15.10 there appears to be a strong relationship between the two predictors; in Table 15.11, the predictors appear to be independent.

TABLE 15.10   Contingency Table*

	Plays golf	Doesn't play golf
Plays tennis	100	0
Doesn't play tennis	0	100

* The data in this contingency table seems to strongly indicate a strong connection between playing golf and playing tennis.

Contingency tables are used throughout statistics as a quick way to both spot relationships between categorical predictors and summarize the a priori and conditional probabilities of various values. The degree of correlation between predictors can be captured via a number of statistical calculations, including the odds ratio and the chi square test. The chi square test is a very powerful way of understanding the degree of dependence between two predictors and also for quantifying the degree of confidence in that relationship.

15.3.2   The chi square test

The chi square (χ^2) test is often used to test to see if there is a relationship between two columns of data in a database—maybe between a predictor column and a prediction column or between two predictors. The test makes use of one of the most basic principles of statistics—that the probabilities of two independent predictors can be multiplied together to get the probability of the values of the predictors occurring simultaneously.

The chi square test measures the difference between the expected number of occurrences of a combination of predictor values if the individual predictors were independent and the number of occurrences that actually occur. The larger the differences are between the numbers expected and those observed, the more likely it is that there is some relationship between the predictors. If there is no difference or the difference is small, then it is likely that the predictors are independent.

The actual equation for the chi square measure is the square of the difference between the expected number of occurrences and the actual number divided by the actual number summed over all the possible combinations of predictor values. The square of the difference is important in the equation in that it allows for both positive and negative differences to contribute to the overall difference calculation. Dividing by the expected number of occurrences

TABLE 15.11   Contingency Table*

	Plays golf	Doesn't play golf
Brown eyes	30	30
Green eyes	20	20
Blue eyes	50	50

* The data in this contingency table indicates that playing golf has no dependence on eye color.

TABLE 15.12   Data Implying a Link between
Playing Tennis and Staying Out of Trouble

Plays tennis	Arrested	Not arrested
Yes	12	108
No	50	260

helps to weight the particular difference in some way relative to the importance of the difference. The best way to see this is in an example.

15.3.3 Sometimes strong relationships are not causal

Consider the example shown in Tables 15.12, 15.13, and 15.14. Looking at the data in those tables in some detail implies a causal relationship that does not, in fact, exist. In this case the data shows that if juveniles play tennis, then they have a much lower chance of being arrested than if they don't play tennis (11 vs. 19 percent). The data is correct, but this interpretation is misleading. In Table 15.13 more data is added, which now breaks up the database by both involvement in tennis as well as the income bracket of the juvenile. This table now tells a very different story even though the data is exactly the same.

When the income predictor is added into the analysis, it becomes clear that the chance of being arrested is exactly the same regardless of whether the juvenile plays tennis once income level is taken into account. The rate for low-income juveniles who do *not* play tennis is 25 percent ($\frac{2}{8}$) and is also 25 percent for the tennis players ($\frac{40}{160}$). In the high-income category the overall arrest record is much lower but is still the same, whether the juvenile plays tennis or not (10 percent = $\frac{10}{100}$). This may be a surprising result since there appeared to be a very strong connection (the U.S. tennis association was probably even hoping for a causal relationship) between playing tennis and preventing juvenile delinquency. Yet the very same data, when looked at in a slightly different way, showed that playing tennis had absolutely no effect on the arrest record of juveniles but that income level did. How did this happen?

Playing tennis appeared to lessen juvenile delinquency because this sport is much more prevalent at higher income levels [from this data, only 5 percent

TABLE 15.13   Correlation between Income, Playing Tennis, and Delinquency*

Income	Plays tennis	Arrested	Not arrested
Low	Yes	2	8
Low	No	40	160
High	Yes	10	100
High	No	10	100

* When another predictor is added to the data, the link between tennis and incidence of arrest comes into question.

TABLE 15.14   Correlation between Income and Delinquency*

Income	Arrested	Not arrested
Low	42	168
High	20	200

* When the same data is viewed solely by income level, a strong connection is found.

($^{10}/_{210}$) of juveniles played tennis in the low-income group but 50 percent ($^{110}/_{220}$) played tennis in the high-income group]. Thus the concentration of tennis-playing juveniles was higher in a subset of the population that was less likely to be arrested. Thus playing tennis wasn't causing less juvenile delinquency; instead, tennis playing was dependent on income level just as juvenile arrests were dependent on income level.

This is just one example of the importance of fully understanding the data and doing some active investigating rather than blindly relying on statistical measures of correlation between predictor and prediction. Table 15.12 seems to imply a strong causal link between playing tennis and staying out of trouble (not being arrested). However, when the data is looked at in more detail, another factor (income) is found to be the real causal factor. The chance of being arrested for tennis players is about 11 percent ($^{12}/_{108}$), while the chances of being arrested for non–tennis players is about 19 percent ($^{50}/_{260}$). When the same data is viewed further broken up into high and low income brackets in Table 15.13, the connection between playing tennis and juvenile delinquency vanishes. With each income level the chance of being arrested is the same whether the juvenile plays tennis or not (25 percent for low income and 10 percent for high income). When the same data is viewed solely by income level, a strong connection is found, as shown in Table 15.14.

15.4   Prediction

In this book the term *prediction* is used for various types of analysis that may elsewhere be more precisely called *regression*. We have done so in order to simplify some of the concepts and to emphasize the common and most important aspects of predictive modeling. Nonetheless regression is a powerful and commonly used tool in statistics, and it will be discussed here.

15.4.1   Linear regression

In statistics prediction is usually synonymous with regression of some form. There are many different types of regression in statistics, but the basic idea is that a model is created that maps values from predictors in such a way that the lowest error occurs in making a prediction. The simplest form of regression is simple linear regression that contains only one predictor and a prediction. The relationship between the two can be mapped on a two-dimensional space and the records plotted for the prediction values along the Y axis and the predictor values along the X axis. The simple linear regression model could then be viewed as the line that minimized the error rate between the actual prediction value and the point on the line (the prediction from the model). Graphically this would appear as shown in Fig. 15.3. The simplest form of regression seeks to build a predictive model that is a line that maps between each predictor value to a prediction value. Of the many possible lines that could be drawn through the data, the one that minimizes the distance between the line and the data points is the one that is chosen for the predictive model.

The predictive model is the thick line shown in Fig. 15.3. The line will take a given value for a predictor and map it into a given value for a prediction. The actual equation would look something like Prediction $= a + b *$ Predictor, which is just the equation for a line $Y = a + bX$. As an example for a bank, the predicted average consumer bank balance might equal $1000 + 0.01 *$ customer's annual income. The trick, as always with predictive modeling, is to find the model that best minimizes the error (in this case across all bank customers). The most common way to calculate the error is the square of the difference between the predicted value and the actual value. Calculated this way, points that are very far from the line will have a great effect on moving the choice of line toward themselves to reduce the error. The values of a and b in the regression equation that minimize this error can be calculated directly from the data relatively quickly.

15.4.2 Other forms of regression

Regression can become more complicated than the simple linear regression we've introduced so far. It can get more complicated in a wide variety of different ways in order to better model particular database problems. However, three main modifications are commonly made:

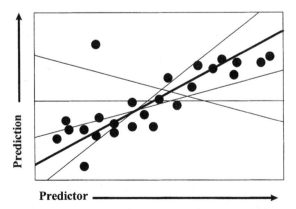

Figure 15.3 Linear regression is similar to the task of finding the line that minimizes the distance to a set of data.

1. More predictors than just one can be used.

2. Transformations can be applied to the predictors.

3. Predictors can be multiplied together and used as terms in the equation.

4. Modifications can be made to accommodate response predictions that just have binary yes/no or 0/1 values.

Adding more predictors to the linear equation can produce more complicated lines that take more information into account and hence make a better prediction. This is called *multiple linear regression* and might result an equation like the following if five predictors $(X_1, X_2, X_3, X_4, X_5)$ were used:

$$Y = a + b_1(X_1) + b_2(X_2) + b_3(X_3) + b_4(X_4) + b_5(X_5)$$

This equation still describes a line but it is now a line in a six-dimensional space rather than the two-dimensional space.

By transforming the predictors by squaring, cubing, or taking their square root, it is possible to use the same general regression methodology and now create much more complex models that are no longer simple shaped lines. This is called *nonlinear regression.* A model of just one predictor might look like this: $Y = a + b_1(X_1) + b_2(X_1^2)$. In many real-world situations analysts will perform a wide variety of transformations on their data just to try them out. If transformed predictors do not contribute to a useful model, their coefficients in the equation will tend toward zero and then they can be removed. The other transformation of predictor values that is often performed is to multiply them together. For instance, a new predictor created by dividing hourly wage by the minimum wage might be a much more effective predictor than hourly wage by itself.

When trying to predict a customer response that is just yes or no (e.g., they bought the product or they didn't, or they defaulted or they didn't), the standard form of a line doesn't work. Since there are only two possible values to be predicted, it is relatively easy to fit a line through them. However, that model would be the same no matter what predictors were being used or what particular data was being used. Typically in these situations a transformation of the prediction values is made in order to provide a better predictive model. This type of regression is called *logistic regression,* and because so many business problems are response problems, logistic regression is one of the most widely used statistical techniques for creating predictive models.

15.5   Some Current Offerings of Statistics Tools

There are a variety of providers of statistical tools packages available today. Although historically strictly the area of the research scientist and savvy business analyst, many of these companies have been redefining themselves with easier-to-use tools that approach a broad audience of business users. SAS Institute has notably redefined itself as not only a purveyor of powerful statistical tools but also as a data warehousing, OLAP, data mining, and applications company. SPSS has expanded its suite of statistical tools with acquisitions of new data mining technologies and powerful new visualization techniques. These trends reflect the fundamental shift of the use of powerful statistical and data mining techniques into the hands of the business end user.

15.5.1   SAS Institute

SAS Institute is the largest of the software providers that provide a full range of statistical tools. Founded in 1976, the company has continued to grow from its first statistical products. SAS products are particularly adept at working with larger databases for analysis and for performing the often required data manipulation and cleansing steps that must be performed before the statistical analysis can begin. They offer perhaps the most comprehensive set of statistical tools to be integrated with OLAP and data warehousing and do offer the low-end JMP software product, which provides a more intuitive and graphical interface to a variety of statistical tools.

15.5.2   SPSS

SPSS is a comprehensive supplier of statistical tools. The company grew out of an academic research project in the late 1960s designed to build a tool to make it easier to run statistical analysis of why people vote. Since that time the company has grown through internal development and acquisition. To date their products include the base set of SPSS tools for statistics and graphing as well as newer packages which include neural networks, CHAID, and the Diamond product for powerful visualization of data.

15.5.3   MathSoft

MathSoft acquired the S-Plus statistical package from StatSci in the mid-1990s, and the package, in turn, is a commercialization of a statistical language called S developed at AT&T. S-Plus is a full-function library of statistical tools built on an object-oriented programming model. In general, S-Plus leads the way in quickly incorporating new statistical techniques and has very high-quality visualization and graphing capabilities tightly integrated with the product. Because of its object-oriented nature, the tool is highly extensible and preferred by those researchers and analysts who want strong control over elaborate algorithms. The tool is not as strong as a high-end, large database product, though, because of the object-oriented nature and extensibility of the code.

16

Artificial Intelligence

In 1983 Edward Feigenbaum and Pamela McCorduck published their book *The Fifth Generation,* which described how the Japanese had set some very serious and very lofty goals for themselves to develop powerful artificial-intelligence systems. It set off a firestorm of interest in artificial intelligence in the United States as well as around the world as researchers, governments, military forces, and businesses scrambled to keep up with the new threat posed by the Japanese. Over two decades later few of these goals were achieved, but in its wake this research and development of artificial intelligence influenced many of the products and ideas in use today.

Feigenbaum and McCorduck's book was not the first major work on the subject of artificial intelligence (AI), but it was a defining event that both actively drove and passively coincided with a major wave or renewed interest in AI. The roots of AI go much further back, easily into the late 1950s, with some quintessential work by Arthur Samuel on a checkers-playing program. And in the summer of 1956 a conference was held at Dartmouth College organized by Marvin Minsky and John McCarthy, who coined the term *artificial intelligence* to describe the conference. Later Minsky and McCarthy would found the AI lab at the Massachusetts Institute of Technology, where a great deal of the research into AI was done in the 1960s.

The term *artificial intelligence* has been defined by the *Encyclopedia of Artificial Intelligence* as follows: "Artificial Intelligence is a field of science and engineering concerned with the computational understanding of what is commonly called intelligent behavior, and with the creation of artifacts that exhibit such behavior."

With the early successes of such systems as Samuel's checkers player (which learned from its mistakes and eventually was able to play to a draw with the 1965 world champion), it was thought that by the late 1960s it would be possible to re-create human intelligence in a machine and probably even move beyond human intelligence to produce machines that could outperform human beings in a wide variety of tasks. There was a great deal of activity at MIT,

Carnegie Mellon University, and Stanford, but by the late 1960s much of the promise of early successes had proved to be misleading. The problems of replicating even the most basic human abilities such as speaking and visual understanding could be done only on small toy problems in laboratory settings.

Much of the work in these early days centered around solving the following problems or reproducing human behavior in these domains:

- *Vision.*   Much effort was spent in having computers be able to reconstruct a three-dimensional model of the world from a two-dimensional picture of some scene. A seminal work was completed in 1975 by Waltz which reported on a computer program that could accurately determine which lines in a line drawing of stacked blocks represented boundaries between blocks and features on the block itself. These line labels could then be used to reconstruct the three dimensional representation of the line drawing.

- *Natural language.*   A computer that could communicate with a human being in the "natural" language of a human rather than a computer language would certainly be a great aid in programming and controlling these systems. An early example of such a system was the Eliza program built in 1966, which enables a computer to mimic a psychotherapist speaking with a patient.

- *Robotics.*   Creating robots that could perform physical tasks that were too dangerous or boring for human beings was considered to be an important commercial application of AI. The simple problems of calculating which forces to apply to each joint in a robot arm in order to achieve smooth motion along the desired path became an important research problem.

- *Game playing.*   Besides checkers, chess, tic-tac-toe, and go were used as fertile problems that, if solved, would result in a step along the path toward a truly artificial intelligence.

- *Planning.*   The problem of breaking down the achievement of a goal into subproblems, each of which needed to be solved in sequence, was an important area of research as the simple initial systems moved out of the lab into more complex real-world problems. An example might be the planning activity that a person might go through to drive down to the local store to buy some milk. Breaking this task down into subtasks such as getting dressed, starting the car, and driving to the store was what was meant by *planning*.

- *Logic.*   Very accurate systems were built for putting together pieces of information to form logical conclusions. For instance, if one knew that birds could fly and also that eagles were birds, then one could logically deduce that eagles could fly.

16.1   Defining Artificial Intelligence

It is important to understand the history of AI and where it came from in order to look at it correctly today. AI has set for itself nothing less than the lofty goal of re-creating human intelligence, and at that task no one has as yet succeeded.

Some of the simplest things that people do (even as infants) cannot yet be replicated by machines. Despite this, AI has had notable successes. Most people are not aware, however, of how much of AI is being used in their daily lives. For instance

- The chess programs and machines sold in stores today make use of AI techniques.
- The character recognition technology that is part of many computer scanners had its origins in the vision research from AI on everything from scene analysis to blocks worlds.
- Some of the most sophisticated user interfaces that utilize human language to access relational databases without using SQL make use of the technology that was developed as part of AI for natural-language understanding.
- Even the spell checker and grammar checker on your word processor is using underlying techniques from AI to correct your language and spelling.

The interesting thing about the successes of AI is that it seems that once an algorithm or technique that was developed within the AI community is successful and widely adopted, it is no longer considered to be AI. Most people like to think of their intelligence as something complicated and not understandable. So whenever something that would otherwise be considered to be intelligent can be packaged up and re-created on a computer, it is generally discounted as not being very intelligent. Only a century ago *intelligence* was often equated with memory (how many sonnets could you recite from memory) and with mathematical calculations. Today, however, storage of information in computer memory and calculation of exceedingly complex mathematical equations can be performed by a $300 personal assistant and a $10 calculator. Even the game of chess, which is considered to be the quintessential game of strategy and complex thinking, is now dominated by powerful computers using simple brute-force algorithms.

Artificial intelligence thus rarely seems to get its due, probably because the goals it has set are so high. Its successes are impressive, but its failures are equally impressive, and thus the interest in AI seems to rise and fall like the tides. With great interest, investment and anticipation in the early 1960s and 1980s were followed by waves of less interest or more pragmatic applications of the technology on smaller better-understood problems. This happened as part of the resurgence of interest in AI in the 1980s, when rule-based expert systems changed the AI game from that of re-creating humanlike intelligence to merely recording it and playing it back in certain situations and for certain problems. By narrowing the focus of what AI could do, useful systems could be produced that would encode human expertise to solve difficult real-world problems. In many ways the more successful AI technologies of today, such as neural networks, have similarly been successful precisely because they have been aimed at more narrowly focused problems. In this way systems have been created that show human levels of intelligence in certain areas such as pattern recognition and prediction. It is important to make a distinction between some different phases of AI.

The first phase was dominated by the search for the basic underlying infrastructure and architecture by which machines could be considered to be intelligent. The second phase was marked by the advent of expert-driven systems in which particular pieces of human knowledge were encoded into the systems. The third phase, which we are in now, represents a significant departure from the first two, in which human intelligence was being re-created. In this more recent phase intelligence is more slowly evolved by connecting artificially intelligent systems to the real world—either through captured real-world data or through direct interaction through mobile robots and agents. In the last section of this chapter we'll discuss more about how this current phase of AI may well put it on a track toward eventual success by solving some of the fundamentally difficult problems in constructing such systems.

It may seem that data mining would be a part of artificial intelligence. And, depending on how you define AI, it might be. In general, though, AI systems have to do with encoding what human beings do into a computer program—effectively trying to find the right recipe for intelligence or even for solving a particular problem. Artificial intelligence deals mostly with systems that are driven by human knowledge. Data mining, statistics, and machine learning, however, are *data-driven* systems—effectively the systems are taught by real-world examples rather than preprocessed ideas. This is a significant difference. Being data-driven means that the systems are easily and automatically built and can quickly be updated. It often also means that they are less brittle—less likely to make very large dumb mistakes like an idiot savant. It also means that these systems are much less costly to build since there is no need for a human expert to be tightly integrated into the loop of building the system.

16.2   Expert Systems

Expert systems are a class of techniques, algorithms, and computer programs within the field of artificial intelligence which seek to provide expert levels of functionality within well-defined domains. They are generally computer programs that are made up of IF-THEN rules that have been extracted from a human expert. Such systems have been built for everything from weather prediction to medical diagnosis to large computer systems configuration. By keeping the fields in which they are deployed narrow, these systems can sometimes be helpful aids to human beings working within these fields. They allow for the expertise of one person to be shared by many and provide for a means of passing expert knowledge on to others that is much more powerful and detailed than what can be captured in more traditional media such as books and diagrams.

One of the most famous expert systems that was actually deployed for commercial applications was Xcon. Xcon was built and used at Digital Equipment Corporation (Digital or DEC) for configuring components for the purchases of large-scale VAX computer systems. It contains almost 10,000 rules and has information about the properties of hundreds of components that go into such systems. The system is a *forward-chaining system,* which means that it begins by matching the *antecedents* in the left-hand side of the rules and activating the *consequents* in the right-hand side of the rule. The request by the customer for a computer system begins the process. The customer has certain requirements of memory, disk storage, processing power, etc. that match on certain rules that, when they fire, enable yet other rules to fire until a very complex configuration is generated that will satisfy the customers needs and also is deliverable by Digital.

Xcon relieves the human expert from having to configure each of these systems by hand and at the same time creates better configurations than would be available by those less skilled than the few experts (fewer redundant or missing components and systems configurations that do not work). Its success opened the doors for other commercial applications of expert systems.

Xcon employed a type of algorithm for combining the information in the rules called *forward chaining.* It was "forward" in the sense that the systems started off with the input information about the customer's purchase and then moved forward (from the antecedents to the consequents) as the rules fired. For instance a simple sequence might be as follows:

- User requests 100 Gbytes of storage space for their existing database.

- This fires a rule: "If more than 10 Gbytes of storage space is requested, then allocate multiple disk subsystems."

- Which fires a rule: "If there are multiple disk subsystems, provide a new controller card for each."

- Which fires a rule: "If there are more than three controller cards, then require the purchase of additional power supplies."

In this short sequence the rule-based system was able to forward-chain from the input request of storage space to the suggestion for additional power supplies and controller boards. Keep in mind that in this example we've shown only one particular pathway through three rules. Every time an antecedent is matched and a new consequent is activated, there may be hundreds of new rules that match that state. Keeping track of all the rules and how they fire is the job of the *inference engine* that is at the heart of all rule-based expert systems.

In contrast to forward chaining through the rules, backward chaining is also possible. In *backward chaining* a hypothesis is proposed and then the rule base is checked to see if there are rules with matching consequents. The antecedents for those rules are then checked out as if they were the new hypotheses to be validated, and the system continues backward until the input data either validates or invalidates the given hypothesis. If the hypothesis is invalidated, then another hypothesis may be proposed and the process started again. These types of systems are most useful for performing diagnostic work where a hypothesis about what is wrong can be made and then the rules can generate antecedents that can be validated either by firing more rules, matching any input data, or asking a user.

Mycin is an expert system developed at Stanford University by E. H. Shortliffe in 1976. It is a backward chaining rule-based expert system that uses a compilation of a wide array of expert medical knowledge in the field of bacterial infections. It contains around 500 rules and can make recommendations on 100 different kinds of infections. It was deployed to assist physicians in the diagnosis of infections (bacteremia and meningitis) and to determine which of a host of different antibiotics would be the best to treat the infections. The system interacts with the physician via a natural-language interface by asking the physician questions about the patient and the patient's symptoms, and then recommending tests. By using backward chaining, the Mycin system is much more user-friendly to the physician since it only asks questions that are relevant to a particular hypothesis (e.g., initial evidence points to *Escherichia coli* so that further questions will be directed at confirming or denying this hypothesis before another is considered). Irrelevant tests and lab work are not requested, and, in general, the system seems to make sense to the physicians using it. A forward-chaining rule system could be difficult for physicians to interact with since it will jump from rule to rule in what may appear to be no particular order.

Despite these successes with rule-based expert systems, there are also some drawbacks, and in general these systems are less widely used today than they were in the late 1980s. Some of the drawbacks include:

- *The system is only as smart as your human expert.* Since the system isn't learning from data directly but rather from knowledge extracted from human experts, any biases or errors in reasoning inherent in the expert's view of the world will be reflected in the system. And because the systems are complex, it is often difficult to detect such errors and correct them even if good data is available.

- *The systems are complex.* Some rule-based systems have grown to thousands of rules in size, and often there are redundancies in the database. Because all the rules can interact with each other, the firing patterns can be very complex as well, which makes it difficult to debug such systems and also makes the systems very fragile in that a small change to one rule may have a major impact on the way other rules behave.

- *The systems are human-intensive.* The majority of the time spent in building these systems is in trying to extract the knowledge from the human experts. Usually this knowledge is not written down or organized in any particular way, and more often than not the expert does not have good reasons for why certain decisions are made. Sometimes they don't know why they perform in a certain way. Consequently, much of the time can be spent in helping the experts better understand how they themselves operate.

Expert systems have had many notable successes, and various modifications of these systems have been used to address some of these problems. Fuzzy logic is one such modification. Even without these fixes, expert systems represented a breakthrough for AI in that for really the first time AI produced systems that could be used in real-world situations and were of benefit and aid to the end user of the tool.

16.3 Fuzzy Logic

One problem with rule-based systems is that they can be somewhat brittle— "brittle" in the sense that they break relatively easily when they are bent toward a slightly different problem. For instance, there may be a very powerful rule that states "If income is high and debt is high, then the loan applicant is a bad risk."

The rule itself begs the question of what is "high"? The term "high" is in the rule rather than a particular number (e.g., $60,000) because the rules were generated by people and for people who wanted to be able to quickly understand what the rules meant and to capture high-level intuitions rather than detailed specifics. The problem is that "high" may mean different things to different people, and it may be interpreted to be a very specific cutoff value (one income is high but another that is only slightly less is no longer considered to be "high"). Because there can be such a sharp cutoff, some valuable information may be lost.

Consider the problem, for instance, in which "high income" is defined to be anything over $100,000 per year and high debt is defined to be when a consumer pays more than 45 percent of their gross income in interest or payout on debt. The rule can then be interpreted as "If people are wealthy but in a lot of debt, then they shouldn't be given the loan." The fact that words such as "high" have been used to make it easy to understand and interpret the rule. The problem is that these words shoehorn continuous information into rigid categories—and mistakes can be made. Consider an applicant Steve whose debt is 55 percent of his gross annual income, which is $99,999.

In the classic rule-based expert system the rule mentioned above would not fire to deny the loan since Steve's income falls just barely below the cutoff for the definition of what is considered to be "high income." This is a problem because his debt is exceedingly high. Thus the rule that should have captured Steve as a bad risk just misses. This is an example of the brittleness of classically built expert systems.

Fuzzy logic is a technique designed to correct these shortcomings of rule-based systems (and classic logic systems in general). The basic idea of fuzzy logic is that there is no precise cutoff between sets or categories and that these boundaries are "fuzzy." A given person is not high-income or low-income but has some representation of varying degree in each of these categories. The value of income in a fuzzy system would, for instance, show partial membership in two different categories. At $99,999 per year, Steve falls just within the definition of middle income and just outside the boundary of high income. In fuzzy logic the boundaries for high and moderate income would overlap.

A graphical way to see this difference is to think of the definitions of the categories as a degree of membership. For the old, brittle way, the graph would show 100 percent membership or 0 percent membership for a given income—basically a "yes" or a "no." This is shown in Fig. 16.1. This provides ease of understanding to the end user but can be misleading when values lie critically close to boundaries where decisions are made.

Instead of this hard cutoff between different categories, fuzzy logic uses truth values between 0.0 and 1.0 to imply the degree of membership that a certain value has in a given category. In Fig. 16.2 this degree of membership is shown for the three discrete values of income. In the example of the $99,999 income, Steve would have a 0.51 truth value for middle income and a truth value of 0.49 for high income. Thus the truth values would capture the fact that Steve was at the boundary rather than truly just middle income.

Fuzzy-logic systems then look a lot like rule-based expert systems except that they have the added advantage of working at a high level of abstraction (e.g., "high," "medium," "low") while preserving the smoothness and lack of brittleness of using numeric systems. Because of this, fuzzy logic systems are easier to build and debug than a comparable rule-based expert system. At least some of this is due to the fact that people can create fuzzy-logic systems using more abstract descriptions without requiring them to create complex mathematical formulas to describe things. Because the fuzzy logic is less brittle, the results will also be better than systems using only traditional rule-based techniques.

When fuzzy logic is actually used to solve a problem, the system itself looks very much like a rule-based expert system. There are a large number of different fuzzy rules that have a left-hand side or *premise* consisting of one or more

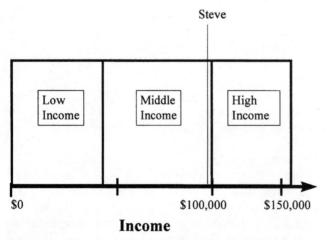

Income

Figure 16.1 Mapping of the real value of income into three categories.

Steve

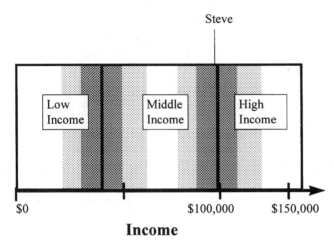

Income

Figure 16.2 Fuzzy logic allows for smooth boundaries between categories so that values at the boundaries can be more fairly judged.

antecedents or constraints and a right-hand side or *conclusion* which may contain one or more consequents. The antecedents in the rule can be combined with both conjunctions (e.g., "tall AND fat") and disjunctions (e.g., "moderately wealthy OR wealthy"). The language of fuzzy logic will include these as well as NOT, VERY, and SOMEWHAT, which each have the following effects on a constraint or a value.

- *AND.* When AND is used, the truth values of the two constraints need to be combined in such a way as to imply that both constraints need to be true. To accomplish this, the fuzzy system takes the minimum truth value from the two constraints. For example, in the rule "If high income AND high debt, then deny credit" if the truth value for Steve for "high income" is 0.49 and for "high debt" is 0.90, then the resulting truth value for the rule would be 0.49.

- *OR.* When OR is used, the truth values of the two constraints need to be combined in such a way as to imply that if either one of the constraints is satisfied, the rule will apply. To accomplish this, the fuzzy system takes the maximum truth value from the two constraints. For example, in the rule "If high income OR high debt, then deny credit," if the truth values are again 0.49 and 0.90, respectively, the truth value for the rule would be 0.90.

- *NOT.* The NOT operator reverses the meaning of the truth value by subtracting the truth value from 1.0. For instance, if the rule were "If income NOT high, then deny credit," then the truth value for the rule for Steve would be 0.51 (1.0 − 0.49).

- *VERY.* The VERY operator is a convenient way to make the constraint on a value more demanding than it would otherwise have to be. For example, in "If VERY high income, then deny credit" normally the truth value for Steve

for this rule would be 0.49 since he had high income. With the VERY operator, the rule is more strict and the truth value for Steve would be considerably less—maybe 0.30 instead.

- *SOMEWHAT.* The SOMEWHAT operator is a convenient way to relax the
  constraint on a value. For instance, even if Steve's income wasn't VERY HIGH
  (truth value of 0.30), it might be SOMEWHAT HIGH (truth value of 0.65).

Graphically all these operators can be viewed as shown in Fig. 16.3. With such
a graph any given value can be mapped into a truth value for a given category.

The truth value or degree of membership in each of three categories can be
shown for Steve's salary of $99,999 by the value at which it intersects the line
representing each category. For instance, the truth value for high and middle
income is around 0.5; for low, it is 0.0. The modifiers NOT, SOMEWHAT, and
VERY have been applied to the high-income category and consequently modify
the truth values.

Using fuzzy logic in a system involves several steps:

Step 1: input data.   The first step deals with converting the input values
into fuzzy values. Figure 16.3 shows a nice way to visualize how continuous
values such as income are translated into discrete categories (high, middle,
low) and how their truth values are calculated. It will be up to the end user in
conjunction with tools for fuzzy systems to define the shapes of the lines on this

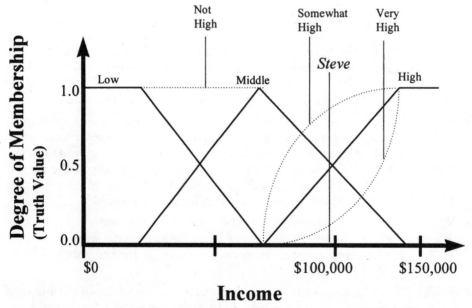

Figure 16.3 Another graphical way to view the fuzzy values for income. This figure includes the
representation of the modifiers.

graph. Once this step is done, the system can automatically convert input data into fuzzy data with membership information.

Step 2: combining evidence. The next step is to see what rules apply to the given situation and combine the evidence. When the rules have been created by the end user, they can then be applied to new situations or against the historical data for testing. The antecedents of the rules will match given values in the current situation, and several rules may be applicable—most of them having different consequents with different truth values. All the results of the applicable rules "vote" for membership in particular categories. A common practice is to sum the truth values for all rules with the particular set in the conclusion.

Step 3: defuzzification. The final step is to translate back from the fuzzy answer into a value that can be used directly (e.g., translating from rules that indicate "high income" with truth value 0.75 and "middle income" with truth value 0.45 to the usable result of $124,000). This process is accomplished by weighting each set (category) by its truth value and multiplying by the mean value of each set. Thus the sets with the highest truth values will have the most impact on the eventual defuzzified value. If the fuzzification graphs are more complex (e.g., if they use SOMEWHAT and "VERY"), the calculation can be somewhat more complex.

Fuzzy systems provide a quick and accurate way for expert users to create, modify, and use expert systems that simulate complex real-world processes or perform prediction and classification within databases. The systems have been used to smooth the operation of physical devices such as the brakes on subway cars and elevators and the shifting in an automatic transmission. They have also been used successfully in classic corporate domains such as finance and health care for assessing risk, detecting fraud, setting product pricing, and even making suggestions for corporate acquisitions. Although probably most popular in Japan, these systems have been deployed more and more often in the United States, and powerful tools for their construction are now being provided by a number of companies around the world.

16.4 The Rise and Fall of AI

From the earliest work in artificial intelligence to the more recent advances, it has been a field with the most challenging of goals—namely, the re-creation of an intelligence in a machine that rivals that of a human being. And depending on how you define it, it can be an amazingly broad field—encompassing everything from the research of physically powerful but intellectually weak robots used in manufacturing to the algorithms and techniques used in today's computer programs for chess.

Those who consider themselves to be in the AI field have often complained that as soon as a difficult AI problem is solved successfully by AI researchers, it fails to still be AI. This is problematic because it means that AI research is never completed successfully. All other fields get the glory, and no credit goes to

AI. This really is not the case. In fact, the problem with getting credit really has to do with scope. AI, by its very name, is very broad in scope and very aggressive. AI will not be truly successful until it captures the goal it set out for itself by the name of artificial intelligence. That implicit goal is to re-create and understand human intelligence as a complete package—not as individual pieces of game-playing programs of special-purpose natural-language or rule-based expert systems. There may be even a more fundamental problem with AI which may not be solved until there is a radical rethinking of what an "artificial intelligence" is and what process is required to achieve it.

This problem is that underneath it all AI, in an effort to make whatever comes out of it be understandable, has required that these systems utilize an underlying framework of explanation. The way that humans explain things to each other is via language and words. Each word can be viewed as a symbol that represents something in the natural world (a chair, running, green, big, etc.). The difficulty with AI is that in many systems the concentration is on how to define and manipulate these symbols within some representation that will allow all the symbols to be used to answer some question or perform some task—effectively to successfully pass what is known as the Turing test.

The *Turing test* is a simple test that Alan Turing described in 1950 that could be used to determine whether a computer could think.

> Set up two rooms and in one place a person who will be the interrogator and in the other place another human and a computer. The interrogator can communicate with the human and the computer by typing into two different terminals (one connected to the computer; the other connected to the other person) but the interrogator is not told which terminal is connected to the computer and which is connected to the other person. If, after a lengthy interrogation, the interrogator cannot determine which is the computer and which is the person, then the computer passes the Turing test and is deemed to be intelligent, and the creation of an artificial intelligence will have been accomplished. To make the test fair, interrogator is allowed to ask any question that comes to mind to try to stump the computer and find some query that would distinguish one from the other. The computer on the other is allowed to do anything it can to mislead the interrogator (including slowing down its responses to questions that it can process more quickly than a human can) and can have access to any knowledge base available.

Even with these loose constraints, no computer has as yet come close to passing the Turing test, and there are some who believe that it will never be possible. One reason given for the difficult time that modern AI systems have in passing the Turing test is that since these systems work with representations of reality in the form of symbols, they often sidestep the difficult issue of how to ground these symbols in reality. This is known as the *symbol grounding problem,* and understanding it helps one understand the limitations and the success of AI.

The symbol grounding problem was the name given to this idea by Stevan Harnad in the mid-1980s. His argument is that it is difficult to say that any machine truly is intelligent when it works only at the symbolic level without grounding those symbols. This grounding may be as simple as mapping symbols to the perceptual inputs that are available to the intellect that is manipu-lating the symbols. He reviews three different thought experiments to make his point that even if a computer could pass the Turing test, it could do this without really having any intelligence whatsoever. The first one, proposed by Searle in 1980, has come to be known as the "Chinese room argument." Here are synopses of the three thought experiments:

- *The Chinese room argument.* Assume that an AI system has been built out of rules that take in human language and manipulate the words as "sym-bols" to create new "symbols" that are then fed back to the interrogator out-side Turing's room. Now assume that the interrogator is communicating in Chinese and inside the room is a human who is processing the input Chinese text by the same rules that the computer program would and producing the correct Chinese text as the answer returned to the interrogator. This system passes the Turing test, but since the human who is manipulating the sym-bols doesn't understand Chinese, they can have no understanding whatso-ever of the questions being asked or the answers they are providing. Thus Searle argues that even if a symbol manipulation system could be created to pass the Turing test, it might well still not have any true understanding or intelligence.

- *Chinese translation from a dictionary.* Imagine that you had to learn Chi-nese as a second language only from a Chinese dictionary with no words from your native language included in it. You could manipulate the symbols and look up one Chinese word and see other symbols that defined it, but none of the symbols would be grounded. It would be a merry-go-round from one word to the next without ever having any true understanding. Learning Chinese in this way might well be an impossible task.

- *Language learning from a Chinese dictionary.* An even harder problem would be to ask one to learn one's first language solely by reading a dictio-nary. In this case none of the words could even be translated into ideas and concepts that were grounded by one's real-world experience. This is posed by Harnad as an impossible task, but he also points out it is often the task that most AI systems try to tackle by building knowledge bases and symbol sys-tems to perform human intelligent(?)like behavior.

Although Harnad does not propose a specific answer for this problem, he does state that perhaps the "grounding" that is needed for these symbolic ideas is true grounding in sensory images (visual, auditory, tactile, etc.). Other researchers have also recognized this as a fundamental problem of artificial intelligence and have suggested that before complex intelligent behavior such as planning and medical diagnosis can be performed, the simplest of intelligent behavior must first be accomplished.

Rod Brooks from the Massachusetts Institute of Technology has argued that in order to build human-level intelligence, we need to make sure that we can create insect-level intelligence first. In effect, we need to walk before we can run. To do this, Brooks creates mobile robots that respond in real-world situations with visual and tactile systems and end up performing quite complex behaviors such as avoiding obstacles, exploration of unknown areas, and even more complex behaviors such as cleaning up empty soda cans around the lab. Brooks' systems are based on simple interacting processes without any specific representation or symbol manipulation. Despite this, these robot creatures display quite sophisticated and intelligent behavior.

Even in particular case studies where AI has been employed at a symbolic level, often simple brute-force approaches driven from sensory input (note that data collected in databases is a form of sensory input about the outside world) outperform sophisticated representational systems.

- Most handwritten character recognition systems now rely on huge quantities of training data (sensory input) to learn from rather than sophisticated representations of visual symbols such as lines, arcs, and circles.
- In a well-documented comparison between a data-driven model and a rule-based expert system built for the U.S. Census Bureau, the data-driven system increased the amount of automated classification by nearly 30 percent in comparison to the rule-based system and required nearly 40-fold fewer staff months to create.
- The best computer chess programs in the world use relatively simple brute-force search of possible moves on very powerful computers, and the ranking of the program seems to increase fairly regularly with how far ahead the computer thinks when deciding when to move.
- The most powerful natural-language processing systems for information retrieval are now built using statistical analysis of language patterns directly from large volumes of textual data rather than from complex representations of grammar and sophisticated parsers.

These are just a few of the successes of AI-like systems that are now being used. The question will be whether AI will redefine itself to address some of these important issues and encompass data-driven and sensory grounded systems like these or whether the major thrust of AI will continue to be the extraction of knowledge from human beings directly in an attempt to create the correct representation of knowledge to support true artificial intelligence.

Data Mining

At this point we have introduced the concepts of the data warehouse, the underlying technologies that make its construction possible, and even many of the currently available products. In the previous section we further discussed how data warehouses are being used for decision support through OLAP and business reporting tools. We also introduced the basic concepts of detecting useful patterns and of building models from the data warehouse through statistical techniques and through artificial intelligence. In this part we explain how these basic ideas about patterns, models, and statistical validation are used in data mining technologies and how these technologies can be deployed to have a real and positive business impact. Having laid the foundation, this part of the book gives a chapter-by-chapter summary of the most important data mining technologies available today:

- *Introduction to Data Mining (Chap. 17)*
- *Decision Trees (Chap. 18)*
- *Artificial Neural Networks (Chap. 19)*
- *Nearest Neighbor and Clustering (Chap. 20)*
- *Fuzzy Logic and Genetic Algorithms (Chap. 21)*
- *Rule Induction (Chap. 22)*
- *Selecting and Using the Right Technique (Chap. 23)*

17

Introduction to Data Mining

17.1 Data Mining Has Come of Age

Have you heard about data mining? Pick up the latest issue of your favorite industry or business magazine, and you may well find an article on "data mining." What is data mining? And why are so many people talking about it in both the computer industry and in direct marketing?

The answer is simple: *Data mining helps end users extract useful business information from large databases.* What makes this definition interesting is the word "large." If the database were small, you wouldn't need any new technology to discover useful information. If, for instance, this were the early 1800s and you were the owner of a general store, you wouldn't need to employ data mining (or direct marketing) since you would probably have only a few hundred customers, each of whom you knew by name. You would probably also know, in great detail, who they were and what they bought. When you've got only a few hundred customers you really don't need much of a computer to mine the data. The best database analysis and predictive models that could possibly be done could be done in the shopkeeper's head.

Today, however, the "shopkeeper" of the 1990s has hundreds of thousands to millions of customers, and for the first time in history the data on these customers is being accumulated at one location where consistent access and consistent storage is being guaranteed: the data warehouse. The metaphors between "data warehouses" and "data mining" can be confusing. The idea that ties them together is that the large data collection in your data warehouse is the "data mountain" presented to data mining tools. Data warehousing allows you to build that mountain. Data mining allows you to sift that mountain down to the essential information that is useful to your business.

What is so new about extracting information from data to make our businesses run better? We've been doing that for years, right? Well, in fact, what you see, as various new data mining products begin to enter the marketplace, is that many of them perform the same types of activities that were performed by the other database products. Once the data warehouse exists, you've got to have ways to look at it and navigate it. If the database is of any reasonable size (typically they are made up of hundreds of millions to billions of records), you can no longer easily access it via a spreadsheet, and to do so you need to move into the realm of the tools created for database professionals. These tools allow you to access your database via a language called *Structured Query Language* (SQL). SQL is the lingua franca of those other brave souls, climbing the data mountain. The problem is that SQL, although standard, is different from the language that most people in marketing speak—sort of like having to communicate your business problem by using only a computer language. You can say what you need to say, but it will be difficult to get the point across, and the result may be so complex that it may be ripe with errors.

The allure of data mining is that it promises to fix the problem of miscommunication between you and your data and allow you to ask of your data complex questions such as: "What has been going on?" or "What is going to happen next and how can I profit?" The answer to the first question can be provided by the data warehouse and multidimensional database technology (OLAP) that allow the user to easily navigate and visualize the data. The answer to the second question can be provided by data mining tools built on some of the latest computer algorithms: decision trees (CART, CHAID, AID), neural networks, nearest neighbor, and rule induction.

17.2   The Motivation for Data Mining Is Tremendous

As an example of the impact that data mining can have on a business, consider the following direct marketing problem: John, a typical cellular phone user, has just decided to not renew his contract with you, his current cellular provider. Why? Because he was just made an offer by the competing provider for a free phone. Since that Motorola phone that he got from you last year was really starting to look like old technology and the competition had the same rate plan as you, John opted for their offer. This is good news for John and good news for John's new cellular provider, but really bad news for John's old provider (you). You invested in John to the tune of $700 to land him as a customer less than one year ago. The sad thing is that if you had only known that John was at risk of leaving, you surely would have invested the extra $100 to upgrade John's phone (John does $350 worth of calling per month). Now that John has signed the contract with the competition, it is too late. The really aggravating thing is that you could have known that John was at risk. If you had used data mining on your customer account database, you could have built a predictive model that would have shown that John, and others like him, are at grave risk of attrition. With this predictive model you could have launched a successful and profitable direct marketing campaign to save your valuable customers.

Today the cellular phone industry looks very much the way the credit card industry looked only a few years ago. The cellular industry is growing at around 50 percent per year, and everyone is scrambling for market share. At the same time margins are dropping as the industry becomes more and more competitive and as the market begins to saturate. What happens when everyone who wants a cellular phone already has one? What happens when the market saturates and everyone starts playing a zero-sum game of trading customers? This is the state of the credit card industry today, and it may foreshadow some of what is to come in the next 5 years for the cellular industry. Specifically, some of the methods and techniques for preventing and reversing customer attrition that are in use today in the credit industry may well make sense for the cellular industry. One of these techniques, data mining, has been employed within the credit industry with very positive results.

The following should sound somewhat familiar to the path the cellular industry has been taking recently. In 1981 116 million credit cards were issued in the United States; and within 10 years since then, over 263 million. In another 10 years, however, it is unlikely that there will be another doubling of this number since there are only 250 million people in the United States and they can carry only so many credit cards with them in their wallets and purses. It is, in fact, the belief of industry analysts that the credit card market has already stopped growing and has been saturated since 1988.

Such a saturated marketplace means that whatever gains are made by one company come only at the expense of another—a zero-sum game. Those customers lost to competitors are called "attriters," and credit card companies can typically lose 1 to 10 percent of their customers to their competition each year. In the long run, the winners are those who eke out fractional improvements in understanding and reacting to their customers' needs. The key attribute of these winning companies is their ability to retain their good customers at minimum cost. Data mining tools that make use of existing customer transactional and demographic data are a necessity for the credit industry and will likely become so for the cellular industry as well. Those companies in the cellular industry who can prepare for this shift to a saturated market will be in the best possible position when it actually occurs.

17.3   Learning from Your Past Mistakes

"Those who cannot remember the past are
condemned to repeat it."
GEORGE SANTAYANA

How does data mining work? It isn't magic. Instead it works the same way a human being does. It uses historical information (experience) to learn. However, in order for the data mining technology to pull the "gold" out of your database, you do have to tell it what the gold looks like (i.e., what business problem you would like to solve). It then uses the description of that "gold" to look for similar examples in the database and uses these pieces of information from the past to develop a predictive model of what will happen in the future.

For instance, let's say that you have a direct marketing program where you would like to make an offer to only the subset of your customers that would be interested in such an offer. Contacting only those customers who would be interested optimizes your profit by maximizing your revenue while minimizing your costs. It also is good news for your prospects and current customers since they are not bothered with offers that don't make sense to them. Examples include mailing out offers for balance transfer to credit card customers, or targeting interested customer segments with niche catalogs for a catalog house selling craft supplies.

The trick to building a successful predictive model is to have some data in your database that describes what has happened in the past. If you have already sent out a small test mailing, you now have some information about what types of customers responded and which ones didn't. Data mining tools are designed to learn from these past successes and failures (just as you would) and then be able to predict what is going to happen next. One of the key differences between you and a data mining tool is that the data mining tool can automatically go through the entire database and find even the smallest pattern that may help in a better prediction. These tools also check for the statistical significance of the pattern and report it back to the user. For instance, if your data mining tool found that 100 percent of the people in the database from one particular zip code with high credit limits had responded to your offer, but only three people who had these characteristics, the data mining tool would report this information with a warning that it was very likely to be an idiosyncrasy of the database rather than a usable predictive pattern.

17.4 Data Mining? Don't Need It— I've Got Statistics . . .

An obvious question at this point is to ask how data mining differs from statistics. After all, people have been using statistics for better targeting of their marketing efforts for many years now.

Statistics has the same general uses and results as data mining. Regression is used in statistics quite often to create models that are predictive of customer behavior, and these models are built from large stores of historical data. The main difference between data mining and statistics is that data mining is meant to be used by the business end user—not the statistician. Data mining effectively automates the statistical process, thereby relieving the end user of some of the burden. This results in a tool that is easier to use. For instance, it may have occurred to you to ask "If most of statistics is a matter of making a guess and then checking it out (a.k.a. hypothesis testing), why don't we just let the computers make those guesses and then test them automatically?"

For this reason data mining tools are often coupled with other tools that make it easier to apply data analysis techniques and understand the results.

These tools then no longer need to be wielded solely by the data analyst but instead by the business user. This may sound like a dangerous idea: giving powerful predictive technologies to end users who may or may not have taken statistics courses on their way to completing their MBAs. Keeping these business users from harm while allowing them to access much of the power of predictive and descriptive data analysis is why data mining is a technology to watch.

17.5 Measuring Data Mining Effectiveness: Accuracy, Speed, and Cost

Those who might like to use a data mining tool have many choices. To make the right one, they need to evaluate it in comparison to existing statistical techniques and also compare between the large number of new data mining products that are currently on the market. Data mining technology is actually quite similar to statistics in the way it builds a predictive model from data. Often the accuracy of that prediction depends more on the correct deployment of the technology and the quality of the data than on the technology itself. The choice of data mining should be driven by the advantages that it brings to the bottom line of the entire business process—not just the statistical predictive accuracy.

Let's now look a little more closely at the complete calculation of profit or return on investment from a targeted marketing offer and contrast it to the way that these targeted marketing offers are now being performed. In the following example we are mailing out offers to customers. If they respond, we make money; if they don't respond, we lose money proportional to the cost of the mailing (and sometimes proportional to the cost of the offer). Let's assume that the size of the targeted customers is fixed (often this is the case because of fixed marketing budgets) and call it the "target size." Then

$$\text{Profit} = \text{revenue} - \text{fixed costs} - \text{variable cost} \times \text{target size}$$

$$\text{Revenue} = \text{responders} \times \text{response value}$$

$$\text{Fixed costs} = \text{marketing design} + \text{production} + \text{infrastructure} + \text{mistakes}$$

The impact of predictive accuracy can be seen in the revenue calculation by noting that in many cases:

$$\text{Responders} = \text{target size} \times \text{prediction accuracy}$$

For a given-size customer or prospect target population, the higher the predictive accuracy of the technique being used, the greater the number of responders that will be captured in that targeted set. It is often argued that data mining techniques such as neural networks will increase the predictive accuracy beyond what can be attained via standard statistical techniques. The reality is, however, that many of the techniques do quite well and their relative success is more often due to data quality and quantity and the skills of the person wielding the tool. There can also be some variation in optimal accuracy among the models from problem to problem in different domains.

The other way that data mining techniques are often measured is by speed. The reasoning is that the faster the tool runs, the larger the data set to which it can be applied. The larger the database is, the better the accuracy of the predictive model will be. Thus many data mining tools are being implemented on parallel computers in order to increase their speed of execution. This improved speed can be substantial (factors of a thousand or more speed-up).

To truly determine which technologies are best, it is helpful to look at the big picture. The big picture includes a much larger business process than just data analysis. The full process includes data collection, data analysis (data mining), predictive model visualization, and the launching of a marketing program against a customer set. Too often data analysis tools are measured only by their predictive accuracy (where it is difficult to distinguish a winner) and their speed. But these systems do not work in isolation. They are part of this much larger picture and tools that provide adequate predictive accuracy and also fit seamlessly into this bigger picture will be the most effective for your business.

The average marketing department that uses predictive data mining or any kind of data analysis goes through the following business process:

- First, the marketing user, having a good understanding of the business, gets an idea for a new marketing program or maybe a question about the performance of a current marketing program. From this idea or question the user needs to build a predictive model in order to launch the marketing program.

- The marketing department makes a request to their analytics department. The analytics department interviews the marketing user in order to understand the business problem, and then, when this is done, the analytics department makes a request to the IT department for a data extract from which to build the model.

- Several days to weeks are spent by the analyst in crafting a model from this extract (getting the extract from the IT department may require days to weeks to achieve by itself), and when the model is complete, it is presented to the marketing department.

- If the marketing department likes the model (i.e., it makes business sense as well as statistical sense), they will launch the program, which often means recoding the predictive model from a statistical format to one that can be executed on their data warehouse where the customer data resides.

Total turnaround time from idea to execution is a minimum of several days and can be up to several months. This can be a problem in rapidly changing markets. A bigger problem than this lengthy processing time is that, with all this transfer of data between the marketing, analytics, and IT departments, there are many possible places where major errors can occur in the translation and movement of that data. This could result in the wrong model being built and the wrong marketing program being launched.

In the banking industry a large mistake was recently made when the analytics department of a large bank requested a "random" sample of customers from the data warehouse. They wanted to build a model to predict which customers would be interested in a new retirement account product. A "randomly" ordered list of customer accounts was returned to the analytics department from which they took the first 100,000 records to build the model and the second 100,000 records to test the model. The model worked quite well on the test data, so a targeted mailing was launched. When the returns came in, the customer response to the promotion was significantly below what was predicted by the model.

When the analytics department finally uncovered the problem, they found that the IT department had sorted the customers by account balance in order to achieve a "random" list. This was not a random list at all—in fact, it was probably worse than if the original "nonrandomized" data had been used. The problem was that all the good customers were at the front of the list, and these were the customers who were used to build the model. Unfortunately, the model was then applied to the general-customer population, whose behavior was significantly different from that of this good-customer subpopulation.

17.6 Embedding Data Mining into Your Business Process

Major errors like the one mentioned above in the banking industry occur more often than not as the data is moved, translated, and recoded from one department to another, and from one piece of hardware and database to another (often from mainframe or large server running a relational data warehouse, to a UNIX workstation running a specialized database for data analysis, to a small extract file that the marketing professional interacts with via Microsoft Excel, Access, or a multidimensional database tool). Avoiding these major errors can be a much more important part of determining predictive accuracy than the subtle differences in accuracy between different technologies.

The cost of this distributed business process is also quite high. There are multiple types of databases, operating systems, and computers on which to maintain and train your staff. There are also costs specific to the model itself, such as having to recode the model back on the mainframe and then spending a significant amount of time retesting the model once it is on the mainframe to make sure that no mistakes were made. It would be much less expensive, much faster, and much less error-prone to have this entire marketing business process more directly under the control of the marketing professional and running seamlessly within the existing data warehouse. In order to achieve this, the data analysis must be (1) embedded into the data warehouse and (2) understandable and usable by the marketing professional. These two criteria can be fulfilled by several of the new data mining technologies more adeptly than existing statistical techniques can. It is the ability of data mining technologies such as decision trees to embed into data warehouses and to provide understandable results to the business end user that provide the greatest improvements in accuracy, speed, and cost that are desirable in such a business system. This is the major difference between data mining and classic statistics.

This "embedded data mining" concept seeks to reduce the errors and costs of the current data analysis system while, for the first time, allowing marketing professionals to truly see what is going on in their database. Data mining needs to be embedded into the data warehouse without the requirement of a data extract. Similarly, the predictive model should be placed back into the data warehouse without the requirement of recoding and retesting it. It can then be applied to any database in the warehouse and used by others as well. It is, in the parlance of data warehousing, "metadata" or data about the data. Additional metadata can be used to create the focused "data mart," which is a high-speed view into the data warehouse that is specifically tailored to make it easy for a businessperson to access and navigate in an otherwise complex data warehouse. These data marts are typically implemented via multidimensional database technology.

17.7   The More Things Change, the More They Remain the Same

"There is nothing new under the sun."
ECCLESIASTES

"Except in the computer industry."
ANONYMOUS

It may seem that all the articles about data mining, and all the new products are just heralding the rediscovery of a great new age of statistics or (since statistics has been in use for decades) just more of the same. But despite the overlap in usage and even technology, data mining is bringing something new to the party—namely, an easy way for business and marketing professionals to access the power of statistics. This is not a small thing.

The real opportunity provided by data mining is that it represents an empowerment of the end user in much the same way that the spreadsheet first empowered the business user in the late 1970s to early 1980s. Before the spreadsheet appeared, business users could run financial analyses, but to do so, they would have to call their finance department, who, in turn, would call the data-processing department and between the two they would try to figure out what the business user wanted to model. The business user would have a usable financial analysis within days or weeks.

Contrast this scenario to what we see today, where business and marketing professionals regularly build and run small financial models themselves without ever calling the data processing or finance organizations. They build these models immediately and interactively by working directly with their modeling tools. Their turnaround time has gone from days and weeks to seconds and minutes, and a whole new way of interacting with their financial data has been born. They are able to gain understanding and intuitions from their data that just were not possible when that data and those models were being built for them by others. They are now in control of how their real business problems are communicated to the database.

This basic promise of the spreadsheet proved to be a powerful force in creating a new functional tool for the business end user. This is also the promise of data mining. To achieve it, however, data mining must be deployed as an embedded technology within the data warehouse. When this is done, there are improvements in accuracy, speed, and cost.

17.8   Discovery versus Prediction

17.8.1   Gold in them thar hills

The image that usually comes to mind when people hear the term "data mining" is that there exists a "mountain" of data and some nugget of gold in the mountain that would otherwise be too costly or too difficult to find without some powerful mining tools. The other metaphor is like looking for a needle in a haystack. In any case, finding either the nugget or the needle is only one piece of what data mining can do for you. Data mining can also take that mountain of data and tell you what your mountain is going to look like next month— specifically, not just where the gold is today but where the gold might be tomorrow. Thus data mining also includes prediction as one of its benefits. If we took the data mining analogy a step further, this second part of data mining would correspond to understanding the tectonics of mountains—how they are changing and moving—not just what they look like today. We will call these two important features of data mining "discovery" when we are looking for an existing useful nugget in our databases and "prediction" when we are seeking to use what we have found to predict what is going to happen next.

17.8.2   Discovery—finding something that you weren't looking for

One of the obvious things about real mining is that when you come across a diamond or a vein of gold, you know that you have found it. You can recognize the important properties of diamonds or gold because they have been discovered before and you know what they look like and feel like, and barring that, you can always take them into the lab to do detailed tests to make sure that they are genuine and that you have not stumbled onto some cubic zirconium or some iron pyrite or fool's gold. In the case of large databases sometimes users are asking the impossible: "Tell me something I didn't know but would like to know." How do you describe the characteristics of this nugget of gold when even the end users don't know exactly what they want?

For instance, how does the data mining tool know that in the telephone industry, losing nearly all revenue from a class of customers over the summer is an important "nugget" of information? How does it know that the nugget of information that "Customers who buy large numbers of your product tend to be the highest revenue customers" is uninteresting since this is an obvious association between number of purchases and total revenue?

Distinguishing between the two nuggets described above will be important for any data mining system to accomplish. Certain algorithms can be employed, however, to help to pull the gold out of the dross and distinguish between the gold and the pyrite. We will talk more about this in the section on discovery and rule induction, but the main idea of how these systems work is by making three measurements: (1) how strong, (2) unexpected, and (3) ubiquitous the association is.

17.8.3 Prediction

Now contrast discovery to prediction. With prediction you, as the end user, have a very specific event or attribute that you would like to find a pattern in association with. For instance, you would like to predict customer attrition. One of the most important parts of predicting customer attrition is in having historical information in your database about which customers have attrited in the past. There may be many interesting patterns in your database—say, between age of your customers and their buying habits—that you might like to discover, but in this case you know very well that attrition is costing you a lot of money and, for now, you will be very pleased to discover the factors contributing to attrition within your database and to predict which of your customers are at risk of attriting in the near future. After you do this, you may also be interested in discovery, but, for now, predicting attrition is the most important problem you have in your business.

A distinction between prediction and discovery is also made in the machine learning field. Here the two ways of building predictive models are called supervised and unsupervised learning. *Supervised learning* is equivalent to learning with a teacher and involves building a model for the specific purpose of optimally predicting some target field in the historical database (the value of which can be used to gauge whether the right or wrong prediction was made). In contrast, *unsupervised learning* does not have any well-defined goal or target to predict (and, thus, no particular supervision over what is a right or wrong answer). Techniques such as clustering and detection of association rules fall into the category of unsupervised learning.

17.9 Overfitting

Originally the term *data mining* was used in the statistical community with a negative connotation—namely, that if you "mined through your data" long enough, eventually you'd find something that looked like a useful pattern. This was also called "fishing"—the idea being that if you fish long enough you will eventually catch something. The difficulty with mining and fishing in this sense is that you've ended up catching something just because you were trying so hard—not that there really were useful, reproducible patterns in your database. Today this idea is generally called *overfitting* rather than data mining.

17.10   State of the Industry

The current offerings in data mining software products emphasize different important aspects of the algorithms and their usage. The different emphases are usually driven by differences in the targeted user and the types of problems being solved. There are four main categories of products:

- Targeted solutions
- Business tools
- Business analyst tools
- Research analyst tools

17.10.1   Targeted solutions

The products in this category have taken the power of data mining and applied it to a particular problem or industry. An example of this type of product is the *HNC Falcon system,* which is a neural-network-based solution that is targeted specifically at the credit card fraud and risk assessment problem. Other targeted examples are the Churn Prophet product from Lightbridge Inc., which has been created specifically for detecting customer "churn" (nonrenewal of contract) in the cellular phone industry.

These systems, because they have been tailored to a particular industry or problem, can automate or eliminate much of the complexity inherent in the data mining algorithms. For instance, in the case of cellular phone customer churn, the emphasis of the product is in producing understandable and actionable results. Because of this focus a particular type of random sampling can be chosen a priori as being most useful across the industry. Or the ROI (return on investment) models can be simplified to match the marketing interventions that are common in the cellular phone company's arsenal—which usually consist of giving something away in order to preserve the customer relationship (e.g., the newest-technology cellular phone in return for a year extension on the contract).

17.10.2   Business tools

The products in this category have been targeted for the business end user with the intention of presenting the power of data mining in a way that is easy enough to use and understandable enough that the business user can get some value from the tool and avoid any mistakes from misusing the product. These products should be likened to a child's sandbox, in which there are many useful things to play with but where, as long as you stay inside the sandbox, the child is relatively safe.

These types of tools usually provide sophisticated, interactive ROI analysis on the predictive models but also automate some of the parts of the algorithm that can get the user into trouble if misused. For instance, random sampling of the database and validation of the model are often automated in these tools, since many mistakes have been made by overly aggressive marketing managers in creating predictive models that are biased on a particular bad "random" sample—and then maybe even validated according to the database from which the model was created.

17.10.3   Business analyst tools

There is also a class of tools provided for users of tools for business applications in which the user wielding the tool has some sense of how data mining works and what some of the different variations accomplish. Typically these tools will have simplified the data mining process to a great degree, probably automating things like sampling, connecting to the database, and validation, but they will also expose to the expert business user a whole host of knobs and controls that affect how the data mining algorithm works. For instance, in a decision tree algorithm these tools would expose the choice of metric for making the splits (either Gini or entropy, etc.). They would also probably allow the user to force splits in the decision tree if the user wanted the split to take place rather than having the algorithm always make the decision.

These tools also present the results in a form that is closer to the data mining algorithm rather than the business end use. For instance, the structure of the neural network or the decision tree would be exposed and available to the user as well as higher-level business views of the results such as segmentation analysis, the construction of descriptive rules, or ROI and profit analysis. In general, these tools will allow the user much greater latitude in how the data mining functions but will, in general, still protect the user from any egregious error. For instance, these tools would either strongly warn the user or prevent the user from using a model that was not statistically valid and had been overfitted to the data.

17.10.4   Research analyst tools

The last class of commercial offerings is targeted at the data mining researcher or statistical analyst who desires the utmost control over the algorithm as well as the greatest latitude in choosing an algorithm. These offerings often include huge libraries of statistical, graphing, and visualization software and will be offered as the cutting edge in technology. These tools will generally be the first to include any new techniques coming out of the research labs or from academia.

From the business user's perspective, these tools should be wielded with extreme caution as they assume that the user has detailed knowledge about how the algorithms work. Consequently the user can easily create models that are significantly below optimal or are statistically invalid.

17.11   Comparing the Technologies

Most of the data mining technologies that are out there today are relatively new to the business community, and there are a lot of them (each technique usually is accompanied by a plethora of new companies and products). Given this state of affairs, one of the most important questions being asked right after "What is data mining?" is "Which technique(s) do I choose for my particular business problem?" The answer is, of course, not a simple one. There are inherent strengths and weaknesses of the different approaches, but most of the weaknesses can be overcome. How the technology is implemented into the data mining product can make all the difference in how easy the product is to use independent of how complex the underlying technology is.

The confusion over which data mining technology to use is further exacerbated by the data mining companies themselves who will often lead one to believe that their product is deploying a brand-new technology that is vastly superior to any other technology currently developed. Unfortunately this is rarely the case, and as we show in the chapters on modeling and comparing the technologies, it requires a great deal of discipline and good experimental method to fairly compare different data mining methods. More often than not, this discipline is not used when evaluating many of the newest technologies. Thus the claims of improved accuracy that are often made are not always defensible.

To appear to be different from the rest, many of the products that arrive on the market are packaged in a way so as to mask the inner workings of the data mining algorithm Many data mining companies emphasize the newness and the black-box nature of their technology. There will, in fact, be data mining offerings that seek to combine every possible new technology into their product in the belief that more is better. In fact, more technology is usually just more confusing and makes it more difficult to make a fair comparison between offerings. When these techniques are understood and their similarities researched, one will find that many techniques that appeared to initially be different when they were not well understood are, in fact, quite similar. For that reason the data mining technologies that are introduced in this book are the basics from which the thousands of subtle variations are made. If you can understand these technologies and where they can be used, you will probably understand better than 99 percent of all the techniques and products that are currently available.

To help compare the different technologies and make the business user a little more savvy in how to choose a technology, we have introduced a high-level system of score cards for each data mining technique described in this book. These score cards can be used by the reader as a first-pass high-level look at what the strengths and weaknesses are for each of the different techniques. Along with the score card will be a more detailed description of how the scores were arrived at, and if the score is low, what possible changes or workarounds could be made in the technique to improve the situation. The scores themselves will be based on the most common forms of the data mining algorithms and implementations, not on a particular implementation or product.

The first of the three score cards is the business score card, which captures the most salient features of the technology that matter most to the business user. At a more detailed level, the applications score card shows which application areas a particular technique performs well in and where it either can't be used or in general needs to be shoehorned into. The third scorecard, the algorithm score card, is the most detailed. It compares the technologies at the lowest levels of the data mining algorithm. How the data mining technology behaves on the algorithm scorecard directly affects the rating it achieves on the business and applications score cards. For instance, a high score in the ability to handle dirty data on the algorithm score card goes a long way toward a high score on the automation measure on the business score card.

17.11.1 Business score card

This score card, shown in Fig. 17.1 and Table 17.1, compares just those things that are possible given the underlying strengths and weaknesses of the particular data mining technique. It does not address issues of implementation—instead assuming that the implementation has been done optimally well so that accuracy and speed are not issues for this particular measure.

The business score card is used to assess business value of the data mining technique. The real-world problems of the business community are thus taken into consideration in evaluating the technique rather than some more academic measure of speed or performance. There are three measures for the most critical factors for building a usable data mining system into the business process. These measures reflect what ends up being some of the most critical aspects of whether a data mining systems is successfully deployed, is just an academic exercise, or becomes a case study in how *not* to implement such a system. The measures that are most critical to business success have to do with

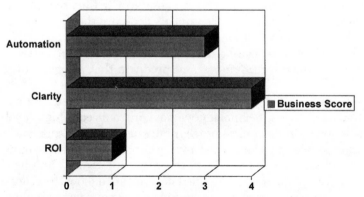

Figure 17.1   The business score card. This measures the overall impact of the data mining technology to a business.

TABLE 17.1   Requirements for Business Score Card Measures

Data mining measure	Description
Automation	Is the technique relatively automated and easy to use, or does it require a lot of expertise in data mining?
Clarity	Are the results that come out of the use of the technique clear and understandable, or are they complex and nonintuitive?
ROI	Is the technique useful for achieving bottom-line results and improved return on investment, or is it mostly an academic tool that is disconnected from day-to-day business requirements?

the ease of deployment and the real-world problems such as avoiding big mistakes as well as achieving major successes. To this end the data mining technique needs to be easy to use and deploy in as automated a fashion as possible (if data mining promises anything, it promises automation). The technique should also readily provide clear understandable answers that make business sense. And finally the technique needs to provide an answer that can be converted into ROI analysis—not just some academic exercise in prediction. These three measures are captured in the business score card as the "automation," "clarity," and "ROI" measures of the data mining technique.

17.11.2   Applications score card

The applications score card, as shown in Fig. 17.2 and Table 17.2, has been developed to aid in the choice of a data mining algorithm when it is to be used for a particular application. Some of the data mining techniques are better suited for one particular application than another mostly in terms of ease of use. For instance, decision trees and even neural networks can be used to generate rules from a database, but in general, if the application is to find all possible association rules or interesting rules in the database, rule induction

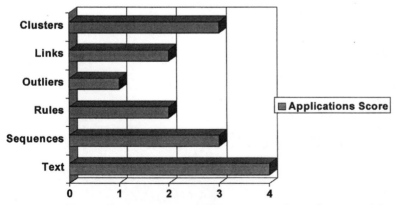

Figure 17.2   The applications score card. This measures the performance of the data mining technology on a variety of key applications.

TABLE 17.2   Requirements for Applications Score Card Measures

Application	Description
Clusters	Can the technique easily be used to perform clustering on input data?
Links	Can the technique be used to find links between records in the database?
Outliers	Can the technique be used to detect abnormal records and predictor values in the database?
Rules	Can the technique be used to efficiently create rules in the database, and does it have a proven technique for combining those rules to make predictions?
Sequences	Can the technique be used for time series or sequential data prediction?
Text	Can the technique be used for the clustering and prediction of textual information?

techniques are going to be the most efficient way to do this. Or consider that text retrieval and processing has been done with decision trees and neural networks but the most conceptually natural choice for this application is the nearest-neighbor algorithm.

17.11.3 Algorithmic score card

As we've stated in this chapter and throughout this book, data mining techniques have classically, and wrongly, been judged solely by their accuracy. And usually this accuracy is measured solely on the basis of a few well-chosen

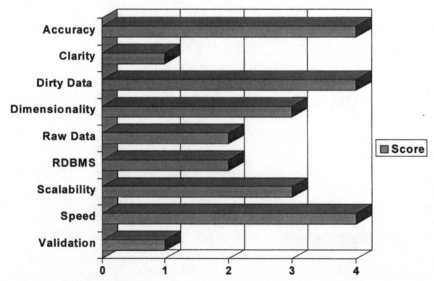

Figure 17.3 The algorithmic score card. This measures the data mining algorithm along several key indicators necessary for a good data mining algorithm.

TABLE 17.3   Requirements for Algorithmic Score Card Measures

Data mining measure	Description
Accuracy	How accurate is the data mining technology at getting the right answer?
Clarity	How clear is the data mining technology at explaining or exposing the model that is being used to make the prediction?
Dirty data	Can the algorithm handle data with missing values and errors in it in a graceful manner?
Dimensionality	How good is the data mining technique at working in high-dimensional spaces where there are many predictors?
Raw Data	Can the technique work with the predictor values pretty much as they appear in the original database, or does a lot of pre-processing need to be performed?
RDBMS	Is the technique amenable to being embedded directly into RDBMS data warehouse systems, or does it need to have proprietary data structures?
Scalability	Does the technique work on large numbers of records, and can it be implemented in parallel to gain performance for large numbers of records?
Speed	Is the data mining algorithm (measured in the time it takes to both build and use the model) inherently fast or slow?
Validation	Does the technique facilitate or automate the validation of the predictive model so that the end user feels confident that the right answer was arrived at?

examples. As we have seen when these techniques are used for real-world applications, a whole host of other factors come in to play in determining the overall effectiveness of the data mining technique, not the least of which is the ability of the technique to keep the user from making big mistakes.

The algorithmic score card, shown in Fig. 17.3 and Table 17.3, has been designed to help show the strengths and weaknesses of each technique on the basis of some very detailed measures at the level of the underlying algorithm itself (i.e., independent of the way the algorithm is implemented or the particular application to which it is being applied). For instance, accuracy is one of the measures used, but what good is the accuracy of the algorithm if it cannot adequately handle data which is corrupted or noisy to some degree or has missing values? Or also consider the fact that overall speed and scalability are critical in allowing the data mining algorithm to run in a reasonable amount of time and on sufficiently large databases but that a very fast technique that runs on 10 Gbytes of data in under 10 min is of little benefit if the extraction and preparation of the data takes more than a month. With these three score cards it should be much easier to see the strengths and weaknesses of each technique from the highest level of business utility down to the lowest level of actual algorithmic implementation. In general, these score cards are needed because there is currently no best answer in the choice of technique. Instead there are only good and bad choices for a particular business application, data store, and corporate infrastructure. The evaluations of these techniques should help you to pick the right one for your particular situation.

18

Decision Trees

18.1   What Is a Decision Tree?

A *decision tree* is a predictive model that, as its name implies, can be viewed as a tree. Specifically, each branch of the tree is a classification question, and the leaves of the tree are partitions of the data set with their classification. For instance, if we were going to classify customers who churn (don't renew their phone contracts) in the cellular telephone industry, a decision tree might look something like that found in Fig. 18.1.

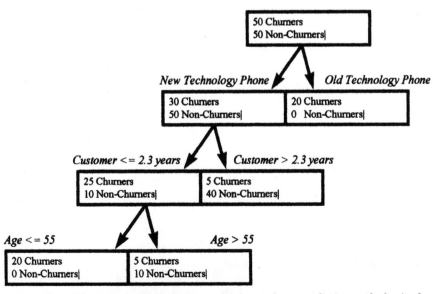

Figure 18.1   A decision tree is a predictive model that makes a prediction on the basis of a series of decisions much like the game of 20 questions.

You may notice some interesting things about the tree.

- It divides up the data on each branch point without losing any of the data (the number of total records in a given parent node is equal to the sum of the records contained in its two children).
- The number of churners and nonchurners is conserved as you move up or down the tree.
- It is pretty easy to understand how the model is being built (in contrast to the models from neural networks or from standard statistics).
- It would also be pretty easy to use this model if you actually had to target those customers who are likely to churn with a targeted marketing offer.
- You may also build some intuitions about your customer base, for example, "customers who have been with you for a couple of years and have up-to-date cellular phones and are pretty loyal."

From a business perspective, decision trees can be viewed as creating a segmentation of the original data set (each segment would be one of the leaves of the tree). Segmentation of customers, products, and sales regions is something that marketing managers have been doing for many years. In the past this segmentation has been performed in order to get a high-level view of a large amount of data—with no particular reason for creating the segmentation except that the records within each segmentation were somewhat similar to each other.

In this case the segmentation is done for a particular reason—namely, for the prediction of some important piece of information. The records that fall within each segment fall there because they have similarity with respect to the information being predicted—not just that they are similar—without "similarity" being well defined. These predictive segments that are derived from the decision tree also come with a description of the characteristics that define the predictive segment. Thus the decision trees and the algorithms that create them may be complex, but the results can be presented in an easy-to-understand way that can be quite useful to the business user.

18.2   Business Score Card

As can be seen in Fig. 18.2 and Table 18.1, decision trees are among the top scorers for data mining techniques applied to business. Because of their tree structure and ability to easily generate rules, they are the favored technique for building understandable models. Because of this clarity they also allow for more complex profit and ROI models to be added easily in on top of the predictive model. For instance, once a customer population is found with a high predicted likelihood to attrite (or leave the vendor), a variety of cost models can be used to see if an expensive marketing intervention should be used because the customers are highly valuable, or whether a less expensive intervention should be used because the revenue from this subpopulation of customers is marginal.

TABLE 18.1   Business Score Card for Decision Trees

Data mining measure	Description
Automation	Decision trees present a very favorable technique for automating most of the data mining and predictive modeling process. They embed automated solutions to such things as preventing overfitting and handling of missing data that most other techniques leave as a burden to the user.
Clarity	The models built by decision trees can be easily viewed as a tree of simple decisions based on familiar predictors or as a set of rules. The user can actually confirm the decision tree model by hand or modify it and direct it on the basis of their own expertise.
ROI	Because decision trees work well with relational databases, they provide well-integrated solutions with highly accurate models.

Because of their high level of automation and the ease of translating decision tree models into SQL for deployment in relational databases, the technology has also proved to be easy to integrate with existing IT processes, requiring little preprocessing and cleansing of the data, or extraction of a special-purpose file specifically for data mining.

18.3   Where to Use Decision Trees

Decision trees are a form of data mining technology that has been around in a form very similar to the technology of today for almost 20 years now, and early versions of the algorithms date back to the 1960s. Often these techniques were originally developed for statisticians to automate the process of determining which fields in their database were actually useful or correlated with the particular problem that they were trying to understand. Partly because of this history, decision tree algorithms tend to automate the entire process of hypothesis

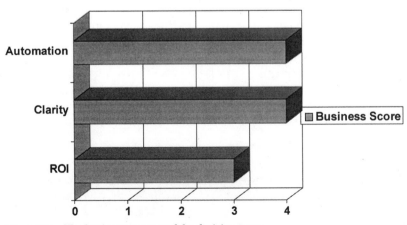

Figure 18.2   The business score card for decision trees.

generation and then validation much more completely and in a much more integrated way than any other data mining techniques. They are also particularly adept at handling raw data with little or no preprocessing. Perhaps also because they were originally developed to mimic the way an analyst interactively performs data mining, they provide a simple-to-understand predictive model based on rules (such as "90 percent of the time credit card customers of less than 3 months who max out their credit limits are going to default on their credit card loans").

Because decision trees score so highly on so many of the critical features of data mining, they can be used in a wide variety of business problems for both exploration and prediction. They have been used for problems ranging from credit card attrition prediction to time series prediction of the exchange rate of different international currencies. There are also some problems where decision trees will not do as well. Some very simple problems in which the prediction is just a simple multiple of the predictor can be solved much more quickly and easily by linear regression. Usually the models to be built and the interactions to be detected are much more complex in real-world problems, and this is where decision trees excel.

18.3.1   Exploration

The decision tree technology can be used for exploration of the data set and business problem. This is often done by looking at the predictors and values that are chosen for each split of the tree. Often these predictors provide usable insights or propose questions that need to be answered. For instance, if you ran across the following in your database for cellular phone churn, you might seriously wonder about the way your telesales operators were making their calls and maybe change the way that they are compensated: "IF customer lifetime < 1.1 years AND sales channel = telesales THEN chance of churn is 65 percent."

18.3.2   Data preprocessing

Another way that the decision tree technology has been used is for preprocessing data for other prediction algorithms. Because the algorithm is fairly robust with respect to a variety of predictor types (e.g., number, categorical) and because it can be run relatively quickly, decision trees can be used on the first pass of a data mining run to create a subset of possibly useful predictors that can then be fed into neural networks and nearest-neighbor and normal statistical routines—which can take a considerable amount of time to run if there are large numbers of possible predictors to be used in the model.

18.3.3   Prediction

Although some forms of decision trees were initially developed as exploratory tools to refine and preprocess data for more standard statistical techniques like logistic regression, they have also been used—and are now increasingly being used—for prediction. This is interesting because many statisticians will still use decision trees for exploratory analysis, effectively building a predictive model as a by-product but then ignore the predictive model in favor of techniques that they are most comfortable with. Sometimes veteran analysts will do this even excluding the predictive model when it is superior to that produced by other techniques. With a host of new products and skilled users now appearing in the industry, this tendency to use decision trees only for exploration now seems to be changing.

18.3.4   Applications score card

Figure 18.3 and Table 18.2 show the applications score card for decision trees. Decision trees are very versatile and have been shown to provide competitive models in a wide variety of application domains.

18.4   The General Idea

The general idea behind decision tree technologies is that these decision trees can be built from historical data. They are a form of supervised learning, although they are often used for exploratory analysis as well.

18.4.1   Growing the tree

The first step in the process is that of growing the tree. Specifically, the algorithm seeks to create a tree that works as perfectly as possible on all the data that is available. Most of the time it is not possible to have the algorithm work perfectly. There is always noise in the database to some degree (there are predictors that are not being collected that have an impact on the prediction target.

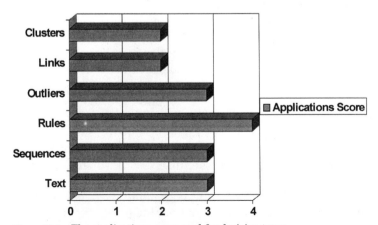

Figure 18.3   The applications score card for decision trees.

TABLE 18.2   Applications Score Card for Decision Trees

Application	Description
Clusters	Decision trees can be used for clustering, but because they are generally supervised learning techniques, the clustering is driven by some particular target prediction.
Links	Like most other techniques, decision trees can be used to find links between predictors in a database, although they are not particularly optimized for it.
Outliers	Outliers can be detected by noting the records that have very different predictors or prediction values within a particular leaf of the tree.
Rules	Rules can easily be translated out of the decision tree in order to make a better explanation.
Sequences	Decision trees have done as well as or better than other techniques in time series prediction.
Text	Decision trees have been used for text classification and information retrieval usually within some lower-dimensional space rather than the actual words of the text (such as topical categories).

The name of the game in growing the tree is to find the best possible question to ask at each branchpoint of the tree. The goal is to have the leaves of the tree be as homogeneous as possible with respect to the prediction value. Thus the question "Are you over 40?" probably does not sufficiently distinguish between those who are churners and those who are not—let's say that the percentage is 40/60. On the other hand, there may be a series of questions that do quite a nice job in distinguishing those cellular phone customers who will churn and those who won't. Maybe the series of questions would be something like "Have you been a customer for less than a year, do you have a telephone that is more than 2 years old, and were you originally landed as a customer via telesales rather than direct sales?" This series of questions defines a segment of the customer population in which 90 percent churn. These are then relevant questions to be asking in relation to predicting churn. The difference between a good question and a bad question has to do with how much the question can organize the data—or in this case, change the likelihood of a churner appearing in the customer segment. If we started off with our population being half churners and half nonchurners, then we would expect that a question that didn't organize the data to some degree into one segment that was more likely to churn than the other wouldn't be a very useful question to ask. On the other hand, a question that was very good at distinguishing between churners and nonchurners—say, that split 100 customers into one segment of 50 churners and another segment of 50 nonchurners—would be considered a good question. In fact, this question would have decreased the "disorder" of the original segment as much as possible.

The processes in decision tree algorithms are very similar when they build trees. These algorithms look at all possible distinguishing questions that could break up the data set into segments that are homogeneous with respect to the prediction values. Some decision tree algorithms may use heuristics in order to pick the questions or even pick them at random. Classification and Regression Trees (CART) picks the questions in a very unsophisticated way—it tries them all. After it has tried them all, CART picks the best one, uses it to split the data into two more organized segments, and then again asks all possible questions on each of those new segments individually.

18.4.2   When does the tree stop growing?

If the decision tree algorithm just continued like this, it could conceivably create more and more questions and branches in the tree so that eventually there was only one record in the segment. To let the tree grow to this size is computationally expensive and also unnecessary. Most decision tree algorithms stop growing the tree when one of three criteria are met:

1. The segment contains only one record or some algorithmically defined minimum number of records. (Clearly, there is no way to break a single-record segment into two smaller segments, and segments with very few records are not likely to be very helpful in the final prediction since the predictions that they are making won't be based on sufficient historical data.)

2. The segment is completely organized into just one prediction value. There is no reason to continue further segmentation since this data is now completely organized (the tree has achieved its goal).

3. The improvement in organization is not sufficient to warrant making the split. For instance, if the starting segment were 90 percent churners and the resulting segments from the best possible question were 90.001 percent churners and 89.999 percent churners, then not much progress would have been or could be made by continuing to build the tree.

18.4.3   Why would a decision tree algorithm prevent the tree from growing if there weren't enough data?

Consider the following example (shown also in Table 18.3) of a segment that we might want to split further because it has only two examples. Assume that it has been created out of a much larger customer database by selecting only those customers aged 27 with blue eyes and with salaries ranging between $80,000 and $81,000.

In this case all the possible questions that could be asked about the two customers turn out to have the same value (age, eye color, salary) except for name.

TABLE 18.3   Decision Tree Algorithm Segment*

Name	Age	Eyes	Salary ($)	Churned?
Steve	27	Blue	80,000	Yes
Alex	27	Blue	80,000	No

* This segment cannot be split further except by using the predictor "name."

It would then be possible to ask a question like "Is the customer's name Steve?" and create the segments which would be very good at breaking apart those who churned from those who did not.

The problem is that we all have an intuition that the name of the customer is not going to be a very good indicator of whether that customer churns or not. It might work well for this particular two-record segment, but it is unlikely to work for other customer databases or even the same customer database at a different time. This particular example has to do with overfitting the model—in this case fitting the model too closely to the idiosyncrasies of the training data. This can be fixed later on, but clearly, stopping the building of the tree short of either one record segments or very small segments in general is a good idea.

18.4.4   Decision trees aren't necessarily finished after they are fully grown

After the tree has been grown to a certain size (depending on the particular stopping criteria used in the algorithm), the CART algorithm has still more work to do. The algorithm then checks to see if the model has been overfit to the data. It does this in several ways using a cross-validation approach or a test set validation approach—basically using the same mind-numbingly simple approach it used to find the best questions in the first place: trying many different simpler versions of the tree on a held-aside test set. The tree that does the best on the held-aside data is selected by the algorithm as the best model. The nice thing about CART is that this testing and selection is all an integral part of the algorithm as opposed to the after-the-fact approach that other techniques use.

18.4.5   Are the splits at each level of the tree always binary yes/no splits?

There are several different methods of building decision trees, some of which can make splits on multiple values at time—for instance, eye color: green, blue, and brown. But recognize that any tree that can do binary splits can effectively partition the data in the same way by just building two levels of the tree: the first, which splits brown and blue from green; and the second, which splits apart the brown and blue split. Either way, the minimum number of questions you need to ask is two.

18.4.6   Picking the best predictors

An obvious question at this point would be how decision trees pick one particular predictor over another one to make a split on the data set (noting here, of course, that it does need to make some kind of a choice since only one predictor is used at each branchpoint of the tree). To do so they create a numeric measure of goodness of split that seems to map in a reasonable way to what they are looking for in terms of decreasing the disorder of the dataset. For instance, we have a general intuition that the split shown in Table 18.4 is a really good one but that the one shown in Table 18.5 is not very helpful.

Name	Churned?
TABLE 18.4 Decision Tree Algorithm Segment*	
Segment 1	
Jim	Yes
Sally	Yes
Steve	Yes
Joe	Yes
Segment 2	
Bob	No
Betty	No
Sue	No
Alex	No

* An example of the best possible split on the data creates two segments, each homogeneous in the values of the prediction.

Name	Churned?
TABLE 18.5 Example of a Split that Makes No Improvements on the Data*	
Segment 1	
Bob	No
Betty	No
Steve	Yes
Joe	Yes
Segment 2	
Jim	Yes
Sally	Yes
Sue	No
Alex	No

* Both segments have mixed values for the prediction.

In the first split we broke the original 8-record segment with 50 percent churners into two 4-record segments—one with 100 percent churners and one with 0 percent churners. In the second split we went from the original 50 percent churner segment into two 50 percent churner segments. Thus in the first split we created a segment in which we could predict churn at a very high confidence level (100 percent); for the second split, we could predict churn no better than we did in the original segment (50 percent) and really wouldn't have made any progress.

There is, in fact, a plethora of different calculations that could be performed to order the predictors and pick the best one. As is described above, the main characteristic of the predictor's split that is used is the change in the densities of the prediction's values after the split is made. One can think about this as effectively reducing the disorder of the original segment into smaller segments that are more orderly (more concentrated in particular prediction values). When the prediction has just two values, one can effectively think of this process as a "teasing apart" of the two values—like a shepherd separating out the black sheep from the white sheep into different holding pens.

18.4.7   Picking the right predictor value for the split

We've got some idea now of what makes a good split and a bad split but there is something we haven't mentioned yet—specifically, that even if you know what predictor to split on, the algorithm still needs to know what value in that predictor to use. For instance, if the algorithm were going to use age as the predictor to split a given segment into two halves, which age value should it use? Age 50? Because that is half way between 0 and the oldest person in your database? Or maybe split on all possible ages and break the segment up into 100 much smaller segments of age 1, 2, 3, . . . , 100? Or just pick a random age? Maybe it doesn't matter that much?

In fact, it does matter, but just as there are ways to measure the efficacy of each predictor in making a split, it is also possible to measure the efficacy of each possible split value of the predictor. Consider that if we ordered our 10 records by age, we would indeed get different types of splits (some more valuable than others) for a given predictor. Consider the example data in Table 18.6.

The best possible split value would have left and right densities with percentage ratios of either 100/0 or 0/100; since these values are not available in the database, the splitting value that most closely approximates these values should be chosen. A likely candidate might be at Sally's age of 46, where the split is 80/20 since the lesser and greater ages surrounding it (age 47 for Bob and age 32 for Joe) are not as good. A case could be made for the split at Steve's age of 27 which results in a 100/38 split—it all depends on the measure in the algorithm that is used to build the decision tree. There are a few things to notice in this simple example:

- Not all possible ages needed to be tested. Only those ages that actually appeared in the database needed to be tried out since any age that wasn't in the database would end up with a split no better than the nearest age that was in the database. For example, if we tried to split on age 51, we would still have the same concentrations of churners on either side of the split as we would for Betty's age of 53 since there is no one in the database who actually was of age 51.

- There is no "perfect" split. No matter what split value is chosen, the segments will always be inhomogeneous with respect to the prediction value. It is, in fact, rare to find a perfect split except on very small amounts of data, and that split probably would not be statistically significant.

- What is considered to be the best split may depend on the particular application. Some splits may be less accurate but apply to more data and be more

TABLE 18.6 Data Table Ordered by Age Showing Probabilities of Positive and Negative Target Predictions (Churn/No Churn) for the Two Resulting Segments at Each Possible Split Value

Name	Age	Churned?	Split value	Left split	Right split
Karen	21	Yes	≤21	100% (1/1)	44% (4/9)
Steve	27	Yes	≤27	100% (2/2)	38% (3/8)
Alex	27	No	≤27	67% (2/3)	43% (3/7)
Joe	32	Yes	≤32	75% (3/4)	33% (2/6)
Sally	46	Yes	≤46	80% (4/5)	20% (1/5)
Bob	47	No	≤47	67% (4/6)	25% (1/4)
Ray	50	Yes	≤50	71% (5/7)	0% (0/3)
Betty	53	No	≤53	62% (5/8)	0% (0/2)
Jim	62	No	≤62	56% (5/9)	0% (0/1)
Sue	68	No	≤68		

statistically significant. And the errors created by each segment might be weighted differently (for instance, it is far more costly to miss a fraudulent phone card user than to be overcautious and double-check a suspicious but harmless set of phone calls).

18.5   How the Decision Tree Works

In the late 1970s J. Ross Quinlan introduced a decision tree algorithm named *ID3*. This was one of the first decision tree algorithms though it was built solidly on previous work on inference systems and concept learning systems from that decade and the preceding decade. Initially ID3 was used for tasks such as learning good game-playing strategies for chess end games. Since then ID3 has been applied to a wide variety of problems in both academia and industry and has been modified, improved, and borrowed from many times over.

ID3 picks predictors and their splitting values on the basis of the gain in information that the split or splits provide. *Gain* represents the difference between the amount of information that is needed to correctly make a prediction both before and after the split has been made (if the amount of information required is much lower after the split is made, then that split has decreased the disorder of the original single segment) and is defined as the difference between the *entropy* of the original segment and the accumulated entropies of the resulting split segments. Entropy is a well-defined measure of the disorder or information found in data. It is further defined in Sec. 18.5.4.

The entropies of the child segments are accumulated by weighting their contribution to the entire entropy of the split according to the number of records they contain. For instance, which of the two splits shown in Table 18.7 would you think decreased the entropy the most and thus would provide the largest gain?

Split A is actually a much better split than B because it separates out more of the data despite the fact that split B creates a new segment that is perfectly homogeneous (0 entropy). The problem is that this perfect zero-entropy segment has only one record in it and splitting off one record at a time will not create a very useful decision tree. The small number of records in each segment (i.e., 1) is unlikely to provide useful repeatable patterns. The calculation (met-

TABLE 18.7   Two Possible Splits for Eight Records with Calculation of Entropy for Each Split Shown*

Candidate	Left split	Right split	Left entropy	Right entropy
Split A	+ + + + −	+ − − − −	$-\frac{4}{5}\lg(\frac{4}{5}) + -\frac{1}{5}\lg(\frac{1}{5}) = 0.72$	$-\frac{1}{4}\lg(\frac{1}{4}) + -\frac{3}{4}\lg(\frac{3}{4}) = 0.72$
Split B	+ + + + + − − −	−	$-\frac{5}{8}\lg(\frac{5}{8}) + -\frac{3}{8}\lg(\frac{3}{8}) = 0.99$	$-\frac{1}{1}\lg(\frac{1}{1}) + -\frac{0}{1}\lg(\frac{0}{1}) = 0$

* The positive and negative values for the prediction target are represented by plus and minus signs, respectively.

ric) that we use to determine which split is chosen should make the correct choice in this case and others like it. The metric needs to take into account two main effects:

- How much has the disorder been lowered in the new segments?

- How should the disorder in each segment be weighted?

The entropy measure can easily be applied to each of the new segments as easily as it was applied to the parent segment to answer the first question, but the second criterion is a bit harder. Should all segments that result from a split be treated equally? This question needs to be answered in the example above where the split has produced a perfect new segment but with little real value because of its size. If we just took the average entropy for the new segments, we would choose split B since in that case the average of 0.99 and 0.0 is around 0.5 We can also do this calculation for split A and come up with an average entropy of 0.72 for the new segments.

If, on the other hand, we weighted the contribution of each new segment with respect to the size of the segment (and consequently how much of the database that segment explained), we would get a quite different measure of the disorder across the two new segments. In this case the weighted entropy of the two segments for split A is the same as before but the weighted entropy of split B is quite a bit higher. (See Table 18.8.)

Since the name of this game is to reduce entropy to as little as possible, we are faced with two different choices of which is the best split. If we average the entropies of the new segments, we would pick split B; if we took into account the number of records that are covered by each split, we would pick split A.

ID3 uses the weighted entropy approach as it has been found, in general, to produce better predictions than just averaging the entropy. Part of the reason for this may be that, as we have seen from the modeling chapter, that the more data that is used in a prediction, the more likely the prediction is to be correct and the more likely the model is to match the true underlying causal reasons and processes that are actually at work in forming the prediction values.

TABLE 18.8   Weighting the Entropy Values for Two Possible Shifts*

Candidate	Left split	Right split	Average entropy	Weighted entropy
Split A	+ + + + −	+ − − − −	$0.72 = (0.72 + 0.72)/2$	$0.72 = (\frac{1}{2}) * 0.72 + (\frac{1}{2}) * 0.72$
Split B	+ + + + + − − − −	−	$0.50 = (0.99 + 0)/2$	$0.89 = (\frac{9}{10}) * 0.99 + (\frac{1}{10}) * 0.0$

* The better of the two possible splits can be chosen when the entropies are weighted by the size of the resulting segments.

18.5.1 Handling high-cardinality predictors in ID3

So far we have shown a simple example for ID3 in which the possible splits on the predictor were solely binary (e.g., male/female, old/young, tall/short). There are other predictors available that have many more values than just two. There are those with a small number of values such as eye color (brown, blue, green) or hair color (blond, brown, black, red), but there are also predictors with a very large number of different values, such as the number of *stockkeeping units* (SKUs) for a grocery store, which are the individual identification numbers assigned to each different product on the store's shelves. A typical grocery store has 60,000 different SKUs at any one time. This large number of values for a given predictor poses a new and unique problem for the ID3 algorithm.

The algorithm itself can be easily modified to accommodate multivalued predictors. The entropy equation can be calculated in the same way within each resulting segment, and the weighted entropy equation can be extended by weighting each new segment by the fraction of the parent segment data that it contains. The problem is that with very large numbers of values for a predictor, these equations, if unaltered, will again favor the formation of many small segments with little or no data contained in them over other splits that have much more substantial amounts of data in each resulting segment. This type of predictor is given the same name as a database column with the same characteristic: high cardinality. In the case of a database this is important because it affects the performance and hence the choice of indexing algorithm. In the case of the decision tree algorithm it is important because it affects the accuracy of the resulting model.

Like many other techniques, ID3 has been improved to handle high-cardinality predictors. A *high-cardinality predictor* is one that has many different possible values and hence many different possible ways of performing a split. We could see one of the classic problems with using a high-cardinality predictor if we used the customer name field as the predictor for churn. This may seem like an obviously dumb thing to do, but keep in mind that most decision trees are sufficiently automated that they can be given any set of predictors and will automatically pick the best one. So while you, as the decision tree user, may be smart enough to keep the customer name out of the analysis, you might forget about many other high-cardinality predictors such as Social Security numbers or even postal zip codes. Eliminating fields is also something we'd like to have the decision tree automate for the user. To do this, the measure for picking the best split that the decision tree is using needs to be improved.

Assume that our measure of performance for picking a split was based on

1. The amount that the disorder (entropy) of the original data segment was reduced.
2. The relative sizes of the resulting segments so that the disorder reduction was weighted to give more weight to the larger resulting segments.

These two criteria solved many of our problems, but the issue of high-cardinality predictors (which is related to the problem in statistics of a large number of degrees of freedom) is actually still unsolved. Consider the following example, where we have split the records by the name of the customer and have created 10 resultant segments from our 10-record database. Since each segment is homogeneous (made up entirely of all churners or nonchurners but containing only one record) the entropy for each resulting segment is 0 (there is now no disorder). All the segments are of equal size, so their weights are identical and thus their weighted entropy is also zero. Thus there is no other split possible that could do any better than this one (including using the prediction field itself as a predictor). This is clearly a problem since our splitting metric would choose customer name as the best predictor to split on in this case, yet using customer name will result in a model that can never be used except on historical data.

To correctly accommodate high-cardinality predictors, the splitting metric used in ID3 can be improved. Instead of just taking the weighted entropy as a measure of the gain of the system, the improved metric takes into account the cardinality of the predictor as well. The new metric is called the *gain ratio,* and unlike the gain, it is relatively smaller if the cardinality of the predictor is high, all other things being equal. It is calculated by figuring out the entropy on the relative sizes of the resulting segments. For instance, in the case of the customer name predictor above, one-tenth of the records falls into each of the new segments. The fractions of the dataset that fall into each segment are just like the fractions of the prediction values within any given segment. Both can be viewed as probabilities:

- The first is the probability that any record from the parent segment falls into a particular child segment.
- The second is the probability that, given that a record has fallen into a given child segment, it has a particular prediction value.

Calculating the entropy on this new set of probabilities is identical to the way it was calculated before—the negative of the summation of each probability multiplied by its logarithm base 2. For the customer name predictor, the gain ratio would be the gain divided by the entropy of the segment sizes. The entropy of the parent segment is 1.0 (since it is maximally disordered, consisting of half-churners and half-nonchurners), the entropy of the child segments, as we said before, is 0.0, so the gain is 1.0 (1.0 − 0.0).

The entropy of the split itself is just

$$3.32 = -\tfrac{1}{10} \lg(\tfrac{1}{10}) - \tfrac{1}{10} \lg(\tfrac{1}{10}) - \tfrac{1}{10} \lg(\tfrac{1}{10}) - \tfrac{1}{10} \lg(\tfrac{1}{10}) - \tfrac{1}{10} \lg(\tfrac{1}{10})$$

$$- \tfrac{1}{10} \lg(\tfrac{1}{10}) - \tfrac{1}{10} \lg(\tfrac{1}{10}) - \tfrac{1}{10} \lg(\tfrac{1}{10}) - \tfrac{1}{10} \lg(\tfrac{1}{10}) - \tfrac{1}{10} \lg(\tfrac{1}{10})$$

The gain ratio is then the gain divided by the entropy of the split or: 0.3 = 1.0/3.32.

To give some idea of how this helps, compare this gain ratio number to the value we would calculate on the previous best split (split A) above. In this case split A split the 10 records evenly into two 5-record segments. The entropy of the split itself would be

$$1.0 = -\tfrac{5}{10} \lg(\tfrac{5}{10}) - \tfrac{5}{10} \lg(\tfrac{5}{10})$$

Since the gain on split A was 0.28, the gain ratio would be 0.28 = 0.28/1.0.

In this case the high-cardinality field (customer name) would still be chosen by the algorithm as the better of the two, but it is a much closer decision than if the gain had been used rather than the gain ratio. However, this is not an optimal choice since it is unlikely that there is any kind of causal relationship between a customer's first name and likelihood to churn. This relationship would be expected to hold up when the tree was tested. With some decision tree techniques such as CART, the metric for choosing splits might also erroneously allow high-cardinality splits to occur, but because a pruning process is used inside the algorithm that tests the tree against held-aside data, it is likely that an erroneous split would be eliminated during this phase of the algorithm.

18.5.2   C4.5 Enhances ID3

C4.5 is an enhancement of the ID3 algorithm that improves the performance of the algorithm in several areas:

- Predictors with missing values can still be used.
- Predictors with continuous values can be used.
- Pruning is introduced.
- Rules can be derived.

Many of these techniques appear in the CART algorithm as well, so we will introduce them by way of CART.

18.5.3   CART definition

Classification and Regression Trees (CART) is a data exploration and prediction algorithm developed by Leo Breiman, Jerome Friedman, Richard Olshen, and Charles Stone and is nicely detailed in their 1984 book *Classification and Regression Trees* (Breiman et al., 1984). These researchers from Stanford University and the University of California at Berkeley showed how this new algorithm could be used on a variety of different problems, such as the detection of chlorine from the data contained in a mass spectrum.

18.5.4   Predictors are picked as they decrease the disorder of the data

In building the CART tree each predictor is picked based on how well it teases apart the records with different predictions. For instance, one measure that is used to determine whether a given split point for a given predictor is better than another is the *entropy metric*. The measure originated from the work done by Claude Shannon and Warren Weaver on information theory in 1949. They were concerned with how information could be efficiently communicated over telephone lines. Interestingly, their results also prove useful in creating decision trees.

The information equation they derived is simply

$$-\sum p \lg(p)$$

where p is the probability of that prediction value occurring in a particular node of the tree. Since p is a probability, it has a minimum value of 0.0 and a maximum value of 1.0. Thus the value of disorder can also go from a minimum of 0.0 to a maximum disorder of 1.0.

For instance, if we had a node in the tree in which we were trying to predict churn or no churn for a cellular telephone company's customers and we had the numbers

- 100 total customers in the node

- 30 who churn

- 70 who don't churn

we would know that the probability of churning in the node is $^{30}/_{100}$ or $p = 0.3$ and that nonchurning is $^{70}/_{100}$ or $p = 0.7$. The disorder measure from Shannon and Weaver would be

$$-0.3 * \lg(0.3) + -0.7 * \lg(0.7) = (-0.3 * -1.74) + (-0.7 * -0.514) = 0.412$$

Consider the optimal node in terms of prediction where every record is of one prediction value or the other:

- 100 total customers in the node

- 100 who churn

- 0 who don't churn

In this case we would hope that the measure of disorder would be lower or, in fact, as low as it can go since this is the best possible node. The value of disorder for this node is, in fact, 0.0:

$$-1.0 * \lg(1.0) + -0.0 * \lg(0.0) = -1.0 * 0.0 + -0.0 * \infty = 0.0$$

At the other extreme, the metric also behaves appropriately. In this case almost no order has been imposed on the node, and the disorder is at a maximum:

- 100 total customers in the node

- 50 who churn

- 50 who don't churn

Here we would expect the disorder measure to be higher so that when choosing predictors and splits, the metric will favor the splits and predictors that are important to the prediction; in the case of decision trees for predictive modeling the entropy measure is

$$-0.5 * \lg(0.5) + -0.5 * \lg(0.5) = -0.5 * -1.0 + -0.5 * -1.0 = 1.0$$

So the worst possible node in a decision tree also corresponds to the maximum disorder value from the entropy equation.

Other metrics that are often used are the *twoing metric* and the *Gini diversity index*. The *Gini value* for a given segment is calculated to be one minus the sum of squared probabilities for each prediction. Thus the Gini value will be greatest when the proportions of each prediction value are equivalent (also the highest entropy) and lowest (equal to zero) when the segment is homogeneous. The Gini metric, like the entropy metric in ID3, is weighted by the probability of the segment (proportionate size of the segment) in order to compare the overall reduction in the Gini value due to a particular split. The *twoing criterion* is similar to the Gini criterion but tends to favor more balanced splits (more equivalent-sized segments), which can be an advantage in avoiding the "dangling" node problem where a split is chosen to create a very small segment while the majority of the records in the parent segment are moved into a nearly equivalent-sized child segment. If the power used in the Gini calculation is raised above 2 (e.g., going from the square of the probabilities to the cube), it tends to also favor more balanced splits.

18.5.5 CART splits unordered predictors by imposing order on them

One of the remaining hard questions for CART is how it determines the split on a predictor with unordered values. For instance, a two-way split on hair color could result in many different possible splits:

- Brown, blond ‖ black, red

- Brown ‖ blond, black, red

- Brown, blond, black ‖ red

- Brown, red ‖ black, blond

Because this is an unordered categorical predictor, there is no order on the values (e.g., brown cannot be less or greater than blond), and the total number of even binary splits that could conceivably be tried can become immense for even moderately high-cardinality predictors. To solve this problem, CART imposes an order on the values which can be proved to dramatically limit the total number of splits that needs to be tried without the possibility of missing the optimal split.

18.5.6   CART automatically validates the tree

One of the great advantages of CART is that the algorithm has the validation of the model and the discovery of the optimally general model built deeply into the algorithm. CART accomplishes this by building a very complex tree and then pruning it back to the optimally general tree on the basis of the results of cross-validation or test set validation. The tree is pruned back according to the performance of the various pruned versions of the tree on the test set data. The most complex tree rarely fares the best on the held-aside data as it has been overfitted to the training data. By using cross-validation, the tree that is most likely to do well on new, unseen data can be chosen.

18.5.7   CART surrogates handle missing data

The CART algorithm is relatively robust with respect to missing data. If the value is missing for a particular predictor in a particular record, that record will not be used in determination of the optimal split when the tree is being built. In effect, CART will utilize as much information as it has on hand in order to make the decision for picking the best possible split.

When CART is being used to predict on new data, missing values can be handled via surrogates. *Surrogates* are split values and predictors that mimic the actual split in the tree and can be used when the data for the preferred predictor is missing. For instance, although shoe size is not a perfect predictor of height, it could be used as a surrogate to try to mimic a split based on height when that information was missing from the particular record being predicted with the CART model.

18.5.8   CHAID

Another equally popular decision tree technology beside CART is CHAID (Chi square Automatic Interaction Detector). CHAID is similar to CART in that it builds a decision tree but differs in the way that it chooses its splits. Instead of the entropy or Gini metrics for choosing optimal splits, the technique relies on the chi square test used in contingency tables to determine which categorical predictor is farthest from independence with the prediction values. Because CHAID relies on the contingency tables to form its test of significance for each predictor, all predictors must be either categorical or coerced into a categorical form via binning (e.g., break up people's ages into 10 bins from 0 to 9, 10 to 19, 20 to 29). Although this binning can have deleterious consequences, the actual accuracy performances of CART and CHAID have been shown to be comparable in real-world direct marketing response models.

18.6   Case Study: Predicting Wireless Telecommunications Churn with CART

Churn in the wireless telecommunications (cellular telephone) market could easily be the industry's number one problem today. Even worse, within months of this writing, the industry will be opened up through a new technology so that the current maximum of two computing cellular providers per region will quickly grow to six or more.

Customer churn is the term used in the cellular telecommunications industry to denote the movement of cellular telephone customers from one provider to another. In many industries this is called *customer attrition,* but because of the highly volatile and growing market and the current limited competition, many customers churn from one provider to another frequently in search of better rates or even for the perks of signing up with a new provider—like receiving a new-technology cellular phone.

The problem is severe in the wireless industry. While other industries like the credit card industry struggle with attrition rates hovering around 5 percent per year, the industry average for the cellular industry is 2.2 percent per month—or about 27 percent of a given carrier's customers are lost each year. Over time it looks even worse. J. D. Power and Associates estimates that 90 percent of cellular users have churned at least once in the last 5 years.

Losing these customers can be very expensive as it costs $300 to $600 to acquire a new customer in sales support, marketing, advertising, and commissions and many of these new customers are less profitable than the ones that were lost. The average monthly bill has decreased from $84 in 1990 to just $52 in 1995. At these rates it takes a wireless company nearly the full year of the initial contract just to recover its costs of acquisition.

Clearly, if a predictive model could be built for churn in the wireless industry, substantial money could be saved by more focused targeting of at-risk customers and by building an understanding of which factors indicated high-risk customers. For instance, consider a moderate-sized cellular phone company of 500,000 customers with the industry-average churn rate of 25 percent. Even if their acquisition costs were uncommonly low, at $300, they could still realize a $7.5 million savings if they could produce a predictive model that would help them reduce churn by only 5 percent.

Because of the high cost of churn and the opportunity to prevent it, several companies have begun to provide targeted applications and consulting to build predictive models specifically for churn in the telecom industry. One such company is Lightbridge Inc. of Burlington, Massachusetts, which uses CART as part of its Churn Prophet (trademark) application for building and deploying predictive models in the telecom industry.

When deployed against a database from one of the largest cellular providers in the region, the CART model produced was able to identify 50 percent of the provider's churners within the first 10 percent of the customer base, thus providing a lift of 5 or an increase in the predicted density of churners of fivefold over a mass marketing approach of targeting churners. The entire lift chart is shown in Fig. 18.4, and a high-level view of the decision tree itself is shown in Fig. 18.5.

Because CART was able to express the rules that were used in the model, the carrier was also able to glean some valuable insights into what caused their customers to be loyal or at risk of churning. For instance, some of these patterns included

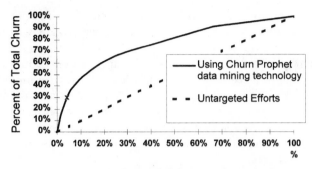

Figure 18.4 Lift chart for the predictive model for cellular phone churn using the CART algorithm through the commercial product Churn Prophet (trademark) from Lightbridge, Inc.

- Subscribers who call Customer Service are more, not less, loyal to the carrier and are less likely to churn.
- Only the first-year anniversary appears to be a vulnerable time for customers. After the customer weathers the first anniversary without churn, the later anniversaries are relatively unpredictive.

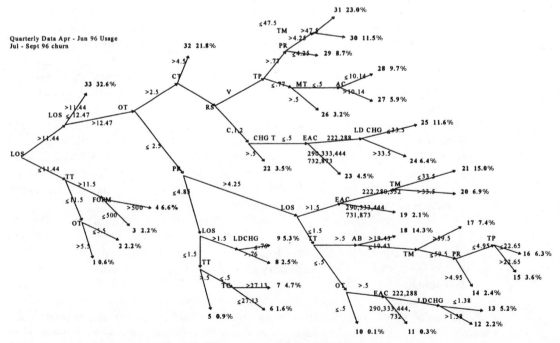

Figure 18.5   A high-level view of the CART tree produced for the cellular churn prediction.

- Several high-value customer segments were found to be at particularly high risk.
- A geographic region of the northeastern United States was discovered to have the beneficial findings of high-value customers as well as lower-than-average churn rates.

18.7   Strengths and Weaknesses

The technology of decision trees spans a wide area that includes algorithms that have been derived from the fields of artificial intelligence, statistics, and hybrids between the two. For instance, ID3 definitively grew out of the field of AI and CHAID, from statistics. CART, on the other hand, grew up somewhere in between.

18.7.1   Algorithm score card

In general, the strengths of the decision tree come from its ability to create understandable models that are highly automated in their construction (specifically with the embedding of techniques to prevent overfitting). The systems respond well to missing and noisy data, although, because the prediction is made by well-defined decisions, there is a chance that dirty or noisy data in a predictor that is used at a branchpoint could lead to an incorrect answer. Overall, though, decision trees receive high marks in the algorithmic score card presented in Fig. 18.6 and Table 18.9.

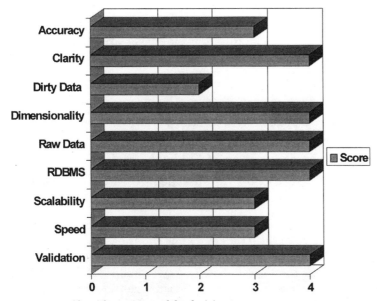

Figure 18.6   Algorithm score card for decision trees.

TABLE 18.9   Algorithm Score Card for Decision Trees

Data mining measure	Description
Accuracy	Although, in practice, decision trees are equal or superior to most other data mining techniques, there are some simple linear problems in which they can produce overly complex models.
Clarity	Because of the representation of the model as a tree, rules can be extracted and the model can be clearly seen.
Dirty data	The algorithm accommodates missing values quite well by either working around them or using surrogates to mimic their effect. Dirty data can sometimes cause the creation of less-than-optimal trees and cause misclassification.
Dimensionality	Decision trees handle large numbers of predictors very well and often are used as a preprocessing step to provide only selected predictors to data mining algorithms such as neural networks which have difficulty with high-dimensional spaces.
Raw data	Decision trees in general and CART in particular require almost no preprocessing of data, although CHAID does require binning.
RDBMS	Decision tree models are easily translated into SQL that can be executed directly on an RDBMS.
Scalability	Highly efficient MPP and SMP implementations of decision trees have been created.
Speed	The model building process of decision trees is comparable to other techniques. The application of the model is faster than most other techniques. The overall model building process is significantly faster as it is more automated than any other data mining or statistical technique.
Validation	Validation is built into most of the decision tree techniques.

18.7.2   State of the industry

The current offerings in decision tree software emphasize different important aspects and use of the algorithm. The different emphases are usually driven because of differences in the targeted user and the types of problems being solved. There are four main categories of products:

- *Business*—those that emphasize ease of use for the business users

- *Performance*—those that emphasize the overall performance and database size

- *Exploratory*—those that emphasize ease of use for the analyst

- *Research*—those tailored specifically for detailed research or academic experimentation

Tools such as Pilot Software's Discovery Server fall into the category of business use. The Pilot Discovery Server (trademark) provides easy-to-use graphical tools to help the business user express their modeling problem and also provides applications such as the Pilot Segment Viewer and Pilot Profit Chart (both trademarks) to allow business end users to visualize the model and perform simple profit/loss models on different targeted marketing applications. A tool that falls into the performance category would be Thinking Machines Corporation's StarTree tool, which implements CART on MPP and SMP computer hardware and has been optimized for large databases and difficult-to-solve problems. Angoss' Knowledge Seeker (trademark) tool, on the other hand, is targeted mostly at the PC user but provides more control to the analyst to specify different parameters that control the underlying CHAID algorithm, if desired. Salford Systems' CART product provides even more control over the underlying algorithms but provides only limited GUI or applications support; however, it is useful to researchers and business analysts who want in-depth analysis and control over their model creation.

19

Neural Networks

19.1   What Is a Neural Network?

When data mining algorithms are discussed these days, people are usually talking about either decision trees or neural networks. Of the two, neural networks have probably been of greater interest through the formative stages of data mining technology. As we will see, neural networks do have disadvantages that can be limiting in their ease of use and ease of deployment, but they do also have some significant advantages. Foremost among these advantages are their highly accurate predictive models, which can be applied across a large number of different types of problems.

To be more precise, the term *neural network* might be defined as an "artificial" neural network. True neural networks are biological systems [also known as (a.k.a.) *brains*] that detect patterns, make predictions, and learn. The artificial ones are computer programs implementing sophisticated pattern detection and machine learning algorithms on a computer to build predictive models from large historical databases. Artificial neural networks derive their name from their historical development, which started off with the premise that machines could be made to "think" if scientists found ways to mimic the structure and functioning of the human brain on the computer. Thus historically neural networks grew out of the community of artificial intelligence rather than from the discipline of statistics. Although scientists are still far from understanding the human brain, let alone mimicking it, neural networks that run on computers can do some of the things that people can do.

It is difficult to say exactly when the first "neural network" on a computer was built. During World War II a seminal paper was published by McCulloch and Pitts which first outlined the idea that simple processing units (like the individual neurons in the human brain) could be connected together in large networks to create a system that could solve difficult problems and display behavior that was much more complex than the simple pieces that made it up. Since that time much progress has been made in finding ways to apply artificial neural networks to real-world prediction problems and improving the performance of the algorithm in general. In many respects the greatest breakthroughs in neural networks in recent years have been in their application to more mundane real-world problems such as customer response prediction or fraud detection rather than the loftier goals that were originally set out for the techniques such as overall human learning and computer speech and image understanding.

19.1.1 Don't neural networks learn to make better predictions?

Because of the origins of the techniques and because of some of their early successes, the techniques have enjoyed a great deal of interest. To understand how neural networks can detect patterns in a database, an analogy is often made that they "learn" to detect these patterns and make better predictions, similar to the way human beings do. This view is encouraged by the way the historical training data is often supplied to the network—one record (example) at a time. Neural networks do "learn" in a very real sense, but under the hood, the algorithms and techniques that are being deployed are not truly different from the techniques found in statistics or other data mining algorithms. It is, for instance, unfair to assume that neural networks could outperform other techniques because they "learn" and improve over time while the other techniques remain static. The other techniques, in fact, "learn" from historical examples in exactly the same way, but often the examples (historical records) to learn from are processed all at once in a more efficient manner than are neural networks, which often modify their model one record at a time.

19.1.2 Are neural networks easy to use?

A common claim for neural networks is that they are automated to a degree where the user does not need to know that much about how they work, or about predictive modeling or even the database in order to use them. The implicit claim is also that most neural networks can be unleashed on your data straight out of the box without the need to rearrange or modify the data very much to begin with.

Just the opposite is often true. Many important design decisions need to be made in order to effectively use a neural network, such as

- How should the nodes in the network be connected?
- How many neuronlike processing units should be used?
- When should "training" be stopped in order to avoid overfitting?

There are also many important steps required for preprocessing the data that goes into a neural network—most often there is a requirement to normalize numeric data between 0.0 and 1.0, and categorical predictors may need to be broken up into virtual predictors that are 0 or 1 for each value of the original categorical predictor. And, as always, understanding what the data in your database means and a clear definition of the business problem to be solved are essential to ensuring eventual success. The bottom line is that neural networks provide no shortcuts.

19.1.3 Business score card

Neural networks are very powerful predictive modeling techniques, but some of the power comes at the expense of ease of use and ease of deployment. As we will see in this chapter, neural networks create very complex models that are almost always impossible to fully understand, even by experts. The model itself is represented by numeric values in a complex calculation that requires all the predictor values to be in the form of a number. The output of the neural network is also numeric and needs to be translated if the actual prediction value is categorical (e.g., predicting the demand for blue, white, or black jeans for a clothing manufacturer requires that the predictor values blue, black and white for the predictor color be converted to numbers). Because of the complexity of these techniques, much effort has been expended in trying to increase the clarity with which the model can be understood by the end user. These efforts are still in their infancy but are of tremendous importance since most data mining techniques including neural networks are being deployed against real business problems where significant investments are made on the basis of the predictions from the models (e.g., consider trusting the predictive model from a neural network that dictates which one million customers will receive a $1 mailing).

These shortcomings in understanding the meaning of the neural network model have been successfully addressed in two ways:

1. The neural network is packaged up into a complete solution such as fraud prediction. This allows the neural network to be carefully crafted for one particular application, and once it has been proven successful, it can be used over and over again without requiring a deep understanding of how it works.

2. The neural network is packaged up with expert consulting services. Here the neural network is deployed by trusted experts who have a track record of success. The experts either are able to explain the models or trust that the models do work.

The first tactic has seemed to work quite well because when the technique is used for a well-defined problem, many of the difficulties in preprocessing the data can be automated (because the data structures have been seen before) and interpretation of the model is less of an issue since entire industries begin to use the technology successfully and a level of trust is created. Several vendors have deployed this strategy (e.g., HNC's Falcon system for credit card fraud prediction and Advanced Software Applications' ModelMAX package for direct marketing).

Packaging up neural networks with expert consultants is also a viable strategy that avoids many of the pitfalls of using neural networks, but it can be quite expensive because it is human-intensive. One of the great promises of data mining is, after all, the automation of the predictive modeling process. These neural network consulting teams are little different from the analytical departments many companies already have in house. Since there is not a great difference in the overall predictive accuracy of neural networks over standard statistical techniques, the main difference becomes the replacement of the statistical expert with the neural network expert. Either with statistics or neural network experts, the value of putting easy-to-use tools into the hands of the business end user is still not achieved.

Figure 19.1 and Table 19.1 show the relative strengths of neural networks from a business user's perspective. Neural networks rate high for accurate models that provide good return on investment but rate low in terms of automation and clarity, making them more difficult to deploy across the enterprise.

19.2   Where to Use Neural Networks

Neural networks are used in a wide variety of applications. They have been used in all facets of business from detecting the fraudulent use of credit cards and credit risk prediction to increasing the hit rate of targeted mailings. They also have a long history of application in other areas such as the military for the automated driving of an unmanned vehicle at 30 mph on paved roads to biological simulations such as learning the correct pronunciation of English words from written text.

19.2.1   Neural networks for clustering

Neural networks of various kinds can be used for clustering and prototype creation. The Kohonen network described in this chapter is probably the most common network used for clustering and segmentation of the database. Typically the networks are used in a unsupervised learning mode to create the clus-

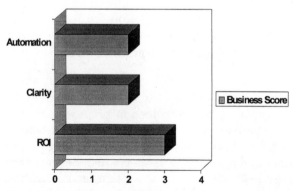

Figure 19.1   Business score card for neural nets.

TABLE 19.1   Business Score Card for Neural Networks

Data mining measure	Description
Automation	Neural networks are often represented as automated data mining techniques. While they are very powerful at building predictive models, they do require significant data preprocessing and a good understanding and definition of the prediction target. Usually normalizing predictor values between 0.0 and 1.0 and converting categoricals to numeric values is required. The networks themselves also require the setting of numerous parameters that determine how the neural network is to be constructed (e.g., the number of hidden nodes). There can be significant differences in performance due to small differences in the neural network setup or the way the data is preformatted.
Clarity	The bane of neural networks is often the clarity with which the user can see and understand the results that are being presented. To some degree the complexity of the neural network models goes hand in hand with their power to create accurate predictions. This shortcoming in clarity is recognized by the neural network vendors, and they have tried to provide powerful techniques to better visualize the neural networks and to possibly provide understandable rules or prototypes to help explain the models.
ROI	Neural networks do provide powerful predictive models and theoretically are more general than other data mining and standard statistical techniques. In practice, however, the gains in accuracy over other techniques are often quite small and can be dwarfed by some of the costs because of careless construction or use of the model by nonexperts. The models can also be quite time-consuming to build.

ters. The clusters are created by forcing the system to compress the data by creating prototypes or by algorithms that steer the system toward creating clusters that compete against each other for the records that they contain, thus ensuring that the clusters overlap as little as possible.

19.2.2   Neural networks for feature extraction

One of the important problems in all data mining is determining which predictors are the most relevant and the most important in building models that are most accurate at prediction. These predictors may be used by themselves or in conjunction with other predictors to form "features." A simple example of a feature in problems that neural networks are working on is the feature of a vertical line in a computer image. The predictors, or raw input data, are just the colored pixels (picture elements) that make up the picture. Recognizing that the predictors (pixels) can be organized in such a way as to create lines, and then using the line as the input predictor, can prove to dramatically improve the accuracy of the model and decrease the time to create it.

Some features such as lines in computer images are things that humans are already pretty good at detecting; in other problem domains it is more difficult to recognize the features. One novel way that neural networks have been used to detect features is to exploit the idea that features are a form of a compression of the training database. For instance, you could describe an image to a friend by rattling off the color and intensity of each pixel on every point in the picture, or you could describe it at a higher level in terms of lines and circles—or maybe even at a higher level of features such as trees and mountains. In either case your friend eventually gets all the information needed to know what the picture looks like, but certainly describing it in terms of high-level features requires much less communication of information than the "paint by numbers" approach of describing the color on each square millimeter of the image.

If we think of features in this way, as an efficient way to communicate our data, then neural networks can be used to automatically extract them. The neural network shown in Fig. 19.2 is used to extract features by requiring the network to learn to re-create the input data at the output nodes by using just five hidden nodes. Consider that if you were allowed 100 hidden nodes, then re-creating the data for the network would be rather trivial—involving simply passing the input node value directly through the corresponding hidden node and on to the output node. But as there are fewer and fewer hidden nodes, that information has to be passed through the hidden layer in a more and more efficient manner since there are less hidden nodes to help pass along the information.

To accomplish this, the neural network tries to have the hidden nodes extract features from the input nodes that efficiently describe the record represented at the input layer. This forced "squeezing" of the data through the narrow hidden layer forces the neural network to extract only those predictors and combinations of predictors that are best at re-creating the input record. The link weights used to create the inputs to the hidden nodes are effectively creating features that are combinations of the input node values.

19.2.3   Applications score card

Figure 19.3 and Table 19.2 show the applications score card for neural networks with respect to how well they perform for a variety of basic underlying

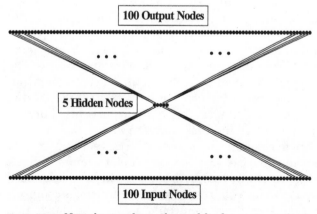

Figure 19.2   Neural networks can be used for data compression and feature extraction.

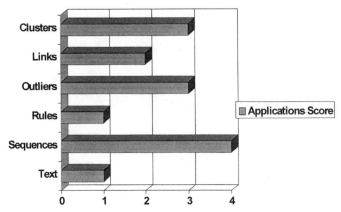

Figure 19.3 Applications score card for neural nets.

applications. Neural networks have been used for just about every type of supervised and unsupervised learning application. Because the underlying model is a complex mathematical equation, the generation of rules and the efficient detection of links in the database is a stretch for neural networks. Also, because of the large number of different words in text-based applications (high

TABLE 19.2   Applications Score Card for Neural Networks

Problem type	Description
Clusters	Although neural networks were originally conceived to mimic neural function in the brain and then used for a variety of prediction and classification tasks, they have also been found useful for clustering. Almost coincidentally, the self-organizing nature of the brain when mimicked in an artificial neural network results in the clustering of records from a database.
Links	Neural networks can be used to determine links and patterns in the database, although to be efficient, neural architectures very different from the standard single hidden layer need to be used. To do this efficiently, a network would generally have as many input nodes as output nodes and each node would represent an individual object that could be linked together.
Outliers	The general structure of the neural network is not designed for outlier detection in the way that nearest-neighbor classification techniques are, but they can be used for outlier detection by simply building the predictive model and seeing which record's actual values correspond to the predicted values. Any large disparity between the actual and predicted could well be an outlier.
Rules	Neural networks do not generate rules either for classification or explanation. Some new techniques are now being developed that would create rules after the fact to try to help explain the neural network, but these are additions to the basic neural network architecture.
Sequences	Because of their strengths in performing predictions for numeric prediction values and regression in general, neural networks are often used to do sequence prediction (like predicting the stock market). Generally a significant amount of preprocessing of the data needs to be performed to convert the time series data into something useful to the neural network.
Text	Because of the large number of possible input nodes (number of different words used in a given language), neural networks are seldom used for text retrieval. They have been used at a higher level to create a network that learns the relationships between documents.

dimensionality), neural networks are seldom used for text retrieval. They do provide some sense of confidence in the degree of the prediction so that outliers which do not match the existing model can be detected.

19.3   The General Idea

19.3.1   What does a neural network look like?

A neural network is loosely based on concepts of how the human brain is organized and how it learns. There are two main structures of consequence in the neural network:

1. The *node*—which loosely corresponds to the neuron in the human brain
2. The *link*—which loosely corresponds to the connections between neurons (axons, dendrites, and synapses) in the human brain

Figure 19.4 is a drawing of a simple neural network. The round circles represent the nodes, and the connecting lines represent the links. The neural network functions by accepting predictor values at the left and performing calculations on those values to produce new values in the node at the far right. The value at this node represents the prediction from the neural network model. In this case the network takes in values for predictors for age and income and predicts whether the person will default on a bank loan.

19.3.2   How does a neural net make a prediction?

In order to make a prediction, the neural network accepts the values for the predictors on what are called the *input nodes*. These become the values for those nodes; these values are then multiplied by values that are stored in the links (sometimes called *weights* and in some ways similar to the weights that are applied to predictors in the nearest-neighbor method). These values are then added together at the node at the far right (the output node), a special thresholding function is applied, and the resulting number is the prediction. In this case, if the resulting number is 0, the record is considered to be a good

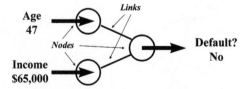

Figure 19.4 A simplified view of a neural network for prediction of loan default.

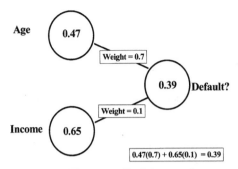

Figure 19.5 The normalized input values are multiplied by the link weights and added together at the output.

credit risk (no default); if the number is 1, the record is considered to be a bad credit risk (likely default).

A simplified version of the calculations depicted in Fig. 19.4 might look like Fig. 19.5. Here the value of age of 47 is normalized to fall between 0.0 and 1.0 and has the value 0.47, and the income is normalized to the value 0.65. This simplified neural network makes the prediction of no default for a 47-year-old making $65,000. The links are weighted at 0.7 and 0.1, and the resulting value after multiplying the node values by the link weights is 0.39. The network has been trained to learn that an output value of 1.0 indicates default and that 0.0 indicates nondefault. The output value calculated here (0.39) is closer to 0.0 than to 1.0, so the record is assigned a nondefault prediction.

19.3.3 How is the neural network model created?

The neural network model is created by presenting it with many examples of the predictor values from records in the training set (in this example age and income are used) and the prediction value from those same records. By comparing the correct answer obtained from the training record and the predicted answer from the neural network, it is possible to slowly change the behavior of the neural network by changing the values of the link weights. In some ways this is like having a grade school teacher ask questions of her student (a.k.a. the *neural network*) and if the answer is wrong, to verbally correct the student. The greater the error, the harsher the verbal correction; thus large errors are given greater attention at correction than are small errors.

For the actual neural network, it is the weights of the links that actually control the prediction value for a given record. Thus the particular model that is being found by the neural network is, in fact, fully specified by the weights and the architectural structure of the network. For this reason it is the link weights that are modified each time an error is made.

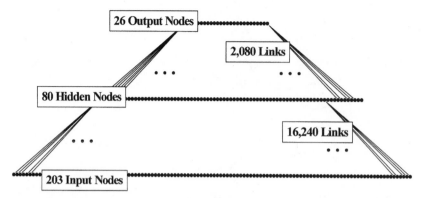

Figure 19.6   The neural network architecture for the NETtalk system was complex.

19.3.4   How complex can the neural network model become?

The models shown in Figs. 19.4 and 19.5 have been designed to be as simple as possible in order to make them understandable. In practice no networks are as simple as these. Figure 19.6 shows a network with many more links and many more nodes. This was the architecture of a neural network system called *NETtalk,* which learned how to pronounce written English words. This drawing shows only some of the nodes and links. Each node in the network was connected to every node in the level above it and below it, resulting in 18,629 link weights that needed to be learned in the network. Note that this network also now has a row of nodes in between the input nodes and the output nodes. These are called "hidden nodes" or the "hidden layer" because the values of these nodes are not visible to the end user in the way that the output nodes are (which contain the prediction) and the input nodes (which just contain the predictor values). There are even more complex neural network architectures that have more than one hidden layer. In practice one hidden layer seems to suffice, however.

19.3.5   Hidden nodes are like trusted advisors to the output nodes

The meanings of the input nodes and the output nodes are usually pretty well understood—and are usually defined by the end user with respect to the particular problem to be solved and the nature and structure of the database. The hidden nodes, however, do not have a predefined meaning and are determined by the neural network as it trains. This poses two problems:

1. It is difficult to trust the prediction of the neural network if the meaning of these nodes is not well understood.

2. Since the prediction is made at the output layer and the difference between the prediction and the actual value is calculated there, how is this error cor-

rection fed back through the hidden layers to modify the link weights that connect them?

The meaning of these hidden nodes is not necessarily well understood, but sometimes after the fact they can be studied to see when they are *active* (have larger numeric values) and when they are not and derive some meaning from them. In some of the early work neural networks were used to learn the family trees of two different families—one was Italian and one was English, and the network was trained to take as inputs either two people and return their relationship (father, aunt, sister, etc.) or given one person and a relationship to return the other person. After training, the units in one of the hidden layers were examined to see if there was any discernible explanation as to their role in the prediction. Several of the nodes did seem to have specific and understandable purposes. One, for instance, seemed to break up the input records (people) into either Italian or English descent, another unit encoded for which generation a person belonged to, and another encoded for the branch of the family that the person came from. Each of these nodes were automatically extracted by the neural network to aid in prediction.

Any interpretation of the meaning of the hidden nodes needs to be done after the fact—after the network has been trained, and it is not always possible to determine a logical description for the particular function for the hidden nodes. The second problem with the hidden nodes is perhaps more serious (if it hadn't been solved, neural networks wouldn't work). Luckily it has been solved.

The learning procedure for the neural network has been defined to work for the weights in the links connecting the hidden layer. A good analogy of how this works would be a military operation in some war where there are many layers of command with a general ultimately responsible for making the decisions on where to advance and where to retreat. The general probably is advised by several lieutenant generals, and each lieutenant general, in turn, is probably advised by several major generals. This hierarchy continues downward through colonels and privates at the bottom of the hierarchy.

This is not too far from the structure of a neural network with several hidden layers and one output node. You can think of the inputs coming from the hidden nodes as advice. The link weight corresponds to the trust that generals have in their advisors. Some trusted advisors have very high weights and some advisors may not be trusted and, in fact, have negative weights. The other part of the advice from the advisors has to do with how competent the particular advisor is for a given situation. The general may have a trusted advisor, but if that advisor has no expertise in aerial invasion and the situation in question involves the air force, this advisor may be very well trusted but the advisor personally may not have any strong opinion one way or another.

In this analogy the link weight of a neural network to an output unit is like the trust or confidence that commanders have in their advisors and the actual node value represents how strong an opinion this particular advisor has about this particular situation. To make a decision, the general considers how trustworthy and valuable the advice is and how knowledgeable and confident all the advisors are in making their suggestions; then, taking all this into account, the general makes the decision to advance or retreat.

In the same way, the output node will make a decision (a prediction) by taking into account all the input from its advisors (the nodes connected to it). In the case of the neural network this decision is reached by multiplying the link weight by the output value of the node and summing these values across all nodes. If the prediction is incorrect, the nodes that had the most influence on making the decision have their weights modified so that the wrong prediction is less likely to be made the next time.

This learning in the neural network is very similar to what happens when the wrong decision is made by the general. The confidence that the general has in all those advisors who gave the wrong recommendation is decreased—and all the more so for those advisors who were very confident and vocal in their recommendations. On the other hand, any advisors who were making the correct recommendation but whose input was not taken as seriously would be taken more seriously the next time. Likewise, any advisors who were reprimanded for giving the wrong advice to the general would then go back to their own advisors and determine which of them should have been trusted less and whom should have been listened to more closely in rendering the advice or recommendation to the general. The changes generals should make in listening to their advisors to avoid the same bad decision in the future are shown in Table 19.3.

This feedback can continue in this way down throughout the organization—at each level, giving increased emphasis to those advisors who had advised correctly and decreased emphasis to those who had advised incorrectly. In this way the entire organization becomes better and better at supporting the general in making the correct decision more of the time.

A very similar method of training takes place in the neural network. It is called *backpropagation* and refers to the propagation of the error backward from the output nodes (where the error is easy to determine as the difference between the actual prediction value from the training database and the pre-

TABLE 19.3   Neural Network Nodes*

General's trust	Advisor's recommendation	Advisor's confidence	Change to general's trust
High	Good	High	Great increase
High	Good	Low	Increase
High	Bad	High	Great decrease
High	Bad	Low	Decrease
Low	Good	High	Increase
Low	Good	Low	Small increase
Low	Bad	High	Decrease
Low	Bad	Low	Small decrease

* The link weights in a neural network are analogous to the confidence that generals might have in their trusted advisors.

diction from the neural network) through the hidden layers and to the input layers. At each level the link weights between the layers are updated so as to decrease the chance of making the same mistake again.

19.3.6   Design decisions in architecting a neural network

Neural networks are often touted as self-learning automated techniques that simplify the analysis process. The truth is that there still are many decisions to be made by the end user in designing the neural network even before training begins. If these decisions are not made wisely, the neural network will likely come up with a suboptimal model. Some of the decisions that need to be made include

- How will predictor values be transformed for the input nodes? Will normalization be sufficient? How will categoricals be entered?
- How will the output of the neural network be interpreted?
- How many hidden layers will there be?
- How will the nodes be connected? Will every node be connected to every other node, or will nodes just be connected between layers?
- How many nodes will there be in the hidden layer? (This can have an important influence on whether the predictive model is overfit to the training database.)
- How long should the network be trained for? (This also has an impact on whether the model overfits the data.)

Depending on the tool that is being used, these decisions may be explicit, where the user must set some parameter value, or they may be decided for the user because the particular neural network is being used for a specific type of problem (like fraud detection).

19.3.7   Different types of neural networks

There are literally hundreds of variations on the backpropagation feedforward neural networks that have been briefly described here. One involves changing the architecture of the neural network to include recurrent connections where the output from the output layer is connected back as input into the hidden layer. These recurrent nets are sometimes used for sequence prediction, in which the previous outputs from the network need to be stored someplace and then fed back into the network to provide context for the current prediction. Recurrent networks have also been used for decreasing the amount of time that it takes to train the neural network. Another twist on the neural net theme is to change the way that the network learns. Backpropagation effectively utilizes a search technique called *gradient descent* to search for the best possible improvement in the link weights to reduce the error. There are, however, many other ways of doing search in a high-dimensional space (each link weight corresponds to a dimension), including Newton's methods and conjugate gradient as well as simulating the physics of cooling metals in a process called *simulated annealing* or in simulating the search process that goes on in biological evolution and using genetic algorithms to optimize the weights of the neural networks. It has even been suggested that creating a large number of neural networks with randomly weighted links and picking the one with the lowest error rate would be the best learning procedure.

Despite all these choices, the backpropagation learning procedure is the most commonly used. It is well understand, is relatively simple, and seems to work in a large number of problem domains. There are, however, two other neural network architectures that are used relatively often. Kohonen feature maps are often used for unsupervised learning and clustering, and radial-basis-function networks are used for supervised learning and in some ways represent a hybrid between nearest-neighbor and neural network classifications.

19.3.8   Kohonen feature maps

Kohonen feature maps were developed in the 1970s and were created to simulate certain human brain functions. Today they are used mostly to perform unsupervised learning and clustering.

Kohonen networks are feedforward neural networks generally with no hidden layer. The networks contain only an input layer and an output layer, but the nodes in the output layer compete among themselves to display the strongest activation to a given record, what is sometimes called a "winner take all" strategy.

The networks originally came about when some of the puzzling yet simple behaviors of the real neurons were taken into effect—namely, that physical locality of the neurons seems to play an important role in the behavior and learning of neurons. The specific features of real neurons were:

- Nearby neurons seem to compound the activation of each other.
- Distant neurons seemed to inhibit each other.
- Particular neurons seemed to have specific tasks that would not overlap with the tasks assigned to other neurons.

Much of this early research came from the desire to simulate the way that vision worked in the brain. For instance, some of the early physiological work showed that surgically rotating a section of a frog's eyeball so that it was upside down would result in the frog jumping up for food that was actually below the frog's body. This led to the belief that the neurons had certain unalterable roles that were dependent on the physical location of the neuron. Kohonen networks were developed to accommodate these physiological features by a very simple learning algorithm:

1. Lay out the output nodes of the network on a two-dimensional grid with no hidden layer.

2. Fully connect the input nodes to the output nodes.

3. Connect the output nodes so that nearby nodes would strengthen each other and distant nodes would weaken each other.

4. Start with random weights on the links.

5. Train by determining which output node responded most strongly to the current record being input.

6. Change the weights to that highest-responding node to enable it to respond even more strongly in the future. This is also known as *Hebbian learning.*

7. Normalize the link weights so that they add up to some constant amount; thus, increasing one weight decreases some other.

8. Continue training until some form of global organization is formed on the two-dimensional output grid (where there are clear winning nodes for each input and, in general, local neighborhoods of nodes are activated).

When these networks were run, in order to simulate the real-world visual system it became obvious that the organization that was automatically being constructed on the data was also very useful for segmenting and clustering the training database. Each output node represented a cluster and nearby clusters were nearby in the two-dimensional output layer. Each record in the database would fall into one and only one cluster (the most active output node), but the other clusters in which it might also fit would be shown and likely to be next to the best matching cluster. Figure 19.7 shows the general form of a Kohonen network.

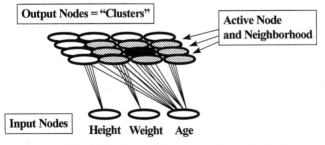

Figure 19.7   The Kohonen network arranges the output nodes in a two-dimensional grid to simulate the positive reinforcement of neighboring neurons in brains.

19.3.9   How does the neural network resemble the human brain?

Since the inception of the idea of neural networks, the ultimate goal for these techniques has been to have them re-create human thought and learning. This has once again proved to be a difficult task—despite the power of these new techniques and the similarities of their architecture to that of the human brain. Many of the things that people take for granted are difficult for neural networks—such as avoiding overfitting and working with real-world data without a lot of preprocessing required. There have also been some exciting successes.

19.3.10   A neural network learns to speak

One successful system for neural networks was the NETtalk system by Sejnowski and Rosenberg. This system was instrumental in launching the current interest in neural networks in the mid-1980s after interest had waned in the late 1960s and throughout the 1970s. NETtalk was a neural network system that learned to speak English once it was given a training database of written words and their phonetic pronunciation. The resulting network could then be applied to test records and the phonetic results piped through to hardware that would actually produce the sounds required to pronounce each word. This provided for a powerful demonstration as listeners could actually hear the improvement in the speaking voice as the system learned—going from nonsensical babbling with the original random weights in the neural net to very understandable speech with few mistakes as the net finished training.

19.3.11   A neural network learns to drive

Another notable and interesting application of neural networks has been their use in learning how to automatically drive unmanned military vehicles. The ALVINN (Autonomous Land Vehicle In a Neural Network) system has learned how to drive a van along roads on which it has been trained at speeds of up to 40 mph. It does this by "watching" the road through a videocamera as a human driver drives along (effectively creating the training set). One interesting problem that needed to be overcome was that because human drivers were so skilled at staying on the road, there were insufficient historical data for ALVINN to learn how to get back on the road if it veered off course slightly. To combat this problem, these records were simulated for the system.

19.3.12   The human brain is still much more powerful

With successes like NETtalk and ALVINN and some of the commercial successes of neural networks for fraud prediction and targeted marketing, it is tempting to claim that neural networks are making progress toward "thinking," but it is difficult to judge just how close we are. Some real facts that we can look at are to contrast the human brain as a computer to the neural network implemented on the computer.

Today it would not be possible to create an artificial neural network that even had as many neurons in it as the human brain, let alone all the processing required for the complex calculations that go on inside the brain. The current estimates are that there are 100 billion neurons in the average person (roughly 20 times the number of people on earth). Each single neuron can receive input from up to as many as 100,000 synapses or connections to other neurons, and overall there are 10,000 trillion synapses.

To get an idea of the size of these numbers, consider that if you had a 10-Tbyte data warehouse (the largest warehouse in existence today), and you were able to store all of the complexity of a synapse in only a single byte of data within that warehouse, you would still require 1000 of these warehouses just to store the synapse information. This doesn't include the data required for the neurons or all the computer processing power required to actually run this simulated brain. The bottom line is that we're still a factor of 1000 away from even storing the required data to simulate a brain. If storage densities on disks and other media keep increasing and the prices continue to decrease, this problem may well be solved. Nonetheless, there is much more work to be done in understanding how real brains function.

19.4 How the Neural Network Works

19.4.1 How predictions are made

In Fig. 19.8 there are three input nodes and one output node. The input nodes—age, gender, and income—have values that are converted to numbers between 0.0 and 1.0. For instance, for age, the 1-year-olds would be converted to 0.0, and 112—the oldest age in the database—would be converted to 1.0. Likewise, male would be converted to 0.0 and female to 1.0. When these values are calculated for a specific record's predictors, they are placed at the input nodes, and then new values are calculated for the next level (the hidden layer) by multiplying the values of the nodes at the input layer by the weights on the links connecting the input nodes to the hidden nodes and then summing them together. For instance, if the input values were 0.4 for age, 0.0 for gender, and 0.8 for income, we'd have a record for a middle-aged male who was relatively wealthy. These predictor values would be multiplied by the weights on the links and then summed at the hidden node to achieve a value of 4.0.

This summed value is then passed through a special conversion filter that turns the value into a number between 0.0 and 1.0. This value is then the output of the hidden nodes and is what is then fed into the output node by the same mechanism (passing the summed weighted node values through this fil-

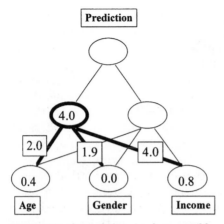

Figure 19.8 One of the simplest possible representations of a neural network that displays full connection between layers and a hidden layer.

ter function). By doing this layer by layer, a very large and complex neural network could be created. In practice, there is almost never a requirement to create such a complex network. One hidden layer is sufficient.

19.4.2 How backpropagation learning works

Backpropagation of errors from the output layer through the hidden layers to modify link weights is by far the most commonly used method for building a neural network model. Since the only thing that can change once the architecture of the model is decided on are the link weights, it is these link weights that are modified so as to improve the predictive accuracy of the model—basically by changing the weights so that in the future the neural network is less likely to make the same error.

If an error is made by the neural network, that error can be measured at the output node as the difference between the value of the output node and the desired output (remember that the desired output is known since this is during the training phase when historical data is used). The bigger the error, the more the weights should be modified; likewise, the greater the output of the hidden node, the larger the change in the weights from that node. These two factors, along with the slope of the filtering function and a learning rate value, are all that are included in the precise calculation of the new weights.

The learning rate controls how quickly the neural network reacts to a particular error. If the rate is high, each error will be treated as very important and the weights will be significantly modified. If the rate is low, the weights will only be nudged in the right direction each time an error is made. Keep in mind that the correct weights will eventually be achieved by small steps (low value for the learning rate parameter), but it could take a very long time for the neural network to arrive at weights that provide a usable predictive model. If a very aggressive learning rate is used (large value), the network will act quickly to correct one mistake but then the next error might require another large jump in the weights that reverses the changes made by the previous error. The high learning rates could lead to a much faster build of a neural network, but they can also result in a neural network that doesn't achieve convergence, and the weights could change rapidly from one value to another with each new error encountered.

19.4.3   Data preparation

The way that the data in the training database is fed into the neural network can have a huge impact on the time it takes to train the network and also on the accuracy of the network. Often the data is preprocessed to a great degree to "spoon-feed" the neural network with a form of the raw data that it can most easily deal with. As an example, consider that when predicting a time series (like the next closing price of a stock on the stock market), the raw data (without any preprocessing) is stored in the database as a series of prices over time at fixed intervals. It might be that the price of the stock is captured every hour on the hour ($30.00 at 11:00 A.M., $31.00 at noon, $28.00 at 1:00 P.M., $30.00 at 2:00 P.M., etc.). This data could be presented to the neural network by allocating one node per hourly data point. A much better way to deliver the same data to the network is to provide not only the actual stock price but also the difference between stock prices from hour to hour (e.g., $1.00, −$3.00, +$2.00 for the previous example). The same data is being presented to the neural network to train with but the encoding of the data as differences in prices will produce a far superior predictive model.

The input nodes of a neural network expect values within the range of 0.0 to 1.0 (sometimes from −1.0 to 1.0). For a predictor to be mapped into one of these ranges, the values must be scaled in some way. If the predictor is a continuous number such as age or income, there are several strategies for doing this.

- *Scaling.*   This technique will divide the least and the greatest values for the predictor by a number so that the difference between the two is 1.0. Then the minimum value can be set to 0.0 and the maximum to 1.0 by adding the appropriate number. For example, predictor values from 100 to 300 can be scaled to fall between 0.0 and 1.0 by dividing each predictor value by 200 and subtracting 0.5.

- *Nonuniform scaling.*   For some predictors, such as annual income, the difference between smaller values (say, between incomes of $50,000 and $150,000) may be much more significant than the difference between much larger values (e.g., incomes of $1,000,000 and $1,100,000). To aid the neural network in making these important distinctions, the scaling may be done in a nonuniform way, by taking the logarithm of the predictor values, for instance.

- *Binning.*   For some numeric predictors, multiple nodes are used to make it easier for the neural network to detect the important and predictive patterns. This is done by breaking the values of the predictor into ranges (effectively throwing them into a fixed number of different bins) and assigning a node to each range that specifies whether the value does or does not fall into that bin (0.0 or 1.0). For example, Fahrenheit temperature could be broken up into the bins: less than 0, 0 to 25, 25 to 50, 50 to 75, and greater than 75°F. One problem with this is that these bins need to be picked out beforehand and may bias the network away from finding important patterns. For instance, by binning temperature values like this, the important distinction between frozen and unfrozen water is masked since 31, 32, and 33°F all fall into the same bin.

- *Thermometer encoding.*   When numeric data is binned into a fixed number of ranges, the input values can be represented by setting to 1.0 the node for which the value falls into or setting to 1.0 all nodes that represent less than that value. This is analogous to mercury rising up in the thermometer. For example, if the temperature were 45°F and the five bins previously described were used, the first three nodes would have values of 1.0 and the last two would have values of 0.0.

- *Time-difference embedding.*   It is almost always a good idea to provide the differences in values over time, as well as the actual values, to the neural network. This effectively provides the first derivative of the value over time to the network—or the rate of change in its value. It can also sometimes be valuable to provide the second derivative as a preprocessing step—which is the rate at which the rate of change is taking place (i.e., is the rate of change accelerating or holding steady).

- *General nonlinear transformations.*   Many researchers will create input nodes that have the square, cube, logarithm, and products of various numeric predictors (e.g., an input node might contain the product of age times income). These nodes can sometimes provide valuable predictors that would otherwise not have been detected by the neural network. If these combinations of predictors are not valuable, the link weights from the nodes should decay to unimportant values. However, adding all the additional nodes for each predictor can make the size of the network much larger and the training time much longer.

Mapping categorical predictors such as eye color is somewhat more difficult than mapping numeric predictors. It is easy enough to map income or weight into a numeric value between 0.0 and 1.0, but it is not clear how to do this for a categorical predictor with a fixed number of values and no ascertainable ordering between the different values (e.g., to ask if "blond" is greater than "brown" doesn't make sense the way it does to ask if one person is older than another). To solve these problems, a number of techniques have been used to encode categorical predictors for neural networks:

- *Numeric encoding.* Each predictor value is randomly assigned a number (e.g., blond = 1, brown = 2, red = 3, black = 4, other = 5), and then these values are scaled to fit between 0.0 and 1.0. One problem with this encoding is that an order has been implicitly placed on the categorical values that may bias the network in the predictive model that is ultimately learned.

- *One-of-N encoding.* In this case each different categorical value gets its own input node (e.g., there would be five input nodes for the predictor hair color). Each node receives a value of 0.0 if that value for that predictor is not present and 1.0 if it is (e.g., of the five nodes for hair color, only one would be 1.0 and the rest would be 0.0).

- *Binary encoding.* Each predictor value is randomly assigned a number, and then these numbers are converted into binary representation (e.g., blond = 1 = 001, brown = 2 = 010, red = 3 = 011, black = 4 = 100, other = 5 = 101). An input node is assigned to each position in the binary string (e.g., three nodes would be required for the binary encoding of hair color).

In addition to transforming the predictor values, other cleansing operations can be performed on the database to help clean up duplicate records and missing values. For instance, the NeuralWare neural net product can replace missing values in predictors with the median value and can compress the database by binning the predictor values for each predictor, thus creating a much smaller number of possible records (prototypes). These prototypes then represent a large number of records by using the average predictor and prediction values.

19.4.4   Combatting overfitting

As with all predictive modeling techniques, some care must be taken to avoid overfitting with a neural network. Neural networks can be quite good at overfitting training data with a predictive model that does not work well on new data. This is particularly problematic for neural networks because it is difficult to understand how the model is working. In the early days of neural networks, the predictive accuracy that was often mentioned first was the accuracy of the training set, and the vaulted or validation set database was reported as a footnote. This was due in part to the fact that—unlike decision trees or nearest-neighbor techniques, which can quickly achieve 100 percent predictive accuracy on the training database—neural networks can be trained forever and still not be 100 percent accurate on the training set. While this is an interesting fact, it is not terribly relevant since the accuracy on the training set is of little interest and can have little bearing on the validation database accuracy.

Perhaps because overfitting was more obvious for decision trees and nearest-neighbor approaches, more effort was placed earlier to add pruning and editing to these techniques. For neural networks, generalization of the predictive model is accomplished by rules of thumb and sometimes in a more methodical way by using cross-validation as is done with decision trees. One way to control overfitting in neural networks is to limit the number of links. Since the number of links represents the complexity of the model that can be produced, and since more complex models have the ability to overfit while less complex ones cannot, overfitting can be controlled by simply limiting the number of links in the neural network. Unfortunately, there are no good theoretical grounds for picking a certain number of links.

In recent books and journal articles on neural networks it has been suggested that the number of links in the network should be either 5 times, twice, or equal to the number of training examples. The NeuralWare software product recommends controlling the number of input nodes to keep 10 to 40 times as many records as there are input nodes.

These rules of thumb can help guide the user in constructing their neural networks but recognize that there are still many caveats. For instance, doubling the size of the training database by making a copy of the records does not help in combating overfitting since no new information is presented by the duplicate records. Likewise, a database that has very different and informative records could support a neural network with many more links than a database with many more records that are very similar. Because of this, it is recommended to always use test set validation or cross-validation. Test set validation can be used to avoid overfitting by building the neural network on one portion of the training database and using the other portion of the training database to detect what the predictive accuracy is on vaulted data. This accuracy will peak at some point in the training, and then, as training proceeds, it will decrease while the accuracy on the training database will continue to increase. The link weights for the network can be saved when the accuracy on the held-aside data peaks. NeuralWare and other products provide an automated function that saves link weights for the network when it is performing at its best on the test set and even continues to search after the minimum is reached.

The number of hidden nodes is also important in determining the number of links in the network and thus also affects the ability of the network to overfit. For this reason there are similar rules for the ratio of the number of hidden nodes to the number of input and output nodes. NeuralWare, for instance, recommends that the number of hidden nodes be two-thirds of the number of input nodes and output nodes. So if you had 23 input nodes and one output node, the recommendation would be $(\%)(23 + 1) = 16$ hidden nodes. They also recommend that with their product that no more than 50 hidden nodes be used, and although NeuralWare allows for any number of hidden layers, it is strongly recommended that only one be used for good performance.

19.4.5 Applying and training the neural network

The application of the neural network to a new database is relatively inexpensive. Each record can be run through the series of multiplications, sums, and filtering functions that make up each node of the neural network. In fact, the neural network can be applied to a database in parallel—in a massively parallel manner where each processor contains a single copy of the neural network and the trained link weights and a subset of the total number of records to be scored. The actual model is just the link weights and the connection pattern between nodes. Because most networks are today fully connected between layers, the architectural structure of the network can be stored by simply noting which layer a given node is in and the link weights connecting it to the next level.

Training the neural network can be much more computationally expensive. Normally the training of the neural network has the following steps:

1. Create an initial network with random weights assigned to the links.

2. Run each record from the training database through the network and use the backpropagation learning algorithm to correct the error.

3. Check for stopping criterion (hopefully using cross-validation to check for overfitting, but training could also be stopped when a prespecified minimum training error is reached).

4. If stopping criterion is not reached, return to step 2 and repeat with the entire training database.

This training technique can go on for quite some time. Each application of the entire database is called a *training epoch,* and it is not uncommon for a network to require hundreds of epochs of training in order to achieve acceptable results. How long it takes depends on a large number of factors such as the difficulty of the problem (how many different spaces represent the predictive concept). The length of training time also depends on the database. Large diverse databases will take longer than small homogeneous databases, but should also provide superior results. As mentioned previously, the learning rate parameter that needs to be specified along with the backpropagation algorithm can have a significant effect on the amount of time for the network to settle in on a consistent model. If the rate is too large, the network may oscillate between values for link weights and never converge. Setting the rate parameter too low is analogous to only being allowed to take baby steps when climbing a mountain. Eventually you'll get to the summit, but it can take a very long time. One attempt at a happy medium between these two techniques is to have the system take very large steps initially and then slowly begin to take smaller and smaller steps as the summit is achieved. This technique is called *simulated annealing* and is described later in this chapter.

19.4.6   Explaining the network

One indictment against neural networks is that it is difficult to understand the model that they have built and also how the raw data affects the output predictive answer. With nearest-neighbor techniques, prototypical records are provided to "explain" why the prediction is made, and decision trees provide rules that can be translated into English to explain why a particular prediction was made for a particular record. The complex models of the neural network are captured solely by the link weights in the network, which represent a very complex mathematical equation.

There have been several attempts to alleviate these basic problems of the neural network. The simplest approach is to actually look at the neural network and try to create plausible explanations for the meanings of the hidden nodes. Sometimes this can be done quite successfully. In the example given at the beginning of this chapter, the hidden nodes of the neural network seemed to have extracted important distinguishing features in predicting the relationship between people by extracting information like country of origin—features that, it would seem, a person would also extract and use for the prediction. But there were also many other hidden nodes, even in this particular example, that were hard to explain and didn't seem to have any particular purpose—except that they aided the neural network in making the correct prediction.

Understanding the behavior of the hidden nodes is probably the most difficult part of the neural network. A simpler question that arises is which, of the many predictors, is actually important in making a given prediction. One might look at the link weights of a given predictor to see whether they were small or large. If all the link weights emanating from an input node were near zero for a given predictor, then that particular predictor would likely be having little impact. If, however, some of the links were unimportant but others were not, this predictor would have likely impact in certain situations but not in others. When there is a hidden layer present, it is too complicated to determine the overall impact of the given predictor since the one strong link might connect to a node in the hidden layer that has strong impact on all output nodes.

Because of this complexity, the impact of various predictors is determined through iterative experimentation in two ways:

1. Build a network from scratch without an input node for the predictor, and compare the predictive accuracy to a network with the predictor. If the predictor has no impact on the prediction, then the accuracy of the network without it will show little degradation in performance. Even if the predictor is highly predictive of the target prediction, the new network could still perform quite well if there were another predictor that was strongly correlated with the removed predictor (e.g., if you removed the average account balance field for a customer record but included the average interest paid on that balance, the network would effectively have two sources of the same information, and the new network would show little degradation in performance).

2. Slightly change the values for a given predictor and see if the output value changes. This is a good test because it indicates not only how important the predictor is but also how sensitive it is to small perturbations that might easily arise in a real database (slightly incorrect data was collected or entered into the system).

NeuralWare provides an "explain" function that will help the user make small perturbations in the values of the predictors (e.g., change an actual predictor value from 5.0 to 5.5 or 4.5) and then records whether that change had any impact on the final output. If the small change had a significant impact on the final output, then that predictor would be considered to be significant. If the output were relatively unchanged despite changes in a particular predictor, then that predictor would be considered to be less significant. This process can be carried out across all the records and the significance averaged.

19.5   Case Study: Predicting Currency Exchange Rates

Neural networks have probably seen their greatest acceptance and application in the financial industry. Applications such as credit card fraud, default (personal bankruptcy), and even customer attrition have all shown successful applications with neural networks. For fraud alone, the dollar amounts to be saved by viable predictive models are staggering. In 1995 the combined losses from credit card fraud and counterfeiting was $1.3 billion. Visa member banks alone lost more than $148 million to counterfeiters in 1994. The good news is that neural network systems have been introduced that reduced that loss by 16 percent to $124 million just one year later.

Despite successes like these in fraud and other applications, the holy grail of the financial applications is still time series prediction: being able to say what is going to happen next—whether it is predicting the closing price of a stock, the market, or even general overall shifts in the market. One particularly difficult prediction is foreign exchange rates between different currencies. In this case study the exchange rate of the Swiss franc to the U.S. dollar is used as an application area to spotlight the power of a neural network.

19.5.1   The problem

One difficulty in predicting any market phenomenon is that you are not the only one trying to do it. In fact, the multiple players, all trying to exploit small niches to make money, are what actually create the market and its behavior. Because of the many people playing in the currency exchange markets, each with mostly the same information but some with slightly more than others (and some probably even playing with "inside information"), the market is commonly thought to be "efficient." Simply stated, the "efficient market hypothesis" is based on the premise that there is little opportunity to exploit the market changes because as soon as a small one occurs that might be predictable, someone probably already beat you to it. It also implies that the price of anything in the market has been efficiently set to the correct value for the current time on the basis of future risk and future possibilities for profit. Because of this, it is generally believed that it is difficult to predict future market behavior based on historical information in any better manner than basically at random. This, of course, does not deter many from trying. It just means that there is good reason to believe that, without information additional to the historical price information, it is a very hard problem.

In the case presented here, 4 years of exchange rate data between the Swiss franc and the U.S. dollar were obtained for the years 1985–1988. Historical data was used to train a neural network to predict whether the exchange rate would rise or fall 30 min into the future. This work was performed by Xiru Zhang of PHZ Partners, Cambridge, Massachusetts.

19.5.2 Implementation

A standard feedforward neural network algorithm (no recurrent paths between nodes of different layers) was used with the backpropagation learning algorithm. Two network architectures were tried. The first had seven input units, seven hidden units, and one output unit; the second had an input layer of seven units, two hidden layers (five units and two units), and a single output unit. Both networks individually, as well as the average of their outputs, were tried. This averaging seemed to improve the performance of either network alone and was tried in an effort to remove any bias inherent in using one particular architecture.

The seven input nodes corresponded to predictors that held the exchange rate values at 30-min intervals over a 3½-h period (210 min). The prediction value corresponded to the positive or negative direction of the exchange rate. The filtering function used at each hidden node and output node took the summed inputs of the node and output a value between −1.0 and 1.0. This choice was made, at least in part, because the output to be predicted was the direction of the exchange rate (1.0 for an upswing and −1.0 for a downturn).

In this case overfitting was corrected for by using the data from 1985 as a cross-validation test set. The data from 1986 and 1987 was used for training the neural network. The cross-validation test set was tested against the neural network to determine when the maximum accuracy was achieved but was never used in the training or modification of the weights of the neural network.

19.5.3 The results

The goal of the neural network system was to simply predict whether the rate would rise, fall, or stay the same (without distinction for how large the change was). If the time series were really a random walk, then one could do no better than 50 percent correct (since the change would go up 50 percent of the time and down 50 percent of the time just by random chance). The neural networks performed much better than just random change. The neural network running with two hidden layers performed slightly better than the single-hidden-layer network, but the averaged output from both networks performed even better. All neural network models outperformed a simple linear model as shown in Table 19.4.

These results were interesting, but it was difficult to tell if the models might actually be useful in practice (i.e., if they were used to make trades in the market). (The saying goes that if you are right even 51 percent of the time, you can become very rich in the stock market.) To get a better idea of how any of the models might perform with actual money being invested, a simulation was created that made realistic assumptions about the cost of making a trade (transaction cost of switching position from short to long), the amount of money that could be borrowed to make a trade (the so-called leverage of a trader), and the perceived risk of lending money, which affects the maximum amount that can be borrowed (the so-called maximum drawdown). With realistic values set for these variables, the model was applied to new data and the simulation of actual trading was performed.

The results showed an ordering of models similar to those observed before, except that in this case the linear model lost money over time while all neural networks made money. One explanation for this was that the neural networks were particularly adept at the correct prediction at times when the market made large changes. Thus the neural networks were more accurate when it mattered the most.

19.6   Strengths and Weaknesses

19.6.1   Algorithm score card

Neural networks are probably the best known techniques for data mining, and part of the reason for this is their excellent ability to provide highly accurate models in a variety of real-world problem situations. They do, however, have some significant limitations in terms of training time, clarity, and dimensionality. Figure 19.9 and Table 19.5 present the algorithm score card for neural networks.

TABLE 19.4   Neural Network Models versus a Simple Linear Model*

Model	Percentage correct	Total return (%)
No model (random guessing)	50.0	—
Linear	52.5	–6.8
Single-hidden-layer network	53.4	9.9
Double-hidden-layer network	54.0	9.8
Averaged network	53.7	11.5

* Two neural network architectures were tried with a single hidden layer and a double hidden layer. Both networks and their averaged output were superior to no model and a simple linear model.

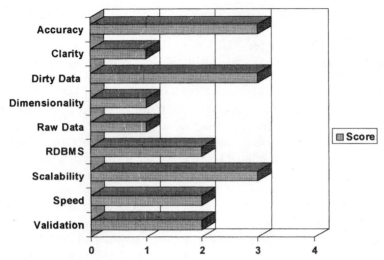

Figure 19.9 Algorithm score card for neural networks.

19.6.2 Some current market offerings

In addition to its wide variety of statistical and visualization tools, SPSS also contains a neural network package: SPSS Neural Connection. The system runs on a PC with a math coprocessor recommended and implements three types of neural networks: Multi-Layer Perceptron, radial basis function, and the Kohonen network. The system also provides three standard statistical tools: multiple regression, closest-class mean classifier, and principal-component-analysis tools. As with other neural network packages, SPSS allows the user to experiment with different architectures and learning models by adjusting such things as the transfer functions, the starting weights, or the number of hidden layers.

The system also has a nice intuitive GUI for allowing the user to create the complete process of data mining by connecting together icons on the screen that represent various stages in the data mining process that allow the user to preprocess the data with four different filtering tools. For the more experienced user, there are also two scripting languages that allow the user to run batch jobs at off-peak hours. The NetAgent scripting language allows the user to create annotated applications that can then be more easily used and understood by others.

NeuralWare provides a wide variety of tools for constructing neural networks and can be counted on to contain the latest innovations in neural network algorithms. Although the system has easy-to-use user interfaces, its scope of detailed control of neural network construction and training make it most valuable to the expert end user looking for optimizing different neural network architectures and training algorithms for particular problems.

HNC Software Inc. has, to date, been one of the most financially successful data mining companies. They offer a neural network technology, but rather than including it in an analyst's workbench or technology toolbox, they have targeted the technology to particular end uses. These include the Falcon Sys-

TABLE 19.5   Algorithm Score Card for Neural Networks

Data mining measure	Description
Accuracy	When used for prediction, neural networks provide highly accurate results in a wide variety of different problem domains.
Clarity	Neural networks are quite opaque in terms of the end user being able to understand the "model" that is being built. Additions have been made to the basic algorithm to perform sensitivity analysis and determine predictor importance, but in general neural networks are far less intuitive models than are decision trees or nearest neighbor.
Dimensionality	Neural networks do not fare well in databases where there are large numbers of predictors. Unimportant predictors are not easily ignored the way they are for decision trees and instead will significantly slow down the time to convergence of the training of the network.
Dirty data	While missing data is not explicitly handled as it is for decision trees, neural networks are relatively robust with respect to missing values or corrupted data.
Raw data	Neural networks require a great deal of preprocessing of the data, not only to convert categoricals and unordered numeric fields but also to aid in the prediction model to be used. How the data is preprocessed can have a very large impact on the accuracy of the resulting model.
RDBMS	The basic building blocks of the neural network are multiplication, addition, and a complex filter function. Since these techniques are used repeatedly in the training of the neural network, inexpensive specialized hardware has been built. Embedding these techniques into database systems is problematic since most database systems are usually optimized for data movement, not numeric calculations.
Scalability	Neural networks have been used on very large databases as well as with very large neural networks trained in parallel on SMP and MPP supercomputers. The parallel algorithm consists of training one network on each processor with a local subset of the training database. Application of neural networks is easily parallelizable.
Speed	Neural networks are relatively fast to apply to data, although they do require significant numeric computation. The time to build the network can be quite long and cannot be as easily bounded in completion as can a decision tree.
Validation	Neural networks were not originally designed to validate the resulting model and measure for overfitting, but systems have been wrapped around the basic algorithm that provide this functionality.

tem for credit card fraud detection, ProfitMax for credit cardholder profitability management, and ProfitMax Bankruptcy for predicting credit cardholder bankruptcy. They also offer targeted applications in retail, insurance, and financial as well as a product for data mining of text for improving advertising effectiveness.

19.6.3   Radial-basis-function networks

Radial-basis-function networks are neural networks that combine some of the advantages of neural networks with some of the advantages of nearest-neighbor techniques. In radial basis functions the hidden layer is made up of nodes that represent prototypes or clusters of records. Just as in Kohonen networks, one of these hidden nodes will become the most active for certain types of records input. These nodes represent the basis functions whose values can be combined in the output layer to create the correct predictions. They are often built before the training is performed on the output layer of the network and are created by using Kohonen networks or other clustering techniques. The best way to think of these hidden nodes is as a specialist that calculates how close a given training example is to the center of each important cluster or prototype. For this reason the hidden nodes are sometimes called "centers."

Once the weights to the hidden nodes are created, training of the output links can be accomplished by standard back propagation. Because the link weights need to be optimized only for the output layer, the training phase for these networks can be much faster than for a similarly sized and architected neural network using backpropagation for all layers.

19.6.4 Genetic algorithms and neural networks

If you think simply about the training process in neural networks, you could view it as a game of trying to find the best possible combination of link weights for a given network architecture (say, the standard three-layer network, fully connected between layers). The network is, in fact, fully defined by the numbers assigned to each link (e.g., for a network with five input nodes, three hidden nodes, and two output nodes, there would be 21 links (5*3 + 3*2) and just 21 numbers that defined the full behavior of the neural network. The trick in training is to find those right numbers. This is what the backpropagation algorithm accomplishes by changing the numbers each time to improve the accuracy of the network.

Backpropagation is not the only way of determining these link weights, however. Genetic algorithms have also been deployed to try to find the best possible link weights. Figure 19.10 shows a population of neural networks evolving. From one generation to the next, some networks do better and some do worse, but over time, the best solution in the population gets better and better.

Genetic algorithms simulate natural evolution on the computer. To do so, they simulate DNA, which in nature describes how to uniquely grow the animal or plant. The analog to DNA in genetic algorithms is the list of numbers that represent the link weights in the neural network. In some ways this list is like a chromosome and each number is like a gene. Taken together, all these simulated genes fully describe how to build the given neural network. In genetic algorithms there are good lists of link weights that represent highly accurate neural networks, and there are poor lists of link weights that represent neural networks that are no more predictive than random guessing. Genetic algorithms generate many different genetic guesses at the right link weights and create a population of different neural networks. Survival-of-the-fittest techniques are then used to weed out the poorly performing networks and reward the more accurate ones.

If a network is particularly accurate, it will be rewarded by allowing it to "reproduce"—making copies of itself with slight variations. These modifications to the link weights are made at randomlike genetic mutations and sometimes result in improved performance. Those that improve continue to be modified until highly accurate link weights are evolved.

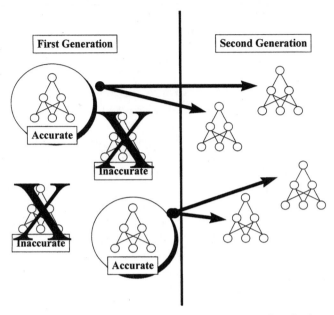

First Generation

Second Generation

Accurate

Inaccurate

Inaccurate

Accurate

Figure 19.10 Genetic algorithms can be used to evolve the best neural network by a process similar to natural selection.

Genetic algorithms have proved to be an interesting way to determine link weights for neural networks, but they have not, as yet, been shown to generate better solutions or even comparable solutions in less time than does backpropagation. They also have a problem of getting "stuck" on a suboptimal solution very early in the training and never being able to find a better one.

19.6.5 Simulated annealing and neural networks

We have used the analogy that backpropagation is similar to what one does in climbing to the top of a hill. It is constantly trying to move in the direction that improves the network as much as possible, similar to the way one would walk in the direction that is most uphill if one were trying to get to the top of the hill most quickly. For neural networks this means modifying the link weights, most which will have the greatest impact on improving the performance of the network.

This art of "hill climbing" is an area that physicists have been interested in for years. In their case they are looking at how metals cool and materials form crystals, but many of the same effects appear in all three areas. Because of the similarities between searching for the optimal neural network and the physics of metals cooling, several simulations have been tried in order to speed up the performance of neural network training. One technique is called *simulated annealing.*

Annealing is the process of cooling a metal or a glass at the right rates of speed in order to minimize the number of defects that are formed in the structure of the material. Simulated annealing borrows the idea of heating and cooling a metal from the real world and applies it to removing the defects from a neural network. The idea is pretty simple: "Make large changes in the weights of the links early on in training, then slowly decrease the amount of change made to the network so that it can zero in on the best solution." Allowing for these large changes in the link weights early on in the training process corresponds to a high temperature in a metal where the metal is just barely solid and is very malleable. Likewise, the neural network is "malleable" in the early part of the training, allowing for the trial of many very different values in the link weights. As time passes, the changes in the link weights become smaller and smaller and the removal of errors is done at finer and finer levels. The process is analogous to looking around the world for the highest mountain ranges before getting into the details of which particular outcropping of rock at the summit of Mount Everest or K2 is a foot higher than the other.

20

Nearest Neighbor
and Clustering

Clustering and the nearest-neighbor prediction technique are among the oldest techniques used in data mining. Most people have an intuition that they understand what clustering is—namely, that like records are grouped or clustered together and put into the same grouping. Nearest neighbor is a prediction technique that is quite similar to clustering; its essence is that in order to determine what a prediction value is in one record, the user should look for records with similar predictor values in the historical database and use the prediction value from the record that is "nearest" to the unknown record.

A simple example of clustering would be the clustering that most people perform when they do the laundry—grouping the permanent-press, dry cleaning, whites, and brightly colored clothes is important because they have similar characteristics. And, it turns out, they have important attributes in common about the way they behave (and can be ruined) in the wash. To "cluster" your laundry, most of your decisions are relatively straightforward. There are, of course, difficult decisions to be made about which cluster your white shirt with red stripes goes into (since it is mostly white but has some color and is permanent-press). When clustering is used in business, the clusters are often much more dynamic—even changing weekly to monthly, and many more of the decisions concerning which cluster a record falls into are difficult.

A simple example of the nearest-neighbor prediction algorithm is that if you look at the people in your neighborhood (in this case those people who are, in fact, geographically near to you), you may notice that, in general, you all have somewhat similar incomes. Thus if your neighbor has an income greater than $100,000, chances are good that you, too, have a high income. Certainly the chances that you have a high income are greater when all your neighbors have incomes over $100,000 than if all your neighbors have incomes of $20,000. Within your neighborhood there may still be a wide variety of incomes possible among even your "closest" neighbors, but if you had to predict someone's income based only on knowledge of their neighbors' incomes, your best chance of being right would be to predict the incomes of the neighbors who live closest to the unknown person.

The nearest-neighbor prediction algorithm works in very much the same way except that "nearness" in a database may consist of a variety of factors other than just where the person lives. When predicting income, it may, for instance, be far more important to know which school(s) someone attended and what degree(s) that person attained. The better definition of "near" might, in fact, be other people that you graduated from college with rather than the people that you live next to.

20.1 Business Score Card

The *business score card* is used to assess business value of the data mining technique. The real-world problems of the business community are thus taken into consideration in evaluating the technique rather than some more academic measure of speed or performance. Three measures are the most critical factors for building a usable data mining system into the business process: automation, clarity, and return on investment. These measures reflect what ends up being some of the most critical aspects of whether a data mining system is successfully deployed, as just an academic exercise, or becomes a case study in how *not* to implement such a system. The performance of nearest-neighbor techniques is displayed in Fig. 20.1 and Table 20.1.

The measures that are most critical to business success have to do with the ease of deployment and real-world problems such as avoiding serious mistakes as well as achieving big successes. To this end, the data mining technique needs to be easy to use and deploy in as automated a fashion as possible (if data mining promises anything, it promises automation). The technique should also readily provide clear understandable answers that make business sense.

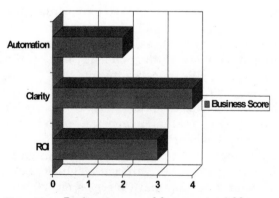

Figure 20.1 Business score card for nearest neighbor.

And last, the technique needs to provide an answer that can be converted into ROI analysis—not just some academic exercise in prediction. These three measures are captured in the business score card as the *automation, clarity,* and *ROI* measures of the data mining technique.

Nearest-neighbor techniques are among the easiest to use and understand because they work in a way similar to the way people think—by detecting closely matching examples. They also perform quite well in terms of automation, as many of the algorithms are robust with respect to dirty or missing data. Last, they are particularly adept at performing complex ROI calculations because the predictions are made at a local level where business simulations could be performed in order to optimize ROI. As they enjoy similar levels of accuracy compared to other techniques, the measures of accuracy such as lift are as good as those from any other method.

20.2   Where to Use Clustering and Nearest-Neighbor Prediction

Clustering and nearest-neighbor prediction are used in a wide variety of applications, ranging from personal bankruptcy prediction to computer recognition of a person's handwriting. These methods are also used every day by people who may not even realize that they are doing any kind of clustering. For instance, we may group certain types of foods or automobiles together (e.g., high-fat foods, U.S.-manufactured cars).

20.2.1   Clustering for clarity

Clustering is a method in which like records are grouped together. Usually this is done to give the end user a high-level view of what is going on in the database.

TABLE 20.1   Business Score Card for Nearest Neighbor

Data mining measure	Description
Automation	Nearest-neighbor techniques are relatively automated, although some preprocessing of the data needs to be performed in converting some predictors into values that can be used in a measure of distance. Unordered categoricals predictors such as eye color (blue, brown, green) need to be defined in terms of the distance from each other when there is a match (e.g., whether a blue-eyed person is a closer match to a green-eyed person than to a brown-eyed person).
Clarity	Excellent for clear explanation of why a prediction was made. A single example or set of examples can be extracted from the historical database for evidence as to why a prediction should or should not be made. The system can also communicate when it is not confident of its prediction.
ROI	Since the individual records of the nearest neighbor are returned directly without altering the database, it is possible to understand all facets of business behavior and thus derive a more complete estimate of the ROI not just from the prediction but from a variety of different factors.

Clustering is sometimes used to mean *segmentation*—which, most marketing people will tell, you is useful for coming up with a bird's-eye view of the business. Two commercial offerings of clustering systems are the PRIZM (trademark) system from Claritas corporation and MicroVision (trademark) from Equifax corporation. These companies have grouped the population by demographic information into segments that they believe are useful for direct marketing and sales. To build these groupings, they use information such as income, age, occupation, housing, and race collectively in the U.S. Census. Then they assign memorable "nicknames" to the clusters. Some examples are shown in Table 20.2.

This clustering information is then used by the end user to tag the customers in their database. Once this is done, the business user can get a quick high-level view of what is happening within the cluster. Once business users have worked with these codes for some time, they also begin to build intuitions about how these different customer clusters will react to the marketing offers particular to their business. For instance, some of these clusters may relate to their business and some of them may not. But given that their competition may well be using these same clusters to structure their business and marketing offers, it is important to be aware of how your customer base behaves in regard to these clusters.

20.2.2   Clustering for outlier analysis

Sometimes clustering is performed not so much to keep records together as to make it easier to see when one record sticks out from the rest. For instance

- Most wine distributors selling inexpensive wine in Missouri and that ship a certain volume of product produce a certain level of profit. A cluster of stores can be formed with these characteristics. One store stands out, however, as producing significantly lower profit. On closer examination it turns out that the distributor was delivering product to but not collecting payment from one of its customers.

- A sale on men's suits is being held in all branches of a department store for southern California. All stores except one with these characteristics have seen at least a 100 percent jump in revenue since the start of the sale. It

TABLE 20.2   Some Commercially Available Cluster Tags

Name	Income	Age	Education	Vendor
Blue Blood Estates	High	35–54	College	Claritas PRIZM*
Shotguns and Pickup	Middle	35–64	High school	Claritas PRIZM*
Southside City	Low	Mix	Grade school	Claritas PRIZM*
Living off the Land	Middle–low	Families with school-age children	Low	Equifax MicroVision*
University USA	Very low	Young–mix	Medium–high	Equifax MicroVision*
Sunset Years	Medium	Seniors	Medium	Equifax MicroVision*

* All trademarks.

turns out that this store had, unlike the others, advertised via radio rather than television.

20.2.3 Nearest neighbor for prediction

One essential element underlying the concept of clustering is that one particular object (whether cars, food, or customers) can be closer to another object than can some third object. It is interesting that most people have an innate sense of ordering placed on a variety of different objects.

Most people would agree that an apple is closer to an orange than it is to a tomato and that a Toyota Corolla is closer to a Honda Civic than to a Porsche. This sense of ordering on many different objects helps us place them in time and space and to make sense of the world. It is what allows us to build clusters—both in databases on computers and in our daily lives. This definition of nearness that seems to be ubiquitous also allows us to make predictions.

The nearest-neighbor prediction algorithm, simply stated, is

> Objects that are "near" to each other will have similar prediction values as well. Thus, if you know the prediction value of one of the objects, you can predict it for its nearest neighbors.

One of the classic places where nearest neighbor has been used for prediction has been in text retrieval. The problem to be solved in text retrieval is one in which end users define a document (e.g., a *Wall Street Journal* article, a technical conference paper) that is interesting to them and they solicit the system to "find more documents like this one," effectively defining a target of "this is the interesting document" or "this is not interesting." The prediction problem is that only a very few of the documents in the database actually have values for this prediction field (viz., only the documents that the reader has had a chance to look at so far). The nearest-neighbor technique is used to find other documents that share important characteristics with those documents that have been marked as interesting. As with almost all prediction algorithms, nearest neighbor can be used for a wide variety of places. Its successful use depends mostly on the preformatting of the data, so that nearness can be calculated, and where individual records can be defined. In the text-retrieval example this was not too difficult—the objects were documents. This is not always as easy as it is for text retrieval. Consider what it might be like in a time series problem—say, for predicting the stock market. In this case the input data is just a long series of stock prices over time without any particular record that could be considered to be an object. The value to be predicted is just the next value of the stock price.

This problem is solved for both nearest-neighbor techniques and for some other types of prediction algorithms by creating training records, taking, for instance, 10 consecutive stock prices and using the first 9 as predictor values and the 10th as the prediction value. Doing things this way, if you had 100 data points in your time series, you could create at least 10 different training records.

You could create even more training records than 10 by creating a new record starting at every data point. For instance, you could take the first 10 data points in your time series and create a record. Then you could take the 10 consecutive data points starting at the second data point, then the 10 consecutive data points starting at the third data point. Even though some of the data points would overlap from one record to the next, the prediction value would always be different. In our example of 100 initial data points, 90 different training records could be created this way, as opposed to the 10 training records created via the other method.

20.2.4   Applications score card

Figure 20.2 and Table 20.3 show the applications score card for the nearest-neighbor technique with respect to how well this technique performs for a variety of basic underlying applications. Given the way the prediction is formed (via distance in an N-dimensional space), it is hard for the system to generate simple rule-like explanations of its predictions. Instead, graphical descriptions and prototypes are more often used. For this reason rules are seldom used for explanation of nearest-neighbor prediction. The technique is clearly closely akin to clustering and in fact could easily be used for unsupervised learning in clustering if that is what is desired.

20.3   The General Idea

The nearest-neighbor algorithm is basically a refinement of clustering in the sense that both techniques use distance in some feature space to create either structure in the data or predictions. The nearest-neighbor algorithm is a refinement since part of the algorithm usually is a way of automatically determining the weighting of the importance of the predictors and how the distance will be measured within the feature space. Clustering is one special case of this where the importance of each predictor is considered to be equivalent.

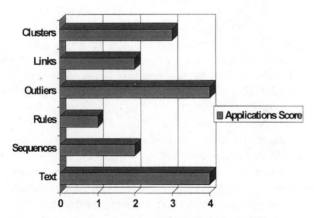

Figure 20.2   Applications score card for nearest neighbor.

TABLE 20.3   Applications Score Card for Nearest Neighbor

Problem type	Description
Clusters	The underlying prediction method for nearest-neighbor technology is nearness in some feature space. This is the same underlying metric used for most clustering algorithms, although for nearest neighbor the feature space is shaped in such a way as to facilitate a particular prediction.
Links	Nearest-neighbor techniques can be used for link analysis as long as the data is preformatted so that predictor values to be linked fall within the same record (e.g., for linking market-basket items together, the individual market items purchased in the same market basket must be recorded within the same record—note that this implies that the records may be variable in length).
Outliers	Nearest-neighbor techniques are particularly good at detecting outliers since they have effectively created a space within which it is possible to determine when a record is out of place.
Rules	One strength of nearest-neighbor techniques is that they take into account all the predictors to some degree, which is helpful for prediction but makes for a complex model that cannot easily be described as a rule. The systems are also generally optimized for prediction of new records rather than exhaustive extraction of interesting rules from the database.
Sequences	Nearest-neighbor techniques have been successfully used to make predictions in time sequences. The time values need to be encoded in records (as is similarly required for neural networks and other techniques).
Text	Most text retrieval systems are based around nearest-neighbor technologies, and most of the remaining breakthroughs in text retrieval come from further refinements of the predictor weighting algorithms and the distance calculation.

To see clustering and nearest-neighbor prediction in use, let's look at an example database in two ways. First, let's try to create our own clusters—which, if useful, we could use internally to help simplify and clarify large quantities of data (and maybe, if we did a very good job, sell these new codes to other business users). Second, let's try to create predictions based on the nearest neighbor.

First take a look at the data. How would you cluster the data in Table 20.4?

If these were your friends rather than your customers (hopefully they could be both) and they were single, you might cluster them according to their com-

TABLE 20.4   A Simple Example Database

ID	Name	Prediction	Age	Balance ($)	Income	Eyes	Gender
1	Amy	No	62	0	Medium	Brown	F
2	Al	No	53	1,800	Medium	Green	M
3	Betty	No	47	16,543	High	Brown	F
4	Bob	Yes	32	45	Medium	Green	M
5	Carla	Yes	21	2,300	High	Blue	F
6	Carl	No	27	5,400	High	Brown	M
7	Donna	Yes	50	165	Low	Blue	F
8	Don	Yes	46	0	High	Blue	M
9	Edna	Yes	27	500	Low	Blue	F
10	Ed	No	68	1,200	Low	Blue	M

patibility with each other, creating your own mini dating service. If you were a pragmatic person, you might cluster your database as follows because you think that marital happiness is dependent mostly on financial compatibility and create three clusters as shown in Table 20.5.

If, on the other hand, you are more of a romantic, you might note some incompatibilities between 46-year-old Don and 21-year-old Carla (even though they both make very good incomes). You might instead consider age and some physical characteristics to be most important in creating clusters of friends. Another way you could cluster your friends would be based on their ages and on the color of their eyes. This is shown in Table 20.6. Here three clusters are created where each person in the cluster is about the same age and some attempt has been made to keep people of like eye color together in the same cluster.

20.3.1 There is no best way to cluster

This example, although simple, points up some important questions about clustering. For instance, is it possible to say whether the first clustering that was performed above (by financial status) was better or worse than the second clustering (by age and eye color)? Probably not, since the clusters were constructed for no particular purpose except to note similarities between some of the records and that the view of the database could be somewhat simplified by using clusters. But even the differences that were created by the two different clusterings were driven by slightly different motivations (financial vs. romantic). In general, the reasons for clustering are just this ill-defined because clusters are used more often than not for exploration and summarization and not as much as for prediction.

20.3.2 How are tradeoffs made when determining which records fall into which clusters?

Note that for the first clustering example, there was a pretty simple rule by which the records could be broken up into clusters—namely, by income. In the

TABLE 20.5   A Simple Clustering of the Example Database

ID	Name	Prediction	Age	Balance ($)	**Income**	Eyes	Gender
3	Betty	No	47	16,543	**High**	Brown	F
5	Carla	Yes	21	2,300	**High**	Blue	F
6	Carl	No	27	5,400	**High**	Brown	M
8	Don	Yes	46	0	**High**	Blue	M
1	Amy	No	62	0	**Medium**	Brown	F
2	Al	No	53	1,800	**Medium**	Green	M
4	Bob	Yes	32	45	**Medium**	Green	M
7	Donna	Yes	50	165	**Low**	Blue	F
9	Edna	Yes	27	500	**Low**	Blue	F
10	Ed	No	68	1,200	**Low**	Blue	M

second clustering example the dividing lines were less clear since two predictors were used to form the clusters (age and eye color). Thus the first cluster is dominated by younger people with somewhat mixed eye colors, whereas the latter two clusters have a mix of older people where eye color has been used to separate them out (the second cluster consists entirely of blue-eyed people). In this case these tradeoffs were made arbitrarily, but when clustering much larger numbers of records, these tradeoffs are explicitly defined by the clustering algorithm.

20.3.3 Clustering is the happy medium between homogeneous clusters and the lowest number of clusters

In the best possible case clusters would be built where all records within the cluster had identical values for the particular predictors that were being clustered on. This would be the optimum in creating a high-level view since knowing the predictor values for any member of the cluster would mean knowing the values for every member of the cluster no matter how large the cluster was. Creating homogeneous clusters in which all values for the predictors are the same is difficult to do when there are many predictors and/or the predictors have many different values (high cardinality). It is possible to guarantee that homogeneous clusters are created by breaking apart any cluster that is inhomogeneous into smaller clusters that are homogeneous. In the extreme, though, this usually means creating clusters with only one record in them, which usually defeats the original purpose of the clustering. For instance, in our 10 record database mentioned above, 10 perfectly homogeneous clusters could be formed of 1 record each, but not much progress would have been made in making the original database more understandable.

The second important constraint on clustering is then that a reasonable number of clusters are formed—where, again, "reasonable" is defined by the user but is difficult to quantify beyond that except to say that just one cluster is unacceptable (too much generalization) and that as many clusters and orig-

TABLE 20.6   A More "Romantic" Clustering of the Example Database to Optimize for Your Dating Service

ID	Name	Prediction	Age	Balance ($)	Income	Eyes	Gender
5	Carla	Yes	21	2,300	High	Blue	F
9	Edna	Yes	27	500	Low	Blue	F
6	Carl	No	27	5,400	High	Brown	M
4	Bob	Yes	32	45	Medium	Green	M
8	Don	Yes	46	0	High	Blue	M
7	Donna	Yes	50	165	Low	Blue	F
10	Ed	No	68	1,200	Low	Blue	M
3	Betty	No	47	16,543	High	Brown	F
2	Al	No	53	1,800	Medium	Green	M
1	Amy	No	62	0	Medium	Brown	F

inal records is also unacceptable. Many clustering algorithms either let users choose the number of clusters that they would like to see created from the database or provide users with a "knob" by which they can create fewer or greater numbers of clusters interactively after the clustering has been performed.

20.3.4   What is the difference between clustering and nearest-neighbor prediction?

The main distinction between clustering and the nearest-neighbor technique is that clustering is what is called an *unsupervised learning* technique and nearest neighbor is generally used for prediction or a *supervised learning* technique. Unsupervised learning techniques are unsupervised in the sense that when they are run, there is no particular reason for the creation of the models the way there is for supervised learning techniques that are trying to perform prediction. In prediction, the patterns that are found in the database and presented in the model are always the most important patterns in the database for performing some particular prediction. In clustering there is no particular sense of why certain records are near to each other or why they all fall into the same cluster. Some of the differences between clustering and nearest-neighbor prediction are summarized in Table 20.7.

20.3.5   What is an *n*-dimensional space?

When people talk about clustering or nearest-neighbor prediction, they often discuss a "space" of *n* dimensions. What they mean is that in order to define what is near and what is far away, it is helpful to have a "space" defined where distance can be calculated. Generally these spaces behave just like the three-dimensional space that we are familiar with, in which distance between objects is defined by euclidean distance (just like figuring out the length of a side in a triangle).

What goes for three dimensions works pretty well for more dimensions as well, which is a good thing since most real-world problems consist of far more

TABLE 20.7   Some of the Differences between the Nearest-Neighbor Data Mining Technique and Clustering

Nearest neighbor	Clustering
Used for prediction as well as consolidation.	Used mostly for consolidating data into a high-level view and general grouping of records into like behaviors.
Space is defined by the problem to be solved (supervised learning).	Space is defined as default *n*-dimensional space, or is defined by the user, or is a predefined space driven by past experience (unsupervised learning).
Generally only uses distance metrics to determine nearness.	Can use other metrics besides distance to determine nearness of two records—for example, linking points together.

than three dimensions. In fact, each predictor (or database column) that is used can be considered to be a new dimension. In the example above the five predictors—age, income, balance, eyes, and gender—can all be construed to be dimensions in an n-dimensional space where n, in this case, equals 5. It is sometimes easier to think about these and other data mining algorithms in terms of n-dimensional spaces because it allows for some intuition as to how the algorithm is working.

Moving from three dimensions to five dimensions is not too large a jump, but there are also spaces in real-world problems that are far more complex. In the credit card industry, card issuers (creditors) typically have over one thousand predictors that could be used to create an n-dimensional space. For text retrieval (e.g., finding useful *Wall Street Journal* articles from a large database, or finding useful Web sites on the Internet), the predictors (and hence the dimensions) are typically words or phrases that are found in the document records. In just one year of the *Wall Street Journal* more than 50,000 different words are used—which translates to a 50,000-dimensional space in which nearness between records must be calculated.

20.3.6   How is the space for clustering and nearest neighbor defined?

For clustering, the n-dimensional space is usually defined by assigning one predictor to each dimension. For the nearest-neighbor algorithm, predictors are also mapped to dimensions, but then those dimensions are literally stretched or compressed according to how important the particular predictor is in making the prediction. The stretching of a dimension effectively makes that dimension (and hence predictor) more important than the others in calculating the distance.

For instance, if you were a mountain climber and someone told you that you were 2 mi from your destination, the distance would be the same whether it were 1 mi north and 1 mi up the face of the mountain or 2 mi north on level ground, but clearly the former route is much different from the latter. The distance traveled straight upward is the most important in figuring out how long it will really take to get to the destination, and you would probably like to consider this "dimension" to be more important than the others. In fact, you, as a mountain climber, could "weight" the importance of the vertical dimension in calculating some new distance by reasoning that every mile upward is equivalent to 10 mi on level ground.

If you used this rule of thumb to weight the importance of one dimension over the other, it would be clear that in one case you were much "farther away" from your destination (11 mi) than in the second (2 mi). In the next section we'll show how the nearest-neighbor algorithm uses the distance measure that similarly weights the important dimensions more heavily when calculating a distance.

20.4 How Clustering and Nearest-Neighbor Prediction Work

20.4.1 Looking at an *n*-dimensional space

Figure 20.3 graphically portrays the data for a given database. Each record has been mapped to a certain point in this rectangular space on the basis of its values for age and income (e.g., old rich people would be in the upper right corner and rich young people would be in the lower right corner).

Although there are some 40 or more data points represented in this image, there are three main clusters of records that could be presented to the end user for a useful high-level view of the database. If you were in the golf equipment business, these might represent important segments of your customer population:

Cluster 1—retirees with modest incomes

Cluster 2—middle-aged weekend golfers

Cluster 3—wealthy youth who have exclusive club memberships

But also note that there is an additional set of records that does not easily fit into any of the existing clusters that seem to be middle-aged but of low income. There are not a lot of data points to support a fourth cluster, but it is possible that this also is an important segment of your customer base—maybe the middle- to low-income blue-collar workers who play leagues at county courses.

The other points that do not fit neatly into one of the three clusters are called *outliers* (because they lie outside the normal cluster region) and don't easily fit into even the nearest cluster (which could be quite far away). The distance between the cluster and a given data point is often measured from the center of mass of the cluster (just like a physical object such as a plate, which has one point where the weight is equal in all directions and can be balanced). The center of mass of the cluster can be calculated by simply calculating the average income and age of each record that falls within the cluster.

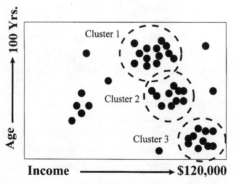

Figure 20.3   Three clusters found in a database of customers.

Clusters can be defined solely by their centers or by their centers with some radius attached in which all points that fall within the radius are classified into that cluster. The center of mass of the cluster can be viewed as the proto-typical record that represents all the records in the cluster. For example, the center of cluster 1 might be a prototypical golfer of age 64.7 years and $33,000 annual income.

This example shows how normal database records could be viewed as being mapped onto an n-dimensional space (where n is some number like 3 to correspond to the three-dimensional space that we live in). In this case the space only has two dimensions and is pretty easy to visualize. If there were three dimensions (e.g., age, income, bank account balance), we could map the data points into a three-dimensional graph. If there were four dimensions (e.g., age, income, bank account balance, eye color), we could still visualize this in three-dimensional space by changing the color of each point to match the color of the person's eyes. Once we get past four dimensions, however, it is hard to visualize all the dimensions at one time the way we can with two, three, or even four dimensions.

Many clustering problems, however, have hundreds to thousands of dimensions, and one caveat for using clustering is that these n-dimensional spaces are quite different from just two dimensions and many of our intuitions about how things behave in two or three dimensions may not hold when n becomes 100 or more. In this case we can see only a few dimensions at a time and thus have only a narrow view of all that is going on inside of the data.

20.4.2   How is "nearness" defined?

Hopefully it is becoming clear that both clustering and nearest-neighbor techniques work within an n-dimensional space where there is some sense of one record being close to or far from another record. How is this "nearness" determined? One way to do this would be to simply say that any record in the historical database that is exactly the same as the record to be predicted is considered "close" and anything else is far away as shown in Table 20.8.

The difficulty with this strategy is twofold:

- It is unlikely that you will find exact matches of records in your database.
- The perfectly matching record might be spurious. Better results can be obtained by taking a vote among several nearby records.

Two other definitions of nearness don't require an exact match. The *Manhattan distance* metric simply adds up the differences between each predictor

TABLE 20.8   A Perfectly Close Match between a Historical Record and a New Record to Be Predicted

ID	Name	Prediction	Age	Balance ($)	Income	Eyes	Gender
5	Carla	Yes	21	2300	High	Blue	F
	Sue	??	21	2300	High	Blue	F

between the historical record and the record to be predicted. The other, called the *euclidean distance,* calculates distance just the way the pythagorean theorem calculated the length of the hypotenuse of a triangle (the square of the hypotenuse is equal to the sum of the squares of the other two sides). This same calculation is used to calculate the distance between two points in n dimensions by squaring the differences of the predictor values for the two records and then taking the square root of that sum. For instance, to calculate the Manhattan distance between Carla and Carl, as shown in Table 20.9, the difference between each predictor (age, balance, income, eyes, and gender) must be calculated. Calculating this difference for their ages (6 years) and their bank balances ($3100 = $5400 − $2300) is relatively straightforward. Calculating the difference between blue eyes and brown eyes is problematic.

One way to resolve this dilemma is to fall back on the exact-match criterion and consider the distance between mismatching eye colors to be 1 and exact matches to be 0. A similar technique could be used for the gender predictor but perhaps something a little bit more sophisticated for the income predictor. In this case there is actually an ordering on the values even though they are not numeric. One solution is to assign numbers to each value (high = 3, medium = 2, and low = 1). In this case since Carl and Carla's incomes are identical, there is no difference contributed to the distance. The distance between the two records is then

$$3108 = 6 + 3100 + 0 + 1 + 1$$

Now there is a new problem. The total distance between the two records is completely dominated by the difference in balances. It almost doesn't matter if all the other predictors are exact matches since the contribution from the balance is in general so much larger. To compensate for this, many clustering systems will normalize the values in each dimension so that the minimum and maximum for each predictor do not vary (e.g., always remaining between 0 and 100).

When the records are normalized like this, the maximum distance contributed by any single predictor is always the same. No one predictor could dominate if this normalization were performed. In this case if the predictor values were normalized between 0 and 100, the maximum difference any given predictor could contribute would be 100 and each predictor would have equal importance in the determination of which records were close to each other. If this were done in the Carl and Carla example, the new distance would be

$$225 = 6 + 19 + 0 + 100 + 100$$

TABLE 20.9   Calculating the Distance between Two Records*

ID	Name	Prediction	Age	Balance ($)	Income	Eyes	Gender
5	Carla	Yes	21	2300	High	Blue	F
6	Carl	No	27	5400	High	Brown	M

* This calculation can be difficult if some of the predictors are categorical.

The difference value of 19 for the balance predictor was calculated by recognizing that the maximum difference in this data set between balances could be 16,543 (a minimum of $0 for Don and Amy and a maximum of $16,543 for Betty). The actual difference in balances between Carl and Carla is $3100, which is 19 percent of that maximum difference of $16,543. By treating each predictor equally, we see that the distance is no longer dependent on particular idiosyncrasies of the measuring units with which the data was recorded (consider that if balance were recorded in Japanese yen rather than dollars, the problem would be even more severe).

20.4.3   Weighting the dimensions: distance with a purpose

Notice that the nice round clusters of data in this first example are easy to spot only visually because of the implicit normalization of the dimensions (the age and income axes show the maximum and minimum within the same distance). We have implicitly decided that the maximum values on our two-dimensional view correspond to the maximum age and income that we have in the database. In this first example let's say that there is a maximum age of 100 and a maximum income of $120,000. In this case the clusters are easy to detect. But let's now say that Bill Gates is an avid golfer and one of our customers and we need to add his customer record to our two-dimensional graph. Because of the large value for income that this new record supplies, the space has effectively been rescaled so that what originally looked like three or four very distinct clusters now looks like one long vertical one with a single outlier (Bill Gates).

What this rescaling has accomplished is to effectively redefine what we implicitly meant by "near" when we defined our clusters. In the previous example, the clustering implicitly placed a great deal of importance on the difference between $10,000 and $20,000 in income. Now with a billionaire to be accounted for, a $20,000 or even a $100,000 difference in income between records is not even noticeable. Only hundreds of millions of dollars' difference in income could be visually recognized on this graph (see Fig. 20.4). Thus simply "normalizing" the age and income dimensions does not help detect useful clusters.

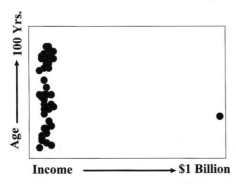

Figure 20.4 Original clusters with Bill Gates' record added.

These same issues also arise within the distance calculations used by the clustering and nearest-neighbor algorithms themselves and are not just limited to these graphical representations. The basic question is as follows: When "near" is defined, how important is each dimension's contribution? The answer is that it depends. It depends on what you are trying to accomplish. Remember the mountain-climbing example where, if you are trying to determine how difficult it will be to get to someplace, you may well want to consider vertical distances up the mountain to be more important than horizontal distances across flat terrain. This is also true in n-dimensional spaces for doing prediction.

For example, if you are using the nearest-neighbor algorithm to predict whether someone is pregnant, then you would expect predictors (dimensions) such as gender and age to have enormous impact on the prediction value. While predictors such as eye color would be expected to have little impact (e.g., blue-eyed people are pregnant as often as brown-eyed people but very few people over 60 or under 10 years old are pregnant). Thus a good algorithm would consider someone to be near in this space if the people are close in age and of the same gender, but differences in eye color would be inconsequential. If, on the other hand, the problem is to predict a genetic disease that is linked to the gene that produces eye color, you would expect eye color to be a key predictor in determining what is near and what is not and would be more heavily weighted.

20.4.4   Calculating dimension weights

There are several automatic ways of calculating the importance of different dimensions. In the case of document classification and topic prediction, the dimensions of the space are often the individual words contained in each document. For instance, there might be a dimension for the word "entrepreneur" that has only two values—a 0 if the word does not occur in the document and a 1 if it does. In the case of text classification the documents either contain or do not contain the word, but not all words (dimensions) are created equal. For instance, the word "the" is so common to so many documents that it is of very little interest if it is matched on. On the other hand, the word "entrepreneur" occurs in only very select documents and if that is the topic the user is looking for, the fact that "entrepreneur" occurs in the document is very significant. The fact that the word "the" occurs in the document is almost completely inconsequential.

The weights for these word dimensions are thus calculated using two methods:

1. The inverse frequency of the word is often used. For example, if the word "the" occurred in 10,000 documents, then it would have a word weight of $\frac{1}{10,000} = 0.0001$; if "entrepreneur" occurred in 100 documents, it might receive a word weight of $\frac{1}{100} = 0.01$.

2. The importance of the word to the topic to be predicted. If the topic the user is looking for is about starting a small business, words such as "entrepreneur"

and phrases like "venture capital" will be given much higher weight than words that otherwise might be important in other contexts, like "tornado."

Data mining in documents is a bit of a special situation in that there are so many dimensions and almost all of the dimensions are binary. For many other business problems there will be binary (e.g., gender), categorical (e.g., eye color), and numeric (e.g., quarterly revenue) dimensions. Each dimension type can be weighted by calculating how relevant that particular predictor is to making the particular prediction. This calculation can be the correlation between the predictor and the prediction columns, or it could be as simple as the conditional probability that the prediction has a certain value given that the predictor has a certain value (i.e., if a predictor existed such that every time it contained a certain value it would correctly predict the prediction value, it would garner a very high weight).

Dimension weights have also been calculated via algorithmic searches where random weights are tried initially and then slowly modified to improve the overall accuracy of the system. Techniques have been used for this such as simple "hill climbing" methods that make a small change to the weight and then keep it if it improves accuracy to genetic algorithms which employ a simulated competition, mutation, and crossover on the weights of the dimensions to use simulated evolution to evolve the dimension weights that do best at lowering the error rate of the entire system. The first-layer weights in a neural network are also a form of dimension weighting that are optimized via the learning algorithms of the neural network.

20.4.5 Hierarchical and nonhierarchical clustering

There are two main types of clustering techniques: those that create a hierarchy of clusters and those that do not. The hierarchical clustering techniques create a hierarchy of clusters from small to big. The main reason for this is that, as was already stated, clustering is an unsupervised learning technique, and as such, there is no absolutely correct answer. For this reason and depending on the particular application of the clustering, fewer or greater numbers of clusters may be desired. With a hierarchy of clusters defined, it is possible to choose the number of clusters that are desired. At the extreme it is possible to have as many clusters as there are records in the database. In this case the records within the cluster are optimally similar to each other (since there is only one) and certainly different from the other clusters. But of course, such a clustering technique misses the point in the sense that the idea of clustering is to find useful patterns in the database that summarize it and make it easier to understand. Any clustering algorithm that ends up with as many clusters as there are records has not helped the user understand the data any better. Thus one of the main points about clustering is that there should be many fewer clusters than there are original records. Exactly how many clusters should be formed is a matter of interpretation. The advantage of hierarchical clustering methods is that they allow the end user to choose from either many clusters or only a few.

The hierarchy of clusters is usually viewed as a tree in which the smallest clusters merge together to create the next highest level of clusters, and those at that level merge together to create the next-highest level of clusters. Figure 20.5 shows how several clusters might form a hierarchy. When a hierarchy of clusters like this is created, the user can determine what the right number of clusters is that adequately summarizes the data while still providing useful information (at the other extreme, a single cluster containing all the records is a great summarization but does not contain enough specific information to be useful).

This hierarchy of clusters is created through the algorithm that builds the clusters. There are two main types of hierarchical clustering algorithms:

- *Agglomerative.* Agglomerative clustering techniques start with as many clusters as there are records where each cluster contains just one record. The clusters that are nearest each other are merged together to form the next-largest cluster. This merging is continued until a hierarchy of clusters is built with just a single cluster containing all the records at the top of the hierarchy.

- *Divisive.* Divisive clustering techniques take the opposite approach from agglomerative techniques. These techniques start with all the records in one cluster, then try to split that cluster into smaller pieces, and then, in turn, try to split those smaller pieces.

Of the two, the agglomerative techniques are the most commonly used for clustering and have more algorithms developed for them. We'll talk about these in

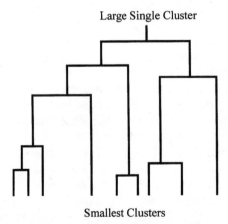

Large Single Cluster

Smallest Clusters

Figure 20.5   Diagram showing a hierarchy of clusters. Clusters at the lowest level are merged together to form larger clusters at the next level of the hierarchy.

more detail in the next section. The nonhierarchical techniques in general are faster to create from the historical database but require that the user make some decision about the number of clusters desired or the minimum "nearness" required for two records to be within the same cluster. These nonhierarchical techniques often are run multiple times, starting off with some arbitrary or even random clustering and then iteratively improving the clustering by shuffling some records around. Or these techniques sometimes create clusters that are created with only one pass through the database, adding records to existing clusters when they exist and creating new clusters when no existing cluster is a good candidate for the given record. Because the definition of which clusters are formed can depend on these initial choices of which starting clusters should be chosen or even how many clusters should be used, these techniques can be less repeatable than the hierarchical techniques and can sometimes create either too many or too few clusters because the number of clusters is predetermined by the user, not solely by the patterns inherent in the database.

Nonhierarchical clustering. There are two main nonhierarchical clustering techniques—both of them can be computed very rapidly on the database but have some drawbacks: (1) *single-pass methods,* in which the database must be passed through only once in order to create the clusters (i.e., each record is read from the database only once); and (2) *reallocation methods,* involving the movement or "reallocation" of records from one cluster to another in order to create better clusters. Reallocation techniques do use multiple passes through the database but are relatively fast in comparison to the hierarchical techniques.

The general algorithm for a single-pass technique is as follows:

1. Read in a record from the database and determine the cluster that it best fits into (using some measure of nearness).

2. If the nearest cluster is still pretty far away (there is no good fit), create a new cluster with this new record in it.

3. Read in the next record.

Since reading in records from the database is often one of the most expensive aspects of the clustering algorithm, the single-pass algorithm can be quite fast. It does have some problems, though, in that it often creates large clusters early in the clustering process and since the decision to create a new cluster is based on which clusters already exist and which records have already been processed, the clusters that are generated are dependent on the order in which the records are structured in the database, and the records that are read first can have a significant effect on which clusters are formed—which is not necessarily what is desired. The ideal would be to have clustering created on the basis of the database as a whole—i.e., the right answer is delivered for the given database independent of the processing steps of the algorithm.

The reallocation algorithms seek to solve this problem of dependence on the order in which the data is processed by readjusting the contents of the clusters to optimize the similarity of records within clusters and the dissimilarity of records between clusters. The general algorithm for a reallocation technique is as follows:

1. Preselect the number of clusters desired.
2. Randomly pick a record to become the center or "seed" for each of these clusters.
3. Go through the database and assign each record to the nearest cluster.
4. Recalculate the centers of the clusters.
5. Repeat steps 3 and 4 until there is a minimum or reallocation of records between clusters.

What actually happens in this technique is that records are initially assigned to clusters which are not particularly good fits (because we initially picked our clusters at random). By recalculating the center of the cluster in step 4, we see that clusters that better match the actual data are formed. One could visualize this as the centers of the clusters (which really define the clusters) moving around in the n-dimensional space moving closer and closer to the centers of high density and away from particular outliers.

Predefining the number of clusters rather than having them driven by the data might seem to be a bad idea as there might be some very distinct and observable clustering of the data into a certain number of clusters which the user might not be aware of. For instance, the user may wish to see their data broken up into 10 clusters, but the data itself partitions very cleanly into 13 clusters. These nonhierarchical techniques will try to shoehorn these extra three clusters into the existing 10 rather than creating 13 which best fit the data. The saving grace for these methods, however, is that, as we have seen, there is no one right answer for how to cluster, so, by arbitrarily predefining the number of clusters, you would seldom end up with the wrong answer. One advantage of these techniques is that users often do have some predefined level of summarization in which they are interested (e.g., "25 clusters is too confusing, but 10 will help to give me an insight into my data"). The fact that greater or fewer numbers of clusters would better match the data is actually of secondary importance.

Hierarchical clustering. Hierarchical clustering has the advantage over nonhierarchical techniques in that the clusters are defined solely by the data (not by the users predetermining the number of clusters) and that the number of clusters can be increased or decreased by simply moving up and down the hierarchy. The hierarchy is created by starting either at the top (one cluster that includes all records) and subdividing (divisive clustering) or by starting at the bottom with as many clusters as there are records and merging (agglomerative clustering). Usually the merging and subdividing are done two clusters at a time. The general algorithm for agglomerative techniques is as follows:

1. Start with as many clusters as there are records, with one record in each cluster.

2. Combine the two nearest clusters into a larger cluster.

3. Continue until only one cluster remains.

The general algorithm for the divisive techniques moves in the reverse direction:

1. Start with one cluster that contains all the records in the database.

2. Determine the division of the existing cluster that best maximizes similarity within clusters and dissimilarity between clusters.

3. Divide the cluster and repeat on the two smaller clusters.

4. Stop when some minimum threshold of cluster size or total number has been reached or when there is only one record in the cluster.

The divisive techniques can be quite expensive to compute. One algorithm separates the cluster into every possible pair of smaller clusters and picks the best split on the basis of the minimum average distance between records within the cluster. For this reason and others, the agglomerative methods are the more prevalent in use today. To better understand how the clustering is really performed, it is necessary to look carefully at how the decision to merge clusters is made for the agglomerative techniques.

This decision can be made in several ways:

1. Join the clusters whose nearest records are as near as possible. This is called the *single-link method.* Because clusters can be joined together on the basis of just a single near pair of records, this technique can create long, snakelike clusters. For this reason it is not as good at extracting classic spherical and compact clusters.

2. Join the clusters whose most distant records are as near as possible. This is called the *complete-link method,* so called because all records within the cluster are linked together within some maximum distance. This technique favors the creation of small compact clusters.

3. Join the clusters where the average distance between all pairs of records is as small as possible. This is called the *group-average link* method. Because it considers all records within the clusters, including the nearest and the most distant, it results in clusters somewhere in between the elongated single-link clusters and the tight complete-link clusters.

4. Join the clusters whose resulting merged cluster has minimum total distance between all records. This is called *Ward's method,* and it tends to produce a symmetric hierarchy and is good at recovering cluster structure but it is sensitive to outliers and has difficulty in recovering elongated clusters.

The main distinction between these techniques is their ability to favor long, scraggly clusters that are linked together record by record, or to favor the detection of the more classic, compact, or spherical cluster that was shown at the beginning of this chapter. It may seem strange to want to form these long snaking chainlike clusters, but in some cases these are the patterns that the user would like to have detected in the database. These are the times when the underlying space looks quite different from the spherical clusters and the clusters that should be formed are not based on the distance from the center of the cluster but rather on the records being "linked" together. Consider the example shown in Fig. 20.6 or 20.7. In these cases there are two clusters that are not very spherical in shape but could be detected by the single-link technique.

When looking at the layout of the data in Fig. 20.6, there appears to be two relatively flat clusters running parallel to each along the income axis. Neither the complete link nor Ward's method would, however, return these two clusters to the user. These techniques rely on creating a "center" for each cluster and picking these centers so as to minimize the average distance between each record and this center. Points that are very distant from these centers would necessarily fall into a different cluster.

What makes these clusters "visible" in this simple two-dimensional space is the fact that each point in a cluster is tightly linked to some other point in the cluster. For the two clusters we see that the maximum distance between the nearest two points within a cluster is less than the minimum distance between the nearest two points in different clusters. In other words, for any point in this space, the nearest point to it is always going to be another point in the same cluster. The center of gravity of a cluster could be quite distant from a given point but every point is linked to every other point by a series of small distances.

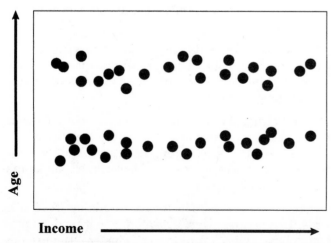

Figure 20.6 An example of elongated clusters which would not be recovered by the complete link or Ward's methods but would be by the single-link method.

20.4.6 Nearest-neighbor prediction

Implicit in the discussion of clustering was that some patterns were being detected in a large database between locations where records existed and where they didn't (in the diagrams the black dots represent the records and the white space represents possible records that don't exist in the database). For prediction with nearest neighbors, the problem becomes a little bit more interesting. In nearest-neighbor prediction there is still the concept of records that exist and don't exist, but there is also the concept of the prediction value of the record. Even in the simplest case where the prediction value is "yes" or "no" (e.g., will customers pay their bills or not), our visualization is somewhat different. There are now three types of points in the diagram: "yes" records, "no" records, and missing records. Our clustering problem in this case now becomes well defined: "Create clusters that are as homogenous as possible so that when used for prediction, they minimize the error rate on test data." This is the essential difference between the unsupervised learning that occurs in clustering and the supervised learning that occurs in the nearest neighbor prediction method.

To visualize the prediction problem, look at Fig. 20.8. There are now two types of records present in the database, represented by a solid circle and a hollow square. For prediction, clusters need to be formed in the database that segregate the squares from the circles. This is supervised learning because the "goodness" of this segregation can be measured by the error rate of the prediction. A good segregation might be made nearly vertically along the middle of the income axis as is shown in Fig. 20.9.

The segregation in Fig. 20.9 between bill payers and defaulters is not too different from a cluster except that in this case the boundaries of that segmentation are very carefully defined to avoid errors. In the bill payer segment of the database, all customers will be predicted to be bill payers. In this case there are

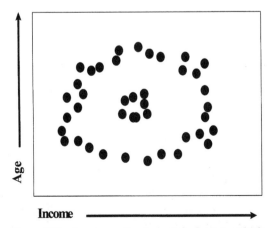

Figure 20.7 An example of nested clusters which would not be recovered by the complete link or Ward's methods but would be by the single-link method.

● Pays Bills
□ Defaults

Figure 20.8 In prediction techniques there are records and missing records as there are in clustering, but in addition, there are different types of records based on the prediction values (represented here by circles and squares).

two records of defaulting customers within the segment, which translates to errors. Thus the prediction on the historical data will not have a 0 percent error rate. In the defaulter segment there are no mistaken predictions made for the historical database, but that does not mean that the error rate will be 0 percent on the test data.

The nearest-neighbor prediction technique makes the prediction for an unclassified record based on the prediction value of the nearest historical

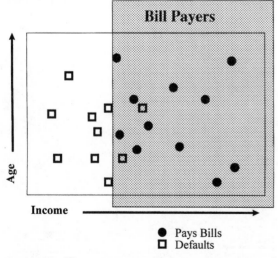

● Pays Bills
□ Defaults

Figure 20.9 The gray area represents a segregation of the database into the customers who pay their bills and those who do not.

record. As mentioned previously, the definition and meaning of "near" can have a dramatic impact on the accuracy of the prediction technique. Once defined, however, we can visualize how the nearest-neighbor technique works in Fig. 20.10. Here unclassified records, denoted by the letters A, B, and C, fall somewhere in the n-dimensional space. The nearest neighbor is then calculated and the prediction is made on the basis of the prediction value of that record.

For the unclassified record A, the nearest neighbor is the record of a customer who has defaulted. Since the customer portrayed in this record has age and income characteristics similar to those of the historical record, this unclassified record will be predicted to have a value of default for the prediction column. For unclassified record B, the decision is not quite as clearcut. In this case record B falls along the boundary between the defaulters and the nondefaulters. It has near neighbors that are both defaulters and nondefaulters. The nearest neighbor, however, is a defaulter, so record B will be predicted to be a defaulter.

20.4.7 *K* nearest neighbors— voting is better

One of the improvements that is usually made to the basic nearest-neighbor algorithm is to take a vote from the *K* nearest neighbors rather than just relying on the sole nearest neighbor to the unclassified record. In Fig. 20.10 we can see that unclassified example C has a nearest neighbor that is a defaulter and yet is surrounded almost exclusively by records that are good credit risks. In this case the nearest neighbor to record C is probably an outlier—which may be incorrect data or some nonrepeatable idiosyncrasy. In either case it is more than likely that C is a nondefaulter yet would be predicted to be a defaulter if the sole nearest neighbor were used for the prediction.

In cases like these a vote of the 9 or 15 nearest neighbors would provide a better prediction accuracy for the system than would just the single nearest

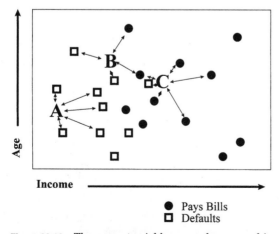

Income

● Pays Bills
□ Defaults

Figure 20.10 The nearest neighbors are shown graphically for three unclassified records: A, B, and C.

neighbor. Usually this is accomplished by simply taking the majority or plurality of predictions from the K nearest neighbors if the prediction column is a binary or categorical or taking the average value of the prediction column from the K nearest neighbors.

Another important aspect of any system that is used to make predictions is that the user be provided with not only the prediction but also some sense of the confidence in that prediction (e.g., the prediction is a defaulter with the chance of being correct 60 percent of the time). The nearest-neighbor algorithm provides this confidence information in a number of ways:

- The distance to the nearest neighbor provides a level of confidence. If the neighbor is very close or an exact match, then there is much higher confidence in the prediction than if the nearest record were a great distance from the unclassified record.

- The degree of homogeneity among the predictions within the K nearest neighbors can also be used. If all the nearest neighbors make the same prediction, then there is much higher confidence in the prediction than if half the records made one prediction and the other half made another prediction.

20.4.8   Generalizing the solution: prototypes and sentries

One of the shortcomings of the nearest-neighbor classification technique is that, in its simplest form, all the original historical database must be preserved in order to use the predictive model. The database is, in fact, the predictive model in effect, which means that the model can be quite large in comparison to the small predictive models generated by decision trees or neural networks.

Another shortcoming of the method is that there is no formal way of preventing overfitting of the model to the historical data since the historical data is completely retained as part of the predictive model. In order to overcome these two shortcomings of the technique, several editing processes have been proposed that remove redundant records from the predictive model and seek to provide a more generalized model that is both smaller and of higher accuracy on held-aside data.

Two of the ways that this editing has been carried out is to form prototypes and sentries that correspondingly represent the center or the boundaries of large numbers of records that have the same prediction value.

- Prototypes are formed by merging nearby historical records together into an averaged record (prototype) that represents both records. The merged record is added to the prototype as long as it does not decrease the overall predictive accuracy of the model below what was achieved with the original historical database.

- Sentries are formed by removing historical records that are not required in order to make an accurate prediction. They represent the boundaries of the

n-dimensional space within which the prediction value is homogeneous. In effect, they act like sentries guarding geographic borders.

Figure 20.11 shows a homogeneous circle of defaulters surrounded by nondefaulters. A single prototype in the center of the circle can adequately represent all the records within the circle and still achieve the same levels of accuracy of prediction. If sentries are used, the records inside of the circle are deleted—again without loss of predictive accuracy. Both the prototype technique and the sentries technique are shown in Fig. 20.12.

20.5 Case Study: Image Recognition for Human Handwriting

20.5.1 The problem

Optical character recognition (OCR) refers to the class of problems that has to do with converting computer-stored images of human handwriting into recognizable letters and numerals. This may at first seem like an almost trivial task, but it turns out to be a particularly difficult task and one that benefits greatly from sophisticated data mining techniques. A typical image and a difficult image are presented in Fig. 20.13. The first image is clearly the number 9; the second image, however, is ambiguous and could be interpreted as either a 4 or a 9. Interestingly there are only three pixels (white or black boxes) that differ between the two images.

The automated recognition of human handwriting is a very valuable endeavor as the U.S. Census alone spends many tens of millions of dollars to have humans read and key in the U.S. Census forms. In an effort to fairly and

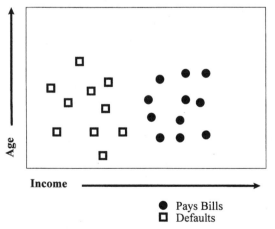

● Pays Bills
□ Defaults

Figure 20.11 One of the shortcomings of the nearest-neighbor method is that it retains all the original database as part of the predictive model, even though much of the data could be compressed and the model simplified.

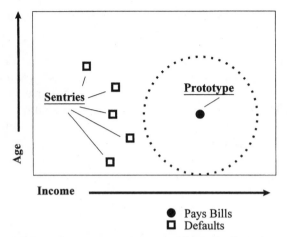

Figure 20.12 Prototypes and sentries dramatically reduce the numbers of records that are needed in order to maintain predictive accuracy and often improve the robustness and generality of the model.

scientifically assess the state of the art in handwritten character recognition, the U.S. Census Bureau and the National Institute of Standards and Technology sponsored a competition among 46 different data mining and statistical classification techniques offered by a variety of commercial and academic organizations. The test was to compare predictive accuracies on the recognition of images of numbers and letters taken from two sets of human handwriting. The first was a set of 223,000 images of printed numbers collected from 2100 U.S. Census employees. This database was used to train the systems. The second database was collected from 500 high-school students; this database was used to test the accuracies of the techniques.

20.5.2   Solution using nearest-neighbor techniques

The nearest-neighbor algorithm was used to perform the predictions on each of the unclassified images in the test database. This was done by comparing the

Computer Image   Ambiguous Image
of a Handwritten 9   of a 9 or a 4

Figure 20.13   An example of two character images from an OCR system.

given test image to every image contained in the training database. The distance metrics included simple counts of the number of mismatching pixels (picture elements) between the two images. The larger the number of corresponding pixels that differed in color between the two images, the greater the distance was determined to be. In the images shown in Fig. 20.13, the distance would have been 3 since only three pixels differ between the two images.

This measure of distance, as well as a more sophisticated method of calculating the amount of "stretching" that would need to be performed on one image in order for it to match the other, was also used. The nearest neighbor was then found in the training database, and the prediction value of that record was assigned to the record in the test database.

Various nearest-neighbor techniques were used with modifications to the distance metric and with greater and lesser degrees of preprocessing of the data (for instance, one nearest-neighbor technique tried to recreate and extract the actual penstrokes from the image). The results of most of the K nearest-neighbor systems were quite good—in the range of at least 95 percent correct (they correctly classified 95 percent of the test images), and some of the techniques were among the best. The overall results of the competition and how some of the other data mining techniques fared is shown in Fig. 20.14.

20.6 Strengths and Weaknesses

When evaluating the strengths and weaknesses of the nearest-neighbor methods, it is important to emphasize the value of being able to use the space metaphor within the grouping of the data. The simplicity of this notion that the prediction algorithm can be based directly on the historical data without signifi-

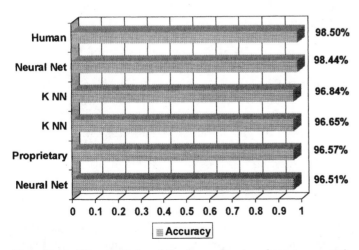

Figure 20.14 The accuracies of the top-performing character recognition systems in the NIST competition (note that even human recognition is not perfect on this difficult database).

cantly altering it is also important. This gives the user an understanding of not just what the predictive model is and how it works but also how it was derived. The fact that the nearest-neighbor models are tied so directly to the historical database may be their greatest advantage. In no other technique would it be possible to view the 10 ($K = 10$) or so records that contributed to the particular prediction. And because the model is tied so directly to the database, as the database increases in size and new records or columns are added, they are automatically incorporated into the model.

Another advantage of having the predictive model tied so closely to the database is that as the infrastructure of the data warehouse is improved through new RDBMS architectures and parallel hardware, the performance advantages will be passed on to the nearest-neighbor algorithm. The nearest-neighbor algorithm is almost a requirement for high-dimensional databases where there are a lot of binary or categorical predictor columns. Thus nearest neighbor is all but the standard for document-retrieval applications and some consumer preference applications (e.g., where there are a huge number of products, only a few of which are purchased by an individual). This ability to work well in these domains does not, however, mean that the method cannot also be correctly applied to problems that are more classically thought of as being in the domain of statistical regression models or neural networks (e.g., nearest-neighbor approaches have been used for time series data prediction as in predicting the stock market or foreign currency exchange rates).

From an IT perspective, the nearest-neighbor techniques represent a small incremental addition to the existing database infrastructure. Nearest neighbor can be implemented via SQL (albeit very slowly) and because for at least the classic implementation there is no training time required (calculating dimension weights or editing to create prototypes or sentries does require significant training time), the user can begin to generate predictions immediately. As the user requirements increase to require higher accuracy rates or simplified modeling via dimension weights, prototypes and sentries can be calculated and used. And from the IT perspective, one weakness of the algorithm, the requirement to retain the entire database as the model, may be viewed as an advantage as IT has found one more ROI-driven raison d'être for its data warehouse.

One weakness of the nearest-neighbor method is that it does not automatically perform overtraining detection and pruning. It will be important to make sure that whatever software product you purchase, it has this built into it on top of the nearest-neighbor algorithms. There is no particular reason why an effective pruning technique could not be implemented, but it should be a requirement for any usable software. Even minor "contaminations" of the training database from the test database can cause serious consequences in the accuracy of the model. Normally the test database is effectively put into a vault where it cannot be used until after the model has been built (not unlike locking up the answers to a college final exam). If the data mining product does not automatically track and keep the databases separated, even the most experienced data analysts can make mistakes.

In one instance when a predictive model was built for the U.S. Census Bureau to build a predictive model to classify the occupation of U.S. citizens, the entire data set was used for calculating the conditional probabilities of each predictor (i.e., the weight of the predictor dimension would be greatest if, every time a value of the predictor occurred, only one value of the prediction occurred). Technically this was breaking the golden rule of keeping the test database separate from the training database, but normally taking general statistics like this across the entire database is acceptable since there are so many records. In this case, however, several predictors had nonnull values only 1 or 2 times out of 100,000 records. Because of this the weights calculated for these predictors were heavily weighted toward the correct prediction in the test database if the one or two records that the nonnull value appeared in happened to come from the test database. The results were that the model performed nearly flawlessly in the lab and had significant degradation when applied to new data.

To avoid embarrassing and costly mistakes like these, it is important that the vaulting of the test database be done within the nearest-neighbor product rather than relying on a process that must be repeated correctly by skilled analysts each time the model is run (even experts can make mistakes). It will also be important to look for products that incorporate generalization and pruning techniques into the nearest-neighbor algorithm as this can cut the size of the predictive model hundreds to thousands of times and make it more reliable and robust to changing data.

20.6.1   Algorithm score card

The nearest-neighbor method gets high marks in a number of categories, but certainly its greatest strength is its simplicity, which directly translates into an easy-to-implement, easy-to-run, and easy-to-understand model. The overall performance on the critical algorithmic dimensions are shown in Fig. 20.15 and Table 20.10.

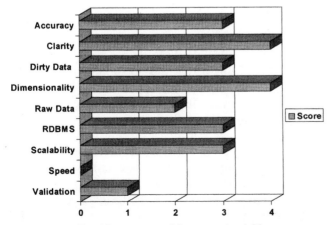

Figure 20.15   Algorithm score card for nearest neighbor.

TABLE 20.10   Algorithm Score Card for Nearest Neighbor

Data mining measure	Description
Accuracy	When used for prediction, nearest-neighbor systems provide highly accurate results.
Clarity	These systems are among the simplest to understand and provide even novice users with clear reasoning and convincing proof of predictions that are made.
Dimensionality	These systems perform very well in problem domains with a huge number of predictors. These high-dimensional spaces can be problematic for other techniques which may require a preprocessing step that decreases the dimensionality.
Dirty data	Data preprocessing for these systems is minimal, although nearest-neighbor systems usually require that missing values have a default value. Corrupted data is handled in a graceful manner.
Raw data	Nearest neighbor does require some preprocessing for categorical data, but handles continuous predictors particularly well.
RDBMS	Because of their simplicity, these systems are easy to integrate into existing data warehouses, although the computational cost of their execution can be quite slow since they can require a great deal of floating-point arithmetic.
Scalability	These systems parallelize quite well and can scale to very large databases but are inherently computationally expensive unless some of the algorithmic refinements are used.
Speed	Nearest-neighbor systems require nearly no time to build the model but can take a very long time to apply the model.
Validation	Although these systems do not have any built-in overtraining detection, they can easily be validated through held-aside or vaulted data. Pruning of the system is much more complex and ad hoc than in other systems.

20.6.2   Predicting future trends

Because of the simplicity of the nearest-neighbor algorithm and the fact that it is already tied so closely to the data warehouse infrastructure, it may not be surprising to see some basic primitives to perform nearest-neighbor prediction begin to be put directly into the database with high-performance indexing and extensions to SQL. There will probably not be a need for a new or extended data type, though; as is true with almost any data mining algorithm, the preferred schemata will likely be those that store the predictor values close to each other on disk. It is also likely that new indexing schemes will be created that allow for fast lookup of nearest neighbors (a data structure called a *K-D tree* is often used). Luckily this is nearly the same indexing structure that is required for geographic databases and has already been implemented seamlessly into existing RDBMS indexing structures by companies like Oracle.

As far as the accuracy of the algorithm itself goes, it is unlikely to see any major breakthroughs in the way the algorithm operates. The nearest-neighbor techniques are among the oldest of any data mining technique, and most of the exciting news that is coming from the technique comes from new areas of application (e.g., using the nearest-neighbor algorithm for stock market prediction or for controlling the motion of robot arms has recently been shown to be as effective as other data mining techniques) and from improved methods of dimension weighting and pruning (e.g., the development of the sentries approach is relatively recent).

Perhaps the most interesting areas for these methods will come from adaptive learning of the dimension weights. Several recent studies have shown that the weights applied to the dimensions can be automatically calculated by a variety of different techniques, including hill-climbing search and genetic algorithms. The power of these techniques is that they operate by trying to optimize the weighting and the generalization of the predictor weights and the pruning of the database on the basis of the predictive accuracy of the model on test data (test set validation or cross-validation).

21

Genetic Algorithms

In 1859 Charles Darwin published his *The Origin of Species* detailing how complex, problem-solving organisms (a.k.a. human beings) could be created and improved through an evolutionary process of random trials, sexual reproduction, and selection. Genetic algorithms are used to create a version of biological evolution on computers. They operate on small computer programs that, just like organisms undergoing natural evolution, are subject to mutation, sexual reproduction, and selection of the most fit. Over time these small programs on the computer improve in their performance in solving a particular problem—eventually achieving a high degree of competence. In 1975 John Holland, of the University of Michigan, published his book *Adaptation in Natural and Artificial Systems,* which for the first time brought together many of the ideas of simulating natural evolution on the computer. It provided several important mathematical analyses as to why simulating evolution on a computer might be a highly optimal way of solving many hard problems. Several other researchers were working on these ideas at the same time, and earlier much of the work of simulated evolution on the computer had been performed, solely for the purpose of understanding genetics and evolution. Holland's book outlined how this process could be used to solve other real-world problems with the techniques of evolution. It is considered to be the seminal book in the field and the one that launched the current field of genetic algorithms in computer science.

Interestingly, the term *genetic algorithms* does not appear in the index or any of the chapters of Holland's book but became the catch phrase for the field sometime later. The term nicely captures the biological aspects as well as the computational aspects of these computer systems. A more inclusive term, however, might be *simulated evolution.* Such a term would capture both the genetic-algorithms-related work (concerning mostly search and optimization of real-world problems), the simulation of evolution on computers solely for the understanding of genetics and evolution, and the field of artificial life, which seeks to produce lifelike systems for the purpose of reproducing complex interactions between simple organisms. In this chapter we'll use the term *genetic algorithms* in this broad sense of simulated evolutionary systems because it is the best-known term—although we recognize that the pure usage of genetic algorithms is generally more focused on optimization and search.

21.1   What Are Genetic Algorithms?

Genetic algorithms loosely refer to these simulated evolutionary systems, but more precisely they are the algorithms that dictate how populations of organisms should be formed, evaluated, and modified. For instance, there is a genetic algorithm that determines how to select organisms for sexual reproduction and another that will determine which organisms will be deleted from the population. They can also define how the genetic material of the simulated chromosome is converted into a computer program that can solve some real-world problem.

The problems that may be solved by genetic algorithms vary from optimizing a variety of data mining techniques such as neural networks and nearest neighbor to the optimization of negotiating strategies for oil rights. The trick in solving these real-world problems often is to determine how to convert the proposed solution to a complex real-world problem into simulated genetic material (usually just an array of numbers) on a computer. A simple example of the application of genetic algorithms, first proposed by Alex Singer, would be a two-gene chromosome that encoded the solution to a simple direct marketing problem: "What is the optimal number of coupons that should be put into a coupon mailer in order to optimize profit?" At first this might seem to be a pretty simple problem to solve—simply mail out as many coupons as possible, thus optimizing the possibility of a consumer both receiving and actually using a coupon. The problem is a made a little bit more complicated, however, because several other factors affect whether a coupon packet mailer makes a profit.

- The more coupons there are, the more the mailer weighs and the higher the mailing costs (thus decreasing profit).

- Any coupon that does not appear in the mailer is not used by the consumer, resulting in lost revenue.

- If there are too many coupons in the mailer, the consumer will be overloaded and not choose to use any of the coupons.

This problem can be encoded into a simple genetic algorithm where each simulated organism has a single gene that represents the "organism's" best guess at the correct number of coupons. These computer programs are as simple as just one number that reflects how many coupons to put into a mailer. The genetic algorithm can proceed with this optimization by creating a population of these single-gene organisms at random and through simulated evolution, modifying the genes, deleting the worst performers and making copies with slight modifications of the best performers. Over time the optimal number of coupons is determined. Figure 21.1 shows a population of these simple coupon organisms, indicating which ones would be deleted in the next generation because their solution was too far from the optimal.

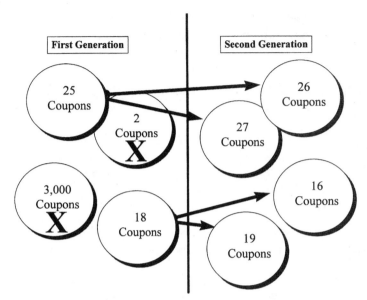

Figure 21.1   Genetic algorithms can be used to evolve the optimal number of coupons to be placed in a mailer.

In this case two simulated organisms in the first generation were deleted because of the low profitability of the mailers they proposed. The other two simulated organisms reproduced similar copies of themselves into the next generation. In this case the problem was so simple that random guessing of numbers and then evaluating those guesses would have sufficed. When the problems become much more complicated, random guessing is not sufficient and the use of genetic algorithms may be the best way to get to the right solution.

21.1.1   How do they relate to evolution?

In many ways genetic algorithms stay true to the processes available in biological evolution—or at least they try to. Some of the analogs in genetic algorithms that appear in natural evolution include

- *Organism*—which represents the computer program being optimized.

- *Population*—the collection of organisms undergoing simulated evolution.

- *Chromosome*—in biology the chromosome or chromosomes contain the genetic makeup of the organisms and fully define how the organism will develop from its genotype (genetic definition) with environmental influences to its phenotype (outward appearance and behavior). In genetic algorithms the chromosome encodes the computer program.

- *Fitness*—the calculation with which an organism's value can be determined for selection and survival of the fittest.

- *Gene*—the basic building block of the chromosome which defines one particular feature of the simulated organism.

- *Locus*—the position on the chromosome that contains a particular gene (e.g., the location that determines eye color).

- *Allele*—the value of the gene (e.g., blue for the locus for eye color).

- *Mutation*—a random change of the value of a gene (allele).

- *Mating*—the process by which two simulated organisms swap pieces of computer program in a simulated crossover.

- *Selection*—the process by which the simulated organisms that are the best at solving the particular problem are retained and the less successful are weeded out by deleting them from computer memory.

Many other important aspects of natural evolution are not mentioned in this list, some of which can be very important. These represent some of the important research areas for genetic algorithms and include topics such as simulations of old age and death, parasites, diploidy (having two copies of each chromosome), overcrowding for finite resources, and geographic constraints on mating patterns. Some of the recent research into these topics has resulted in surprisingly good results and is covered at the end of this chapter.

21.1.2 Genetic algorithms, artificial life, and simulated evolution

It may be confusing to keep straight a number of different topics that are discussed quite often with respect to genetic algorithms. Here are some of the other fields that overlap with genetic algorithms and how they differ:

- *Artificial life.* A field of computer science that simulates evolution and natural processes on computers generally for the purpose of creating complex lifelike behaviors. Examples include the automated growth of realistic-looking plants and the realistic flocking, schooling, and herding behaviors of large numbers of simulated organisms.

- *Simulated evolution.* A field of computer science and biology that simulates evolution and biological systems on the computer for the purpose of better understanding how evolution works. An example would be the simulation of an extremely simple single-gene organism to understand the effects of recessive genes.

- *Simulated systems, emergent systems, and complex systems.* Systems that are constructed from simple preformed organisms that don't evolve but do interact with each other for the purpose of understanding large-scale effects over time (i.e., the evolution of the system is of more interest than any evolution of an organism)—for example, a system that models telephone customers and how they react to rate changes and competitors' offers over time in order to understand how to optimize calling rates.

- *Cellular automata.* Systems that create quite complex macro behavior through the interaction of very simple predefined rules. Cellular automata have been used for everything from creating artwork to random-number generation.

- *Optimization systems.* A system used for the express purpose of optimizing the solution to some well-defined problem. Genetic algorithms are typically used for these kinds of systems as well as hill-climbing and simulated annealing algorithms.

21.1.3 How can they be used in business?

Although they would have to be classified generally as an emerging science, genetic algorithms have a wide variety of uses in business. There are three main areas to which they can be applied:

- *Optimization.* Given a business problem with certain variables and a well-defined definition of profit, a genetic algorithm can be used to automatically determine the optimal values for the variables that optimize the profit.

- *Prediction.* Genetic algorithms have been used as metalevel operators that are used to help optimize other data mining algorithms. For instance, they have been used to optimize the weights in a neural network or to find the optimal association rules in market-basket analysis.

- *Simulation.* Sometimes a specific business problem is not well defined in terms of what the profit is or whether one solution is better than the other. The business person instead just has a large number of entities (usually customers or competitors) that they would like to simulate via simple interaction rules over time.

21.1.4 Business score card

Although several companies now provide products that utilize genetic algorithms, these products are still in their infancy for use in the business community. In some successful implementations they have been used with a great deal of consulting resources or on well-defined problems that map easily into places where they have been used before. Perhaps their greatest strength is their inherent clarity and simple use of generating a proposed solution and then testing it via survival of the fittest (which can be viewed as a form of statistical hypothesis testing and cross-validation).

Figure 21.2 and Table 21.1 show the business score card for genetic algorithms. Some of the advantages that these systems offer to the business community are that they scale extremely well to parallel software and hardware systems and in general are fun to use. They can be slow when wielded by a naïve user and can get stuck in suboptimal solutions even when wielded by experienced users.

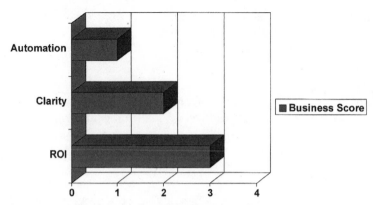

Figure 21.2   Business score card for genetic algorithms.

21.2   Where to Use Genetic Algorithms

At heart, genetic algorithms are optimization techniques. They are systems that take difficult-to-solve and very complex problems and come up with a pretty good solution without a lot of detailed understanding about the problem except how to evaluate a good solution. They can be applied to an incredibly diverse set of problems and will come up with solutions superior to random guessing and often better solutions than could be achieved via hill-climbing techniques. Beyond that, though, it is difficult to characterize where the application of genetic algorithms is appropriate as much depends on how the problem is encoded and how effective the fitness function is at evaluating whether a solution is good or bad.

At the other end of the scale, a genetic algorithm can almost never replace or outperform a well-thought-out algorithm designed specifically to solve one particular problem. For example, backpropagation will work better and faster to train neural networks, and simple rules-of-thumb optimization techniques can solve the traveling-salesperson problem (described below) much better and

TABLE 21.1   Business Score Card for Genetic Algorithms

Data mining measure	Description
Automation	Genetic algorithms are relatively automated once the fitness function and how the problem will be encoded into simulated genetic material on the computer are defined. These two processes can, however, be quite difficult. The good news is that even suboptimal encoding schemes can still result in useful solutions.
Clarity	When genetic algorithms are used to optimize existing data mining techniques, they cannot afford any further clarity than is inherent in the underlying technique. They do provide a good sense of clarity in the optimization procedure, although it can be difficult to tell how near the proposed solution is to the true optimum.
ROI	One of the great advantages of genetic algorithms is that because the problem solution being optimized can be fairly general (as long as you can define the fitness function, it can be optimized), many different factors relating to overall ROI of the entire business process can be taken into account at the same time.

more quickly than can genetic algorithms. Their use then comes often as a replacement for the time involved in detailed analysis of a given problem—which in business may mean quite a few problems that are quite complex but so new that there is no precedent for a previous well-thought-out solution. In cases like these, genetic algorithms provide optimized solutions where no optimization was performed before.

There are probably four key attributes for a business problem that could benefit from the application of genetic algorithms:

1. The value from various proposed solutions can be well defined.

2. The problem is complex and cannot be solved directly.

3. The problem is relatively new and not well understood, and no one has yet been able to determine other optimization techniques to be used for its solution.

4. The problem involves a large number of variables working together but can be modeled through simpler processes working together to produce a large-scale effect.

If these four key attributes occur in the problem that you are trying to solve, then genetic algorithms may be a good technique to try. If any of the attributes are not present, then some other technique probably exists and is preferable. For instance, if the proposed solution cannot be defined as good or bad, it will not be possible for the system to evolve to a better solution. If the problem is simple, then it is likely that there will be better and faster direct methods; and if the problem—even if complex—has been actively researched, then there are also probably better solutions available. The last attribute is not necessarily a requirement, but it does seem to be a common theme among successful applications of genetic algorithms. For instance, it is often the case that you can model the behavior of an individual customer but not be able to understand the overall behavior (and profit) of a dynamic system that includes all your customers.

21.2.1 Genetic algorithms for optimization

Genetic algorithms are one of a variety of techniques known as *optimization techniques*. These techniques are built to take a given well-defined problem and find ways to optimize the performance on the problem. In some ways genetic algorithms have some similarities with early applications of neural networks in which neural networks (especially those by Hopfield and Tank) were used to optimize some classically difficult problems. One of these problems is the traveling-salesman problem. The problem is posed somewhat like a riddle: "What is the shortest distance that a salesperson can travel to make sales calls on exactly one customer in each of a number of different cities?" For only a few cities, this is a relatively easy problem; for many more cities, it is very difficult. Figure 21.3 shows the typical optimization problem for a few cities and then for many cities.

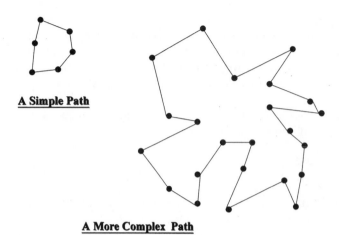

A Simple Path

A More Complex Path

Figure 21.3 The traveling-salesman problem. For tours of 50 cities or less, reasonably good tours can be constructed by hand. For hundreds of cities, optimal solutions are nearly impossible to produce.

21.2.2   Genetic algorithms for data mining

The use of genetic algorithms for data mining has a variety of forms, but in general their application is made on top of an existing data mining technique such as neural networks or nearest-neighbor classification. To see how this will work, remember that most of the data mining techniques that have been introduced in this book boil down to an optimization problem. For neural networks, it is the problem of finding the optimal link weights for the optimal network architecture. For nearest neighbor, it is a matter of finding the optimal importance weights to be applied to each predictor. For decision trees, which are usually created via a greedy search algorithm, it is the optimization problem of finding the best predictors and values to split on and in optimizing the pruning of the decision tree. Genetic algorithms can be used with cross-validation as the fitness function to define the optimal predictive models for data mining. To date it has not, however, been shown that using genetic algorithms provides either faster or better solutions than do the search algorithms specific to the individual data mining technique.

21.2.3   Applications score card

Figure 21.4 and Table 21.2 show the applications score card for genetic algorithms. Since genetic algorithms are very general-purpose search techniques, they are used for applications only in combination with other data mining techniques. For this reason the score here represents the success that genetic algorithms have shown with data mining techniques in general, although much depends on the data mining technique that is chosen.

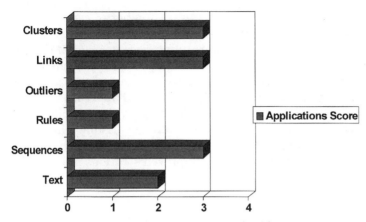

Figure 21.4   Applications score card for genetic algorithms.

21.3   The General Idea

21.3.1   Do genetic algorithms guess the right answer?

It may seem to this point that genetic algorithms are a panacea. They seem able to provide an optimal solution with little more than defining what "good" is (the fitness) and how to translate the problem into a form compatible with the genetic algorithms (mutation, crossover, etc.). While they are applicable to a wide variety of problems, genetic algorithms are not black magic. They work similarly to biological evolution by making small changes in the organism and when the answer is better, that answer is retained and something else is tried.

Genetic algorithms in no sense guess the best answer; rather, they slowly build up to it. Take, for example, the coupon mailing example. If completely

TABLE 21.2   Applications Score Card for Genetic Algorithms

Problem type	Description
Clusters	Genetic algorithms have been used directly to find optimal clusters based on a well-defined profit measure.
Links	Genetic algorithms can be used directly for link analysis by producing a population of rules and determining their values either directly by statistical calculations across the population or locally by incrementally keeping track of how often the rule applies.
Outliers	Genetic algorithms by themselves don't detect outliers.
Rules	Genetic algorithms by themselves do not create rules.
Sequences	Genetic algorithms have been used to optimize nearest-neighbor classification systems for predicting sequences in time series.
Text	Genetic algorithms have been used to optimize word weights and numbers of neighbors (k) for nearest-neighbor classification systems for text.

blind guessing were used to determine the optimal number of coupons for a mailer, it would be unlikely that random guessing would ever arrive at the optimal solution given that there are an infinite number of possible values that could be tried. If, on the other hand, a solution were proposed and then compared to a lesser solution and a greater solution and the best of the three was kept, slow but steady progress would be made. This second approach is a simplified version of a search technique called "hill climbing," which is comparable to what genetic algorithms perform—although genetic algorithms have some additional advantages over straight hill-climbing approaches, they share with these approaches the advantage of ratcheting improved solutions in place and making continuous progress.

21.3.2 Are genetic algorithms fully automated?

Since evolution is a natural biological process that is automatic, it might be tempting to believe the same of genetic algorithms. This is not the case. A great deal of work needs to be done in setting up the genetic algorithm systems before the systems can be started. Once this is done, however, the process is relatively automatic.

The pieces that need to be defined up front are the fitness function and the encoding of the problem solution into simulated genetic code. In the following examples the fitness function and the encodings are described to give an idea of the variety of ways that this is done.

21.3.3 Cost minimization: traveling salesman

One problem which has been a touchstone for comparing various implementations of genetic algorithms and other optimization algorithms is the "traveling-salesman problem." As described previously, this problem requires that the salesperson take the shortest path through a number of cities while visiting each city only once. The fitness function is relatively trivial to compute; it is simply the total distance traveled. Encoding of the cities into the chromosome is done in a variety of ways. Table 21.3 shows the different kinds of encoding methods that are possible.

- *Path encoding.* The simplest way is to create an array that represents the path taken and lists one city after the other. For instance, the chromosome on

TABLE 21.3 Different Encoding Strategies Used to Encode Three Different Paths of Cities Labeled A, B, C, D, and E

Encoding strategy	A=>B=>C=>D=>E	A=>C=>B=>D=>E	B=>E=>C=>A=>D
Path encoding	A|B|C|D|E	A|C|B|D|E	B|E|C|A|D
Ordinal encoding	1|1|1|1|1	1|2|1|1|1	2|4|2|1|1
Rank encoding	1|2|3|4|5	1|3|2|4|5	4|1|3|5|2

the computer would be simply an array of city names. The order of the cities in the array would represent the path taken through the cities. This is a simple encoding, but it can lead to nonviable solutions after standard crossover during reproduction and mutation (e.g., some cities might be visited multiple times and others might not be visited at all).

- *Ordinal encoding.*   The value of the gene would correspond to the selection in a list of cities. As the chromosome is traversed, each city is picked from the list of cities and is not replaced. This system has the advantage of always producing a valid crossover between two chromosomes, but it does have the disadvantage of breaking up useful subpaths in a relatively random way.

- *Rank encoding.*   Another encoding would be to have each element of the array (analogous to a locus in a chromosome) represent a city. The value of the array slot (allele) would be the order in which the city was visited. This technique has the advantage of always providing viable organisms after crossover or mutation and also preserving beneficial subinformation.

21.3.4   Cooperation strategies: prisoner's dilemma

The "prisoner's-dilemma problem" is a simplification of a complex negotiation and cooperation problem in the social sciences. Posed in the 1950s, it has been debated and written about as an abstraction of these negotiation practices, including everything up to the brinksmanship and cost analysis associated with an arms race. The problem is as follows. There are two prisoners who have been captured, and the authorities have some minimal evidence against them. The authorities are willing to cut a deal and lessen the sentence of one of the prisoners if that prisoner is willing to turn over evidence on the other one. If, however, they both turn over evidence on each other, they will be both be given more severe sentences than if they both remained silent. The problem is that the two prisoners are in different cells and cannot communicate, so both must decide independently if they are willing to trust the other to remain silent and receive a lesser sentence.

The scenario is not too different from two superpowers deciding on whether to escalate a world conflict, knowing that a world war would be deleterious to all concerned but that if they could have first strike to disable a counterstrike, their position would be improved. Multiple games can be played out with less dire consequences with the result that each "prisoner" can begin to build a model of how the other prisoner will react. For instance, if one prisoner will always remain silent no matter what, then it is optimal for the other prisoner to always turn over evidence (defect). If, on the other hand, a prisoner will always turn over evidence, it makes sense for the other prisoner to always do the same.

Robert Axelrod of the University of Michigan used this game to see if a genetic algorithm could evolve a superior strategy over the course of many games. To do this, Axelrod solicited a variety of strategies from human experts who had studied the game. The optimal strategy appeared to be to start off by remaining silent (cooperating with your fellow prisoner) but then reciprocating in kind (defecting) if the prisoner turned evidence (defected) on you the last time the game was played. This was named the "tit for tat" strategy because it initiated cooperation but returned bad behavior in kind. Axelrod calculated the fitness of the evolved strategy in two ways using the scoring for the various outcomes as shown in Table 21.4:

- Each evolved strategy competed against eight of the human-generated strategies, and the overall payoff was averaged across all the competitions.
- Each evolved strategy competed against others in the population, and the overall payoff was averaged across all the competitions.

The strategy was encoded into the simulated chromosome by creating a mapping between the outcomes of the three previous games and the current action. For instance, the three previous games could have been CC CD DD (where C stands for cooperation and D stands for defection and the first letter of each pair represents the action of the first prisoner). The three games could have occurred in 64 possible ways; thus the chromosome must encode an action for each of these possibilities (whether to defect or cooperate). The 64 possible three-game scenarios were encoded as a location in an array (the locus of the simulated chromosome), and the value (allele) of the array was the action that the organism would take (either cooperate or defect). Thus a sequence of 64 letters could completely determine the actions for all possible three-game scenarios. A chromosome might look like the following:

cdccdcdcddcdcdcccdcdcdcccddcdcccdcdcdcdcdcdcdcdcdcdcccdcddcdcddccdc

21.4   How the Genetic Algorithm Works

21.4.1   The overall process

The following steps generally occur in a computer system using genetic algorithms:

1. Define the problem to be solved, providing a way to encode the problem in a chromosome and a way to measure the goodness of the solution encoded in the chromosome.

TABLE 21.4   Prisoner's Dilemma as an Optimization Problem*

Prisoner 1	Prisoner 2	Prisoner 1's payoff	Prisoner 2's payoff
Cooperates	Cooperates	3	3
Defects	Cooperates	5	0
Cooperates	Defects	0	5
Defects	Defects	1	1

* The prisoner's dilemma is a classic optimization problem of cooperation and conflict, in which defection is an optimal strategy only if the other player attempts to cooperate.

2. Initialize a population of chromosomes with random values.

3. Evaluate the fitness of each organism in the population using the previously defined fitness function.

4. Allow the multiple copies of the genetic material of the best chromosomes to be made, and delete the organisms that are less fit.

5. Allow the new population of organisms to undergo mutation and sexual reproduction.

6. Evaluate the fitness of each organism in the population using the previously defined fitness function.

7. Stop if any of the following criteria are met:
   a. A solution has been found that is good enough.
   b. The system has run for the prespecified number of generations.
   c. The system has stopped making progress towards improvement.

8. If no stopping criterion is met, then return to step 4.

This process is conducted across the entire population of organisms in what is called a *generation*. Multiple generations are run with sometimes hundreds, to thousands or hundreds of thousands of organisms. Because there are so many organisms, it can be difficult to understand what is taking place within the system. Even the most basic questions such as whether the system is making progress are sometimes difficult to answer. To answer the questions several statistics are often gathered about the system to determine how it is doing:

- Average fitness of the population
- The highest fitness achieved so far
- The generation in which the highest-fitness organism occurred
- The last generation where an improvement was made
- Some measure of the diversity of the organisms in the population
- A visualization of the organism (e.g., mapping between the chromosome and the actual path for the traveling-salesperson problem)
- The average and variance of alleles for each gene.

More sophisticated measures can be used as well, including tracking of the lineage of each organism, which can sometimes be useful in understanding how sexual reproduction and genetic crossover combine two less-fit individuals into a highly fit organism.

21.4.2 Survival of the fittest

Evolution makes progress in producing successively better organisms by selectively weeding out those organisms that are less fit. From a biological perspective, this means that those organisms that are most healthy and strong (presumably because of their genetic makeup) are the most likely to pass on their genetic material. If the chromosomes in an organism have a flaw that creates an organism that is less likely to survive, then that genetic material is weeded out of the gene pool for that species.

The same is true for genetic algorithms. Here the genetic material is made up of numbers that dictate how to solve a particular problem (whether this is the order of cities in the traveling-salesman problem or the best customer attributes for targeted marketing). If a particular gene causes a particularly bad solution to the problem being solved, it will lower the fitness for the individual, and the genetic material that contributed to the poor solution will be weeded out of the population.

Survival of the fittest is analogous to starting off at the base of a mountain with a small search party of mountain climbers. The mountain has never been climbed before, so the path and the location of the top are not known (let's say there is a white-out blizzard that keeps search party members from seeing more than a few feet in front of them). The organisms in your simulated population are analogous to your search party members, and their current heights are analogous to the fitness function that gives some idea of how close to the summit one is. Genetic mutation is something like taking small steps around where you currently stand and then accepting those steps that improve your position.

Survival of the fittest is then like reallocating the members of the search party to the higher areas of elevation once they are determined. If, for instance, there are some searchers standing on the side of the mountain, some on the plain, and some in the valley, then the best way to make it to the top of the mountain is to relocate some of the people from the lowest positions to the higher elevations and allow them to start to slowly wander around from there (if they are already in the valley, it will take them a lot longer to find the top of the mountain than if they are already near the summit). This reallocation of trials from the low performers to the high performers is exactly what survival of the fittest does. By doing so, it increases the chance that small perturbations to the current location via mutation are more likely to cause an even more fit organism.

This reallocation of trials can be based directly on how fit the organism is. For instance, if organism A provides a solution to the problem at hand that is twice as good as that of another organism, then perhaps that organism should receive twice as many progeny. Calculating the number of progeny in the next generation as proportionate to the fitness is a common way of accomplishing survival of the fittest. Another way that this can be accomplished is by even more closely simulating natural processes and allowing organisms to compete. In this case two simulated organisms in the population would pair off, and the organism that was more fit would be able to make a copy of itself in the next generation; the loser and its genetic material would disappear from the population in the next generation.

To better simulate natural processes and allow for some randomness in these processes, the number of progeny in the next generation may be a probabilistic function of the fitness of the organism, so that the more fit individual would be more likely to win the competition but the less fit organism could "get lucky" sometimes. Often randomness is sprinkled into the genetic operators (in addition to mutation) for the same reason that you wouldn't move all members of your search party to the current highest known elevation because you realize that some paths that don't look promising at the current time may lead to the eventual mountain peak, while others which look very promising may run into a dead end or a false peak a few steps down the road.

21.4.3   Mutation

Mutation makes changes in the genetic material of your simulated organisms in a random way. As we've seen, survival of the fittest makes sure that as things are learned about the space that the genetic algorithm is searching, that information is passed on and taken advantage of in succeeding generations. Survival of the fittest by itself without some active exploration will not likely lead to a very good solution. This would be analogous to randomly assigning search party members to various sites on the mountain and then moving everyone to stand on the single site that was the best so far. Mutation is analogous to taking small steps around the current solution to see if some small perturbation is better.

In genetic algorithms there are several major ways of performing mutation. In general, there is one overriding mutation rate that is set for the entire system (e.g., 0.001 would mean that 1 out of every 1000 genes would be mutated). Following are the major ways that mutation is accomplished.

- *Random bit mutation.*   The genetic material is viewed as bits from a computer science perspective and for each bit in each organism a coin is tossed. If it comes up heads, then the bit is flipped. For instance, the allele for a given gene could be the number 7. In binary this would be 111; if the second bit were mutated, the new value would be 101, which is the number 5.

- *Random gene mutation.*   In this case the allowable alleles for a given gene are known and the entire gene is mutated to some other valid value. For instance, the hair color gene might have five values (brown, blond, red, black, auburn). In the chromosome these might be encoded as the numbers (0,1,2,3,4), which would require 3 bits to represent (000, 001, 010, 011, 100). In this case random bit mutations could result in alleles that have no meaning (e.g., 101 does not map to a hair color). These nonsensical alleles could be weeded out through selection, but it would be more efficient to have a more sophisticated gene-level mutation.

- *Creep mutation.*   In this case the genes are modified by some small perturbation rather than truly random changes. For instance, a gene with a value of 6 might be modified to be a 5 or a 7 (effectively creeping away from the original value) as opposed to truly random mutation, where large jumps in values are possible (e.g., a single-bit mutation could change 0000 to 1000, representing a change in value from 0 to 8). Likewise, creep mutation makes it easy to change values that might otherwise be difficult to modify via single-bit mutation. Consider that 0111 is the number 7 and 1000 is the number 8 but it would require the mutation of all 4 bits in order for this small modification to be made.

- *Heuristic mutation.* In some cases heuristics or rules of thumb are known which can be applied to chromosomes that can dramatically improve the fitness of the organism. An example is found in the traveling-salesman problem; when certain small portions of the overall path are found to be tangled, a fairly straightforward algorithm can be used to "mutate" these chromosomes into shorter paths.

21.4.4 Sexual reproduction and crossover

Most higher organisms contain a pair of chromosomes rather than just one. They are known as *diploid organisms,* rather than *haploid,* which have just one copy. The two copies of the same genes are received one from the mother and one from the father during sexual reproduction. These two copies have different alleles, and often this mixing of genes from two parents can create organisms with the good traits from both. It can also result in organisms with bad traits from both, but these will be quickly weeded out of the population by selection.

In natural systems the exact behavior of diploidy is very complex and has to take into account things like dominant and recessive genes. In most genetic algorithms diploidy and true sexual reproduction is not used; rather, a simpler process for sharing genes between parents is used. It is called *crossover* and, like diploidy, has its analog in biology. Crossover, as its name implies, is the crossing over of the single chromosome between the two parents so that the progeny still has just one chromosome, but some of the genes are from one parent and some of the genes are from the other. Figure 21.5 shows a stylized view

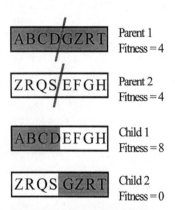

Parent 1
Fitness = 4

Parent 2
Fitness = 4

Child 1
Fitness = 8

Child 2
Fitness = 0

Figure 21.5 Crossover. Most genetic algorithms utilize crossover between like chromosomes to create new organisms that hopefully have the best parts of each.

of how this crossover could create progeny that are both superior and inferior to their parents. In this case the organisms have greatest fitness when the genes create the letter sequence ABCDEFGH.

For some time the belief has been that crossover and other operators such as mutation need to be done at the bit level rather than at the allele level in order to achieve the most effective search and the best possible answer. This is no longer believed to be the case.

21.4.5   Exploration versus exploitation

When searching either on a mountain or within a fitness function for genetic algorithms, a fundamental tradeoff must be made as to whether to allocate the majority of resources to the spots that currently seem best with the chance that currently less productive areas may have been abandoned too early and a real opportunity was missed. In genetic algorithms this tradeoff translates into how severe the selection criteria are. For instance, one extreme form of survival of the fittest would take the most fit organism from the population and fully populate the next generation with only its genetic material. This would likely be a mistake since it is unlikely that the most fit individual at the earliest part of the evolution would necessarily be along the right track for the optimal solution. The other extreme would be to use no selection criterion at all and just let the system randomly try solutions via massive mutation.

This tradeoff between exploiting current knowledge about where good and bad solutions are and the exploration of radically new solutions is encapsulated in genetic algorithms in what is know as the "one-armed-bandit problem." The problem is as follows:

> You are in Las Vegas, and standing before you are two one-armed-bandit machines (the slot machines where you pull the lever and the coins come out of the bottom if you win). The owner of the casino, who is a friend of yours, has told you that one of the machines pays out 20 percent of the time and the other machine only pays out 10 percent of the time. This friend won't tell you which is which but gives you an hour before closing in order to make as much money as you can.
>
> Once you know which machine pays out more, you'd like to spend all of your remaining time using that machine. Your predicament is that you can never really be sure which one it is. The more times you pull the handle, the more sure you become, but it also means the more pulls you've wasted on the lower-payoff machine if you have guessed wrong. For instance, if you pulled both handles 5 times and one machine paid out and the other didn't, would you be willing to pull the handle solely of that first machine that paid out? Probably not, because there would still be a good chance that the other machine just had an unlucky run but is really the higher-payoff machine.

This is the same problem faced in genetic algorithms where one organism may initially look better than the other but long term, a less fit organism may lead to the best solution. Luckily the one-armed-bandit problem has been analyzed, and the optimal strategy turns out to be to exponentially increase the number of trials on the better of the two machines as time goes on but to never completely give up some small experiments on the other machine. Thus, for instance, if the first machine paid out better throughout the evening than the second machine, a reasonable strategy to optimize the amount of money made by the end of the night would be to stop every 5 min, check to see which machine was paying out better, and then double the rate at which that machine is tried. This is shown in Table 21.5. In this case machine 1 appears to be paying out better, so more and more trials are allocated to it over time. Slot machine 2 is tried less and less frequently.

Since the one-armed-bandit problem is identical to the exploitation and exploration decisions needed for selection and reproduction in the genetic algorithm, the same exponential allocation of trials can be applied. Conveniently, this is exactly what reproduction by survival of the fittest provides.

21.4.6 The schema theorem

One argument made about the power of genetic algorithms is that they search the problem space in parallel because of the way they process what are called *schemas*. To understand what is meant by a schema, consider again the simple alphabet problem posed in Fig. 21.5 where the optimal chromosome is the letter sequence ABCDEFGH. In this case there are eight genes, and for every letter that is placed in the right alphabetical position, the fitness is increased. Thus there seem to be subsets of chromosomes that are shared among many different chromosomes. These shared patterns are called *schemas*. For instance, the chromosomes

ABDCEDFB

AEDCEDGG

AFHCBDAF

TABLE 21.5   Optimizing Winnings between Two Slot Machines*

Time period	Trials 1 : 2 ratio	Payout (%)		Better machine
		1	2	
1	1 : 1	0	0	1
2	2 : 1	15	13	1
3	4 : 1	35	8	1
4	8 : 1	28	12	1
5	16 : 1	23	11	1
6	32 : 1	21	10	1
7	64 : 1	20	11	1

* To optimize winnings between two slot machines, trials are exponentially increased to the machine that appears to be better.

share the common pattern A**C*D**, where the * represents any possible allele. They also share the pattern A******* and ***C*D** and several others. The pattern A******* contributes and increases in fitness over any other schema with an allele locked into place in the first position, with the rest of the alleles allowed to be any value. Because of the fitness function, an organism that contains the A******* pattern will have a higher fitness than one that contains a B******* or an H******* pattern. The implicit parallelism of these systems comes from the ability of the total population to evaluate these patterns and effectively come up with an average measure of goodness for the pattern.

The schema theorem states that the observed best patterns or schemas in the population will receive an exponentially increasing number of trials (via replication and selection of the genetic material) over successive generations. As we've seen from the one-armed-bandit example, this exponential allocation of trials is the optimal way to balance the tradeoff between exploration and exploitation.

21.4.7 Epistasis

In the alphabet example the schema processing seems to make a lot of sense—once a letter is correctly found in a given position in the chromosome, increase its density in the population and effectively lock it in place as one step toward the correct answer. Most problems are not this simple and suffer from what is known as *epistasis*. In epistatic systems the value of one gene can affect the meaning of the other. When epistasis is present, it is not possible to "lock down" the correct value for one gene and then move onto the next; instead, all the genes values must be found as they depend on each other. Consider, for example, the traveling-salesman problem, in which there is no "correct" answer for a given gene value. The gene can take on the same value and be either detrimental or incremental to the fitness of the organism dependent on the ordering of the city tour as determined by the other gene values.

Because of epistasis, some of the value of the schema theorem is more theoretical than practical. In these cases allocating exponentially increasing trials can cause the population to converge to like values very quickly, and it has been shown that there are "GA deceptive" problems in which a schema that may have a high overall fitness may actually be deleterious to finding the eventual right solution. This happens because the effects of other genes are not fully taken into account and the population is led toward a solution that is suboptimal.

21.4.8 Classifier systems

Genetic algorithms have been used directly to try to build machine learning systems. These systems generate simple rules that chain together to solve a more complex problem, each rule doing some form of classification of an input state and an output state. These systems, called *classifier systems,* have been used on problems as simple as letter sequence prediction to playing poker and simulating the behavior of an organism seeking to navigate through a simulated forest to find food.

A typical classifier system has many small rules that chain together to produce a more complex rule. For instance, in chess there could be a very large number of rules that take the current state of the chessboard and propose a move. To keep a strategy in mind, they also store the state of a given strategy on a message list which is additional information that can be used in deciding what to do next (for instance, normally it would be the right move to acquire the opponent's queen, except if there is a larger series of moves that is being played out to achieve checkmate of the opponent). A simple encoding of a classifier for chess might include a gene for every board position, and the value of the gene would be the type of chess piece positioned there. Then two more genes could be used to denote the piece to move and the final position. The general structure of the classifier would be "If board = state defined in classifier, then move piece to position specified." If the classifier were defined this way, it would be far too costly to construct all the possible classifiers, which would be larger than all the possible board positions. To accommodate this difficulty, classifier systems will leave some conditions as undecided. So, for instance, rather than specifying in detail the entire board state, the classifier may specify only three or four key positions and leave the rest unspecified—effectively using wildcard characters that will match any piece at a given location. These wildcard characters and the particular gene values are determined by a genetic algorithm which allocates increased trials to successful classifiers and deletes the unsuccessful ones. In practice, chess is too hard a game for classifiers to solve. One of the main reasons is that, because of the length of the game, it is not clear how to allocate credit to the individual moves. For instance, if in a given game a classifier allowed the capture of an opponent's queen but the overall game were lost, should that classifier be considered to be of high fitness or of low fitness? There are two different schools of thought on how to determine this:

- The *Michigan approach* utilizes an algorithm called the "bucket brigade," in which the fitness is determined by the last classifier that fires and either loses or wins the game. That reward or punishment is then passed backward in an attenuated fashion to all the classifiers that contributed to that game. The reward or punishment is passed backward in much the same way a bucket of water used to be passed from one person to the next in a long line of people when putting out a fire. The major indictment of this technique is that it can take a tremendously long time to pass the reward or punishment backward in a timely manner, especially since the genetic algorithm is zeroing in on beneficial schemas at an exponential rate.

- In the *Pitt approach,* the organism that is evolved is the collection of rules (classifiers) required to fully play the entire game of chess rather than the organism to be evolved serving as just a single rule among a long chain of rules. This view matches our intuitions a bit better, since now the learning and evolving organism can be viewed as one self-contained entity, and the credit assignment problem is simplified to assigning credit to the best-performing organism and allowing the internals of the organism to determine how to allocate credit internally.

21.4.9   Remaining challenges

Although genetic algorithms have met with some success, there has yet to be an evolved intelligence on anyone's computer. Instead, these systems tend to move fairly predictably toward the optimization of the fitness function. In order to improve, these systems face several challenges:

- *Premature convergence.*   The exponential allocation of trials to the more fit organism is both a curse and a blessing. Although it allows the system to quickly hone in on a successful solution, more often than not it causes the population to converge so that there is very little diversity in the population and effectively new areas and ideas are not explored.

- *Too many parameters.*   In most systems a very large number of parameters need to be set before the evolution can begin. These parameters include things like population size, mutation rate, number of generations, selection algorithm, and crossover algorithm. Often these parameters are set by trial and error by the user of the system and if not set correctly, can have a decided negative effect on the performance of the system.

21.4.10   Sharing: a solution to premature convergence

A possible solution to the problem of premature convergence may be offered through a new technique in genetic algorithms called *sharing.* The need for sharing is as follows. On a perfectly parallel computer (i.e., with unlimited processing power), it has been shown that the optimal performance of the genetic algorithm will be achieved by using the largest population possible. The performance of large populations, however, can be crippled by premature convergence of the population to a suboptimal solution. Convergence of too many individuals to the same genetic material is equivalent to reduction of population without reduction of expense. Thus the power of large populations and parallel computing can be nullified if this problem is not solved.

Genetic algorithms exploit past experience by copying and slightly altering organisms that have had past success. Natural selection provides a force tending to push a population toward domination by many copies of a single, relatively fit organism. In the standard genetic algorithm, there is no force specifically working against this domination, and the fate of most populations, after several generations, is domination by many copies of nearly identical organisms. Once this "total convergence" to a single solution has occurred, crossover can no longer generate variation in the population; remaining is mutation, a slower, "blind" source of variation. After total convergence, the search for better solutions is effectively stopped.

Use of a large population alone can slow convergence somewhat, but convergence can progress exponentially quickly, so that doubling the population size does not necessarily double the time to total convergence. In nature, however, the population of a single type of organism does not continue to increase without limit. As a single type of organism multiples to a large subpopulation, this subpopulation consumes more of certain resources present in the environment, and these resources become scarce. The individual organisms must then compete with each other for these scarce resources, causing all organisms to suffer from want. Growth of this subpopulation is then slowed, and finally settles around some "carrying capacity," at which the number of organisms of a particular type is in equilibrium with the availability of the resources that they consume. Simulation of this effect, called *sharing,* can be added to the standard genetic algorithm by supposing abstract resources that all organisms exploiting a particular niche must compete for or share. If there are too many organisms within a niche, the shortage of these resources decreases the fitness of all the organisms within the niche. It is assumed that two organisms that are adjacent in the search space will consume more of the same resources than will two organisms that are far apart in the search space. The effect is accomplished by multiplying an organism's base fitness by a sharing factor, which decreases the fitness depending on how many other organisms have similar genetic makeup.

In practice, the sharing technique has provided improved solutions more quickly and kept the population from converging while maintaining useful search and allocation of trials to the most fit. The approach does require additional computation during the fitness evaluation phase, but this is more than made up for by the avoidance of premature convergence.

21.4.11   Metalevel evolution: the automation of parameter choice

The second large problem for genetic algorithms is the number of parameters that control the behavior of the system that must be set by hand. It appears that neither general rules for these parameters nor analytical equations will be available to calculate them for particular problems (the reason for this is that so much of how parameters such as mutation rate are set depends on the particulars of the fitness function and the genetic encoding, which vary substantially between different problems). Another possible solution is to try to encode some of these parameters that control evolution directly into the genetic material itself. This has been termed "metalevel evolution" since the processes that control the evolution are themselves evolving.

The seeming disadvantage of this approach is that the size of the search space for can be dramatically increase (2^{640} times more possible solutions to search in some research). The hoped-for advantage of these systems is that they will be less brittle and more likely to display innovative solutions to given evolutionary optimization problems. This seems to be borne out in research which showed that evolutionary systems that encode the mutation rate directly into the chromosome provide performance equivalent to standard evolutionary systems despite the increase in the size of the search space. Such systems also prove to be more robust as changes in the difficulty of the problem are introduced.

Metalevel operators encoded as genes do have precedents in biology. For instance, it has been found that one-third of all mutations in a given chromosome occur at only one site—far different from the idea that background radiation and other factors contribute to a consistent mutation rate across all genes.

In genetic algorithms both mutation rates and crossover points have been encoded by genes within the chromosome undergoing evolution. There have also been proposals for metalevel classifiers in classifier systems that would aid in the allocation of credit between lower-level classifiers, thus vastly speeding up the bucket-brigade algorithm but doing so within the evolutionary paradigm.

21.4.12 Parallel implementation

Genetic algorithms are highly parallelizable. In general, one organism is allocated to each processor or virtual processor on a parallel machine. Fitness is evaluated locally on that processor, and those organisms that do not achieve the required fitness can be deleted and replaced with the genetic material of more-fit individuals. Mutation and crossover can likewise by accommodated by local, efficient computation once the mating chromosomes have been moved onto a single processor. All parallel computers accommodate this sort of interprocessor communications.

21.5 Case Study: Optimizing Predictive Customer Segments

To get an idea of how one might encode a business problem into a simulated chromosome for a genetic algorithm to operate on, consider the simple database we have used for other examples (shown in Table 21.6). In this case let's define the problem as determining the optimal combination of income, eye color, and age range that optimizes total profit. Profit will be defined as 1 percent times the account balance minus a $10 cost per customer for handling the account. The trick, then, is not just to find the predictive rules that correspond to high account balance but to also trade this off against the cost of handling the account (an added constraint that would probably not be taken into consideration by most data mining techniques).

The definition of the customer segment can be encoded in four simulated genes:

TABLE 21.6   An Example Customer Database that Can Be Used with a Genetic Algorithm to Optimize Profit

ID	Name	Prediction	Age	Balance ($)	Income	Eyes	Gender
1	Amy	No	62	0	Medium	Brown	F
2	Al	No	53	1,800	Medium	Green	M
3	Betty	No	47	16,543	High	Brown	F
4	Bob	Yes	32	45	Medium	Green	M
5	Carla	Yes	21	2,300	High	Blue	F
6	Carl	No	27	5,400	High	Brown	M
7	Donna	Yes	50	165	Low	Blue	F
8	Don	Yes	46	0	High	Blue	M
9	Edna	Yes	27	500	Low	Blue	F
10	Ed	No	68	1,200	Low	Blue	M

- Gene 1—contains the lower bound of the age constraint
- Gene 2—contains the upper bound of the age constraint
- Gene 3—contains the income-level constraint
- Gene 4—contains the eye color constraint

So a chromosome that defines blue-eyed medium-income individuals between the ages of 50 and 65 would look as follows: |50 | 65 | medium | blue|. The fitness function can be easily calculated by constructing a SQL query on the basis of the values of the genetic material and then subtracting the cost from the revenue.

Note, though, that right off the bat there are a few small problems with our definition of the chromosome. For instance, after mutation and crossover it could be possible for the lower bound of the age constraint to exceed the upper bound. This is easily solved by redefining genes 1 and 2 to be just bounds on the age and leaving it up to the calculation in the fitness function to determine which bound is lower than the other.

This representation also has the effect of limiting the segment to consist of only customers of a single eye color and income level. It is possible, for instance, that the optimal segment consists of customers of two different eye colors and multiple income levels. This can be solved by allocating three genes to each eye color and income level. Each gene will represent high, medium, and low incomes and brown, blue, and green eye colors. The value will be a yes or no (binary value) indicating whether that particular attribute should be included

TABLE 21.7   A Better Genetic Representation for Encoding the Customer Profit Optimization Problem

Gene	1	2	3	4	5	6	7	8
Meaning	Age-bound	Age-bound	Income high?	Income medium?	Income low?	Eyes blue?	Eyes brown?	Eyes green?
Example 1	20	56	Yes	Yes	No	Yes	No	Yes
Example 2	13	85	No	No	Yes	Yes	No	No
Example 3	42	35	Yes	No	No	Yes	Yes	Yes

in defining the segment. This new chromosome and several examples are shown in Table 21.7. Typically the alleles for these chromosomes would be converted to numbers to conserve space on the computer (i.e., no = 0, yes = 1).

Once the genetic encoding is defined, a population of random organisms is created and their fitness is evaluated. To keep things simple in this example, we will be using local competition and mating algorithms to effect survival of the fittest, although there are many other ways that this could be accomplished. To do this, the organisms are laid out next to each other on a two-dimensional grid (thus each organism has a neighbor to the left, right, to the above, and below). To effect selection, the following steps are followed:

1. *Competition.*   Each organism exchanges fitness values and genetic material with its neighbor to the right. If the neighbor is more fit than the current organism, then the genetic material of the current organism is replaced by that of its neighbor, thus creating the effective "death" of one organism and the replication of the other.

2. *Mating.*   Each organism now takes genetic material from its neighbor above and performs a crossover of genetic material at a randomly chosen gene location (locus).

3. *Mutation.*   The genes of the new crossed-over organism are now evaluated one by one and with probability 0.001 that the gene has its value changed to some other allowable allele.

4. *Repeat.*   Repeat but randomly change the neighbor that is used for the competition and the mating steps (e.g., use the left neighbor this time around for the competition step).

Since the fitness is defined on the basis of profit, the system will slowly converge on that combination of customer attributes that consistently provides the highest profit. There is some chance that a customer segment will be defined with less than the optimal profit and that it could dominate the population, but for this simple problem the random effect of mutation will keep the system exploring new attribute combinations. Also note that throughout the population a variety of suboptimal but nonetheless interesting segments will be created which could be culled from the population and saved as well. Effectively, this genetic algorithm is doing rule induction in a general-purpose way.

21.6   Strengths and Weaknesses

21.6.1   Algorithm score card

It is difficult to directly evaluate genetic algorithms via the algorithm score card since this score card has been developed to compare the strengths of various data mining algorithms; genetic algorithms are mostly used for general-purpose optimization. Their use for data mining only comes in conjunction with the optimization of some other data mining technique. With that caveat, genetic algorithms can be extremely useful in complex business situations where much is known about the value and cost of various parts of a complex business process but there is no other way to model it. In these cases genetic algorithms can provide substantially improved return on investment with a given data mining algorithm. The algorithm score card is shown in Fig. 21.6 and Table 21.8.

21.6.2 State of the marketplace

The genetic algorithms marketplace is still in its infancy, consisting mostly of small consulting shops or small practices within the larger consulting houses. Because the market is new, the players are extremely volatile, with new ones arriving and older ones disappearing at regular intervals.

21.6.3 Predicting future trends

Genetic algorithms will become more prevalent in the future, as real-world problems to be solved become more complex; also, because of highly dynamic marketplaces, there is less time to carefully analyze a problem to determine an optimal heuristic or analytical solution. Genetic algorithms will play an important role here, especially as data mining solutions move from being evaluated by predictive accuracy to evaluation by return on investment or profit across the entire business process. For this reason there will also be more and more evolutionary systems created solely for modeling complex behavior.

These systems will be constructed from large numbers of simple agents that each have some slightly different behavior and preferences. These agents will

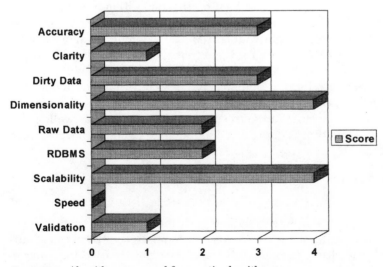

Figure 21.6 Algorithm score card for genetic algorithms.

TABLE 21.8   Algorithm Score Card for Genetic Algorithms

Data mining measure	Description
Accuracy	Genetic algorithms can produce accurate results when applied in novel areas, but in general, once the problem is well understood, more specialized learning procedures will produce more accurate results.
Clarity	It can be difficult to understand how a genetic algorithm arrived at its answer. These systems can have large populations that are randomly generated; thus different runs can produce very different results.
Dimensionality	Genetic algorithms are often the optimization and search method of choice in very high-dimensional spaces.
Dirty data	Because they are so adaptive, genetic algorithms can sometimes work better with dirty data and missing values than can other systems.
Raw data	Oftentimes genetic algorithms require a good deal of preprocessing of data so that it can be used by the fitness function.
RDBMS	To date genetic algorithms have stayed farther away from the mainstream business processes. Although they could become well integrated, they have not as yet.
Scalability	Genetic algorithms scale extremely well to parallel processing environments.
Speed	Genetic algorithms can be slow, especially when premature convergence is avoided through increased mutation rates.
Validation	The validity depends on the method used in the fitness evaluation. Generally this would be a modified version of cross-validation.

likely represent consumers or business prospects where individual behavior is relatively well understood but the dynamics and profitability of the entire system are not. These will be systems that will not necessarily evolve the genetic material of the agents but instead evolve at a macro level over time.

Genetic algorithms will continue to borrow more and more from biology and natural evolution as it is better understood. In this chapter we have discussed the tremendous benefits of using sharing to prevent premature convergence and in doing so have learned something about both natural and simulated evolution. There are other things that can be and have been borrowed from nature.

- Including parasites that sap the fitness from the host organism has also been shown to prevent premature convergence.

- Diploidy and recessive genes have been incorporated.

- Selection via competition and breeding in local neighborhoods rather than interbreeding across the entire population has been shown to avoid premature convergence and encourage speciation (two organisms are considered to be of different species if their progeny are not fit enough to survive).

- Simulations of newtonian physics have led to the evolution of creature that evolve to learn locomotion on both land and in the water.

- Computer code itself allowing tremendous latitude in the genetic organism to find powerful and creative solutions to difficult problems is being developed. In this case the LISP computer language can be used in the genetic material, and modified mutation and crossover have led to programs able to do everything from park a simulated truck to create desirable artwork.

As more is learned about genetic algorithms, more will be learned about natural genetics and evolutionary systems. We expect that this will be a fruitful place to watch for new products in the coming years.

22

Rule Induction

Rule induction is one of the major forms of data mining and is perhaps the most common form of knowledge discovery in unsupervised learning systems. It is also perhaps the form of data mining that most closely resembles the process that most people associate with data mining, namely, "mining" for gold through a vast database. The gold in this case would be a rule that is interesting—that tells you something about your database that you didn't already know and probably weren't able to explicitly articulate (aside from saying "show me things that are interesting"). Rule induction on a database can be a massive undertaking in which all possible patterns are systematically pulled out of the data and then accuracy and significance calculated, telling users how strong the pattern is and how likely it is to occur again. In general, these rules are relatively simple; for instance, for a market basket database of items scanned in a consumer market basket, you might find interesting correlations in your database such as

- If bagels are purchased, then cream cheese is purchased 90 percent of the time and this pattern occurs in 3 percent of all shopping baskets.

- If live plants are purchased from a hardware store, then plant fertilizer is purchased 60 percent of the time and these two items are bought together in 6 percent of the shopping baskets.

The rules that are pulled from the database are extracted and ordered to be presented to the user according to the percentage of times that they are correct and how often they apply.

The bane of rule induction systems is also its strength—that it retrieves all possible interesting patterns in the database. This is a strength in the sense that it leaves no stone unturned, but it can also be viewed as a weakness because the user can easily become overwhelmed with such a large number of rules that it is difficult to look through all of them. You almost need a second pass of data mining to go through the list of interesting rules that have been generated by the rule induction system in the first place in order to find the most valuable gold nugget among them all. This overabundance of patterns can also be problematic for the simple task of prediction; because all possible patterns are culled from the database, there may be conflicting predictions made by equally interesting rules. Automating the processes of culling the most interesting rules and of combing the recommendations of a variety of rules are well handled by many of the commercially available rule induction systems on the market today; such automation is also an area of active research.

22.1   Business Score Card

Rule induction systems are highly automated and are probably the best data mining techniques for exposing all possible predictive patterns in a database. They can be modified for use in prediction problems, but the algorithms for combining evidence from a variety of rules comes more from rules of thumb and practical experience.

In comparing data mining techniques along an axis of explanation, neural networks would be at one extreme of the data mining algorithms and rule induction systems at the other end. Neural networks are extremely proficient at saying exactly what must be done in a prediction task (e.g., whom do I give credit to or whom do I deny credit to) with little explanation. Rule induction systems, when used for prediction, on the other hand, are like having a committee of trusted advisors, each with a slightly different opinion as to what to do but relatively well-grounded reasoning and a good explanation for why it should be done.

The business score card for rule induction shown in Fig. 22.1 and Table 22.1 reflects the highly automated way in which the rules are created, which makes it easy to use the system. This approach can suffer from an overabundance of interesting patterns, which can make it complicated in order to make a prediction that is directly tied to return on investment (ROI).

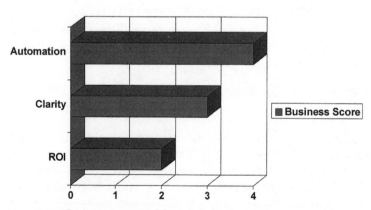

Figure 22.1   Business score card for rule induction systems.

TABLE 22.1   Business Score Card for Rule Induction Systems

Data mining measure	Description
Automation	Rule induction systems tend to be highly automated in the construction ordering and presentation of the rules. The user is often required to wade through large numbers of rules that are proposed as interesting in order to actually determine whether the rule is important.
Clarity	The rules themselves are generally simple and easy to understand, although why they occur may not be as easy to distill. Also, because of the large number of rules that are returned to the end user, some of the clarity of the system can be lost as the user is overwhelmed with obscure rules that don't make sense or obvious rules that were already known.
ROI	Although rule induction systems can be used for prediction, they are most often used for unsupervised learning to find out things that are not already known. It is even more difficult to quantify the return on investment for "interesting" rules than to calculate for other supervised learning techniques that are targeted at well-known prediction problems where ROI is better understood.

22.2   Where to Use Rule Induction

22.2.1   What is a rule?

In rule induction systems the rule itself comes in the simple form of "if this and this and this, then this." For example, a rule that a supermarket might find in their data collected from scanners would be "If pickles are purchased, then ketchup is purchased." Or

- If paper plates, then plastic forks
- If dip, then potato chips
- If salsa, then tortilla chips

For the rules to be useful, two pieces of information must be supplied as well as the actual rule:

1. *Accuracy*—how often is the rule correct?
2. *Coverage*—how often does the rule apply?

Just because the pattern in the database is expressed as a rule does not mean that it is true all the time. Thus, just as in other data mining algorithms, it is important to recognize and make explicit the uncertainty in the rule. This is what the accuracy of the rule means. The *coverage* of the rule relates to how much of the database the rule "covers" or applies to. Examples of these two measures for a variety of rules are shown in Table 22.2.

In some cases accuracy is called the "confidence" of the rule and coverage is related to another measure called the "support." Accuracy and coverage appear to be the preferred ways of naming these two measurements. To see why both coverage and accuracy are important, consider the following examples. The rules themselves consist of two halves. The left side is called the *antecedent* and the

TABLE 22.2   Examples of Rule Accuracy and Coverage*

Rule	Accuracy (%)	Coverage (%)
If breakfast cereal purchased, then milk will be purchased.	85	20
If bread purchased, then swiss cheese will be purchased.	15	6
If 42 years old and purchased pretzels and purchased dry roasted peanuts, then beer will be purchased.	95	0.01

* Both accuracy and coverage are important in determining the usefulness of a rule. The first rule is a pattern that occurs quite often and is right more often than not. The second rule is almost never wrong but also is almost never applicable.

right side, the *consequent*. The antecedent can consist of just one condition or multiple conditions which must all be true in order for the consequent to be true at the given accuracy. Generally the consequent is just a single condition (e.g., prediction of purchasing just one grocery store item) rather than multiple conditions. Thus rules such as "If x and y, then a and b and c are uncommon."

22.2.2   What to do with a rule

When the rules are mined out of the database, they can be used either for better understanding the business problems that the data reflects or performing actual predictions against some predefined prediction target. Since there is both a left side and a right side to a rule (antecedent and consequent), they can be used in several ways for your business.

1. *Target the antecedent.*   In this case all rules that have a certain value for the antecedent are gathered and displayed to the user. For instance, a grocery store may request all rules that have nails, bolts, or screws in the antecedent in order to try to understand whether discontinuing the sale of these low-margin items will have any effect on other higher-margin items. For instance, maybe people who buy nails also buy expensive hammers but wouldn't do so at the store if the nails were not available.

2. *Target the consequent.*   In this case all rules that have a certain value for the consequent can be used to understand what is associated with the consequent and perhaps what affects the consequent. For instance, it might be useful to know all the interesting rules that have "coffee" in their consequent. These may well be the rules that affect the purchases of coffee and that a store owner may want to put close to the coffee in order to increase the sale of both items. Or it might be the rule that the coffee manufacturer uses to determine in which magazine to place their next coupons.

3. *Target based on accuracy.*   Sometimes the most important thing for a user is the accuracy of the rules that are being generated. Highly accurate rules of 80 or 90 percent imply strong relationships that can be exploited even if they have low coverage of the database and occur only a limited number of times. For instance, a rule that has only 0.1 percent coverage and an accuracy of 95 percent can be applied only one time out of 1000 but will very

likely be correct. If this one time is highly profitable, then it can be worthwhile. This, for instance, is how some of the most successful data mining applications work in the financial markets—looking for that limited amount of time in which a very confident prediction can be made.

4. *Target based on coverage.*   Sometimes users want to know what the most ubiquitous rules are or those rules that are most readily applicable. By looking at rules ranked by coverage, they can quickly get a high-level view of what is happening within their database most of the time.

5. *Target based on "interestingness."*   Rules are interesting when they have high coverage and high accuracy and deviate from the norm. There have been many ways in which rules have been ranked by some measure of interestingness so that the tradeoff between coverage and accuracy can be made.

Since rule induction systems are so often used for pattern discovery and unsupervised learning, it is less easy to compare them. For example, it is very easy for just about any rule induction system to generate all possible rules; it is, however, much more difficult to devise a way to present those rules (which could easily be in the hundreds of thousands) in a way that is most useful to the end user. When interesting rules are found, they usually have been created to find relationships between many different predictor values in the database, not just one well defined target of the prediction. For this reason it is often much more difficult to assign a measure of value to the rule aside from its interestingness. For instance, it would be difficult to determine the monetary value of knowing that if people buy breakfast sausage, they also buy eggs 60 percent of the time. For data mining systems that are more focused on prediction for things such as customer attrition, targeted marketing response, or risk, it is much easier to measure the value of the system and compare it to other systems and other methods for solving the problem.

22.2.3   Caveat: Rules do not imply causality

It is important to recognize that even though the patterns produced from rule induction systems are delivered as if-then rules, they do not necessarily mean that the left side of the rule (the "if" part) causes the right side of the rule (the "then" part) to happen. Purchasing cheese does not cause the purchase of wine even though the rule "if cheese, then wine" may be very strong.

This is particularly important to remember for rule induction systems because the results are presented as "if this, then that" as many causal relationships are presented.

22.2.4   Types of databases used for rule induction

Typically rule induction is used on databases with either fields of high cardinality (many different values) or many columns of binary fields. The classic case of this is the supermarket basket data from store scanners that contains individual product names and quantities and may contain tens of thousands of different items with different packaging that create hundreds of thousands of stockkeeping units (SKU) identifiers.

Sometimes the concept of a record is not easily defined within the database—consider the typical star schema for many data warehouses that store the supermarket transactions as separate entries in the fact table. The columns in the fact table represent some unique identifiers of the shopping basket (so that all items can be noted as being in the same shopping basket), such as the quantity, the time of purchase, or whether the item was purchased with a special promotion (sale or coupon). Thus each item in the shopping basket has a different row in the fact table. This layout of the data is not typically the best for most data mining algorithms, which would prefer to have the data structured as one row per shopping basket and each column to represent the presence or absence of a given item. This can be an expensive way to store the data, however, since the typical grocery store contains 60,000 SKUs or different items that could come across the check-out counter. This structure of the records can also create a very high-dimensional space (60,000 binary dimensions) which would be unwieldy for many classic data mining algorithms such as neural networks and decision trees. As we'll see, several tricks are played to make this computationally feasible for the data mining algorithm while not requiring a massive re-organization of the database.

22.2.5   Discovery

The claim to fame of these rule induction systems is much more so for knowledge discovery in unsupervised learning systems than it is for prediction. These systems provide both a very detailed view of the data where significant patterns that occur only a small portion of the time and can be found only when looking at the detail data as well as a broad overview of the data where some systems seek to deliver to the user an overall view of the patterns contained in the database. These systems thus display a nice combination of both micro and macro views:

1. *Macro level.*   Patterns that cover many situations are provided to the user to be used very often and with great confidence, and can also be used to summarize the database.

2. *Micro level.*   Strong rules that cover only a very few situations can still be retrieved by the system and proposed to the end user. These may be valuable if the situations that are covered are highly valuable (maybe they apply only to the most profitable customers) or represent a small but growing subpopulation, which may indicate a market shift or the emergence of a new competitor (e.g., customers are being lost only in one particular area of the country where a new competitor is emerging).

22.2.6   Prediction

After the rules are created and their interestingness is measured, there is also a call for performing prediction with the rules. Each rule by itself can perform prediction—the consequent is the target, and the accuracy of the rule is the accuracy of the prediction. But because rule induction systems produce many rules for a given antecedent or consequent, there can be conflicting predictions with different accuracies. This is an opportunity to improve the overall performance of the systems by combining the rules. This can be done in a variety of ways by summing the accuracies as if they were weights or just by taking the prediction of the rule with the maximum accuracy.

Table 22.3 shows how a given consequent or antecedent can be part of many rules with different accuracies and coverages. From this example, consider the prediction problem of trying to predict whether milk was purchased solely on the basis of the other items that were in the shopping basket. If the shopping basket contained only bread, then from the table we would guess that there was a 35 percent chance that milk was also purchased. If, however, bread and butter and eggs and cheese were purchased, what would be the prediction for milk then? Would the answer 65 percent chance of milk because the relationship between butter and milk is greatest at 65 percent? Or would all the other items in the basket increase even further the chance of milk being purchased to well beyond 65 percent? Determining how to combine evidence from multiple rules is a key part of the algorithms for using rules for prediction.

22.2.7   Applications score card

The applications scorecard for rule induction systems is shown in Fig. 22.2 and Table 22.4. Rule induction systems are designed to extract rules from a database as well as links. They are less often used for outlier or cluster analysis.

TABLE 22.3   **Accuracy and Coverage in Rule Antecedents and Consequents***

Antecedent	Consequent	Accuracy (%)	Coverage (%)
Bagels	Cream cheese	80	5
Bagels	Orange juice	40	3
Bagels	Coffee	40	2
Bagels	Eggs	25	2
Bread	Milk	35	30
Butter	Milk	65	20
Eggs	Milk	35	15
Cheese	Milk	40	8

* A single antecedent can predict multiple consequents just as many different antecedents can predict the same consequent.

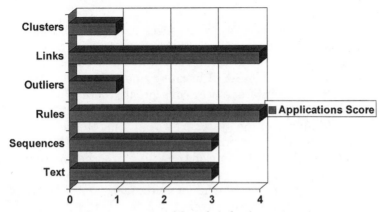

Figure 22.2 Applications score card for rule induction systems.

22.3 The General Idea

The general idea of a rule classification system is that rules are created to show the relationship between events captured in your database. These rules can be simple, with just one element in the antecedent; or they might be more complicated, with many column value pairs in the antecedent, all joined together by a conjunction (item 1 and item 2 and item 3 . . . must all occur for the antecedent to be true).

The rules are used to find interesting patterns in the database, but they are also used at times for prediction. Two main things are important to understanding a rule:

TABLE 22.4 **Applications Score Card for Rule Induction Systems**

Problem type	Description
Clusters	Although rule induction systems have been used to summarize data through high-level macro rules, they are not mutually exclusive in the way that they divide the data the way that clustering systems typically are.
Links	Association rule systems are a specific type of rule induction systems that have been specifically designed to perform link analysis.
Outliers	Rule induction systems are not typically used to perform outlier analysis but can be used for finding small but interesting subpopulations in the database.
Rules	Rule induction systems excel at extracting rules from a database and making them understandable to the end user.
Sequences	Rule induction systems can be used for uncovering sequence information, although using them for prediction is more difficult.
Text	Because rule induction systems are often used in high-dimensional spaces like those found in text prediction applications, the techniques are very similar.

- *Accuracy*—the probability that if the antecedent is true, then the precedent will be true. *High accuracy* means that this is a rule that is highly dependable.

- *Coverage*—the number of records in the database that the rule applies to. *High coverage* means that the rule can be used very often and also that it is less likely to be a spurious artifact of the sampling technique or idiosyncrasies of the database.

From a business perspective, accurate rules are important because they imply that there is useful predictive information in the database that can be exploited—namely, that there is something far from independent between the antecedent and the consequent. The lower the accuracy, the closer the rule comes to just random guessing. If the accuracy is significantly below that of what would be expected from random guessing, then the negation of the antecedent may well in fact be useful (for instance, people who buy denture adhesive are much less likely to buy fresh corn on the cob than normal).

From a business perspective, *coverage* implies how often you can use a useful rule. For instance, you may have a rule that is 100 percent accurate but is applicable in only 1 out of every 100,000 shopping baskets. You can rearrange your shelf space to take advantage of this fact, but it will not make you much money since the event is not very likely to happen. Table 22.5 displays the tradeoff between coverage and accuracy.

An analogy between coverage and accuracy and making money is the following from betting on horses. Having a high-accuracy rule with low coverage would be like owning a racehorse that always won when racing but could race only once a year. In betting, you could probably still make a lot of money on such a horse. In rule induction for retail stores, it is unlikely that finding one rule between mayonnaise, ice cream, and sardines that seems to always be true will have much of an impact on your bottom line.

22.3.1 How to evaluate the rule

One way to look at accuracy and coverage is to see how they relate to some simple statistics and how they can be represented graphically. In statistics, coverage is simply the a priori probability of the antecedent occurring. The accuracy is just the probability of the consequent conditional on the precedent. So, for instance, if we were looking at the following database of supermarket basket scanner data, we would need the following information in order to calculate the

TABLE 22.5   Rule Coverage versus Accuracy*

	Accuracy low	Accuracy high
Coverage high	Rule is rarely correct but can be used often	Rule is often correct and can be used often
Coverage low	Rule is rarely correct and can be used only rarely	Rule is often correct but can be used only rarely

* Both coverage and accuracy will have an impact on how valuable the rule is.

accuracy and coverage for a simple rule (let's say milk purchased implies eggs purchased).

- $T = 100$ = total number of shopping baskets in the database
- $E = 30$ = number of baskets with eggs in them
- $M = 40$ = number of baskets with milk in them
- $B = 20$ = number of baskets with both eggs and milk in them

Accuracy is then just the number of baskets with eggs and milk in them divided by the number of baskets with milk in them. In this case that would be $20/40 = 50\%$. The coverage would be the number of baskets with milk in them divided by the total number of baskets. This would be $40/100 = 40\%$. This can be seen graphically in Fig. 22.3.

Note that we haven't used E, the number of baskets with eggs in these calculations. One way that eggs could be used would be to calculate the expected number of baskets with eggs and milk in them in reference to the independence of the events. This would give us some sense of how unlikely and how special the event is that 20 percent of the baskets contain both eggs and milk. Remember from the statistics section that if two events are independent (have no effect on one another), the product of their individual probabilities of occurrence should equal the probability of the occurrence of them both together.

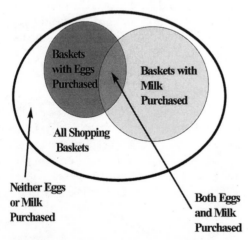

Figure 22.3 Graphically the total number of shopping baskets can be represented in a space, and the number of baskets containing eggs or milk can be represented by the area of a circle. Coverage of the rule "If milk, then eggs" is just the relative size of the circle corresponding to milk. The degree of accuracy is the size of the overlap between the two relative to the circle representing milk purchased.

If the purchase of eggs and milk were independent of each other, we would expect that $0.3 \times 0.4 = 0.12$ or 12% of the time we would see shopping baskets with both eggs and milk in them. The fact that this combination of products occurs 20 percent of the time would be out of the ordinary if these events were independent. In other words, there is a good chance that the purchase of one affects the other, and the degree to which this is the case could be calculated through statistical tests and hypothesis testing.

22.3.2 Conjunctions and disjunctions

There is no particular reason why the antecedent part of the rule cannot be more complex than just a single item or predictor value. For instance, there may be a useful rule that shows that if three products are purchased together, then it is highly likely that a fourth will also be purchased. There is no theoretical limit to the number of constraints that could be tied together by "and" in the antecedent. There are, however, several practical limits, the main one of which is that the coverage of the rule decreases dramatically as the number of constraints in the antecedent is increased. To see this graphically, consider the diagram in Fig. 22.4.

Every time a new constraint is added to the rule, the coverage can become much smaller, especially for constraints that do not overlap very much. In the example given for grocery shopping, for instance, the number of people purchasing soda and potato chips may have a large overlap and thus high coverage. The overlap between other products may be much smaller; for instance, a box of low-fat, low-sugar, organic granola and a bag of potato chips are less likely to find themselves in the same shopping baskets. Every time a constraint is added to the antecedent of the rule, the coverage of the rule is decreased. It can also be

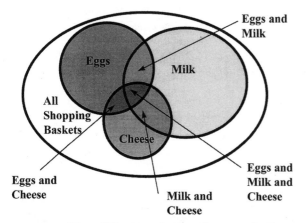

Figure 22.4 Many different product purchases can be shown graphically. Each overlapping area represents the logical AND or conjunction of two products being in the same market basket.

dramatically increased. It could also be possible, for example, to use a logical OR or disjunction of the constraints to form a new rule rather than the logical AND or conjunction of the constraints. If a disjunction is used, the coverage of the rule can increase with additional constraints in the antecedent. For instance, the rule "If diet soda or regular soda or beer, then potato chips" will cover many more shopping baskets than will just one of the constraints by themselves and many more than all of the constraints together as a conjunction.

Although rules that are created from a disjunction of constraints are perfectly acceptable and understandable, the generation of rules is usually limited to conjunctions of constraints when they are being generated since the addition of conjunctive constraints decreases or limits the coverage it helps to bound the search for interesting rules. The disjunction of constraints happens implicitly between different conjunctive rules. For instance, the two rules

1. If milk, then eggs.
2. If cheese, then eggs.

can be separately generated by the data mining system but used together to effectively cover all instances in which either milk or cheese was purchased. In some rule induction systems the rules will be generated as conjunctions of constraints and then later combined together as disjunctions afterward.

22.3.3 Defining "interestingness"

One of the biggest problems with rule induction systems is the sometimes overwhelming number of rules that are produced, most of which have no practical value or interest. Some of the rules are so inaccurate that they cannot be used; some have so little coverage that, although they are interesting, they have little applicability; and finally, many of the rules capture patterns and information that the user is already familiar with. To combat this problem, researchers have sought to measure the usefulness or interestingness of rules.

Certainly any measure of interestingness would have something to do with accuracy and coverage. We might also expect it to have at least the following four basic behaviors:

1. Interestingness = 0 if the accuracy of the rule is equal to the background accuracy (a priori probability of the consequent). The example in Table 22.6 illustrates this point; in this case a rule for attrition is no better than just guessing the overall rate of attrition.

TABLE 22.6   Uninteresting Rules

Antecedent	Consequent	Accuracy (%)	Coverage (%)
\<No constraints\>	Then customer will attrite	10	100
If customer balance > $3000	Then customer will attrite	10	60
If customer eyes = blue	Then customer will attrite	10	30
If customer Social Security number = 144 30 8217	Then customer will attrite	100	0.000001

2. Interestingness increases as accuracy increases (or decreases with decreasing accuracy) if the coverage is fixed.

3. Interestingness increases or decreases with coverage if accuracy stays fixed.

4. Interestingness decreases with coverage for a fixed number of correct responses (remember that accuracy equals the number of correct responses divided by the coverage).

Various measures of interestingness that have these general characteristics are used. They are used for pruning back the total possible number of rules that might be generated and then presented to the user.

Table 22.6 shows a rule table which compares no rule for attrition (which by default has the a priori probability or background rate) to other rules with the same accuracy (10 percent) or rules with high accuracy but very low coverage and can almost never be used. These would *not* be interesting rules.

22.3.4 Other measures of usefulness

Although coverage and accuracy are probably the two most important aspects of a rule, especially for prediction (one tells you how often you will be right, and the other tells you how often you can guess), there are still other measures that could be taken into account. For instance, one other measure that is often used is the "support" of a rule, which is the percentage of times the entire rule (both antecedent and consequent) occurs. This can be calculated as just the accuracy multiplied by the coverage, but the support is often quoted by itself to give an indication of the overall frequency of a given rule in the database.

Another measure is to capture coverage not as a probability or percentage but as the total number of records that match the given antecedent. There is good reason to capture coverage as a number of records rather than a probability because the statistical variance in the rule based on sampling will be dependent on the number of records, not the fraction of the database that it covers. Thus, if coverage is presented as a fraction (say, 30 percent), this number does not convey whether this means $\frac{3}{10}$ or $\frac{3000}{10,000}$. If the coverage is reported as 3 versus 3000, then the user gets a good idea of how much variance can be expected in the coverage and accuracy of the rule. Two rules could have the same coverage when measured by proportion but very different levels of confidence. This other measure of variance can be easily calculated from the first by multiplying the coverage as a probability by the total size of the database used for training.

One other measure that has been used throughout statistics and throughout other data mining techniques is comparison of the given pattern to random chance. This would be our "out of the ordinary" measure. As in statistics, two events are considered independent if the product of their probabilities is equal to the probability of both events occurring together. This fact is put to good use in the chi square statistic, and it could also be used in rule induction systems. For instance, the rule "If milk and eggs, then bread" may look very interesting with a support of 30 percent and an accuracy of 60 percent, but it may also not be very out of the ordinary. The support for this rule would be $0.3 \times 0.6 = 0.18$ (this rule is found 18 percent of the time in the database). If, however, eggs occur in 60 percent of the baskets, milk in 70 percent, and eggs in 40 percent of the baskets, then, by just random chance, if these events were completely independent of each other, we would expect the probability of the three events occurring together to be 0.17 ($0.6 \times 0.7 \times 0.4$), which is nearly equivalent to the actual frequency of these events in the database. Thus, although we have found a rule with high accuracy and high coverage, it may not be of much interest because it merely reflects the random independent events in the database—not any connection between the events, as the rule implies. Another important measure is that of simplicity of the rule. This is important solely for the end user. Complex rules, as powerful and as interesting as they might be, may be difficult to understand or to confirm via intuition. Thus the user has a desire to see simpler rules and consequently this desire can be manifest directly in the rules that are chosen and supplied automatically to the user.

Finally, a measure of novelty is also required during the creation of the rules—so that rules that are redundant but strong are less favored to be searched than are rules that may not be as strong but cover important examples that are not covered by other strong rules. For instance, there may be few historical records to provide rules on a little-sold grocery item (e.g., mint jelly), and they may have low accuracy but since there are so few possible rules, even though they are not interesting, they will be "novel" and should be retained and presented to the user for that reason alone.

To summarize, then, these are the important measures by which rules should be presented to the end user:

1. *Accuracy*—answers the question of how often the rule will supply the correct prediction
2. *Coverage*—answers the question of how often the rule can be used for prediction (and how sensitive it would be to the sample taken to create it)
3. *Support*—answers the question of how frequently the rules (both antecedent and consequent) occur
4. *Significance*—tells the user how unlikely this pattern would be compared to random chance of independent events
5. *Simplicity*—helps the user build intuitions and confirm the rule via intuitions
6. *Novelty*—helps the user find rules that may occupy regions of the predictive space where few other rules are

22.3.5   Rules versus decision trees

Decision trees also produce rules but in a very different way than rule induction systems. The main difference between the rules that are produced by decision trees and rule induction systems is as follows:

Decision trees produce rules that are mutually exclusive and collectively exhaustive with respect to the training database, while rule induction systems produce rules that are not mutually exclusive and might be collectively exhaustive.

In plain English, this means that for a given record, there will be a rule to cover it and there will only be one rule for rules that come from decision trees. There may be many rules that match a given record from a rule induction system, and for many systems it is not guaranteed that a rule will exist for each and every possible record that might be encountered (although most systems do create very general default rules to capture these records). The reason for this difference is the way in which the two algorithms operate. Rule induction seeks to go from the bottom up and collect all possible patterns that are interesting and then later use those patterns for some prediction target. Decision trees, on the other hand, work from a prediction target downward in what is known as a "greedy" search, looking for the best possible split on the next step (i.e., greedily picking the best one without looking any further than the next step). Although the greedy algorithm can make choices at the higher levels of the tree which are less than optimal at the lower levels of the tree, it is very good at effectively squeezing out any correlations between predictors and the prediction. Rule induction systems, on the other hand, retain all possible patterns, even if they are redundant or do not aid in predictive accuracy.

For instance, consider that in a rule induction system, if there were two columns of data that were highly correlated (or, in fact, just simple transformations of each other), they would result in two rules whereas in a decision tree, one predictor would be chosen and then, since, the second one was redundant, it would not be chosen again. An example might be the two predictors' annual charges and average monthly charges (average monthly charges being the annual charges divided by 12). If the amount charged were predictive, then the decision tree would choose one of the predictors and use it for a split point somewhere in the tree. The decision tree effectively "squeezed" the predictive value out of the predictor and then moved onto the next. A rule induction system would, on the other hand create, two rules, perhaps something like

- If annual charges >12,000, then default = true 90% accuracy.
- If average monthly charges >1000, then default = true 90% accuracy.

In this case we've shown an extreme case in which two predictors were exactly the same, but there can also be less extreme cases. For instance, height might be used rather than shoe size in the decision tree, whereas both would be presented as rules in a rule induction system.

Neither one technique or the other is necessarily better, although having a variety of rules and predictors helps with the prediction when there are missing values. For instance, if the decision tree did choose height as a split point but that predictor was not captured in the record (a null value) but shoe size was, the rule induction system would still have a matching rule to capture this record. Decision trees do have ways of overcoming this difficulty by keeping "surrogates" at each split point that most closely replicate the split as does the chosen predictor. In this case shoe size might have been kept as a surrogate for height at this particular branch of the tree. One other thing that decision trees and rule induction systems have in common is the fact that they both need to find ways to combine and simplify rules. In a decision tree this can be as simple as recognizing that if a lower split on a predictor is more constrained than a split on the same predictor further up in the tree, both don't need to be provided to the user—only the more restrictive one. For instance, if the first split of the tree is age ≤50 years and the lowest split for the given leaf is age ≤30 years, then only the latter constraint needs to be captured in the rule for that leaf.

Rules from rule induction systems are generally created by taking a simple high-level rule and adding new constraints to it until the coverage gets so small as to unmeaningful. This means that the rules actually have families or what is called "cones of specialization," where one more general rule can be the parent of many more specialized rules. These cones then can be presented to the user as high-level views of the families of rules and can be viewed in a hierarchical manner to aid in understanding.

22.4   How Rule Induction Works

22.4.1   Constructing rules

The way that rules are constructed is somewhat similar to the way trees are generated for decision trees, except for one major difference. In decision trees only the best possible constraint is added to the tree, while when constructing rules, all possible constraints are added to the existing rule. There are a variety of ways of growing rules, keeping track of which rules to expand and how to prune and organize the rules once they are created. In general, constraints in the form of new conjunctions are added to the rule as either specific values for categorical (low-cardinality) predictors or as constraints based on particular intervals for a continuous ordered predictor. Although the algorithms are varied, they have several main steps in common:

1. Preprocess the data so that each predictor has well-defined intervals rather than continuous values.
2. Generate initial rules from the data of just one constraint.
3. From the records, generate rules that have an additional constraint from the given rules.
4. Keep the group of rules that are good candidates to have added constraints.
5. Continue adding constraints onto the rules until the stopping criteria have been met for all rules.
6. Organize the rules on the basis of their usefulness (i.e., accuracy, coverage, support, significance, simplicity, and novelty) to the end user.

In the first step the data is preprocessed so that both categorical and continuous predictors have a small number of different values; these values are then the constraints that can be added to the rule one at a time to create more complex rules. This step is also sometimes used in decision tree algorithms when "prebinning" of the predictor needs to be done.

Generation of the initial rules is performed simply by picking each value of each predictor in each record and pairing it with all other predictor value pairs. These pairs of values represent the first pass of simple if-then rules. From these rules it is possible to determine which rules are good candidates for expanding with new constraints. Usually these are the rules that pass some minimum threshold of accuracy and coverage.

For instance, if a rule has very low accuracy (e.g., apple purchases predict waffle purchases 0.1 percent of the time), it is much less likely that the rule will become much more accurate with additional constraints (although this is possible). An even better threshold to employ for determining which rules should be considered finished and which ones should continue to be expanded is to look at the coverage and the support. Adding constraints can at best not affect the coverage and support of a given rule but most likely they will significantly decrease these variables. Adding constraints can never increase the coverage or support for a rule. If a rule has a low enough coverage, it may not make sense to expand the rule since there will be some minimal coverage after which the rule is of no value even if it is of high accuracy (i.e., if the rule is never used, then it doesn't matter what the accuracy is). When the support for the rule grows small, then there are few historical records to substantiate the rule and the rule itself may be entirely spurious and an artifact of random noise or statistical variations due to the small sample. As an example, consider the example database we've been using throughout these chapters. In this case the initial rules would be created between two columns of the database. To keep this simple, let's just look at the income, eyes, and gender columns and create rules with income and eye color in the antecedent and gender in the consequent. Since there are three different values for income and eyes and two different values for gender, there is a possibility of $3 \times 3 \times 2$ or 18 different rules with two constraints in the antecedent. This would represent all different combinations of the values of the predictors and it would correctly account for the fact that even if the order of the constraints in the rule were changed, the rule would still be the same and be counted only once. For instance, the two rules

- If medium income and brown eyes, then female
- If brown eyes and medium income, then female

are equivalent even though the order of the constraints is changed in the antecedent. Table 22.8 shows the number of different rules that could be created with two constraints in the antecedent from the historical data in Table 22.7. Interestingly, the number of rules is only 8 rather than the 18 possible rules that were predicted. The reason for this is that many of the possible rules

TABLE 22.7   Example Historical Database

ID	Name	Prediction	Age	Balance ($)	Income	Eyes	Gender
1	Amy	No	62	0	Medium	Brown	F
2	Al	No	53	1,800	Medium	Green	M
3	Betty	No	47	16,543	High	Brown	F
4	Bob	Yes	32	45	Medium	Green	M
5	Carla	Yes	21	2,300	High	Blue	F
6	Carl	No	27	5,400	High	Brown	M
7	Donna	Yes	50	165	Low	Blue	F
8	Don	Yes	46	0	High	Blue	M
9	Edna	Yes	27	500	Low	Blue	F
10	Ed	No	68	1,200	Low	Blue	M

TABLE 22.8   The Possible Rules Generated with Two Constraints in Antecedent and Gender in Consequent

Rule number	Antecedent	Antecedent	Consequent	Supporting records
1	Low income	Blue eyes	Female	2
2	Low income	Blue eyes	Male	1
3	Medium income	Brown eyes	Female	1
4	Medium income	Green eyes	Male	2
5	High income	Brown eyes	Female	1
6	High income	Brown eyes	Male	1
7	High income	Blue eyes	Female	1
8	High income	Blue eyes	Male	1

never occurred in the actual database. Part of this is due to the very small sample that is being used to make the point, but this does come into play relatively often during real-world rule induction on much larger databases. In a real-world database there could easily be hundreds of predictors, each with 100 different values. This would result in nearly 10 billion ($100 \times 100 \times 100 \times 100 \times 100$) possible rules if just four of the predictors were used for the antecedent.

The bottom line on rule generation is thus twofold:

- The number of different possible rules can quickly grow to be enormous.
- The number of actual rules will be much smaller since many of the possible rules do not actually occur in the data.

After these rules are generated, it is possible to add further constraints to the rules by adding in other predictors. Since these rules come from an example 10-record database, the support for each of them is very small—either one or two records, which is far below what would be considered to be statistically significant. If, however, the rules had greater support, they could be expanded with additional constraints from other predictors. In the limit if the algorithm did not halt for low support, the system could create rules that contained every value for every predictor and so constrain the space that only one record from the historical database was captured by each rule. The accuracy would be 100 percent, but the system would suffer from overfitting and would produce rules that did not generalize well. The required thresholds for support and coverage are, in fact, attempts to limit overfitting in the generation of the rules, and the rules with the greatest support are the most likely to generalize to new situations.

22.4.2   A brute-force algorithm
for generating rules

The algorithm described above proceeds by adding on constraints to existing rules and then measuring their accuracy, coverage, and support. There are a host of heuristic methods by which this addition of new constraints can be performed, but as computers speed up and disk and memory space become cheaper, brute-force approaches are becoming more and more appealing. The simplest brute-force algorithm would be as follows:

1. Generate all predictor/value pairs for each record as the first set of rules.
2. Count the number of occurrences for each rule and the antecedent by itself.
3. Calculate the accuracy, coverage, and support and eliminate those rules that do not pass the required minimum threshold.
4. For each record, see which rules apply to it and add an additional constraint (predictor value) to the rule from the record.
5. Return to step 1 until the rules are too complex or no rule passes the minimum coverage or support thresholds.

This algorithm may seem to be very computationally expensive, but it can be efficiently implemented via a sorting or hashing algorithm. This is particularly efficient when performed on a parallel computer and makes full use of parallel processing. The algorithm is performed in parallel by first producing all new rules for a given record based on the previous rules (just go through each rule associated with the given record and add a constraint from the available predictor values). Now take this new list of possible rules and tag it with the record number that it was generated from. Then sort all these newly formed rules so that rules with the same exact precedent and antecedent are next to each other. Because each new rule from a given record is next to the same rule generated from another record (due to sorted order), all the values needed to be counted in order to compute the accuracy, coverage, and support can be easily computed via a running sum (something that is very efficiently performed on massively parallel computers).

The thresholds can then be applied to these new rules, and those that pass can then be sorted again according to the record number from which they came, and when they are local to that record the next set of rules can be generated. Thus any system that has optimized sorting routines can perform this rule generation very quickly.

22.4.3   Combining evidence

To combine the "recommendations" from multiple matching rules, consider a problem with three possible prediction values (A,B,C) and several rules that match the existing conditions for the prediction. This is shown in Table 22.9. The question, given these conflicting predictions, is which prediction should be made.

The prediction could be calculated in several ways. The simplest would be to take the maximum accuracy afforded by rule group 2 for the rule that predicts value C with 90 percent accuracy. Another way to do this would be to add up all the accuracies (as either percentages or probabilities) and use that as total evidence. These values are shown in the last row in the table, and using this technique for combining evidence would lead to a different answer, namely, that prediction B had the greatest amount of accumulated evidence, although no one particular rule had an accuracy above 80 percent. Clearly, one of the problems with this way of combining evidence is that there is no longer an easy way to evaluate the prediction as a simple probability. The last row has accumulated accuracies of greater than 100 percent, which means that they can no longer be interpreted as probabilities.

There are other techniques for accumulating evidence; one such technique divides the accuracy of one rule by the combined accuracies of all other rules with the same antecedent but different consequents (all rules that would match for a given record but make different predictions) and then takes the logarithm of that value. This ratio of accuracies is useful because it will be greater than 1 when the accuracy of one rule is greater than that of all other rules combined and the log will be positive; otherwise the log will be negative. To make a prediction, these evidence values are then summed together for all rules that match the given record and the prediction is made on the basis of the prediction with the highest total evidence.

22.5   Case Study: Classifying U.S. Census Returns

Every 10 years the U.S. Census Bureau needs to calculate and then report the number of, and changes in, occupations and industries within the United

TABLE 22.9   Combining Evidence*

Rule group with same antecedent	Prediction accuracy (%)		
	A	B	C
1	60	20	30
2	40	50	90
3	20	80	10
Summed evidence	120	150	130

* Several rules may be applicable in the prediction for a given record. This table shows the chance of each of three possible predictive values based on each rule (remember that a given antecedent can occur in several rules with different consequents).

States. This is done via information collected from the long form of the U.S. Census, which asks residents a number of detailed questions about who they are, where they work, and what they do for a living. Although there is some numeric data such as age and categorical data such as type of company, the majority of the information collected is in the form of free text response to the following questions:

1. What kind of business or industry was this?
2. What kind of work is this person doing?
3. What are the person's most important activities or duties?

The respondents were free to write anything that they wished in response, and as a result there was a great deal of slang and even profanity captured in the text. All this information was entered into a database and, on the basis of the information, one of 232 different industry categories and 504 occupation categories needed to be assigned. Example industry categories included sporting goods, photographic equipment and supplies, and motor vehicles and equipment. Example occupation categories included construction painters, supervisors, and carpenter apprentices.

The historical database from which the rules were mined consisted of 132,247 records consisting of several numeric and categorical predictors and three predictors that contained a list of some 10 or fewer words from the free-text responses. This free text corresponded to some 50,000 different words in the database. The total concept space could be viewed as consisting of binary dimensions of either the presence or absence of a single word in a given document. This would lead to a 50,000-dimensional space that would have been unwieldy to find predictive patterns in. Making the conservative assumption of just 10 words per record, the total number of possible rules with two constraints in the antecedent would have been $(50,000)^{10}$. In reality, when some 65,000 records were used to create the rules, only 4.5 million rules were generated. This is certainly still a large number of rules, but much smaller than the total number of possible rules. Despite the brute-force algorithm used, the accuracies for all these rules were computed in under 10 minutes on a massively parallel computer.

The prediction task was performed by generating all possible rules with single and double constraints in the antecedent, and the accuracy was used to determine which of the many industry and occupation values would be assigned. In this case a hybrid model between the typical rule-based prediction and nearest-neighbor prediction was used whereby all rules present in a given record in the historical database were generated but only those rules that matched a given record in the database were used to accumulate evidence. In this case three methods were used to accumulate evidence:

1. *MAX.* The matching rule with the highest accuracy was used to assign the industry and occupation value (i.e., evidence was not accumulated across multiple matching rules).

2. *SUM.*   The accuracies of all rules that matched were summed together for each industry and occupation category, and the category with the largest sum was assigned to the new record.

3. *ERROR.*   A novel approach was used to accumulate evidence from multiple rules that avoids the disadvantages of the summation of evidence which would overreward multiple weak rules.

The system was implemented on a massively parallel computer and utilized a form a nearest-neighbor prediction to determine which rules were relevant to be applied to the given unknown record. The results of the system showed that the automated system that induced predictive rules from the database outperformed an expert system that had rules hand-crafted by human experts. The rule induction system was able to correctly classify 60 percent of the incoming census forms, while the expert system was able to classify only 47 percent.

This application showed not only how automated rule generation could be used to improve and automate the solution to a heretofore human-intensive problem but also how generated rules could be used in conjunction with a nearest-neighbor data mining approach to improve the overall performance of the system. The system also provided a good real-world test for the use of massively parallel computing to generate useful rules from the database in an exhaustive and brute-force approach. This case was written up in detail and provides an excellent overview of not only rule-based data mining but also the nearest-neighbor technique. See Creecy (1992) for the details.

22.6   Strengths and Weaknesses

Rule induction systems have been shown to be relatively easy to understand, relatively easy to deploy, and to display great utility for both discovery and prediction. Because the systems extract all interesting patterns, they are not brittle or sensitive to missing values or noisy data. In some ways rule induction systems are similar to making a decision via committee—many members vote and the plurality offer the decision. For rule-based systems, the many rules all contributing to the final prediction ensure that a single rule or a misstep by a greedy algorithm will not cause an incorrect prediction to be made. This decision by consensus does have the downside, however, of obscuring the simplicity of the individual rule which offers the very understandable and defensible conditional probability as the reason for the decision being made.

Overall rule induction systems are well suited to a variety of tasks and nearly as well automated as some of the more advanced decision tree algorithms. For some high-dimensional domains such as market basket analysis, where small correlations can be extremely important, rule induction systems outperform all others. The algorithm score card for the rule induction systems is shown in Fig. 22.5 and Table 22.10.

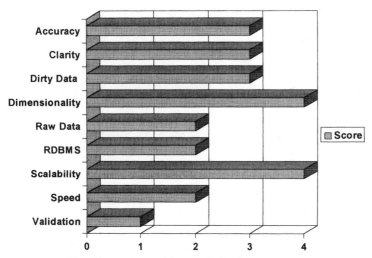

Figure 22.5   Algorithm score card for rule induction systems.

TABLE 22.10   Algorithm Score Card for Rule Induction System

Data mining measure	Description
Accuracy	When rule induction systems are used for prediction, their predictive accuracies can be among the best. However, because the accumulation of evidence from multiple matching rules is still more art than science and the lack of a process for accomplishing cross-validation the systems can offer surprising results if they are not carefully deployed.
Clarity	Rule-based systems are relatively understandable for the rules themselves, but the sheer number of rules can overwhelm the user. The clarity of predictions can also be obscured since the accumulation of evidence utilizes many rules, all of which influence determination of the prediction.
Dimensionality	Because they construct rules independently, rule induction systems can accommodate very high-dimensional concept spaces and dimensions with high cardinality. Although more dimensions slow down the process, the increase in time is usually linear with the number of predictor values that must be tried in the rules.
Dirty data	Rules work well at overcoming missing values and dirty data in general.
Raw data	These systems may require some preprocessing of numeric data into bins or intervals initially but are no worse than any of the decision tree algorithms and are better than most of the neural network algorithms.
RDBMS	Rule induction systems generally utilize algorithms that are difficult to implement directly within an RDBMS without a database extract. The rules themselves can be deployed against an RDBMS via SQL, but those techniques that use accumulated evidence for prediction can be more difficult and less efficient to implement.
Scalability	Rule systems scale well with larger numbers of records and dimensionality. They also map well to parallel computer architectures.
Speed	These systems can be slow, even on parallel hardware, although in general this is because they are extracting all possible patterns from the database rather than just those patterns for a particular prediction target. The application of the rules can be very fast.
Validation	These systems seldom have built-in cross-validation or test set validation. Some of the more sophisticated systems do use statistical tests and Bonferroni-like adjustments for repeated trials.

22.7   Current Offerings and Future Improvements

There are several commercial offerings of rule induction systems, including those from Information Discovery, Attar Software, and from IBM. In the future, look for these rule systems to become better at visually displaying the large numbers of rules and of clustering the rules and producing hierarchies. Don't hold out too much hope for a breakthrough on what "interestingness" means since this is very much still an art and very dependent on what individual end users think they want. Also look for some breakthroughs in algorithms for more deterministically generating all possible rules and for algorithms that are more easily embedded into the data warehouse.

It is also possible that some time in the near future a more general notion of the commonalities among prediction and discovery algorithms will emerge so that the lines between techniques such as nearest neighbor, rule induction, and decision trees will begin to blur. For instance, the case study discussed in this chapter showed a nice hybrid approach between rule induction and nearest neighbor. With some of the new features of decision trees where multiple trees are created or surrogates are used, the commonalities between these algorithms are becoming more noticeable than the differences.

23

Selecting and Using
the Right Technique

So far a variety of data mining techniques and algorithms have been presented, and some of their strengths and weaknesses have been discussed. In this chapter these strengths and weaknesses will be reviewed, and it will be shown how these data mining techniques fit into the bigger picture of an efficient business information process across the enterprise.

23.1 Using the Right Technique

The bottom line in picking a data mining technology and then an actual product really depends on whether the product can deliver real value to the business. This always translates to the bottom-line profit, increased revenue, decreased cost, or return on investment. If the technique and tool do not provide one of these four assets in a measurable way, it is unlikely that anyone in your business will have time to mine their data. Data mining needs to be more than finding interesting patterns in large databases if it is to be successfully deployed in your business.

23.1.1 The data mining process

To start off, let's look at the overall data mining process that has been proposed by those in the research community. They have argued that data mining (the actual generation of predictive models and patterns) is just one step along a much larger process of turning data into knowledge. The following steps have been proposed (note that this is in some contrast to the simpler set of steps that have been proposed here to date).

Figure 23.1 shows the technology-centric view of the data mining process that focuses on optimizing the data preprocessing but ignores many of the steps required for deploying a truly successful business application. This view of data mining shows how to move from raw data to useful patterns to knowledge. The better the data mining tool, the more automated and painless the transition from one step to the next.

23.1.2 What all the data mining techniques have in common

In order to make an intelligent selection among data mining tools and technologies, it will be helpful to categorize areas where they differ. To more clearly see this, and because there is so much overlap, one of the best ways to see the valid distinctions between the algorithms is to see what is similar. For instance, although they differ in how they accomplish them, each data mining algorithm has the following:

- *Model structure.*   The structure that defines the model (i.e., is it a decision tree, a neural network, or a nearest neighbor). This is the perceived model since the actual instantiation of the model might just be SQL queries in the case of decision trees and rule-based systems, or mathematical equations in the case of statistical regression.

- *Search.*   The manner in which the algorithm amends and modifies the model over time as more data is made available (e.g., neural networks search through link-weight space via the backpropagation algorithm, whereas the genetic algorithm searches through random permutation and genetic recombination).

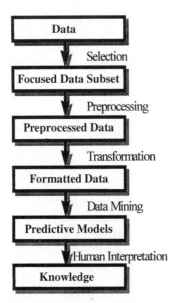

Figure   23.1 The technology-centric view of the data mining process.

■ *Validation.* The determination, by the algorithm, of a valid model. For instance, CART decision trees use cross-validation to determine the optimal level of growth of the tree. Neural networks don't have a specific validation technique to determine termination, but cross-validation is often used outside the neural network.

This description of the data mining algorithms should already be helpful because it makes more obvious how genetic algorithms are somewhat different from the other techniques mentioned as data mining algorithms. Genetic algorithms do not have any inherent model structure; instead, they are merely the optimization strategy for whatever model structure is defined to be encoded into the genetic material. The chromosome itself is not the model structure, but the interpretation of the chromosome is. This distinction is made even in biology by calling the genetic material the *genotype* and what it grows (is translated) into the *phenotype*. Because the genetic algorithm really is a search strategy without a model structure, genetic algorithms can be used in combination with any of the other data mining techniques. In Table 23.1 the data mining algorithms are categorized by these three features: structure, search, and validation.

By organizing the algorithms by these three features, it is clear that some of the major differences reflect the use of validation. Some techniques do not have it built in at all, some validate directly against the data, and some use statistical significance tests to calculate the best model. Although helpful, this view glosses over some important features that can make all the difference. For

TABLE 23.1   Comparing the Data Mining Algorithms

Algorithm	Structure	Search	Validation
CART	Binary tree	Splits chosen by entropy or Gini metric	Cross-validation
CHAID	Multiway split tree	Splits chosen by chi square test and Bonferroni adjustment	Validation performed at time of split selection
Neural network	Forwardpropagation network with non-linear thresholding	Backpropagation of errors	Not applicable
Genetic algorithms	Not applicable	Survival of the fittest on mutation and genetic crossover	Usually cross-validation
Rule induction	"If then" rule	Add new constraint to rule and retain it if it matches the "interestingness" criterion on the basis of accuracy and coverage	Chi square test with statistical significance cutoff (P value set to low value to combat the multiple comparisons or "fishing" problem)
Nearest neighbor	Distance of prototype in n-dimensional feature space	Usually there is no search	Cross-validation used for reported accuracy rates but not for algorithm termination

instance, it is quite difficult for a decision tree to represent a simple linear boundary between two prediction values efficiently when that boundary is not orthogonal to one of the axes of one of the predictors. In fact, the model structure used can be critical as to whether the problem can be solved at all in a reasonable amount of time.

23.1.3   Cases in which decision trees are like nearest neighbors

Consider also some of the similarities between the data mining algorithms. For instance, decision trees are doing a kind of nearest-neighbor match. If, for instance, a decision tree were fully grown, there could be a branchpoint for every predictor/value pair for every record in the database (e.g., at the first level all values of a predictor would represent different branches; at the next level, all values for the next predictor would be used). If such a tree were created and not pruned, then each leaf would effectively be executing an exact match between the record being classified and the training record that was used to build the tree.

If a slightly modified tree in which some predictors were not used were built, this would correspond to the nearest-neighbor algorithm, where those missing predictors were given a dimension weight of zero. The parallels are so close between the two algorithms that a decision-tree-like structure is often used to speed up the detection of the nearest neighbors of a record that has no prediction value.

Remember also that there are multiple records in the leaf of the decision tree that may not all be of the same prediction value (nonhomogeneous leaf). These records represent the K nearest neighbors of any record that is classified into that leaf. With the simplest K nearest-neighbor algorithm, each neighbor gets to cast a vote as to the prediction of the unpredicted record. Typically the predicted value is the majority vote in binary predictors, the plurality vote in multiple valued categoricals, and the average in the case of continuous-ordered predictors. This is, in fact, exactly what the probability measure inside the leaf of the decision tree gives you for each of these types of predictions.

23.1.4   Rule induction is like decision trees

Rule induction is very similar to decision trees except that the rules that are produced in rule induction do not partition the database into mutually exclusive subsets. No record from the training database will ever be classified by more than one rule in a decision tree algorithm, but a given training record may match any number of rules in a rule induction system—including no rules at all.

Decision trees create the most efficient and smallest possible set of rules that will create an optimal predictive model. If there is overlap between two predictors, the better of the two would be picked, whereas in the rule induction system both could well be represented and the fact that one was slightly less accurate or had slightly lower coverage would be captured as data along with the rule.

A decision tree, because it is focused on a particular prediction problem, is not as efficient as rule induction systems at finding all possible "interesting" rules, but decision trees can be used in a slightly different way in order to accomplish this. They just need to be given each possible predictor/value combination as the target and see what rules arise. Again, the best links between predictor values and prediction values will be captured in the tree and the others will be automatically discarded. Effectively using decision trees to find interesting combinations would be building a new tree for each prediction/value pair—which could be quite slow, but would automatically have done much of the filtering out of less interesting rules, which is a major postprocessing step of rule induction systems.

Just as it is a bit of a stretch to use decision trees to perform rule induction, it is somewhat awkward to use rule systems as prediction systems. When rule systems are used for prediction, multiple rules may match a given unpredicted record, each perhaps having a different prediction, accuracy, and coverage. Usually there are heuristic methods for combining the evidence of these multiple rules in order to arrive at a final prediction value. Normally the combining of sources of evidence is not an issue for decision tree algorithms since each record would match only one rule (because the rules are mutually exclusive). This all changes with some of the newer techniques that are now being used for decision trees where multiple trees may be grown on different random samples of the training database. When multiple trees are used, a given record could fall into multiple leaves and hence have multiple rules that match it. The multiple-trees algorithm for decision trees then combines evidence in ways that are quite similar to those of the rule induction systems, by averaging the predictions across the trees.

23.1.5 Could you do link analysis with a neural network?

One of the oldest algorithms for training neural networks is Hebbian learning, which was created in an effort to simulate normal neuron firing patterns. Links between biological neurons appear to be strengthened when two neurons fire together often. Hebbian learning simulates this effect by increasing the link weight between two nodes in a neural network when they are both in an excited state at the same time. This learning algorithm could then also be used to find links between products in a shopping basket. To accomplish this, one could construct a neural network with only an input layer and one node for each item in the shopping basket. The nodes would be fully connected with each other, so if there were N different possible items in a shopping cart, there would be N nodes and approximately $N^2/2$ links. If there were a large number of SKUs, the number of links could get quite large (e.g., 100,000 SKUs is not unreasonable and would translate to a 100,000-node network with nearly 5 billion links). In general, it would be much more efficient to create the links between products via the more efficient association rules, which in this case would require only one read of the database from disk, while the neural network might require multiple passes through the database before the link weights converge.

23.2   Data Mining in the Business Process

If we look at the way many of the data mining products are deployed, we may see a very similar cycle in which data from the data warehouse is mined for important information about the customers or about some action to take against customers or competitors (e.g., making an offer of your new product at a reduced price to those customers who you predict will be price-sensitive). When that action is taken, there is generally some response (reaction) in the marketplace (e.g., the customer either buys or does not buy the product). That reaction is data that then needs to be captured and entered into the data warehouse. When data mining is used for nonexploratory reasons, or whenever supervised learning techniques are used, this customer reaction provides a fairly well defined target column within the database which relates to the business process. The target must have the following attributes in order to be successful with data mining:

- The target has value. It has some relationship to bottom-line business value (e.g., stopping loss through attrition or fraud, increasing revenue through cross-selling). Predicting customer weight from their buying habits might have value, or it might not. To be a suitable target, it would need to have well-defined business value.

- The target is actionable. It is believed that certain actions can be taken to influence the target. For instance, if retirement age is the main predictor of employee attrition, there is probably little you can do about how old your employees are; on the other hand, improving health care coverage is something that could be effective.

- The effect of action can be captured. If a good predictive model is created and an action is created but the effect on the customer cannot be measured, then there is little way to measure value, but also there is no way to tell the exact impact of the action and to have that information fed back into the system so that the next model could be further improved.

The data path between the target, the action, and the customer reaction is captured in Fig. 23.2. For data mining to work for predictive modeling and as part of the business process, the target to be predicted must be well defined and have a presence in the historical database in order for it to be useful for the predictive model. In order for the predictive model to have business value, the target must be actionable and the customer reaction to that action must be captured back into the data warehouse. A typical example of action and reaction would be

In a credit card balance transfer offer, the target is the customer response to the offer which had been previously sent out to a small random sample of the customer base. The results of this mailing were captured in the database. In this case the target has well-defined value (the credit card company should at least know how much needs to be transferred per account, at what interest rate, and how long it must stay as debt in order to be profitable) and is actionable (through the mailing of the offer), and customer reaction is easily captured in the data warehouse because they either accept or do not accept the offer.

23.2.1 Avoiding some big mistakes in data mining

The technology-centered view of the data mining process emphasizes getting the model right with the assumption that the predictive product has been well defined and that the data that has been captured to date is well understood. This is not always the case. We believe that this view of the process is helpful for the data processing itself but is too limited to help in the actual evaluation of what data mining can do to better enable business. The steps in this technology-centered process, which appear to be just small steps toward getting to the hard work of data mining, are often as hard as and frequently much more time-consuming than the data mining itself, and if they are not well considered in the selection of the data mining tool and technology, they may well render the actual predictive model and patterns inconsequential because they will not be usable within the larger business context.

23.2.2 Understanding the data

As an example, consider the analytics group at a bank which requested from their information technology (IT) group an extract of 100,000 random bank customers whom they targeted for a cross-selling program of a new bank product. When the data was extracted from the data warehouse by IT and run through the data mining tools, a highly accurate targeted marketing model was found. However, when deployed, the model dramatically underperformed

Figure 23.2 A broader view of where data mining fits into the complete business process.

expectations. In retracing their steps, the analytics group asked IT how the randomization for the 100,000 records had been performed. The answer: the customers were sorted by account balance (in order to "randomize" them) and then the first 100,000 were delivered as the subset! Thus, this study provided a highly selective set of customers that was far from representative of the general customer population. From the IT perspective, this was a fair "random" subset. From the analysts perspective, this was far from random.

This disconnect between the owners of the data and the owners of the data mining analysis causes significant errors to occur that can cause devastating losses. Disconnects between those who understand the business problem and those performing the analysis can be even worse. Consider a real-world case in the credit card industry in which an outsourcing company building attrition models used a neural network to predict the attrition. They, like the aforementioned bank, needed historical time series data from the original data source in order to train the neural network. Even though the analysts actually performed the extract, they inadvertently switched the meaning of time in the time series data. The net result was that the neural net achieved very high rates in the lab, but when actually deployed in a targeted mailing, the response rate was half of what was expected. Because the time series information had been reversed, the neural network had been using current information in order to predict past information rather than using historical information to predict the future. Despite the magnitude of the error, the error was not detected until the program was deployed and the validation against real customers began. There were two contributing factors to the error occurring:

1. The opacity of the neural network made it difficult to understand how the data was being processed and thus notice, for instance, that what should have been the oldest information seemed to be having the most impact on the model rather than the most recent information, as would be expected.

2. Although the same people who built the model also handled the data, the fact that the data had to be extracted, copied, and preprocessed allowed the inversion of the meaning of the time series information to occur. If the data had been kept in the data warehouse with a competent and up-to-date data dictionary and metadata store, the actual misunderstanding of the data could have been avoided.

Defining the business model.   Another source of error that can occur happens when the business problem is not fully understood by those responsible for the data handling or the analysis itself.

Consider, for instance, the statistical analyst posed with the problem of predicting customer attrition (churn) in the cellular phone industry. In this case the predictive problem is communicated in a very simple and direct way, but the overall business problem is not communicated. The new marketing program saves the attriters by offering a cellular phone as a giveaway. If only the likelihood of churn is taken into account in building the model, the program could have a negative impact on the bottom line by giving away free cellular phones (at a cost of $100 each) to save low-value customers who spend only $10 per month on their cellular service to begin with. If the owner of the business problem doesn't adequately communicate this requirement to the analyst, mistakes like these can happen.

In another case in the insurance industry, the CEO of a major homeowners' insurance company was concerned about the total payout that was going to be required after a hurricane devastated a certain county in Florida. The CEO's request to the IT department was to determine how many policies were issued for the county and to calculate the total downside if all the homeowners collected. The query was run and the figure posted to the CEO. When the claims came in, however, the total payout was almost twice what had been estimated.

The problem turned out to be that the IT department had calculated the value on the basis of how many policies were issued in the devastated county—which was actually quite low since the main sales office was in an adjoining county. Calculation of the actual number should have been based on the home mailing address of the policyholder, not where the policy was issued.

The benefits of exposing the data mining tools to those familiar with the business can bring in substantial upside when done correctly. When the business problem, revenue, and ROI are fully taken into consideration and reflected throughout the business information process, creative and highly profitable business solutions can be the outcome.

Consider, for instance, that the data mining tools were easy enough to use so that a product marketing manager (with an M.B.A. but no Ph.D. in statistics) could use them and the data mining process were tightly integrated with the existing data warehouse, so that end users could interact with the data themselves—and that the resulting predictive modeling could be visualized in an intuitive way through OLAP technology. Then the business end user could perform this entire process in a tightly integrated way that avoids many of the disconnects that currently occur.

In one situation when the business end users felt comfortable in using data mining tools, they were able to recognize a targeted marketing opportunity that was available to them that they would otherwise not have been aware of. Specifically, a prescription drug manufacturer was interested in knowing what effect the sales calls of his salesforce was having on doctors' prescription rates of a particular brand of antidepressant drug. When the data mining was performed, it was learned that for all the physicians who prescribed large amounts of the drug, the salesforce had no effect except to keep the physician at the desired level of prescribing.

These physicians were the customers that the pharmaceutical company was most interested in because they represented only a small portion of the total number of physicians but the bulk of the prescriptions. If the predictive modeling had been done in the typical way, the analysis would have ended there, with the result that there was no way to increase prescriptions of the drug through sales interventions. In this case, however, the results were presented in a visual form in which the various subpopulations of physicians were broken up into segments of the total population, each segment representing physicians at about the same level of prescriptions. Through this visualization it was possible to see that, although there was really very little to do for the problem as originally posed, there was still business opportunity.

In this case there were physicians who could be influenced by sales interventions and by the dropping off of free samples. These physicians turned out to be the low-volume physicians who wrote only a few prescriptions per month—perhaps because they were overlooked by other competing salesforces, or perhaps because they relied more heavily on the salesperson for information than an expert in the field who might already be highly competent in that particular drug. They were more easily affected by the sales interventions.

From a business perspective, they represented an opportunity because the segment contained so many low-volume physicians that they represented a significant amount of total revenue. The only problem was that, although they could be affected by the sales interventions, their volumes did not warrant the hundred dollars and more cost of a salesperson's visit. There was, however, a way to exploit this segment—through low-cost direct mail. By allowing the marketing manager to directly interact with the predictive model and understand the answers, a wholly new marketing plan was developed to exploit this previously ignored customer niche.

Cases like these where money can be made and other cases where money can be lost, not because of a lack of a good predictive modeling algorithm but because of the lack of clarity and exposure to larger business issues, compel us to propose a more holistic view of the data mining process as is shown in Fig. 23.3.

A business-centric view of the data mining process relies on the data mining product to automate much of the predictive modeling process. Here the focus is on the business problem definition, ROI, and understanding of the data rather than the preprocessing and reformatting which are central to the technology centric process.

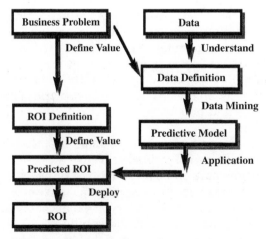

Figure 23.3 The business-centric view of the data mining process.

The major differences between technology-centric and business-centric data mining processes is a matter of focus. The business-centric view assumes that "data mining" is fairly self-contained and automated once the business problem and data are understood. The overall allocation of resources might be quite different between the two approaches. With the business-centric view, a great deal of effort will be put in up front in the definition of the business problem, the definition of the actual prediction, and understanding of the data, while much of the effort in the technology-centric view will be focused on the logistics of data processing and movement and the human-intensive cycle of trying out different data mining technologies.

23.3   The Case for Embedded Data Mining

As you look at different tools for data mining, keep in mind whether your business needs are really so well understood and your data warehouse so well constructed that you can concentrate on just the technology or whether you do have to look at the bigger picture of the business process and how data mining fits into it.

When evaluating data mining technology, the first thing to look for is whether the model is capable of creating accurate predictions for the types of problems that are common to your business. But be forewarned that accuracy by itself will not guarantee success. In fact, when well implemented, data mining algorithms tend to provide similar results on real-world business problems. Figure 23.4 shows that the normal way of judging data mining tools is by the accuracy of the predictive model that they create. Because, the reasoning goes, you don't know which one will do best on a given problem, the tool you use should provide a large number of different techniques that can be tried out on the problem and the best result selected at the end. If these are the two axes by

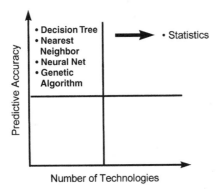

Figure 23.4 Evaluation of data mining tools based solely on predictive accuracy and numbers of algorithms is misguided since statistical tools already provide an even larger set of predictive modeling algorithms with comparable predictive accuracies.

which data mining product should be judged, then there is already a clear winner: statistics.

Statistical methods for prediction and validation have been in use for decades; they produce comparable accuracy results to the newer data mining techniques, and because they have been in development for so long, most statistical tool packages such as SAS, SPSS, and SPlus have a wide variety of different algorithms to choose from. If, however, you believe (as has been shown in several good head-to-head comparisons) that the type of technique can make only a small difference in the accuracy, then you are relegated to working with statistical toolsets or deciding to reevaluate what the differences are with data mining technologies and how they should be measured. Our recommendation is that they should be measured along the lines of what matters to the business-centric process, not the technology-centered process.

In Fig. 23.5 the comparable accuracies of these techniques has been confirmed by a fair test of prediction accuracy held by the U.S. government. While this test did not explicitly use decision trees or rule induction for this task, the task of character prediction from images is representative of the high-dimensional data mining problems that are encountered in the business world.

23.3.1   The cost of a distributed business process

One source of major mistakes in building and deploying a data mining model is in the copying, transfer, and reformatting of data outside the data store (data

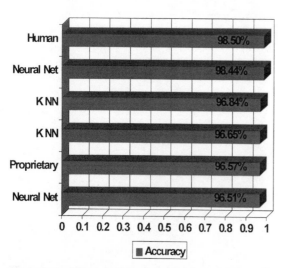

Figure 23.5 Although there have not been many well-proctored head-to-head comparisons of neural networks to nearest-neighbor techniques, the U.S. Census Bureau and National Institute of Standards and Technology held a competition for handwritten digit prediction from images. Twenty-nine groups participated. The top six performers on this task are shown here all with very comparable performance.

warehouse) in which the original data dictionary and metadata are stored. This process can be costly as well in terms of the amount of time taken to perform data mining to the degree where a meaningful measure of ROI can be taken.

The example shown in Fig. 23.6 and Table 23.2 is not atypical for companies in well-established industries with relatively static marketplaces and competition. These companies have had need for predictive modeling and general data mining for some time and have, over time, created a department of analysts that work with the marketing and sales departments as well as IT or the owner of the enterprise-level data. Typically there are three main players in these systems: IT, the analysts, and the business end user. Each of the players is usually separated from the others by

- *Physical distance.* They may well be in different buildings or even cities.

- *Technology distance.* Each will have a different preferred platform for hardware and operating system.

- *Data distance.* Each will have a different preferred set of tools for data manipulation and storage.

- *Skills distance.* Each will have a different set of skills in which they are expert and prefer to use these skills rather than learn those of another player.

Because of this variety of distances, the time it can take from an end user coming up with a good idea to a model being built, tested, and deployed (see Table 23.3 for a list of these deployment stages) can easily be months. For these static industries, this may be acceptable. For many industries, 3 months is a huge

Real World

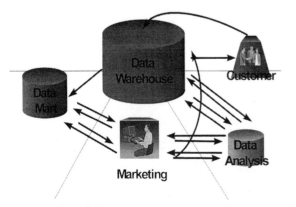

Figure 23.6 A typical data-driven business process (even after the data warehouse is completed) consists of multiple steps between multiple servers and data extracts, preprocessing, and conversions.

TABLE 23.2   Stages in a Typical Data-Driven Business Process*

Stage of process	Activity	Time for completion
Exploratory	Business user works with the OLAP data mart to build intuitions about the business and the data and propose possible marketing programs.	Minutes to hours
Definition	Business user works with a statistical analyst to try to understand the business process and determine what data to request for extraction.	Days
Extraction	Statistician requests extract of the required data from the data warehouse into a format usable by statistical tools.	Weeks
Analysis	Statisticians use the extract database to build predictive models based on the understood business model.	Weeks
Confirmation	The predictive model recommended by the statisticians is returned to the business end user along with a guess at level of accuracy. Assumptions for the predictive model are reviewed by the business end user and the anticipated results evaluated.	Days
Recoding	The statistical model built on the proprietary database is recoded to work on the original data warehouse data structures. The model must be completely retested in this new environment.	Weeks
Deployment	The new model is run against the detail customer information in the data warehouse, and a marketing program is launched.	Weeks
Collection	Customers react to the marketing program, and the data is captured to enrich the warehouse.	Weeks

* There are many stages of activity between the time that a business end user comes up with a marketing program and the time that the program is deployed against the customer. The time between the initial concept development and the actual deployment can be substantial because of the number of different parties involved in the process.

open window of time in which the competition can respond or take the lead and present a new campaign toward your customer base. The ideas of targeted marketing of a seasonal campaign is giving way to the ideas of the "continuous campaign," where smaller targeted campaigns are constantly being launched and their results captured and added to the data warehouse in a process of continual improvement.

23.3.2   The best way to measure a data mining tool

As we've just seen, many current views toward data mining are penny-wise and dollar-foolish. The systems are highly optimized for seeking out the last fraction of a percent in accuracy when, in fact, the market is moving so quickly that the likelihood that any predictive model could remain that accurate over time is very unlikely (for this reason, even current debates over large data or small data and massive parallel processing hardware can become a moot point)—or worrying about the accuracy of the system to boost the profit by a small fraction when the database itself is corrupted because of data copying and transfers or when the business model is ill-defined and the highly predictive model nonetheless leads in a misguided business direction. While predictive accuracy is what data mining is all about, there are really three key measures that must be made in order to fully evaluate a data mining tool. These three measures should be the golden rules for data mining tool development:

1. *Accuracy.* The data mining tool must produce a model that is as accurate as possible but recognize that small perceived improvements in accuracy between different techniques may be phantom effects caused by fluctuations in random sampling (even if you use the entire database for your model), or may be effects that are washed out in the dynamics of the marketplace in which you deploy your models.

2. *Explanation.* The data mining tool needs to be able to "explain" how the model works to the end user in a clear way that builds intuition and allows intuitions and common sense to be easily tested and confirmed. It should also allow for the explanation of the profit or ROI calculation in a clear manner.

3. *Integration.* The data mining tool must integrate with the current business process and data and information flow in the company. Requiring copies of data to be made and massive preprocessing of the data create many points of process where errors can occur. With tight integration, many fewer possible points of error are created.

TABLE 23.3 Deployment Stages for a Marketing Program*

Stage of process	User	Database	Software	Hardware
Exploratory	Business end user	Multidimensional database extract	Windows or Web OLAP applications	PC connected to small NT or UNIX platform
Definition	Statistician	NA	NA	NA
Extraction	IT staff or DBA	Data warehouse or operational data store	SQL, COBOL	Mainframe or large multiprocessor hardware
Analysis	Statistician	Proprietary database or flat file	Sophisticated statistical analysis tools	UNIX or NT server
Confirmation	Business end user	Proprietary database or flat file	Visualization applications from statistics tool	PC
Recoding	IT staff, DBA, or statistician	Data warehouse or operational data store	SQL, COBOL	Mainframe or large multiprocessor hardware
Deployment	IT staff, DBA, or statistician	Data warehouse or operational data store	SQL, COBOL, campaign management, and mailing applications	Mainframe or large multiprocessor hardware
Collection	IT staff, DBA, or statistician	Data warehouse or operational data store	SQL, COBOL	Mainframe or large multiprocessor hardware

* The stages of deployment for a marketing program often mean that a wide variety of tools, database formats, operating systems, and hardware configurations must be used as the process moves between the business user, analytics, and IT. Every transition between systems is costly in terms of both effort and time and because mistakes may be made.

When these three requirements are well met, the data mining tools will produce highly profitable models that are likely to remain stable over long periods of time. Figure 23.7 shows how two additional measures (explanation and integration) can be used once accuracy has been achieved.

23.3.3   The case for embedded data mining

With these new rules for effective data mining within the business process, several changes have to be made for data mining to achieve these goals. Copying the database, for instance, is often done because many algorithms require preformatting of the data by hand before the tools can be launched, and the flat file extracts are often made in order to increase the speed of the model building process. To avoid this, the data mining process needs to be embedded into the hardware, software, and DBMS where the data is being stored. This may mean writing the data mining algorithm in SQL for a relational database system, or writing stored procedures or special access functions for new data types. Independent of the way it is accomplished, the key will be to have a data mining system that does not require data extracts and minimizes any preprocessing of the columns of the database (whether instantiated or via views). And finally, a data mining system that is fully integrated will make as much use as possible of existing data dictionary information and other metadata and conform the metadata that it produces to that which can be accommodated by the current data store.

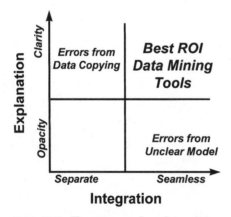

Figure 23.7   The measures for a data mining product should first be directed at achieving acceptable levels of accuracy but then be designed to fit seamlessly into your existing business process by providing explanation of the results and integration with your existing IT data process.

To achieve quality explanation from the data mining system, several routes can be taken:

- Create powerful special-purpose visualization tools.

- Display the data mining results in visualization objects that are less powerful but are familiar and reuse a user interface metaphor that the user is already familiar with and currently uses in solving the business problem targeted for data mining.

Both strategies are valid, but clearly the second approach, if successful, makes it easiest on the end user. They don't have to learn about another tool, and they can compare and contrast the data mining results within a metaphor about which they have already built intuitions.

Fulfilling both the integration and explanation requirements for data mining requires that the data mining system embed into the existing data storage (data warehouse) infrastructure and that the explanation facility embed into existing data navigation tools and applications that are familiar to the end user.

To date several companies with data mining products have begun to achieve this goal of embedded data mining. Pilot Software was the first to achieve embedding in the data warehouse as well as in an OLAP system. Cognos and Business Objects have both recently announced tree-based data mining systems as additions to their OLAP product line. Other data mining companies such as DataMind have achieved the embedded technology via partnerships with data warehousing vendors such as Red Brick and with OLAP providers such as Arbor. The database vendors themselves have also begun creating the infrastructure for data mining to be performed efficiently within the database. These include Informix (with data mining extensions through DataBlades to its Universal Server architecture) and Tandem and Red Brick through its partnership with DataMind.

As an example of how this can be done, Pilot Software's Discovery Server embeds the data mining engine directly into any RDBMS via executing a decision tree algorithm in SQL against any existing database, whether it is fully normalized, denormalized, or anywhere in between. No extract of the database is ever made, and the predictive model is stored in tables within the RDBMS as metadata. The model can then be applied to predict on new data entirely within the database system. In order to achieve a high degree of explanation for the predictive model, the decision tree is reformatted as a segmentation and embedded as a hierarchical dimension in a multidimensional database view. This provides business end users the common metaphor of segmentation to visualize the predictive model and the power of a full OLAP engine to navigate, drill down, drill up, etc. on the predictive model as well as any other dimension. This model is shown in Fig. 23.8.

23.4   How to Measure Accuracy, Explanation, and Integration

23.4.1   Measuring accuracy

When comparing data mining for prediction, the single most important measure by which the system is judged is the accuracy with which the system makes future predictions. For unsupervised learning systems such as clustering, or association rule mining, head-to-head measures are more difficult since the benefits of the result can depend on the particular circumstances in which the tool is used.

When prediction is performed in data mining, the most common ways of measuring the benefits from the system are the following:

- *Accuracy.*   Accuracy is the percentage of total predictions which were correct. For a multiple-valued prediction or a binary prediction, this is easily calculated as being either right or wrong. A continuous ordered prediction (such as predicting income) could be accomplished by defining some threshold within which the prediction must come of the actual value in order for it to be considered correct (e.g., predicting personal income within $10,000 is considered a correct prediction).

- *Error rate.*   The error rate is the other side of accuracy, and it simply measures the percentage of predictions that were wrong. Error rates are often

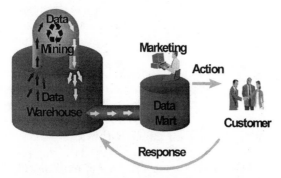

Figure 23.8   By embedding data mining into the data warehouse, no extracts of the data need to be performed, thus avoiding a host of possible errors and pre-processing steps. By embedding the results of the data mining into an OLAP data mart as a new dimension in a multidimensional view, the data mining results become understandable and usable by the business end user.

preferred when the accuracy levels are very high and it is easier to see improvement when looking at the error rates. For instance, moving from 99.0 percent accuracy to 99.5 percent accuracy may seem less substantial an improvement than moving from 50 percent accuracy to 75 percent accuracy. In both cases, however, the error rate was cut in half (a dramatic improvement).

- *Error rate at rejection.* Often when making a prediction the data mining algorithm will provide both the prediction and the confidence that the prediction is correct. Consider the K nearest-neighbor algorithm when all K neighbors unanimously make the same prediction as opposed to just a majority. The prediction might be the same in both cases, but in the unanimous case the confidence in the prediction is much higher. By using the confidence, the predictions can be ordered and the least confident predictions rejected (i.e., don't make a prediction). By using confidence, much higher accuracy rates can be achieved. For instance, the accuracy rate might be doubled if 80 percent of the predictions are rejected.

- *Mean-squared error.* For continuous, ordered predictions, the degree of mismatch between the prediction and the actual value can be captured by subtracting the two values and squaring the result. This "squared error" can then be averaged over all predictions to give an estimate of how much the prediction would be off for a given prediction. The squaring is performed both to more severely weight very bad misses and to make sure that all errors are positive and sum together when the average is taken. For example, if the prediction for one record were 20 and the prediction were 15, the mean squared error would be $25 = (15–20)^2$.

- *Lift.* Lift measures the degree to which the prediction model increased the density of responses for a given subset of the database over what would be achieved by no model (random selection). The performance improvement is usually measured for lift by stating the percentage of the population for which the prediction will be used and the lift for that subset. For instance, if the normal density of response in the population to a targeted mailing were 10 percent but by focusing in on just the top quarter of the population predicted to respond by the predictive model, the response were increased to 30 percent, then the lift would be 3 for the first quartile (quarter of the database, lift = 3 = 30%/10%). Since this method for measuring lift gives only a limited view of the improvement for one particular subset of the entire population, sometimes the area between the response curve for the predictive model and random marketing is used.

- *Profit or ROI.* The truly best way to measure the benefits of a system is to calculate the maximum profit or return on investment (ROI) possible from the predictive model. If a profit or ROI model is available for the business problem, this calculation will dramatically simplify any guesses as to what size of subpopulation should be used.

23.4.2   Measuring explanation

Once the accuracy of the data mining technique has been assessed, it will be important to the explanation facilities built into the technique or product. Things to look for include

- *Automated rule generation.*   Regardless of the technique, it is often possible to generate rules that explain the predictive model. Although the rules themselves cannot be guaranteed to be causal or entirely capture the particular business problem of interest, they can nonetheless be useful in understanding the model.

- *OLAP integration.*   Check to see if the results are embedded in an existing OLAP navigation environment. OLAP can often provide new ideas into how the data is to be used and to confirm intuitions about the model.

- *Model validation.*   The data mining system should aid in the automated validation of the model, whether by test set or cross-validation, and be able to allow the user to view both more complex and more general models and their performance on vaulted data.

23.4.3   Measuring integration

A variety of factors go into the integration of the data mining process into the existing business and IT processes. Mostly these requirements are necessary for facilitating the integration of data mining into existing processes with minimal disruption or requirement of new hardware or software or data storage. The critical pieces to watch for fall into the following categories.

- *Proprietary data extracts.*   To achieve the best data mining performance, it will be important to find data mining tools that accommodate your data as it resides in your enterprise. Tools that require copying of the data and transforming it into flat files or other formats run the risk of introducing errors and greatly increase the complexity of getting and keeping up-to-date data from the data warehouse.

- *Metadata.*   It will be tremendously beneficial if the predictive model is stored as metadata in the data warehouse as well as the actual scoring of records in the database by the predictive model. On the other end, it will be beneficial to the data mining algorithms if they are able to access existing metadata structures.

- *Predictor preprocessing.*   Many current techniques require the end user to significantly modify the predictors in the database (e.g., converting values to between 0.0 and 1.0 for neural networks). Make sure that either the tool is able to do this automatically and still achieve acceptable levels of accuracy or that easy-to-use tools are available for performing this data manipulation and feeding it into the data mining tool.

- *Predictor and prediction types.*   Be sure that the tool easily handles all common types of predictors in a seamless and understandable way, with respect to ordered versus categorical, to high-cardinality columns (e.g., postal zip code), and continuous values versus binary values.

- *Dirty data.*   Sometimes your data can mislead you. Either it does not have sufficient useful information in it, sometimes it is just plain wrong in a random way, and sometimes it is just plain wrong in a way that significantly affects the accuracy of the resulting predictive model. For the most part, data mining techniques handle dirty data gracefully and do the best they can with whatever information is available. Cross-validation and test set validation of the database go a long way toward finding and eliminating errors in the database. However, there are still cases where data can be misleading in both the training data and the test data, and thus even cross-validation can let errors slip through. These are usually due to transformation errors which can be mostly avoided if a proprietary data extract is not required.

- *Missing values.*   Another form of noise that you can find in the database is missing values. All tools should handle missing values either by working around them (ignoring records that have missing values for critical predictors) or by trying to re-create them (e.g., by using the average value in place of the missing value or by predicting the missing value on the existing predictors without missing values).

- *Scalability.*   The tool should be able to handle both large and small databases by providing a robust and automated sampling routine as well as taking advantage of parallel processing hardware and RDBMS implementations.

23.5 What the Future Holds for Embedded Data Mining

Once the data mining process becomes easy enough to use and seamlessly integrated into business processes and the general data and information flow around the enterprise, there will be new applications and synergies that will make data mining an even more critical requirement for any fully functioning data warehouse. Here are just a few:

- Use data mining to improve the multidimensional database. One difficulty of OLAP and MDBs is that it can be difficult to determine which columns in the original data store should become dimensions in the multidimensional database, especially when users may not be aware that they are actually important to their business perspectives. Data mining will be used here to create a predictive modeling dimension for the MDB or provide a ranking of importance of the different columns of data based on some business specific prediction target.

- Use data mining to improve the data warehouse structure. One difficulty in moving from raw transaction-level data to the data warehouse is determining which data is relevant to the majority of business questions. Data mining will be used as a first-pass cut at what raw data is important from a business perspective and should be added to the data warehouse.

- Multidimensional databases and summary data will enhance data mining performance. The more data, the better for any data mining technique, so even though the most obscure and interesting patterns come at the detail level of data, the preprocessing of data into summary information and even the use of metadata such as roll-up hierarchies in dimensions can be important extra information that could be used to benefit data mining. Even directly mining a summary MDB without detail data will be fruitful and far more efficient than looking for patterns by hand in the MDB, as as is currently performed in an ad hoc way in OLAP systems.

5

Data Visualization and Overall Perspective

This is the final part of the book. It contains two chapters:
Chap. 24, "Data Visualization," and Chap. 25, "Putting It All Together."
Chapter 24 finishes the discussion on data warehousing and data
mining by looking at an emerging and powerful technology of data
visualization—presenting the results of an interactive analysis in a
visual, easy-to-understand fashion.

Chapter 25, as its title indicates, attempts to put together all the
different technologies that are discussed throughout the book in
a holistic picture of how to leverage the power and capabilities of a
data warehouse. A view of data warehousing trends and direction is
also discussed in this chapter.

24

Data Visualization

As databases grow ever bigger and as computer hardware grows more powerful in creating and storing the data and presenting it to the end user, there are even greater requirements for tools which provide visualization of data. This need arises from the fact that, while computers have grown and continue to grow at rates of an order-of-magnitude increase every few years, the system that eventually needs to process the information that comes out of the computers has remained a constant. That constant is the maximum bandwidth with which human beings can absorb information. No matter how large the database and no matter how fast the computer, in the end, the information must flow through the tightest of bottlenecks—the speed at which the human brain can absorb and process new information. Data visualization seeks to combat this problem by utilizing the new-found computer power to make it easier for the human being to absorb information. These systems allow the end user to take high-level views of the data and build and confirm intuitions based on these views.

In one of the scenes from the futuristic science fiction movie *Alien,* the character Ripley, played by Sigourney Weaver, sits down at a computer display and tries to translate a message sent to her from an alien ship. To do so she sits at the computer console and begins to decipher the message by looking at it in the computer binary code of 1s and 0s. After a long time of looking for patterns in the hundreds of thousands of 1s and 0s that pass by her screen, she finally recognizes the pattern for what it is—a warning beacon of imminent danger. Unfortunately, by the time she finally comprehends the data, it is too late and the alien is let loose on her ship.

The problem for Ripley was that, although she was looking at the data, she was not looking at it in a way that could easily and quickly reveal to her the basic message (i.e., that this was a warning, not a welcome). The details of the message were irrelevant if this high-level message was missed. She was down in the details of the data but had missed the big picture. This is a good (but fictional) example of what can happen without data visualization. Looking at data—whether from your data warehouse to detect fraud or from a crashed alien ship—can be time-critical, and trying to decipher it by looking at it in binary is about the worst thing you can do. The volumes of data are overwhelming, and the human visual systems and brain are not equipped to work with the data in this form. Using data visualization would have allowed much faster processing of the data and in many cases the ability to see patterns in the data that would not be possible in any other way. If you think of your data warehouse as a mountain of data ready to be mined, then try to imagine getting a grasp of a real mountain—say, Mount McKinley—by viewing it as a listing of elevation and position coordinates across the mountain for every square foot of its >7000 mi^2 of area. With this information it would be easy to say what the exact elevation for the mountain was at any given latitude and longitude, but it would be most difficult to make even the most basic intuitions about the overall shape of the mountain, such as whether it was high or had multiple peaks. A simple photograph—or better yet, a low resolution three-dimensional computer model—could contain far fewer bits of information but could convey these critical meanings about the mountain. If you can think of the terabytes of data in your data warehouse as contributing to a mountain, then you can see how visualization of your data can be critically helpful for quickly conveying the general structure of your data mountain.

24.1   Data Visualization Principles

Throughout this chapter we will discuss visualization of data and sometimes specifically representations of the patterns in that data or the predictive models themselves. In general, much of data visualization has to do with finding a mapping between very high-dimensional spaces that exists in the database or the predictive model and the two-dimensional space that exists on the computer screen.

There is some latitude in how dimensionality can be expressed on a computer screen. For instance, three dimensions are mapped onto the screen, and even four dimensions can readily be expressed through the use of color. But fundamentally the information is passing through a two-dimensional device, and whenever many more than two dimensions are passed through it, difficulties can arise. For instance, it has been argued that even though three-dimensional graphs are commonplace in desktop applications and software tools, it is still fundamentally difficult to "see" what is going on in the three-dimensional graph unless the graph is animated and the user can flip it and turn it to see around obscuring features. Thus information "animation" has been born and techniques like dynamic rotation and fly-through have been enabled so that users can interact with the simulated three-dimensional view in much the same way they would if they were holding the object in their hands or navigating over the data terrain on foot or by plane.

The use of color is also problematic, given the number of colorblind people using computers today. And for data mining this could be critical—if someone is red/green colorblind and color-coded stop/go tags are added to the visualization.

Historically data visualization has come from three areas (and not surprisingly from folks being overwhelmed by data):

- Simulations of natural phenomena on the computer
- Statistics
- Data collected from natural systems

The first category includes the simulations that have been performed on super-computers that range from simulating the smog buildup over Los Angeles to the simulation of the propagation of faults at the atomic level that could result in structural failure of an airplane wing. These systems create their own data by simulating natural processes.

In statistics data often comes not from a physical system or its simulation but from much higher-dimensional spaces generated by human data collection—such as all 100 of the test results that define information about a cancer patient. In general, statisticians like to see data compressed into distributions which show the high-level view of the expected value and the variance or a two-dimensional scatterplot that can show the relationship between two predictors.

Data collected from natural systems would include the visualization of an MRI (magnetic resonance imaging) or CAT (computerized axial tomography) scan data. The data was collected from a process that actually occurred in nature, so for that reason it should be relatively easy to visualize—but because of the detailed nature of the data, even more can be done than could be seen in nature. The data can be used to re-create the three-dimensional structures but can also be used to show internal structures based on density that could not otherwise be seen. Such visualizations will have a knob which controls the density of the object to be visualized and can, for example, be set to filter out all structures except for bone, muscle, or skin from a person's MRI.

Most good data visualization allows the user some key abilities:

- Ability to compare data
- Ability to control scale (look from a high level or drill down to detail)
- Ability to map the visualization back to the detail data that created it
- Ability to filter data to look only at subsets or subregions of it at a given time.

As a result, data visualization is used in a number of places within data mining:

- As a first-pass look at the "data mountain" that provides the user some idea of where to begin mining
- As a way to display the data mining results and predictive model in a way that is understandable to the end user
- As a way of providing confirmation that the data mining was performed the correct way (e.g., to confirm intuitions and common sense at a very high level)

- As a way to perform data mining directly through exploratory analysis, allowing the end user to look for and find patterns so efficiently that it can be done in real time by the end users without using automated data mining techniques

24.2   Parallel Coordinates

The real problem with most attempts to show large numbers of dimensions on a computer screen is that the dimensions are drawn perpendicular or orthogonal to each other. The problem with this is that, although it works well in the physical world of three dimensions, it doesn't work that well when trying to map even three dimensions into the two dimensions of the computer. Some data is obscured by other data values because one dimension is drawn either into or out from the screen. The more dimensions you have, the more data is obscured, and anything beyond three dimensions doesn't make intuitive sense to the end user.

In a seminal paper in 1985 Alfred Inselberg proposed a solution. If the problem with visualizing all the dimensions is that they are drawn perpendicular to each other, then why not draw them parallel to each other instead? By doing so, an unlimited number of dimensions could be shown in a two-dimensional space, and there would be no obscuring of the data. To get an idea of how this would work, consider a simple three-dimensional space: age, income, eye color; and a number of records. Each record can be represented as a point in the three-dimensional space made up by the dimensions of age, income, and eye color.

To make this simpler, let's do the following mapping of eye color onto numeric values: unknown = 0, blue = 1, brown = 2, green = 3. Then a customer record could be described by three values such as 28, 40, and 2, which would represent a 28-year-old making $40,000 per year and having brown eyes. This form of encoding the records is analogous to the x,y,z coordinates that would be assigned to data points in a physical three-dimensional space that would fully specify the exact location of an object. If these records were to be represented in parallel coordinates space, they might look like that shown in Fig. 24.1.

In Fig. 24.1 the record is shown by specifying the values for each of the dimensions (predictors) in the record. Interestingly, the representation of the record itself is now a polygonal line with segments connecting from one parallel dimension to the other—rather than the point that would have been represented in a normal three-dimensional view where the dimensions were drawn perpendicular to each other.

24.3   Visualizing Neural Networks

The visualization of neural networks generally deals with the representation for the link weight. Normally this is done by graphically drawing out the neural network architecture with nodes and lines and denoting the strength of the link by the width of the line representing it. The activation of the node as well as the

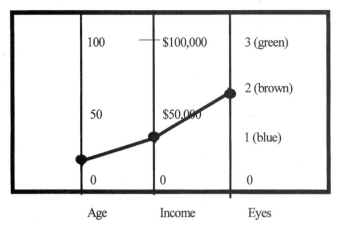

Figure 24.1   A simple view of mapping a record onto a parallel coordinates representation.

negative or positive value of the link can be color-coded. Often the neural networks are shown in this structure as they learn over time. Another visualization technique that is used is the Hinton diagram, named after Geoffrey Hinton, one of the best known of the most recent group of neural network researchers. In the Hinton diagram each link weight is represented by a square and the size of the square represents the magnitude of the weight. Its color represents the sign of the link weight. Hinton diagrams are very useful for looking into a neural network to try to discern what role each node is playing in the final output and which input nodes have the most influence. It was this kind of analysis that allowed Hinton to understand the function of the hidden nodes in the neural network that he had produced to predict family relationships.

24.4   Visualization of Trees

The most common visualization of decision trees is simply to draw out the tree and the splitting decisions and at each branch point in the tree, draw a box which contains the relevant information at that level of subdivision. Such information would include

- The number of records—or relative proportion of records
- The proportion of each prediction value (either as a density, histogram, or smooth plot).
- Some estimate of the error

These values are often written out as text and shown graphically as color. Because the trees can become so large in size, sophisticated ways of zooming in and zooming out on particular sections are provided, enabling the user to view the entire tree or look at just one section in particular detail. Sometimes just the leaves of the tree are displayed as a segmentation of the database, and the split points are concatenated into rules. Such a segmentation viewer provides a more compact way of visualizing the data and quickly building intuitions (compare the tree display and segment viewer in the review of available products).

24.5 State of the Industry

24.5.1 Advanced Visual Systems

Advanced Visual Systems (AVS) offers AVS/Express as a multiplatform application development environment for both UNIX and Windows. It contains all the basic data visualization tools such as basic graphing capabilities as well as state-of-the-art visualization techniques for displaying high-dimensional data and for rendering and volume visualization. The user can easily build visualization applications through an object-oriented graphical design package that allows the user to visually connect modules that process data and feed it through a variety of visualization tools.

A variety of different products are offered within that AVS family for data visualization:

- *Data Visualization Kit,* which includes objects, data structures, and function libraries for preprocessing data (e.g., scaling, thresholding) and a variety of visualization techniques for both scalar and vector data

- *Graphics Display Kit,* which includes a library of rendering techniques for viewing two- and three-dimensional images (including light source position, object rotation, probing of data points)

- *User Interface Kit,* which allows the user to quickly construct user interfaces for both Motif (UNIX) and windows platforms

- *Database Kit,* which allows access to data in relational databases for data extraction for visualization and some limited ability to control tables and views within the database

In Fig. 24.2 a screen dump from AVS shows a way of visualizing currency exchange rates between different countries. Laying out the two axes of countries like this is a common technique that is used to show the relationships between different values of a categorical predictor (such as countries or, as we'll see in another example, between items in a shopping cart). This graphic quickly and easily allows the user to detect a high or low exchange rate between different countries and to compare the rates among many different countries.

24.5.2 Alta Analytics

Alta Analytics has a visualization tool for very high-dimensional spaces of high-cardinality categorical data. The visualization lays out differing categori-

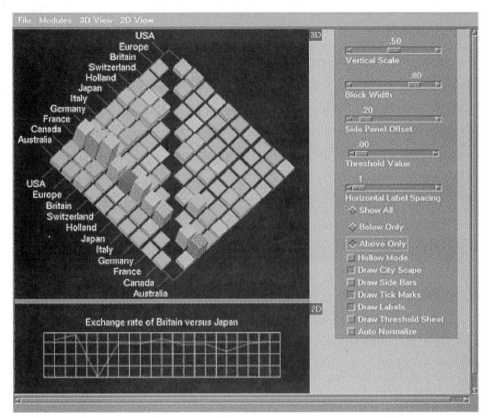

Figure 24.2   Advanced Visual Systems provides a visualization of exchange rates between countries.

cal values from, say, market-basket analysis at different points around a circle and then draws lines between the points showing the degree of association. For market-basket analysis, the strength of the line would indicate the number of times that the two items appeared in the same shopping basket.

This technique can also be used for following links between entities, for instance, in tracking down the links of transactions in

- *Money laundering*—where each entity might be a person or organization that handles transactions of money. Recognizing that certain questionable businesspeople constantly do business with certain banks that then make questionable loans to new businesses that lose money can prompt an investigator to find the links.

- *Espionage*—where each entity would be a person and the links would represent which people they associate with and whom their associates associate with. Often the immediate associates are not questionable, but following these links of who knows whom can provide valuable information.

In addition to these, Netmap has been used for fraud detection, message and traffic pattern tracking, the tracking of drugs and other contraband, terrorism, and detecting embezzlement.

24.5.3   Business Objects

Business Objects includes a tree visualization tool with their data mining tool. The visualization allows the user to graphically see the size and shape of the decision tree and to quickly understand the population size and densities of prediction values in each node within the tree, both numerically and with color.

Figures 24.3 to 24.5 show some of the features that Business Objects provides for visualizing the decision tree in their product. Figure 24.3 shows how a segmentation of the customer base into three segments can be analyzed to determine the effect of gender on each particular segment. By using simple bar charts it is possible to quickly visualize whether there is a dramatic difference in the concentration of male or female customers in each of the three segments.

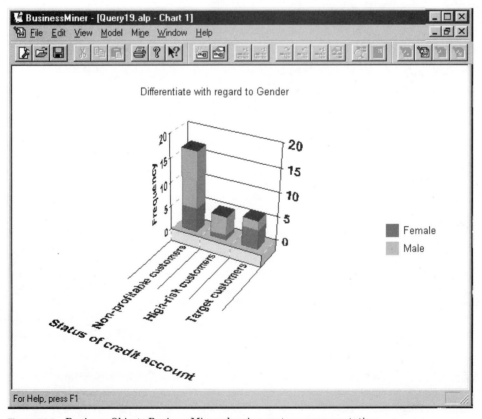

Figure 24.3   Business Objects BusinessMiner showing customer segmentation.

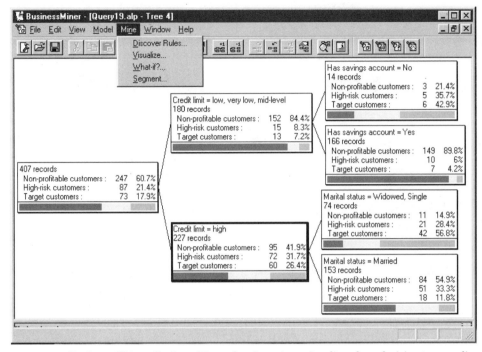

Figure 24.4 Business Objects BusinessMiner showing a tree visualizer for a decision tree predictive model.

The tree visualizer shown in Fig. 24.4 is similar to those provided by other vendors, such as Cognos and Angoss. Since the trees to be viewed can sometimes be quite large, it is important to have the ability to zoom out to a high level to see the overall structure of the tree. Likewise, many users like the ability to perform "what if" analysis on the nodes of the tree at any level to see what would happen if some other predictor or predictor value were used as the splitting value. Figure 24.5 shows such "what if" analysis being performed. Note that the decision tree algorithm is capable of providing the best possible splitting criterion to the end user, but sometimes users prefer to use less optimal predictors if they are more familiar with them.

24.5.4 IBM

IBM provides a wide variety of visualization services, among which are some of the most creative commercially available. These include

- Parallel coordinates
- Diamond
- The Visual Data Explorer

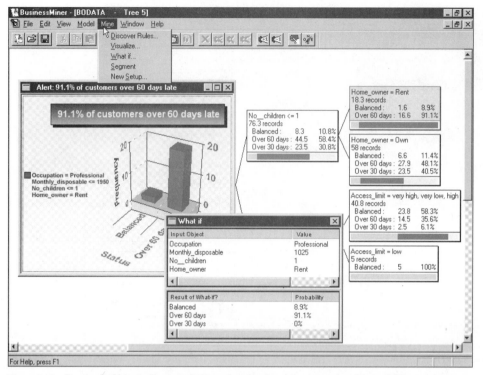

Figure 24.5 Business Objects BusinessMiner showing how the tree visualizer can be used to perform "what if" analysis.

Figures 24.6 and 24.7 show two screens from IBM's data mining visualization tools. Figure 24.6 maps the number and average age of vehicles to a map of Texas. The user can quickly see how many vehicles there are in each zip code (note that it is easy to detect the large cities of Dallas, San Antonio, Houston, and Austin) and their average age which has been mapped to a color bar. Figure 24.7 shows how some complex biological data about mushrooms has been mapped to a three dimensional space. In this case the data is unordered categorical, where the three axes represent physical aspects of each type of mushroom, and color is used to display whether the mushrooms are poisonous (red) or edible (blue).

24.5.5 Pilot software

As part of Pilot's Discovery Server tool for data mining in relational databases, several visualization techniques are utilized to display the results of the data mining. Quadrant charts can be used as well as ranking analysis and Pareto 80/20 analysis to discover tradeoffs between the cost and the value of various marketing promotions. For data mining in particular, two visualization tools are employed:

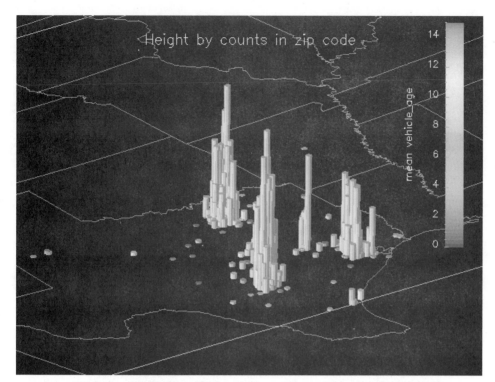

Figure 24.6 Using visualization from IBM to display number and age of vehicles in Texas.

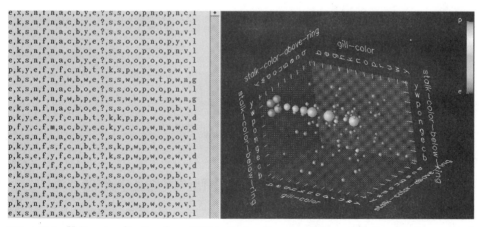

Figure 24.7 Using visualization from IBM to find patterns and characteristics of poisonous and edible mushrooms.

- *Pilot Segment Viewer*—allows the user to visualize the size, makeup, and ranked order of response of each customer segment for a particular marketing offer

- *Pilot Profit Chart*—allows the user to visualize the profit or lift gained from the predictive data mining for a particular marketing offer

Figures 24.8 to 24.10 show screen dumps of the Pilot Segment Viewer and the Pilot Profit Chart tools. The top bar in the Segment Viewer screen represents all the customers in the database as they have been broken up into segments of those most likely and least likely to respond to marketing offers. The second colored bar is an enlarged view of the segmentation displayed in the first segment bar, which is useful when there are many segments or when the segments are very small.

The segment bar encodes the size of the actual customer segment proportionate to the size in the segment bar and encodes the likelihood of response via color. In general, hotter colors like red and yellow are used to indicate "hot" segments where response is predicted to be quite high, while cooler colors are used for segments that are either at the normal average response rate or predicted to be below normal. By using the segment bar, marketers can quickly get

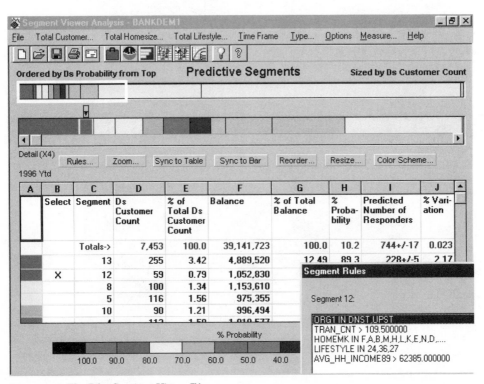

Figure 24.8   The Pilot Segment Viewer™.

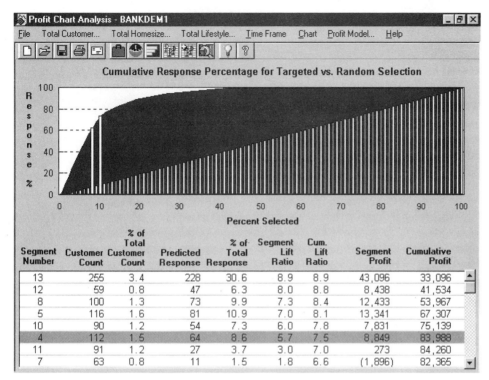

Figure 24.9 The Pilot Profit Chart™.

an understanding of how large the market opportunity is and how well the data mining system is doing at the prediction. Detailed information can also easily be gained on each segment by clicking on the segment, and the row in a table of numeric descriptions of the data is highlighted and the rule describing the characteristics of the customers in the segment is produced.

The Pilot Profit Chart is shown in Figs. 24.9 and 24.10. The top half of the screen displays a response graph which shows the percentage of expected maximum response as a function of the percentage of the customer population to whom the marketing offer is made. For instance, if there were 100 customers, of whom 10 would respond, then, if all 100 customers were given the marketing offer, all 10 of the possible responses would surely be captured (100 percent receive offer, 100 percent of possible response is captured). The normal response curve when no predictive modeling is used is shown by the diagonal line. This line shows that, all things being equal, if no model is used and 50 percent of the customers are made the offer, 50 percent of the possible response will be captured (some of the responses were missed in the 50 percent of the customers who were not made the offer).

The preferred response, and the one obtained by a good predictive model, is represented by the higher curved line. In this case 10 percent of the customers

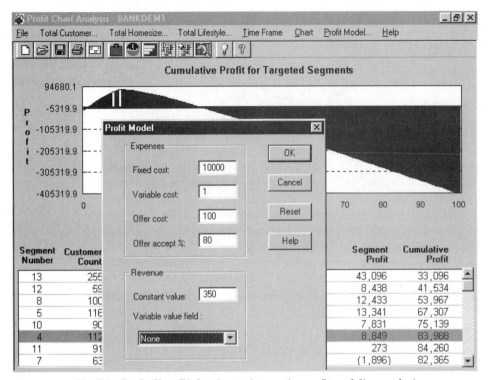

Figure 24.10   The Pilot Profit Chart™ showing an interactive profit modeling analysis.

can be made the offer, but now nearly 80 percent of the possible responders can be captured. This happens because the segments that are predicted to be most dense in responders are presented first on the horizontal axes. In this case segment 4 has been selected in the table of detailed information, and its position and width are shown above in the response chart. By viewing such a chart, a business end user can quickly ascertain how much better the current predictive model is than a mass mailing would be. This difference is captured in the area between the higher curved response curve from the predictive model and the diagonal line representing no model or mass marketing techniques.

The final question as to which customer segments to actually make the offer is presented in Fig. 24.4. This screen is still the profit chart, but now a graph of profit is displayed rather than a graph of response. By looking at the graph it is easy to see that the profit peaks at one point when the most dense segments are captured, but eventually the profit turns to loss as marketing dollars are spent on less and less productive segments. With a quick look, the marketing manager can judge the general profit possible from a marketing offer and generally the size and makeup of the customer segments that should be targeted. In this tool the cost and revenue values can be modeled interactively to accommodate changes in the way the offer is deployed or the customer value is derived.

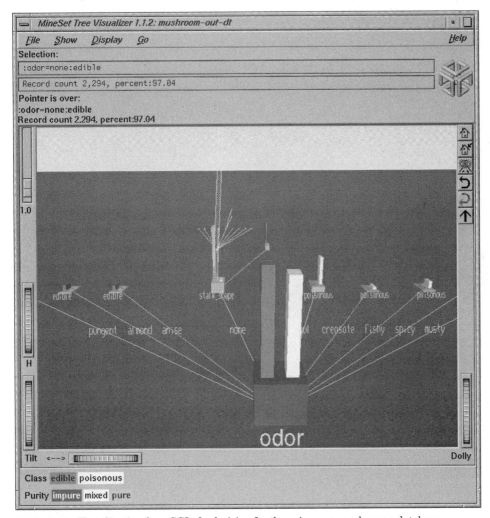

Figure 24.11   Visualization from SGI of a decision for the poisonous mushrooms database.

24.5.6   Silicon Graphics

Silicon Graphics provides a sophisticated data mining toolkit with associated visualization software that includes

- A rule visualizer
- A tree visualizer that allows for dynamic fly-through of the data.
- A map visualizer that displays two predictors for each spot on the map (via color and height)
- A sophisticated scatter visualizer
- Evidence visualizer

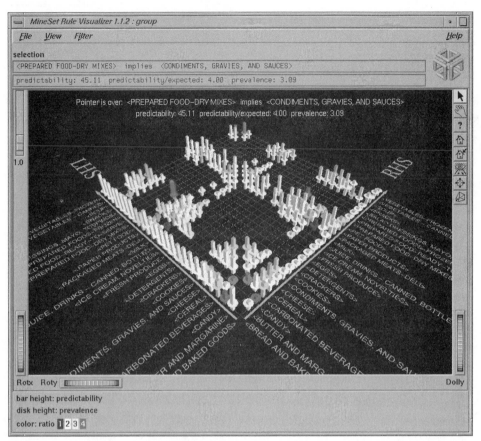

Figure 24.12   Visualization from SGI of the relationships between the purchases in market basket analysis.

These visualization tools complement their powerful array of data mining algorithms and tools and allow the user to more fully exploit the models built with the data mining toolset. Figure 24.11 shows a visualization from SGI of a decision tree built from a poisonous mushrooms database similar to that shown in Fig. 24.7, and Fig. 24.12 presents a two dimensional graph showing the relationships between product purchases at supermarkets.

Chapter

25

Putting It All
Together

Chapter 1 has described a profound shift in both the computing and business paradigm. The computing paradigm shift toward distributed client/server environments, World Wide Web, content-rich information processing, and data warehousing and related technologies is a reflection on and the result of a significant shift in the way business is conducted.

The business paradigm shift can be summarized as the shift from automation to information and knowledge processing. The traditional view of information technology (IT) as the means of automation is being replaced by a realization that in today's global and highly competitive business environment the IT has another, potentially much more important, role to play outside business automation; and that is as a provider of information.

The problem is that although the proliferation of desktop technologies now enables almost any business manager to manipulate quite large amounts of data and perform quite complex calculations, much of this is ineffective and the current infatuation with the technologies hides the fact that we often do not know which questions to ask, or which questions can be asked.

Indeed, if automation is concerned with the efficiency of predictable, repetitive tasks, information is a level above automation and is fundamentally derived from an act of comparison. Generating a monthly sales report is an act of automation unless there is some comparative process which is added (e.g., actual vs. forecast). Information always prompts action, and the computer used to process and analyze information is transformed from a giant calculator to a giant logical machine.

Most businesses have realized the majority of benefits that might be derived from automation, and attention is turning to other ways in which competitive advantage might be leveraged. Many businesses are starting to realize that information might be the ultimate weapon with which they can realize a sustainable competitive advantage.

533

Data warehousing and related technology, discussed in this book, represent a first tentative step in a movement that will eventually make the current commercial use of information technologies look quite modest.

Relating data warehousing more directly to the business, we can say that the administrative and production side of business has been very well served during the past 30 years. The new wave in computing is more concerned with the active, creative side of the business. Sales, marketing, and distribution are desperate for systems which deliver competitive advantage to the business. Efficiency is no longer the key to business success; flexibility and responsiveness have taken its place. When we add to this the emergence of a worldwide communications infrastructure, then the situation starts to look quite interesting. Within a few years we will see many business transactions conducted through this infrastructure, with the potential for a real-time mode of business operation. Those organizations that have harnessed the power of information will have a massive competitive advantage over their rivals, and key to this will be an effective data warehousing strategy.

The use of IT for information can meet some serious barriers in many organizations. The justification of IT spent for automation is quite straightforward—it is almost always based on cost saving. Justification of spending on data warehousing technologies is not so easy, since there is no simple equivalent cost saving calculation that can be made. This issue is perhaps the greatest threat for most companies who might wish to use these technologies. The creative use of information technology will separate those organizations which have a vision and those which do not.

So as you approach the end of the book, let's take a look at several issues raised in this introduction. Most of these issues had been discussed at various levels of detail throughout the book, but focusing our attention on these issues here should confirm a clear view of what a data warehouse is and is not and what pitfalls to watch out for. Additionally, although we don't have a crystal ball, we are making a reasonable attempt to analyze data warehousing trends to describe what to expect in this area in the next few years.

25.1   Design for Scalability

Looking at the current state of the industry, it is clear that strategic applications need to rapidly scale up to the amount of data they manage, the number of users they support, and the types of functionality they include. And a data warehouse acts as a magnifying glass for the issues related to scalability.

Handling this growth successfully requires expanding and even changing the way we think about systems and applications. If we traditionally used designed functionality to classify applications as OLTP, OLCP (on-line complex processing), OLAP, data warehousing, and so on, today we focus our attention on whether a given application, system, or an environment can scale and adapt as organizational needs increase and change. In this context, we can classify applications and systems as scalable and unscalable. And, it should be quite clear by now, that a data warehouse, a data mart, or even an operational data store *must* be scalable. With this understanding in hand, we analyzed and explained the value, attributes, and issues related to scalable parallel computing platforms like SMP and MPP, and parallel scalable database management systems (Chaps. 3 to 7). Since the scalability of a system is a function of the scalability of each its components, then it is clear that the last component of a total scalable solution—an application—has to be scalable as well.

Methodology for building scalable applications.   The question is how to develop applications that will effectively take advantage of the underlying scalable hardware and parallel database software. The answer includes an understanding that a new technique, a new methodology, is needed. This understanding is not new; indeed, whenever a new technology is introduced, a new design technique usually comes along to help adapt to leverage the new technology. For example, this happened with the introduction of relational database technology, graphical application environments, and client/server architecture, to name just a few.

Fundamentally, when you want to build a scalable solution that can grow incrementally, you must *think, design,* and *implement* incrementally as well. Of course, often this is easier said than done. Nevertheless, several approaches to the scalable application development have emerged in recent months. They all have a lot in common, so we'll briefly discuss a generic methodology for building scalable applications. This methodology consists of the following phases:

- *Business analysis phase.*   The main focus of this phase is to understand the business needs of the organizations, the current and projected volumetric, and the requirements for performance and capacity of the application. One result of this phase is a clear identification of the scalability requirements and the issues affecting potential scalability thresholds. The key point is that in a traditional approach the bulk of analysis is focused on the current situation and the current set of requirements; in scalable methodology, the focus is on the future growth.

- *Architectural design phase.*   The phase in which the business requirements collected in the previous phase are transformed into a tangible architectural construct. To design a scalable architecture, you have to ensure that each layer of the architecture is scalable; this includes not only the hardware but also all software components (middleware, interprocess communications, networking protocols, directories, security components, backup and recovery mechanisms, etc.). Remember that the application needs drive the design decisions! This phase includes development of *performance assurance metrics,* which should guide the selection of the hardware and software. The most difficult part of the design in this phase is the application, since it's the developer's responsibility to design a scalable solution. Since every application is different, we can only offer a set of guidelines aimed at helping designers to think "scalably":

⇨ Use a components-based (applets, objects, etc.) approach as opposed to a monolithic application design.

⇨ Use the right balance between the degree of granularity and the number of components; too many components will limit scalability as well (inter-component communications may become excessive and result in a serious bottleneck).

⇨ Chose a design that does not have an inherent bottleneck. An example of such an inherent bottleneck can be a shared resource that can become overloaded as the number of its users grows. This warning does not imply a recommendation not to use shared resources—on the contrary, resource sharing is beneficial to application design. But understanding the potential bottleneck may help you avoid overloading the resource (e.g., by providing additional instances of the resource, replicating data and process to other system nodes for load balancing, or partitioning the workload across several shared resources).

■ *Incremental implementation phase.* Designing an application to be scalable is the necessary but not sufficient requirement for success. A scalable application must also be built and deployed incrementally. That is, an application is not built all at once, but rather broken into multiple small development cycles, each of which adds to the scope and scale of the application. This iterative development phase is appropriate for scalable application development not only because typically these applications are too big in the first place; by definition, scalable applications will continually grow and adapt to user and business requirements, and incremental deployment will follow those changing requirements as they occur.

Scalability and the Internet.   The scalability issue has become apparent with the advent of the World Wide Web. As vendors and organizations embrace the Internet as a ubiquitous channel for business transactions, the design for scalability is no longer an option, but a necessity. To put it simply, the Internet means more access by more users to more data from more sources. By developing an application for the Web deployment, you may find yourself in a situation where the user population grows at the same rate as the Web itself. This means that the need for scalability for all applications may be intensified. And, this is especially true for data warehouses that already push the limits of hardware, database, and application scalability.

25.2 Data Quality

As a strategic means to transform data into information and knowledge, a data warehouse magnifies the GIGO (garbage in, garbage out) principle. The quality of data obtained from a data warehouse represents one of the many risks that must be managed when designing, developing, and operating a data warehouse.

Data quality is the state of completeness, validity, consistency, timeliness, and accuracy that makes data appropriate for a specific use. Areas affected by data quality include the major business domains first discussed in Chap. 1:

- *Decision support.* If the data quality is questionable, wrong decision can be made, and the users will lose faith in the data warehouse capabilities.

- *Customer retention.* Sophisticated customer retention programs begin with modeling those customers who have defected, to identify patterns that led to their defection. These models are then applied to the current customers to identify likely defectors so that preventive actions can be initiated. To accomplish this, it is necessary to have detailed profiles of each customer, with as many accurate variables as possible. Inaccurate data leads to inaccurate profiles, resulting in weaker retention programs.

- *Sales and customer service.* In today's highly competitive environment, superior customer service creates the sales leaders. When information is properly aggregated and delivered to front-line sales and service professionals, customer service is greatly enhanced. Inaccurate customer information leads to ineffective promotions, missed cross-sales opportunities, and annoyed and unsatisfied customers.

- *Marketing.* Marketing depends heavily on accurate information to execute retention campaigns, lifetime value analysis, trending, targeted promotions, etc. Indeed, only by having a complete customer profile can promotions be targeted, and targeting dramatically increases response rates and thus decreases campaign costs. Direct mail costs are directly proportional to the accuracy of customer data.

- *Risk assessment and fraud detection.* An accurate business information base significantly reduces the risk of doing business. For example, a mail order retailer can analyze payment patterns from different customers at the same address, identifying potentially fraudulent practices by an individual using different names. An insurance company can identify its complete relationship with a client who may have different kinds of policies totaling more than an acceptable level of exposure. A bank can identify fiscally related companies that may be in financial jeopardy before extending a loan.

In short, you can develop a "state of the art" data warehouse infrastructure, but if the data in the warehouse does not meet quality characteristics required to support decision making, the data warehouse effort will fail. This is a significant risk, and we recommend a prudent approach that recognizes that some data quality imperfection will always be present, and that some data quality problems present greater risks than others. By adapting this approach you can focus on applying limited resources to solve high-risk problems instead of attempting to solve every data issue. Ideally, data quality risks are identified early in the data warehouse development effort, but the proposed approach can also be applied to postimplementation situations.

As an example of a source of inaccurate data, consider that data warehouses often evolve by putting existing data captured from legacy transaction systems to new DSS applications. This use of data was unforeseen when the transaction systems were originally built. Therefore, it is reasonable to expect that the data delivered by the transaction systems reflects a different set of data quality characteristics than are required by the new DSS applications.

The recommended approach adheres to a total quality management (TQM) philosophy of continuous improvement, but uses risk as a criterion for prioritizing and focusing the quality improvement efforts.

The risk-based approach to improve data quality consists of three key elements:

- Define the user's expectations for the data. These expectations are defined using metadata and data quality metrics that measure the characteristics of data (i.e., accuracy, legibility, completeness, consistency, timeliness) appropriate for each use.

- Define risk in terms of what can cause the data quality to fail to meet expectations for specific uses, and initiate actions or projects to minimize the risk. Costs can be expressed in terms of lost funding, lost production, lost assets, or legal liability.

- Risks are identified throughout the life cycle of data managed in the data warehouse, and approaches for mitigating risk vary depending on the phase of the life cycle in which the risk is identified. The data quality process improvements should be made as close to the source of data input and update as possible (i.e., in the operational transaction system).

- Incorporate a data quality assurance and certification process as an integral practice for proactively analyzing and detecting potential data quality problems. The objective is to integrate data quality assurance into procedures for acquiring, maintaining, and archiving data rather than treating it as a separate activity. The process' results should be reviewed and evaluated to determine how data quality management practices can be improved.

25.3   Implementation Notes

This section discusses some implementation considerations as they apply to the operational data stores, data marts, and star schemas.

25.3.1   Operational data stores (ODSs)

When data is extracted from the primary legacy systems, it may be stored for safekeeping and for querying before performing any summarization. This nonsummarized, queryable, and long-lasting form of the legacy data is in fact the ODS.

Indeed, when the data is a direct image of the original legacy base-level records, it is not summarized. Capturing this base-level data means that you can only roll the data upward; it is not possible to descend to a lower level.

Base-level records from legacy systems take on many different forms. Base-level data generally consists of transactions or a snapshot of the transaction taken at the end of the reporting interval (usually daily). In both cases, the base-level record looks remarkably similar. The record consists of key entries and textual and numeric measured values. These base-level records are almost always just one step away from being both dimensional and queryable. That one step consists of cleaning up the key values so that they point to clean dimensions. The essence of this cleanup effort is as follows: if a key value refers to a central, common business dimension such as customer, product, or geography, use a corporationwide key value that points to the respective dimension table recognizable by the other data sources in the data warehouse.

As a result of this initial cleanup, the base-level records start to become queryable because they can be tied via a simple star join to the primary dimensions of the surrounding business. Additionally, these records will be much easier to deal with in the future because some of the data processing needed to tie these records to other data in the data warehouse has already been done.

25.3.2 Data marts

As was discussed in Chap. 6, the data mart must not be an independent quick and dirty data warehouse. Instead, it should be a single subject area implemented within the framework of an overall plan. A data mart can be loaded with data extracted directly from legacy sources. A data mart does not have to be downloaded formally from a larger centralized enterprise data warehouse.

The key to a successful data mart strategy was defined by Ralph Kimball as follows—for any two data marts in an enterprise, the common dimensions must conform to the *equality and roll-up rule,* which says that these dimensions are either the same or one is a strict roll-up of another.

Thus in a retail store chain, if the purchase order database is one data mart and the sales database is another data mart, the two data marts will form a coherent part of an overall enterprise data warehouse if their common dimensions (e.g., time and product) conform. The time dimensions from both data marts might be at the individual day level. Or perhaps the purchase order time dimension is at the day level but the sales time dimension is at the week level. Because days roll up to weeks, the two time dimensions are conformed. The time dimensions would not be conformed if one time dimension were weeks and the other time dimension were, say, fiscal quarter. The resulting data marts could not usefully coexist in the same application.

The advantage of conformed dimensions is that the two data marts don't have to be on the same system and don't even need to be created at the same time. Once both data marts are running, an application spanning the two subject areas can request data simultaneously from both (in a single query or separate queries depending on implementation).

To reiterate, the key to a successful data mart strategy is the development of an overall scalable data warehouse architecture. The key step in that architecture is identifying the common dimensions. Once the common dimensions have been identified, the development of separate data marts must be managed under this common dimensional framework.

25.3.3   Star schema

Contrary to a popular opinion that the star schema (discussed in Chap. 9) is not extensible and cannot readily accommodate changes in database design requirements, we agree with the opinion of experts like Ralph Kimball that this data model is extremely robust. It can withstand serious changes to the content of the database without requiring existing applications to be rewritten. Specifically, new dimensions can be added to the design, existing dimensions can be made more granular, and new facts and dimensional attributes can also be added to the schema.

The key to an extensible star schema implementation is building the fact table at a granular level. (Of course, one caveat here is that if aggregates are not stored in the database, the price for this dynamic flexibility may be reduced performance.) For example, the fact table may represent daily sales of individual products in individual stores. If all three primary dimensions (time, product, and store) are expressed in low-level atomic units, they can roll up to any conceivable level. If, on the other hand, the data was preaggregated along the time dimension into weeks, it would be difficult to provide a reliable quarterly report without returning to a primary database daily extract and building a new database incompatible with the old.

In general, a correctly designed star schema provides standard, convenient hooks for extending the database to meet new requirements. Many extensions can be implemented without changing any previous application and rewriting the SQL code.

25.4   Making the Most of Your Warehouse

Our entire existence is a process of gathering, analyzing, understanding, and acting on the information. Information (and energy) are at the core of everything around us. Data warehousing has emerged as a recognition of the value and role of information. In fact, a data warehouse is the means for strategic data usage. It is a platform with integrated data of improved quality to support many DSS and EIS applications and processes within an enterprise. Data warehousing improves the productivity of corporate decision makers through consolidation, conversion, transformation, and integration of operational data, and provides a consistent view of an enterprise.

Therefore, it is extremely important to view and implement a data warehouse not as an IT initiative, but as a strategic tool for the business to achieve and sustain a competitive advantage. An approach often taken is to design a data warehouse as a technology exercise that is focused on delivering known reports to the business community. Another approach is to build a warehouse as a multidimensional OLAP platform. In both cases, current business needs are satisfied, but future needs may require significant reengineering efforts. And this is not necessarily a scalability issue. A report-focused data warehouse my be perfectly scalable, but would need to be changed in order to accommodate OLAP-style analysis. Both report-focused and OLAP data warehouses will most likely have to be changed in order to implement data mining and data visualization. In light of this view, we strongly recommend that a data warehouse design follows the architecture framework depicted in Fig. 25.1, and incorporates all business usage into a cohesive framework.

In other words, a data warehouse should easily integrate all business analysis activities, including reporting, OLAP, data mining, and data visualization. Integrating reporting, OLAP, and data mining into a data warehouse is a strategic imperative. It requires a clear vision of the business trends and an in-depth understanding of the relevant technologies. In practice, this means that, in addition to the development activities associated with building a data warehouse, you should constantly analyze, evaluate, research, and assess the state of technology. Indeed, if technologies such as data mining can provide you with a significant competitive advantage, you cannot afford to fall behind your competitors, who may discover and implement a new technique that would immediately yield a tangible financial benefit.

25.5   The Data Warehousing Market

In order to analyze the data warehousing market, first let's look at what products are not applicable to data warehousing. In reality, it is hard to define a product that cannot be viewed as a potential data warehousing product. It is

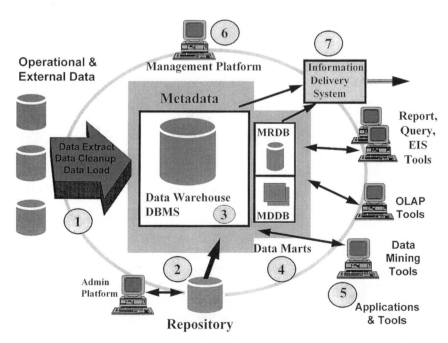

Figure 25.1   Data warehouse architecture framework.

not surprising, therefore, that the total data warehousing market for 1997 has been estimated by several industry analysts at $9 billion. Almost every vendor company has repositioned products to be data warehousing products. Both potential users of data warehousing technology and the companies who sell it, see data warehousing as a huge opportunity, but from differing angles. The purchasers hope that it will allow rich micromarkets to be discovered within their business domain so that they can exploit them more effectively. Warehouse technology suppliers can see the rush to build data warehouses and hope that they will sell many data warehouse products along the way.

As with any market, there are those companies who will attract a larger market share than the others. For data warehousing, industry analysts predict that the top market players for the next few years will be the major database vendors. The reason—they have the most to lose. The database that drives the warehouse is perhaps one of the largest cash value products in the market. Many of these vendors have responded intelligently to the needs of the data warehouse market by providing additional products or partial rewrites of their code to bring the performance of the DBMS up to a more acceptable level for data warehousing.

This approach has two goals—it provides the database vendors with large new opportunities, and it also prevents some of the newer vendors with data-warehouse-specific options from capturing too much of the market. For example, data-warehouse-specific products from companies like VMark and Red Brick are next-generation databases specifically written with query performance (i.e., data warehousing) in mind. It remains to be seen whether these companies will capture a significant amount of market share, or some of them will be absorbed by the product line of the major vendor, repackaged, and sold as that vendor's next-generation database.

Another interesting phenomenon is the emergence of an industrial-strength object-relational database systems. Again, most of the major database vendors are extremely active in this area, not only because of the interesting opportunities in the areas of text search, digital video, and spatial data but also because of the industry realization that current data under management (in legacy systems, OLTP, and data warehouses) is only about 15 percent of the total available data. The ability to store and manipulate rich, complex data types via user-defined or vendor-provided functions will likely result in the clear business need to manage and analyze this complex data as an extension of a data warehouse.

Another large opportunity in data warehousing appears to be in the area of data cleanup, sourcing, and transformation tools. Only a few vendors (e.g., Informatica, Constellar, Prism, Carleton, ETI, Vality, all discussed in Chap. 10) are present in this space, but the demand for robust, enterprisewide automated solutions is already very large and growing. These vendors appear on almost every other vendor's list of third-party support. As the data warehousing market increases, these relatively small companies will either grow rapidly or be absorbed by some larger company.

Finally, a large growth segment of the data warehousing market is the analytical segment, occupied by vendors producing products such as query and reporting tools, OLAP tools, and data mining tools. This is also the most turbulent market because

- The tools themselves are undergoing a significant consolidation toward a more sophisticated solution. For example, query and reporting tools are being merged with OLAP tools to provide a combined functionality.

- Data mining is still a relatively new area of technology with a very large revenue opportunity. Many data mining techniques are still not mature enough as they are applied to solving business problems. The tool's development and usage often require an extremely high level of expertise in statistics, artificial intelligence, machine learning, and the like, and the companies building these tools are often small and lack business (sales and marketing) skills.

- Large tools and database vendors are moving aggressively into OLAP and data mining space by either developing their own or aggressively acquiring best-of-breed solutions (e.g., IBM's Intelligent Miner, Informix's MetaCube, Platinum's Prodea, Oracle's Express).

We should expect some significant realignments and consolidations in this segment of the data warehousing market.

In light of all these considerations, what should an organization embarking on a data warehouse project do? One option is to look for a total-solution provider, while another is to shop around for the best-suited or the best-of-breed combination.

Total-solution provider.   There are a handful of vendors who are able to offer a complete solution under a single banner. They provide complete support from design through development to implementation. The major RDBMS vendors such as IBM, Oracle, Software AG, Sybase, and Informix, plus vendors like SAS Institute and NCR, are among the main competitors in the single-vendor market.

Many single-vendor solutions have some inherent weaknesses, especially in the area of data cleanup, transformation, metadata management, replication, and data bridging capabilities. The total-solution provider will undoubtedly bring in business partners for this area. The strengths of the single-vendor solutions are also apparent. Their products are able to offer very high levels of integration and cooperation. Information exchange between components of the solution is easily managed, and a consistent look and feel can be maintained throughout. These are all important factors when considering how the total environment will function within the organization.

Multivendor approach.   The best-of-breed idea is diametrically opposed to the single-vendor solution. The aim is to build an environment that fits the requirements of the organization. There is no compromise between databases and tools to support it, and the selected products are those which are best able to fulfill the criteria for functionality and price. Unfortunately, building a best-of-breed solution requires a large effort, and there is much more risk involved. Conversely, if a fully functioning solution can be found, the results can be very powerful.

As we stated over and over again, the key to success here is to follow an architected, holistic approach to data warehouse development. The first task is to adopt a framework which describes the way in which the organization needs to progress. This architecture framework is a key to integrating different products into a cohesive environment. Remember that inadequate integration is the most common reason for failure of best-of-breed solutions.

Another important point to consider here is the overall expense of buying best-of-breed solutions. The purchase of separate products does reduce the bargaining power for license costs, and the management of a number of suppliers can prove to be difficult—especially when something doesn't work as anticipated. A nice by-product of the best-of-breed approach is the ability to develop the knowledge base that can be used as a basis for any future changes.

25.6   Costs and Benefits

As we stated throughout the book, data warehouse usage includes locating the right information; presentation of information in an easy-to-understand form of reports, graphs, and 3-D images; testing of hypothesis; discovery of information and new knowledge; and sharing not only the results of the analysis but also the process of the analysis itself with knowledge workers and domain experts.

The design, development, management, and usage of a data warehouse is a time-consuming and often expensive proposition. Many industry observers agree that the average implementation cost of a data warehouse for a large company is about $2 to $5 million. This includes the hardware, software, infrastructure, and a large data modeling effort. Also, the bulk of this cost is spent on solving critical data quality and integration problems that most likely need to be solved, anyway.

While this cost may seem overly high, the benefits and the return on investment outweigh the cost by a very significant margin. Using better tools to access data can reduce outdated, historical data. Likewise, users can obtain the data when they need it most, often during business decision-making processes, not on a schedule predetermined months earlier by the technology organization and computer operations staff.

Data warehouse architecture can enhance overall availability of business intelligence data, as well as increase the effectiveness and timeliness of business decisions.

Tangible benefits.   A successfully implemented data warehouse can realize some significant tangible benefits. For example, conservatively assuming an improvement in out-of-stock conditions in the retailing business that leads to a 1 percent increase in sales can mean a sizable cost benefit (e.g., even for a small retail business with $200 million in annual sales, a conservative 1 percent improvement in sales can yield additional annual revenue of $2 million or more). In fact, several retail enterprises claim that data warehouse implementations have improved out-of-stock conditions to the extent that sales increases range from 5 to 20 percent. This benefit is in addition to retaining customers who might not have returned if, they had to do business with other retailers because of out-of-stock problems.

Other examples of tangible benefits of a data warehouse initiative include the following:

- Improved product inventory turns.

- Costs of product introduction are decreased with improved selection of target markets.

- More cost-effective decision making is enabled by separating (ad hoc) query processing from running against operational databases.

- Better business intelligence is enabled by increased quality and flexibility of market analysis available through multilevel data structures which may range from detailed to highly summarized. For example, determining the effectiveness of marketing programs allows the elimination of weaker programs and enhancement of stronger ones.

- Enhanced asset and liability management means that a data warehouse can provide a "big" picture of enterprisewide purchasing and inventory patterns, and can indicate otherwise unseen credit exposure and opportunities for cost savings.

Intangible benefits.   In addition to the tangible benefits outlined above, a data warehouse provides a number of intangible benefits. Although they are more difficult to quantify, intangible benefits should also be considered when planning for the data warehouse. Examples of intangible benefits include

- Improved productivity, by keeping all required data in a single location and eliminating the rekeying of data

- Reduced redundant processing, support, and software to support overlapping decision support applications

- Enhanced customer relations through improved knowledge of individual requirements and trends, through customization, improved communications, and tailored product offerings.

- Enablement for business process reengineering—the data warehouse can provide useful insights into the work processes themselves, resulting in developing breakthrough ideas for the reengineering of those processes.

Benefits reported in IDC study.   But probably the best evidence of the benefits of data warehousing is found in the IDC study conducted in 1996. As we reported in Chap. 1, some of the reasons for seeing large financial returns in data warehousing implementations include

- Ability to focus on business processes and perform a complete financial analysis of these processes, thus enabling organizations to make decisions based on the understanding of the entire system rather than using rough estimates based on incomplete data.

- Ability to rationalize and automate the process of building an integrated enterprisewide information store rather than developing many individual decision support systems and the corresponding infrastructure.

- The hardware, software, and storage costs related to the development, deployment, and maintenance of large informational data stores continue to decline.

- The benefits of data warehousing can be easily extended to strategic decision making, which can yield very large and tangible benefits.

- Ability to simultaneously understand and manage both the macro and micro perspectives of the organization can save organizations countless hours of manual work and can help avoid making costly mistakes that can be a result of assumptions made on incomplete or incorrect data.

The IDC study concluded that an average 3-year return on investment in data warehousing reached *401* percent, with over 90 percent of the surveyed companies reporting a 40+ percent ROI, half of the companies reporting over 160 percent ROI, and one-quarter showing returns greater than *600* percent!

25.6.1 Big data—bigger returns

The strategic value of a data warehouse is that it contains detailed information about your customers and your markets, the information you could exploit to increase your profits and improve return on investment (ROI).

However, one obstacle to fully utilize this information in a timely and cost-effective manner is the fact that critical information about market trends and your customers is in essence hidden from you by the sheer volume of data available.

The truth of the matter is that if you don't take advantage of this information, your competition will, and in a crowded or saturated market small improvements in marketing efficiency can correspond to large swings in market share. In a situation where there are too many players in the game and too few payers to go around, many companies choose to downsize—do more with less—but as you will see, our message is to do more with more, to get more business with more of the data you've been storing.

As an example, consider the problem of customer attrition in the credit card industry: the loss of business because customers move to the competition. In 1981 there were 116 million credit cards issued in the United States, and 10 years later there were over 263 million. By 2001, however, it is unlikely that there will be another doubling of this number, since there are only 250 million people in the United States, and they can physically carry only a small number of cards in their wallets and purses. In fact, it is the belief of industry analysts that the credit card market has already stopped growing and in fact has been saturated since 1988.

Such a saturated market means that whatever gains are made by one issuer come only at the expense of another—it is now a zero-sum game. Those customers lost to competitors are called "attriters," and companies can typically lose 1 to 10 percent of their customers to their competition each year. In this way the credit card market is becoming much like the stock market, where an advantage of even a fraction of a percent can be worth millions of dollars. In the long run, the key attribute of the winning companies will be their ability to retain their good customers at minimum cost. That's where the high-performance analytical and prediction data mining tools discussed throughout this book are becoming a necessity, not a luxury.

Traditionally, the measure of strength of a company's marketing programs has been the number of people reached through them. For example, in a customer-retention program, the number of potential attriters saved would be studied; and in a fraud-reduction program, the number of fraud cases found. In general, the results of running marketing programs have often been measured in terms of something called "lift"—a number that, for a targeted customer list of a given size, indicates how many more customers respond to this targeted list than to a nontargeted list of the same size. For example, if a credit card company were able to produce a mailing list of 100,000 customers, where 35 percent of them were soon going to attrite, and if normally 5 percent of their customers attrited, then the lift for that targeted list of customers would be 7. However, lift measures the proportion of people reached, and does not balance the costs of reaching them against the benefits of retaining them. Indeed, the credit card issuer isn't just trying to retain people; it's trying to generate profit. Instead of measuring the number of people reached through a program, the credit card issuer must instead show that the return on the investment in the attriter-retention program is worthwhile. The real decision point is to compare the marketing program against the best alternative use of the money to be invested in running the program. The standard measure to use when considering investments is the *net present value* (NPV) of the investment, which is the sum of the discounted cash flows from that investment. But since it can be difficult to get information needed to calculate NPV, the return on investment (ROI) is often used. Although ROI is related to NPV, it is a simpler calculation than NPV, and is a form of lift. The ROI for a marketing program is calculated as "The sum over all responding customers of the offer times the revenue per customer all divided by the fixed costs and the sum of the variable costs over all of the customers." (A more detailed discussion can be found in App. B.)

Both research and experience show that in many marketing situations small changes in lift or in predictive accuracy can have dramatic increases in ROI. These changes in predictive accuracy can be accomplished by picking either (1) the right data mining method or (2) the right data source. Of the two, a much greater impact on the model is the diversity, quality, and to some degree the amount of data used to build the predictive model.

This may seem to be a compelling reason to use as large a database as possible, but again even this decision should be based on ROI. For example, moving from 10 Gbytes of data to 100 Gbytes will have associated costs of increased storage and increased time in building and executing the predictive model. For a typical targeted marketing problem, the small increase in the lift may not warrant the additional cost. The true advantage of the data warehouse for mining data then comes from its location as a single repository of enterprise data that is clean, is organized, and contains as much varied information as possible. This high-quality data is and will continue to have dramatic impact on the effectiveness of predictive models.

25.6.2 Law of diminishing returns

In looking across the industry at the way we are using the data warehouse and data mining, we are, as users and technology providers, beginning to learn some general rules about what works and what doesn't work. One of these rules that seems to be extractable from a variety of different domains within data storage, presentation, and data mining is the rule of diminishing returns. In general, this rule states that the incremental effort required on a task results in less and less incremental return or value over time. We usually think of this as portrayed on a graph as shown in Fig. 25.2.

The basic law of diminishing returns dictates that unless effort is free, there will be some point at which the value added from additional effort will not be compensated by the cost of the effort. We can see this rule in effect in several areas that we have talked about in this book:

1. The initial effort in using a data mining tool results in a significantly accurate model. Further playing with the model over time and trying many models requires as much effort but results in only small incremental gains, if any.

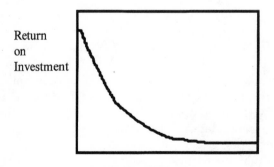

Invested effort over time =>

Figure 25.2   The basic law of diminishing returns.

2. An initial sample of a database that is much smaller than the total database can be used very quickly to build a predictive model; using larger and larger subsets of the database initially produces improved models, but the improvement decreases dramatically.

Note that the law of diminishing returns or its sister (Pareto) law of 80/20 (20 percent of the effort garners 80 percent of the return) does not state that increased value (or revenue) cannot be attained by further effort. The laws merely make explicit the fact that once again the cost, in addition to the value, must also be taken into account. From a direct marketer's point of view, this is an obvious result when targeting customers for a promotion. Targeting customers is, in fact, a realization of the 80/20 principle (the recognition that marketers are willing to leave 20 percent of the revenue uncollected if they can save 80 percent of the cost).

From the perspective of data mining, the law of diminishing returns takes a slightly different turn. The question then is "In a highly competitive or saturated market that is quickly changing, can you afford to spend six months finely crafting a predictive model to help target your marketing program?" Even two decades ago, taking 6 months to build and deploy a predictive model might have been just fine; 5 years ago 2 months may have been the right thing to do. Today, however, many markets are so volatile and changing that if a model takes longer than a month to build and deploy, some opportunity is missed. In these rapidly changing markets the predictive models must be deployed quickly. For this reason the rule of diminishing returns can be employed to get a pretty good model out quickly before the market changes. We see in the future that the whole idea of "launching a marketing program" may well be supplanted by the idea of a continuous program marketing program with continuous small tests, data gathering, model building, and deployment as part of an overall process of continuous improvement.

25.7 A Unifying View of Business Information

The more you learn about a particular field of technology, the more clearly you can see the commonalities, and as you progress, you also see the important differences among various technologies in the field. This is the situation we find ourselves in when studying and understanding the field of data warehousing. To illustrate this point, let's consider what is the same between a variety of different technologies by asking the question "How are the following alike?"

- Relational databases
- Query and reporting
- Multidimensional databases
- Data mining

Each of these technologies have data as a common component, and in some way transforms that data into useful information so that business decisions can be made. The combination of these technologies provides a powerful new force for decision support within the business enterprise: the data warehouse. These technologies can be considered as filters that take data in some form and automatically create new and useful information.

Relational databases store data, but it would be difficult to argue that they help to create new information for the business. Query and reporting tools, however, allow the user to view the data in a way that useful business information can be garnered without resorting to writing SQL queries or even deciphering the highly optimized naming conventions that your IT department came up with for column names. Instead, business users can now look at a report that shows how their business works. The end user no longer needs to understand or write SQL, but if the report generates a question that is not captured in the report, it is impossible for the business user to get an answer to the question without requesting the creation of a new report. Multidimensional databases solve this problem.

Multidimensional databases have allowed business end users, for the first time, access to their database in a way that is both flexible (they can ask most any query they desire and get the answer quickly) and safe. Safety is, in fact, a key attribute of multidimensional databases since within a multidimensional database the business end user has, in effect, a sandbox in which to play and not get hurt. The major difference is that to the business end user the multidimensional database makes intuitive sense as a language of navigation. How is data mining different, then, from multidimensional databases? In the sense that data mining also seeks to create useful business information from data, the process and the goals are the same. The difference has to do with the level of automation. Consider a simple definition of data mining as a process that detects interesting and predictive patterns of useful information from a large database. For instance, data mining could find for you a customer segment of blond-haired, blue-eyed, middle-aged men with incomes over $100,000 who were likely to purchase your new special limited-edition surfboard. Data mining found the pattern in the database, but couldn't you have done the same by navigating in a multidimensional database? Or by issuing SQL queries? You most definitely could have. In fact, for some data mining algorithms such as K-nearest neighbor, decision trees, and some genetic algorithm simulations, this is very much what the algorithms do automatically. The key is twofold: (1) doing discovery and prediction is a radical change in the way we do business, and (2) a data mining tool performs this function in an automated way which is much more efficient (and precise) than you could have done by yourself.

In some ways, we begin to see this evolution from the data storage and transactional access that RDBMSs provide, to the quick navigation of multidimensional databases, to the efficient automated detection of that which is interesting and useful. This evolution is driven by the need to become better and more efficient at detecting new valuable patterns and extracting new knowledge.

These new technologies, then, are not so much breakthrough as they are the normal evolutionary steps in refining and automating a new useful business process. In today's highly competitive and fast-changing markets, this evolution from data to information must now be performed at an increasingly rapid pace in order just to keep up.

25.8   What's Next

Clearly, a data warehouse is not at the end of the information era, but just a beginning. Yes, we believe that there is life beyond data warehousing! From 100,000 ft, this new information space may include a distributed data warehouse and data marts, operational data stores (ODSs), complex analysis of rich, arbitrarily defined data types, a ubiquitous utilization of the Internet and the World Wide Web for information delivery and universal access, and finally, a new architectural construct—the *corporate information factory* (CIF), which can receive, clean up, and transform all available legacy, internal operational, purchased external, and reference data, in order to produce a whole spectrum of information products for various information users. This section discusses some of these data warehousing trends.

25.8.1   Distributed warehouse environments

It has been the experience of the authors that in large corporations, a data warehouse will likely be implemented in a distributed environment. The concept of dividing applications across distinct computing platforms which are interconnected through the use of a repository and middleware technologies is the cornerstone of a widely accepted client/server computing model. One extension of this model is the concept of the distributed-object model, in which individual components can be made available as services on any number of platforms. Of course, the World Wide Web is the ultimate in the distributed computing environment (at least as far as a potential number of nodes or users are concerned). In fact, the theoretical data warehousing computing model is becoming increasingly distributed. For example, Fig. 25.3 illustrates a hypothetical global financial services firm that has deployed an enterprisewide distributed data warehouse of financial information. The primary repository of the integrated information resides in New York, and is accessed by local financial analysts. Regional data marts contain information pertinent to the regions, and are populated by using replication technologies. Some regions don't have local data marts (e.g., northeastern Europe and the U.S. West Coast), and their analytical tools access the appropriate data stores remotely.

The technologies needed to support the theory include data marts, synchronous and asynchronous messaging middleware, data replication techniques, heterogeneous database gateways, data and access security, systems and application management systems, and the World Wide Web. All these technologies are rapidly evolving to be able to support distributed environments including distributed data warehouses.

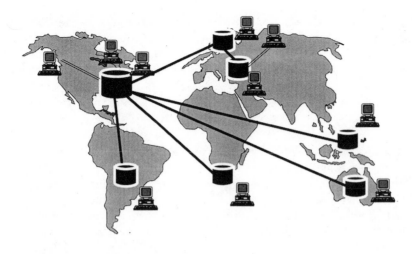

—————————— **Replication**

═══════════ **Remote Access**

Figure 25.3   Global distributed data warehouse.

25.8.2 Using the Internet or intranet for information delivery

Even a surface analysis of the information technology industry indicates that the two most pervasive themes in computing have been the Internet/WWW and data warehousing. From a marketing perspective, a marriage of these two giant technologies is a natural and unavoidable event. The reason for this trend is simple—the compelling advantages in using the Web for access are magnified even further in a data warehouse. This magnification has been facilitated by the maturity in scalable database technology, rapidly improving network bandwidth and transmission rates, availability of robust OLAP and data mining tools, digital telephony, and efficient and cost-effective storage devices, to name just a few.

We already stated that the value of the information in data warehouses is extraordinary. If you look at the revenue potential of a purchased data (e.g., ACNielsen, Schaumburg, Ill., which provides data on over one million consumer products to consumer packaged goods manufacturers, retailers, and brokers) you'll see multi-million-dollar revenue streams selling this data via static magnetic media or using on-line access. The interesting fact is that, by some estimates, the industry has so far extracted approximately 1 percent of the value from these warehouses. This is mostly because of technical, logistical, security, and management difficulties of deploying data warehouses to large numbers of users across organizational boundaries while relying on conventional client/server technology.

Fortunately, some of the challenges of deploying decision support applications are being addressed by Internet technology. The intranet movement has resulted in a drastic decrease in the capital intensity and project expense of creating and deploying applications on the Web. Today, corporations can set up a RDBMS server, DSS server, and Web server in a single location, build a decision support application using standard tools, and then immediately deploy to hundreds or even thousands of users anywhere on the corporate intranet. Application maintenance, code upgrades, and security privileges are now administered centrally. New users can be brought on line quickly and with minimal effort, and support of the client software, operating system, and network components can be outsourced much more easily.

Another argument for the Internet or intranet deployment of data warehouses is the realization that the customer does not necessarily need to own and maintain the data warehouse in order to obtain useful insight from it. There are whole classes of decision support reports that can be obtained using data collected by transaction providers or syndicators. To obtain this insight in an economical and practical fashion, the data must be centrally captured and maintained by the service originator, then distributed back to customer firms in the form of a commercial DSS offering. We can see these widely deployed data warehouses as the killer applications of the Web.

As an example, consider deploying a single relational OLAP application such as the Sabre computer reservation system to thousands of client firms via the Web. As the result, consumers can now perform travel planning and purchase tickets over the Web (http://www.travelocity.com/). The goal of this deployment is to automate travel budgeting, booking, and data analysis to help corporations control travel expenses and better manage quality. Consider how many corporations would like to take advantage of this opportunity and at the same time cut the inefficiencies from their travel processes.

The implications are awesome. This single application would likely have 100 to 500 times as many users as would the typical modern data warehouse. The value-in-use of this system would be proportional to the number of users, and far exceed many data warehousing efforts performed to date. A conservative estimate would place the recoverable waste in a $20 million company's travel budget at $20,000 annually, implying billions of dollars in potential savings for a system broadly deployed. Providers of a data warehouse application like this would benefit either from selling the DSS service or by using it to obtain greater market share for their transaction services.

There are thousands of data warehousing applications, including banking, purchasing, travel, insurance, supply chain, credit card, market research, real estate, investment analysis, telecommunications, federal, defense, municipal, and more, worth selling via the Web, and a ready and willing customer base of millions. The result is a consumer market for decision support, with billions of dollars in revenue for those companies capable of making the transition and providing solutions for the new medium.

Web access to a data warehouse should be an open solution, allowing the use of any Web browser or Web servers. Obviously, the look and feel of the client presentation can be enhanced with Java applets to build more powerful applications and utilize JavaScript and JavaBeans. Any Web authoring tool can be used for the page design. As a bonus, Web browsers incorporate as standard features many attributes that are especially useful in analytical applications, including local caching of pages, which drastically improves the response time for repetitive analyses; viewing of partial results as the page is loaded, which is particularly useful for speed-of-thought analysis; and asynchronous processing, data compression, and data encryption-features that may not be included in client/server OLAP, query, or reporting tools. In short, Web access can be an extremely cost-effective way to provide widespread connection, achieving remarkable economies of scale.

Issues.   Web access offers some clear advantages over existing architectures, but there are some very clear issues and concerns. To deal with these issues successfully, one has to understand the general usage patterns of Web users. The list of issues includes

- *Security.*   The availability of sensitive company information practically to everybody on the Web is a serious concern. Of course, encryption schemes and secure servers have reduced the exposure, but still the most secure solution is to use Intranets and hide the valuable information behind robust firewalls.

- *Performance.*   This issue is the result of a potentially significant increase in the user base. Designing for scalability should help, but sometimes an underlying technology presents a formidable obstacle. One specific technology in question relates to the way corporate databases talk to the Web. The CGI (Common Gateway Interface) protocol for message passing to and from Web servers is inefficient (e.g., single-threaded) and requires writing code in C, a step backward in a drive toward 4GL tools for higher developer productivity. There are alternatives to gateways and CGI, including Java scripts and servlets (see Chap. 13) that help solve this particular problem.

- *Statelessness.*   The interaction between a Web browser and a Web server is *stateless,* meaning that the familiar client/server notion of a connection to a data source just doesn't exist in the Web. The Web server acts as a message-passing server, responding to messages it receives and, in turn, contacting other resources on the network or replying to the Web browser. If each query to a database through a Web browser required a connection and log-in to the database, the accumulated overhead would have a severe negative impact on the database server and consequently on the user. This particular problem has a number of solutions. One is to employ the Web gateways using the CGI API—when the user generates a query, product-specific tags are inserted into HTML and passed to the Web server. These are then passed to the Web gateway, which generates the request in the API of the data server. The process is reversed on the way back to the user, passing the returned data to the Web gateway, which converts it to HTML and sends it to the Web server.

By maintaining the connection to the data sources from the server and keeping track of each client messaging in from the Web browsers, the data or the analytic (OLAP) engines control the whole interaction, which circumvents the stateless problem of the Web.

- *Functionality.*   This issues is more evident on the example of the OLAP drill-down—a common manipulation technique that creates a series of analyses, each containing more detail about all or part of the previous analysis. This is often displayed as a series of overlapped windows in step fashion, lending a handy visual metaphor to the process. This memory of previous analyses is often referred to as a "context" of the interaction. Reproducing this in a Web browser requires some elaborate designs; for example, the Web gateways for these products will have to produce much more complex pages that look like overlapped windows. This may have performance implications as well.

- *Presentation.*   Data visualization is a key element of analytical processing. The standard method for displaying graphics with Web browsers now is to broadcast the images from the server, which could be prohibitively slow. In order to draw charts dynamically at the client, based on a small burst of data from the server, additional capabilities need to be built into the products, most likely involving charting applets developed in Java or Microsoft's ActiveX.

To optimize a data warehouse for the Web, designers have to deal with security, performance, persistence (stateless nature of HTTP), and complexities of the multitiered architecture. Some of these issues are not new, and had been successfully addressed in distributed client/server architectures. Therefore, we can offer the following suggestions:

- Design your data warehouse very carefully, try to avoid the usual pitfalls, and focus on scalability and integration; this includes an understanding and efficient exploitation of multithreading (remember that CGI, for example, is not multithreaded).

- Minimize the number and size of data transmissions per access. Consider not using or reducing the number of frames (remember, each frame is probably a separate transmission); also, think about generating dynamic pages, and transmitting changes only.

- Use more server-based processing, including stored procedures and server-side functions.

- Ensure that the server is extensible. This is especially important in the Web environment, where thin clients prevail. So, plan to use Java applets, but pay close attention to servlets. To enable server-based processing, you may want to look for solutions that support user-defined functions and data types.

- Design applications that can take advantage of the Web environment, but don't blindly duplicate the rich user interface of a "fat" client.

- Don't forget to consider and design for high availability and load balancing.

The technologies supporting the Internet and the Web continue to advance very rapidly. Therefore, when you evaluate data warehousing products for the Web access, keep in mind that the features you see in the current release should not be the deciding factor—in order to stay competitive, vendors will continue to improve their products' Web capabilities significantly, sometimes even radically. It is clear that the Web is here to stay and can play a valuable role in data warehousing, even in the short term.

25.8.3 Object-relational databases

One of the latest trends in database management space has been toward what's been called by various vendors a *universal server* or a *universal database*. This is the trend toward ultimate extensibility in database management systems. The need for this extensibility is clear—data stored in relational database systems today (alphanumeric data) represent about 15 percent of all data under management. The voice, image, and video data stored in proprietary structures, the text data stored in word-processor files, and complex data types such as spatial data and time series data cannot be stored and manipulated in a traditional RDBMS. The types of manipulations required is beyond a simple compare operation; the business needs for processing abstract data types include various scalar and specialized functions as well. In other words, the business is looking for a robust solution for the content management. For example, if a database stores spatial data, a coordinate comparison is a primitive operation, but the ability to compare two trajectories and determine which one is shorter should also be performed as a primitive operation (e.g., both EQUAL and LESS THAN operations should be supported). Another example may include an astronomy application that processes images, in order to find the images containing the darkest shade of blue first.

Some of these problems can be solved by object-oriented databases, which implement a persistent storage for objects to be manipulated via a object-oriented programming language. However, given the investment and the amount of data stored in relational database systems, an acceptable business solution should provide the capabilities of the content management via Structured Query Language (SQL). This not only enables content management by extending the capabilities of a relational DBMS but also provides robust, recoverable, scalable, and persistent storage and management capabilities for complex data objects (Dr. Michael Stonebreaker offers the classification shown in Fig. 25.4).

The approaches and technologies used to dramatically extend the capabilities of relational database management systems follow the directions set by the emerging SQL3 standard that allows a relational DBMS to store, manage, and operate on both data objects and the methods encapsulated into these objects. The requirements for such an extensible object-relational system can be summarized as follows:

- Support, store, and manipulate arbitrary complex data objects (use-defined data types).

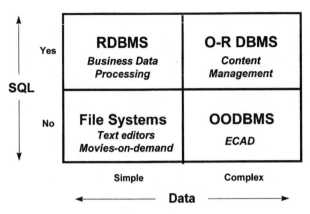

Figure 25.4   The market for rich data types.

- Support, preserve, and possibly extend the behavior of the complex data objects by supporting and rapidly adapting new methods via user-defined functions (UDFs).

- Support key object properties of the complex data objects, including method encapsulation, inheritance, and function overloading.

- Recognize and support user-defined data types and user-defined functions as a part of standard SQL expressions.

- Extend the DBMS engine and the optimizer to be aware of the new data types and functions; thus, the engine can optimize a query execution plan on the basis of the relative cost of the new functions and operations.

- Extend the DBMS engine to support specialized, data-type-specific index structures in order to facilitate the cost-based optimization.

The architecture approach to implementing such an object-relational system is to include the extensibility features into add-on modules that can be plugged into the database engine using a well-defined API (application programming interface). That is the approach that most major RDBMS vendors are taking with their existing products. Although there are some differences among vendor implementations, Informix's DataBlades, Oracle's Data Cartridges, and IBM Relational Extenders are examples of this approach.

Regardless of the design differences, the trend toward object-relational database technology is one of the most significant ones affecting the database and data warehousing markets. Indeed, the object-relational design coupled with the ability to manage complex, abstract, user-defined data types and functions opens up large, previously unheard-of opportunities. Imagine, for example, a data warehouse of spatial data obtained from the earth-observing satellites. Not only can we store the 2-D and 3-D images; we can also perform complex analytical functions using SQL and user-defined functions on that data as if it were traditional relational data. A data warehouse of x-ray, MRI, and CAT scan images can provide an invaluable tool to perform in-depth multidimensional analysis and discover previously unknown symptoms of or reasons for a rare illness. The list of these opportunities is practically endless.

25.8.4 Very large databases (VLDBs)

The subject of VLDB is directly related to data warehousing. We can define a VLDB as a database with a size of >100 Gbytes. But, even if you define a VLDB as a >500-Gbyte database, you can be sure that over time an average data warehouse will grow to reach this point and beyond.

Clearly, any database whose size exceeds 100 Gbytes presents a number of challenges to its designers as well as to the underlying hardware, software, and database technologies. The ability to scale up and speed up query processing, the ability to back up and recover such a database, and the question of high availability and systems management in such an environment are some of these challenges.

The advent of data warehousing is accelerating the growth of databases toward a VLDB processing, and emphasizing the importance of technology and design when dealing with a VLDB. Some of the factors behind the inevitable growth of database sizes include

- The Web, with its large and growing user base, and the rich information content that needs to be stored and processed.

- Object-relational database technology, with its processing of the complex data types. Integrating multimedia objects into a database increases its size in the orders of magnitude.

- The maturity and high-value potential of data mining techniques cause companies to accumulate more data on the their customer base to transform the company from a mass market company to a mass customization to a "market of one." In retail, capturing customer demographics, preferences, and detail market basket content can easily result in a terabyte (1 Tbyte) of data captured and stored on a daily basis.

- Dropping disk storage prices make the economic implications of a VLDB implementation increasingly attractive.

The examples of rapidly growing VLDB market can be found in health care, manufacturing, direct marketing, and many other areas.

Of course, these are just a few major trends that affect and are affected by data warehousing. Developments in *intelligent agents, simulation systems,* and *smart objects,* to name just a few, are as important and will have a major impact on the way we do business, build systems, and process information.

25.9   Conclusion

We have discussed the second generation of information technology that plays a primary role in the advent of the information age. This has pushed data warehousing to the forefront of the business and technology agenda as the supporting infrastructure for the corporate decision-making process. Reorganizing corporate information for the data warehouse presents an ideal and unique opportunity to get the house of data in order. This opportunity should be embraced by all organizations planning to survive and win competitively in the new information age.

Data warehouse design is based on iterative prototyping, since most organizations require feedback loops with users to provide input for design throughout the initial stages. Experience from data warehousing pioneers has demonstrated that a "big bang" approach will fail. The approach that actually works is iterative but holistic; that is, you should use the principle of "think big but start small." A successful data warehouse project is the one that depends on the initial design being scalable and flexible. Clear evidence from early projects has shown that the only certainty in data warehousing projects is that they will continue to grow.

Organizations planning to implement a data warehouse will require significant foresight. The market is still immature, and there is a steep learning curve in adapting new technologies and the new way of thinking. But the industry consensus is that data warehousing is the most significant trend to emerge in the information technology space for a decade, presenting compelling arguments for all corporations to move beyond using IT purely for automation.

Looking into the near future, we see data warehousing as significantly different from the models presented by today's solution providers. There is a possibility that both OLTP and data warehouses will coexist using the same database. The resulting corporate information factories will make the data available for a variety of information products, including a real-time analysis of transactions as they occur.

Complex data types such as text, voice, image, and spatial and time series will be also stored and available for analysis in new data warehouses. Combined database volumes will reach tens and hundreds of terabytes. Some of this data will be made available over the World Wide Web. The information on almost any subject may be obtained (purchased) through this channel, including customer information lists on art, music, and other topics. The purchased information will then be used to more finely tune the marketing strategies of the company.

In conclusion, we see that the information age is here, and it brings with it many surprises, not all of them welcome. Those who miss opportunities will be left behind. But those who manage to survive the day and implement a successful warehouse using the right combination of products will find themselves in an enviable position of sustained competitive advantage. Thus, the future for data warehousing looks bright. It will clearly continue to be one of the drivers for commercial growth for several years and allow companies to compete on levels entirely different from those of today.

Appendix

A

Glossary

access method A method used to move data between the main storage and peripheral devices (e.g., I/O devices such as tapes or disks). Access can be sequential (records are accessed one after another in the order in which they appear in the file), random (individual records can be referred to in any order), and dynamic (both sequential and random access is allowed).

accuracy A measure of a predictive model that reflects the proportionate number of times that the model is correct when applied to data.

Advanced Interactive eXecutive (AIX) IBM's version of the UNIX operating system.

Advanced Peer-to-Peer Networking (APPN) Data communication support that routes data in a network between two or more APPC systems that are not directly attached.

Advanced Program-to-Program Communications (APPC) Peer-level data communication support, based on SNA's logical unit type 6.2 protocols.

alert An error message sent to a central network control point (e.g., SSCP) at a host system.

American National Standard Code for Information Interchange (ASCII) The code, developed by ANSI, for information exchange between data-processing systems, data communication systems, and associated equipment. The ASCII character set consists of 7-bit characters plus one bit for parity check.

American National Standards Institute (ANSI) An organization sponsored by the Computer and Business Equipment Manufacturers Association for establishing voluntary industry standards.

antecedent One of the constraints on the left-hand side of a rule from a rule-based expert system or rule induction system.

API See **application programming interface**.

APPC See **Advanced Program-to-Program Communications**.

application program (1) A program written for or by a user that performs the user's work; (2) a program used to connect and communicate with stations on a network.

application programming interface (API) The formally defined programming language interface between a program (system control program, licensed program) and its

561

user. In VTAM, API is the interface through which a program interacts with the access method.

Application Requester (AR)   In DRDA, the source of a request sent to a remote relational database management system.

application server (AS)   In DRDA, the target of a request from an AR.

APPN   See **Advanced Peer-to-Peer Networking**.

architecture-neutral distribution format (ANDF)   A way to develop and distribute software independently from the hardware architecture platform on which the software is intended to run.

artificial intelligence   The scientific field concerned with the creation of intelligent behavior in a machine.

artificial neural network (ANN)   See **neural network**.

AS/400   Application System/400—a family of IBM's midrange computers.

association rule   A rule in the form of "if this, then that" that associates events in a database; for example, the association between purchased items at a supermarket.

asynchronous processing   A series of operations that are done separately from the job or transaction in which they were requested.

asynchronous transmission   In data communication, a method of transmission in which the sending and receiving of data is controlled by control characters rather than by a timing sequence.

back-end program   In CICS, a program that is initiated by the front-end program in order to support an LU6.2 conversation.

backpropagation   One of the most common learning algorithms for training neural networks.

batch   In contrast with interactive, a group of jobs to be run on a computer sequentially, with little or no operator intervention.

binary code   A binary data representation for discrete data. Each distinct category is assigned an integer value and coded as a standard binary string.

binary large object (BLOB)   Very large (up to several gigabytes in size) binary representation of an image data type.

Binary Synchronous Communications (BSC)   A data communications line protocol that uses a standard set of transmission control characters and control character sequences to send binary-coded data over a communication line. Contrast with **synchronous data-link control**.

BIND   A request to activate a session between two logical units.

binning   The process of breaking up continuous values into bins. Usually done as a preprocessing step for some data mining algorithms; for example, breaking up age into bins for every 10 years.

boundary function   In SNA (1) the capability of a subarea node to provide protocol support for adjacent peripheral nodes, such as transforming network addresses to local addresses, performing session sequence numbering, or providing session-level pacing support; (2) a component that provides these capabilities.

bridge   A means (device) of connecting two similar environments at relatively low protocol levels (such as two LANs at the logical-link level).

brute-force algorithm   A computer technique that exhaustively uses the repetition of very simple steps repeated in order to find an optimal solution. They stand in contrast to complex techniques that are less wasteful in moving toward an optimal solution but are harder to construct and are more computationally expensive to execute.

bucket brigade   A commonly used form of credit allocation for classifier systems in which credit for correct solutions is passed backward to all the contributing steps along the way to that solution.

buffer   A portion of storage for temporarily holding input or output data.

cardinality   The number of different values a categorical predictor or OLAP dimension can have. High-cardinality predictors and dimensions have large numbers of different values (e.g., postal zip codes); low-cardinality fields have few different values (e.g., eye color).

Carrier Sense Multiple Access with Collision Detection or Collision Avoidance (CSMA/CD, CSMA/CA)   Popular LAN networking protocols.

CART   Classification and regression trees. A type of decision tree algorithm that automates the pruning process through cross-validation and other techniques.

Causality   The property that one event reliably causes another to happen.

CCITT   The International Telephone and Telegraph Consultative Committee.

CHAID   Chi square automatic interaction detector. A decision tree that uses contingency tables and the chi square test to create the tree.

change-direction protocol   A data flow control function in which the sending logical unit stops sending requests, signals the receiver using the change-direction indicator, and prepares to receive requests.

channel   A path along which signals can be sent, e.g., System/390 data channels.

channel-attached   A device attached directly to the computer channel.

Character Data Representation Architecture (CDRA)   In DRDA, the architecture that defines codes to represent characters and conversion to or from these codes.

CICS (Customer Information Control System)   A teleprocessing and transaction management system which runs as a VTAM application.

classification   The assignment of a value to a record that previously had an undetermined value. Generally used to refer to this process when the value is categorical.

classifier system   A rule-based system that learns to solve complex tasks through the use of genetic operators and a credit allocation procedure (generally the bucket brigade).

client   A system entity (combination of hardware and software components) which requests particular services to be done on its behalf from another entity: the server.

cluster controller   A channel-attached or link-attached device that can control the input/output operations of more than one device connected to it (e.g., IBM 3174).

clustering   The technique of grouping records together according to their locality and connectivity within the n-dimensional space. This is an unsupervised learning technique.

collinearity   The property of two predictors showing significant correlation without a causal relationship between them.

commit   The process that causes the changes to the protected resources to become permanent. See also **syncpoint**.

Common Gateway Interface (CGI)   In WWW, an interface designed to allow access from the client application directly to the remote relational database.

communication controller   Communication hardware that operates under the control of the network control program (NCP) and manages communication lines, cluster controllers, workstations, and routing of data through the network.

complex instruction set computing (CISC)   The opposite of RISC (reduced instruction set computing), a computer system architecture that utilizes a relatively large set of complex instructions, in which each instruction requires more than one CPU cycle to execute.

conditional probability   The probability of an event happening given that some event has already occurred. For example, the chance of a person committing fraud is much greater given that the person had previously committed fraud.

Configurator   In the SYBASE Navigation Server, a tool used for up-front planning and ongoing management of the Navigation Server configuration.

congestion   An overload condition caused by traffic in excess of the network's capabilities.

consequent   The result of the right-hand side of a rule. The consequences of the rule being true.

Control Server   A component of the SYBASE Navigation Server that acts as a front-end request processor.

conversation   The logical connection between a pair of transaction programs for serially sharing a session between two type 6.2 logical units. Conversations are delimited by brackets to gain exclusive use of a session.

CORBA (Common Object Request Broker Architecture)   An architecture developed by the Object Management Group (OMG) to provide portability and interoperability of objects over a network of heterogeneous systems. CORBA defines an object-oriented switching mechanism—the object request broker—for the messages passed between objects.

coverage   A number that represents either the number or the percentage of times that a rule can be applied.

cross-validation and test set validation   The process of holding aside some training data which is not used to build a predictive model and to later use that data to estimate the accuracy of the model on unseen data simulating the real-world deployment of the model.

cryptography   The practice of transforming data to conceal its meaning.

CS-Library   A library of routines that are useful to both client and server applications. All Client-Library applications will include at least one call to CS-Library. Client-Library routines use a structure which is located in CS-Library. CS-Library is included with both the Open Client and Open Server products.

CT-Library A call-level interface also used to write client applications. Client Library is new to System 10 and is designed to accommodate cursors and other advanced features in the SYBASE 10.0 product line. Advanced programming features such as asynchronous programming and callback events are supported. Connection processing, and error and message handling have all been improved.

data mining The process of efficient discovery of nonobvious valuable information from a large collection of data.

database cursor A mechanism for accessing the results of a SQL select statement one row at a time. Using cursor applications can process each row individually rather than having to process the entire set of rows returned by the select statement.

database device In SYBASE, a logical device that is mapped to a raw disk partition or an operating system file.

database management system (DBMS) A software system that controls and manages the data to eliminate data redundancy and to ensure data integrity, consistency, and availability, among other features.

database mirroring The DBMS capability to maintain a duplicate of the database and the transaction log each on separate devices.

data channel A device that connects a processor and main storage with I/O control units.

Data Definition Language (DDL) A part of the Structured Query Language (SQL) that consists of the commands responsible for the creation or deletion of the database objects.

data-flow-control (DFC) layer The SNA layer within a half-session that controls whether the half-session can send, receive, or concurrently send and receive RUs (request/response units); groups related RUs into RU chains; delimits transactions through the use of brackets; controls the interlocking of the requests and responses, generates sequence numbers; and associates requests with responses.

data-link-control (DLC) layer The SNA layer that consists of the link stations that schedule data transfer over a link between two nodes and perform error control for the link.

Data Manipulation Language (DML) A part of the Structured Query Language (SQL) that consists of the operators responsible for the data manipulation (e.g., SELECT, DELETE, UPDATE, INSERT).

data server interface (DSI) An open-client connection from a replication server to a data server that maps to a connection.

data stream A continuous stream of defined format data elements being transmitted, or intended to be transmitted.

DB-Library A call-level interface used to write client applications. DB-Library includes a bulk copy library and a special two-phase commit library.

decipher To return enciphered data to its original form.

decision trees A class of data mining and statistical methods that form treelike predictive models.

definite response A protocol that directs the receiver of the request to unconditionally return a positive or negative response to that request.

Digital Network Architecture (DNA)   A network architecture developed by Digital Equipment Corporation.

directory services   Services for resolving user identifications of network components to network routing information.

Distributed Computing Environment (DCE)   The standards-based environment developed by the Open Software Foundation (OSF) that provides interoperability and portability across heterogeneous distributed systems.

distributed data management (DDM)   An architecture that allows application programs or users on one system to access data stored on remote systems.

distributed management environment (DME)   A standards-based computing environment proposed by the OSF that provides a distributed management solution for the DCE.

Distributed Relational Database Architecture (DRDA)   A connection architecture developed by IBM to provide access to relational databases distributed across various (IBM) platforms.

distributed request   An extension of the distributed unit of work (DUW) method of accessing distributed relational data in which a single SQL statement may reference data residing in different systems; distributed request support includes unions and joins across distributed DBMSs.

distributed transaction processing (DTP)   A type of transaction processing that is characterized by synchronous communication between partners, accomplished via LU6.2 protocols.

distributed unit of work (DUW)   A method of accessing distributed relational data in which each SQL statement may reference only one system location, but the unit of work may consist of several SQL statements that can read and write data from several distributed DBMSs.

document interchange architecture (DIA)   Protocols within the transaction services layer, used by distributed office application processes for data interchange.

duplex   Simultaneous two-way independent data transmission in both directions.

EBCDIC   Extended binary-coded decimal interchange code.

embedded data mining   An implementation of data mining in which the data mining algorithms are embedded into existing data stores and information delivery processes rather than requiring data extraction and new data stores.

emulator high-level language application programming interface (EHLLAPI)   An API that provides a way for users to access the 3270 host presentation space.

encipher   To scramble or convert data prior to transmission in order to hide the meaning of the data from an unauthorized user.

entropy   A measure often used in data mining algorithms that measures the disorder of a set of data.

epistasis   The complex interaction of many factors. Usually refers to the effect the value of one gene can have on the interpretation of the value of another gene in genetic algorithm systems.

error rate   A number that reflects the rate of errors made by a predictive model. It is one minus the accuracy.

Ethernet   LAN architecture that uses CSMA/CD for media access control.

event control block (ECB)   A control block used to represent the status of an event.

event callback model   A presentation logic technique used in some graphical user interface (GUI) routines to handle events.

event loop model   A presentation logic technique used in some GU routines to handle events.

exception response   A protocol that directs the receiver to return a response only if the request is unacceptable or cannot be processed.

exit routine   Special-purpose user-written routine.

expert system   A data-processing system comprising a knowledge base (rules), an inference (rules) engine, and a working memory.

exploratory analysis   The processes and techniques for general exploration of data for patterns in preparation for more directed analysis of the data.

factor analysis   A statistical technique which seeks to reduce the number of total predictors from a large number to only a few "factors" that have the majority of the impact on the predicted outcome.

Fiber Distributed Data Interchange (FDDI)   High-performance networking standard based on the token-passing technique used in the fiberoptic cable.

field   The structural component of a database that is common to all records in the database. Fields have values. Also called *features, attributes, variables, table columns,* or *dimensions.*

finite-state machine   An architectural entity that can be placed in a limited number of defined states as the result of applying allowed input sequences.

flow control   The process of managing the rate at which data traffic passes through a network.

formatted data object content architecture (FDOCA)   An architected collection of constructs used to interchange formatted data.

front-end program   In CICS, a program that is responsible for starting an LU6.2 conversation with the back-end program.

full duplex   See **duplex**.

function shipping   A CICS facility that allows certain CICS functions, requested in one CICS system, to access resources on another, remote CICS system.

fuzzy logic   A system of logic based on the fuzzy-set theory.

fuzzy set   A set of items whose degree of membership in the set may range from 0 to 1.

fuzzy system   A set of rules using fuzzy linguistic variables described by fuzzy sets and processed using fuzzy-logic operations.

general data stream (GDS)   Data and commands that are defined by length and identification bytes.

genetic algorithm   A method of solving optimization problems using parallel search, based on Darwin's biological model of natural selection and survival of the fittest.

genetic operator   An operation on the population member strings in a genetic algorithm which are used to produce new strings.

Gini metric   A measure of the disorder reduction caused by the splitting of data in a decision tree algorithm. Gini and the entropy metric are the most popular ways of selected predictors in the CART decision tree algorithm.

graphical user interface (GUI)   An interface used by display workstations to interface with end users, which provides a consistent API and a standard look and feel. Microsoft's Windows, OSF/Motif, Sun's Open Look, and OS/2 Presentation Manager are some of the most popular GUIs.

half-duplex   In data communications, alternate, one-way-at-a-time, independent transmissions.

Hebbian learning   One of the simplest and oldest forms of training a neural network. It is loosely based on observations of the human brain. The neural net link weights are strengthened between any nodes that are active at the same time.

hill-climbing search   A simple optimization technique that modifies a proposed solution by a small amount and then accepts it if it is better than the previous solution. The technique can be slow and suffers from being caught in local optima.

host processor   In SNA, a processor in which a telecommunication access method resides.

HTML (HyperText Markup Language)   A document formatting language used to build WWW pages.

HTTP (HyperText Transport Protocol)   Communications protocol used on the World Wide Web to transmit HTML-encoded pages.

hypothesis testing   The statistical process of proposing a hypothesis to explain the existing data and then testing to determine the likelihood of that hypothesis being the explanation.

ID3   One of the earliest decision tree algorithms.

independence (statistical)   The property of two events displaying no causality or relationship of any kind. This can be quantitatively defined as occurring when the product of the probabilities of each event is equal to the probability of both events occurring.

intelligent agent   A software application which assists a system or a user by automating a task. Intelligent agents must recognize events and use domain knowledge to take appropriate actions on the basis of those events.

Interclient Communications Conventions Manual (ICCM)   A set of specifications published by the X Consortium that allow client applications to communicate and work together.

Interface Definition Language (IDL)   A language used to define interfaces to interconnect clients and servers; examples include RPC IDL in the OSF's DCE and ORB IDL in CORBA.

Internet Protocol (IP)   A part of the TCP/IP protocol suite that performs data packet segmentation and routing.

intersystem communications (ISC)   In CICS, a way of providing communications between two CICS systems residing in different processors by using the ACF/VTAM access method. Contrast with CICS multiregion operations (MRO).

interval categorical predictor   A type of predictor whereby a sense of numerical difference is conveyed between values. For example, 30 years old is 5 years older than 25 years old as opposed to a predictor that had values of first, second, third, fourth, etc.

ISQL (Interactive Structured Query Language)   SYBASE interface to the SQL Server.

knowledge discovery   A term often used interchangeably with *data mining.*

Kohonen network   A type of neural network in which the nodes learn as local neighborhoods and locality of the nodes is important in the training process. They are often used for clustering.

layer   An architectural grouping of related functions that are logically separated from the functions of the other layers.

lift   A number representing the increase in response from a targeted marketing application using a predictive model over the response rate achieved when no model is used.

link   The combination of the link connection and link stations that join adjacent nodes in the network.

link connection   The physical equipment that provides two-way communication between link stations.

link station   The combination of hardware and software that allows a node to attach to, and provide control for, a link.

local area network (LAN)   The physical connection that allows information exchange among devices (typically, personal computers) located on the same premises.

Log Transfer Manager (LTM)   A component of SYBASE Replication Server that facilitates replication of changes throughout the replicated sites.

logical unit (LU)   A port through which an end user accesses an SNA network in order to communicate with another end user.

logical unit of work (LUW)   A work that is performed between the start of a transaction and COMMIT or ROLLBACK of the same transaction.

loose consistency   In SYBASE Replication Server, the data consistency protocol implemented via replication (contrast with *tight consistency,* which is based on the two-phase commit protocol).

LU6.2   Logical unit type 6.2—a special type of logical unit that supports Advanced Program-to-Program Communications (APPC) between programs in a distributed processing environment. APPC/LU6.2 is characterized by peer-to-peer communication support, comprehensive end-to-end error processing, optimized data transmission flow, and a generic application programming interface.

machine learning   A field of science and technology concerned with building machines that learn. In general, it differs from artificial intelligence in that learning is considered to be just one of a number of ways of creating an artificial intelligence.

management services   In SNA, one type of network service in the network control point and physical units (PUs) that provide functions for problem management, performance, accounting, configuration, and change management.

mapped conversation   In APPC, a type of conversation in which the data can be sent and received in a user-defined format, while the data transformation is performed by APPC/LU6.2.

massively parallel processors (MPPs)   A computing architecture based on a distributed-memory shared-nothing approach.

memory-based reasoning (in data mining)   A technique for classifying records in a database by comparing them with similar records that are already classified. A variant of nearest-neighbor classification.

message unit   A generic term for the unit of data processed by a communication system.

metropolitan area network (MAN)   A network using a city infrastructure to connect nodes within the geographic limits of a city.

middleware   A generic term that defines a set of run-time software services designed to insulate clients and servers from the knowledge of environment-specific communications and data access mechanisms.

MIME (Multimedia Internet Mail Enhancements)   A freely available standardized method of sending and receiving attachments.

minimum-description-length principle   The idea that the least complex predictive model (with acceptable accuracy) will be the one that best reflects the true underlying model and performs most accurately on new data.

model   A description that adequately explains and predicts relevant data but is generally much smaller than the data itself.

modem   A device that modulates and demodulates signals transmitted over data communication facilities in order to convert digital signals into and from an analog form.

motif   A popular window manager selected by the Open Software Foundation for the presentation management in its version of the open-system environment.

nearest neighbor   A data mining technique that performs prediction by finding the prediction value of records (near neighbors) similar to the record to be predicted.

negative response   A response indicating that a request did not arrive successfully or was not processed successfully by the receiver.

network address   An address that identifies a link, a link station, or a network-addressable unit.

Network File System (NFS)   Popular method of accessing remote files in a UNIX system environment (developed by Sun Microsystems).

network operating system (NOS)   A generic term for the operating-system-level software used to manage and control networks.

NetView   An IBM product used to monitor, manage, and diagnose a network.

neural network   A computing model based on the architecture of the human brain. A neural network consists of multiple simple processing units connected by adaptive weights.

node   An endpoint of a link in a neural network, or a junction common to two or more links.

nominal categorical predictor   A predictor that is categorical (finite cardinality) but in which the values of the predictor have no particular order. For example, red, green, blue are values for the predictor *eye color.*

object   A named unit that consists of a set of characteristics that are encapsulated within the object and describe the object and data; certain characteristics of an object are inherited from its *parents* and can be inherited to its *children;* operations valid for the object are stored together with the object as its methods; in computer architecture, an object can be anything that exists in and occupies space in storage (e.g., programs, files, libraries) and on which operations can be performed.

Object Request Broker (ORB) A key component of CORBA—an object-oriented message-switching mechanism designed to provide portability and interoperability of objects over a network of heterogeneous systems.

Occam's razor A rule of thumb used by many scientists that advocates favoring the simplest theory that adequately explains (or predicts) an event. This is more formally captured for machine learning and data mining as the minimum-description-length principle.

on-line analytical processing (OLAP) Computer-based techniques used to analyze trends and perform business analysis using multidimensional views of business data.

Open Look A popular window manager that is used primarily by the members of UNIX International (UI).

Open Network Computing (ONC) UNIX International's architecture for an open distributed computing environment.

Open Software Foundation (OSF) Not-for-profit technology organization that intends to develop an open computing environment by selecting technology solutions from its members.

ordinal categorical predictor A categorical predictor (i.e., having a finite number of values) in which the values have order but do not convey meaningful intervals or distances between them. Examples are the values high, middle, and low for the income predictor.

OS/2 (Operating System/2) A multiprogramming, multitasking operating system, developed for the PS/2 family of personal computers.

OSI (Open Systems Interconnection) A layered architecture that is designed to allow for interconnection between heterogeneous systems.

outlier analysis A type of data analysis that seeks to determine and report on records in the database that are significantly different from expectations. The technique is used for data cleansing, spotting emerging trends, and recognizing unusually good or bad performers.

overfitting (overtraining) The effect in data analysis, data mining, and biological learning of training too closely on limited available data and building models that do not generalize well to new unseen data. At the limit, overfitting is synonymous with rote memorization where no generalized model of future situations is built.

pacing A technique by which a receiver controls the rate of transmission by the sender.

packet A data transmission information unit, consisting of a group of data and control characters.

packet switching The process of routing and transferring data by means of addressed packets.

parallel sessions Two or more concurrently active sessions between two logical units using different pairs of network addresses.

positive response A response indicating that a request has been successfully processed.

predictor   The column or field in a database that could be used to build a predictive model to predict the values in another field or column. Also called *variable, independent variable, dimension,* or *feature.*

prediction   (1) The column or field in a database that currently has unknown value that will be assigned when a predictive model is run over other predictor values in the record. Also called *dependent variable, target,* or *classification.* (2) The process of applying a predictive model to a record. Generally, *prediction* implies the generation of unknown values within time series. Throughout this book prediction is used to mean any process for assigning values to previously unassigned fields, including classification and regression.

predictive model   A model created or used to perform prediction. In contrast to models created solely for pattern detection, exploration, or general organization of the data.

Presentation Manager (OS/2 PM)   An OS/2 component that provides graphical API.

principal components analysis   A data analysis technique that seeks to weight the importance of a variety of predictors so that they optimally discriminate between various possible predicted outcomes.

prior probability   The probability of an event occurring without dependence on (conditional to) some other event. In contrast to conditional probability.

protocol boundary   A synonym for the architecturally defined application program interface.

queued attach   In OS/2 APPC, an incoming allocate request that is queued by the Attach Manager until the transaction program issues an appropriate APPC verb.

queuing   A store-and-forward communication mechanism often employed by messaging middleware.

radial-basis-function networks   Neural networks that combine some of the advantages of neural networks with those of nearest-neighbor techniques. In radial basis functions the hidden layer is made up of nodes that represent prototypes or clusters of records.

RAS programs   Reliability, availability, and serviceability programs that facilitate problem determination.

Recommendation X.21   The Consultative Committee on International Telephone and Telegraph (CCITT) recommendations for a general-purpose interface between data terminal equipment and data circuit equipment for synchronous operations on a public data networks.

Recommendation X.25   The Consultative Committee on International Telephone and Telegraph (CCITT) recommendations for an interface between data terminal equipment and packet-switched networks.

record   The fundamental data structure used for performing data analysis. Also called a *table row* or *example.* A typical record would be the structure that contains all relevant information pertinent to one particular customer or account.

reduced instruction set computing (RISC)   The opposite of CISC (complex instruction set computing), a computer system architecture that utilizes a relatively small set of computer instructions in which each instruction is "simple" enough to require one CPU cycle to execute.

regression A data analysis technique classically used in statistics for building predictive models for continuous prediction fields. The technique automatically determines a mathematical equation that minimizes some measure of the error between the prediction from the regression model and the actual data.

reinforcement learning (in data mining) A training model in which an intelligence engine (e.g., neural network) is presented with a sequence of input data followed by a reinforcement signal.

relational database (RDB) A database built to conform to the relational data model; includes the catalog and all the data described therein.

Remote Data Access (RDA) A proposed ANSI standard to access remote relational databases.

remote procedure call (RPC) A connectionless method of communication between two programming systems in which a requester (client) issues an RPC to execute a procedure on a remote system (server).

remote request The form of SQL distributed processing where the application runs on a system different from the one housing the RDB. Contains a single SQL statement referencing data located at a single site.

remote unit of work (RUW) The extension of the remote request form of SQL distributed processing in which multiple SQL statements may reference data located at a single remote site.

Replication Server Interface (RSI) An asynchronous interface from one Replication Server to another.

Replication Server Manager (RSM) A GUI-based administration tool for managing the Replication Server system.

Replication Server System Database (RSSD) The SYBASE System Catalog for the Replication Server.

response A binary prediction field that indicates response or nonresponse to a variety of marketing interventions. The term is generally used when referring to models that predict response or to the response field itself.

Rhapsody Workflow management software developed by AT&T.

rollback The process of restoring protected resources to the state at the last commit point.

SA Companion The SYBASE front-end tool for SQL Server administration tasks.

sampling The process by which only a fraction of all available data is used to build a model or perform exploratory analysis. Sampling can provide relatively good models at much less computational expense than using the entire database.

segmentation The process or result of the process that creates mutually exclusive collections of records that share similar attributes in either unsupervised learning (such as clustering) or supervised learning for a particular prediction field.

sensitivity analysis The process which determines the sensitivity of a predictive model to small fluctuations in predictor value. Using this technique, end users can gauge the effects of noise and environmental change on the accuracy of the model.

Schema Server A component of the SYBASE Navigation Server used to control the Global Directory.

server A system entity (combination of hardware and software components) which performs particular services on behalf of another entity—a client.

server-requestor programming interface (SRPI) An API used by requestor and server programs to communicate with a PC or hosts.

session A logical connection between two network-addressable units that allows them to communicate.

session-level pacing In SNA, a flow control technique that permits the receiver to control the data transfer rate.

shared-nothing architecture A computing architecture for parallelizing work in a computer system where multiple processors, each with its own private memory and disk, are interconnected and communicate via messages.

simulated annealing An optimization algorithm loosely based on the physical process of annealing metals through controlled heating and cooling.

Split Server A component of SYBASE Navigation Server used primarily to process join requests in parallel systems.

SQL Debug The SYBASE source-level debugger for Transact-SQL code.

stored procedure An advanced design technique employed by SYBASE to allow a collection of SQL statements and flow-control directives (e.g., IF, THEN, ELSE) to be parsed, verified, compiled, bound, and stored at the DBMS server. Stored procedures are invoked by client applications in a fashion similar to RPC and provide a significant performance improvement over a traditional embedded SQL.

Structured Query Language (SQL) A standard for the nonnavigational data access and definition language used in relational databases.

Subscription In SYBASE Replication Server, a technique that allows all or parts of data tables to be replicated to the subscribers of that data. It uses a subscription resolution engine (SRE) to match primary data with the subscription for that data.

supervised learning (in data mining) A class of data mining and machine learning applications and techniques in which the system builds a model based on the prediction of a well-defined prediction field. This is in contrast to unsupervised learning, where there is no particular goal aside from pattern detection.

support The relative frequency or number of times a rule produced by a rule induction system occurs within the database. The higher the support, the better the chance of the rule capturing a statistically significant pattern.

SYBASE Backup Server A component of SYBASE System 10 designed specifically to perform backup operations.

SYBASE Navigation Server A component of SYBASE System 10 that is designed to provide database scalability and performance by taking advantage of SMP and MPP computing architectures.

SYBASE OmniSQL Server The SYBASE gateway product (an Open Server application) designed to provide a transparent access to distributed heterogeneous databases.

SYBASE Open Client A programmable client component (a set of library routines and the corresponding APIs such as DB-Lib and CT-Lib) of Sybase's suite of client server products.

SYBASE Open Server   A programmable server component of Sybase's suite of client/server products.

SYBASE Replication Server   A SYBASE System 10 component that implements and manages database replication.

SYBASE SQL Monitor   A SYBASE System 10 tool used to monitor SYBASE SQL Server performance.

symmetric multiprocessing (SMP)   A computer architecture in which several tightly coupled CPUs share a common memory and common workload.

synchronization level   In APPC, the specification indicating that the conversation allows no synchronization (SYNCLEVEL = NONE), and supports confirmation exchanges (SYNCLEVEL = CONFIRM) or full synchronization (SYNCLEVEL = SYNCPT).

synchronous data-link control (SDLC)   A communication protocol for managing synchronous code-transparent, serial-by-bit information transfer over a link connection.

synchronous transmission   In data communication, a method of transmission in which the sending and receiving of characters is controlled by timing signals.

syncpoint   (1) A point in time when all protected resources accessed by an application are consistent. (2) An LU6.2 verb that causes all changes to protected resources to become permanent, and, therefore, the resources are consistent. See also **commit**.

System Services Control Point (SSCP)   In SNA, a central location point within an SNA network for managing the configuration, coordinating network operator and problem determination requests, and providing directory support and other session services for end users.

Systems Network Architecture (SNA)   The description of the logical structure, formats, protocols, and operational sequences for transmitting information through and controlling configuration and operation of networks.

Systems Network Architecture Distributed Services (SNADS)   An IBM architecture that defines a set of rules to receive, route, and send electronic mail (e-mail) across networks.

targeted marketing   The marketing of products to select groups of consumers who are more likely than average to be interested in the offer.

terminal   In data communication, a device capable of sending and receiving information.

threads   A unit of context management under the control of a single process that can be implemented within the server process or via operating system services.

time series forecasting   The process of using a data mining tool (e.g., neural networks) to learn to predict temporal sequences of patterns, so that, given a set of patterns, it can predict a future value.

timesharing option (TSO)   A feature of an operating system [e.g., Multiple Virtual Storage (MVS)] that provides conversational timesharing of system resources from remote stations.

Top End   A transaction monitor developed by the NCR Corporation to provide transaction management in the open systems (UNIX-based) distributed environment.

Transact-SQL   Sybase's proprietary programming and control language.

transaction   In communications, a unit of processing and information exchange between a local program and a remote program that accomplishes a particular action or result.

Transaction Monitor/Transaction Manager (TPM)   Software system that provides control and management functions to support transaction execution, synchronization, integrity, consistency, atomicity, and durability.

transaction program (TP)   In APPC, a program that uses the APPC API to communicate with a partner transaction program on a remote system.

transaction routing   In CICS, a facility that allows CICS transactions, initiated on a local CICS system, to be executed on a remote CICS system.

Transmission Control Protocol/Internet Protocol (TCP/IP)   Communication protocol popular because of its openness and easy interoperability features.

Threshold Manager   A feature of SYBASE System 10 that monitors the amount of free space available on a particular database segment, and executes a predefined stored procedure when a threshold is reached.

triggers   In a DBMS, triggers can be viewed as a special type of stored procedure that have the ability to initiate (trigger) certain user-defined actions based on a particular data-related event; triggers are often used to implement referential integrity constraints.

Tuxedo   A transaction monitor developed by AT&T to provide transaction management in the UNIX system distributed environment.

two-phase commit (2PC)   A protocol that ensures the integrity and consistency of all protected resources affected by a distributed transaction.

unit of work   The amount of processing that is executed from the time the transaction is started to the time the transaction is ended.

Universal Resource Locator (URL)   A format used to specify addresses on the World Wide Web.

unsupervised learning   A data analysis technique in which a model is built without a well-defined goal or prediction field. The systems are used for exploration and general data organization. Clustering is an example of an unsupervised learning system.

verb   In APPC, an LU6.2 command, defined in the APPC API.

Virtual Machine/System Product (VM/SP)   An IBM-licensed program, which is an operating system that manages the resources of a real processor to provide virtual machines to end users.

Virtual Telecommunications Access Method (VTAM)   An IBM-licensed program that controls communication and data flow in an SNA network.

visualization   Graphical display of data and models which helps the user understand the structure and meaning of the information contained in them.

VTAM application program   A program that (1) has identified itself to VTAM by opening an ACB and (2) can issue VTAM macro instructions.

WAIS (wide area information server)   A program that allows relatively easy searching and retrieval from indexed text databases on remote computers.

Web Browser   A client/server program that lets users navigate and view documents on the World Wide Web. Examples include Mosaic (invented at the National Center for Supercomputing Applications at the University of Illinois) and Netscape.

wide area network (WAN)   A network connecting nodes located across large geographic areas.

workstation   A terminal or personal computer at which a user can run applications.

World Wide Web (WWW)   A network of computers that presents information graphically through a hypertext-based system that lets users search for related "pages" globally by pointing and clicking with a mouse.

XA Interfaces   X/Open proposed standards for the portable application programming interfaces between transaction managers and resource managers (DBMS).

X/Open   Nonprofit organization founded to develop standards for interoperability between unlike systems. Its specifications for system interoperability and portability are listed in the X/Open Portability Guide (currently in its fourth issue: XPG4).

X Window System   A distributed presentation management system developed by MIT for UNIX-based environments.

X.21   See **Recommendation X.21**.

X.25   See **Recommendation X.25**.

B

Big Data—Better Returns: Leveraging Your Hidden Data Assets to Improve ROI

B.1 Introduction

Whether you work on Wall Street or in Wal-Mart, American Express or American Airlines, your company is probably generating and storing hundreds of gigabytes to terabytes of data each year. These data often contain detailed information about your customers and your markets, information you could exploit to increase your profits and improve your return on investment. The problem is that you can't fully utilize these data. The reason is that because there are so many of them, you are unable to analyze them in a timely and cost-effective manner. What should be one of your most valuable assets is being underutilized. The critical information about market trends and your customers is, in essence, hidden from you by the sheer volume of data available.

Now, for the first time, several new technologies have converged to provide a cost-effective solution to this problem. Harnessed with data-mining technologies that automatically sift through large databases, the new generation of parallel processing database machines allows users to not only utilize the large quantities of data that they have been warehousing, but also to capitalize on them by creating solutions that can be tied directly to return on investment (ROI). This appendix reviews which of these new methods work best and how they can be used to exploit the hidden assets of the corporate data warehouse. We will illustrate their impact on ROI using a case study from the banking industry.

This paper, by Thinking Machines Corporation, appeared under the title "Leveraging Your Hidden Assets to Improve ROI: A Case Study in the Credit Card Business," by Mario Bourgoin and Stephen Smith, in *Artificial Intelligence in the Capital Markets,* R. Freedman, R. Klein, and J. Lederman, eds., Probus Publishing, Chicago, 1995.

The case we present is the application of these data-mining techniques to preventing customer attrition for a large credit card issuer. Attrition is becoming a particularly important problem for credit card issuers because the current credit card market is saturated, making it very difficult to acquire new customers. What new customers there are often come at a high price—most often they must be enticed with special offers, such as a low APR or the waiver of the yearly fee. In this credit card attrition case, the credit card issuer was losing 7 percent of its customer base per year to the competition. To even maintain the status quo it needed to acquire that many new customers through expensive offers, whereas recognizing a future attriter could often mean retaining that customer at much less cost.

The data in this case were large both in the number of customer records (millions of customers) and in the number of fields of detailed data about each customer (approximately 500). Because of the amount of data, much of it was hidden—fields in records and customer records were ignored. These data were hidden not because the issuer was unaware of their existence but because older data analysis technologies were not able to put them to effective use. The issuer's computer systems could not build models that were complex enough to draw information from hundreds of fields, so only a small fraction of them were used. Even if all the fields could have been used, it would still not have been possible to process the millions of records quickly enough. This unused and hidden information is often what is necessary to effectively decide what is fact and what is artifact: what customer traits and patterns really matter and are predictive and which ones are idiosyncrasies of the data used for analysis.

The credit card issuer in this case was able to identify those customers that it could cost-effectively save by applying the new technologies to its hidden data. The issuer was able to find patterns it had never before encountered in its customer data by using fields that had previously been ignored, and it was able to determine which of these patterns could be depended on by verifying that they existed in parts of the database which had never been used in the past.

By using this case study we show how four basic questions about the use of these new data-mining techniques can be answered:

- *When should I look to use these new technologies?* We outline the problem facing credit card issuers and motivate the effort to use hidden assets.

- *How will I know which method is better?* We explore how hidden assets can improve the returns from an attriter retention program and show how to compare methods to find the one that provides the best ROI.

- *What's different about these methods?* We show how the new technologies actually work where conventional technologies fail to make effective use of the hidden data.

- *How can I be sure these methods will give me the right answer?* We show how the utilization of the hidden data will increase the confidence that can be placed on the answers derived with these new technologies.

B.1.1   Case study: retaining your valuable customers

While companies have been able to generate, acquire, and store data for many years now, the new technologies to actually put it to work require a change in the way business is done. Businesses can now be driven more directly by the information that can be found in the data and less driven by marketing speculation and hunches. These valuable hidden assets now exist, but if your business is doing well without using them, why change now? The obvious answer is that if you don't change your competition will, and in a crowded or saturated market small improvements in marketing efficiency can correspond to large swings in market share. The credit card industry is currently in that situation: there are too many players in the game and too few payers to go around. In such a competitive situation many companies choose to downsize—do more with less. But as you will see, our message is to do more with more—get more business with more of the data you've been storing. This section looks at the problem of attrition in the credit card industry: the loss of business because customers move to the competition.

In 1981 there were 116 million credit cards issued in the United States, and within 10 years there were over 263 million. By 2001, however, it is unlikely that there will be another doubling of this number since there are only 250 million people in the United States and they can only physically carry a small number of cards in their wallets and purses. In fact, it is the belief of industry analysts that the credit card market has already stopped growing and has been saturated since 1988.

Such a saturated marketplace means that whatever gains are made by one issuer come only at the expense of another—it is now a zero-sum game. Those customers lost to competitors are called *attriters,* and companies can typically lose 1 to 10 percent of their customers to the competition each year. In this way the credit card market is becoming much like the stock market. It is a very competitive game where even an advantage of a fraction of a percent can be worth millions of dollars. In the long run, the winners will be those who can eke out fractional improvements in understanding and reacting to their customers' needs. The key attribute of these winning companies will be their ability to retain their good customers at minimum cost. High-performance analytical and prediction tools that can make use of hidden data assets are becoming a necessity, not a luxury.

As a testimony to this belief, consider the credit card company Advanta in Horsham, Pennsylvania. They use proprietary prediction and classification techniques to micromarket their existing customers and find high-quality new ones. For instance, while an average customer mailing for a major credit card might include one or two different types of cards with different rates and terms, Advanta might target as many as 30 different customer segments with different card offers in a single mailing. Their success is notable:

- While the industry has been increasing receivables at a rate of 6 percent over the last 5 years, Advanta has increased receivables at a rate of 35 to 40 percent each year.

- While the industry average customer balance is $1200, Advanta achieves nearly twice that level.

- While the average credit card is used 10 to 15 percent of the time for charged purchases, Advanta's customers favor their card more than twice as often (35 percent). [*Wall Street Journal,* April 8, 1993]

The success of card issuers such as Advanta is predicated on pulling more of the purchase dollars from each customer and also on finding and retaining those customers that are most lucrative. The best customers are those who don't default yet keep high revolving balances and are not constantly shopping for the lowest interest rate; they are called *revolvers.* Others do not keep a balance but generate fees through transactions; they are called *transactors.* Finding out which of hundreds of millions of potential customers are the lucrative ones is a difficult task. In contrast, it is a trivial task to know which of your current customers are the lucrative ones because you have a large store of past information about them. For this same reason it is much easier and less expensive to retain a current customer than to acquire a new one. Your large historical database of customer information can be put to use not only to determine the good customers but also to predict whether they are likely to attrite. A customer headed for attrition can often be successfully retained. The trick is that you need to act before the customer actively attrites by canceling the card or passively attrites by not using the card or by paying off the balance. After customers have attrited, it is often too late to win them back.

Retaining a potential attriter requires using one of several different strategies. Which one is most likely to be successful depends on the particular customer. Some customers attrite solely for monetary reasons, such as no membership fee or a lower interest rate on a competing card. Some customers look for convenience (Is it accepted everywhere? Is there a low monthly payment? Are late payments penalized?). Others, such as transactors (who fully pay off their balance every month), are not motivated by lower interest rates, and still others, called *credit-limited revolvers*—who are at the limit of their available credit line—look for an increase in their credit limit.

There are four main strategies for dealing with potential attriters once they have been recognized. They are, listed in order of expense, as follows:

1. *Education.*   Make the customer aware of all the services provided by your card.

2. *Bonus.*   Provide additional product points on linked products, like airline travel miles or credit for the next car purchase.

3. *Price.*   Lower the APR or waive the membership fee for a year.

4. *Do nothing.*   Let the member attrite or proactively drop the member if the calculated ROI is unfavorable.

Clearly, in all cases of attrition, acting preemptively is far more effective than allowing the customer to attrite, but it is equally important to take the right action for the right customer. For the customers who do not take advantage of the card, the solution is cheap: educate them about the perks that you offer and the other uses of your product. But each of the other strategies costs something, and using the wrong strategy will result in the loss of the customer's business. For instance, waiving the membership fee might be important for a transactor but would be ineffective for a credit-limited revolver.

So, it is important not only to target likely attriters but also to recognize the kind of offer that each customer will respond to. In this game of small margins, no company can afford to not target its customers with the most effective and least expensive offer. And the expense is not just the cost of the offer but also the costs of the mailing itself, which can be substantial. In the case where a mailing is used to convey the offer, the final expense may be close to a dollar per envelope (depending on the type of mailing done, including printing and design costs). With telemarketing, the costs are even higher, since a human operator must be paid. With all of these variables to consider (customer response, offer cost, attrition risk, credit risk, and so on), how can a credit card issuer know which offers can be profitably made to which customers? The answer is to build a predictive model with these new data-mining tools and to calculate the return on investment.

B.2   The Return on Investment

Once you know that you will need to change your business to get more business, you need to know what you will get out of such an effort. Perhaps you don't need to use those hidden assets to retain your customers, or perhaps you can turn to standard data analysis tools to get better models. But how will you know what's better for you? How will you justify the costs of retaining customers? That requires knowing the benefits of this retention, and the best measure of those benefits is the return on the investment. This section introduces a method based on ROI as a means of measuring the performance of a technology on a prediction problem.

Traditionally, the measure of goodness of a company's marketing programs has been the number of people they reach. For example, an attriter retention program would look at the number of potential attriters saved, a fraud reduction program would measure the number of fraud cases found, and a product marketing program would report the number of positive responses made. Because of this method of measuring benefit, the results of running marketing programs have often been measured in terms of something called *lift*. Lift is a number that indicates how many times more dense in responders a targeted customer list of given size is than a nontargeted list of the same size. For example, if a credit card company was able to produce a mailing list of 100,000 customers, 35 percent of whom were soon going to attrite, and if normally 5 percent of the customers would attrite, then the lift for that targeted list of customers would be 7. For the attrition retention program, lift is:

$$\text{Lift} = \frac{\text{Attriters Found in Program Population, \%}}{\text{Attriters Found in General Population, \%}}$$

This lift reflects the proportion of desired customers present in the group that's selected for the program's offer.

In our case study the credit card issuer was initially no different from the competition in that it used lift to gauge how well a given marketing program would perform. The question was: "What is the best lift that your models can achieve?" Its current programs, built using conventional techniques, were able to achieve a lift of 5—considered to be a very respectable number for a targeted marketing program.

Lift can be an appropriate measure in the right circumstances, but in this case, it didn't match the credit card issuer's situation. In order for such a program to be worthwhile, the revenue it generates has to cover the costs both for developing the predictive model from the historical database and for running that model over the entire database, and then for actually making the offer to the customer. That's not what lift measures.

Lift measures the proportion of people reached and does not balance the costs of reaching them against the benefits of retaining them. For example, the credit card issuer in this case study was losing 70,000 of each million customers to the competition. If it could mail to 100 people but be certain that each and every one was a future attriter, its high lift would indicate a huge benefit to the program. It would have a lift of over 14, the largest lift possible. But to retain those 100 future attriters, it would also have had to pay the fixed costs of processing the million customers to pick out those 100 and the fixed costs involved in the printing. It would also have lost the vast majority of its future attriters, having only targeted those that it were sure were going to attrite. This may sound similar to the story about the man who lost his pen while walking down a dark city street but who looked for it only under the one street lamp, because that was where he could see best! Fortunately, common sense prevails, and seldom if ever would a mere 100-customer offer be mailed out, regardless of the lift.

The lifts obtained on the credit card issuer's problem by different prediction methods has been compared—specifically the comparison of predictions from SAS GLIM (a standard statistical technique), Darwin StarNet (neural network tool), and Darwin StarTree (Classification and Regression Trees tool). For each method it was found that, while lift does allow for some comparisons between methods, it provides no guide as to the return that could be had from using a given method.

The problem with just using lift as a measure is that it misses the main goal of the marketing project. The credit card issuer isn't just trying to retain people—it's trying to generate revenue. Instead of measuring the number of people reached through a program, the credit card issuer must instead show that the return on the investment in the attrition retention program is worthwhile. When considering the return of a program, the comparison is not to the size of the business created, as important as that number might look on a report. Rather, it's the best alternative use of the money to be invested in running the program. If investing in T-bills provides a better return than running a program, then it might be appropriate to go that route . . . unless a better investment exists. The standard measure to use when considering investments is the *Net Present Value* (NPV) of the investment, which is the sum of the discounted cash flows from that investment. But it can be difficult to get the information needed to calculate NPV, and for the kind of application being considered—attriter retention—most of the costs are relatively immediate. In this appendix, we use the return on investment as a stepping stone to get to a simple evaluation formula. It will be seen that ROI is a form of lift and is related to NPV.

Lift is an easy formula to calculate, which is one of its main attractions. In comparison, calculating the true ROI can be complicated. But, we can make things simpler by realizing that there are two kinds of costs: fixed costs, such as those of running a model over the entire database, and variable costs, such as those of making an offer to a customer. In that case, the ROI from our credit card issuer's use of a prediction in a program could be:

$$\text{ROI} = \frac{\substack{\text{Sum over responding customers} \\ (\text{Balance Actually Retained} \times \text{Customer APR})}}{\text{Fixed Costs} + \text{Variable Costs} \times \text{Customers in Program}}$$

which is the ratio of the total of the finance charges on balances retained to the total costs of running the program. Looking at this formula, we can see that one way to maximize the revenue from finance charges would be to put all customers into the program and thereby eliminate the fixed costs. This can, however, be very expensive due to the variable costs associated with each customer. To optimize ROI the issuer must then determine which reduced set of customers would optimally amortize the fixed cost and trade off the variable costs for the return.

This is where a good prediction can help the most, by reducing the variable costs of the program while minimizing the impact on the expected return. The variable cost is the cost of making an offer to a customer, such as waiving the yearly fee or cutting the APR. On the other hand, the fixed costs are untouched by the prediction, and they are the costs of actually having an attriter retention program, including the cost of creating a prediction. They are fixed because they are incurred regardless of the number of customers in the program, and they are an important factor when evaluating the returns from small numbers of customers.

If ROI is so obviously the right measure, why then doesn't everybody use it? One of the reasons is that it can be difficult to get good estimates of the numbers required for its calculation (e.g., the balances that will be retained by each customer). In this case study, we introduce a simpler formula for comparing different prediction technologies. The formula allows us to move away from the details of a particular program, but retains the essential feature of ROI, accounting for costs that provide a realistic comparison. To make the simplification, we will assume three things:

1. That the retention rate will be the same for all predictions. Then, the retention rate can be factored out by assuming that all potential attriters can be retained if they are targeted.

2. That the average balance retained per identified attriter will be the same for all predictions. Then, the actual amount retained can be replaced by the number of attriters identified.

3. That the fixed costs will be proportional to the size of the database being processed. Then, the processing costs will be comparable between testing a method and actually using it.

If the actual data for these factors are available, it is better to use them to calculate the ROI, but when they are not, we have found that the following formula works quite well for identifying the method that produces the best returns.

The preceding assumptions allow us to use a simpler formula that in practice is closely related to ROI and which will be called the R-Score:

$$R\text{-Score} = \frac{\text{Correctly Identified Attriters}}{F/V \text{ Ratio} + \text{Customers in Program}}$$

With this formulation, the F/V Ratio is the ratio of the fixed costs of the program to the variable cost per customer. It can be seen that this formula is related to lift, except that it includes costs and has a maximum at a point that is different from lift.

What does this mean in practice? The R-Scores on the credit card issuer's problem were obtained by different prediction methods. In this case, the F/V Ratio is 2000. When examining the results of the comparison, one should look for the high point in each prediction's R-Score curve because that is the point of highest return when using that prediction. That point corresponds to a targeted subset of the full customer database which, in turn, represents the size of the investment necessary to achieve that return.

It was found that the best R-Score of 0.134 was achieved by Darwin StarTree and requires making an offer to 4 percent of the customers. The next-best R-Score of 0.125 was achieved by Darwin StarNet and requires making an offer to 5 percent of the customers. Finally, the highest R-Score, for SAS GLIM, was 0.103 and requires making an offer to 11 percent of the customers. The R-Score of a mass mailing (Mass) was also calculated for illustrative purposes only. It showed that it is not possible to achieve a good R-Score by randomly choosing customers to include in the program. In the next section, we show that the advantage enjoyed by the Darwin StarTree and StarNet models is made possible by leveraging vast quantities of data that were not accessible to the standard statistical techniques.

B.2.1   Methods that use hidden data

Today, the use of statistics in the business community is increasing. More than ever, normal company operations acquire large amounts of data which, if correctly analyzed for causal patterns and used for prediction, can be worth millions of dollars in profits. This is especially true for the banking and credit industries, in which data are accumulated and stored at the rate of hundreds of gigabytes per year. The data include everything from personal spending patterns to what was purchased. These companies now have the opportunity to utilize this stored historical data to make predictions and find useful patterns.

In the banking and credit industries there are other important problems in addition to attrition. For instance, VISA alone loses approximately $800 million dollars per year due to fraud, and for many credit card companies the cost of default (personal bankruptcy) is even higher than that of fraud. The ability to predict these events can allow companies to take corrective action or to limit their losses. Many companies currently use statistical models to perform these predictions, but the state of the art for these systems is generally limited to simple linear models and to workstations. This forces these companies to use small samples of data from their databases and somehow choose, in advance, what data will allow them to solve their problem. Clearly, if some of the newer techniques were applied and could improve the prediction accuracy by only a small amount, it could mean savings of millions of dollars.

With the understanding that even a small but significant improvement in predictive accuracy can be very important, it makes sense to use some of the more sophisticated modeling tools on these types of problems. These tools include standard regression and other generalized linear models from statistics and nonparametric or "segmentation" techniques such as Classification and Regression Trees (CART), artificial neural networks (ANN), and Memory-Based Reasoning (MBR).

B.2.2   How can I do better than statistics?

Traditional statistical techniques, such as regression, often can't handle very large databases or thousands of fields because it is computationally infeasible. They may also have other problems, such as an oversensitivity to peculiar records in the databases, called *outliers,* that are markedly different from others with similar predicted behavior. This may be because of data-entry errors or may reflect a tiny but real fraction of the database to be predicted. Unfortunately, nonrobust statistical techniques may dramatically alter the prediction model in order to accommodate a single outlier at the expense of greatly reduced prediction accuracy for many other records. The result can be correct prediction on the outlier with incorrect prediction on the majority of the records.

Traditional statistics also often require that the data analyst have some idea of the *shape* of the model that is to be built. This often means using common sense and human intuition to determine which variables are important and in what combinations they are to be used. In contrast, the new methods are *adaptive*. They can adapt to large databases by isolating outliers. They can automatically determine what variables are influential and can find those combinations that are important. This allows them to leverage large databases to find small patterns and explore thousands of variables to identify valuable combinations.

The Classification and Regression Trees (CART) method derives its name from the treelike structure that it builds as a model. These trees work much like the child's game of 20 questions, where one child asks questions to determine the kind of object another child has in mind. In this case, the tree asks questions about cardmembers to determine which ones are likelier to attrite. Each question in the tree represents a choice between values of a particular variable that break a large group of cardmembers into two smaller groups.

For instance, there might be a choice between those members with more than $1000 monthly balances and those with less than that amount. Those with less than $1000 could be transactors while those with more could be revolvers. As with the child's game, each question's answer provides a bit of information about cardmembers and leads to other, more appropriate questions. For revolvers, the next-best question to determine whether someone will attrite might be whether the monthly balance has been decreasing, but for transactors, those who always pay off their monthly balance, the next-best question might be whether the monthly volume of transactions has been decreasing. Eventually, enough questions will have been asked of the cardmembers to place each one in a group of people who will reliably do much the same as each another: stay or attrite.

Because CART uses tests on the database to find its questions, it can be robust in the face of outliers, by isolating them with a single question. And because it searches for the best variable to use in the groups created by answers to questions based on other variables, it automatically finds combinations of variables.

The artificial neural network (ANN) method has often been spoken about with lofty analogies to the human brain. What ANNs really do is arithmetically combine the evidence provided by the variables of a record to make deductions about that record. What differentiates ANNs from linear regression methods is that neural networks, like CART, automatically determine how to combine the variables to produce the answer. They do this by being trained on a dataset and learning how to combine the variables, just as CART learns the questions to ask.

The Memory-Based Reasoning (MBR) method derives its name from the creation of a prediction model that consists of a large memory of previously classified examples. It makes decisions about unknown records by determining which known records are most similar and then predicting based on the behavior of those most closely matching known records. It differs from other methods in that all of the original records that were used to build the model are retained unmodified. While this is expensive in terms of computer memory, it can be the most flexible and robust approach to solving a problem. It also provides a good and simple method for model explanation by providing, to the user, a prototype of similar customer behavior from the historical database.

B.2.3 Gaining confidence in your predictive models

Because the new methods use large databases and thousands of variables, they can find small patterns and unusual answers in the data—not all of which are necessarily useful for predicting future customer behavior. How then can you know whether a predictive model is spurious and has zeroed in on nonpredictive artifacts in the data? The answer, once again, lies in exploiting the massive quantities of data that are available but heretofore have been effectively hidden from use. By using large amounts of data not only to build your predictive models but also to test them, you can get a fair reading on whether the methods have found fact or artifact.

B.2.4 How to feel confident in betting a million dollars on your model

After you've got your answer, how can you be sure that it is correct? If your prediction tells you that in order to optimize ROI you should send out a million-customer mailing at $1 per piece of mail, how do you know that some gross error hasn't been made in the way that the model has been built? You are making a $1-million investment based on a software prediction tool and your historical database. Does this preclude a large error from occurring? Should you trust that the model has been built correctly and that your database is not biased or corrupted? For $1 million you are probably betting your career on this being a targeted market with an improved response level over mass mailing. You'd like to be sure that you've got it right.

In today's marketing programs, product and campaign managers often rely on particular analysts as experts. Over time, certain human analysts build up expertise and marketing people begin to build confidence in particular people independent of the method or tools that that particular person is employing. These analysts, in turn, build up confidence by working with tools that they are familiar with or by using their own domain of knowledge to build models directly. Many of the newer model-building tools that are now available are more automated and may be very different from the tools that veteran analysts are familiar with—they have no sense of familiarity with the tools, yet the new tools often give better results. How then can these tools provide the same levels of security and confidence at these higher levels of performance?

Two of the most important ways are by sticking to the data and sticking to the revenue model. By *sticking to the data* we mean that models should be supported by and derived from the facts in your historical database, not built solely from intuition or human bias. By *sticking to the revenue model* we mean that models should be judged by how they perform at the bottom line and in terms of ROI. As we have already seen, it is easy to be misled by other ways of measuring the performance of your model.

B.2.5   Sticking to the revenue model

By *sticking to the revenue model* we mean that you should always consider that the real goal of using any of these predictive systems in industry is to provide and improve ROI—not necessarily to detect fraud or to target a mailing. This sounds simple, but it is often the case in the credit card industry that the unwritten rule "accrue new members while minimizing risk" is the only guiding principle for growth. And even though this, in turn, sounds simple, it is a much sounder principle than the one that it replaced: "accrue new members at any cost."

As straightforward as these rules are, there can be pitfalls. For example, when a credit card company waives its annual membership fee, it may find that it is extremely successful in recruiting new members but that many of these members become *latent attriters,* or cardholders who never officially discontinue their membership but seldom if ever use their cards. These latent attriters do cost the company money and resources in supporting them even at minimum levels. At best, the bank would like to induce these members to begin fully utilizing their cards or, at worst, the bank would like to cut them loose.

Even though the cost model for the attrition problem is somewhat complex, there are other problems whose cost models are even more complicated. For instance, in the case of balance transfer (BT) offers, which are currently quite common in the credit industry, a credit card company that knows its member to have a balance on one or more other cards will try to induce that customer to move the balance from those other cards to its card. The company will likely do this by offering lower interest rates or some other kind of incentive. The effectiveness of these programs is again routinely judged by response and risk. If a campaign achieves a 5 percent response rate with low-risk candidates, it is often considered to be a success. By looking at the revenue model, however, you can see that high response and low risk are only part of the equation. Additional questions are needed: "How much money was transferred?" "How long did the transferred money stay in the new account?" and more subtle questions, like "Did the balance transfer offer itself affect otherwise low-risk members such that by accepting the offer they now have a higher risk of personal bankruptcy?"

The revenue models become ever more complicated now that the credit card industry has become more and more competitive. These BT campaigns often interplay with other campaigns of other cards. For instance, the incentive from one BT campaign may be a cash-back bonus of 0.1 percent or accrual of frequent-flier miles. If you couple that program with a loan program of another card that allows no-interest payments for the first month, you may find savvy cardholders who take advantage of both programs to the issuers' detriment. Cardholders will borrow against this no-interest loan, balance-transfer this debt into their other account (accruing the cash-back bonus) and then immediately pay off the BT amount with the original money borrowed from the first account. They accrue no finance charges by paying off immediately and can make a significant amount of money through the cash-back bonus of the BT offer.

These are likely to be low-risk individuals who are all too willing to respond to any BT campaign and transfer large amounts of money—they are, however, quite obviously not the customers to target. What might have seemed like a great campaign when risk, response, and even amount of response were considered turns out to be a gross money loser for the bank. How then to measure? Each case is different, but the moral of the story is that before you begin to target your market you must make sure you truly have confidence in your model and can prove that achieving growth in that market will have a positive impact on your bottom line. By sticking to the revenue model you can be sure that you have not wasted your efforts in targeting your market.

B.2.6 Sticking to the data

Many of the clients that we have worked with in the banking industry typically have 1000 or more different fields of data stored for each of their customers. These data consist of everything from home address, age, and birth date to time-series information like the account balance for the last 18 months. Strangely, many of these fields are not used. Some have been ignored because they were determined at some point to not be of any predictive value, some have been discarded because they were felt to be corrupted, and some have been discarded for intuitive reasons (such as "the middle initial of the client's name has no causal relationship to credit risk"). On the whole, however, these fields have been discarded because they produced models that were too computationally expensive to calculate or too unwieldy to effectively evaluate and improve on. For instance, if it takes over a week to build a model and get an answer to your question, you may well have forgotten what the question was by the time you get an answer. It has been argued, in fact, that it is better to use simpler models that can be used interactively (thus building up an intuition about the database) than it is to use more complicated (and perhaps higher-performance) models that require days to run and thus limit the interactive nature of building the model. To achieve this interactive ability, many companies are willing to pay a very high price—often ignoring most of the thousands of fields of detailed data to concentrate on only 15 or so.

The problem with working with fewer fields is that some important information may be lost. And in the competitive markets where these models are now being built, this may be the difference between winning and losing. The data analyst is then left with a quandary: "If they use all of the data, then they are left with a task that takes so long to process that experiments cannot be carried out in a timely manner. If they limit the amount of data that they use, they risk missing important information that might confer the incremental improvement in prediction that can make all the difference." The solution that we propose is, of course, to move to new methods that build models in a more automated and regular manner and make use of massively parallel computing hardware. Then you can stick to the data without having to make prior assumptions about what is or isn't useful and still be able to build predictive models in a nearly interactive manner (within an hour rather than days).

If you don't stick to the data, what's the worst that can happen when you make prior assumptions about the data? Well, you can certainly miss important information for your model, but you may also find that unless you have the ability to work directly with the data without either eliminating some of it or preprocessing it, you may miss an important pattern of corrupted data that leads to a big mistake. We have found that such cases seem to happen more frequently than you would expect—especially when either large amounts of data are compressed or all of the data is used but with long cycle times for experimental model building.

In one such case a client had nearly 1000 fields of detailed data about each of its customers. In order to process this data on a workstation or mainframe the number of fields was compressed down to less than 50 and then a predictive model with a neural network running on a workstation was built. The results showed that a substantial savings could be had in reversing customer attrition by using the targeted marketing mailing lists produced from this model (typically such a result would increase the density of response in the first 10 percent of the mailing campaign by 5 to 10 times). When the original uncompressed data was used with the Darwin StarTree tool, each piece of detailed data was laboriously tested and added to the model in an automated process, a procedure that would swamp a mainframe but that took under an hour on a parallel computer (in this case a 64-node Connection Machine). The result was a model that delivered perfect prediction. It was never wrong.

Clearly, this was too good to be true. So over several days the code of the algorithm and the algorithm itself was checked and rechecked for bugs that could cause this kind of result. Finally, when all possible errors in the hardware and software were ruled out, the only remaining source of problems appeared to be the data itself. Sure enough, when the StarTree predictive model was evaluated, it turned out that the classification was trivially simple: for a given record, if a certain field corresponding to credit risk was included and held a certain categorical value, then the record was predicted to be that of a future attriter. The question then was why this field was so predictive.

To determine the answer to these questions, the data dictionary (which contains the plain-English explanations of how the fields' data were collected and what they mean) was consulted, but nothing out of the ordinary was found about that particular field. However, when the owners of the data were consulted, it was determined that this particular field actually contained the answer to the attrition question—it was tainted with future information which had been easily and systematically exploited by the StarTree tool when it was run on all of the data.

The predictive models that were built on the mainframe had been compressed to such a degree that this information was no longer directly available to them and could not be fully exploited. Thus, the models had not been able to detect this corruption in the database, although they had been exploiting it to a small degree. Had this not been a case of corrupted data these systems might well have missed crucial predictive information. In fact it was discovered only later in working with this same client (after months of building and fine tuning the models) that yet another source of future information had been incorporated into the mainframe models but was not detected by the algorithms. Had they been able to stick to all of the data from the beginning without having to make arbitrary judgments about which fields were important, they could have avoided these problems and detected early on any corruption of the dataset.

B.2.7   If you've got something valuable, put it in a vault

In the preceding paragraphs we've shown a few examples of where good models can go wrong through lack of data, overuse of human intuition, and just not having the tools to handle large databases. How then to overcome these problems? How can you gain confidence in your model? How can you understand it? We propose a methodology for building your predictive models that should eliminate all but the most egregious (and unlikely) forms of errors, the cornerstone of which follows:

When you are building your model, set aside some data with which to later test it. Put it in a virtual vault and seal it in tight until the time when you are ready to evaluate your model.

The reason for thinking of putting the dataset in a vault is that if you were to use this vaulted test database at any time during the period in which you are building your model, you might find that your choice of model is affected by how well you perform on the test database. If you are not careful you will find that the model becomes tailored to the idiosyncrasies of that particular test database and that the performance on new data (that you might be basing a large-dollar decision on) may be significantly different.

For instance, consider the task of direct-marketing a product to customers. The product might be anything from a money-market fund to a low-interest credit card loan. Your task is to optimize ROI by targeting your audience to those who are most likely to respond and not wasting the mailing and marketing costs on those who are unlikely to respond to your offer. To assist you in targeting your market you have a database of 20 million of your current customers,

10 percent of whom you have sent out mailings to in the past, and you know whether or not they responded to that particular offer. You now want to take some portion of that 2-million-record database and use part of it to build your model and part of it test your model.

Typically, however, when you build your model you get very good results on the database on which you build it, but far lesser results on new data. This is because many models, as they become more complex, begin to home in on the idiosyncrasies of the patterns in a particular dataset rather than on the general patterns that would be predictive for any new data. For this reason it is important that the test data not be used in picking or affecting the model. If that were to happen, then the performance of the test data would no longer be an unbiased indicator of future performance, which would result in a suboptimal predictive model being chosen and the calculation of a suboptimal ROI point.

The good news is that when test data are adequately vaulted and used for evaluation of the model, it is rare that the predicted performance level and ROI differ substantially from what is achieved with an actual marketing campaign. For instance, one large credit card company that we have worked with has found that as long as it has correctly tested its model on historical data, it has never experienced dramatically different results when applying that model to a real marketing campaign.

B.2.8 Require your model to explain itself

In addition to testing your model, another way to increase your faith in a model's performance is to get some semblance of an idea of what is going on inside the model. How is it making its predictions? Do they seem logical and driven by the data, or are they haphazard and exploiting portions of the data that are idiosyncratic to the training and testing datasets? Can you understand the model, or is it just a black box?

The desire for understanding models is so great, and the costs of mistakes so large, that many companies in the banking industry not only limit the size of the database that they utilize, but they also limit the sophistication of their models. In statistics there are sophisticated nonlinear models (models where the change in the value being predicted increases or decreases by differing amounts based on the value of the given data field) and much simpler linear models (where the change in the value of the predicted field is constant for constant incremental changes in the given data field). Linear models are much more intuitively appealing in that for any given change in the data field (predictor field) a corresponding change occurs in the predicted field. For instance, every dollar spent on mailing for mass marketing results in 50 cents of response. If you spend $1 million you receive $500,000. If you spend $10 you receive $5.

Linear models are thus fairly easy to understand, but unfortunately many predictive relationships, especially in business, are not linear. For instance, high-risk credit card customers may be those whose last monthly purchases were both relatively high (as they go on a final buying spree before filing personal bankruptcy) and relatively low (as they finally reach their credit limit and now finally have to pay their bills). This nonlinear relationship between monthly credit card usage and personal bankruptcy could not be captured by a simpler model.

There is also a cost in using complicated models—there is always the chance that if the model is not correctly built and tested it may exploit idiosyncrasies of the database and not generalize to new data. One way to combat this problem is to limit oneself to very simple models. The other way is to use as powerful a model as possible and to rely on stringent testing to be sure that it is a viable one and to rely on the structure of the model to provide confidence and understanding rather than restricting it to an unnecessarily simple and, consequently, less-powerful model.

Another way to gain confidence in a model, besides testing, is to be able to understand it—to see if it makes sense in terms of what is in the data. There are several sophisticated modeling techniques that allow not only for complex models to be built but also for the predictions from those models to be explained. In the case of decision-tree models such as StarTree, rules can be extracted and interpreted so that the values and the fields that were used in making the prediction can be explicitly read. In addition, information can be retrieved that explains how often in the historical database a particular rule would have corresponded to a correct prediction and how many examples in the database it would have classified.

By looking at the decision tree and the rules extracted from it, the user can begin to gain some insight into how these predictions were made and the structure of the prediction problem. This can, of course, be an important feature for detecting problems in the database or the model design, as was shown previously in the case where future information was mistakenly included in the training data.

Another example where understanding and visualizing the predictive model allowed for a better understanding of a client's customers and markets occurred when using StarTree to predict and cluster which customers would represent the majority of the purchases of a given product over a year's duration. When this clustered data was then graphed three-dimensionally (dimensions were customer segment, amount of product purchased, and the month) it could be easily recognized that the clustered data was also broken up into a subpopulation of customers that had never been seen before by the manufacturer. There was a segment of the population, larger than 10 percent, that almost completely stopped purchasing the product in the summer months, only to then begin purchasing again late in the fall. Before the data had been clustered and viewed in this way, this particular customer behavior had never been seen before.

Memory-Based Reasoning models also yield ways of supplying explanations by providing the nearest—or several nearest—neighboring examples or prototypes. Since these examples come directly from the database and are, in general, unaltered, they provide solid evidence as to why a prediction was made. The neural networks models, in general, are less able to explain themselves, though some new methods have been developed to perform sensitivity analysis to determine which of the input fields are most critical in the prediction. There has also been some recent work in extracting rules from neural networks, though this is still preliminary.

B.3   Conclusions

For years, many companies have been paying the expense of storing on tape the vast databases produced by their operations, waiting for the time when they would be able to put them to use. In general these data assets have remained effectively hidden because neither the software techniques nor the computer hardware has been available to take full advantage of them in a cost-effective manner. Now, however, the combination of massively parallel computer technology and new data-analysis methods, such as Classification and Regression Trees and artificial neural networks, create a new approach that makes the use of these databases viable.

We argue in this appendix, through a specific case study of credit card membership attrition, that these new approaches improve the return on investment by allowing more sophisticated predictive models to be built that make use of as large a section of the database as desired and that, because they are data-driven, remove the inherent bias of preselected fields and compressed databases. This is possible because massively parallel computer technologies can rapidly extract the required parts of the databases, process them, produce the needed results, and validate them—all within hours, so that the results can be had nearly interactively.

We also issue a warning that the power of these new technologies must be used with discretion and understanding. These new predictive models must be judged by return on investment, not just on response or increased market share, and they must also be rigorously tested and understood as best as possible—as has always been the case for predictive methods. However, when these caveats are heeded and care is taken, these technologies can provide significantly increased return on investment for a wide variety of prediction problems, and they have the further advantage of providing high-confidence results that can be established by testing predictions on large segments of real data.

Dr. E. F. Codd's 12 Guidelines for OLAP

Dr. E. F. Codd, the father of the relational model, has formulated a list of 12 guidelines and requirements as the basis for selecting OLAP systems. Users should prioritize this suggested list to reflect their business requirements and consider products that best match those needs:

1. *Multidimensional conceptual view.* A tool should provide users with a multidimensional model that corresponds to the business problems and is intuitively analytical and easy to use.

2. *Transparency.* The OLAP system's technology, the underlying database and computing architecture (client/server, mainframe gateways, etc.), and heterogeneity of input data sources should be transparent to users to preserve their productivity and proficiency with familiar front-end environments and tools (e.g., MS Windows, MS Excel).

3. *Accessibility.* The OLAP system should access only the data actually required to perform the analysis. Additionally, the system should be able to access data from all heterogeneous enterprise data sources required for the analysis.

4. *Consistent reporting performance.* As the number of dimensions and the size of the database increases, users should not perceive any significant degradation in performance.

5. *Client/server architecture.* The OLAP system has to conform to client/server architectural principles for maximum price/performance, flexibility, adaptivity, and interoperability.

6. *Generic dimensionality.* Every data dimension must be equivalent in both structure and operational capabilities.

7. *Dynamic sparse matrix handling.* The OLAP system has to be able to adopt its physical schema to the specific analytical model that optimizes

sparse matrix handling to achieve and maintain the required level of performance.

8. *Multiuser support.* The OLAP system must be able to support a workgroup of users working concurrently on a specific model.

9. *Unrestricted cross-dimensional operations.* The OLAP system must be able to recognize dimensional hierarchies and automatically perform associated roll-up calculations within and across dimensions.

10. *Intuitive data manipulation.* Consolidation path reorientation (pivoting), drill-down and roll-up, and other manipulations should be accomplished via direct point-and-click, drag-and-drop actions on the cells of the cube.

11. *Flexible reporting.* The ability to arrange rows, columns, and cells must exist in a fashion that facilitates analysis by intuitive visual presentation of analytical reports.

12. *Unlimited dimensions and aggregation levels.* Depending on business requirements, an analytical model may have a dozen or more dimensions, each of which has multiple hierarchies. The OLAP system should not impose any artificial restrictions on the number of dimensions or aggregation levels.

Ten Mistakes for Data Warehousing Managers to Avoid

This appendix has been adapted from Ramon Barquin, Allan Paller, and Herb Edelstein, *Ten Mistakes to Avoid for Data Warehousing Managers,* The Data Warehousing Institute, Washington, D.C., 1995.

Mistake 1: Starting with the Wrong Sponsorship Chain

A data warehousing project without the right sponsorship chain (see Table D.1) is like an automobile with insufficient gasoline and oil, and a linkage problem between the steering wheel and the wheels.

The right sponsorship chain includes two key individuals above the data warehousing manager (the person who leads the data warehousing project). At the top is an executive sponsor with a great deal of money to invest in effective use of information. Corporate presidents, vice presidents of marketing, and vice presidents of research and development often fit the bill. A good sponsor, however, is not the only person required in the reporting chain above the warehousing manager. When a data warehousing project fails, the cause can sometimes be traced to the lack of a key individual—often called the project "driver" because this is the person who keeps the project moving in the right direction and ensures that the schedule is kept—between the sponsor and the data warehousing manager. A good driver is a businessperson with three essential characteristics: (1) must have already earned the respect of the other executives, (2) has a healthy skepticism about technology, and (3) is decisive but flexible.

Mistake 2: Setting Expectations that Cannot Be Met

Data warehousing projects have at least two phases. Phase 1 is the selling phase in which you attempt to persuade people that, by investing in your proj-

TABLE D.1   Price Paid When Certain Sponsorship Elements Are Missing

Problem with sponsorship chain	Price paid by the project
Sponsor is an IT executive rather than a business executive outside IT	Project is seen as a technology experiment rather than a strategic investment in the business
Sponsor has a limited budget	Every unexpected technical challenge is a crisis, as budget dollars are hard to get; project gains reputation as "problem-prone" and a "budget buster"
There is no driver; DW manager reports directly to sponsor	No one on the project has authority to broker peace among competing data definitions; sponsor soon tires of data definition wars and withdraws support
Driver has not earned the respect of peers at the executive level	Content of data warehouse is not trusted, in part because no one can vouch for the validity of the definitions used
Driver is excited rather than skeptical about technology	Project is viewed as a technical experiment (or toy); most businesspeople avoid it
Driver is indecisive or unwilling to act quickly	Project slows, executive support dissolves, interest fades, users find alternative solutions

ect, they can expect to get wonderful access to the right data through simple, graphical delivery tools. Phase 2 is the struggle to meet the expectations you have raised in phase 1. Sadly, it is not uncommon for overeager project managers to make claims that their data warehouse will give people throughout the enterprise easy access to all the information they need, when they need it, in the right format. Along with that promise (explicit or implied) comes a bill for $1 to $7 million dollars. Business executives who hear those promises and see those budgets cannot help but have high expectations. But users do not get all the information they need. All data warehousing is, by necessity, domain-specific, which that means it focuses on a particular set of business information. Worse still, many warehouses are loaded with summary information—not detail. If a question asked by an executive requires more detail or requires information from outside the domain, the answer is often "we haven't loaded that information, but we can; it will just cost (a bunch) and take (many) weeks."

Mistake 3: Engaging in Politically Naive Behavior

A common error made by many data warehousing managers is promoting the value of their data warehouse with arguments to the effect of "This will help managers make better decisions." When a self-respecting manager hears those words, the natural reaction is "This person thinks we have not been making good decisions and that his/her system is going to 'fix' us." From that point on, that manager is very, very hard to please.

Those IT professionals who have been in the industry for at least 10 years know that the objective of data warehousing is similar to the one that fueled the fourth-generation language boon of the late 1970s, and the DSS/EIS activities of the 1980s—giving users better access to important information. While 4GL products have had a long and useful life, the DSS/EIS activities had a quick rise and even quicker fall, probably because DSS/EIS initiatives were often promoted as change agents that would improve business and enable better management decisions. Most people will support the concept of a data warehouse when it is presented without the fanfare as the place people can go to get useful information.

Mistake 4: Loading the Warehouse with Data Just Because It Is Available

Some inexperienced data warehousing managers send a list of tables and data elements to end users along with a request asking which of those data elements should be included in the warehouse. Sometimes, the users are asked to categorize the elements as "essential," "important," or "nice to have." Typically, the results are very long lists of marginally useful information that radically expands the data warehouse storage requirements and slows the responsiveness.

Loading extraneous data leads to very large databases, which are difficult to manage and support, and which take too long to load. Additional hardware required to support this load can be justified only when all data is useful for the decision-making process; otherwise, it becomes a very expensive and inefficient white elephant.

Mistake 5: Believing that Data Warehouse Database Design Is the Same as Transactional Database Design

Since the goals of transaction processing systems differ from the goals of data warehouses, the database designs must be different as well. In transaction processing, the goal is speed to access and update a single record or a few records. Data warehousing is fundamentally different. The goal here is to access aggregates—sums, averages, trends, and more. Another difference is the user. In transaction systems, a query will be used tens of thousands of times. In data warehousing, an end user may formulate a query that may be used only once. Data warehousing databases are often denormalized to enable easy navigation for infrequent users. Transaction processing databases are often normalized to ensure speed and data integrity.

An even more fundamental difference is in content. Where transactional systems usually contain only the basic data, data warehousing users increasingly expect to find aggregates and time series information already calculated for them and ready for immediate display. (This has been an impetus behind the multidimensional database market.)

Mistake 6: Choosing a Data Warehouse Manager Who Is Technology-Oriented Rather than User-Oriented

One data warehousing user complained that the biggest mistake made on a large data warehousing project was to put a "propeller head" as a data warehousing manager. This user-hostile project manager made so many people angry that the entire project was in jeopardy of being canceled.

Although many technologists make excellent project managers, remember that data warehousing is a service business and making clients angry is a near-perfect method of destroying a service business.

Mistake 7: Focusing on Traditional, Internal Record-Oriented Data, and Ignoring the Potential Value of External Data and of Text, Images, and—Potentially—Sound and Video

A study conducted by the White House in the early 1980s showed that senior-level management in over 50 large companies rely on outside data (news, telephone calls from associates, etc.) for more than 95 percent of all the information they use, and the higher people are in the organization, the less value they place on internal data. Because of this preferential treatment of external data, senior executives sometimes see data warehousing as irrelevant. It is not that they are uninterested in key operating indicators; they just don't have time to bury themselves in the sort of detailed data a warehouse provides. Thus, a data warehouse that makes every piece of internal data available to senior management will likely be seen as only marginally useful. Therefore, it is imperative to extend the project focus to include external data.

In addition, consider expanding the forms of information available through the warehouse. Today, data warehousing solutions employ data visualization techniques and multimedia, and they often present the information in the form of images, full-motion video, and sound.

Mistake 8: Delivering Data with Overlapping and Confusing Definitions

The Achilles heel of data warehousing is the requirement to gain consensus on data definitions. Conflicting definitions each have champions, and they are not easily reconciled, especially if the definitions reflect the way some organizational units operate (e.g., "sales" can be defined differently by the finance and marketing departments). Solving this problem is one of the most important tasks of the data warehousing project. If it is not solved, users will not have confidence in the information they are getting. Worse, they may embarrass themselves by using the wrong data, in which case they will inevitably blame the data warehouse.

Mistake 9: Believing the Performance, Capacity, and Scalability Promises

Recently, CEOs from three companies—a manufacturer, a retailer, and a service company—have reported an identical problem. Within four months of getting started, each had to purchase at least one additional processor of a size equal to or larger than the largest computer they had originally purchased for the data warehouse. They simply ran out of power.

Bigger problems may lie in wait on the software side. Often, counting on a promise of a powerful (and expensive) parallel database system may be a mistake since the software may not always perform as advertised. Problems with performance and scalability can also come from front-end applications that can use nonscalable tools (or nonscalable design) to fail in delivering an acceptable performance.

An even more common capacity problem arises in networking, with abundant examples of network saturation. Network overloads are a very common surprise in client/server systems in general and in data warehousing systems in particular.

Mistake 10: Believing that Once the Data Warehouse Is Up and Running, Your Problems Are Finished

Each happy data warehouse user asks for new data and tells others about the great new tool. And they, too, ask for new data to be added, and want it immediately. At the same time, each performance or delivery problem results in a high-pressure search for additional technology or a new process.

Thus, the data warehousing team needs to maintain high energy levels over long periods of time. A common error is to place data warehousing in the hands of project-oriented people who believe that they will be able to set it up once and have it run itself.

Data warehouses need to be intensely nurtured for at least a year after their initial launch. Even after that, without a dynamic leader, they can easily lose their momentum and their sponsorship. Data warehousing is a journey, not a destination.

Mistake 11: Focusing on Ad Hoc, Data Mining, and Periodic Reporting

As you can see, this is mistake number 11. It is true that believing that there are only 10 mistakes is also a mistake.
                    R. BARQUIN ET AL.

This is a subtle error, but an important one. Fixing it may transform a data warehousing manager from a data librarian into a hero.

The natural progression of information in a data warehouse is (1) extract the data from legacy systems, clean it, and feed it to the warehouse; (2) support ad hoc reporting until you learn what people want; and then (3) convert the ad hoc reports into regularly scheduled reports. This is the natural progression, but it isn't the best one. It ignores the fact that managers are busy and that reports are liabilities rather than assets unless the recipients have time to read the reports. Reports are like inventory; if they are not used, they just generate costs.

Alert systems can be a better approach and they can make a data warehouse mission-critical. Alert systems monitor the data flowing into the warehouse and inform all key people with a need to know, as soon as a critical event takes place. One key to an effective alert system is infrequency—if alerts are sent too often, they become a burden rather than an asset. To determine the contents and the thresholds of that critical information, one must fully understand what's going on in the mind of the businessperson who will receive the alert. Data warehousing drivers and managers with solid ties to senior managers are in the best position to do that job well.

Bibliography

Here are books that are specifically concerned with data warehousing, data mining, OLAP, and decision support and that appear to be aimed primarily at practitioners. Also listed are several books that are good for a person with a general systems background who may not be familiar with some of the core technologies used to build these systems.

Ackley, D. H., *A Connectionist Machine for Genetic Hillclimbing,* Kluwer Academic Publishers, Norwell, Mass., 1987.

Adriaans, Pieter, and Dolf Zantiage, *Data Mining,* Addison-Wesley, Reading, Mass., 1996.

Agresti, A., *Categorical Data Analysis,* Wiley, New York, 1990.

Aiken, Peter, *Data Reverse Engineering: Slaying the Legacy Dragon,* McGraw-Hill, New York, 1995.

Anahory, Sam, and Dennis Murray, *Data Warehousing in the Real World,* Addison Wesley Longman, Reading, Mass., 1997.

Anderberg, M., *Cluster Analysis for Applications,* Academic Press, New York, 1973.

Anderson and Rosenfeld, eds., *Neurocomputing,* MIT Press, Cambridge, Mass., 1988.

Barquin, Ramon, and Herb Edelstein, eds., *Building, Using, and Managing the Warehouse,* Prentice-Hall, Upper Saddle River, N.J., 1997.

Barquin, Ramon, and Herb Edelstein, eds., *Planning and Designing the Data Warehouse,* Prentice-Hall, Englewood Cliffs, N.J., 1996.

Berry, Michael, and Gordon Linoff, *Data Mining Techniques: For Marketing, Sales and Customer Support,* Wiley, New York, 1997.

Berson, Alex, *Client / Server Architecture,* 2d ed., McGraw-Hill, New York, 1996.

Berson, Alex, and George Anderson, *SYBASE and Client / Server Computing,* 2d ed., McGraw-Hill, New York, 1996.

Bigus, Joseph P., *Data Mining with Neural Networks,* McGraw-Hill, New York, 1996.

Bischoff, Joyce, and Ted Alexander, eds., *Data Warehouse: Practical Advice from the Experts,* Prentice-Hall, Upper Saddle River, N.J., 1997.

Blattberg, Robert C., Rashi Glazer, and John D. C. Little, eds., *The Marketing Information Revolution,* Harvard Business School Press, Cambridge, Mass., 1994.

Bontempo, Charles J., and Cynthia Saracco, *Database Management: Principles and Products,* Prentice-Hall, Englewood Cliffs, N.J., 1996.

Booker, L. B., D. E. Goldberg, and J. H. Holland, *Classifer Systems and Genetic Algorithms,* 1989.

Brackett, Michael H., *Data Sharing,* Wiley, New York, 1994.

Brackett, Michael H., *The Data Warehouse Challenge,* Wiley, New York, 1996.

Breiman, L., J. Friedman, R. Olshen, and C. Stone, *Classification and Regression Trees,* Chapman and Hall, New York, 1984, 1993.

Brodie, Michael L., and Michael Stonebraker, *Migrating Legacy Systems: Gateways, Interfaces, and the Incremental Approach,* Morgan Kaufmann, San Francisco, 1995.

Burleson, Donald, *High Performance Oracle Data Warehousing,* Coriolis Group, 1997.

Cabena, Perter, *Discovering Datamining: From Concept to Implementation,* Prentice-Hall, Upper Saddle River, N.J., 1997.

Chen, H., "Machine Learning for Information Retrieval: Neural Networks, Symbolic Learning, and Genetic Algorithms," *Journal of the American Society for Information Science,* 1995.

Corey, Michael, and Michael Abbey, *Oracle Data Warehousing,* McGraw-Hill, New York, 1996.

Creecy, R., B. Masand, S. Smith, and D. Waltz, "Trading MIPS and Memory for Knowledge Engineering," *Communications of the ACM,* August, 1992.

Dasrathy, B. V., ed., *Nearest Neighbor (NN) Norms: NN Pattern Classification Techniques,* IEEE Computer Society Press, Los Alamitos, Calif., 1990.

Data Warehousing for Dummies, IDG Books, San Mateo, Calif., 1997.

Dawkins, R., *The Blind Watchmaker,* W. W. Norton and Company, New York, 1986.

Dawkins, Richard, *The Selfish Gene,* Oxford University Press, New York, 1989.

Devlin, Barry, *Data Warehouse: From Architecture to Implementation,* Addison-Wesley, Reading, Mass., 1997.

Dhar, Vasant, and Roger Stein, *Intelligent Decision Support Methods: The Science of Knowledge Work,* Prentice-Hall, Upper Saddle River, N.J., 1997.

Dhar, Vasant, and Roger Stein, *Seven Methods for Transforming Corporate Data into Business Intelligence,* Prentice-Hall, Upper Saddle River, N.J., 1997.

Dyer, Robert, and Ernest Forman, *An Analytic Approach to Marketing Decisions,* Prentice-Hall, Englewood Cliffs, N.J., 1995.

Fayyad, Usama M., Gregory Piatetsky-Shapiro, Padhraic Smyth, and Ramasamy Uthurusamy, *Advances in Knowledge Discovery and Data Mining,* MIT Press, Cambridge, Mass., 1995.

Fogel, L. J., A. J. Owens, and M. J. Walsh, *Artificial Intelligence Through Simulated Evolution,* Wiley, New York, 1966.

Frakes, W., and R. Baeza-Yates, eds., *Information Retrieval, Data Structures and Algorithms,* Prentice-Hall, Englewood Cliffs, N.J., 1992.

Freedman, R., R. Klein, and J. Lederman, eds., *Artificial Intelligence in the Capital Markets,* Probus Publishing, Chicago, 1995.

Gill, Harjinder, and Prakash Rao, *The Official Client/Server Computing Guide to Data Warehousing,* Que, Englewood Cliffs, N.J., 1996.

Gleick, J., *Chaos: Making a New Science,* Penguin Books, New York, 1987.

Gonick, L., and W. Smith, *The Cartoon Guide to Statistics,* HarperPerennial, New York, 1993.

Gray, J., and A. Reuter, *Transaction Processing Concepts and Techniques,* Morgan Kaufmann, San Francisco, 1993.

Groth, Robert, *Data Mining: A Hands On Approach for Business Professionals,* Prentice-Hall, Upper Saddle River, N.J., 1997.

Gupta, Vivek R., *Data Warehousing with MS SQL Server Unleashed,* Sams, Englewood Cliffs, N.J., 1997.

Hackathorn, Richard D., *Web Farming for the Data Warehouse,* Morgan Kaufmann, San Francisco, 1998.

Hackney, Doug, *The Seven Deadly Sins of Data Warehousing,* Addison Wesley Longman, Reading, Mass., 1997.

Hackney, Doug, *Understanding and Implementing Successful Data Marts,* Addison Wesley Longman, Reading, Mass., 1997.

Hammergren, Thomas C., *Data Warehousing: Building the Corporate Knowledgebase,* International Thomson Computer Press, 1997.

Hammergren, Thomas C., *Official Sybase Data Warehousing on the Internet,* International Thomson Computer Press, 1997.

Hofstadter, D., *Godel, Escher, Bach: An Eternal Golden Braid,* Random House, New York, 1979.

Holland, J., *Adaptation in Natural and Artificial Systems,* University of Michigan Press, Ann Arbor, Mich., 1975.

Humphreys, Patrick, et al., *Implementing Systems for Supporting Management Decisions,* Chapman & Hall, New York, 1996.

Inmon, W. H., *Building the Data Warehouse,* 2d ed., QED Publishing Group, Wellesley, Mass., 1996.

Inmon, W. H., Claudia Imhoff, and Greg Battas, *Building the Operational Data Store,* Wiley, New York, 1996.

Inmon, W. H., Claudia Imhoff, and Ryan Sousa, *Corporate Information Factory,* Wiley, New York, 1997.

Inmon, W. H., John Zachman, and Jonathon Geiger, *Data Stores, Data Warehousing, and the Zachman Framework,* McGraw-Hill, New York, 1997.

Inmon, W. H., J. D. Welch, and Katherine Glassey, *Managing the Data Warehouse,* Wiley, New York, 1997.

Inmon, W. H., and Richard D. Hackathorn, *Using the Data Warehouse,* Wiley, New York, 1994.

Kearns, M., and U. Vazirani, *An Introduction to Computational Learning Theory,* MIT Press, Cambridge, Mass., 1994.

Kelly, Brian W., *AS/400 Data Warehousing: The Complete Implementation Guide,* CBM Books, 1996.

Kelly, Sean, *Data Warehousing in Action,* Wiley, New York, 1997.

Kelly, Sean, *Data Warehousing: The Route to Mass Customization,* Wiley, New York, 1994.

Kimball, Ralph, *The Data Warehouse Toolkit,* Wiley, New York, 1996.

Kirkpatrick, S., C. D. Gelatt, and M. P. Vecchi, "Optimization by Simulated Annealing," *Science,* **220**: 671–680 (1983).

Kosko, B., *Fuzzy Thinking, the New Science of Fuzzy Logic,* Hyperion, New York, 1993.

Koza, J., *Genetic Programming,* MIT Press, Cambridge, Mass., 1992.

Larsen, R., and M. Marx, *An Introduction to Mathematical Statistics and its Applications,* 2d ed., Prentice-Hall, Englewood Cliffs, N.J., 1986.

Love, Bruce, *Enterprise Information Technologies: Designing the Competitive Company,* Van Nostrand Reinhold, New York, 1993.

Mattison, Rob, *Data Warehousing and Data Mining for Telecommunications,* Artech House, 1997.

Mattison, Rob, *Data Warehousing: Strategies, Tools and Techniques,* McGraw-Hill, New York, 1996.

Mitchell, Tom, *Machine Learning,* McGraw-Hill, New York, 1997.

O'Neil, Patrick, *Database: Principles, Programming, Performance,* Morgan Kaufmann, San Francisco, 1994.

O'Neil, Bonnie, *Oracle Data Warehousing Unleashed,* Sams, Englewood Cliffs, N.J., 1997.

Paller, Alan, *The IS Book: Information Systems for Top Management,* Dow Jones-Irwin, Homewood, Ill., 1990.

Parsaye, Kamran, and Mark Chignell, *Intelligent Database Tools and Applications,* Wiley, New York, 1993.

Piatetsky-Shapiro, G., and W. Frawley, *Knowledge Discovery in Databases,* MIT Press, Cambridge, Mass., 1991.

Poe, Vidette, *Building a Data Warehouse for Decision Support,* Prentice-Hall, Englewood Cliffs, N.J., 1996.

Poolet, Michelle A., and Michael D. Reilly, *Data Warehousing with Microsoft SQL Server,* Que, Englewood Cliffs, N.J., 1997.

Quinlan, J., *C4.5: Programs for Machine Learning,* Morgan Kaufmann, San Francisco, 1988.

Raden, Neil, *Performance Is Everything,* Wiley, New York, 1997.

Redman, Thomas C., *Data Quality for the Information Age,* Artech House, 1996.

Rich, E., *Artificial Intelligence,* McGraw-Hill, New York, 1983.

Rumelhart, D., and J. McClelland, *Parallel Distributed Programming,* MIT Press, Cambridge, Mass., 1986.

Sauter, Vicki L., *Decision Support Systems,* Wiley, New York, 1996.

Shannon, C., and W. Weaver, *The Mathematical Theory of Communication,* University of Illinois Press, Champaign, Ill., 1949.

Shapiro, S., ed., *Encyclopedia of Artificial Intelligence,* 2d ed., Wiley, New York, 1992.

Shepard, D., *The New Direct Marketing,* Irwin, Homewood, Ill., 1995.

Silverston, Len, Inmon, W. H., and Graziano, Kent, *The Data Model Resource Book: A Library of Logical Data Models and Data Warehouse Designs,* Wiley, New York, 1997.

Simon, Alan R., *Strategic Database Technology: Management for the Year 2000,* Morgan Kaufmann, San Francisco, 1995.

Singh, Harry S., *Data Warehousing: Concepts, Technology, and Applications,* Prentice-Hall, Upper Saddle River, N.J., 1997.

Sprague, Ralph H., and Hugh Watson, *Decision Support for Management,* Prentice-Hall, Englewood Cliffs, N.J., 1996.

Stanfill, C., and D. Waltz, "Toward Memory Based Reasoning," *Communications of the ACM,* **29**(2): 1213–1228 (1986).

Stonebraker, M., ed., *Readings in Database Design,* Morgan Kaufmann, San Francisco, 1994.

Tanler, Richard, *The Intranet Data Warehouse: Tools and Techniques for Connecting Data Warehouses to Intranets,* Wiley, New York, 1997.

Thomsen, Erik, *OLAP Solutions: Building Multidimensional Information Systems,* Wiley, New York, 1997.

Turban, Efraim, *Decision Support Systems and Expert Systems,* Prentice-Hall, Englewood Cliffs, N.J., 1995.

Watson, Hugh J., George Houdeshel, and Rex Kelly Rainer, *Building Executive Information Systems and Other Decision Support Applications,* Wiley, New York, 1997.

Weiss, Sholom M., and Nitin Indurkhya, *Predictive Data Mining: A Practical Guide,* Morgan Kaufmann, San Francisco, 1997.

Widrow, Rumelhart, and Leht, "Neural Networks: Applications in Industry, Business, and Science," *Communications of the ACM,* **37**(3) (1994).

Wilkinson, R. A., et al., *The First Census Optical Character Recognition Systems Conference Proceedings,* National Institute of Standards and Technology, Technical Report #NISTIR 4912, Gaithersburg, Md., August 1992.

Winston, P., *Artificial Intelligence,* Addison-Wesley, Reading, Mass., 1993.

Winter, R. A., and S. A. Brobst, "An Introduction to Parallel Database Technology," *Enterprise Systems Journal,* August, 1994.

Yazdani, Sima, and Shirley Wong, *Data Warehousing with Oracle: An Adminstrator's Handbook,* Prentice-Hall, Upper Saddle River, N.J., 1997.

Zelazny, Gene, *Say It with Charts,* Dow Jones-Irwin, Homewood, Ill., 1985.

Zhang, Xiru, "Non-Linear Predictive Models for Intra-Day Foreign Exchange Trading," in *Intelligent Systems in Accounting, Finance and Management,* vol. 3, Wiley, New York, 1994, pp. 293–302.

Index

ABOUT THE AUTHORS

ALEX BERSON is an internationally recognized information technology architect with over 20 years of experience in various areas of information technology, including distributed client/server computing, database systems, parallel computing systems, object technology, data communications, and machine learning. He has successfully designed and implemented several large-scale data warehousing projects for major financial services companies. He is the author of several best-selling McGraw-Hill books, including *Client/Server Architecture/2E* and *Sybase and Client/Server Computing/2E*.

STEPHEN J. SMITH is a director and architect responsible for the creation and delivery of two data mining products over the last decade—one for parallel supercomputers and the second for data warehouses with multidimensional databases. He is a well-respected expert in the field of data mining and its integration with the data warehouse.